THE MINSTER

SPANISH
DICTIONARY

THE MINSTER

SPANISH

DICTIONARY

MINSTER BOOKS

First published in 1976 by
The Hamlyn Publishing Group Limited
Published in 1983 by Newnes Books,
Michelin House, 81 Fulham Road,
London SW3 6RB

This 1992 edition reprinted exclusively for MINSTER BOOKS

ISBN 0 600 36565 4

Printed at Thomson Press (India) Ltd.
Faridabad (Haryana)

Foreword

This dictionary aims to give concise and accurate definitions of 24,000 of the most important words in use in the English and Spanish languages today.

A pronunciation system based on the International Phonetic Alphabet is used (see *Key to symbols used in pronunciation*), indicating the pronunciation of all headwords in both sections of the dictionary.

Modern technical, commercial, and informal usage is given particular attention, in preference to outmoded terms or other expressions not in common contemporary use. Definitions are numbered in order to distinguish senses, and abbreviations are used to indicate use in specific technical, scientific, or commercial fields (see *Abbreviations used in the Dictionary*). An additional feature is the inclusion of idiomatic expressions and phrases, so necessary for the understanding and use of the foreign language.

This dictionary, with its emphasis on modernity, together with its compact form and clear typeface, should prove indispensable in the home, at school, in the office, and abroad.

Abbreviations used in the Dictionary

adj	adjective	*indef art*	indefinite article	*pol*	politics
adv	adverb	*inf*	informal	*poss*	possessive
anat	anatomy	*infin*	infinitive	*pref*	prefix
arch	architecture	*interj*	interjection	*prep*	preposition
aux	auxiliary	*invar*	invariable	*pron*	pronoun
aviat	aviation	*lit*	literature	*rel*	religion
bot	botany	*m*	masculine	*s*	singular
cap	capital	*math*	mathematics	*sci*	science
comm	commerce	*med*	medical	*sl*	slang
conj	conjunction	*mil*	military	*tab*	taboo
cul	culinary	*min*	minerals	*Tdmk*	trademark
def art	definite article	*mod*	modal	*tech*	technical
derog	derogatory	*mot*	motoring	*Th*	theatre
dom	domestic	*mus*	music	*US*	United States
educ	education	*n*	noun	*v*	verb
fam	familiar	*naut*	nautical	*vi*	intransitive verb
fml	formal	*neg*	negative	*v imp*	impersonal verb
game	cards, chess, etc.	*neu*	neuter	*vr*	reflexive verb
gram	grammar	*pers*	person	*vt*	transitive verb
geog	geography	*phot*	photography	*zool*	zoology

Key to symbols used in pronunciation

English

Vowels

i:	m*ee*t	u	p*u*t	ai	fl*y*		θ	*th*in
i	b*i*t	u:	sh*oo*t	au	h*ow*		ð	*th*en
e	g*e*t	ʌ	c*u*t	ɔi	b*oy*		ŋ	si*ng*
æ	h*a*t	ə	*a*go	iə	h*ere*		j	*y*es
ɑ:	h*ear*t	ɔ:	s*ir*	ɛə	*air*		ʃ	*sh*ip
ɔ	h*o*t	ei	l*a*te	uə	p*oor*		ʒ	mea*s*ure
ɔ:	*ough*t	ou	g*o*				tʃ	*ch*in
							dʒ	*g*in

Consonants

' indicates that the following syllable is stressed, as in *ago* (ə'gou).
ˌ placed under an *n* or *l* indicates that the *n* or *l* is pronounced as a syllable, as in *button* ('bʌtn̩) and *flannel* ('flænl̩).

Spanish

Vowels

i	*i*sla	o	libr*o*	j	*y*a		θ	*z*orro
e	m*e*sa	u	*u*no	ʎ	e*ll*a		β	de*b*er
a	*a*la			ɲ	se*ñ*or		ð	co*d*o
				tʃ	*ch*ulo			

Consonants

' indicates that the following syllable is stressed, as in *uno* ('uno).

The Spanish alphabet treats *CH, LL,* and *Ñ* as separate letters following *C, L,* and *N*. When these letters occur within a word, they will follow *-cz-, -lz-,* or *-nz-,* e.g. *saña* after *santuario, resollar* after *resolver,* etc.

Plurals of almost all Spanish nouns are regularly formed by the addition of *-s* or *-es*. The few irregular plurals are shown immediately after the part of speech, e.g. **rubí** . . . *nm, pl* **rubíes**. Nouns that do not change in the plural are marked as invariable, e.g. **tocadiscos** . . . *nm invar* record-player.

Feminine forms of nouns are not shown when they can be derived in a regular way from the masculine form. Both masculine and feminine forms are shown when different translations are required, e.g. *hijo* son, *hija* daughter. When the same word may be both an adjective and a noun, the gender of the noun is given only when it is fixed. Thus, **mamífero** . . . *adj,nm* (mammal) indicates that the word is an adjective or a masculine noun; **mellizo** . . . *adj,n* (twin) indicates that the word is an adjective or a masculine or feminine noun (*el mellizo, la melliza*).

Adverbs derived from adjectives are not shown unless the formation is irregular or unless a translation different from that of the adjective is required. Spanish adverbs are regularly formed by the addition of *-mente* to adjectives (*-mente* being added to the feminine form of the adjective if the adjective has both masculine and feminine endings), e.g. *fácil, fácilmente, rápido, rápidamente.*

A swung dash (~) before a change of part of speech indicates that the part of speech refers to the headword, not the preceding subentry shown in heavy type.

Radical-changing verbs, which change their stem vowels when these vowels are stressed, are immediately followed by an indication of the vowel change, e.g. **acertar (ie), aprobar (ue), despedir (i)**. These changes are summarized in Table I below.

Irregular verbs are followed by an asterisk in the headword list in both sections of the dictionary. Table II below summarizes spelling changes that affect a large number of verbs ending in *-cer, -cir, -ger,* etc. In Table III are listed major verbs whose irregularities are not covered in the other tables.

English irregular verbs

Infinitive	Past Tense	Past Participle	Infinitive	Past Tense	Past Participle
abide	abode *or* abided	abode *or* abided	draw	drew	drawn
arise	arose	arisen	dream	dreamed *or* dreamt	dreamed *or* dreamt
awake	awoke *or* awaked	awoke *or* awaked	drink	drank	drunk
be	was	been	drive	drove	driven
bear[1]	bore	borne *or* born	dwell	dwelt	dwelt
beat	beat	beaten	eat	ate	eaten
become	became	become	fall	fell	fallen
begin	began	begun	feed	fed	fed
bend	bent	bent	feel	felt	felt
bet	bet	bet	fight	fought	fought
beware[2]			find	found	found
bid	bid	bidden *or* bid	flee	fled	fled
bind	bound	bound	fling	flung	flung
bite	bit	bitten *or* bit	fly	flew	flown
bleed	bled	bled	forbid	forbade *or* forbad	forbidden *or* forbid
blow	blew	blown	forget	forgot	forgotten *or* forgot
break	broke	broken			
breed	bred	bred	forgive	forgave	forgiven
bring	brought	brought	forsake	forsook	forsaken
build	built	built	freeze	froze	frozen
burn	burnt *or* burned	burnt *or* burned	get	got	got
			give	gave	given
burst	burst	burst	go	went	gone
buy	bought	bought	grind	ground	ground
can	could		grow	grew	grown
cast	cast	cast	hang[3]	hung *or* hanged	hung *or* hanged
catch	caught	caught			
choose	chose	chosen	have	had	had
cling	clung	clung	hear	heard	heard
come	came	come	hide	hid	hidden *or* hid
cost	cost	cost	hit	hit	hit
creep	crept	crept	hold	held	held
crow	crowed *or* crew	crowed	hurt	hurt	hurt
cut	cut	cut	keep	kept	kept
deal	dealt	dealt	kneel	knelt	knelt
dig	dug *or* digged	dug *or* digged	knit	knitted *or* knit	knitted *or* knit
do	did	done	know	knew	known

Infinitive	Past Tense	Past Participle	Infinitive	Past Tense	Past Participle
lay	laid	laid	shear	sheared	sheared or shorn
lead	led	led			
lean	leant or leaned	leant or leaned	shed	shed	shed
leap	leapt or leaped	leapt or leaped	shine	shone	shone
learn	learnt or learned	learnt or learned	shoe	shod	shod
leave	left	left	shoot	shot	shot
lend	lent	lent	show	showed	shown
let	let	let	shrink	shrank or shrunk	shrunk or shrunken
lie	lay	lain			
light	lit or lighted	lit or lighted	shut	shut	shut
lose	lost	lost	sing	sang	sung
make	made	made	sink	sank	sunk
may	might		sit	sat	sat
mean	meant	meant	sleep	slept	slept
meet	met	met	slide	slid	slid
mow	mowed	mown	sling	slung	slung
must			slink	slunk	slunk
ought			slit	slit	slit
panic	panicked	panicked	smell	smelt or smelled	smelt or smelled
pay	paid	paid			
picnic	picnicked	picnicked	sow	sowed	sown or sowed
put	put	put	speak	spoke	spoken
quit	quitted or quit	quitted or quit	speed	sped or speeded	sped or speeded
read	read	read			
rid	rid or ridded	rid or ridded	spell	spelt or spelled	spelt or spelled
ride	rode	ridden	spend	spent	spent
ring	rang	rung	spill	spilt or spilled	spilt or spilled
rise	rose	risen	spin	spun	spun
run	ran	run	spit	spat or spit	spat or spit
saw	sawed	sawn or sawed	split	split	split
say	said	said	spread	spread	spread
see	saw	seen	spring	sprang	sprung
seek	sought	sought	stand	stood	stood
sell	sold	sold	steal	stole	stolen
send	sent	sent	stick	stuck	stuck
set	set	set	sting	stung	stung
sew	sewed	sewn or sewed	stink	stank or stunk	stunk
shake	shook	shaken	stride	strode	stridden
shall	should		strike	struck	struck

English irregular verbs

Infinitive	Past Tense	Past Participle	Infinitive	Past Tense	Past Participle
string	strung	strung	wake	woke	woken
strive	strove	striven	wear	wore	worn
swear	swore	sworn	weave	wove	woven or wove
sweep	swept	swept	weep	wept	wept
swell	swelled	swollen or swelled	will	would	
			win	won	won
swim	swam	swum	wind	wound	wound
swing	swung	swung	wring	wrung	wrung
take	took	taken	write	wrote	written
teach	taught	taught			
tear	tore	torn			
tell	told	told			
think	thought	thought			
throw	threw	thrown			
thrust	thrust	thrust			
traffic	trafficked	trafficked			
tread	trod	trodden or trod			

[1] when *bear* means *give birth to,* the past participle is always *born.*

[2] used only in the infinitive or as an imperative.

[3] the preferred form of the past tense and part participle when referring to death by hanging is *hanged.*

Table I

infinitive	Change	Occurs in
acertar, atender	*e* to *ie*	1, 2, 3 *s*, 3 *pl* present indicative and present subjunctive
aprobar, mover	*o* to *ue*	1, 2, 3 *s*, 3 *pl* present indicative and present subjunctive
dormir	(1) *o* to *ue*	1, 2, 3 *s*, 3 *pl* present indicative and present subjunctive
	(2) *o* to *u*	1, 2 *pl* present subjunctive; 3 *s*, 3 *pl* preterite
pedir	*e* to *i*	1, 2, 3 *s*, 3 *pl* present indicative; present subjunctive; 3 *s*, 3 *pl* preterite
sentir	(1) *e* to *ie*	1, 2, 3 *s*, 3 *pl* present indicative and present subjunctive
	(2) *e* to *i*	1, 2 *pl* present subjunctive; 3 *s*, 3 *pl* preterite

Spanish verb tables

Table II

Infinitive ending in	Change	Occurs in
-car	c to qu before e	present subjunctive; 1 s preterite
-cer, -cir	(1) c to z before a,o (e.g. vencer, esparcir)	1 s present indicative; present subjunctive
	(2) c to zc before a,o	1 s present indicative; present subjunctive
-gar	g to gu before e	present subjunctive; 1 s preterite
-ger, -gir	g to j before a,o	1 s present indicative; present subjunctive
-guir	gu to g before a,o	1 s present indicative; present subjunctive
-llir, -ñir	omit i after ll or ñ	3 s, 3 pl preterite
-quir	qu to c before a,o	1 s present indicative; present subjunctive
-uir	i to y	1, 2, 3 s, 3 pl present indicative; present subjunctive; 3 s, 3 pl preterite
-zar	z to c before e	present subjunctive; 1 s preterite

Table III

Infinitive	Present Indicative (1,3 s)	Preterite (1 s)	Future	Past Participle
andar	ando, anda	anduve	andaré	andado
caber	quepo, cabe	cupe	cabré	cabido
caer	caigo, cae	caí	caeré	caído
dar	doy, da	di	daré	dado
decir	digo, dice	dije	diré	dicho
erguir	yergo, yergue	erguí	erguiré	erguido
errar	yerro, yerra	erré	erraré	errado
estar	estoy, está	estuve	estaré	estado
haber	he, ha	hube	habré	habido
hacer	hago, hace	hice	haré	hecho
ir	voy, va	fui	iré	ido
oír	oigo, oye	oí	oiré	oído
oler	huelo, huele	olí	oleré	olido
poder	puedo, puede	pude	podré	podido
poner	pongo, pone	puse	pondré	puesto
querer	quiero, quiere	quise	querré	querido
reducir	reduzco, reduce	reduje	reduciré	reducido
reír	río, ríe	reí	reiré	reído
saber	sé, sabe	supe	sabré	sabido
ser	soy, es	fui	seré	sido
tener	tengo, tiene	tuve	tendré	tenido
traer	traigo, trae	traje	traeré	traído
valer	valgo, vale	valí	valdré	valido
venir	vengo, viene	vine	vendré	venido
ver	veo, ve	vi	veré	visto

A

a (a) *prep* 1 to, at. 2 in, on. 3 by, by means of.

abad (a'βað) *nm* abbot. **abadesa** *nf* abbess. **abadía** *nf* abbey.

abajo (a'βaxo) *adv* below, down, downstairs. **¡abajo!** *interj* down with! **de abajo** *adj* lower.

abalanzar (aβalan'θar) *vt* 1 balance. 2 hurl, throw. **abalanzarse** *vr* rush forward.

abandonar (aβando'nar) *vt* 1 desert, leave. 2 abandon. 3 give up. **abandonarse** 1 let oneself go. 2 give way to, yield to. **abandonado** *adj* 1 abandoned. 2 neglected. **abandono** *nm* 1 abandonment. 2 neglect.

abanicar (aβani'kar) *vt* fan. **abanico** *nm* fan.

abaratar (aβara'tar) *vt* lower the price, cheapen. *vi* become cheaper. **abaratamiento** *nm* reduction in price.

abarcar (aβar'kar) *vt* include, take in.

abarrotar (aβarro'tar) *vt* fill to capacity.

abastecer* (aβaste'θer) *vt* supply, provide. **abastecedor** *nm* supplier. **abastecimiento** *nm* supply. **abasto** *nm* provisions.

abatir (aβa'tir) *vt* 1 knock down, demolish. 2 humble. 3 prostrate. **abatido** *adj* depressed, low, prostrated. **abatimiento** *nm* 1 demolition. 2 depression.

abdicar (aβði'kar) *vt,vi* abdicate.

abedul (aβe'ðul) *nm* birch.

abeja (a'βexa) *nf* bee. **abejar** *nm* beehive. **abejorro** *nm* bumblebee.

aberración (aβerra'θjon) *nf* aberration.

abertura (aβer'tura) *nf* opening, hole.

abeto (a'βeto) *nm* 1 fir. 2 fir cone.

abierto (a'βjerto) *v* see **abrir**. *adj* 1 open. 2 honest, sincere.

abismo (a'βismo) *nm* abyss. **abismal** *adj* abysmal.

abjurar (aβxu'rar) *vt* forswear.

ablandar (aβlan'dar) *vt,vi* soften. **ablandarse** *vr* 1 moderate. 2 mellow. 3 relent.

abnegarse (ie) (aβne'garse) *vr* 1 deny oneself. 2 be unselfish.

abobado (aβo'βaðo) *adj* stupid, silly.

abochornar (aβotʃor'nar) *vt* 1 overheat. 2 shame, embarrass. **abochornarse** *vr* 1 blush. 2 get overheated.

abofetear (aβofete'ar) *vt* slap, hit.

abogar (aβo'gar) *vi* 1 plead. 2 advocate. **abogado** *nm* 1 lawyer. 2 solicitor.

abolengo (aβo'lengo) *nm* ancestry.

abolir (aβo'lir) *vt* abolish. **abolición** *nf* abolition.

abollar (aβo'ʎar) *vt* dent. **abolladura** *nf* dent.

abominar (aβomi'nar) *vt* abominate. **abominable** *adj* abominable. **abominación** *nf* abomination.

abonar (aβo'nar) *vt* 1 guarantee, stand surety for. 2 subscribe to. 3 fertilize (earth). **abonado** *adj* reliable, trustworthy. *nm* 1 subscriber. 2 season-ticket holder. **abono** *nm* 1 subscription. 2 guarantee. 3 fertilizer.

abordar (aβor'ðar) *vt* board (a ship, etc.). *vi* come into port.

aborigen (aβo'rixen) *adj,n* Aborigine, Aboriginal.

aborrecer* (aβorre'θer) *vt* hate. **aborrecimiento** *nm* hatred.

abortar (aβor'tar) *vt,vi* abort. **aborto** *nm* 1 miscarriage, abortion. 2 failure.

abotonar (aβoto'nar) *vt* button up.

abovedado (aβoβe'ðaðo) *adj* arched.

abrasar (aβra'sar) *vt* 1 burn. 2 parch, waste. **abrasarse** *vr* burn (with heat, passion, etc.). **abrasivo** *adj* abrasive.

abrazar (aβra'θar) *vt* embrace, hug. **abrazo** *nm* embrace.

abrelatas (aβre'latas) *nm invar* tin-opener.

abrevar (aβre'βar) *vt* water (an animal, land, etc.). **abrevadero** *nm* drinking trough.

abreviar (aβre'βjar) *vt* 1 shorten, abbreviate. 2 hurry. **abreviatura** *nf* abbreviation.

abrigar (aβri'gar) *vt* shelter, protect, cover. **abrigo** *nm* 1 overcoat. 2 shelter.

abril (a'βril) *nm* April.

abrillantar (aβriʎan'tar) vt polish, burnish.

abrir (a'βrir) vt 1 open. 2 reveal. 3 unfold.

abrochar (aβro'tʃar) vt 1 fasten. 2 button.

abrogar (aβro'gar) vt repeal. **abrogación** nf repeal.

abrumar (aβru'mar) vt 1 weigh down. 2 crush, overwhelm. **abrumarse** vr become foggy. **abrumador** adj 1 exhausting. 2 overwhelming.

abrupto (a'βrupto) adj 1 abrupt, steep. 2 rough.

absceso (aβs'θeso) nm abscess.

ábside ('aβsiðe) nm apse.

absolución (aβsolu'θjon) nf 1 rel absolution. 2 pardon.

absoluto (aβso'luto) adj absolute, complete. **en absoluto** absolutely, by no means.

absolver (ue) (aβsol'βer) vt absolve, pardon, acquit.

absorber (aβsor'βer) vt absorb, soak up. **absorbente** adj absorbent. **absorción** nf absorption. **absorto** adj 1 absorbed, lost in thought. 2 amazed.

abstemio (aβs'temjo) adj abstemious.

abstenerse (aβste'nerse) vr abstain.

abstinencia (aβsti'nenθja) nf abstinence.

abstracto (aβs'trakto) adj abstract. **abstracción** nf abstraction.

abstraer (aβstra'er) vt abstract, remove. **abstraer de** do without, exclude. **abstraerse** vr be preoccupied. **abstraído** adj 1 withdrawn. 2 absent-minded.

absurdo (aβ'surðo) adj absurd.

abuelo (a'βwelo) nm grandfather. **abuela** nf grandmother.

abultar (aβul'tar) vt enlarge, swell. vi be bulky. **abultamiento** nm 1 swelling. 2 bulkiness.

abundar (aβun'dar) vi be plentiful, abound. **abundancia** nf abundance. **abundante** adj abundant.

aburrir (aβur'rir) vt 1 bore. 2 tire. **aburrido** adj boring, dull. **aburrimiento** nm boredom.

abusar (aβu'sar) vt 1 impose upon. 2 misuse. **abuso** nm 1 abuse. 2 imposition.

abyecto (a'βjekto) adj vile, abject.

acá (a'ka) adv 1 here. 2 now, at this time. **acá y allá** here and there.

acabar (aka'βar) vt finish, complete. vi 1 end. 2 die. **acabar de** have just.

academia (aka'ðemja) nf academy. **académico** adj academic.

acaecer (akae'θer) vi happen.

acalorar (akalo'rar) vt 1 make warm. 2 excite, inflame. **acalorarse** vr become hot or heated.

acampar (akam'par) vi camp.

acantilado (akanti'laðo) adj 1 (of a cliff) steep. 2 rocky. nm cliff.

acaparar (akapa'rar) vt 1 monopolize. 2 hoard.

acariciar (akari'θjar) vt caress, stroke.

acarrear (akarre'ar) vt 1 transport. 2 cause (damage, harm). **acarreo** nm transport, haulage.

acaso (a'kaso) adv perhaps. nm chance. **por si acaso** just in case.

acatar (aka'tar) vt respect, revere. **acatamiento** nm respect.

acaudalar (akauða'lar) vt 1 hoard. 2 acquire. **acaudalado** adj well-off, wealthy.

acaudillar (akauði'ʎar) vt lead, command.

acceder (akθe'ðer) vi accede. **acceder a** agree to. **accesión** nf agreement.

acceso (ak'θeso) nm 1 entry, access. 2 med attack.

accidente (akθi'ðente) nm accident. **accidental** adj accidental.

acción (ak'θjon) nf action. **accionista** nm,f shareholder.

acebo (a'θeβo) nm holly.

acechar (aθe'tʃar) vt 1 spy on. 2 ambush. **acecho** nm 1 spying. 2 ambush.

aceite (a'θeite) nm 1 oil. 2 olive oil. **aceitoso** adj oily. **aceituna** nf olive.

acelerar (aθele'rar) vt accelerate. **acelerarse** vr hurry. **acelerador** nm accelerator.

acentuar (aθen'twar) vt 1 stress, accentuate. **acento** nm accent.

aceptar (aθep'tar) vt accept. **aceptable** adj acceptable. **aceptación** nf acceptance.

acequia (a'θekja) nf irrigation ditch.

acera (a'θera) nf pavement.

acerbo (a'θerβo) adj 1 sharp, sour. 2 harsh.

acerca (a'θerka) prep **acerca de** about, concerning.

acercar (aθer'kar) vt bring near. **acercarse (a)** vr approach. **acercamiento** nm 1 approach. 2 reconciliation.

acero (a'θero) nm steel.

acérrimo (a'θerrimo) adj 1 very strong. 2 obstinate.

acertar (ie) (aθer'tar) vt 1 hit (target). 2 find. 3 succeed. vi be successful. **acertar a** happen to. **acertado** adj 1 correct. 2 well-aimed.

acertijo (aθer'tixo) nm riddle.

ácido ('aθiðo) adj,nm acid.

acierto (a'θjerto) nm 1 success. 2 knack. 3 good shot.

aclamar (akla'mar) vt applaud, acclaim.

aclarar (akla'rar) vt 1 clarify, explain. 2 rinse (clothes). vi clear. **aclaración** nf explanation.

aclimatizar (aklimati'θar) vt acclimatize

acné (ak'ne) nm acne.

acobardar (akoβar'ðar) vt intimidate, frighten.

acoger (ako'xer) vt 1 welcome. 2 accept. **acogerse** vr take refuge. **acogedor** adj 1 (of a room) friendly, welcoming. 2 cosy. **acogida** nf welcome.

acolchar (akol'tʃar) vt 1 quilt. 2 pad.

acólito (a'kolito) nm acolyte.

acometer (akome'ter) vt 1 attack. 2 attempt. 3 overcome. **acometida** nf attack.

acomodar (akomo'ðar) vt 1 adapt. 2 find room for. 3 arrange. vi suit. **acomodarse** vr 1 comply. 2 agree. **acomodación** nf 1 adaptation. 2 accommodation. **acomodado** adj suitable, convenient. 2 wealthy.

acompañar (akompa'nar) vt accompany, escort. **acompañamiento** nm 1 accompaniment. 2 following. **acompañante** nm 1 escort. 2 accompanist.

acondicionar (akondiθjo'nar) vt 1 prepare. fix. **acondicionarse** vr condition oneself. **bien/mal acondicionado** adj in good/bad condition.

acongojar (akongo'xar) vt sadden.

aconsejar (akonse'xar) vt advise. **aconsejarse** vr seek advice.

acontecer* (akonte'θer) vi happen. **acontecimiento** nm event.

acoplar (ako'plar) vt join, couple. **acoplarse** vr make up, become friends again.

acordar (ue) (akor'ðar) vt 1 decide. 2 harmonize. 3 remind. vi agree. **acordarse** vr 1 agree. 2 remember. **acorde** adj agreed. nm mus chord.

acordeón (akorðe'on) nm accordion.

acordonar (akorðo'nar) vt cordon off.

acorralar (akorra'lar) vt round up (animals, etc.).

acortar (akor'tar) vt shorten. **acortarse** vr be very shy.

acosar (ako'sar) vt 1 persecute, pursue. 2 harass. **acoso** nm 1 pursuit. 2 persecution.

acostar (ue) (akos'tar) vt 1 lay down. 2 put to bed.

acostumbrar (akostum'brar) vt accustom. vi be in the habit. **acostumbrarse a** vr become used to. **acostumbrado** adj usual.

acotar (ako'tar) vt 1 mark out. 2 limit. 3 survey.

acre[1] ('akre) adj 1 bitter. 2 acrid, pungent.

acre[2] ('akre) nm acre.

acrecentar (ie) (akreθen'tar) vt increase. **acrecentamiento** nm 1 increase. 2 growth.

acreditar (akreði'tar) vt 1 do credit to. 2 prove. **acreditado** adj reputable.

acreedor (akree'ðor) nm creditor.

acribillar (akriβi'ʎar) vt 1 riddle with holes. 2 wound.

acróbata (a'kroβata) nm,f acrobat.

acta ('akta) nf 1 minutes (of a meeting, etc.). 2 record. 3 certificate.

actitud (akti'tuð) nf attitude.

activar (akti'βar) vt stimulate, make active.

actividad (aktiβi'ðað) nf activity, bustle. **activo** adj 1 active. 2 lively. nm comm assets.

acto ('akto) nm act, deed.

actor (ak'tor) nm actor.

actriz (ak'triθ) nf actress.

actual (ak'twal) adj present, actual. **actualidad** nf 1 present (time). 2 pl current affairs. **actualmente** adv really and truly.

actuar (ak'twar) vt operate, work. vi act, work. **actuación** nf Th performance. **actuario** nm law clerk.

acuarela (akwa'rela) nf watercolour.

acuario (a'kwario) nm aquarium.

acuático (a'kwatiko) adj aquatic.

acuciar (aku'θjar) vt incite, urge. **acucioso** adj keen.

acuclillarse (akukli'ʎarse) vr crouch, squat.

acudir (aku'ðir) vi attend, come to.

acueducto (akwe'ðukto) nm aqueduct.

acuerdo (a'kwerðo) nm agreement.

acumen (a'kumen) nm talent.

acumular (akumu'lar) vt collect, gather. **acumulación** nf accumulation. **acumulador** adj accumulative. nm storage battery.

acuñar (aku'nar) vt 1 mint, coin (money). 2 wedge.

acuoso (a'kwoso) adj aqueous, watery.

acurrucarse (akurru'karse) vr curl up, crouch, huddle.

acusar (aku'sar) vt 1 accuse, charge. 2 comm acknowledge. **acusación** nf accusation. **acusado** adj accused. nm law accused person, defendant.

acústico (a'kustiko) adj acoustic.

achacar (atʃa'kar) vt attribute.

achaque (a'tʃake) nm illness.

achicar (atʃi'kar) vt 1 make smaller. 2 belittle. 3 naut bale out. **achicarse** vr 1 get smaller. 2 humble oneself.

achicoria (atʃi'korja) nf chicory.

achicharrar (atʃitʃar'rar) vt 1 scorch, overheat. 2 inf annoy.

adalid (aða'lið) nm leader.

adaptar (aðap'tar) vt 1 adapt. 2 adjust. **adaptabilidad** nf adaptability. **adaptable** adj adaptable. **adaptación** nf adaptation.

adecuado (aðe'kwaðo) adj 1 adequate. 2 suitable.

adefesio (aðe'fesjo) nm 1 inf folly, nonsense. 2 ridiculous person or sight.

adelantar (aðelan'tar) vt 1 move forward, advance. 2 speed up. vi 1 progress. 2 (of a clock) be fast. 3 mot overtake. **adelantarse** vr go forward. **adelantado** adj advanced. **adelantamiento** nm advance. **adelante** adv forward(s), on. **de hoy en adelante** in future. **adelanto** nm advancement, progress.

adelgazar (aðelga'θar) vt make thin. vi grow thin or slim.

ademán (aðe'man) nm 1 gesture, motion. 2 pl manners.

además (aðe'mas) adv besides, furthermore. **además de** prep in addition to.

adentro (a'ðentro) adv within, inside.

adepto (a'ðepto) adj adept. nm follower.

aderezar (aðere'θar) vt 1 adorn. 2 prepare. 3 repair. **aderezo** nm 1 preparation. 2 seasoning, dressing.

adeudar (aðeu'ðar) vt owe (money, etc.). vi become related by marriage.

adherir (ie) (aðe'rir) vi adhere, stick. **adherirse a** vr stick, adhere to. **adherencia** nf adherence. **adhesión** nf 1 adhesion. 2 support. **adhesivo** adj sticky. nm adhesive.

adición (aði'θjon) nf addition. **adicional** adj extra.

adicionar (aðiθjo'nar) vt add.

adicto (a'ðikto) adj addicted. nm 1 supporter. 2 addict.

adiestrar (aðjes'trar) vt train, teach. **adiestrarse** vr practise.

adinerado (aðine'raðo) adj wealthy.

adiós (a'ðjos) interj,nm goodbye.

adivinar (aðiβi'nar) vt 1 prophesy, foretell. 2 guess. **adivinación** nf 1 prophecy, divination. 2 guesswork. **adivinanza** nf 1 riddle. 2 prophecy. 3 guess. **adivino** nm fortuneteller.

adjetivo (aðxe'tiβo) nm adjective.

adjudicar (aðxuði'kar) vt 1 award. 2 adjudicate.

adjuntar (aðxun'tar) vt attach, enclose. **adjunto** adj attached, enclosed. nm 1 addition. 2 enclosure.

administrar (aðminis'trar) vt control, administer. **administración** nf administration. **administrativo** adj administrative.

admirar (aðmi'rar) vt admire, respect. **admirarse de** vr be surprised at. **admirable** adj admirable. **admiración** nf admiration. **admirador** adj admiring. nm admirer.

admisible (aðmi'siβle) adj admissible, allowable. **admisión** nf 1 admission. 2 acceptance.

admitir (aðmi'tir) vt 1 admit. 2 accept, allow.

adobar (aðo'βar) vt 1 prepare, dress (food, etc.). 2 pickle.

adolecer* (aðole'θer) vi fall ill. **adolecer de** suffer from.

adolescencia (aðoles'θenθja) nf adolescence. **adolescente** adj,n adolescent.

adónde (a'ðonde) conj where. **¿adónde?** adv where?

adoptar (aðop'tar) vt adopt. **adopción** nf adoption. **adoptivo** adj adopted.

adorar (aðo'rar) vt adore. **adorable** adj adorable. **adoración** nf adoration.

adormecer* (aðorme'θer) vt send to sleep, lull. **adormecerse** vr go to sleep.

adornar (aðor'nar) vt adorn.

adquirir (ie) (aðki'rir) vt obtain, acquire.

adquisición (aðkisi'θjon) nf 1 acquisition. 2 purchase. **adquisitivo** adj acquisitive.

adrede (að'reðe) adv on purpose, intentionally.

adscribir (aðskri'βir) vt appoint, assign.

aduana (a'ðwana) nf customs. **aduanero** nm customs officer.

aducir* (aðu'θir) vt offer as proof.

adueñarse (aðwe'narse) vr take possession.

adular (aðu'lar) vt flatter. **adulación** nf flattery.

adulterar (aðulte'rar) vt adulterate. vi commit adultery. **adulterino** adj adulterous. **adulterio** nm adultery.

adulto (a'ðulto) adj,n adult.

adusto (a'ðusto) adj 1 (of a country or region) very hot. 2 grave. 3 stern.

advenedizo (aðβene'ðiθo) adj 1 foreign, strange. 2 upstart.

advenimiento (aðβeni'mjento) nm arrival, advent.

adverbio (að'βerβjo) nm adverb.

adversario (aðβer'sarjo) n adversary. **adversidad** nf adversity, misfortune. **adverso** adj 1 unfavourable. 2 opposite.

advertir (ie) (aðβer'tir) vt 1 notice. 2 warn, advise. **advertencia** nf 1 warning. 2 preface.

adyacente (aðja'θente) adj adjacent.

aéreo (a'ereo) adj aerial.

aerodinámica (aerodi'namika) *nf* aerodynamics.

aeronáutica (aero'nautika) *nf* aeronautics. **aeronáutico** *adj* aeronautical.

aeroplano (aero'plano) *nm* aeroplane.

aeropuerto (aero'pwerto) *nm* airport.

aerosol (aero'sol) *nm* aerosol.

afabilidad (afaβili'ðað) *nf* affability, friendliness. **afable** *adj* affable, pleasant.

afamado (afa'maðo) *adj* famous.

afán (a'fan) *nm* 1 effort. 2 anxiety. 3 eagerness.

afanar (afa'nar) *vt* 1 urge, press. 2 *inf* steal, pinch. **afanarse** *vr* 1 exert oneself. 2 work hard. **afanoso** *adj* 1 hectic. 2 hard.

afección (afek'θjon) *nf* 1 affection. 2 disease.

afectar (afek'tar) *vt* 1 affect. 2 pretend. 3 *law* encumber. **afectado** *adj* affected. **afectivo** *adj* affective. **afecto** *nm* 1 affection. 2 emotion. **afecto a** 1 affectionate towards. 2 subject to. **afectuoso** *adj* affectionate.

afeitar (afei'tar) *vt* shave. **afeitarse** *vr* make up one's face. **afeite** *nm* cosmetics, make-up.

afeminado (afemi'naðo) *adj* effeminate.

aferrar (ie) (afer'rar) *vt* 1 seize. 2 moor. **aferrarse** *vr* 1 cling, stick. 2 *naut* anchor. **aferramiento** *nm* 1 seizing, capture. 2 *naut* mooring.

Afganistán (afganis'tan) *nm* Afghanistan. **afgano** *adj,n* Afghan.

afianzar (afjan'θar) *vt* 1 fasten. 2 support. 3 guarantee. **afianzarse** *vr* 1 steady oneself. 2 become strong.

afición (afi'θjon) *nf* 1 fondness. 2 inclination. 3 hobby. **la afición** the fans. **aficionado** *adj* 1 keen, interested. 2 amateur. *nm* 1 fan. 2 enthusiast.

aficionarse (afiθjo'narse) *vr* 1 take a liking for. 2 become a follower of.

afilar (afi'lar) *vt* 1 sharpen. 2 grind. **afilador** *nm* sharpener.

afiliarse (afi'ljarse) *vr* join, become a member.

afín (a'fin) *adj* 1 near to. 2 related. *nm* relation by marriage.

afinar (afi'nar) *vt* 1 polish, perfect. 2 *mus* tune.

afinidad (afini'ðað) *nf* 1 affinity. 2 relationship.

afirmar (afir'mar) *vt* 1 affirm, state. 2 make firm. **afirmarse** *vr* steady onself. **afirmativo** *adj* affirmative.

aflicción (aflik'θjon) *nf* affliction, grief.

afligir (afli'xir) *vt* 1 afflict. 2 sadden. **afligirse** *vr* grieve.

aflojar (aflo'xar) *vt,vi* loosen, slacken.

afluencia (aflu'enθja) *nf* 1 crowd. 2 fluency. 3 abundance. **afluente** *nm geog* tributary. *adj* 1 flowing. 2 fluent. 3 abundant.

afluir (aflu'ir) *vi* flow.

afónico (a'foniko) *adj* hoarse, voiceless.

aforrar (afor'rar) *vt* line (clothes, etc.). **aforrarse** *vr* wrap oneself up. **aforro** *nm also* **forro** lining (of clothes).

afortunado (afortu'naðo) *adj* lucky, happy.

afrenta (a'frenta) *nf* 1 insult. 2 disgrace. **afrentar** *vt* insult. **afrentarse** *vr* be ashamed.

África ('afrika) *nf* Africa. **África del Sur** South Africa. **africano** *adj,n* African.

afrontar (afron'tar) *vt* 1 confront. 2 bring face to face.

afuera (a'fwera) *adv* out(side). **afueras** *nf pl* suburbs, outskirts.

agacharse (aga'tʃarse) *vr* stoop, crouch.

agalla (a'gaʎa) *nf* 1 *zool* gill. 2 *pl* tonsils. 3 *pl inf* cheek, guts.

agarrar (agar'rar) *vt* seize, clutch. *vi* take hold. **agarro** *nm* grasp, hold. **agarradero** *nm* handle.

agarrotar (agarro'tar) *vt* 1 tighten. 2 strangle. **agarrotarse** *vr med* become numb.

agasajar (agasa'xar) *vt* treat well, entertain. **agasajo** *nm* 1 present, gift. 2 convivial entertainment.

agazapar (agaθa'par) *vt inf* grab. **agazaparse** *vr* 1 crouch. 2 hide.

agencia (a'xenθja) *nf* 1 agency. 2 office. **agencia de turismo** or **viajes** travel agency. **agente** *nm* agent. **agente de bolsa** stockbroker. **agente de inmobiliario** estate agent.

agenda (a'xenda) *nf* notebook, diary.

ágil ('axil) *adj* agile. **agilidad** *nf* agility.

agitar (axi'tar) *vt* 1 wave. 2 stir up, excite. 3 shake. **agitación** *nf* 1 waving. 2 excitement. 3 movement. **agitado** *adj* 1 excited. 2 agitated.

aglomerar (aglome'rar) *vt* crowd together.

agobiar (ago'βjar) *vt* bow or bend down, weigh down. **agobio** *nm* weight, burden.

agolparse (agol'parse) *vr* rush or crowd together.

agonía (ago'nia) *nf* 1 agony. 2 torment.

agonizar (agoni'θar) *vt inf* bother, urge. *vi* be dying.

agosto (a'gosto) *nm* August.

agotar (ago'tar) *vt* 1 exhaust. 2 drain. **agotado** *adj* worn out. **agotador** *adj* exhausting. **agotamiento** *nm* exhaustion.

agraciar (agra'θjar) *vt* adorn.

agradar (agra'ðar) *vt,vi* please. **agradable** *adj* pleasant.

agradecer* (agraðe'θer) *vt* **1** thank. **2** be grateful for. **agradecido** *adj* grateful. **agradecimiento** *nm* gratitude.

agrado (a'graðo) *nm* **1** pleasure. **2** liking.

agrandar (agran'dar) *vt* make larger.

agravar (agra'βar) *vt* increase, make worse.

agraviar (agra'βjar) *vt* offend, insult. **agravio** *nm* **1** wrong. **2** offence.

agredir (agre'ðir) *vt* attack, assault.

agregado (agre'gaðo) *nm* **1** aggregate. **2** assistant.

agresión (agre'sjon) *nf* aggression. **agresivo** *adj* aggressive. **agresor** *nm* attacker.

agrícola (a'grikola) *adj* agricultural. **agricultor** *nm,f* farmer.

agricultura (agrikul'tura) *nf* agriculture.

agrietar (agrje'tar) *vt* **1** crack. **2** chap.

agrimensor (agrimen'sor) *nm* surveyor. **agrimensura** *nf* surveying.

agrio ('agrjo) *adj* **1** bitter, sour. **2** rough.

agrupar (agru'par) *vt* gather together. **agruparse** *vr* come together.

agua (a'gwa) *nf* water. **agua dulce** fresh water. **aguas abajo** downstream. **aguas arriba** upstream. **entre dos aguas** undecided, sitting on the fence.

aguacate (agwa'kate) *nm* avocado pear.

aguacero (agwa'θero) *nm* shower, downpour.

aguantar (agwan'tar) *vt* **1** tolerate, bear. **2** hold up. **aguante** *nm* tolerance, patience, fortitude.

aguar (a'gwar) *vt* **1** water down (wine, etc.). **2** spoil.

aguardar (agwar'ðar) *vt* **1** wait for. **2** expect.

aguardiente (agwar'ðjente) *nm* liquor.

aguarrás (agwar'ras) *nm invar* turpentine.

agudeza (agu'ðeθa) *nf* **1** sharpness. **2** keenness. **3** wit. **agudo** *adj* **1** sharp. **2** acute. **3** witty.

agüero (a'gwero) *nm* omen, sign.

aguijar (agi'xar) *vt* **1** goad. **2** urge, encourage. *vi* hurry.

aguijón (agi'xon) *nm* **1** goad. **2** sting.

águila ('agila) *nf* eagle.

aguinaldo (agi'naldo) *nm* Christmas present.

aguja (a'guxa) *nf* **1** needle. **2** hand (of a watch, etc.). **3** spire. **4** *pl* railway points.

agujero (agu'xero) *nm* hole.

aguzar (agu'θar) *vt* **1** sharpen. **2** encourage.

ahí (a'i) *adv* there. **de ahí** so, thus. **por ahí** over there, somewhere.

ahijada (ai'xaða) *nf* **1** goddaughter. **2** protégée. **ahijado** *nm* **1** godson. **2** protégé.

ahincar (ain'kar) *vt* urge. **ahincarse** *vr* hurry. **ahínco** *nm* effort.

ahogar (ao'gar) *vt* **1** drown. **2** suffocate. **3** stifle, repress. **ahogarse** *vr* drown.

ahora (a'ora) *adv* now. *conj* now then. **ahora mismo** at this very moment.

ahorcar (aor'kar) *vt* hang.

ahorrar (aor'rar) *vt* **1** save (money). **2** avoid (trouble). **ahorrativo** *adj* thrifty. **ahorro** *nm* economy, saving.

ahuecar (awe'kar) *vt* hollow.

ahumar (au'mar) *vt* **1** smoke (fish, etc.). **2** make smoky. *vi* give out smoke. **ahumarse** *vr* taste smoky.

ahuyentar (aujen'tar) *vt* **1** frighten off. **2** drive away. **ahuyentarse** *vr* flee.

aire ('aire) *nm* **1** air, atmosphere. **2** appearance. **3** jaunty bearing. **4** tune. **aire acondicionado** air conditioning. **airoso** *adj* **1** airy. **2** windy. **3** jaunty.

aislar (ai'slar) *vt* **1** isolate. **2** insulate. **aislación** *nf* insulation. **aislado** *adj* **1** isolated. **2** insulated. **aislamiento** *nm* **1** isolation. **2** insulation.

ajar (a'xar) *vt* crease, crumple.

ajedrez (axe'ðreθ) *nm* chess.

ajeno (a'xeno) *adj* **1** foreign, alien. **2** belonging to another.

ajo ('axo) *nm* **1** garlic. **2** *inf* shady business.

ajuar (a'xwar) *nm* dowry, trousseau.

ajustar (axus'tar) *vt* **1** adjust. **2** fit. **3** settle. **ajuste** *nm* **1** fitting. **2** adjustment.

ajusticiar (axusti'θjar) *vt* execute.

al (al) contraction of **a el**.

ala ('ala) *nf* **1** wing. **2** brim (of a hat).

alabar (ala'βar) *vt* praise. **alabarse** *vr* boast. **alabanza** *nf* praise.

alabastro (ala'βastro) *nm* alabaster.

alacena (ala'θena) *nm* larder.

alacrán (ala'kran) *nm* scorpion.

alacridad (alakri'ðað) *nf* alacrity, readiness.

alambicar (alambi'kar) *vt* **1** distil. **2** examine carefully. **alambique** *nm* still.

alambre (a'lambre) *nm* wire. **alambrada** *nf* barbed wire, wire fence.

alameda (ala'meða) *nf* **1** poplar grove. **2** tree-lined walk.

álamo ('alamo) *nm* poplar.

alarde (a'larðe) *nm* display, show. **alardeo** *nm* boasting.

alargar (alar'gar) *vt* **1** lengthen. **2** reach for.

hand. **3** make last. **4** stretch out. **alargarse** vr get longer.

alarido (ala'riðo) nm yell, shout.

alarmar (alar'mar) vt alarm. **alarma** nf alarm.

alba ('alβa) nf dawn.

albahaca (alβa'aka) nf basil.

albañil (alβa'ɲil) nm mason, bricklayer.

albaricoque (alβari'koke) nm apricot.

albatros (al'batros) nm albatross.

albedrío (elβe'ðrio) nm **1** free will. **2** whim.

albergar (alβer'gar) vt **1** shelter. **2** lodge. **albergue** nm **1** shelter. **2** lodging. **albergue para jóvenes** or **albergue juvenil** youth hostel.

albor (albor) nm dawn.

albornoz (albor'noθ) nm bathrobe.

alborotar (alβoro'tar) vt disturb, excite. vi make a noise. **alborotarse** vr become excited. **alboroto** nm disturbance, row, uproar.

alborozar (alβoro'θar) vt gladden. **alborozarse** vr rejoice.

álbum ('alβum) nm album.

alcachofa (alka'tʃofa) nf artichoke.

alcahuete (alka'wete) nm **1** go-between. **2** procurer.

alcalde (al'kalde) nm mayor.

alcance (al'kanθe) nm **1** reach. **2** range, scope. **3** chase. **4** intelligence. **al alcance** within reach.

alcantarilla (alkanta'riʎa) nf sewer, drain.

alcanzar (alkan'θar) vt **1** reach. **2** catch up. **3** obtain. **4** hit. **5** live in the time of. vi reach.

alcázar (al'kaθar) nm **1** castle. **2** fortress. **3** naut quarterdeck.

alcoba (al'koβa) nf **1** bedroom. **2** alcove.

alcohol (alko'ol) nm alcohol. **alcohólico** adj,n alcoholic.

alcornoque (alkor'noke) nm **1** cork tree. **2** inf idiot.

aldaba (al'ðaβa) nf **1** doorknocker. **2** bolt.

aldea (al'dea) nf village.

aleación (alea'θjon) nf alloy.

alegar (ale'gar) vt allege, state. **alegato** nm **1** allegation. **2** law plea.

alegoría (alego'ria) nf allegory. **alegórico** adj allegorical.

alegrar (ale'grar) vt **1** make happy. **2** excite, stir up. **alegrarse** vr **1** be happy. **2** inf get tight.

alegre (a'legre) adj happy, cheerful. **alegría** nf happiness, joy.

alejar (ale'xar) vt remove, move away. **alejarse** vr move away. **alejamiento** nm removal.

Alemania (ale'manja) nf Germany. **alemán** adj,nm German. nm German (language).

alentar (ie) (alen'tar) vi breathe. vt encourage. **alentarse** vr be encouraged. **alentado** adj **1** brave. **2** haughty.

alerce (a'lerθe) nm larch.

alergia (aler'xia) nf allergy. **alérgico** adj allergic.

alero (a'lero) nm eaves.

alerta (a'lerta) nm alert. adj watchful. interj look out!

aleta (a'leta) nf **1** small wing. **2** zool fin.

aleve (a'leβe) adj treacherous. **alevosía** nf treachery. **alevoso** adj treacherous.

alfabeto (alfa'βeto) nm alphabet. **alfabeto morse** morse code. **alfabético** adj alphabetical.

alfarero (alfa'rero) nm potter. **alfarería** nf pottery.

alféizar (al'feiθar) nm window ledge.

alférez (al'fereθ) nm mil second lieutenant

alfil (al'fil) nm game bishop.

alfiler (alfi'ler) nm **1** pin. **2** brooch.

alfombra (al'fombra) nf carpet.

alforja (al'forxa) nf **1** saddle bag. **2** rucksack.

alga ('alga) nf seaweed.

algarabía (algara'βia) nf **1** Arabic. **2** din, garbled noise.

algazara (alga'θara) nf hubbub, clamour.

álgebra ('alxebra) nf algebra.

álgido ('alxiðo) adj **1** icy cold. **2** culminating (point).

algo ('algo) pron something. adv rather, a bit.

algodón (algo'ðon) nm cotton. **algodón hidrófilo** cotton wool.

alguacil (algwa'θil) nm bailiff.

alguien (al'gjen) pron someone, somebody.

alguno (al'guno) adj some, any. pron **1** some. **2** someone, somebody. **3** pl a few, some.

alhaja (a'laxa) nf **1** jewel. **2** treasure.

alhelí (ale'li) nm wallflower.

aliar (ali'ar) vt ally. **aliado** adj allied. nm ally. **alianza** nf alliance.

alicates (ali'kates) nm pl pliers.

alienar (alje'nar) vt **1** law transfer property. **2** alienate. **alienación** nf alienation. **alienado** adj insane.

aliento (a'ljento) nm **1** breath. **2** spirit, courage.

aligerar (alixe'rar) vt **1** lighten. **2** shorten.

alimentar (alimen'tar) vt **1** feed. **2** encourage. **alimentación** nf feeding, food. **alimenticio** adj nourishing. **alimento** nm food.

7

aliñar (ali'ɲar) vt 1 adorn. 2 cul prepare, season. **aliño** nm cul condiment.

alinear (aline'ar) vt line up.

alisar (ali'θar) vt smooth down, polish. **alisador** nm 1 polisher (person). 2 smoothing tool.

alistar (alis'tar) vt 1 list. 2 mil enlist. 3 prepare.

aliviar (ali'βjar) vt 1 lighten, relieve. 2 quicken. **alivio** nm 1 relief. 2 ease.

alma ('alma) nf 1 soul, spirit. 2 person. **con el alma en la boca** scared to death.

almacén (alma'θen) nm 1 warehouse. 2 store, shop. 3 pl department store. **almacenaje** nm storage. **almacenista** nm wholesaler.

almanaque (alma'nake) nm almanac.

almeja (al'mexa) nf clam.

almendra (al'mendra) nf almond. **almendro** nm almond tree.

almiar (al'mjar) nm haystack.

almíbar (al'miβar) nm syrup.

almidón (almi'ðon) nm starch. **almidonar** vt starch.

almirante (almi'rante) nm admiral. **almirantazgo** nm admiralty.

almohada (almo'aða) nf pillow, cushion.

almorzar (**ue**) (almor'θar) vi lunch.

almuerzo (al'mwerθo) nm lunch, snack.

alojar (alo'xar) vt lodge. **alojarse** vr lodge, stay. **alojamiento** nm lodging(s).

alondra (a'londra) nf lark.

Alpes ('alpes) nm pl Alps.

alpinista (alpi'nista) nm,f sport mountaineer. **alpinismo** nm mountaineering.

alquilar (alki'lar) vt 1 rent. 2 let. 3 hire. **se alquila** to let, for hire. **alquiler** nm 1 letting. 2 hire. 3 rent.

alquimia (al'kimja) nf alchemy. **alquimista** nm alchemist.

alquitrán (alki'tran) nm tar. **alquitranado** adj tarred. nm tarmac.

alrededor (alreðe'ðor) adv around. **alrededor de** prep around, about. **alrededores** nm pl 1 surroundings. 2 outskirts.

altar (al'tar) nm altar.

altavoz (alta'βoθ) nm loudspeaker.

alterar (alte'rar) vt change, alter. **alterarse** vr 1 get upset. 2 get angry. **alteración** nf 1 alteration. 2 disturbance.

altercar (alter'kar) vi argue, quarrel.

alternar (alter'nar) vt,vi alternate. vi be sociable, get around. **alterno** adj.

alternativa (alterna'tiβa) nf alternative, choice. **tomar la alternativa** go through a ceremony

to become a fully qualified bullfighter. **alternativo** adj 1 alternative. 2 alternate.

alteza (al'teθa) nf 1 height. 2 highness (title).

altibajos (alti'βaxos) nm pl ups and downs.

altisonante (altiso'nante) adj 1 pretentious. 2 pompous.

altitud (alti'tuð) nf 1 height. 2 geog altitude.

altivez (alti'βeθ) nf arrogance. **altivo** adj arrogant.

alto¹ ('alto) adj 1 high. 2 tall. 3 loud. adv 1 high (up). 2 loudly. nm 1 height. 2 hill. 3 upper floor (of a building). 4 mus alto. **las altas horas** the small hours. **altura** nf 1 height. 2 top.

alto² ('alto) nm, interj mil halt. **hacer alto** stop.

alubia (a'luβja) nf French bean, kidney bean.

alucinación (aluθina'θjon) nf hallucination.

alud (a'luð) nm avalanche.

aludir (alu'ðir) vi mention, refer.

alumbrar (alum'brar) vt illuminate, light up. vi 1 give light. 2 have a baby. **alumbrado** nm lighting. **alumbramiento** nm 1 lighting. 2 childbirth.

aluminio (alu'minjo) nm aluminium.

alumno (a'lumno) nm 1 pupil. 2 law ward.

alusión (alu'sjon) nf allusion.

alzar (al'θar) vt 1 raise, lift. 2 hoist. **alzarse** vr get up, rise. **alza** nf rise (in price, etc.). **alzada** nf 1 height (of a horse). 2 law appeal. **alzado** adj 1 raised. 2 (of a price) fixed. **alzamiento** nm raising, rise.

allá (a'ʎa) adv there. **más allá** further on, beyond.

allanar (aʎa'nar) vt 1 level, flatten. 2 smooth away (a difficulty, etc.). 3 break into (a house, etc.). **allanarse** vr 1 level off. 2 collapse. 3 submit, give way.

allegado (aʎe'gaðo) adj near, close. nm relative.

allegar (aʎe'gar) vt 1 gather. 2 draw near. **allegarse** vr approach, arrive.

allende (a'ʎende) adv beyond.

allí (a'ʎi) adv there. **por allí** over there, that way.

ama ('ama) nf mistress of the house.

amabilidad (amabili'ðað) nf kindness. **amable** adj kind. **amador** (ama'ðor) adj loving, fond of.

amaestrar (amaes'trar) vt 1 train. 2 tame.

amainar (amai'nar) vi lessen, moderate.

amalgamar (amalga'mar) vt 1 amalgamate. 2 mix. **amalgamación** nf amalgamation.

amanecer* (amane'θer) vi dawn. nm dawn, daybreak.

anca

amansar (aman'sar) *vt* **1** tame. **2** appease.
amante (a'mante) *nm* lover. *nf* mistress. *adj* loving.
amapola (ama'pola) *nf* poppy.
amar (a'mar) *vt* love.
amargar (amar'gar) *vt* **1** embitter. **2** make sour. *vi* be or taste bitter. **amargo** *adj* **1** bitter. **2** tart. **amargor** *nm also* **amargura** *nf* bitterness.
amarillo (ama'riʎo) *adj* yellow.
amarrar (amar'rar) *vt* fasten, moor. **amarradero** *nm* moorings. **amarre** *nm* fastening.
amartillar (amarti'ʎar) *vt* hammer.
amasar (ama'sar) *vt* **1** knead. **2** prepare. **amasador** *nm* baker. **amasijo** *nm* **1** kneading. **2** mixture, hotchpotch. **3** plot, scheme.
ámbar ('ambar) *nm* amber.
ambición (ambi'θjon) *nf* ambition. **ambicioso** *adj* ambitious.
ambiente (am'bjente) *nm* **1** atmosphere. **2** environment. *adj* surrounding.
ambiguo (am'bigwo) *adj* ambiguous. **ambigüedad** *nf* ambiguity.
ámbito ('ambito) *nm* **1** boundary. **2** sphere, range.
ambos ('ambos) *adj,pron* both.
ambulancia (ambu'lanθja) *nf* ambulance.
ambulante (ambu'lante) *adj* itinerant, travelling.
amedrentar (ameðren'tar) *vt* frighten.
amenazar (amena'θar) *vt,vi* threaten. **amenaza** *nf* threat. **amenazador** *adj* threatening.
amenguar (amen'gwar) *vt* **1** lessen. **2** dishonour.
amenizar (ameni'θar) *vt* make pleasant.
ameno (a'meno) *adj* pleasant, agreeable.
América (a'merika) *nf* America. **América del Norte/Sur** North/South America. **América Latina** Latin America. **americano** *adj,n* American.
ametralladora (ametraʎa'ðora) *nf* machine gun.
amiba (a'miba) *nf* amoeba.
amígdala (a'migðala) *nf* tonsil. **amigdalitis** *nf* tonsillitis.
amigo (a'migo) *nm* **1** friend. **2** boyfriend. **amigo por correspondencia** *nm* penfriend. *adj* friendly.
amilanar (amila'nar) *vt* terrify, scare.
aminorar (amino'rar) *vt* lessen, reduce.
amistad (amis'tað) *nf* **1** friendship. **2** *pl* friends.
amnesia (am'nesja) *nf* amnesia. **amnesia temporal** *nf med* blackout.

amnistía (amnis'tia) *nf* amnesty.
amo ('amo) *nm* **1** master. **2** owner. **3** *inf* boss.
amodorrarse (amoðo'rarse) *vr* become drowsy.
amolar (ue) (amo'lar) *vt* **1** grind, sharpen. **2** annoy.
amoldar (amol'dar) *vt* **1** mould. **2** adapt.
amonestar (amones'tar) *vt* **1** warn. **2** advise. **amonestación** *nf* **1** warning. **2** marriage banns.
amontonar (amonto'nar) *vt* **1** pile up. **2** accumulate. **amontonamiento** *nm* accumulation, piling up.
amor (a'mor) *nm* **1** love. **2** lover.
amoral (amo'ral) *adj* amoral.
amordazar (amorða'θar) *vt* **1** muzzle. **2** gag.
amorfo (a'morfo) *adj* shapeless, amorphous.
amoroso (amo'roso) *adj* **1** loving. **2** gentle.
amortiguar (amorti'gwar) *vt* **1** soften. **2** deaden. **3** moderate. **amortiguador** *nm* shock absorber.
amortizar (amorti'θar) *vt* **1** amortize. **2** redeem, recover.
amotinar (amoti'nar) *vt* incite, stir up. **amotinarse** *vr* mutiny.
amparar (ampa'rar) *vt* **1** shelter. **2** protect. **ampararse** *vr* take shelter. **amparo** *nm* shelter, refuge.
ampliar (am'pljar) *vt* **1** enlarge, extend. **2** amplify. **ampliación** *nf phot* enlargement. **amplio** *adj* **1** wide. **2** roomy.
amplificar (amplifi'kar) *vt* amplify. **amplificador** *nm* amplifier.
ampolla (am'poʎa) *nf* **1** bubble. **2** *med* blister. **3** *med* phial.
amputar (ampu'tar) *vt* amputate. **amputación** *nf* amputation.
amueblar (amwe'βlar) *vt* furnish.
anacronismo *nm* anachronism.
anagrama (ana'grama) *nm* anagram.
anales (a'nales) *nm pl* annals.
analfabeto (analfa'βeto) *adj* illiterate. **analfabetismo** *nm* illiteracy.
análisis (a'nalisis) *nm invar* analysis. **analítico** *adj* analytic(al).
analizar (anali'θar) *vt* analyse. **analizador** *nm* analyst.
analogía (analo'xia) *nf* analogy.
ananás (ana'nas) *nm* pineapple.
anaquel (ana'kel) *nm* shelf.
anarquía (anar'kia) *nf* anarchy. **anarquista** *nm, f* anarchist.
anatomía (anato'mia) *nf* anatomy.
anca ('anka) *nf* rump, haunch.

9

anciano (an'θjano) adj old. nm old man. **ancianidad** nf old age.

ancla ('ankla) nf anchor. **anclar** vi drop anchor.

ancho ('antʃo) adj wide, broad. nm width. **a sus anchas** at one's ease. **anchura** nf 1 width. 2 freedom. **anchuroso** adj wide, spacious.

anchoa (an'tʃoa) nf anchovy.

andadas (an'daðas) nf pl tracks, trail. **volver a las andadas** go back to one's old ways.

Andalucía (andalu'θia) nf Andalusia. **andaluz** adj,n Andalusian.

andamio (an'damjo) nm 1 scaffold, platform. 2 scaffolding.

andar* (an'dar) vi 1 walk, move. 2 (of a machine, etc.) work, go. **¡anda!** go on! get along! **andar en 1** be engaged in. 2 tamper with. nm walk, gait.

andas ('andas) nf pl portable platform.

andén (an'den) nm railway platform.

Andorra (an'dorra) nf Andorra. **andorrano** adj,n Andorran.

andrajo (an'draxo) nm rag. **andrajoso** adj tattered, ragged.

anduve (an'duβe) v see **andar.**

anécdota (a'nekðota) nf anecdote.

anegar (ane'gar) vt 1 drown. 2 flood. **anegarse** vr be drowned. **anegación** nf 1 drowning. 2 flooding.

anejo (a'nexo) adj attached, joining.

anemia (a'nemja) nf anaemia. **anémico** adj anaemic.

anestésico (anes'tesiko) adj,nm anaesthetic. **anestesista** nm,f anaesthetist.

anexar (anek'sar) vt annex.

anfibio (an'fiβjo) adj amphibious. nm amphibian.

anfiteatro (anfite'atro) nm amphitheatre.

anfitrión (anfitri'on) nm host.

ángel ('anxel) nm angel. **angelical** adj also **angélico** angelic.

anglicano (angli'kano) adj,n Anglican.

angosto (an'gosto) adj narrow. **angostura** nf narrowness.

anguila (an'gila) nf eel.

ángulo ('angulo) nm 1 angle. 2 bend. **anguloso** adj angular.

angustiar (angus'tjar) vt 1 grieve. 2 distress. **angustia** nf anguish.

anhelar (ane'lar) vi 1 med pant, gasp. 2 be eager to. vt desire. **anhelo** nm desire.

anidar (ani'ðar) vi (of birds) nest. vt shelter.

anillo (a'niʎo) nm ring. **anillo de boda** wedding ring.

ánima ('anima) nf soul.

animal (ani'mal) nm animal, beast. adj animal.

animar (ani'mar) vt enliven, encourage. **animarse** vr cheer up. **animado** adj lively.

ánimo ('animo) nm 1 soul, spirit. 2 courage. 3 intention. **¡ánimo!** courage! come on!

animoso (ani'moso) adj lively, spirited, courageous.

aniquilar (aniki'lar) vt annihilate, destroy.

anís (a'nis) nm aniseed.

aniversario (aniβer'sarjo) nm anniversary.

ano ('ano) nm anus.

anoche (a'notʃe) adv last night.

anochecer* (anotʃe'θer) vi grow dark. nm nightfall.

anomalía (anoma'lia) nf anomaly.

anónimo (a'nonimo) adj anonymous. nm unknown person.

anormal (anor'mal) adj abnormal.

anotar (ano'tar) vt note down.

ansiar (an'sjar) vt long for, desire. **ansia** nf 1 anxiety. 2 desire. **ansiedad** nf worry, anxiety.

antagonismo (antago'nismo) nm antagonism. **antagonista** nm,f opponent.

antaño (an'taɲo) adv 1 last year. 2 formerly.

antártico (an'tartiko) adj Antarctic. nm Antarctic.

ante[1] ('ante) prep before, in the presence of.

ante[2] ('ante) nm suede.

anteayer (antea'jer) adv the day before yesterday.

antecedente (anteθe'ðente) nm antecedent. adj preceding.

antecesor (anteθe'sor) adj former. nm predecessor.

antelación (antela'θjon) nf precedence. **con antelación** in advance.

antemano (ante'mano) adv **de antemano** in advance, beforehand.

antena (an'tena) nf 1 antenna. 2 aerial.

antenatal (antena'tal) adj antenatal.

anteojo (ante'oxo) nm 1 small telescope. 2 pl spectacles, glasses.

antepasado (antepa'saðo) nm ancestor. adj previous.

antepecho (ante'petʃo) nm 1 parapet. 2 window sill.

anteponer* (antepo'ner) vt 1 put in front. 2 prefer.

anterior (ante'rjor) adj 1 former, preceding. 2 fore, front.

antes ('antes) adv 1 before, formerly. 2 rather, sooner. **antes de** prep before. **cuanto antes** as soon as possible.

antiaéreo (antja'ereo) adj anti-aircraft.

antibiótico (anti'bjotiko) adj,nm antibiotic.

anticiclón (antiθi'klon) nm anticyclone.

anticipar (antiθi'par) vt bring forward, advance. **anticiparse** vr 1 happen early. 2 anticipate. **anticipación** nf 1 anticipation. 2 foretaste. **anticipado** adj premature. **anticipo** nm 1 foretaste. 2 comm advance.

anticoncepcional (antikonθepθjo'nal) adj birth-control.

anticonceptivo (antikonθep'tivo) adj,nm contraceptive.

anticuado (anti'kwaðo) adj old-fashioned.

antídoto (an'tiðoto) nm antidote.

antiguo (an'tigwo) adj 1 old, ancient. 2 former. 3 senior. nm pl ancients. **antigüedad** nf 1 antiquity. 2 antique.

antílope (an'tilope) nm antelope.

Antillas (an'tiʎas) nf pl West Indies.

antipatía (antipa'tia) nf dislike. **antipático** adj disagreeable, unpleasant.

antisemítico (antise'mitiko) adj anti-Semitic.

antiséptico (anti'septiko) adj,nm antiseptic.

antisocial (anti'soθjal) adj antisocial.

antítesis (an'titesis) nf invar antithesis.

antojarse (anto'xarse) vr want, take a fancy to.

antojo (an'toxo) nm 1 whim. 2 anat birthmark. 3 pl cravings.

antología (antolo'xia) nf anthology.

antorcha (an'tortʃa) nf torch.

antro ('antro) nm 1 cave. 2 den.

antropófago (antro'pofago) adj,nm cannibal.

antropología (antropolo'xia) nf anthropology. **antropólogo** nm anthropologist.

anual (a'nwal) adj yearly, annual. **anualidad** nm annuity. **anuario** nm yearbook.

anublar (anu'βlar) vt 1 cloud over. 2 obscure. **anublarse** vr cloud over, darken.

anudar (anu'ðar) vt 1 knot. 2 join.

anular (anu'lar) vt cancel. **anulación** nf cancellation.

anunciar (anun'θjar) vt announce, proclaim. **anunciador** nm announcer. **anuncio** nm announcement, advertisement.

anzuelo (an'θwelo) nm 1 (fish) hook. 2 bait.

añadir (aɲa'ðir) vt add. **añadidura** nf addition.

añejo (a'ɲexo) adj very old.

añicos (a'ɲikos) nm pl bits, fragments.

año ('aɲo) nm year. **tener...años** be...years old.

añorar (aɲo'rar) vt long for. vi be homesick.

añoranza nf 1 homesickness, nostalgia. 2 longing.

apacentar (ie) (apaθen'tar) vt graze.

apacible (apa'θiβle) adj 1 gentle. 2 peaceful.

apaciguar (apaθi'gwar) vt pacify, calm.

apagar (apa'gar) vt 1 put out, extinguish. 2 switch off. **apagado** adj 1 extinguished. 2 dull, lifeless. 3 muffled. **apagón** nm blackout, power cut.

apalear (apale'ar) vt beat, thrash.

apañado (apa'ɲaðo) adj skilful, clever.

aparador (apara'ðor) nm sideboard.

aparato (apa'rato) nm 1 machine. 2 apparatus. 3 show, display. **aparatoso** adj showy.

aparecer (apare'θer) vi appear. **aparecido** nm ghost.

aparejar (apare'xar) vt 1 prepare. 2 saddle (a horse). **aparejador** nm foreman. **aparejo** nm 1 preparation. 2 gear, equipment. 3 harness.

aparentar (aparen'tar) vt pretend, feign.

aparente (apa'rente) adj 1 apparent, seeming. 2 visible, evident.

aparición (apari'θjon) nf 1 appearance. 2 publication. 3 apparition.

apariencia (apari'enθja) nf 1 appearance, look(s). 2 probability.

apartado (apar'taðo) adj separated, distant. nm 1 post-office box. 2 spare room. 3 paragraph. 4 box number.

apartamento (aparta'mento) nm apartment, flat.

apartar (apar'tar) vt 1 separate. 2 remove. **apartarse** vr 1 separate. 2 move away. **apartamiento** nm 1 separation. 2 isolation. **aparte** adv aside, separately. nm 1 aside. 2 (new) paragraph. **aparte de** prep apart from.

apasionar (apasjo'nar) vt 1 stir, rouse deeply. **apasionarse** vr get excited or worked up. **apasionado** adj 1 passionate. 2 enthusiastic. **apasionamiento** nm passion.

apatía (apa'tia) nf apathy. **apático** adj apathetic.

apear (ape'ar) vt get down. **apearse** vr dismount, get down.

apedrear (apeðre'ar) vt stone. vi hail. **apedreamiento** nm 1 stoning. 2 hail.

apelar (ape'lar) vi 1 law appeal. **apelación** nf appeal.

apellido (ape'ʎiðo) nm 1 surname. 2 nickname. **apellido de soltera** maiden name.

apenar (ape'nar) vt 1 grieve. 2 cause pain.

apenas (a'penas) adv scarcely, hardly.

apéndice (a'pendiθe) nm appendix. **apendicitis** nf appendicitis.

apercibir (aperθi'βir) vt 1 prepare. 2 warn. 3 notice, observe.

aperitivo (aperi'tiβo) nm aperitif.

apero (a'pero) nm 1 equipment. 2 tools.

apertura (aper'tura) nf opening.

apestar (apes'tar) vt 1 med infect. 2 inf annoy. vi stink.

apetecer* (apete'θer) vt long for. vi attract, have appeal. **apetecible** adj attractive.

apetito (ape'tito) nm 1 appetite. 2 desire.

ápice ('apiθe) nm apex, summit.

apiñar (api'ñar) vt group together. **apiñarse** vr crowd together.

apio ('apjo) nm celery.

apisonadora (apisona'ðora) nm steam-roller.

apisonar (apiso'nar) vt roll (flat).

aplacar (apla'kar) vt placate, calm.

aplanar (apla'nar) vt flatten, make even.

aplastar (aplas'tar) vt crush, flatten.

aplaudir (aplau'ðir) vt applaud, clap. **aplauso** nm applause.

aplazar (apla'θar) vt 1 postpone. 2 summon (a meeting, etc.). **aplazamiento** nm 1 postponement. 2 summons.

aplicar (apli'kar) vt apply. **aplicarse** vr 1 be applicable. 2 apply oneself. **aplicación** nf application.

aplomo (a'plomo) nm self-possession, assurance.

apocar (apo'kar) vt make smaller, reduce.

apodar (apo'ðar) vt nickname. **apodo** nm nickname.

apoderar (apoðe'rar) vt authorize. **apoderarse de** vr take possession of.

apogeo (apo'xeo) nm peak, summit.

apolillarse (apoli'ʎarse) vr be moth-eaten.

apoplejía (aople'xia) nf apoplexy.

aportar (apor'tar) vt 1 bring, contribute. 2 cause.

aposentar (aposen'tar) vt lodge. **aposento** nm lodging.

apostar (ue) (apos'tar) vt,vi bet.

apóstol (a'postol) nm apostle.

apóstrofo (a'postrofo) nm gram apostrophe.

apoyar (apo'jar) vt support. **apoyar en** vi lean against, rest on. **apoyarse en** vr lean on, be supported by. **apoyo** nm support.

apreciar (apre'θjar) vt 1 appreciate. 2 value. **apreciación** nf appreciation, appraisal. **aprecio** nm 1 comm estimate. 2 esteem, appreciation.

aprehender (apreen'der) vt 1 seize. 2 understand. **aprehensible** adj understandable.

apremiar (apre'mjar) vt 1 urge, press. 2 force. **apremio** nm 1 pressure. 2 law summons.

aprender (apren'der) vt learn. **aprendiz** nm 1 novice. 2 apprentice. **aprendizaje** nm apprenticeship.

aprensión (apren'sjon) nf apprehension, nervousness. **aprensivo** adj 1 apprehensive, worried. 2 nervous.

apresar (apre'sar) vt seize, capture.

aprestar (apres'tar) vt 1 prepare. 2 size. **apresto** nm 1 preparation. 2 sizing.

apresurar (apresu'rar) vt hurry.

apretar (ie) (apre'tar) vt 1 tighten. 2 squeeze in. 3 worry, annoy. 4 grit (the teeth). vi 1 get worse. 2 be too tight. **apretarse** vr squeeze together. **apretado** adj 1 difficult, dangerous. 2 mean. ¡**aprieta**! interj nonsense!

aprieto (a'prjeto) nm 1 squeeze, press, crush. 2 difficulty.

aprisa (a'prisa) adv quickly.

aprisionar (aprisjo'nar) vt imprison.

aprobar (ue) (apro'βar) vt 1 approve. 2 pass (an exam). **aprobación** nf 1 approval. 2 pass (in an exam). **aprobado** adj approved. nm pass mark or certificate.

apropiar (apro'pjar) vt adapt, make suitable. **apropiarse** vr appropriate. **apropiado** adj appropriate, suitable.

aprovechar (aproβe'tʃar) vt profit by, use. vi 1 be useful. 2 progress. **aprovecharse** vr take advantage of, profit by, use. **aprovechado** adj 1 diligent. 2 economical. 3 unscrupulous. **aprovechamiento** nm use, exploitation.

aproximar (aproksi'mar) vt bring nearer. **aproximarse a** vr approach. **aproximación** nf 1 approximation. 2 nearness. **aproximado** adj approximate.

aptitud (apti'tuð) nf aptitude. **apto** adj suitable, fitting.

apuesta (a'pwesta) nf bet.

apuntar (apun'tar) vt 1 point. 2 note. 3 sharpen. 4 Th prompt. vi begin to appear. **apuntado** adj pointed. **apunte** nm 1 note. 2 prompter. 2 cue.

apurar (apu'rar) vt 1 tech purify. 2 drain, drink up. 3 examine carefully. 4 annoy. **apurarse** vr worry. **apuro** nm 1 hardship. 2 difficulty.

aquejar (ake'xar) vt med afflict.

aquel, aquella (a'kel, a'keʎa) adj 1 that. 2 pl those. **aquél, aquélla** pron 1 that. 2 the one. 3 the former. 4 pl those. nm inf charm.

aquí (a'ki) adv here. **de aquí en adelante** from now on. **de aquí** hence. **por aquí** this way.

aquietar (akje'tar) vt quieten, calm.

aquilatar (akila'tar) vt test, examine closely.

Arabia (a'raβja) nf Arabia. **Arabia Saudita** Saudi Arabia. **árabe** adj Arab, Arabic. nm,f Arab. nm Arabic (language). **arábigo** adj Arab, Arabic.

arado (a'raðo) nm plough.

arancel (aran'θel) nm tax, tariff.

araña (a'raɲa) nf spider. **araña de luces** chandelier.

arañar (ara'ɲar) vt scratch. **arañazo** nm scratch.

arar (a'rar) vt plough.

arbitrar (arβi'trar) vt,vi 1 arbitrate, judge. 2 referee. **arbitraje** nm arbitration. **arbitrario** adj arbitrary.

arbitrio (ar'βitrjo) nm 1 free will. 2 means. 3 law decision. 4 pl taxes.

árbitro ('arβitro) nm referee, umpire.

árbol ('arβol) nm 1 tree. 2 shaft, axle. 3 naut mast. **árbol de Navidad** Christmas tree. **arboleda** nf grove.

arbusto (ar'βusto) nm bush.

arca ('arka) nf box, chest.

arcada (ar'kaða) nf 1 arcade. 2 pl nausea.

arcaico (ar'kaiko) adj archaic.

arce ('arθe) nm maple.

arcilla (ar'θiʎa) nf clay.

arco ('arko) nm 1 arch, archway. 2 arc. 3 bow. **arco iris** rainbow.

archiduque (artʃi'ðuke) nm archduke. **archiduquesa** nf archduchess.

archipiélago (artʃi'pjelago) nm archipelago.

archivo (ar'tʃiβo) nm archives, records.

arder (ar'ðer) vt,vi burn.

ardid (ar'ðið) nm trick, crafty plan.

ardiente (ar'ðjente) adj 1 burning. 2 ardent, passionate.

ardilla (ar'ðiʎa) nf squirrel.

ardor (ar'ðor) nm 1 ardour. 2 heat, warmth. **ardoroso** adj 1 hot. 2 fiery.

arduo ('arðwo) adj hard, arduous.

área ('area) nf area.

arena (a'rena) nf 1 sand. 2 arena. **arena movediza** quicksand. **arenal** nm sandy ground.

arengar (aren'gar) vt harangue.

arenque (a'renke) nm herring.

argamasa (arga'masa) nf 1 plaster. 2 mortar.

Argelia (ar'xelja) nf Algeria. **argelino** adj,n Algerian.

Argentina (arxen'tina) nf Argentina. **argentino** adj,n Argentinian.

argolla (ar'goʎa) nf 1 large metal ring. 2 doorknocker.

argüir (ar'gwir) vt 1 deduce. 2 indicate. 3 reproach. vi argue.

argumento (argu'mento) nm 1 argument. 2 Th plot. **argumentador** adj argumentative.

aridez (ari'ðeθ) nf 1 dryness. 2 barrenness, sterility. **árido** adj dry, arid.

arisco (a'risko) adj 1 shy. 2 unsociable. 3 wild.

aristocracia (aristo'kraθja) nf aristocracy. **aristócrata** nm,f aristocrat. **aristocrático** adj aristocratic.

aritmética (arit'metika) nf arithmetic.

armar (ar'mar) vt 1 arm, equip. 2 prepare. 3 cause. **armarse** vr 1 arm oneself. 2 prepare oneself. **arma** nf 1 arm, weapon. **armada** nf 1 fleet. 2 navy. **armado** adj armed. **armadura** nf 1 armour. 2 framework. **armamento** nm armament.

armario (ar'marjo) nm 1 cupboard. 2 wardrobe.

armazón (arma'θon) nf 1 frame(work). 2 tech skeleton.

armisticio (armis'tiθjo) nm armistice.

armonía (armo'nia) nf harmony. **armónico** adj harmonic, harmonious. **armonioso** adj harmonious.

armónica (ar'monika) nf harmonica.

aro ('aro) nm 1 hoop. 2 ring. 3 rim.

arpa ('arpa) nf harp. **arpicordio** nm harpsichord.

arpón (ar'pon) nm harpoon.

arquear (arke'ar) vt arch, bend. **arqueo** nm bending, arching.

arqueología (arkeolo'xia) nf archaeology. **arqueológico** adj archaeological. **arqueólogo** nm archaeologist.

arquero (ar'kero) nm archer.

arquetipo (arke'tipo) nm archetype.

arquitectura (arkitek'tura) nf architecture. **arquitecto** nm architect.

arrabal (arra'βal) nm 1 suburb. 2 pl outskirts.

arraigar (arrai'gar) vi take root, become established.

arrancar (arran'kar) vt 1 pull up, extract. 2 tear or snatch away. vi start, set off.

arranque (ar'ranke) nm 1 jerk, wrench. 2 mech start. 3 outburst.

arrasar (arra'sar) vt 1 demolish, flatten. 2 fill to the top. vi (of weather) clear up.

arrastrar (arras'trar) vt 1 drag. 2 carry along. **arrastrarse** vr creep, crawl. **arrastre** nm 1 dragging. 2 haulage.

arrebatar

arrebatar (arreβa'tar) *vt* 1 snatch. 2 charm. 3 move deeply. **arrebatarse** *vr* get carried away. **arrebatamiento** *nm* 1 seizure. 2 rapture. **arrebato** *nm* 1 fit of rage. 2 ecstasy.

arrebujarse (arreβu'xarse) *vr* wrap oneself up.

arreciar (arre'θjar) *vi* 1 grow worse. 2 increase in intensity. **arreciarse** *vr* grow stronger.

arrecife (arre'θife) *nm* 1 reef. 2 causeway.

arreglar (arre'glar) *vt* 1 arrange. 2 mend, put right. 3 smarten up, tidy. **arreglarse** *vr* 1 come to terms. 2 work out. **arreglo** *nm* 1 arrangement. 2 rule, order.

arremeter (arreme'ter) *vt,vi* attack.

arrendar (ie) (arren'dar) *vt* 1 let. 2 rent. **arrendador** *nm* 1 landlord. 2 tenant. **arrendamiento** *nm* 1 letting. 2 rent.

arreos (ar'reos) *nm pl* 1 trappings, adornment. 2 equipment.

arrepentirse (ie) (arrepen'tirse) *vr* repent. **arrepentimiento** *nm* repentance.

arrestar (arres'tar) *vt* arrest. **arresto** *nm* 1 arrest. 2 boldness.

arriba (ar'riβa) *adv* 1 above, overhead. 2 up, upwards. 3 upstairs. **de arriba abajo** from head to foot. **arriba de** *prep* above. ¡arriba! *interj* long live! up with!

arribar (arri'βar) *vi* arrive. **arribar a** reach.

arriendo (ar'rjendo) *nm* 1 letting. 2 rent.

arriesgar (arrjes'gar) *vt* 1 risk. 2 endanger.

arrimar (arri'mar) *vt* draw or bring near. **arrimarse** *vr* 1 come close. 2 lean on. **arrimo** *nm* support.

arrinconar (arrinko'nar) *vt* 1 lay aside. 2 corner. **arrinconarse** *vr* withdraw.

arrobamiento (arroβa'mjento) *nm* rapture, trance.

arrodillarse (arroði'λarse) *vr* kneel (down).

arrogancia (arro'ganθja) *nf* arrogance. **arrogante** *adj* arrogant, proud.

arrojar (arro'xar) *vt* 1 throw. 2 give out, emit. **arrojarse** *vr* hurl oneself. **arrojo** *nm* daring.

arrollar (arro'λar) *vt* 1 roll (up). 2 sweep away. 3 overwhelm.

arropar (arro'par) *vt* 1 cover. 2 wrap up. 3 tuck up (in bed).

arrostrar (arros'trar) *vt* confront, face up to.

arroyo (ar'rojo) *nm* 1 stream. 2 gutter.

arroz (ar'roθ) *nm* rice.

arrugar (arru'gar) *vt* 1 wrinkle. 2 crease, crumple. **arruga** *nf* 1 wrinkle. 2 crease.

arruinar (arrui'nar) *vt* spoil, ruin.

arrullar (arru'λar) *vt* lull to sleep. *vi* coo.

arrurruz (arrur'ruθ) *nm* arrowroot.

14

arsénico (ar'seniko) *nm* arsenic.

arte ('arte) *nm,f* 1 art. 2 craft, skill. 3 workmanship. **no tener arte ni parte en** have nothing at all to do with.

artefacto (arte'fakto) *nm* 1 appliance. 2 artefact.

arteria (arte'ria) *nf* artery.

artesano (arte'sano) *nm* craftsman. **artesanía** *nf* craftsmanship.

Artico ('artiko) *nm* Arctic. **ártico** *adj* arctic.

articular (artiku'lar) *vt* 1 articulate. 2 join up. **articulación** *nf* 1 articulation. 2 joint.

artículo (ar'tikulo) *nm* 1 article, report. 2 thing, commodity. 3 *pl* goods.

artificial (artifi'θjal) *adj* artificial.

artificio (arti'fiθijo) *nm* 1 art, craft. 2 appliance. 3 trick, cunning.

artillería (artiλe'ria) *nf* artillery.

artimaña (arti'maɲa) *nf* trick, trap.

artista (ar'tista) *nm,f* artist. **artístico** *adj* artistic.

artritis (ar'tritis) *nf* arthritis.

arzobispo (arθo'βispo) *nm* archbishop. **arzobispado** *nm* archbishopric.

as (as) *nm* ace.

asa ('asa) *nf* handle.

asado (a'saðo) *adj* roast(ed). **poco asado** underdone. *nm* roast (of meat). **asador** *nm cul* spit.

asalariado (asala'rjaðo) *adj* paid, wage-earning. *nm* wage-earner.

asaltar (asal'tar) *vt* 1 attack, storm. 2 (of an idea) come suddenly. **asalto** *nm* 1 attack. 2 *sport* round.

asamblea (asam'blea) *nf* assembly, meeting.

asar (a'sar) *vt* 1 roast. 2 *inf* pester.

asbesto (as'βesto) *nm* asbestos.

ascendencia (asθen'denθja) *nf* ancestry, origin.

ascender (ie) (asθen'der) *vi* 1 ascend. 2 be promoted. *vt* promote. **ascendiente** *nm,f* ancestor. *nm* influence.

ascensión (asθen'sjon) *nf* 1 ascent. 2 promotion. **ascenso** *nm* promotion.

ascensor (asθen'sor) *nm* lift, elevator.

asco ('asko) *nm* 1 disgust. 2 loathing. **dar asco (a)** disgust, sicken.

ascua ('askwa) *nf* ember. **estar en ascuas** be on tenterhooks.

asear (ase'ar) *vt* 1 adorn. 2 tidy, clean. **asearse** *vr* tidy oneself. **aseado** *adj* 1 smart. 2 tidy.

asechar (ase'tʃar) *vt* ambush. **asechanza** *nf* trap.

asediar (ase'ðjar) vt 1 besiege. 2 pester, bother. **asedio** nm siege.

asegurar (asegu'rar) vt 1 secure, fasten. 2 guarantee. 3 affirm. 4 insure.

asemejarse (aseme'xarse) vr resemble, be alike.

asentar (ie) (asen'tar) vt 1 place. 2 seat. 3 establish. 4 note down. vi be suitable. **asentarse** vr sit down.

asentir (ie) (asen'tir) vi agree, assent. **asentimiento** nm assent.

aseo (a'seo) nm cleanliness, tidiness.

asequible (ase'kiβle) adj 1 obtainable. 2 reasonable.

aserrar (ie) (aser'rar) vt saw. **aserradero** nm sawmill. **aserrín** nm sawdust.

aserto (a'serto) nm assertion.

asesinar (asesi'nar) vt murder, assassinate. **asesinato** nm assassination, murder. **asesino** nm assassin, murderer.

asesorar (aseso'rar) vt advise.

asestar (ases'tar) vt 1 aim. 2 strike.

asfalto (as'falto) nm asphalt.

asfixiar (asfik'sjar) vt suffocate. **asfixia** nf suffocation.

así (a'si) adv so, thus, in this way. **así así** so-so. **así como** the same way as, just as. **así que** as soon as, immediately.

Asia (a'sia) nf Asia. **asiático** adj,nm Asian, Asiatic.

asidero (asi'ðero) nm 1 hold. 2 handle. 3 excuse.

asiduo (a'siðwo) adj regular, constant.

asiento (a'sjento) nm 1 seat, place. 2 site. 3 stability. 4 sediment. 5 buttocks.

asignar (asig'nar) vt assign. **asignación** nf 1 allocation. 2 portion. 3 salary.

asignatura (asigna'tura) nf educ subject.

asilo (a'silo) nm 1 asylum. 2 shelter. 3 home, institution.

asimilar (asimi'lar) vt assimilate. **asimilación** nf assimilation.

asimismo (asi'mismo) adv similarly, in the same way.

asir (a'sir) vt seize, take hold of. vi take root. **asirse** vr take hold.

asistir (asis'tir) vt 1 serve, attend. 2 help, assist. vi be present, attend. **asistencia** nf 1 attendance, presence. 2 help. **asistenta** nf 1 char. 2 daily help. **asistente** nm assistant.

asma ('asma) nf asthma.

asno ('asno) nm donkey, ass.

asociar (aso'θjar) vt associate. **asociarse** vr join, associate oneself. **asociación** nf 1 association. 2 partnership. **asociado** adj associated. nm member.

asolar (aso'lar) vt lay waste, destroy.

asolear (asole'ar) vt put in the sun. **asolearse** vr sunbathe.

asomar (aso'mar) vt show. vi begin to show, appear.

asombrar (asom'brar) vt 1 astonish. 2 shade, darken. **asombro** nm 1 amazement. 2 wonder. **asombroso** adj amazing.

aspecto (as'pekto) nm 1 aspect. 2 appearance, look.

áspero ('aspero) adj 1 rough. 2 harsh. **aspereza** nf 1 roughness. 2 harshness.

aspersión (asper'θjon) nf sprinkling, spray.

aspirar (aspi'rar) vt breathe in. vi aspire. **aspirador de polvo** nm vacuum cleaner.

aspirina (aspi'rina) nf aspirin.

asqueroso (aske'roso) adj 1 disgusting. 2 awful.

asta ('asta) nf 1 spear. 2 shaft. 3 horn. **a media asta** at half mast.

asterisco (aste'risko) nm asterisk.

astil (a'stil) nm 1 pole. 2 handle. **astilla** nf splinter.

astillero (asti'ʎero) nm shipyard.

astringir (astrin'xir) vt 1 constrict. 2 med bind. **astringente** adj,nm astringent.

astro ('astro) nm star.

astrología (astrolo'xia) nf astrology. **astrólogo** nm astrologer.

astronauta (astro'nauta) nm,f astronaut. **astronáutica** nf astronautics.

astronomía (astrono'mia) nf astronomy. **astronómico** adj astronomical. **astrónomo** nm astronomer.

astucia (as'tuθja) nf 1 cleverness. 2 cunning.

astuto (as'tuto) adj 1 clever. 2 crafty.

asumir (asu'mir) vt assume.

asunto (a'sunto) nm 1 subject, matter. 2 business. **asuntos a tratar** agenda.

asustar (asus'tar) vt frighten.

atacar (ata'kar) vt 1 attack. 2 fasten, attach. **atacador** adj attacking. n attacker.

atado (a'taðo) nm bundle, roll.

atajar (ata'xar) vt intercept, stop. vi take a short cut. **atajo** nm short cut.

ataque (a'take) nm attack. **ataque aéreo** air-raid. **ataque cardíaco** heart attack. **ataque fulminate** med stroke.

atar (a'tar) vt tie, lace.

atardecer* (atarðe'θer) vi get dark. nm dusk.

atareado (atare'aðo) *adj* busy.

atascar (atas'kar) *vt* 1 stop (a leak, etc.). 2 block, clog up. **atascarse** *vr* get stuck. **atasco** *nm* obstruction.

ataúd (ata'uð) *nm* coffin.

ataviar (ata'βjar) *vt* adorn. **atavío** *nm* attire.

ateísmo (ate'ismo) *nm* atheism.

atención (aten'θjon) *nf* 1 attention. 2 kindness, courtesy. 3 *pl* courtesies.

atender (le) (aten'der) *vt,vi* attend.

atenerse* (ate'nerse) *vr* **atenerse a** 1 abide by. 2 rely on.

atento (a'tento) *adj* 1 attentive. 2 polite. **atento a** in view of.

atenuar (ate'nwar) *vt* lessen, diminish.

ateo (a'teo) *adj* atheistic. *nm* atheist.

aterrar¹ (le) (ater'rar) *vt* demolish.

aterrar² (ater'rar) *vt* frighten.

aterrizar (aterri'θar) *vi* aviat land. **aterrizaje** *nm* landing.

aterrorizar (aterrori'θar) *vt* 1 terrify. 2 terrorize.

atesorar (ateso'rar) *vt* hoard.

atestar (le) (ates'tar) *vt* 1 stuff, fill. 2 crowd.

atestiguar (atesti'gwar) *vt* testify.

ático ('atiko) *nm* attic.

atisbar (atis'βar) *vt* spy on, watch.

atizar (ati'θar) *vt* 1 poke. 2 stir up, excite. 3 slap. **atizador** *nm* poker.

Atlántico (a'tlantiko) *nm* Atlantic.

atlas (a'tlas) *nm* atlas.

atleta (a'tleta) *nm, f* athlete. **atlético** *adj* athletic. **atletismo** *nm* athletics.

atmósfera (at'mosfera) *nf* atmosphere. **mala atmósfera** atmospherics. **atmosférico** *adj* atmospheric.

atolondrar (atolon'drar) *vt* 1 bewilder. 2 amaze.

átomo ('atomo) *nm* atom. **atómico** *adj* atomic.

atónito (a'tonito) *adj* astonished.

atontado (aton'taðo) *adj* 1 bewildered. 2 *inf* silly.

atormentar (atormen'tar) *vt* 1 torment. 2 torture.

atornillar (atorni'ʎar) *vt* screw, fasten.

atracar (atra'kar) *vt* 1 hold up, attack. 2 moor. 3 stuff (with food). **atracarse** *vr* gorge oneself. **atraco** *nm* robbery.

atracción (atrak'θjon) *nf* 1 attraction, charm. 2 *pl Th* entertainment. **atractivo** *adj* attractive.

atraer* (atra'er) *vt* attract.

atrancar (atran'kar) *vt* bar (a door). *vi* stride along.

atrapar (atra'par) *vt* 1 trap. 2 seize.

atrás (a'tras) *adv* 1 behind. 2 past. 3 back, backwards. **atraso** *nm* 1 delay. 2 backwardness.

atravesar (le) (atraβe'sar) *vt* 1 cross, go through. 2 lay across.

atreverse (atre'βerse) *vr* dare, risk. **atrevido** *adj* bold, daring. **atrevimiento** *nm* boldness.

atribuir* (atriβu'ir) *vt* attribute. **atributo** *nm* attribute.

atrocidad (atroθi'ðað) *nf* atrocity.

atropellar (atrope'ʎar) *vt* 1 trample over, run over. 2 do hurriedly. **atropello** *nm* 1 outrage. 2 accident.

atroz (a'troθ) *adj* atrocious, savage.

atún (a'tun) *nm* tunny.

aturdir (atur'ðir) *vt* 1 daze. 2 bewilder. **aturdido** *adj* bewildered, silly. **aturdimiento** *nm* daze, confusion.

audacia (au'ðaθja) *nf* audacity. **audaz** *adj* audacious, daring.

audible (au'ðiβle) *adj* audible.

audición (auði'θjon) *nf* 1 hearing. 2 audition.

audiencia (au'ðjenθja) *nf* audience.

audífono (au'ðifono) *nm* hearing aid.

audiovisual (audiovisu'al) *adj* audiovisual.

auge ('auxe) *nm* 1 peak, zenith. 2 increase.

aula ('aula) *nf* 1 classroom. 2 lecture theatre. **aula magna** assembly hall.

aullar (au'ʎar) *vi* howl. **aullido** *nm* howl.

aumentar (aumen'tar) *vt,vi* increase. **aumento** *nm* increase, rise.

aun (a'un) *adv* even. **aún** *adv* still, yet.

aún (a'un) *adv* still, yet.

aunar (au'nar) *vt* join.

aunque (a'unke) *conj* (al)though, even though.

áureo ('aureo) *adj* gold(en).

aureola (aure'ola) *nf* halo.

auricular (auriku'lar) *adj* of the ear. *nm* 1 little finger. 2 receiver. 3 *pl* headphones.

ausencia (au'senθja) *nf* absence. **ausente** *adj* absent. *nm,f* absentee.

auspicios (aus'piθjos) *nm pl* 1 auspices. 2 patronage, protection.

austero (aus'tero) *adj* austere, severe, harsh. **austeridad** *nf* austerity.

Australia (aus'tralja) *nf* Australia. **australiano** *adj,nm* Australian.

Austria ('austrja) *nf* Austria. **austríaco** *adj,nm* Austrian.

auténtico (au'tentiko) *adj* authentic, real.

autístico (au'tistiko) *adj* autistic.

auto¹ ('auto) *nm* car.

auto² ('auto) *nm* 1 decree. 2 *law* sentence. 3 mystery play. 4 *pl law* proceedings.

autobiografía (autoβiogra'fia) nf autobiography. **autobiográfico** adj autobiographical.

autobús (auto'bus) nm bus.

autocar (auto'kar) nm mot coach.

autodisciplina (autodisθi'plina) nf self-discipline.

autoescuela (autoes'kwela) nf driving school.

autoexpresión (autoekspre'sjon) nf self-expression.

autógrafo (au'tografo) adj,nm autograph.

automático (auto'matiko) adj automatic.

automatización (automatiθa'θjon) nf automation.

automóvil (auto'moβil) nm automobile, car. **automovilista** nm,f motorist.

autonomía (autono'mia) nf autonomy. **autónomo** adj autonomous.

autopista (auto'pista) nf motorway.

autopsia (au'topsja) nf autopsy, post-mortem.

autor (au'tor) nm 1 author. 2 creator.

autorizar (autori'θar) vt 1 authorize. 2 approve. **autoridad** nf 1 authority. 2 show, pomp. **autoritario** adj authoritarian.

autorretrato (autorre'trato) nm self-portrait.

autoservicio (autoser'viθio) nm self-service restaurant.

autostop (auto'stop) nm hitch-hiking. **hacer el autostop** hitch-hike. **autostopista** nm,f hitch-hiker.

auxiliar (auksi'ljar) vt help, assist. adj auxiliary. nm,f assistant. **auxilio** nm help.

avalancha (aβa'lentʃa) nf avalanche.

avalorar (aβalo'rar) vt estimate, appraise.

avance (a'βanθe) nm 1 advance. 2 comm balance.

avanzar (aβan'θar) vt advance. vi advance, go forward.

avaricia (aβa'riθja) nf greed, miserliness. **avaricioso** adj greedy, miserly. **avaro** adj miserly, mean.

avasallar (aβasa'ʎar) vt dominate, subdue. **avasallarse** vr submit.

ave ('aβe) nf bird. **aves de corral** poultry.

avecinarse (aβeθi'narse) vr approach.

avellana (aβe'ʎana) nf hazelnut.

avena (a'βena) nf oats.

avenencia (aβe'nenθja) nf agreement.

avenida (aβe'niða) nf avenue.

avenir* (aβe'nir) vt bring together, reconcile. **avenirse** vr come to an agreement, be reconciled.

aventajado (aβenta'xaðo) adj outstanding, exceptional.

aventura (aβen'tura) nf 1 adventure. 2 risk. **aventurero** adj adventurous. nm adventurer.

avergonzar* (aβergon'θar) vt 1 shame. 2 embarrass. **avergonzarse** vr be ashamed.

avería¹ (aβe'ria) nf aviary.

avería² (aβe'ria) nf 1 mech breakdown. 2 damage. **averiado** adj 1 damaged. 2 faulty.

averiguar (aβeri'gwar) vt find out, ascertain. **averiguación** nf 1 discovery. 2 investigation.

avestruz (aβes'truθ) nm ostrich.

aviación (aβja'θjon) nf 1 aviation. 2 air force.

aviador (aβja'dor) nm airman, pilot.

ávido ('aβiðo) adj 1 avid, eager. 2 greedy. **avidez** nf 1 greed. 2 eagerness.

avinagrado (aβina'graðo) adj sour, acid.

avión (a'βjon) nm (aero)plane, aircraft. **avión a reacción** jet. **por avión** by airmail.

avisar (aβi'sar) vt 1 inform. 2 advise. **aviso** (a'βiso) nm 1 piece of information, tip. 2 advice.

avispa (a'βispa) nf wasp.

avivar (aβi'βar) vt 1 enliven, stimulate. 2 stoke. **avivarse** vr revive.

aya ('aja) nf child's nurse.

ayer (a'jer) adv 1 yesterday. 2 in the past. nm 1 yesterday. 2 past.

ayo ('ajo) nm tutor.

ayudar (aju'ðar) vt help, assist. **ayuda** nf help, assistance. **ayudante** nm helper, assistant.

ayunar (aju'nar) vi fast. **ayuno** nm fast, fasting.

ayuntamiento (ajunta'mjento) nm 1 town council. 2 town hall. 3 sexual intercourse.

azada (a'θaða) nf hoe.

azafata (aθa'fata) nf aviat stewardess.

azafrán (aθa'fran) nm cul saffron.

azahar (aθa'ar) nm orange blossom.

azar (a'θar) nm 1 fate. 2 chance. **al azar** at random.

azogue (a'θoge) nm mercury, quicksilver.

azorar (aθo'rar) vt 1 alarm, upset. 2 embarrass.

azotar (aθo'tar) vt whip, beat. **azote** nm 1 whip, lash. 2 scourge. 3 spank.

azotea (aθo'tea) nf flat roof.

azúcar (a'θukar) nm sugar. **azúcar fina** castor sugar. **azucarado** adj sweet, sugary.

azucena (aθu'θena) nf lily.

azufre (a'θufre) nm sulphur.

azul (a'θul) adj,nm blue. **azul marino** navy blue.

azulejo (aθu'lexo) nm tile.

B

baba ('baβa) nf saliva, spit. **babero** nm bib.
babor (ba'βor) nm naut port (side).
babosa (ba'βosa) nf slug.
bacalao (baka'lao) nm cod.
bacía (ba'θia) nf 1 basin. 2 shaving bowl.
bacteria (bak'teria) nf 1 germ. 2 pl bacteria.
bache ('batʃe) nm pothole.
bachiller (batʃi'ʎer) nm educ bachelor. **bachillerato** nm 1 final school examination, baccalaureate. 2 bachelor's degree.
bahía (ba'ia) nf geog bay.
bailar (bai'lar) vi dance. **baile** nm dance. **baile clásico** ballet.
bajar (ba'xar) vi fall, come down. vt lower, bring or take down. **baja** nf fall, drop. **bajada** nf 1 slope. 2 descent. **bajamar** nm low tide.
bajo ('baxo) adj 1 low. 2 small. 3 (of a person) short. adv below. prep under. **bajeza** nf 1 lowliness. 2 baseness.
bajón (ba'xon) nm 1 bassoon. 2 decline.
bala ('bala) nf 1 bullet. 2 bale.
balada (ba'laða) nf ballad.
balancear (balanθe'ar) vt,vi 1 balance. 2 rock, sway. **balance** nm 1 balance. 2 stocktaking. **balanceo** nm 1 balancing. 2 swaying. **balanza** nf scales.
balar (ba'lar) vi bleat.
balazo (ba'laθo) nm 1 shot. 2 wound.
balbucear (balβuθe'ar) vi stammer, stutter. **balbuceo** nm stammer.
balcón (bal'kon) nm balcony.
balde[1] ('balde) nm large bucket.
balde[2] ('balde) nm **de balde** free of charge. **en balde** in vain.
baldío (bal'dio) nm waste land. adj 1 wild. 2 barren.
baldosa (bal'dosa) nf flagstone, paving tile.
balística (ba'listika) nf ballistics. **balístico** adj ballistic.
balneario (balne'arjo) nm spa.
balón (ba'lon) nm 1 (foot)ball. 2 comm bale. **baloncesto** nm basketball. **balonvolea** nf volleyball.
balsa[1] ('balsa) nf raft.
balsa[2] ('balsa) nf pond.
bálsamo ('balsamo) nm balsam, comfort.
Báltico ('baltiko) nm Baltic.
ballena (ba'ʎena) nf whale.

ballesta (ba'ʎesta) nf crossbow. **ballestero** nm archer.
ballet (ba'le) nm ballet.
bambolear (bambole'ar) vi sway, reel.
bambú (bam'bu) nm bamboo.
banca ('banka) nf 1 bench. 2 comm banking.
bancarrota (banka'rota) nf bankruptcy. **hacer bancarrota** go bankrupt.
banco ('banko) nm 1 bench, seat. 2 bank.
banda ('banda) nf 1 band, strip. 2 gang, group. **bandada** nf flock.
bandeja (ban'dexa) nf tray.
bandera (ban'dera) nf 1 flag. 2 banner. 3 ensign. **banderilla** nf (bullfighting) dart. **banderillero** nm bullfighter who places the darts.
bandido (ban'diðo) nm bandit, outlaw.
bando ('bando) nm 1 proclamation. 2 faction, side.
bandolero (bando'lero) nm bandit.
banjo ('banxo) nm banjo.
banquete (ban'kete) nm banquet, feast.
bañar (ba'nar) vt bathe. **bañarse** (ba'narse) vr 1 have a bath. 2 swim. **bañador** nm bathing costume. **bañera** nf bathtub. **baño** nm bath.
bar (bar) nm bar, snack bar.
barajar (bara'xar) vt shuffle. **baraja** nf pack of cards.
barandilla (baran'diʎa) nf rail, railing.
barato (ba'rato) adj cheap. **baratija** nf 1 trinket. 2 trifle. 3 pl junk. **baratura** nf cheapness.
barba ('barβa) nf beard.
bárbaro ('barβaro) adj 1 barbarous, savage. 2 sl terrific, marvellous. nm barbarian. **barbaridad** nf 1 barbarity. 2 inf huge amount.
barbilla (bar'βiʎa) nf chin.
barbudo (bar'βuðo) adj bearded.
barca ('barka) nf small boat. **barca de pasaje** ferry boat.
Barcelona (barθe'lona) nf Barcelona. **barcelonés** adj of Barcelona. nm inhabitant of Barcelona.
barco ('barko) nm ship, boat.
barnizar (barni'θar) vt varnish. **barniz** nm 1 varnish. 2 gloss.
barómetro (ba'rometro) nm barometer.
barón (ba'ron) nm baron. **baronesa** nf baroness. **baronet** nm baronet.
barquillo (bar'kiʎo) nm 1 wafer. 2 cornet.
barra ('barra) nf 1 bar. 2 small loaf.
barraca (bar'raka) nf 1 hut. 2 cottage. 3 booth.
barranco (bar'ranko) nm ravine, gorge.

barrenar (barre'nar) vt drill, bore. **barrena** nf drill.

barrer (bar'rer) vt sweep.

barrera (bar'rera) nf barrier. **barrera de peaje** tollgate.

barricada (barri'kada) nf barricade.

barril (bar'ril) nm barrel.

barrio ('barrjo) nm district, quarter.

barro ('barro) nm mud. **barroso** adj muddy.

bártulos ('bartulos) nm pl belongings, gear.

barullo (ba'ruʎo) nm 1 confusion. 2 row.

basar (ba'sar) vt base, found. **basarse en** vr be based on. **base** nf base, foundation.

básico ('basiko) adj basic, fundamental.

bastante (bas'tante) adj enough. adv 1 enough, sufficiently. 2 fairly.

bastar (bas'tar) vi be enough, suffice.

bastardear (bastarðe'ar) vi degenerate. vt adulterate. **bastardilla** nf italics. **bastardo** nm,adj bastard.

bastidor (basti'ðor) nm frame. **entre bastidores** offstage.

basto ('basto) adj 1 rude. 2 coarse. nm pack saddle.

bastón (bas'ton) nm stick.

bastos ('bastos) nm pl game clubs.

basura (ba'sura) nf rubbish, litter. **basurero** nm dustman.

bata ('bata) nf 1 dressing-gown. 2 overall.

batalla (ba'taʎa) nf battle.

batea (ba'tea) nf 1 trough. 2 punt.

batería (bate'ria) nf 1 battery. 2 mus percussion instruments. **batería de cocina** kitchen utensils.

batir (ba'tir) vt 1 beat. 2 clap. 3 knock down. 4 defeat. 5 cul whisk. **batirse** vr fight. **batido** nm 1 batter. 2 milk shake. **batidor** nm whisk, beater. **batiente** nm frame (of door, etc.).

batuta (ba'tuta) nf baton. **llevar la batuta** be in control.

baúl (ba'ul) nm trunk.

bautizar (bauti'θar) vt baptize, christen. **bautismo** nm baptism, christening. **bautizo** nm christening party.

baya ('baja) nf berry.

bayeta (ba'jeta) nf 1 baize. 2 rag, cloth.

bayoneta (bajo'neta) nf bayonet.

baza ('baθa) nf game trick. **meter baza** interfere.

bazar (ba'θar) nm bazaar.

beato (be'ato) adj 1 pious, devout. 2 blessed.

beber (be'βer) vt,vi drink. **bebida** nf drink.

beca ('beka) nf grant, scholarship.

becerro (be'θerro) nm 1 bullock. 2 yearling.

bedel (be'ðel) nm warden, porter.

béisbol ('beisβol) nm baseball.

Belén (be'len) nf Bethlehem. **belén** nm 1 crib. 2 crèche. 3 confusion.

Bélgica ('belxika) nf Belgium. **belga** adj,n Belgian.

bellaco (be'ʎako) adj 1 cunning. 2 wicked. nm rogue.

belleza (be'ʎeθa) nf beauty. **bello** adj 1 beautiful. 2 fine.

bellota (be'ʎota) nf acorn.

bemol (be'mol) nm mus flat.

bendecir* (bende'θir) vt 1 bless. 2 praise. **bendición** nf blessing. **bendito** adj blessed, holy.

beneficiar (benefi'θjar) vt,vi profit, be of benefit (to). **beneficio** nm 1 benefit. 2 gain. **beneficioso** adj profitable, beneficial.

benemérito (bene'merito) adj worthy, honourable.

beneplácito (bene'plaθito) nm consent.

benevolencia (benevo'lenθia) nf kindness, benevolence. **benevolente** adj also **benévolo** kind, benevolent.

benignidad (benigni'dad) nf kindness. **benigno** adj 1 kind. 2 (of weather) mild.

beodo (be'oðo) adj drunk.

berberecho (berβe'retʃo) nm cockle.

berenjena (beren'xena) nf aubergine.

bermejo (ber'mexo) adj 1 bright red. 2 ginger.

berrear (berre'ar) vi bellow, howl. **berrido** nm bellow, howling.

berrinche (ber'rintʃe) nm tantrum.

berro ('berro) nm watercress.

berza ('berθa) nf cabbage.

besar (be'sar) vt kiss. **beso** nm kiss.

bestia ('bestja) nf 1 beast, animal. 2 stupid or ignorant person. adj inf foolish, stupid. **bestial** adj 1 bestial. 2 inf marvellous, great.

betún (be'tun) nm 1 shoe polish. 2 bitumen.

Biblia ('biβlia) nf Bible. **bíblico** adj Biblical.

bibliografía (biβliogra'fia) nf bibliography. **bibliográfico** adj bibliographic(al).

biblioteca (biβlio'teka) nf library. **bibliotecario** nm librarian.

bíceps ('biθeps) nm invar biceps.

bicicleta (biθi'kleta) nf bicycle.

bicho ('bitʃo) nm 1 insect. 2 small animal.

bien (bjen) adv 1 well, right. 2 quite, very. 3 easily. nm 1 good. 2 advantage. 3 gain. 4 pl property, possessions. **bien que** conj though, although.

bienal (bje'nal) adj biennial.

bienaventurado (bjenaβertu'raðo) adj 1 fortunate. 2 blessed.

bienestar (bjenes'tar) nm 1 comfort. 2 well-being.

bienhechor (bjene'tʃor) nm benefactor.

bienio ('bjenjo) nm period of two years.

bienvenida (bjenβe'niða) nf welcome. **dar la bienvenida a** vt welcome.

biftec (bif'tek) nm steak.

bifurcarse (bifur'karse) vr branch off, fork. **bifurcación** nf junction.

bigamia (bi'gamja) nf bigamy.

bigote (bi'gote) nm moustache.

bilingüe (bi'lingwe) adj bilingual.

billar (bi'ʎar) nm billiards.

billete (bi'ʎete) nm 1 ticket. 2 banknote. 3 letter. **billete de abono** season ticket. **billete de ida y vuelta** return ticket. **billete sencillo** single ticket. **sacar un billete** buy a ticket.

binóculo (bi'nokulo) nm binoculars.

biografía (biogra'fia) nf biography. **biográfico** adj biographical.

biología (biolo'xia) nf biology. **biológico** adj biological. **biólogo** nm biologist.

biombo ('bjombo) nm screen.

bióxido (bi'oksido) nm dioxide. **bióxido de carbono** carbon dioxide.

bisagra (bi'sagra) nf hinge.

bisiesto (bi'sjesto) adj **año bisiesto** nm leap year.

bisturí (bistu'ri) nm scalpel.

bizarría (biθar'ria) nf 1 gallantry, valour. 2 splendour, show. **bizarro** adj 1 brave. 2 splendid. 3 dashing.

bizcar (biθ'kar) vi squint. **bizco** adj cross-eyed.

bizcocho (biθ'kotʃo) nm small cake, biscuit.

blanco ('blanko) adj 1 white. 2 blank. nm 1 whiteness, white. 2 blank. 3 target. **blanca** nf minim. **blancura** nf whiteness. **dar en el blanco** be on target. **quedarse en blanco** not have a clue.

blandir (blan'dir) vt,vi wave.

blando ('blando) adj 1 soft. 2 gentle. 3 mild. **blandura** nf 1 softness. 2 tenderness.

blanquear (blanke'ar) vt 1 whiten, bleach. 2 whitewash. **blanqueo** nm bleaching.

blasfemar (blasfe'mar) vi blaspheme, swear. **blasfemia** nf blasphemy, oath.

blasón (bla'son) nm 1 coat of arms. 2 heraldry.

blindar (blin'dar) vt protect with armour. **blindado** adj armour-plated. **blindaje** nm armour.

bloquear (bloke'ar) vt block, obstruct. **bloque** nm 1 block. 2 blockage. 3 bloc. **bloqueo** nm blockade.

blusa ('blusa) nf 1 blouse. 2 overall.

bobada (bo'βada) nf 1 nonsense. 2 foolishness. **bobería** nf stupidity. **bobo** adj foolish, silly. nm idiot.

bobina (bo'bina) nf reel.

boca ('boka) nf 1 mouth. 2 opening. **a la boca de** at the start of. **a boca de jarro** 1 without restraint. 2 at point-blank range. **boca abajo/arriba** face down/up.

bocacalle (boka'kaʎe) nf entrance to a street.

bocadillo (boka'ðiʎo) nm sandwich. **bocado** nm 1 mouthful. 2 bite.

bocina (bo'θina) nf 1 trumpet. 2 mot horn.

bochorno (bo'tʃorno) nm hot and sultry weather. **¡qué bochorno!** what an embarrassment! **bochornoso** adj 1 sultry. 2 thundery. 3 embarrassing.

boda ('boða) nf wedding, marriage.

bodega (bo'ðega) nf 1 wine cellar. 2 storeroom. 3 bar.

bofetada (bofe'taða) nf 1 slap. 2 blow.

boga ('boga) nf vogue, fashion.

bohemio (bo'emjo) adj,nm 1 Bohemian. 2 gypsy.

boicotear (boikote'ar) vt boycott. **boicot** nm boycott.

boina ('boina) nf beret.

bola ('bola) nf 1 ball. 2 fib. **bola de nieve** snowball.

bolero (bo'lero) nm 1 type of dance. 2 short jacket.

boleto (bo'leto) nf 1 ticket. 2 pass. 3 document. **boletín** nm bulletin. **boletín meteorológico** weather forecast. **boletín de noticias** news bulletin. **boletín de precios** price list.

bolígrafo (bo'ligrafo) nm ballpoint pen.

Bolivia (bo'liβja) nf Bolivia. **boliviano** adj,n Bolivian.

bolsa ('bolsa) 1 bag. 2 purse. **bolsa de agua** hot-water bottle. **bolsillo** nm pocket. **bolso** nm 1 handbag. 2 purse.

bollo ('boʎo) nm roll, bun.

bomba ('bomba) nf 1 pump. 2 bomb. **bomba de gasolina** petrol pump. **bomba de mano** grenade. **bomba nuclear** nuclear bomb.

bombardear (bombarðe'ar) vt bombard, shell. **bombardeo aéreo** nm bombardment, air-raid.

bombero (bom'bero) nm fireman.

bombilla (bom'biʎa) nf 1 light bulb. 2 globe. 3 glass tube.

bombo ('bombo) *adj* stunnned, surprised. *nm* 1 drum. 2 great praise.

bombón (bom'bon) *nm* 1 sweet, chocolate. 2 *inf* beauty (girl).

bondad (bon'dað) *nf* 1 goodness. 2 kindness. **bondadoso** *adj* 1 kind. 2 warm-hearted.

bonito (bo'nito) *adj* pretty, nice.

bono ('bono) *nm* 1 bond. 2 certificate. 3 voucher.

boquerón (boke'ron) *nm* 1 opening, large hole. 2 a variety of anchovy. **boquete** *nm* gap, small hole.

boquiabierto (bokja'βjerto) *adj* gaping, openmouthed.

boquilla (bo'kiʎa) *nf* 1 mouthpiece. 2 nozzle.

borboll(e)ar (borβo'ʎar) *vi* bubble. **borbollón** *nm* 1 bubbling. 2 spluttering.

borbotar (borβo'tar) *vi* 1 bubble. 2 boil. **borbotón** *nm* 1 bubbling. 2 boiling.

bordar (bor'ðar) *vt* embroider. **bordado** *nm* embroidery.

bordear (borðe'ar) *vt* 1 edge round. 2 border. **borde** *nm* 1 border, edge. 2 rim.

bordillo (bor'điʎo) *nm* kerb.

bordo ('borðo) *nm naut* board. **a bordo** on board.

borra (borra) *nf* 1 thick wool. 2 nap. 3 stuffing.

borracho (bor'ratʃo) *adj,nm* drunk. **borrachera** *nf* 1 drunkenness. 2 drinking bout.

borrar (bor'rar) *vt* erase, rub out. **goma de borrar** *nf* rubber. **borrador** *nm* 1 rough copy. 2 scribbling pad.

borrasca (bor'raska) *nf* squall, storm. **borrascoso** *adj* stormy.

borrico (bor'riko) *nm* ass, donkey.

borrón (bor'ron) *nm* stain, blot. **borroso** *adj* 1 stained. 2 smudged. 3 blurred.

bosque ('boske) *nm* wood, forest.

bosquejar (boske'xar) *vt* 1 sketch. 2 draft. **bosquejo** *nm* sketch, outline.

bostezar (boste'θar) *vi* yawn. **bostezo** *nm* yawn.

bota ('bota) *nf* 1 boot. 2 wineskin.

botánica (bo'tanika) *nf* botany. **botánico** *adj* botanical. **botanista** *nm,f* botanist.

botar (bo'tar) *vt* 1 throw. 2 bowl. *vi* bounce.

bote[1] ('bote) *nm* 1 blow, bump. 2 bounce.

bote[2] ('bote) *nm* 1 tin can. 2 jar.

bote[3] ('bote) *nm* boat.

botella (bo'teʎa) *nf* bottle.

botica (bo'tika) *nf* chemist's shop. **boticario** *nm* chemist.

botija (bo'tixa) *nf* round earthenware pot. **botijo** *nm* earthenware jug with spout.

botín (bo'tin) *nm* loot.

botón (bo'ton) *nm* 1 button. 2 switch, knob. 3 bud. **botón de camisa** stud. **botones** *nm invar* pageboy.

bóveda ('boβeða) *nf* 1 vault. 2 cave. 3 dome.

bovino (bo'βino) *adj* bovine.

boxear (bokse'ar) *vi* box. **boxeador** *nm* boxer. **boxeo** *nm* boxing.

boya ('boja) *nf* buoy. **boyante** *adj* buoyant.

bozal (bo'θal) *nm* muzzle.

bracero (bra'θero) *nm* 1 labourer. 2 helper.

braga ('braga) *nf* 1 hoist, sling. 2 *pl* breeches. 3 *pl* (woman's) underpants.

bramar (bra'mar) *vi* roar, bellow. **bramido** *nm* roar, bellow.

brasa ('brasa) *nf* glowing cinder. **brasero** *nm* brazier.

Brasil (bra'sil) *nm* Brazil. **brasileño** *adj,nm* Brazilian.

bravío (bra'βio) *adj* 1 savage. 2 wild.

bravo ('braβo) *adj* 1 brave, courageous. 2 fierce. *interj* well done! **bravura** *nf* 1 bravery. 2 ferocity.

brazada (bra'θaða) *nf* 1 arm movement. 2 stroke. **brazado** *nm* armful.

brazalete (braθa'lete) *nm* bracelet.

brazo ('braθo) *nm* 1 arm. 2 branch. **a brazo partido** with bare fists. **brazo derecho** right-hand man.

brea ('brea) *nf* pitch, tar.

brebaje (bre'βaxe) *nm* brew, potion.

brécoles ('brekoles) *nm pl* broccoli.

brecha ('bretʃa) *nf* breach, opening.

bregar (bre'gar) *vi* 1 struggle. 2 quarrel. **brega** *nf* fight.

Bretaña (bre'tana) *nf* Brittany. **bretón** *adj,nm* Breton.

breve ('breβe) *adj* brief, short. *nm rel* papal brief. *nf mus* breve. **en breve** soon, before long. **brevedad** *nf* brevity.

brezal (bre'θal) *nm* heath, moor. **brezo** *nm* heather.

bribón (bri'βon) *adj* 1 lazy. 2 dishonest. *nm* scoundrel.

brida ('briða) *nf* 1 bridle. 2 rein.

brigada (bri'gaða) *nm* sergeant-major. *nf* brigade, squad.

brillar (bri'ʎar) *vi* 1 shine. 2 sparkle. **brillante** *adj* 1 shining, bright. 2 brilliant. **brillo** *nm* 1 brilliance, shine. 2 sparkle.

brincar (brin'kar) vi 1 jump. 2 skip, hop. **brinco** nm jump, leap.

brindar (brin'dar) vt offer. vi drink a person's health. **brindis** nm invar toast.

brío ('brio) nm spirit, go. **brioso** adj 1 lively, spirited. 2 vigorous.

brisa ('brisa) nf breeze.

británico (bri'taniko) adj,nm British.

brocha ('brotʃa) nf 1 brush. 2 paintbrush.

broche (brotʃe) nm 1 fastener, clip. 2 brooch.

broma ('broma) nf 1 joke. 2 fun, merriment. **broma pesada** practical joke. **en broma** as a joke. **bromista** nm,f joker, practical joker.

bromear (brome'ar) vi joke.

bronca ('bronka) nf 1 row. 2 fuss.

bronce ('bronθe) nm bronze. **bronceado** adj 1 bronzed. 2 tanned.

bronco ('bronko) adj 1 rough. 2 harsh.

bronquial (bronki'al) adj bronchial. **bronquitis** nm bronchitis.

broqueta (bro'keta) nf skewer.

brotar (bro'tar) vi 1 bud. 2 spring up. 3 appear. **brote** nm 1 bud, shoot. 2 outbreak. 3 rash.

bruja ('bruxa) nf witch. **brujo** nm wizard.

brújula ('bruxula) nf compass.

bruma ('bruma) nf mist. **brumoso** adj misty.

bruno ('bruno) adj dark brown.

bruñir (bru'ɲir) vt polish. **bruñido** adj 1 polished. 2 shiny. nm shine.

brusco ('brusko) adj 1 brusque, abrupt. 2 sharp.

Bruselas (bru'selas) nf Brussels.

brutal (bru'tal) adj brutal, savage. **brutalidad** nf brutality, cruelty. **bruto** adj 1 brute. 2 rough, coarse. nm brute. **en bruto** min 1 uncut. 2 crude.

buba ('buβa) nf tumour.

bucear (buθe'ar) vi dive. **buceo** nm diving.

bucle ('bukle) nm ringlet, curl.

buche ('butʃe) nm 1 zool crop. 2 stomach.

budismo (bu'ðismo) nm Buddhism. **budista** adj,n Buddhist.

buenaventura (bwenaβen'tura) nf 1 good luck. 2 fortune.

bueno ('bweno) adj also **buen** before nm s 1 good. 2 sound. 3 right. 4 proper, suitable. interj,conj 1 well. 2 all right. **a buenas** willingly. **buena voluntad** goodwill. **¡buenas!** hello! **buenas noches** good night. **buenas tardes** good afternoon, good evening. **buenos días** good morning. **de buenas a primeras** 1 straightaway. 2 suddenly.

buey (bwej) nm ox.

búfalo ('bufalo) nm buffalo.

bufanda (bu'fanda) nf scarf.

bufar (bu'far) vi 1 spit. 2 snort.

buhardilla (bwar'ðiʎa) nf 1 attic. 2 skylight.

búho ('buo) nm 1 owl. 2 inf hermit.

buitre ('bwitre) nm vulture.

bujía (bu'xia) nf 1 candle. 2 sparking plug.

bula ('bula) nf rel papal bull.

bulbo ('bulβo) nm bulb.

Bulgaria (bul'garia) nf Bulgaria. **búlgaro** adj,nm Bulgarian. nm Bulgarian (language).

bulto ('bulto) nm 1 bulk, size. 2 bundle. 3 med lump. **a bulto 1** carelessly. 2 roughly. **de bulto** important.

bulla ('buʎa) nf confusion, racket.

bullicio (bu'ʎiθio) nm 1 bustle. 2 noise. **bullicioso** adj 1 noisy. 2 bustling.

bullir (bu'ʎir) vi 1 boil. 2 bustle. 3 bubble.

buñuelo (bu'ɲwelo) nm 1 bun. 2 doughnut. 3 fritter.

buque ('buke) nm ship, boat. **buque de vapor** steamship.

burbujear (burbuxe'ar) vi bubble. **burbuja** nf bubble.

burdel (bur'ðel) nm brothel.

burgués (bur'ges) adj bourgeois, middle class. **burguesía** nf middle class.

burlar (bur'lar) vt 1 trick. 2 cheat. **burlarse** vr joke. **burlarse de** mock. **burla** nf 1 jeer. 2 joke.

burocracia (buro'kraθja) nf bureaucracy. **burócrata** nm,f bureaucrat, public official. **burocrático** adj bureaucratic.

burro ('burro) nm donkey.

buscar (bus'kar) vt search, look for. **busca** nf search. **buscador** nm searcher. **en busca de** in search of.

búsqueda ('buskeða) nf search.

busto ('busto) nm bust.

butaca (bu'taka) nf 1 armchair. 2 seat.

buzo ('buθo) nm diver.

buzón (bu'θon) nm pillar-box, letterbox.

C

cabal (ka'βal) adj 1 exact. 2 perfect. 3 right.

cábala ('kaβala) nf 1 intrigue. 2 guess.

cabalgar (kaβal'gar) vt,vi ride. **cabalgada** nf troop of horses. **cabalgador** nm horserider.

caballa (ka'βaʎa) nf mackerel.

caballero (kaβa'ʎero) nm 1 horseman. 2

gentleman. **3** knight. **caballeresco** adj chivalrous.

caballete (kaβa'λete) nm **1** ridge. **2** easel. **3** furrow. **4** bridge (of the nose). **5** trestle.

caballo (ka'βaλo) nm **1** horse. **2** horsepower. **3** knight. **4** game queen. **a caballo** on horseback. **caballo de balancín** rocking-horse. **caballo de carreras** racehorse. **caballo padre** stallion. **caballería** nf **1** horse, mount. **2** cavalry. **caballito** nm pony.

cabaña (ka'βaɲa) nf **1** cabin, hut. **2** flock.

cabaret (kaβa're) nm **1** cabaret. **2** nightclub.

cabás (ka'βas) nm satchel.

cabecear (kaβeθe'ar) vi **1** shake one's head in negation. **2** nod sleepily. **cabeceo** nm nodding. **cabecera** nf **1** head (of a table, etc.). **2** bedside. **3** title, heading.

cabecilla (kaβe'θiλa) nm,f ringleader.

cabello (ka'βeλo) nm hair. **cabelludo** adj hairy.

caber* (ka'βer) vi **1** fit, have enough room. **2** be possible. **no cabe duda** there is no doubt.

cabestro (ka'βestro) nm halter.

cabeza (ka'βeθa) nf **1** head. **2** chief, leader. **3** top, summit. **cabeza de turco** scapegoat. **romperse la cabeza** rack one's brains. **cabezada** nf **1** blow on the head. **2** nod. **dar cabezadas** nod off to sleep. **cabezudo** adj big-headed.

cabida (ka'βiða) nf space, area.

cabildo (ka'βildo) nm **1** rel chapter. **2** town council.

cabina (ka'βina) nf cabin. **cabina de teléfono** telephone kiosk.

cabizbajo (kaβiθ'βaxo) adj downhearted, dejected.

cable ('kaβle) nm cable, wire.

cablegrafiar (kaβlegra'fjar) vi cable. **cablegrama** nm cable(gram).

cabo ('kaβo) nm **1** end. **2** handle. **3** stump, stub. **4** strand. **5** chief. **6** corporal. **7** pl bits and pieces, accessories. **al cabo de** at the end of. **llevar a cabo** carry out, finish.

cabra ('kaβra) nf nanny goat. **cabrero** nm goatherd.

cabria ('kaβrja) nf hoist, crane.

cacahuete (kaka'wete) nm peanut.

cacao (ka'kao) nm cocoa, cacao.

cacarear (kakare'ar) vi crow, cackle. vt boast about.

cacería (kaθe'ria) nf hunting, hunt.

cacerola (kaθe'rola) nf (sauce)pan, casserole.

cacique (ka'θike) nm **1** chief, local leader. **2** despot.

caco ('kako) nm **1** pickpocket, thief. **2** coward.

cacto ('kakto) nm cactus.

cacharrería (katʃarre'ria) nf crockery. **cacharro** nm **1** earthenware pot. **2** piece of junk.

cachete (ka'tʃete) nm **1** blow, slap. **2** cheek, plump cheek.

cachivache (katʃi'βatʃe) nm **1** kitchen pot. **2** worthless fellow. **3** useless article, junk.

cacho ('katʃo) nm small piece, crumb.

cachorro (ka'tʃorro) nm puppy, cub.

cada ('kaða) adj invar each, every.

cadáver (ka'ðaβer) nm body, corpse.

cadena (ka'ðena) nf **1** chain, link. **2** sequence, series.

cadencia (ka'ðenθja) nf cadence, rhythm.

cadera (ka'ðera) nf anat hip.

cadete (ka'ðete) nm cadet.

caducar (kaðu'kar) vi **1** become senile. **2** expire, go out of date. **caduco** adj **1** senile. **2** out of date, expired, invalid.

caer* (ka'er) vi **1** fall down, go down, collapse, drop. **2** (of clothes) suit, fit. **3** be located, lie. **caer en** or **sobre** fall upon. **caer en la cuenta** realize, understand.

café (ka'fe) nm **1** coffee. **2** cafe. **café con leche** white coffee. **café solo** black coffee.

cafeína (kafe'ina) nf caffeine.

cafetera (kafe'tera) nf coffee pot.

cafetería (kafete'ria) nf coffee bar, cafe.

caí (ka'i) v see **caer**.

caída (ka'iða) nf **1** fall, drop, downfall. **2** slope. **3** fold, hanging. **la caída del sol** sunset.

caigo (ka'igo) v see **caer**.

caimán (kai'man) nm alligator.

caja ('kaxa) nf **1** box, chest. **2** safe, cashbox, cash desk. **caja de ahorros** savings bank. **cajero** nm cashier. **cajetilla** nf packet (of cigarettes, etc.). **cajita** nf small box. **cajón** nm large box, crate.

cal (kal) nm min lime.

calabaza (kala'βaθa) nf pumpkin, gourd. **dar calabazas a 1** reject amorous proposals (of a man). **2** fail (a student in an exam).

calabozo (kala'βoθo) nm **1** prison cell. **2** dungeon.

calamar (kala'mar) nm squid.

calambre (ka'lambre) nm cramp.

calamidad (kalami'ðað) nf calamity, misfortune.

calar (ka'lar) vt **1** soak, go through. **2** penetrate. **3** tech do fretwork. **4** inf understand, size up. vi **1** (of water, etc.) soak in. **2** leak.

calavera (kala'βera) nf skull.

calcar (kal'kar) vt trace, copy. **calco** nm tracing.

calce ('kalθe) nm rim (of a wheel), tyre.

calceta (kal'θeta) nf 1 stocking. 2 fetter. **calcetero** nm hosier. **calcetín** nm sock.

calcinar (kalθi'nar) vt burn, blacken.

calcio ('kalθjo) nm calcium.

calcular (kalku'lar) vt calculate. **calculadora** nf computer, calculating machine.

cálculo ('kalkulo) nm 1 calculation, estimate. 2 med gallstone, stone.

calda ('kalda) nf 1 heating. 2 pl hot springs.

caldera (kal'dera) nf cauldron, boiling pan. **calderilla** nf coppers, small change.

caldo ('kaldo) nm 1 broth, soup. 2 gravy. 3 dressing, sauce. 4 pl comm oil, wine, vegetable juices.

calefacción (kalefak'θjon) nf heating. **calefacción central** central heating.

calendario (kalen'darjo) nm calendar.

calentar (ie) (kalen'tar) vt heat, warm. **calentarse** vr 1 warm oneself. 2 become heated or excited. **calentura** nf med fever.

calibrar (kali'βrar) vt measure, guage. **calibre** nm 1 gauge. 2 calibre. 3 diameter (of tube, etc.).

calidad (kali'ðað) nf 1 quality. 2 character. **en calidad de** in the capacity of.

cálido ('kaliðo) adj hot, warm.

caliente (kal'jente) adj warm, hot, heated.

calificar (kalifi'kar) vt 1 qualify. 2 assess, judge. **calificación** nf 1 qualification. 2 class, assessment. **calificado** adj 1 qualified. 2 well-known.

cáliz ('kaliθ) nm chalice, cup.

calmar (kal'mar) vt calm, soothe. **calmarse** vr calm down. **calma** nf calm, peace. **calmante** adj soothing. nm sedative. **calmoso** adj calm, tranquil.

calor (ka'lor) nm 1 heat, warmth. 2 excitement.

caloría (kalo'ria) nf calorie.

caluroso (kalu'roso) adj 1 warm, hot. 2 excited, enthusiastic.

calvo ('kalβo) adj 1 bald. 2 bare, barren. **calvicie** nf baldness.

calzar (kal'θar) vt 1 put on (shoes). 2 wear (shoes). 3 wedge, block. **calza** nf 1 wedge. 2 stocking. 3 pl breeches. **calzada** nf road, drive. **calzado** adj wearing shoes, shod. nm footwear.

calzón (kal'θon) nm shorts, pants. **calzón de baño** bathing trunks. **calzoncillos** nm pl underpants.

callar (ka'ʎar) vt,vi keep silent. **callarse** vr become quiet, stop talking. **callado** adj 1 quiet, reserved. 2 silent.

calle ('kaʎe) nf road, street. **abrir** or **hacer calle** clear the way. **callejón** nm alley, side street. **callejuela** nf side street, passage.

callo ('kaʎo) nm 1 med corn, callus. 2 pl cul tripe. **calloso** adj hard, callous.

cama ('kama) nf bed, bedstead. **cama de campaña/matrimonio/soltero** camp/double/single bed.

camaleón (kamale'on) nm chameleon.

cámara ('kamara) nf 1 room, chamber, hall. 2 camera.

camarero (kama'rero) nm waiter, steward.

camarilla (kama'riʎa) nf 1 small room. 2 pol lobby. 3 clique.

camarín (kama'rin) nm 1 dressing room. 2 niche.

cambiar (kam'bjar) vt exchange, convert. vi alter, change. **cambiante** adj changing, variable. nm moneychanger. **cambio** nm 1 change, alteration. 2 exchange. **en cambio** on the other hand, instead.

camello (ka'meʎo) nm camel.

caminar (kami'nar) vi walk, travel. **caminante** nm traveller, walker. **camino** nm 1 road, path. 2 route, way. **ponerse en camino** set out.

camión (ka'mjon) nm lorry, wagon.

camisa (ka'misa) nf 1 shirt. 2 jacket, casing. 3 casing, wrapper. **dejar sin camisa** leave penniless. **camiseta** nf vest. **camisón** nm nightshirt.

campamento (kampa'mento) nm camp.

campana (kam'pana) nf 1 bell. 2 bell-shaped object. **campanada** nf 1 peal (of a bell). 2 scandal. **campanario** nm belfry, bell tower.

campante (kam'pante) adj 1 outstanding. 2 inf self-satisfied, proud.

campaña (kam'paɲa) nf 1 countryside. 2 campaign.

campeón (kampe'on) nm champion. **campeón de venta** bestseller.

campo ('kampo) nm 1 country(side). 2 field, ground. 3 camp. 4 sphere, range. **campesino** adj country, rustic. nm countryman, peasant. **campestre** adj rural, country.

can (kan) nm 1 dog. 2 trigger.

cana ('kana) nf white or grey hair.

Canadá (kana'ða) nm Canada. **canadiense** adj,n Canadian.

canal (ka'nal) nm 1 canal. 2 channel. 3 pipe, tube. **canalón** nm gutter, spout, drainpipe.

canalla (ka'naʎa) nf mob, rabble. nm swine, scoundrel.

canapé (kana'pe) nm 1 sofa, couch. 2 cul canapé.

Canarias (ka'narjas) nf pl Canaries. **canario** adj of the Canaries. nm inhabitant of the Canaries.

canario (ka'narjo) nm canary.

cancelar (kanθe'lar) vt cancel, wipe out. **cancelación** nf cancellation.

cáncer ('kanθer) nm 1 cancer. 2 cap Cancer.

canciller (kanθi'ʎer) nm chancellor.

canción (kan'θjon) nf song, lyric. **cancionero** nm song book.

candado (kan'daðo) nm padlock.

candela (kan'dela) nf candle. **candelero** nm candlestick, lamp.

candente (kan'dente) adj red-hot, burning.

candidato (kandi'ðato) nm candidate. **candidatura** nf candidature.

cándido ('kandiðo) adj simple, innocent. **candidez** nf simplicity, innocence.

candil (kan'dil) nm oil lamp.

candor (kan'dor) nm sincerity, simplicity. **candoroso** adj sincere, open.

canela (ka'nela) nf cinnamon.

canelón (kane'lon) nm 1 spout, gutter. 2 icicle.

cangrejo (kan'grexo) nm crab.

canguro (kan'guro) nm kangaroo.

caníbal (ka'niβal) adj,n cannibal.

canilla (ka'niʎa) nf 1 anat shin. 2 tech bobbin. 3 tap, spout.

canjear (kanxe'ar) vt exchange, swap. **canje** nm exchange.

cano ('kano) adj 1 grey-haired. 2 ancient, venerable.

canoa (ka'noa) nf canoe.

canon ('kanon) nm 1 rule. 2 rel canon. 3 mus canon.

canónigo (ka'nonigo) nm rel canon. **canónico** adj canonical.

cansar (kan'sar) vt tire, weary. **cansado** adj 1 tired. 2 tiresome. **cansancio** nm fatigue.

cantar (kan'tar) vt,vi 1 sing, chant. 2 inf squeal, confess. nm 1 song. 2 singing.

cántara ('kantara) nf 1 large pitcher. 2 liquid measure.

cántaro ('kantaro) nm jug, pitcher. **llover a cántaros** rain cats and dogs.

cantera (kan'tera) nf quarry. **cantería** nf 1 quarrying. 2 masonry. **cantero** nm 1 quarryman. 2 stonemason.

cantidad (kanti'ðað) nf quantity, portion.

cantimplora (kantim'plora) nf water bottle, canteen.

cantina (kan'tina) nf buffet, canteen.

canto[1] ('kanto) nm 1 singing. 2 song.

canto[2] ('kanto) nm 1 edge, border. 2 stone, pebble. **de canto** on edge, edgeways.

cantor (kan'tor) nm singer. adj singing.

caña ('kaɲa) nf 1 reed, stalk. 2 shin, bone. 3 beer glass, tumbler.

cañada (ka'ɲaða) nf ravine, glen.

cáñamo ('kaɲamo) nm hemp.

caño ('kaɲo) nm pipe, sewer. **cañería** nf piping, drain.

cañón (ka'ɲon) nm 1 tube, pipe, shaft. 2 gun, cannon. 3 barrel (of a gun, etc.). 4 canyon.

caoba (ka'oβa) nf mahogany.

caos ('kaos) nm chaos. **caótico** adj chaotic.

capa ('kapa) nf 1 cloak. 2 layer, coating.

capacidad (kapaθi'ðað) nf 1 capacity. 2 ability, talent.

capar (ka'par) vt 1 castrate. 2 reduce.

capataz (kapa'taθ) nm foreman.

capaz (ka'paθ) adj 1 large, roomy. 2 capable.

capellán (kape'ʎan) nm chaplain.

capilar (kapi'lar) adj,nm capillary.

capilla (ka'piʎa) nf chapel, choir.

capital (kapi'tal) nm comm capital. nf capital (city). adj capital, principal.

capitán (kapi'tan) nm captain, chief. **capitanear** vt lead.

capitular (kapitu'lar) vi 1 make an agreement. 2 mil surrender.

capítulo (ka'pitulo) nm 1 chapter (of a book, etc.). 2 meeting (of a council, etc.). 3 rel chapter.

capote (ka'pote) nm 1 long cloak. 2 inf scowl. 3 cape (of a bullfighter).

capricho (ka'pritʃo) nm whim, fancy. **caprichoso** adj capricious.

cápsula ('kapsula) nf cartridge case, capsule.

captar (kap'tar) vt 1 gain, attract. 2 get control over.

capturar (kaptu'rar) vt capture, arrest. **captura** nf capture, seizure.

capucha (ka'putʃa) nf 1 hood. 2 circumflex accent.

capuchina (kapu'tʃina) nf nasturtium.

capullo (ka'puʎo) nm 1 cocoon. 2 bud.

cara ('kara) nf 1 face. 2 appearance. 3 cheek, boldness. 4 outside, surface. **cara adelante/ atrás** forwards/backwards. **cara o cruz** heads or tails. **hacer cara a** face up to.

carabina (kara'βina) nf rifle, carbine. **carabinero** nm rifleman.

caracol (kara'kol) nm 1 snail. 2 curl (of hair). 3 spiral.

carácter (ka'rakter) nm 1 character. 2 nature, type.

característico (karakte'ristiko) adj characteristic.

caramelo (kara'melo) nm toffee, sweet.

carátula (ka'ratula) nf theatre, stage.

caravana (kara'βana) nf 1 caravan. 2 group, band.

carbohidrato (karβoi'δrato) nm carbohydrate.

carbón (kar'βon) nm 1 coal. 2 carbon paper.

carbonero (karβo'nero) nm coalman. adj coal. **carbonería** nf coalyard.

carburador (karβura'δor) nm carburettor.

cárcel (ʹkarθel) nf prison. **carcelero** nm jailer.

carcomer (karko'mer) vt eat away, undermine. **carcomerse** vr become worm-eaten, decay. **carcoma** nf 1 woodworm. 2 gnawing anxiety. **carcomido** adj worm-eaten, rotten.

cardar (kar'δar) vt tech card, comb. **carda** nf 1 tech card, carding. 2 inf reprimand.

cardenal (karδe'nal) nm 1 cardinal. 2 bruise.

cardíaco (kar'δiako) adj cardiac.

cardinal (karδi'nal) adj principal, cardinal.

cardo (ʹkarδo) nm thistle.

carear (kare'ar) vt confront, compare. **carear a face towards. **carearse** vr meet, come face to face.

carecer* (kare'θer) vi lack, need. **carecimiento** nm lack, need. **carencia** nf lack, shortage.

carestía (kares'tia) nf 1 scarcity. 2 famine. 3 high price or cost.

careta (ka'reta) nf mask, veil.

cargar (kar'gar) vt 1 load, burden. 2 charge. 3 inf annoy. vi 1 be loaded. 2 bear, shoulder a load. 3 lean, incline, turn. **cargarse (de)** vr 1 burden oneself (with). 2 be abundant (with). 3 (of sky) become dark. **carga** nf 1 load, burden. 2 charge. 3 loading. 4 duty, tax. **cargadero** nm loading bay. **cargador** nm 1 loader, stoker. 2 tech charger. **cargamento** nm load, cargo.

cargo (ʹkargo) nm 1 load, burden. 2 comm debit, charge. 3 role, duty. 4 accusation, charge. **estar a cargo** be in charge.

cariarse (ka'rjarse) vr (of teeth) decay.

caribe (ka'riβe) adj,n Caribbean. **(Mar) Caribe** Caribbean (Sea).

caricatura (karika'tura) nf caricature.

caricia (ka'riθja) nf caress.

caridad (kari'δaδ) nf charity.

cariño (ka'riɲo) nm affection, love. **cariñoso** adj affectionate, tender.

caritativo (karita'tiβo) adj charitable.

cariz (ka'riθ) nm appearance, look.

carmesí (karme'si) adj,nm crimson.

carnal (kar'nal) adj of the flesh, carnal.

carnaval (karna'βal) nm carnival.

carne (ʹkarne) nf flesh, meat.

carnicería (karniθe'ria) nf 1 butcher's (shop), slaughterhouse. 2 carnage, slaughter. **carnicero** adj 1 carnivorous. 2 cruel. nm butcher.

carnívoro (kar'niβoro) adj carnivorous.

caro (ʹkaro) adj 1 dear, beloved. 2 expensive. adv dear(ly).

carpeta (kar'peta) nf file, folder. **dar carpetazo a** shelve, do nothing about.

carpintería (karpinte'ria) nf 1 carpentry. 2 carpenter's (shop). **carpintero** nm carpenter.

carrera (kar'rera) nf 1 run, race. 2 course, row (of bricks, etc.). 3 career, profession. 4 ladder (in stocking, etc.). 5 course (of study).

carretear (karrete'ar) vt cart, haul. **carreta** nf cart, wagon. **carrete** nm spool, reel.

carretera (karre'tera) nf road, highway.

carril (kar'ril) nm 1 rut, furrow. 2 lane, track, rail.

carro (ʹkarro) nm 1 cart, car. 2 carriage (of a typewriter).

carroña (kar'roɲa) nf carrion.

carroza (kar'roθa) nf 1 coach, carriage. 2 float.

carta (ʹkarta) nf 1 letter. 2 charter, document. 3 map. 4 card. **poner las cartas boca arriba** lay one's cards on the table.

cartel (kar'tel) nm placard, poster. **cartelera** nf hoarding, notice board.

cartera (kar'tera) nf 1 wallet. 2 briefcase. 3 ministerial post.

cartílago (kar'tilago) nm cartilage.

cartón (kar'ton) nm 1 cardboard. 2 box, carton. 3 cartoon.

cartucho (kar'tutʃo) nm 1 cartridge. 2 paper cone.

casa (ʹkasa) nf 1 house, home. 2 flat. 3 building. 4 firm, business. **casa y comida** board and lodging. **en casa** at home. **poner casa** set up house.

casar (ka'sar) vt 1 marry off, give in marriage. 2 pair, join. **casarse con** marry, get married. **casamiento** nm marriage.

cascabel (kaska'βel) nm 1 small bell. 2 inf scatterbrain.

cascada (kas'kaδa) nf cascade, waterfall.

cascar (kas'kar) *vt* **1** crack, split. **2** *inf* beat, wipe the floor with. *vi inf* chatter. **cascarse** *vr* **1** break. **2** *inf* break down in health.

cáscara ('kaskara) *nf* shell, peel, bark.

casco ('kasko) *nm* **1** helmet. **2** skull. **3** broken piece of china, etc.). **4** cask, barrel. **5** hoof. **6** *pl* brains. **cascote** *nm* rubble.

caserío (kase'rio) *nm* **1** group of houses, settlement. **2** country house.

casero (ka'sero) *adj* of the house, domestic. *nm* **1** landlord. **2** caretaker.

casi ('kasi) *adv* almost.

casilla (ka'siʎa) *nf* **1** cabin, hut. **2** pigeonhole, section.

caso ('kaso) *nm* case, event, matter. **en tal caso** in such a case. **en todo caso** in any case. **hacer caso a** notice, heed.

caspa ('kaspa) *nf* dandruff, scab.

casta ('kasta) *nf* **1** race, caste. **2** kind, class.

castaña (kas'taɲa) *nf* **1** chestnut. **2** bun (in the hair). *nm* chestnut tree. **castaño** *adj* brown, chestnut-coloured.

castañuela (kasta'ɲwela) *nf* castanet.

castellano (kaste'ʎano) *adj,nm* Castilian, Spanish.

castidad (kasti'ðað) *nf* chastity.

castigar (kasti'gar) *vt* punish, chastise. **castigo** *nm* punishment.

Castilla (kas'tiʎa) *nf* Castile.

castillo (kas'tiʎo) *nm* castle.

castizo (kas'tiθo) *adj* **1** pure. **2** traditional, authentic. **3** purebred, racially pure.

casto ('kasto) *adj* chaste, pure.

castor (kas'tor) *nm* beaver.

castrar (kas'trar) *vt* **1** castrate. **2** prune.

castrense (kas'trense) *adj* military.

casual (ka'swal) *adj* accidental, chance. **casualidad** *nf* chance, accident. **por casualidad** by chance.

casucha (ka'sutʃa) *nf* hovel, slum.

cataclismo (kata'klismo) *nm* cataclysm.

catadura[1] (kata'ðura) *nf* tasting, sampling.

catadura[2] (kata'ðura) *nf inf* looks, face, mug.

catálogo (ka'talogo) *nm* catalogue.

Cataluña (kata'luɲa) *nf* Catalonia. **catalán** *adj,nm* Catalan, Catalonian. *nm* Catalan (language).

catar (ka'tar) *vt* **1** taste, try. **2** examine, see.

catarata (kata'rata) *nf* **1** waterfall. **2** *med* cataract.

catarro (ka'tarro) *nm* catarrh, common cold.

catástrofe (ka'tastrofe) *nf* catastrophe. **catastrófico** *adj* catastrophic.

catecismo (kate'θismo) *nm* catechism.

cátedra ('kateðra) *nf* **1** lectureship. **2** subject for study. **3** lecture room.

catedral (kate'ðral) *nf* cathedral.

categoría (katego'ria) *nf* category, class. **categórico** *adj* categorical, downright.

cátodo ('katoðo) *nm* cathode.

católico (ka'toliko) *adj* **1** (Roman) Catholic. **2** true, right. *nm* (Roman) Catholic.

catorce (ka'torθe) *adj* fourteen.

catre ('katre) *nm* cot, camp bed.

cauce ('kauθe) *nm* bed (of a river, etc.), ditch.

caución (kau'θjon) *nf* **1** caution. **2** security.

caucho ('kautʃo) *nm* rubber.

caudillo (kau'ðiʎo) *nm* chief, leader.

causar (kau'sar) *vt* cause, create. **causa** *nf* **1** cause, reason. **2** trial.

cautela (kau'tela) *nf* **1** wariness, caution. **2** cunning. **cauteloso** *adj* **1** cautious. **2** cunning.

cautivar (kauti'βar) *vt* **1** capture. **2** charm, captivate. **cautivo** *nm* captive.

cauto ('kauto) *adj* cautious, careful.

cavar (ka'βar) *vt* dig (over). *vi* (of a wound) go deeply. **cava** *nf* cultivation. **cavadura** *nf* excavation.

caverna (ka'βerna) *nf* cave, cavern. **cavernoso** *adj* cavernous, deep.

cavidad (kaβi'ðað) *nf* cavity.

cavilar (kaβi'lar) *vt* think deeply about. **caviloso** *adj* suspicious, brooding.

cayado (ka'jaðo) *nm* stick, crook.

cayó (ka'jo) *v* see **caer.**

cazar (ka'θar) *vt* **1** hunt, chase. **2** catch. **3** *inf* trick. **caza** *nf.* **1** hunting. **2** hunt. **3** game. **cazador** *nm* hunter.

cazo ('kaθo) *nm* ladle.

cazoleta (kaθo'leta) *nf* **1** small pan. **2** bowl (of a pipe). **3** guard (of a sword).

cazuela (ka'θwela) *nf* stewpot, casserole.

cebada (θe'βaða) *nf* barley. **cebadal** *nm* barley field.

cebar (θe'βar) *vt* **1** feed up, fatten. **2** prime, charge (a gun, etc.). *vi* (of a nail, etc.) go in. **cebarse (en)** *vr* **1** vent one's anger (on). **2** devote oneself (to). **cebo** *nm* **1** feed. **2** bait.

cebolla (θe'βoʎa) *nf* **1** onion. **2** bulb (of a flower). **cebollana** *nf* chive.

cebra ('θeβra) *nf* zebra.

cecear (θeθe'ar) *vi* lisp.

ceder (θe'ðer) *vt* give up, yield. *vi* **1** give in. **2** diminish, abate. **3** sag, give way.

cédula ('θeðula) *nf* document, certificate.

cegar (ie) (θe'ɣar) vt 1 make blind. 2 block, close up. vi become blind. **ceguedad** or **ceguera** nf blindness.

ceja ('θexa) nf 1 eyebrow. 2 rim, edging. 3 cloud cap. 4 mountain peak. **fruncir las cejas** knit one's brows. **quemarse las cejas** burn the midnight oil.

celar (θe'lar) vt watch over carefully, check on. **celada** nf 1 ambush. 2 helmet. **celador** nm watchman, attendant.

celda ('θelda) nf cell.

celebrar (θele'βrar) vt 1 celebrate. 2 hold, conduct (a meeting, etc.). 3 praise, welcome. vi rel say mass. **celebrarse** vr take place.

célebre ('θeleβre) adj 1 famous. 2 witty, amusing.

celebridad (θeleβri'ðað) nf 1 celebrity, fame. 2 celebration, festivity.

celeridad (θeleri'ðað) nf speed.

celeste (θe'leste) adj celestial, heavenly.

celibato (θeli'βato) nm 1 celibacy. 2 inf bachelor. **célibe** adj unmarried, single. nm,f unmarried person.

celo ('θelo) nm 1 zeal, enthusiasm. 2 zool rut, heat. 3 pl jealousy. **dar celos a** make jealous. **tener celos (de)** be jealous (of). **celosía** nf 1 lattice, blind. 2 jealousy. **celoso** adj 1 zealous. 2 jealous.

celta ('θelta) adj,n Celtic, Celt. nm Celtic (language).

célula ('θelula) nf bot, zool cell.

cementerio (θemen'terjo) nm cemetery.

cemento (θe'mento) nm cement.

cenar (θe'nar) vi have one's evening meal. vt have for supper, dine on. **cena** nf evening meal, supper.

cenefa (θe'nefa) nf edging, border.

cenicero (θeni'θero) nm ashtray.

ceniza (θe'niθa) nf ash, cinder.

censo ('θenso) nm 1 census. 2 leasehold, mortgage.

censurar (θensu'rar) vt 1 censure, criticize, blame. 2 pol censor. **censura** nf 1 criticism, blame. 2 censorship. **censurable** adj blameworthy.

centellear (θenteʎe'ar) vi flash, twinkle. **centella** nf spark, flash (of lightning, etc.). **centelleo** nm sparkle, flashing.

centena (θen'tena) nf hundred.

centenal (θente'nal) nm also **centenar** nm hundred. **a centenares** by the hundred(s). **centenario** adj,nm centenary.

centeno (θen'teno) nm rye.

centésimo (θen'tesimo) adj hundredth.

centígrado (θen'tiɣraðo) adj centigrade.

céntimo ('θentimo) adj hundredth. nm cent, hundredth part of a peseta.

centinela (θenti'nela) nm,f guard, sentry.

centrar (θen'trar) vt centre. **central** adj central. nf head office, headquarters. **centro** nm 1 centre, middle. 2 goal, objective.

centuria (θen'turja) nf century.

ceñir (i) (θe'ɲir) vt 1 surround, girdle. 2 shorten, abbreviate. **ceñirse** vr 1 put on. 2 limit oneself, tighten one's belt.

ceño ('θeɲo) nm frown. **fruncir el ceño** frown. **ceñudo** adj frowning.

cepa ('θepa) nf 1 stump, stock (of a vine, etc.). 2 origin, stock.

cepillar (θepi'ʎar) vt 1 brush. 2 plane down, smooth. **cepillo** nm 1 brush. 2 tech plane. **cepillo de dientes** toothbrush.

cera ('θera) nf wax.

cerámico (θe'ramiko) adj ceramic. **cerámica** nf ceramics, pottery.

cerca ('θerka) adv near. **cerca de 1** near to, close by. 2 almost, about. **cercanía** nf 1 nearness. 2 suburbs, outskirts. **cercano** adj near, approaching.

cercar (θer'kar) vt enclose, fence in. **cerca** nf wall, fence. **cercado** nm 1 enclosure. 2 fence.

cerco ('θerko) nm 1 ring, hoop. 2 enclosure, circle. 3 frame, casing.

Cerdeña (θer'ðeɲa) nf Sardinia.

cerdo ('θerðo) nm pig, pork.

cereal (θere'al) adj,nm cereal.

cerebro (θe'reβro) nm brain. **cerebral** adj cerebral, brain.

ceremonia (θere'monja) nf ceremony. **ceremonial** adj ceremonial. **ceremonioso** adj ceremonious, formal.

cereza (θe'reθa) nf cherry. **cerezal** nm cherry orchard. **cerezo** nm cherry tree.

cerilla (θe'riʎa) nf match.

cerner (ie) (θer'ner) vt 1 sieve, sift. 2 watch carefully. **cernerse** vr 1 hover, threaten. 2 waddle.

cero ('θero) nm nothing, zero.

cerrar (ie) (θer'rar) vt 1 close, shut. 2 block, obstruct. 3 stop, turn off. 4 enclose. 5 close, complete. vi 1 close, shut. 2 close in. **cerrarse** vr 1 close up. 2 cloud over. 3 stand firm, be determined. **cerrar con llave** lock, bolt. **cerrado** adj 1 closed. 2 obscure. 3

cloudy. 4 secretive, quiet. **cerradura** *nf* 1 locking, shutting. 2 bolt. **cerraja** *nf* lock, bolt.

cerril (θer'ril) *adj* rough, rocky.

cerro (θerro) *nm* 1 hill. 2 *zool* spine, neck.

cerrojo (θer'roxo) *nm* bolt, lock.

certeza (θer'teθa) *nf* certainty. **certidumbre** *nf* certainty, conviction.

certificar (θertifi'kar) *vt* certify, register. **certificado** *adj* certified, registered. *nm* 1 certificate. 2 registered letter.

cervato (θer'βato) *nm* fawn.

cerveza (θer'βeθa) *nf* beer. **cervecería** *nf* brewery.

cerviz (θer'βiθ) *nf* 1 nape of the neck. 2 cervix.

cesar (θe'sar) *vt* cease, stop. *vi* 1 cease, stop. 2 leave one's job, quit. **cesación** *nf* stoppage, cessation. **cesante** *adj* out of work.

césped (θespeð) *nm* lawn, grass.

cesta (θesta) *nf* 1 basket, hamper. 2 racquet. **cesto** *nm* large basket.

cetro (θetro) *nm* sceptre, power.

cía (θia) *nf* hip bone.

cianuro (θja'nuro) *nm* cyanide.

cicatriz (θika'triθ) *nf* scar.

ciclo (θiklo) *nm* cycle. **cíclico** *adj* cyclic(al).

ciclón (θi'klon) *nm* cyclone.

ciego (θjego) *adj* blind. *nm* blind person.

cielo (θjelo) *nm* 1 sky, heaven. 2 roof. **¡cielos!** *interj* heavens!

ciénaga (θjenaga) *nf* marsh, swamp.

ciencia (θjenθja) *nf* science. **científico** *adj* scientific. *nm* scientist.

cieno (θjeno) *nm* mud. **cienoso** *adj* muddy.

ciento (θjento) *adj,nm also* **cien** hundred. **centésimo** *adj,nm* hundredth.

cierre (θjerre) *nm* 1 closing, shutting. 2 fastener, clasp.

cierto (θjerto) *adj* 1 certain, sure. 2 a certain (person or thing). **por cierto** certainly.

ciervo (θjerβo) *nm* stag, deer.

cierzo (θjerθo) *nm* north wind.

cifra (θifra) *nf* 1 number, figure. 2 amount. 3 code, cipher. 4 abbreviation.

cigarro (θi'garro) *nm* cigar. **cigarrillo** *nm* cigarette.

cigüeña (θi'gweɲa) *nf* stork.

cilindro (θi'lindro) *nm* cylinder. **cilíndrico** *adj* cylindrical.

cima (θima) *nf* 1 top (of a tree, etc.). 2 summit (of a mountain, etc.).

cimentar (ie) (θimen'tar) *vt* lay the foundations, establish. **cimiento** *nm* foundation, basis.

cinc (θink) *nm* zinc.

cincel (θin'θel) *nm* chisel. **cincelador** *nm* sculptor, stone cutter.

cinco (θinko) *adj,nm* five.

cincuenta (θin'kwenta) *adj,nm* fifty.

cinchar (θin't∫ar) *vt* secure a saddle on (a horse). **cincha** *nf* girth (of a saddle). **cincho** *nm* belt, iron hoop.

cine (θine) *nm* cinema.

cínico (θiniko) *adj* 1 cynical. 2 impudent. *nm* cynic.

cinta (θinta) *nf* ribbon, tape, strip.

cintura (θin'tura) *nf* 1 waist. 2 belt, girdle. **cinturón** *nm* belt. **cinturón de seguridad** *nm* safety belt.

ciprés (θi'pres) *nm* cypress tree.

circo (θirko) *nm* circus.

circuito (θir'kwito) *nm* circuit.

circulación (θirkula'θjon) *nf* 1 circulation. 2 traffic, movement.

circular (θirku'lar) *vt* pass round. *vi* circulate, move about. *adj* circular, round.

círculo (θirkulo) *nm* circle, ring.

circuncidar (θirkunθi'ðar) *vt* circumcise. **circuncisión** *nf* circumcision. **circunciso** *adj* circumcised.

circunferencia (θirkunfe'renθja) *nf* circumference.

circunflejo (θirkun'flexo) *nm* circumflex.

circunscribir (θirkunskri'βir) *vt* circumscribe, limit.

circunstancia (θirkun'stanθja) *nf* circumstance. **circunstancial** *adj* circumstantial. **circunstante** *adj* surrounding. *nm,f* bystander, onlooker.

ciruela (θi'rwela) *nf* plum. **ciruelo** *nm* plum tree.

cirugía (θiru'xia) *nf* surgery. **cirujano** *nm* surgeon.

cisco (θisko) *nm* 1 *min* slack. 2 *inf* hubbub, row.

cisma (θisma) *nm* schism, disagreement.

cisterna (θis'terna) *nf* cistern, tank.

cita (θita) *nf* 1 appointment, date. 2 quotation.

citar (θi'tar) *vt* 1 make an appointment. 2 quote. 3 *law* summon.

ciudad (θju'ðað) *nf* city, town. **ciudadano** *adj* city, civic. *nm* citizen, city dweller. **ciudadela** *nf* citadel.

cívico (θiβiko) *adj* civic, patriotic.

civil (θi'βil) *adj* civil.

civilizar (θiβili'θar) *vt* civilize. **civilización** *nf* civilization.

cizalla (θi'θaʎa) nf **1** wire cutters, shears. **2** (metal) shavings, filings.

clamar (kla'mar) vi,vt cry out, clamour. nm cry, shout. **clamoroso** adj noisy, loud.

clandestino (klandes'tino) adj secret.

clara ('klara) nf **1** white (of an egg). **2** bald patch.

claraboya (klara'βoja) nf skylight.

clarear (klare'ar) vt,vi brighten, light up. **clarearse** vr **1** be transparent. **2** inf reveal secrets.

clarete (kla'rete) nm light red wine, rosé.

claridad (klari'ðað) nf **1** clarity, brightness. **2** pl home truths, nasty remarks.

clarificar (klarifi'kar) vt clarify, illuminate. **clarificación** nf clarification.

clarín (kla'rin) nm bugle.

clarinete (klari'nete) nm clarinet.

claro ('klaro) adj **1** clear, bright. **2** (of colours) light. **3** distinct, clear. adv clearly. nm **1** opening, gap. **2** skylight. **¡claro que sí!** of course! **poner en claro** explain, clarify.

clase ('klase) nf **1** class, type. **2** class, lesson. **3** classroom. **clase media** middle class.

clásico ('klasiko) adj classic(al). nm **1** classic. **2** classicist.

clasificar (klasifi'kar) vt classify, sort. **clasificación** nf classification.

claudicar (klauði'kar) vi **1** limp. **2** hesitate, back down.

claustro ('klaustro) nm **1** cloister. **2** council. **3** faculty.

claustrofobia (klaustro'foβja) nf claustrophobia.

cláusula ('klausula) nf clause.

clavar (kla'βar) vt **1** nail, knock in. **2** fix, fasten. **3** inf cheat. **clava** nf club, truncheon. **clavado** adj nailed, fixed. **clavija** nf peg, plug. **clavo** nm nail, stud. **dar en el clavo** hit the nail on the head.

clave ('klaβe) nf **1** key (to problem, etc.). **2** mus clef. nm harpsichord.

clavel (kla'βel) nm carnation.

clavícula (kla'βikula) nf collar bone.

clemencia (kle'menθja) nf mercy. **clemente** adj merciful.

clérigo ('klerigo) nm priest, clergyman. **clerical** adj clerical. **clero** nm clergy.

cliente ('kljente) nm client, customer. **clientela** nf clients, patients, clientèle.

clima ('klima) nm climate. **climático** adj climatic.

clínica ('klinika) nf clinic, nursing home. **clínico** adj clinical.

cloaca (klo'aka) nf sewer, drain.

cloro ('kloro) nm chlorine.

clorofila (kloro'fila) nf chlorophyll.

coacción (koak'θjon) nf coercion. **coactivo** adj coercive.

coagular (koagu'lar) vt coagulate, clot, congeal.

coartada (koar'taða) nf alibi.

coartar (koar'tar) vt restrict, limit.

cobarde (ko'βarðe) adj cowardly. nm,f coward. **cobardía** nf cowardice.

cobertizo (koβer'tiθo) nm shed.

cobijar (koβi'xar) vt cover, shelter. **cobijo** nm shelter.

cobrar (ko'βrar) vt **1** recover, regain. **2** charge, earn. **3** gain. vi collect one's salary, draw wages. **cobrarse** vr med recover.

cobre ('koβre) nm **1** copper. **2** mus brass.

cocer* (ko'θer) vt,vi cook. **cocido** adj cooked. nm stew.

cocinar (koθi'nar) vt,vi cook. **cocina** nf **1** kitchen. **2** cookery. **cocinero** nm cook.

coco ('koko) nm **1** coconut. **2** maggot, grub. **3** bogeyman. **4** inf face, mug.

coche ('kotʃe) nm **1** car. **2** coach, carriage. **coche-cama** nm, pl **coches-cama** sleeping car. **cochero** nm coachman.

cochino (ko'tʃino) adj dirty, rotten. nm pig, swine.

codear (koðe'ar) vt,vi elbow, nudge.

codeína (koðe'ina) nf codeine.

códice ('koðiθe) nm manuscript.

codiciar (koði'θjar) vt greatly desire, covet. **codicia** nf greed. **codicioso** adj greedy.

código ('koðigo) nm **1** code. **2** law, rules.

codo ('koðo) nm **1** elbow. **2** angle, bend. **hablar por los codos** talk a great deal, talk nineteen to the dozen.

codorniz (koðor'niθ) nf quail.

coerción (koer'θjon) nf coercion, restraint.

cofia ('kofja) nf white cap, coif.

cofradía (kofra'ðia) nf fraternity, association.

cofre ('kofre) nm chest.

coger (ko'xer) vt **1** seize, grasp. **2** take, catch. **3** obtain, get. vi fit, have room. **cogida** nf **1** gathering. **2** fruit harvest. **3** (in bullfighting) goring. **cogido** nm fold, crease.

cogote (ko'gote) nm nape of the neck.

cohete (ko'ete) nm rocket.

cohibir (koi'βir) vt check, restrain. **cohibirse** vr feel embarrassed or shy. **cohibición** nf restraint, inhibition. **cohibido** adj restricted, shy.

coincidencia (koinθi'ðenθja) nf coincidence. **coincidente** adj coincidental.

cojear (koxe'ar) vi 1 limp. 2 wobble. 3 inf go astray. **cojera** nf lameness. **cojo** adj 1 lame. 2 wobbly, shaky.

cojín (ko'xin) nm cushion.

cok (kok) nm coke.

col (kol) nf cabbage. **col de bruselas** Brussels sprout.

cola ('kola) nf 1 tail, end. 2 train (of a dress, etc.). 3 queue. 4 glue.

colaborar (kolaβo'rar) vi collaborate, help. **colaboración** nf collaboration.

colapso (ko'lapso) nm collapse, breakdown.

colar (ue) (ko'lar) vt 1 strain, filter. 2 bleach. vi go through. **colarse** vr 1 slip through, steal in. 2 slip up, make an error. **colada** nf washing. **coladero** nm colander, sieve.

colcha ('kolt∫a) nf bedspread.

colchón (kol'tʃon) nm mattress.

colear (kole'ar) vi wag (a tail).

colección (kolek'θjon) nf collection. **colectivo** adj collective. **colectividad** nf whole, sum total, collectivity.

colega (ko'lega) nm colleague.

colegio (ko'lexjo) nm school, college. **colegial** adj school, college. nm schoolboy.

cólera ('kolera) nf anger. nm cholera. **colérico** adj angry.

coleta (ko'leta) nf 1 pigtail. 2 postscript.

colgar (ue) (kol'gar) vt,vi hang. **colgadero** nm hanger, peg. **colgadizo** adj hanging. **colgante** adj hanging. nm pendant.

coliflor (koli'flor) nf cauliflower.

colilla (ko'liʎa) nf butt, cigarette end.

colina (ko'lina) nf hill.

colindar (kolin'dar) vi be adjacent. **colindante** adj neighbouring.

colisión (koli'sjon) nf collision, crash.

colmar (kol'mar) vt 1 fill to the top, heap. 2 fulfill. **colmado** adj abundant, overflowing.

colmena (kol'mena) nf (bee)hive.

colmillo (kol'miʎo) nm tooth, fang, tusk.

colmo ('kolmo) nm highest point, limit.

colocar (kolo'kar) vt 1 place, put, arrange. 2 place in a job. **colocación** nf employment.

colonia (ko'lonja) nf colony.

Colonia (ko'lonja) nf Cologne. **agua de colonia** nf toilet water.

colonizar (koloni'θar) vt colonize. **colonia** nf colony. **colonización** nf colonization.

coloquio (ko'lokjo) nm conversation, talk.

color (ko'lor) nm 1 colour, colouring. 2 paint, dye. **coloración** nf coloration. **colorado** adj 1 coloured, esp. red. 2 (of a joke) obscene, blue.

colorar (kolo'rar) vt colour, dye.

colorear (kolore'ar) vt 1 colour, dye. 2 gloss over, whitewash, put in a favourable light. vi grow red. **colorete** nm rouge. **colorido** nm colour(ing). **colorín** nm 1 vivid colour. 2 linnet.

colosal (kolo'sal) adj colossal.

columna (ko'lumna) nf column, pillar.

columpiar (kolum'pjar) vt swing. **columpiarse** vr 1 sway. 2 waddle. **columpio** nm swing.

collar (ko'ʎar) nm necklace, collar.

comadre (ko'maðre) nf 1 godmother. 2 midwife. 3 go-between. 4 friend, neighbour.

comadreja (koma'ðrexa) nf weasel.

comadrona (koma'ðrona) nf midwife.

comandante (koman'dante) nm commander. **comandancia** nf command, headquarters.

comandita (koman'dita) nf sleeping partnership. **socio comanditario** nm sleeping partner.

comarca (ko'marka) nf region, district.

comba ('komba) nf 1 bend, curve. 2 skipping rope. **combadura** nf curve or camber (in a road, etc.).

combatir (komba'tir) vt attack, fight, struggle against. vi fight. **combate** nm combat, fight. **combatiente** nm combatant.

combinar (kombi'nar) vt combine, join. **combinación** nf 1 combination. 2 scheme, plan. 3 underskirt.

combustible (kombus'tible) adj combustible. nm fuel.

comedia (ko'meðja) nf comedy, play. **comediante** nm (comic) actor.

comedido (ko'meðiðo) adj moderate, courteous.

comedor (kome'ðor) nm dining room.

comendador (komenda'ðor) nm knight commander.

comentar (komen'tar) vt comment on, criticize. **comentario** nm commentary. **comentarista** nm commentator. **comento** nm comment.

comenzar (ie) (komen'θar) vt,vi begin, commence.

comer (ko'mer) vt 1 eat, feed, consume. 2 fade, corrode. vi eat, have a meal. **comerse** vr eat up, swallow.

comercio (ko'merθjo) nm 1 commerce, business. 2 dealings, intercourse. **comercial**

adj commercial. **comerciante** *nm* dealer, merchant.

comestible (komes'tiβle) *adj* edible. **comestibles** *nm pl* provisions, groceries.

cometa (ko'meta) *nf* kite. *nm* comet.

cometer (kome'ter) *vt* commit. **cometido** *nm* task, commitment.

cómico ('komiko) *adj* comic(al). *nm* comedian.

comida (ko'miða) *nf* **1** food. **2** meal, lunch.

comienzo (ko'mjenθo) *nm* beginning.

comillas (ko'miλas) *nf pl* inverted commas, quotation marks.

comino (ko'mino) *nm* cumin (seed).

comisaría (komisa'ria) *nf* police station, commissariat. **comisario** *nm* commissary, head of police.

comité (komi'te) *nm* committee.

comitiva (komi'tiβa) *nf* retinue, procession.

como ('komo) *adv* **1** like, as, in the same way. **2** about, approximately. *conj* **1** as, since. **2** if. **tan pronto como** as soon as.

cómo *adv* how, why, in what way. *interj* what, eh. **el por qué y el cómo** the why and the wherefore.

comodidad (komoði'ðað) *nf* comfort, convenience, advantage.

cómodo ('komoðo) *adj* comfortable, convenient.

compacto (kom'pakto) *adj* compact, dense.

compadecer* (kompaðe'θer) *vt* pity. **compadecerse (de)** *vr* sympathize (with).

compadre (kom'paðre) *nm* **1** godfather. **2** friend, pal.

compañero (kompa'nero) *nm* **1** companion, comrade, partner. **2** (one of a) pair. **compañía** *nf* company, society.

comparar (kompa'rar) *vt* compare. **comparación** *nf* comparison. **comparativo** *adj* comparative.

comparecer* (kompare'θer) *vi* appear in court.

compartimiento (komparti'mjento) *nm* **1** compartment. **2** division.

compartir (kompar'tir) *vt* share, divide.

compás (kom'pas) *nm* **1** rhythm, time. **2** *math* compass(es). **3** *naut* compass.

compatible (kompa'tiβle) *adj* compatible. **compatibilidad** *nf* compatibility.

compeler (kompe'ler) *vt* compel.

compendio (kom'pendjo) *nm* summary, compendium. **en compendio** briefly.

compensar (kompen'sar) *vt* compensate, balance. **compensación** *nf* compensation. **compensatorio** *adj* compensatory.

competir (i) (kompe'tir) *vi* compete, rival.

competencia *nf* **1** competition, rivalry. **2** competence. **3** field, province. **competente** *adj* appropriate, apt, adequate. **competición** *nf* contest. **competidor** *nm* competitor, rival.

compilar (kompi'lar) *vt* compile. **compilación** *nf* compilation.

compinche (kom'pintʃe) *nm f* pal, chum.

complacer* (kompla'θer) *vt* please, help. **complacerse** *vr* be pleased to. **complacencia** *nf* pleasure, willingness. **complaciente** *adj* helpful, pleasing.

complejo (kom'plexo) *adj,nm* complex.

complementario (komplemen'tarjo) *adj* complementary. **complemento** *nm* complement.

completar (komple'tar) *vt* complete. **completo** *adj* complete, full, perfect.

complicar (kompli'kar) *vt* complicate, muddle. **complicarse** *vr* become confused or complicated. **complicación** *nf* complication. **complicado** *adj* complicated, complex.

cómplice ('kompliθe) *nm,f* accomplice.

complicidad (kompliθi'ðað) *nf* complicity.

complot (kom'plot) *nm* plot, intrigue.

componer* (kompo'ner) *vt* **1** compose, make up. **2** repair. **3** prepare, arrange. **4** settle (a quarrel, etc.). **componerse** *vr* **1** dress up. **2** consist.

comportar (kompor'tar) *vt* tolerate, bear. **comportarse** *vr* behave. **comportamiento** *nm* behaviour. **comporte** *nm* **1** conduct. **2** bearing, carriage.

composición (komposi'θjon) *nf* **1** composition. **2** settlement (of a quarrel, etc.). **3** arrangement. **compositor** *nm* composer.

comprar (kom'prar) *vt* buy, bribe. **compra** *nf* buying, purchase. **ir de compras** go shopping. **comprador** *nm* shopper.

comprender (kompren'der) *vt,vi* **1** include, comprise. **2** understand. **comprensible** *adj* understandable. **comprensión** *nf* **1** inclusion. **2** understanding. **comprensivo** *adj* **1** inclusive. **2** understanding.

compresa (kom'presa) *nf* **1** compress. **2** sanitary towel. **compresión** *nf* compression.

comprimir (kompri'mir) *vt* squeeze, compress. **comprimirse** *vr* control oneself.

comprobar (ue) (kompro'βar) *vt* prove, check. **comprobación** *nf* proof, checking.

comprometer (komprome'ter) *vt* **1** promise. **2** risk. **comprometerse** *vr* **1** compromise oneself. **2** undertake, promise. **comprometido** *adj* **1** embarrassing. **2** committed.

compromiso *nm* 1 commitment, obligation. 2 engagement, agreement. 3 awkward situation.

compuerta (kom'pwerta) *nf* floodgate, sluice, hatch.

computar (kompu'tar) *vt* calculate. **computador** *nm* computer.

comulgar (komul'gar) *vt* give communion. *vi* take communion.

común (ko'mun) *adj* common, general. *nm* 1 community. 2 toilet. **por lo común** generally. **comunal** *adj* communal.

comunicar (komuni'kar) *vt* 1 communicate, transmit. 2 (of two rooms, etc.) connect. **communicarse** *vr* 1 be in touch, correspond. 2 connect. **comunicación** *nf* 1 communication. 2 message.

comunidad (komuni'ðað) *nf* community.

comunión (komu'njon) *nf* communion.

comunismo (komu'nismo) *nm* communism. **comunista** *adj,n* communist.

con (kon) *prep* 1 with, by means of. 2 in the company of. 3 in spite of. 4 to, towards. **con que** *conj* 1 and so. 2 whereupon. **con tal que** provided that.

cóncavo ('konkaβo) *adj* concave. *nm* hollow.

concebir (i) (konθe'βir) *vt* conceive, imagine. *vi med* conceive. **concebible** *adj* imaginable.

conceder (konθe'ðer) *vt* concede, grant.

concejo (kon'θexo) *nm* council. **concejal** *nm* councillor. **concejil** *adj* municipal.

concentrar (konθen'trar) *vt* concentrate. **concentración** *nf* concentration.

concepción (konθep'θjon) *nf* 1 conception, idea. 2 *med* conception.

concepto (kon'θepto) *nm* 1 idea, opinion. 2 heading.

concerniente (konθer'njente) *adj* concerning.

concertar (ie) (konθer'tar) *vt,vi* harmonize, agree.

conciencia (kon'θjenθja) *nf* 1 conscience, conscientiousness. 2 awareness. **concienzudo** *adj* conscientious.

concierto (kon'θjerto) *nm* 1 agreement. 2 *mus* concert, concerto.

conciliar (konθi'ljar) *vt* 1 reconcile. 2 gain. *adj* of a council. **concillio** *nm* 1 councillor. 2 council, assembly.

conciso (kon'θiso) *adj* concise.

concluir (konklu'ir) *vt* 1 conclude, finish. 2 deduce, decide. *vi* end, finish. **conclusión** *nf* conclusion.

concordar (ue) (konkor'ðar) *vt,vi* agree. **concordancia** *nf* agreement. **concorde** *adj* agreed.

concretar (konkre'tar) *vt* bring together, make concrete. **concretarse** *vr* 1 become definite. 2 confine oneself. **concreto** *adj* concrete, definite.

concubina (konku'βina) *nf* concubine.

concurrir (konkur'rir) *vi* 1 meet, come together. 2 contribute. 3 coincide. **concurrido** *adj* crowded.

concurso (kon'kurso) *nm* 1 contest, competition. 2 meeting. 3 help, cooperation.

concha ('kontʃa) *nf* shell.

condado (kon'daðo) *nm* county, earldom. **conde** *nm* earl.

condecorar (kondeko'rar) *vt* decorate (a person). **condecoración** *nf* decoration, medal.

condenar (konde'nar) *vt* 1 condemn, convict. 2 block up. **condenarse** *vr* blame oneself. **condenación** *nf* condemnation. **condenado** *adj* condemned.

condensar (konden'sar) *vt* condense. **condensador** *nm* condenser.

condescender (kondesθen'der) *vi* 1 condescend. 2 comply, agree, consent. **condescendencia** *nf* acquiescence.

condición (kondi'θjon) *nf* 1 condition, nature. 2 position, rank. 3 condition, requirement.

condicionar (kondiθjo'nar) *vt* condition, determine. **condicionado** *adj* conditioned.

condimentar (kondimen'tar) *vt* season, flavour. **condimento** *nm* seasoning.

condiscípulo (kondis'θipulo) *nm* schoolfellow.

conducir (kondu'θir) *vt* 1 transport. 2 guide. 3 conduct, direct. *vi* 1 *mot* drive. 2 be suitable. **conducirse** *vr* behave, conduct oneself. **conducción** *nf* 1 transportation. 2 guiding. 3 contracting of services. **conducción a la izquierda** left-hand drive.

conducta (kon'dukta) *nf* 1 management. 2 conduct, behaviour.

conducto (kon'dukto) *nm* 1 conduit. 2 pipe. **conductor** *nm tech* conductor.

conduje (kon'duxe) *v* see **conducir.**

conduzco (kon'duθko) *v* see **conducir.**

conectar (konek'tar) *vt tech* 1 connect. 2 switch on.

conejo (ko'nexo) *nm* rabbit. **conejillo de Indias** *nm* guinea pig.

conexión (konek'sjon) *nf* 1 *tech* connection, coupling. 2 relationship.

confabularse (kanfaβu'larse) *vr* scheme, plot.

confeccionar (konfekθjoˈnar) *vt* **1** make, prepare. **2** *med* concoct.

confederar (konfeðeˈrar) *vt* confederate, ally. **confederarse** *vr* confederate. **confederación** *nf* confederation, confederacy.

conferenciar (konferenˈθjar) *vi* confer, consult. **conferencia** *nf* **1** meeting, conference. **2** lecture, talk. **3** trunk call. **conferencia cumbre** summit conference.

conferir (**ie**) (konfeˈrir) *vt* **1** confer, grant. **2** consult.

confesar (konfeˈsar) *vt,vi* acknowledge, confess. **confesar de plano** confess everything. **confesarse** *v* **1** confess. **2** *rel* make confession. **confesarse de sus pecados** confess one's sins. **confesión** *nf* confession. **confesional** *adj* confessional. **confesionario** *nm* confessional.

confiar (konˈfjar) *vi* have faith, trust. *vt* entrust. **confiar en** trust in. **confiar al azar** leave to chance. **confianza** *nf* **1** trust. **2** self-assurance. **3** familiarity.

confidencia (konfiˈðenθja) *nf* secret or confidential information. **confidencial** *adj* confidential.

confidente (konfiˈðente) *nm,f* confidant.

configurar (konfiguˈrar) *vt* fashion, dispose, shape. **configuración** *nf* configuration, shape.

confinar (konfiˈnar) *vt* **1** confine. **2** exile, banish. **confinar con** border on. **confín** *adj* bordering. *nm* **1** border. **2** *pl* confines.

confirmar (konfirˈmar) *vt* confirm, prove.

confiscar (konfisˈkar) *vt* confiscate. **confiscación** *nf* confiscation.

confitar (konfiˈtar) *vt* **1** coat with sugar. **2** preserve in syrup. **confite** *nm* sweet. **confitería** *nf* confectioner's factory or shop.

conflicto (konˈflikto) *nm* conflict.

confluir (konfluˈir) *vi* **1** run or flow together. **2** *inf* gather, meet.

conformar (konforˈmar) *vt* adjust, make agree. **conformar con** agree with. **conformarse** *vr* **1** conform. **2** resign oneself. **conforme** *adj* **1** alike. **2** in agreement. *nm* written endorsement at the bottom of a document. **conforme a** in accordance with. **todo queda conforme estaba** everything remains as it was.

confortar (konforˈtar) *vt* **1** encourage. **2** comfort. **confortable** *adj* **1** encouraging. **2** comforting. **conforte** *nm* **1** encouragement. **2** comfort.

confrontar (konfronˈtar) *vt* **1** bring face to face. **2** compare. **confrontar con** *vi* **1** border on. **2**
confront. *vr* face up to, confront. **confrontación** *nf* **1** confrontation. **2** comparison.

confundir (konfunˈdir) *vt* **1** mix up, confuse. **2** mistake. **confusión** *nf* confusion, perplexity. **confuso** *adj* **1** mixed up. **2** blurred, indistinct. **3** bewildered.

congelar (konxeˈlar) *vt* **1** freeze. **2** congeal. **congelarse** *vr* **1** become frozen. **2** be frostbitten.

congestión (konxesˈtjon) *nf* congestion. **congestionarse** *vr* become congested. **se le congestionó la cara** he got red in the face.

conglomerarse (konglomeˈrarse) *vr* bring together.

congoja (konˈgoxa) *nf* distress.

congratular (kongratuˈlar) *vt* congratulate. **congratularse** *vr* **1** congratulate oneself. **2** be glad. **congratulación** *nf* congratulation.

congregar (kongreˈgar) *vi* congregate. **congregación** *nf* congregation.

congreso (konˈgreso) *nm* *pol* conference, assembly.

cónico (ˈkoniko) *adj* conical.

conjeturar (konxetuˈrar) *vt* guess, conjecture. **conjetura** *nf* conjecture.

conjugar (konxuˈgar) *vt* **1** bring together, combine. **2** *gram* conjugate. **conjugación** *nf* conjugation.

conjunto (konˈxunto) *adj* **1** joint. **2** joined. **3** allied, united. *nm* whole. **en conjunto** as a whole.

conjurar (konxuˈrar) *vi* **1** ally oneself with another by oath. **2** conspire. *vt* **1** take an oath, swear in. **2** exorcise. **conjurarse** *vr* ally oneself by oath.

conmemorar (konmemoˈrar) *vt* commemorate.

conmigo (konˈmigo) *pron 1st pers s* with me, with myself.

conmoción (konmoˈθjon) *nf* **1** commotion, agitation. **2** upheaval, riot. **conmoción cerebral** cerebral concussion.

conmutar (konmuˈtar) *vt* exchange.

cono (ˈkono) *nm* cone.

conocer* (konoˈθer) *vt* **1** know. **2** understand. **3** distinguish, recognize. **4** be acquainted with. **conocer de nombre** know by name. **conocerse** *vr* **1** be acquainted with. **2** understand oneself. **se conoce que** it is known that, it is clear that. **conocer de** or **en** know about. **conocer de** or **en una causa** try a case. **conocedor** *adj,nm* expert. **conocido** *adj* wellknown. *nm* acquaintance. **conocimiento** *nm* **1** knowledge. **2** understanding. **3** *med* consciousness. **perder el conocimiento** lose consciousness.

conozco (ko'noθko) *v* see **conocer.**

conque ('konke) *conj* so, then. *nm inf* condition, terms.

conquistar (konkis'tar) *vt* 1 conquer. 2 gain the affection of, win over. **conquista** *nf* 1 conquest. 2 conquered person or object. **conquistador** *adj* conquering. *nm* 1 conqueror. 2 *inf* lady-killer.

consabido (konsa'βiðo) *adj* aforementioned.

consagrar (konsa'grar) *vt* 1 consecrate, declare sacred. 2 dedicate, devote.

consanguíneo (konsan'gineo) *adj* related by blood. **consanguinidad** *nf* blood relationship.

consciente (kons'θjente) *adj* conscious.

consecuencia (konse'kwenθja) *nf* 1 result, outcome. 2 importance. **en** or **por consecuencia** consequently. **ser de consecuencia** be of importance. **traer** or **tener consecuencia** have consequences.

consecuente (konse'kwente) *adj* 1 subsequent, following. 2 consequential.

consecutivo (konseku'tiβo) *adj* consecutive.

conseguir (konse'gir) *vt* attain, secure, bring about.

consejo (kon'sexo) *nm* 1 advice. 2 council. **consejo de guerra** court-martial. **consejero** *nm* 1 adviser. 2 member of a council.

consentir (ie) (konsen'tir) *vt* 1 permit, allow. 2 pamper. *vi* agree. **consentir en** consent to. **consentirse** *vr* begin to crack or give way. **consentido** *adj* 1 pampered, spoiled. 2 complaisant.

conserje (kon'serxe) *nm* doorkeeper.

conservar (konser'βar) *vt* 1 preserve, save. 2 conserve, maintain. **conservarse** *vr* 1 be kept, remain. 2 take good care of oneself. **conserva** *nf* 1 preserved food. 2 *naut* convoy. **conservas alimenticias** tinned food. **conservación** *nf* preservation. **conservativo** *adj* preserving.

conservador (konserβa'ðor) *adj* 1 preserving. 2 *pol* conservative. *n* 1 keeper, curator. 2 *pol* conservative.

considerar (konsiðe'rar) *vt* 1 think about. 2 take into account. **considerable** *adj* 1 worthy of consideration. 2 of considerable size. **consideración** *nf* 1 consideration. 2 *rel* subject for meditation. **en consideración** under consideration. **ser de consideración** be important. **tener** or **guardar consideraciones** show consideration.

consignar (konsig'nar) *vt* 1 consign. 2 deposit for safe keeping. **consignación** *nf* consignment. **consigna** *nf* left-luggage office.

consigo (kon'sigo) *pron 3rd pers s* 1 with him. 2 with her. 3 with you. 4 with one, with oneself.

consiguiente (konsi'gjente) *adj* consequent.

consistir (konsis'tir) *vi* consist. **consistir en** consist of. **consistencia** *nf* consistency, firmness. **consistente** *adj* consistent.

consolar (ue) (konso'lar) *vt* console, comfort. **consolarse** *vr* be consoled. **consolación** *nf* consolation, comfort.

consonante (konso'nante) *adj* 1 rhyming. 2 harmonious. *nm* consonant.

consorcio (kon'sorθjo) *nm comm* partnership, consortium.

consorte (kon'sorte) *nm,f* 1 consort, associate. 2 spouse.

conspicuo (kons'pikwo) *adj* conspicuous, evident.

conspirar (konspi'rar) *vi* conspire, plot. **conspiración** *nf* conspiracy, plot.

constante (kons'tante) *adj* constant. **constancia** *nf* constancy.

constar (kons'tar) *vi* 1 be certain, be clear. 2 be recorded, be on record. **constar de** consist of. **constar en** be recorded in or on. **consta que es así** it's clear that it's so.

constiparse (konsti'parse) *vr* catch a cold. **constipación** *nf med* cold. **estar constipado** have a cold.

constituir* (konstitu'ir) *vt* constitute, compose. **constitución** *nf* constitution.

construir (konstru'ir) *vt* 1 construct. **construcción** *nf* construction.

consuelo (kon'swelo) *nm* consolation, alleviation.

cónsul ('konsul) *nm* consul.

consultar (konsul'tar) *vt,vi* consult. **consulta** *nf* consultation.

consumado (konsu'maðo) *adj* 1 consummate. 2 complete.

consumir (konsu'mir) *vt* 1 consume, destroy. 2 eat up. **consumirse** *vr* be destroyed. **consumido** *adj* 1 consumed. 2 *inf* emaciated, wasted. **consumo** *nm* consumption.

contabilidad (kontaβili'ðað) *nf* 1 calculability. 2 accounting. **contable** *nm* accountant.

contacto (kon'takto) *nm* contact.

contado (kon'taðo) *adj* 1 counted. 2 few, limited. **de contado** immediately. **pago al contado** *nm* cash payment. **contador** *nm* 1 counter. 2 cashier, bookkeeper. 3 *tech* meter. **contador de aparcamiento** parking meter.

contagiar (konta'xjar) *vt* 1 transmit a contagious disease to. 2 pervert. **contagio** *nm* contagion, infection.

contaminar (kontami'nar) *vt* contaminate. **contaminación** *nf* contamination.

contar (ue) (kon'tar) *vt* 1 count. 2 relate, tell. **contar una historia** tell a story.

contemplar (kontem'plar) *vt* contemplate.

contemporáneo (kontempo'raneo) *adj,nm* contemporary.

contender (ie) (konten'der) *vt* 1 contend, fight. 2 dispute, debate. **contendedor** *nm* contender.

contener (ie) (konte'ner) *vt* contain. **contención** *nf* 1 containment. 2 contest.

contentar (konten'tar) *vt* satisfy, make happy. **ser de buen contentar** be easy to please. **contento** *adj* content, satisfied.

contestar (kontes'tar) *vt* 1 reply to. 2 confirm, support. **contestar una carta** answer a letter. **contestable** 1 debatable. 2 answerable. **contestación** *nf* 1 reply. 2 debate.

contexto (kon'teksto) *nm* context.

contienda (kon'tjenda) *nf* 1 contest, fight. 2 dispute.

contigo (kon'tigo) *pron* 2nd pers s fam with you.

contiguo (kon'tigwo) *adj* contiguous, adjoining. **contigüidad** *nf* contiguity.

continente (konti'nente) *adj* continent. *nm* 1 container. 2 bearing, air. 3 continent. **continencia** *nf* continence.

contingente (kontin'xente) *adj* contingent, possible. **contingencia** *nm* contingency, possibility.

continuar (konti'nwar) *vt* continue. *vi* last, endure. **continuarse** *vr* extend oneself, be continued. **se continuar á** to be continued. **continuación** *nf* continuation. **a continuación de** immediately after. **continuo** *adj* continuous.

contorno (kon'torno) *nm* 1 outline. 2 *inf* neighbourhood. **en contorno** all around.

contra ('kontra) *prep* 1 against. 2 facing, opposite. **contra viento y marea** against all odds. **en contra** in opposition.

contrabajo (kontra'βaxo) *nm mus* double bass.

contrabando (kontra'βando) *nm* 1 act of smuggling. 2 contraband.

contracción (kontrak'θjon) *nf* contraction.

contradecir* (kontraðe'θir) *vt* contradict. **con-**

tradicción *nf* contradiction. **contradictorio** *adj* contradictory.

contraer (kontra'er) *vt* contract.

contrafuerte (kontra'fwerte) *nm* buttress.

contrahacer (kontraa'θer) *vt* imitate.

contrahecho (kontra'etʃo) *adj* deformed.

contramaestre (kontrama'estre) *nm* 1 *naut* warrant officer. 2 foreman.

contrapesar (kontrape'sar) *vt* 1 counterbalance. 2 compensate for.

contrariar (kontra'rjar) *vt* oppose, contradict. **contrariedad** *nf* setback, misfortune. **contrario** *adj* 1 opposed. 2 harmful. *nm* 1 opponent. 2 adversary. **en contrario** in opposition. **por lo contrario** on the contrary.

contrarrestar (kontrarres'tar) *vt* 1 counteract, offset. 2 *sport* return (the ball).

contrasentido (kontrasen'tiðo) *nm* inconsistency, nonsense.

contrastar (kontras'tar) *vt* 1 resist, oppose. 2 stamp with a hallmark. *vi* contrast. **contraste** *nm* 1 opposition. 2 contrast. **marca de contraste** *nf* hallmark.

contrato (kon'trato) *nm* contract.

contravenir (ie) (kontraβe'nir) *vt* contravene.

contribuir (kontriβu'ir) *vt,vi* contribute. **contribución** *nf* 1 contribution. 2 tax.

controversia (kontro'βersja) *nf* controversy.

contumacia (kontu'maθja) *nf* 1 obstinate disobedience. 2 contempt of court.

convalecer* (könβale'θer) *vi* 1 convalesce, recover. **convalecencia** *nf* 1 convalescence. 2 convalescent hospital.

convencer* (könβen'θer) *vt* convince. **convencerse** *vr* be convinced.

convención (könβen'θjon) *nf* convention.

convenir (ie) (könβe'nir) *vt* agree, be agreed. **me conviene** it suits me. **convenible** *adj* compliant. **conveniencia** *nf* 1 usefulness. 2 advantage. **conveniente** *adj* 1 convenient. 2 conformable. **convenio** *nm* agreement, contract.

convento (kon'βento) *nm* convent.

converger (konver'xer) *vi also* **convergir** 1 converge. 2 concur. **convergencia** *nf* convergence. **convergente** *adj* convergent.

conversar (könβer'sar) *vi* 1 converse, talk. 2 live with others. **conversar en** or **sobre** converse on. **conversador** *adj* sociable. **conversación** *nf* conversation.

convertir (ie) (könβer'tir) *vt* convert. **conversión** *nf* 1 conversion. 2 convergence.

convicción (könβik'θjon) *nf* belief, conviction.

convidar (konβi'ðar) vt invite. **convidar a uno con** treat someone to. **convite** nm invitation.

convincente (konβin'θente) adj convincing.

convivencia (konβi'βenθja) nf coexistence.

convocar (konβo'kar) vt convoke, call together.

convoy (kon'βoj) nm convoy.

conyugal (konju'gal) adj conjugal, matrimonial. **cónyuge** ('konjuxe) nm,f spouse.

coñac (ko'nak) nm cognac, brandy.

cooperar (koope'rar) vi cooperate. **cooperación** nf cooperation. **cooperativa** nf cooperative.

coordinar (koorði'nar) vt coordinate.

copa ('kopa) nf 1 glass. **tomarse unas copas** have a few drinks.

Copenhague (kope'nage) nf Copenhagen.

copete (ko'pete) nm 1 tuft or lock of hair. 2 crest, tuft of feathers. **de alto copete** aristocratic.

copia ('kopja) nf 1 abundance, plenty. 2 copy, transcript.

copiar (ko'pjar) vt transcribe, record. **copiador** adj copying. nm 1 copier. 2 copybook. **copiante** nm,f copyist.

copla ('kopla) nf 1 lit couplet. 2 stanza. **coplas de ciego** doggerel rhymes.

copo ('kopo) nm 1 spinning yarn. 2 snowflake.

coque ('koke) nm coke.

coraje (ko'raxe) nm 1 courage. 2 irritation.

coraza (ko'raθa) nf armour.

corazón (kora'θon) nm heart. **con el corazón en la mano** sincerely. **dar** or **decir el corazón** have a premonition.

corbata (kor'βata) nf necktie.

Córcega ('korθega) nf Corsica.

corchea (kor'tʃea) nf mus quaver.

corchete (kor'tʃete) nm hook and eye, clasp.

corcho ('kortʃo) nm cork.

cordel (kor'ðel) nm thin rope, string. **a cordel** in a straight line.

cordero (kor'ðero) nm lamb.

cordial (kor'ðjal) adj 1 invigorating. 2 affectionate. **cordialidad** nf 1 affection. 2 sincerity.

cordillera (korði'ʎera) nf chain of mountains.

cordón (kor'ðon) nm string. **cordón umbilical** umbilical cord.

Corea (ko'rea) nf Korea. **coreano** adj,n Korean. nm Korean (language).

coreografía (koreogra'fia) nf choreography.

corneta (kor'neta) nf bugle. **corneta de llaves** cornet.

cornudo (kor'nuðo) adj 1 horned. 2 cuckolded. nm cuckold.

coro ('koro) nm chorus.

coronar (koro'nar) vt crown. **corona** nf crown. **coronación** nf coronation.

coronel (koro'nel) nm colonel.

coronilla (koro'niʎa) n crown, top of the head.

corpóreo (kor'poreo) adj corporeal.

corral (kor'ral) nm farm yard.

correa (kor'rea) nf leather strap. **correa de ventilador** fan belt.

corrección (korrek'θjon) nf correction.

corredor (korre'ðor) nm 1 sport runner. 2 comm agent, broker. 3 corridor.

corregir (i) (korre'xir) vt correct. **corregirse** vr reform oneself.

correo (kor'reo) nm 1 courier. 2 post, mail. **correo urgente** special delivery.

correr (kor'rer) vi 1 run, flow. 2 go, pass. vt cover, travel over. **correrse** vr move.

corresponder (korrespon'der) vi 1 correspond. 2 be fitting, match, go with. 3 concern. 4 respond, reply. **a quien corresponda** to whom it may concern. **corresponderse** vr 1 correspond. 2 agree. 3 be fond of each other. **correspondencia** nf 1 correspondence, letters. 2 contact. 3 agreement. **corresponsal** nm newspaper correspondent.

corrida (kor'riða) nf running. **corrida de toros** bullfight.

corrido (kor'riðo) adj exceeding the specified weight.

corriente (kor'rjente) adj 1 running. 2 current. 3 everyday, standard. nf current, flow. **agua corriente** nf running water. **al corriente** up-to-date, informed.

corroborar (korroβo'rar) vt corroborate.

corroer (korro'er) vt corrode.

corromper (korrom'per) vt corrupt, rot. vi inf smell bad. **corromperse** vr go bad, become corrupted.

corrosión (korro'sjon) nf corrosion.

corrupción (korrup'θjon) nf 1 corruption. 2 stench.

cortar (kor'tar) vt cut. **cortarse** vr 1 cut oneself. 2 become embarrassed or tongue-tied. **cortante** adj cutting, sharp. **corte** nm 1 cutting edge. 2 act of cutting. 3 cut.

corte ('korte) nf royal court.

cortejar (korte'xar) vt court. **cortejo** nm 1 courtship. 2 entourage.

cortés (kor'tes) adj gracious, courteous.

cortesía (korte'sia) nf courtesy.

corteza (kor'teθa) nf rind.

cortijo (kor'tixo) nm 1 farm. 2 farmhouse.

cortina (kor'tina) nf curtain. **cortina de hierro** iron curtain. **cortina de humo** smokescreen.

corto ('korto) adj short. **corto de vista** short-sighted.

corvo ('korβo) adj curved.

cosa ('kosa) nf thing. **cosa de oír/ver** something worth listening to/seeing.

cosecha (ko'setʃa) nf harvest.

coser (ko'ser) vt sew. **coserse la boca** not speak a word.

cosquillas (kos'kiʎas) nf tickling, ticklishness.

costa ('kosta) nf coast.

costado (kos'taðo) nm 1 side. 2 pl lineage.

costar (ue) (kos'tar) vi cost. **costa** or **coste** nf cost.

costilla (kos'tiʎa) nf rib.

costra ('kostra) nf 1 crust. 2 med scab.

costumbre (kos'tumbre) nf custom, habit. **de costumbre** usual, usually.

costura (kos'tura) nf sewing.

cotejar (kote'xar) vt compare.

cotidiano (koti'ðjano) adj daily.

coto ('koto) nm 1 reserved hunting grounds. 2 landmark.

coyuntura (kojun'tura) nf 1 anat joint. 2 opportunity, occasion.

coz (koθ) nf 1 kick. 2 insult.

cráneo ('kraneo) nm skull.

crear (kre'ar) vt 1 create. 2 invent. 3 found. **creación** nf creation. **creador** nm creator.

crecer* (kre'θer) vi grow. **crecerse** vr 1 increase. 2 acquire greater confidence. **creces** nf pl increase. **con creces** adv amply. **crecido** adj numerous. **crecimiento** nm 1 growth. 2 increase in value.

credenciales (kreðen'θjales) nf pl credentials.

crédito ('kreðito) nm 1 credit. 2 belief. **carta de crédito** nf credit card.

credo ('kreðo) nm creed. **en un credo** in an instant.

crédulo ('kreðulo) adj credulous.

creer* (kre'er) vt,vi 1 believe. 2 think. **¡ya lo creo!** interj of course! **creíble** adj credible.

crema ('krema) nf 1 cream. 2 cream of society. adj 1 beige. 2 best.

crepúsculo (kre'puskulo) nm twilight.

crespo ('krespo) adj 1 crispy. 2 curly.

cresta ('kresta) nf crest.

creyente (kre'jente) adj believing. nm,f believer.

cría ('kria) nf 1 act of breeding. 2 young animal. 3 litter, brood.

criado ('krjaðo) n servant. adj brought up, bred. **bien criado** well-bred.

criar (kri'ar) vt 1 create. 2 breed. 3 suckle, nurse. **criar carnes** put on weight. **crianza** nf 1 breeding. 2 lactation. **criatura** nf 1 creature. 2 new-born baby.

cribar (kri'βar) vt screen, sift. **criba** nm screen, sieve.

crimen ('krimen) nm 1 serious crime. 2 inf wicked deed. **criminal** adj,n criminal.

cripta ('kripta) nf crypt.

crisálida (kri'saliða) nf 1 pupa. 2 cocoon.

crisantemo (krisan'temo) nm chrysanthemum.

crisis ('krisis) nf invar crisis.

crisol (kri'sol) nm crucible.

crispar (kris'par) vt 1 cause to twitch or contract. 2 irritate, annoy. **crisparse** vr twitch.

cristal (kris'tal) nm crystal, glass. **cristal hilado** fibre glass. **cristalería** nf 1 glassworks. 2 glassware. **cristalino** adj crystalline.

cristiano (kris'tjano) adj Christian. n 1 Christian. 2 person. **cristiandad** nf Christianity.

Cristo ('kristo) nm Christ.

criterio (kri'terjo) nm criterion.

criticar (kriti'kar) vt 1 criticize. **crítica** nf criticism. **crítico** adj critical. n critic.

cromo ('kromo) nm chromium, chrome.

crónica ('kronika) nf 1 chronicle. 2 news report.

cronista (kro'nista) nm,f chronicler.

cronología (kronolo'xia) nf chronology. **cronológico** adj chronological.

croquis ('krokis) nm invar rough draft, sketch.

cruce ('kruθe) nm crossing. **cruce a nivel** level crossing. **cruce de peatones** pedestrian crossing.

crucificar (kruθifi'kar) vt 1 crucify. 2 molest, torment. **crucifijo** nm crucifix. **crucifixión** nf crucifixion.

crudo ('kruðo) adj crude.

cruel (kru'el) adj cruel. **crueldad** nf cruelty.

cruento (kru'ento) adj bloody.

crujir (kru'xir) vi crackle. **crujido** nm crackling.

crustáceo (krus'taθeo) nm crustacean.

cruz (kruθ) nf cross. **en cruz** crosswise.

cruzar (kru'θar) vt 1 cross. 2 lay across. **cruzarse** vr 1 cross each other, intersect. 2 cross oneself, make the sign of the cross. **cruzarse de brazos** be idle. **cruzada** nf crusade. **cruzado** adj 1 crossed. 2 cross-bred. nm crusader.

cuaderno (kwa'ðerno) nm notebook.

cuadra ('kwaðra) nf stable.

cuadrado (kwaˈðraðo) *nm* square.
cuadragésimo (kwaðraˈxesimo) *adj* fortieth.
cuadrante (kwaˈðrante) *adj* squaring. *nm* quadrant.
cuadrar (kwaˈðrar) *vt* square.
cuadro (ˈkwaðro) *nm* 1 square. 2 painting, picture. **en cuadro** square-shaped.
cuadrúpedo (kwaˈðrupeðo) *adj,nm* quadruped.
cuajar (kwaˈxar) *vt* 1 congeal, thicken. 2 ornament excessively. *vi* become set or established. **cuajarse** *vr* 1 thicken. 2 fill with.
cual (kwal) *pron* 1 which. 2 he who. **a cual más** equally.
cualidad (kwaliˈðað) *nf* quality.
cuan (kwan) *adv* how.
cuando (ˈkwando) *adv* when. **de cuando** or **de vez en cuando** from time to time. **¿de cuándo acá?** since when?
cuantía (kwanˈtia) *nf* quantity.
cuanto (ˈkwanto) *adj* 1 as much as. 2 how much. **¿cuántos?** how many? **por cuanto** inasmuch as.
cuarenta (kwaˈrenta) *adj,nm* forty.
cuaresma (kwaˈresma) *nf* Lent.
cuartear (kwarteˈar) *vt* quarter, cut up.
cuartel (kwarˈtel) *nm* 1 quarter. 2 *mil* barracks.
cuatro (ˈkwatro) *adj,nm* four. **cuarto** *adj* fourth. *nm* 1 quarter. 2 room. **cuarto de baño** bathroom.
cuba (ˈkuβa) *nf* barrel. **estar hecho una cuba** be drunk.
Cuba (ˈkuβa) *nf* Cuba. **cubano** *adj,nm* Cuban.
cubículo (kuˈβikulo) *nm* cubicle.
cubierta (kuˈβjerta) *nf* 1 cover. 2 *naut* deck. 3 *mot* bonnet.
cubierto (kuˈβjerto) *adj* covered. *nm* 1 place at a table. 2 set of knife, fork, and spoon. 3 meal. **a bajo cubierto** under cover. **precio del cubierto** cover charge.
cubo (ˈkuβo) *nm* bucket.
cubrir (kuˈβrir) *vt* 1 cover. 2 protect. **cubrirse** *vr* 1 put on one's hat. 2 protect oneself against a risk.
cucaracha (kukaˈratʃa) *nf* cockroach.
cuclillas (kuˈkliʎas) *adv* in a squatting position, sitting on one's heels.
cuclillo (kuˈkliʎo) *nm* 1 cuckoo. 2 cuckold.
cuchara (kuˈtʃara) *nf* spoon. **cucharada** *nf* spoonful. **cucharadita** *nf* teaspoonful. **cucharón** *nm* ladle.
cuchichear (kutʃitʃeˈar) *vi* whisper. **cuchicheo** *nm* 1 whisper. 2 whispering.
cuchilla (kuˈtʃiʎa) *nf* 1 large knife. 2 cutting

tool. **cuchillada** *nf* slash, knife wound. **cuchilla de afeitar** razor blade. **cuchillería** *nf* 1 cutlery shop. 2 cutlery. **cuchillo** *nm* knife.
cuello (ˈkweʎo) *nm* 1 neck. 2 collar.
cuenca (ˈkwenka) *nf* 1 bowl. 2 eye socket. 3 *geog* basin.
cuenta (ˈkwenta) *nf* 1 count, calculation. 2 *comm* account, bill. 3 report. **a cuenta y riesgo de uno** at one's own risk.
cuento (ˈkwento) *nm* 1 tale, story. 2 *inf* exaggerated talk, fuss. 3 *pl* trouble.
cuerda (ˈkwerða) *nf* 1 cord. 2 chord.
cuerdo (ˈkwerðo) *adj* sane. *nm* sane person.
cuerno (ˈkwerno) *nm* horn.
cuero (ˈkwero) *nm* 1 hide, skin. 2 leather.
cuerpo (ˈkwerpo) *nm* body. **cuerpo estatal** public body. **cuerpo extraño** foreign body.
cuervo (ˈkwerβo) *nm* raven.
cuesta (ˈkwesta) *nf* sloping ground. **a cuestas** on one's back.
cuestión (kwesˈtjon) *nf* 1 question, issue. 2 dispute, quarrel. **cuestionar** *vt* question, argue about. *vi* argue.
cueva (ˈkweβa) *nf* 1 cave. 2 cellar.
cuidado (kwiˈðaðo) *nm* 1 care, carefulness. 2 fear, worry. **¡cuidado!** *interj* beware!
cuidar (kwiˈðar) *vt* take care of, pay attention to. **cuidar de que** take care that. **no cuidarse de** take no notice of.
culebra (kuˈleβra) *nf* snake.
culebrear (kuleβreˈar) *vi* wriggle, zigzag.
culo (ˈkulo) *nm* backside, bottom.
culpar (kulˈpar) *vt* blame, condemn. **culparse** *vr* take the blame. **culpa** *nf* 1 blame, fault. 2 guilt. **culpable** *adj* 1 guilty. 2 blameworthy. *nm,f* culprit.
cultivar (kultiˈβar) *vt* 1 cultivate. 2 practise, improve. **cultivador** *nm* cultivator, grower. **cultivación** *nf* cultivation. **cultivo** *nm* 1 cultivation. 2 crop.
culto (ˈkulto) *adj* 1 cultivated. 2 cultured. *nm* cult. **rendir culto a** worship.
cultura (kulˈtura) *nf* culture, learning.
cumbre (ˈkumbre) *nf* summit, peak.
cumpleaños (kumpleˈaɲos) *nm invar* birthday.
cumplir (kumˈplir) *vt* fulfil, realize. **cumplir años** reach an age. ~*vi* fulfil one's duties.
cúmulo (ˈkumulo) *nm* 1 heap, accumulation. 2 *sci* cumulus.
cuna (ˈkuna) *nf* 1 cradle. 2 place of origin, birthplace. 3 lineage, family.
cundir (kunˈdir) *vi* spread, expand.
cuneta (kuˈneta) *nf* ditch.

cuña

cuña ('kuɲa) nf wedge.

cuñado (ku'ɲaðo) nm brother-in-law.

cuño ('kuɲo) nm tech stamp, die-stamp.

cuota ('kwota) nf 1 quota. 2 dues. **cuota del gremio** union dues.

cupe ('kupe) v see **caber.**

cupón (ku'pon) nm coupon.

cura ('kura) nm priest. **cura párroco** parish priest.

curar (ku'rar) vi recover, get well. vt 1 treat, apply a remedy. 2 cure. **curarse** vr 1 recover, be cured. 2 take treatment (for a wound). **cura** nf cure, remedy. **curación** nf curing. **primera curación** first aid. **curado** adj 1 cured. 2 hardened, tanned.

curioso (kuri'oso) adj 1 curious. 2 neat, clean. 3 careful. n curious person. **curiosidad** nf curiosity.

cursar (kur'sar) vt 1 frequent. 2 send out, dispatch. 3 study.

cursi ('kursi) adj inf in bad taste, flashy, cheap. n flashy, pretentious person.

curso ('kurso) nm 1 course, direction. 2 educ year. **curso acelerado** crash course.

curtir (kur'tir) vt 1 tan. 2 harden. **curtirse** vr 1 harden. 2 become accustomed to. **curtido** adj tanned, hardened. nm tanning. **estar curtido en** 1 be skilled at. 2 be hardened to. **curtidor** nm tanner.

curva ('kurβa) nf curve.

curvo ('kurβo) adj curved.

cúspide ('kuspiðe) nf peak, summit.

custodiar (kusto'ðjar) vt 1 take care of. 2 guard. **custodia** nf custody. **custodio** nm custodian, guardian.

cutis ('kutis) nm invar human skin, complexion.

cuyo ('kujo) pron 1 whose. 2 of which, of whom.

CH

chabacano (tʃaβa'kano) adj in bad taste. **chabacanería** nf 1 vulgarity. 2 vulgar remark.

chafar (tʃa'far) vt 1 flatten. 2 crumple. 3 spoil, make a mess of. **chafar a uno** cut someone short.

chal (tʃal) nm shawl.

chalado (tʃa'laðo) adj inf crazy, dotty.

chalán (tʃa'lan) nm 1 dealer, seller. 2 horse dealer. 3 inf crafty businessman, shady dealer.

chaleco (tʃa'leko) nm waistcoat.

chambelán (tʃambe'lan) nm chamberlain.

champaña (tʃam'paɲa) nm champagne.

champú (tʃam'pu) nm shampoo.

chamuscar (tʃamus'kar) vt singe, scorch.

chancear (tʃanθe'ar) vi joke, make jokes about.

chanchullo (tʃan'tʃuʎo) nm inf crooked deal.

chantaje (tʃan'taxe) nm blackmail.

chanza ('tʃanθa) nf joke. **en** or **de chanza** in fun.

chapa ('tʃapa) nf sheet, plate.

chaparro (tʃa'parro) adj squat, short, and fat.

chapotear (tʃapote'ar) vt moisten (with sponge, etc.). vi splash. **chapoteo** nm 1 moistening. 2 splashing.

chapucero (tʃapu'θero) adj 1 rough, crude. 2 clumsy, amateurish. nm clumsy person.

chapuzar (tʃapu'θar) vt plunge into water.

charca ('tʃarka) nf pool. **charco** nm puddle.

charlar (tʃar'lar) vi chat, gossip. **charla** nf talk, chatter. **charlador** adj also **charlatán** talkative, chattering. n chatterbox. **charladuría** nf gossip, small talk.

charol (tʃa'rol) nm 1 varnish. 2 patent leather. **darse charol** brag.

charro ('tʃarro) adj 1 vulgar, coarse. 2 flashy, in bad taste.

chasco ('tʃasko) nm 1 prank, trick. 2 disappointment.

chasquear (tʃaske'ar) vt 1 disappoint. 2 trick, make a fool of.

chato ('tʃato) adj 1 flat-nosed. 2 blunt, flattened. nm small glass, glass (of wine).

chaval (tʃa'βal) nm inf lad, kid.

Checoslovaquia (tʃekoslo'βakja) nf Czechoslovakia. **checoslovaco** adj,n Czechoslovak. **checoslovaca** nm Czech (language).

cheque ('tʃeke) nm cheque. **cheque de viajero** traveller's cheque.

chicle ('tʃikle) nm chewing gum.

chico ('tʃiko) adj 1 small. 2 very young. nm 1 youngster, lad. 2 inf old chap.

chichón (tʃi'tʃon) nm lump, swelling.

chiflar (tʃi'flar) vi whistle, hiss. vt 1 mock in public. 2 inf drink, gulp down. **chiflarse** vr become crazy. **chifla** nf whistle. **chiflado** adj crazy. **chifle** nm whistle.

chile ('tʃile) nm chili.

Chile ('tʃile) nm Chile. **chileno** adj,n also **chileño** Chilean.

chillar (tʃi'ʎar) vi shriek, howl, scream. **chillador** adj howling, shrieking. **chillería** nf 1 noisy row. 2 scolding. **chillido** nm scream.

chimenea (tʃime'nea) nf 1 chimney. 2 fireplace.

chimenea francesa fireplace with mantelpiece.

chimpancé (tʃimpan'θe) nm chimpanzee.

china ('tʃina) nf chinaware.

China ('tʃina) nf China. **chino** adj,n Chinese. nm Chinese (language).

chinche ('tʃintʃe) nf bedbug.

chingar (tʃin'gar) vt inf drink too much or too frequently. **chingarse** vr get drunk.

Chipre ('tʃipre) nf Cyprus. **chipriota** adj,n also **chipriote** Cypriot.

chiripa (tʃi'ripa) nf stroke of luck.

chirriar (tʃir'rjar) vi 1 creak. 2 chirp. **chirriadero** adj 1 creaking. 2 chirping. **chirrido** nm chirping.

chisme ('tʃisme) nm 1 contrivance, gadget. 2 piece of gossip.

chismoso (tʃis'moso) adj gossiping. nm gossip.

chispear (tʃispe'ar) vi 1 spark. 2 sparkle. 3 drizzle. **chispa** nf 1 spark. 2 sparkle. 3 small amount.

chisporrotear (tʃisporrote'ar) vi spark. **chisporroteo** nm inf sparking.

chistar (tʃis'tar) vi mumble, mutter. **no chistar** not say a word. ¡**chist**! interj sh!

chiste ('tʃiste) nf joke.

chocar (tʃo'kar) vt 1 shock, surprise. vi 1 shock, be surprising. 2 collide, crash.

chocolate (tʃoko'late) nm chocolate.

choque ('tʃoke) nm 1 jolt, crash. 2 shock. 3 dispute, conflict.

chorizo (tʃo'riθo) nm spicy pork sausage.

chorrear (tʃorre'ar) vi 1 gush, spurt. 2 drip. **chorreo** nm gushing, dripping. **chorro** nm gush.

choza ('tʃoθa) nf hovel, hut.

chubasco (tʃu'βasko) nm 1 shower. 2 adversity, difficulties.

chuleta (tʃu'leta) nf cutlet, chop.

chulo ('tʃulo) adj 1 amusing. 2 proud. 3 bold, outspoken. nm amusing, easy-going person.

chunga ('tʃunga) nf inf fun, joking. **chungar** vi tell jokes, banter.

chupar (tʃu'par) vt suck, absorb, take in. **chuparse** vr become lean.

churro ('tʃurro) nm 1 cul fritter. 2 inf mess.

chusma ('tʃusma) nf rabble, riffraff.

D

dádiva ('daðiβa) nf present, gift.

dado ('daðo) nm game die. **dados falsos** loaded dice.

daga ('daga) nf dagger.

dama ('dama) nf 1 lady. 2 mistress, lover. 3 game queen. 4 pl game draughts.

damasco (da'masko) nm damask.

damnificar (damnifi'kar) vt harm, injure.

danés (da'nes) adj Danish. nm 1 Dane. 2 Danish (language).

Danubio (da'nuβjo) nm Danube.

danzar (dan'θar) vi,vt dance. **danza** nf dancing, dance. **danzante** nm dancer.

dañar (da'ɲar) vt damage, harm. **dañarse** vr get hurt. **dañoso** adj bad, harmful.

dar (dar) vt give. **darse** vr 1 surrender. 2 exist, occur. 3 regard oneself. **dar** a look out on, overlook. **dar como** or **por** consider, regard. **dar con** 1 meet. 2 find, discover. **lo mismo da** it makes no difference. **darse cuenta** notice, realize.

dardo ('darðo) nm dart.

dársena ('darsena) nm inner harbour, dock.

data ('data) nf 1 date. 2 comm item.

dátil ('datil) nm bot date.

dato nm piece of information, fact.

de (de) prep 1 of. 2 from.

debajo (de'βaxo) adv underneath. **debajo de** prep underneath.

debatir (deβa'tir) vt debate, dispute. **debate** nm debate.

deber (de'βer) vt owe. vi must, ought. **deberse a** be due to, be on account of. ~nm 1 duty. 2 debt.

débil ('deβil) adj weak.

debilitar (deβili'tar) vt weaken. **debilidad** nf weakness.

débito ('deβito) nm debt, debit.

decadencia (deka'ðenθja) nf decadence, decline. **decadente** adj decadent, declining.

decaer (deka'er) vi decline. **decaído** adj 1 declining. 2 sad. **decaído de ánimo** in low spirits. **decaimiento** nm decline.

decano (de'kano) nm dean.

decapitar (dekapi'tar) vt behead.

decena (de'θena) nf unit of ten.

decencia (de'θenθja) nf 1 decency. 2 cleanliness.

decenio (de'θenjo) nm decade.

decente (de'θente) adj 1 decent. 2 tidy, clean. 3 respectable.

decepción (deθep'θjon) nf disappointment. **decepcionar** vt disappoint.

decidir (deθi'ðir) vt 1 decide. 2 convince. **decidirse** vr make up one's mind.

décimo ('deθimo) adj tenth. **décima** nf tenth. **decimal** adj,nm decimal.

decimoctavo (deθimok'tavo) adj eighteenth.

decimocuarto (deθimo'kwarto) adj fourteenth.

decimonoveno (deθimono'βeno) adj also **decimonono** nineteenth.

decimoquinto (deθimo'kinto) adj fifteenth.

decimoséptimo (deθimo'septimo) adj seventeenth.

decimosexto (deθimo'seksto) adj sixteenth.

decimotercio (deθimo'terθjo) adj thirteenth.

decir (de'θir) vt,vi say, tell. **a decir verdad** truthfully. **¡diga!** hello (on the telephone).

decisión (deθi'sjon) nf 1 decision. 2 determination. **decisivo** adj decisive..

declamar (dekla'mar) vi speak out. vt declaim, recite. **declamación** nf declamation, recital.

declarar (dekla'rar) vt 1 declare, state. 2 law find. **declararse** vr 1 declare oneself, make one's opinion known. 2 propose to (a girl).

declinar (dekli'nar) vi decline, decay. vt 1 decline, refuse. 2 gram inflect. **declinación** nf 1 decline, falling off. 2 gram declension.

declive (de'kliβe) nm 1 slope, incline. 2 comm slump.

decorar (deko'rar) vt decorate, adorn. **decoración** nf decoration. **decorador** nm decorator. **decorativo** adj decorative.

decoro (de'koro) nm 1 respect. 2 propriety, decorum.

decrecer (dekre'θer) vi decrease.

decrépito (de'krepito) adj decrepit.

decretar (dekre'tar) vt decree. **decreto** nm decree.

dedal (de'ðal) nm thimble.

dédalo ('deðalo) nm maze.

dedicar (deði'kar) vt dedicate, devote.

dedillo (de'ðiʎo) nm little finger. **saber al dedillo** know perfectly.

dedo ('deðo) nm 1 finger, toe. 2 small amount, drop. **estar a dos dedos de** be within an ace of.

deducir (deðu'θir) vt deduce. **deducción** nf deduction. **deductivo** adj deductive.

defender (ie) (defen'der) vt defend. **defendido** nm law defendant. **defensa** nf defence.

defensa pasiva civil defence. **defensivo** adj defensive.

deferencia (defe'renθja) nf deference.

deferir (ie) (defe'rir) vt law refer, relegate. **deferir a** defer to.

deficiencia (defi'θjenθja) nf deficiency. **deficiente** adj deficient.

déficit ('defiθit) nm, pl **déficits** or **deficits** 1 deficit. 2 shortage.

definir (defi'nir) vt define. **definición** nf definition. **definido** adj definite. **definitivo** adj definitive. **en definitivo** finally, in short.

deformar (defor'mar) vt 1 disfigure. 2 distort. **deformarse** vr become deformed, get out of shape. **deformación** nf deformation. **deforme** adj deformed, abnormal.

defraudar (defrau'ðar) vt 1 cheat, deceive. 2 disappoint. **defraudar impuestos** evade taxes. **defraudación** nf deceit. **defraudador** adj fraudulent.

defunción (defun'θjon) nf death.

degenerar (dexene'rar) vi 1 degenerate. 2 decline, get worse.

degollar (ue) (dego'ʎar) vt 1 cut the throat. 2 law behead. **degollación** nf 1 throat-cutting. 2 beheading. **degolladero** nm 1 throttle. 2 slaughterhouse. 3 scaffold.

degradar (degra'ðar) vt degrade. **degradación** nf degradation. **degradante** adj degrading.

degustar (degus'tar) vt taste, sample.

dehesa (de'esa) nf pasture.

deidad (dei'ðað) nf deity.

deificar (deifi'kar) vt deify.

dejar (de'xar) vt 1 leave, forsake. 2 allow, let. **dejar de 1** stop, leave off. 2 fail to, neglect to. **dejarse** vr neglect oneself. **dejarse de 1** stop (doing something). 2 let oneself be (heard, deceived, persuaded, etc.).

del (del) contraction of **de el**.

delantal (delan'tal) nm apron.

delante (de'lante) adv ahead, in front. **delante de** in front of, before.

delatar (dela'tar) vt 1 denounce. 2 betray. **delator** nm informer.

delegar (dele'gar) vt delegate. **delegación** nf delegation. **delegado** adj delegated. nm delegate.

deleitar (delei'tar) vt delight. **deleitarse** vr br delighted. **deleite** nm delight.

deletrear (deletre'ar) vt 1 explain, spell out. 2 interpret.

deleznable (deleθ'naβle) adj 1 brittle. 2 frail, weak.

delfín (del'fin) nm dolphin.

delgado (del'gaðo) adj 1 thin, slender. 2 delicate. **delgadez** nf 1 thinness. 2 delicateness.

deliberar (deliβe'rar) vt 1 discuss. 2 debate. **deliberación** nf deliberation.

delicado (deli'kaðo) adj 1 delicate. 2 dainty. **delicadez** nf 1 debility, weakness. **delicadeza** nf 1 delicacy. 2 refinement. 3 tactfulness.

delicia (de'liθja) nf delight. **delicioso** adj delightful.

delimitar (delimi'tar) vt delimit.

delincuencia (delin'kwenθja) nf delinquency. **delincuencia de menores** juvenile delinquency. **delincuente** adj,n criminal.

delinear (deline'ar) vt 1 outline, draw lines around. **delineante** nm draughtsman.

delirar (deli'rar) vi be delirious, rave.

delito (de'lito) nm crime.

demacrarse (dema'krarse) vr waste away. **demacración** nf emaciation. **demacrado** adj emaciated.

demagogia (dema'goxja) nf demagogy.

demandar (deman'dar) vt 1 request. 2 ask, question. 3 law petition.

demarcar (demar'kar) vt demarcate. **demarcación** nf demarcation.

demás (de'mas) adj other, rest, remaining. pron **los demás, las demás** the others.

demasía (dema'sia) nf excess.

demasiado (dema'sjaðo) adj,adv too much.

demencia (de'menθja) nf insanity.

democracia (demo'kraθja) nf democracy. **demócrata** adj democratic. nm,f democrat. **democrático** adj democratic.

demoler* (demo'ler) vt demolish.

demonio (de'monjo) nm devil, demon.

demorar (demo'rar) vt delay. vi linger. **demora** nf delay, procrastination.

demostrar (ue) (demos'trar) vt 1 prove. 2 demonstrate. **demostración** nf 1 demonstration. 2 proof.

denegar (ie) (dene'gar) vt refuse, deny. **denegación** nf refusal.

denigrar (deni'grar) vt debase, denigrate. **denigración** nf denigration.

denominar (denomi'nar) vt name, designate.

denotar (deno'tar) vt indicate, express.

denso ('denso) adj dense.

dentado (den'taðo) adj 1 having teeth. 2 toothed, jagged.

dental (den'tal) adj dental.

dentera (den'tera) nf 1 nervousness, jitters. 2 envy, jealousy.

dentífrico (den'tifriko) nm toothpaste, dentifrice. **pasta dentífrica** nf toothpaste.

dentista (den'tista) nm,f dentist.

dentro ('dentro) adv within, inside. **dentro de** inside.

denunciar (denun'θjar) vt 1 denounce, report. 2 accuse. **denuncia** nf 1 accusation. 2 report.

departamento (departa'mento) nm department.

depender (depen'der) vi depend. **dependencia** nf dependence, reliance.

deplorar (deplo'rar) vt regret, deplore.

deponer* (depo'ner) vt 1 lay down, lay aside. 2 depose. vi law give evidence.

deportar (depor'tar) vt deport. **deportación** nf deportation.

deporte (de'porte) nm sport. **deportista** adj sporting, sports. nm,f sportsman.

depositar (deposi'tar) vt deposit, put away.

depósito (de'posito) nm deposit.

depravar (depra'βar) vt corrupt. **depravación** nf.corruption. **depravado** adj depraved, bad. nm depraved person.

depreciar (depre'θjar) vt lessen in value.

depresión (depre'sjon) nf 1 depression. 2 sunken place, hollow.

deprimir (depri'mir) vt 1 press down. 2 depress, sadden. **deprimido** adj depressing, saddening.

depurar (depu'rar) vt purify.

derecha (de'retʃa) nf 1 right hand. 2 pol right wing. **¡derecha!** mil right turn! **a la derecha** to the right.

derecho (de'retʃo) adj 1 right, right-hand. 2 straight, upright. 3 right, just. nm law.

derivar (deri'βar) vt derive. **derivación** nf derivation, origin.

derogar (dero'gar) vt repeal, abolish.

derramar (derra'mar) vt 1 spill. 2 scatter, spread. **derramarse** vr spill, overflow.

derretir* (derre'tir) vt melt. **derretido** adj 1 melted. 2 inf deeply in love.

derribar (derri'βar) vt 1 demolish, tear down. 2 knock down (a person). **derribo** nm demolition.

derrochar (derro'tʃar) vt squander. **derrochador** adj,nm spendthrift. **derroche** nm waste, extravagance.

derrotar (derro'tar) vt 1 defeat. 2 tear, (clothing). 3 ruin. **derrota** nf disaster, defeat. **derrotado** adj 1 defeated. 2 shabby.

derrumbar (derrum'bar) vt 1 hurl down. 2 knock down. **derrumbarse** vr 1 be flung down. 2 collapse, fall down.

desabotonar (desaβoto'nar) vt unbutton. vi bot bloom. **desabotonarse** vr come undone.

desabrigar (desaβri'gar) vt remove the clothing from. **desabrigado** adj 1 unclothed. 2 lightly dressed. **desabrigo** nm lack of clothing or protection.

desabrochar (desaβro'tʃar) vt unfasten, unbutton.

desacato (desa'kato) nm disrespect, contempt.

desacertar (ie) (desaθer'tar) vi be wrong, make a mistake. **desacierto** nm blunder.

desacomodar (desakomo'ðar) vt inconvenience, put out. **desacomodado** adj 1 badly off. 2 unemployed.

desaconsejar (desakonse'xar) vt advise or counsel against. **desaconsejado** adj ill-advised. nm imprudent person.

desacordar (ue) (desakor'ðar) vt put out of tune. **desacordarse** vr get out of tune. **desacorde** adj discordant.

desacostumbrar (desakostum'brar) vt **desacostumbrar a** break (someone) of a habit. **desacostumbrarse** vr break a habit.

desacreditar (desakreði'tar) vt discredit.

desacuerdo (desa'kwerðo) nm disagreement, discord.

desafecto (desa'fekto) adj disaffected, indifferent.

desafinar (desafi'nar) vi 1 be out of tune. 2 inf speak out of turn:

desafío (desa'fio) nm challenge.

desagradar (desagra'ðar) vt displease, upset, bother. **desagradarse** vr be unpleasant, be disagreeable. **desagradable** adj unpleasant, disagreeable. **desagradecido** adj ungrateful. **desagrado** nm displeasure.

desagraviar (desagra'βjar) vt make amends to, apologize to. **desagravio** nm righting of a wrong, amends.

desaguar (desa'gwar) vt drain. vi 1 drain away. 2 (of a river) empty into the sea. **desaguadero** nm drain.

desagüe (de'sagwe) nm 1 drainage. 2 drain.

desahogar (desao'gar) vt 1 relieve. 2 console. **desahogarse** vr 1 (of emotions) give free rein to. 2 make oneself comfortable, relax. **desahogado** adj 1 impudent. 2 comfortable. **desahogo** nm 1 ease, relief. 2 freedom. 3 impudence.

desahuciar (desau'θjar) vt 1 evict, throw out. 2 deprive of hope. **desahucio** nm eviction.

desairar (desai'rar) vt disregard, treat with contempt, snub. **desairado** adj 1 unattractive, shabby. 2 unsuccessful. **desaire** nm snub.

desajustar (desaxus'tar) vt disarrange. **desajustarse** vr 1 disagree. 2 get out of order. **desajuste** nm 1 disorder. 2 disagreement.

desalentar (ie) (desalen'tar) vt 1 make breathless, cause to gasp. 2 discourage. **desalentarse** vr become discouraged.

desaliño (desa'liɲo) nm 1 slovenliness, uncleanliness. 2 carelessness.

desalojar (desalo'xar) vt remove, eject. vi evacuate. **desalojamiento** nm evacuation.

desalquilar (desalki'lar) vt vacate, leave. **desalquilarse** vr become vacant. **desalquilado** adj vacant.

desamor (desa'mor) nm indifference.

desamparar (desampa'rar) vt abandon. **desamparado** adj helpless, abandoned. **desamparo** nm 1 desertion. 2 defencelessness.

desangrar (desan'grar) vt 1 bleed. 2 impoverish. **desangrarse** vr lose much blood.

desanimar (desani'mar) vt discourage. **desanimarse** vr become discouraged. **desánimo** nm 1 discouragement. 2 lifelessness.

desanudar (desanu'ðar) vt untie.

desapacible (desapa'θiβle) adj unpleasant.

desaparecer (desapare'θer) vt hide. vi disappear. **desaparición** nf disappearance.

desapercibido (desaperθi'βiðo) adj unnoticed.

desapretar (ie) (desapre'tar) vt loosen.

desaprobar (ue) (desapro'βar) vt disapprove of.

desaprovechar (desaproβe'tʃar) vt misuse, waste. vi lose ground. **desaprovechado** adj unproductive.

desarmar (desar'mar) vt,vi disarm. **desarme** nm disarmament.

desarraigar (desarrai'gar) vt uproot. **desarraigado** adj rootless.

desarreglar (desarre'glar) vt disarrange, upset. **desarreglado** adj 1 disorderly. 2 out of order. **desarreglo** nm disorder.

desarrollar (desarro'ʎar) vt 1 unroll. 2 develop, grow. **desarrollo** nm development, unfolding.

desarrugar (desarru'gar) vt smooth out.

desasir (desa'sir) vt undo, loosen. **desasirse** vr 1 get clear of. 2 free oneself of.

desasosegar (ie) (desasose'gar) vt disturb. **desasosiego** nm uneasiness, disquiet.

desastre (de'sastre) nm disaster. **desastrado**

adj 1 unlucky. 2 ragged, shabby. **desastroso** *adj* disastrous.

desatar (desa'tar) *vt* unfasten, undo. **desatarse** *vr* become undone, break loose.

desatender (ie) (desaten'der) *vt* 1 pay no attention to. 2 ignore. **desatención** *nf* 1 inattention. 2 discourtesy. **desatentado** *adj* absent-minded. **desatento** *adj* discourteous.

desatinar (desati'nar) *vt* bewilder, confuse. *vi* 1 talk nonsense. 2 act foolishly. **desatino** *nm* 1 foolishness, silliness. 2 foolish act, blunder.

desavenir (ie) (desaβe'nir) *vt* cause disagreement between. **desavenirse con** disagree with. **desavenencia** *nf* disagreement, quarrel. **desavenido** *adj* contrary, opposing, on bad terms.

desaventajado (desaβenta'xaðo) *adj* 1 inferior. 2 unfavourable.

desayunar (desaju'nar) *vi* have breakfast. **desayuno** *nm* breakfast.

desazón (desa'θon) *nf* 1 lack of flavour. 2 discomfort. 3 uneasiness, annoyance. 4 itch. **desazonar** *vt* 1 remove the flavour from (food). 2 annoy, displease.

desbandarse (desβan'darse) *vr* 1 *mil* disband. 2 flee in disorder.

desbarajustar (desβaraxus'tar) *vt* confuse, throw into disorder. **desbarajuste** *nm* disorder, confusion.

desbaratar (desβara'tar) *vt* 1 spoil, ruin. 2 squander, waste. **desbaratarse** *vr* 1 get out of order. 2 lose one's temper, become unbalanced. **desbarate** *nm* 1 destruction. 2 waste.

desbordar (desβor'ðar) *vt* pass, exceed. *vi* overflow. **desbordarse** *vr* overflow.

descabezar (deskaβe'θar) *vt* 1 behead. 2 *inf* surmount.

descalabro (deska'laβro) *nm* extreme misfortune, defeat.

descalificar (deskalifi'kar) *vt* disqualify.

descalzar (deskal'θar) *vt* take off (the shoes). **descalzo** *adj* barefooted.

descamisado (deskami'saðo) *adj* very poor, destitute. *nm* ragamuffin.

descansar (deskan'sar) *vi* rest, take a break. *vt* 1 lean on, rest on. 2 help, aid. **descanso** *nm* 1 rest time, break. 2 relief.

descarado (deska'raðo) *adj* shameless, brazen.

descargar (deskar'gar) *vt,vi* 1 unload, empty. 2 unburden. 3 (of electricity) discharge. **descargarse** *vr* 1 unburden. 2 relinquish obliga-

tions. **descarga** *nf* unloading. **descargo** *nm* 1 unloading. 2 discharge of debt.

descargue (des'karge) *nm* unloading of goods.

descartar (deskar'tar) *vt* leave out, lay aside.

descender (ie) (desθen'der) *vi* 1 descend. 2 flow, run. *vt* bring down, lower. **descendencia** *nf* descent, lineage. **descendiente** *nm,f* descendant. **descenso** *nm* 1 descent. 2 fall, decline.

descentralizar (desθentrali'θar) *vt* decentralize.

descerrajar (desθerra'xar) *vt* force a lock, break open.

descifrar (desθi'frar) *vt* decipher.

descolgar (ue) (deskol'gar) *vt* lower, take down, get down.

descolorar (deskolo'rar) *vt* discolour.

descomedido (deskome'ðiðo) *adj* excessive, immoderate.

descomponer (ue) (deskompo'ner) *vt* 1 break down into parts. 2 decompose. 3 disturb, put out of order. **descomponerse** *vr* 1 decompose. 2 break down. **descomposición** *nf* decomposition. **descompuesto** *adj* 1 broken, faulty. 2 angry, discourteous.

desconcertar (ie) (deskonθer'tar) *vt* 1 put out of order, damage. 2 disconcert, embarrass. **desconcierto** *nm* disorder, confusion.

desconectar (deskonek'tar) *vt* disconnect.

desconfiar (deskon'fjar) *vi* 1 lack confidence. 2 be distrustful. **desconfiado** *adj* distrustful. **desconfianza** *nf* mistrust.

desconocer (deskono'θer) *vt* 1 not to know, be ignorant of. 2 fail to recognize, ignore. **desconocido** *adj* unknown.

desconsiderado (deskonsiðe'raðo) *adj* inconsiderate.

desconsolar (ue) (deskonso'lar) *vt* grieve, distress. **desconsuelo** *nm* grief.

descontar (ue) (deskon'tar) *vt* 1 deduct. 2 discount.

descontento (deskon'tento) *adj* dissatisfied.

descorazonar (deskoraθo'nar) *vt* discourage. **descorazonarse** *vr* become disheartened.

descorchar (deskor't∫ar) *vt* uncork (a bottle). **descorchador** *nm* corkscrew.

descortés (deskor'tes) *adj* discourteous. **descortesía** *nf* discourtesy.

descrédito (des'kreðito) *nm* discredit.

describir (deskri'βir) *vt* describe. **descripción** *nf* description. **descriptivo** *adj* descriptive.

descuajar (deskwa'xar) *vt* 1 liquefy. 2 discourage, dishearten. 3 pull out, uproot.

descubierto (desku'βjerto) *adj* 1 exposed. 2 hatless.

descubrir (desku'βrir) *vt* 1 discover. 2 uncover. **descubridor** *n* discoverer. **descubrimiento** *nm* discovery.

descuento (des'kwento) *nm* discount.

descuidar (deskwi'ðar) *vt* 1 neglect, be careless about. 2 relieve from care. 3 divert the attention of. *vi* be careless. **¡descuida!** don't worry. **descuidado** *adj* 1 neglected. 2 negligent. **descuido** *nm* 1 neglect. 2 negligence.

desde (desðe) *prep* from. **desde luego** of course.

desdecir* (desðe'θir) *vi* 1 be unworthy of. 2 not suit, clash. **desdecirse** *vr* retract, take back.

desdén (des'ðen) *nm* disdain, scorn. **al desdén** with studied neglect. **desdeñar** *vt* disdain, scorn.

desdicha (des'ðitʃa) *nf* 1 misfortune. 2 misery, unhappiness. **desdichado** *adj* unfortunate, wretched.

desdoblar (desðo'βlar) *vt* 1 unfold, spread out. 2 make two of, split.

desdorar (desðo'rar) *vt* tarnish.

desear (dese'ar) *vt* desire, want.

desecar (dese'kar) *vt* dry up.

desechar (dese'tʃar) *vt* scrap, cast aside.

desembalar (desemba'lar) *vt* unpack (goods).

desembarazar (desemba'raθar) *vt* remove an impediment, clear the way. **desembarazarse** *vr* free oneself of. **desembarazado** *adj* unobstructed. **desembarazo** *nm* 1 disencumbrance. 2 ease.

desembarcar (desembar'kar) *vt,vi* land, put ashore.

desembocar (desembo'kar) *vi* flow, empty.

desembolsar (desembol'sar) *vt* pay out.

desembragar (desembra'gar) *vt* release, disengage. *vi mot* declutch.

desembrollar (desembro'ʎar) *vt* disentangle.

desempeñar (desempe'ɲar) *vt* 1 recover pawned or pledged property. 2 free from debt or obligation. 3 perform (a role, duty).

desempleo (desem'pleo) *nm* unemployment. **desempleado** *adj* unemployed.

desencantar (desenkan'tar) *vt* disillusion. **desencanto** *nm* disillusionment.

desenfado (desen'faðo) *nm* 1 ease, freedom, lack of inhibition. 2 disrespect.

desenfrenar (desenfre'nar) *vt* unbridle. **desenfrenarse** *vr* give oneself up to evil or vice. **desenfreno** *nm* unruliness, licentiousness.

desenganchar (desengan'tʃar) *vt* unfasten.

desengañar (desenga'ɲar) *vt* free from illusions, disabuse. **desengañarse** *vr* see things as they really are. **¡desengáñate!** don't deceive yourself! **desengañado** *adj* disillusioned. **desengaño** *nm* disillusionment.

desenlace (desen'laθe) *nm* end, outcome.

desenredar (desenre'ðar) *vt* 1 disentangle. 2 clear up confusion, straighten out. **desenredarse** *vr* get out of a jam. **desenredo** *nm* disentanglement.

desenrollar (desenro'ʎar) *vt* unroll.

desentenderse (ie) (desenten'derse) *vr* 1 pretend to have no interest in or knowledge of (something). 2 take no part in.

desenterrar (ie) (desenter'rar) *vt* 1 unearth. 2 recall.

desentonar (desento'nar) *vi* be out of tune.

desentrañar (desentra'ɲar) *vt* 1 disembowel. 2 puzzle out, unravel.

desenvainar (desembai'nar) *vt* draw (a sword).

desenvoltura (desembol'tura) *nf* 1 naturalness, ease, confidence. 2 brazenness.

desenvolver (ue) (desembol'βer) *vt* unroll. 2 evolve, develop.

deseo (de'seo) *nm* desire, want.

desequilibrar (desekili'βrar) *vt* put out of balance. **desequilibrarse** *vr* become mentally unbalanced. **desequilibrado** *adj* mentally unbalanced. **desequilibrio** *nm* lack of equilibrium.

desertar (deser'tar) *vt,vi* desert. **desertar el hogar** leave home. **deserción** *nf* desertion. **desértico** *adj* deserted. **desertor** *nm* deserter.

desesperar (desespe'rar) *vi* despair, have no hope. *vt* drive to despair. **desesperarse** *vr* be exasperated. **desesperación** *nf* despair.

desestimar (desesti'mar) *vt* undervalue.

desfachatez (desfatʃa'teθ) *nf* brazenness, impudence.

desfalcar (desfal'kar) *vt* embezzle.

desfallecer* (desfaʎe'θer) *vt* weaken. *vi* 1 get weak. 2 faint. **desfallecer de ánimo** lose heart. **desfallecido** *adj* 1 weak. 2 faint. **desfallecimiento** *nm* 1 weakness. 2 faintness.

desfavorable (desfaβo'raβle) *adj* unfavourable.

desfigurar (desfigu'rar) *vt* disfigure, alter.

desfilar (desfi'lar) *vi* parade. **desfiladero** *nm* long narrow pass. **desfile** *nm* parade. **desfile de modelos** fashion show.

desgajar (desga'xar) *vt* 1 break off, tear off.

desganarse (desga'narse) *vr* 1 lose one's

appetite. 2 lose interest. **desgana** nf 1 loss of appetite. 2 reluctance, disinclination.

desgarrar (desgar'rar) vt 1 tear, rip. 2 break (the heart).

desgastar (desgas'tar) vt 1 wear away, erode. 2 corrode.

desgraciar (desgra'θjar) vt 1 displease. 2 ruin, spoil. **desgraciarse** vr be spoiled, be ruined. **desgracia** nf misfortune. **desgraciado** adj 1 unfortunate. 2 graceless.

deshabitado (desaβi'taðo) adj uninhabited.

deshacer* (desa'θer) vt undo. **deshacerse** vr 1 be undone or destroyed. 2 become impatient.

deshelar (ie) (dese'lar) vt thaw, melt.

desheredar (desere'ðar) vt disinherit.

deshidratar (desiðra'tar) vt dehydrate.

deshielo (de'sjelo) nm thawing, melting.

deshilar (desi'lar) vt 1 unravel. 2 (of meat) shred. **deshilarse** vr fray, become worn.

deshilvanado (desilβa'naðo) adj (of speech, writing, etc.) disjointed, disconnected.

deshinchar (desin'tʃar) vt 1 deflate. 2 reduce swelling. **deshincharse** vr 1 deflate. 2 lose one's vanity.

deshojar (deso'xar) vt 1 defoliate. 2 pull petals off a flower. **deshojarse** vr 1 defoliate. 2 (of flower) lose petals.

deshonesto (deso'nesto) adj dishonest.

deshonrar (deson'rar) vt dishonour. **deshonra** nf dishonour. **tener a deshonra** consider dishonourable. **deshonrable** adj shameless. **deshonroso** adj dishonourable.

deshora (de'sora) **a deshora** adv 1 at an inconvenient time. 2 at the wrong time.

deshuesar (deswe'sar) vt 1 bone (meat). 2 stone (fruit).

desidia (de'siðja) nf carelessness.

desierto (de'sjerto) adj deserted. nm desert.

designar (desig'nar) vt designate. **designación** nf designation. **designio** nm plan, design.

desigual (desi'gwal) adj unequal.

desilusión (desilu'sjon) nf disillusionment.

desilusionar (desilusjo'nar) vt disillusion. **desilusionarse** vr become disillusioned.

desinfectar (desinfek'tar) vt disinfect.

desinflar (desin'flar) vt deflate.

desinterés (desinte'res) nm disinterest.

desistir (desis'tir) vi desist.

desleal (desle'al) adj disloyal.

desligar (desli'gar) vt 1 untie. 2 unravel.

deslinde (des'linde) nm fixing of limits, delimitation.

deslizar (desli'θar) vi,vt slide, skid.

deslucido (deslu'θiðo) adj tarnished, dull.

deslumbrar (deslum'brar) vt dazzle.

desmán (des'man) nm excess, outrage.

desmandarse (desman'darse) vr 1 be insolent. 2 (of animals) break away from the group.

desmantelar (desmante'lar) vt dismantle.

desmayarse (desma'jarse) vr faint, pass out. **desmayado** adj (of colour) faint, pale. **desmayo** nm faintness, weakness.

desmedirse (i) (desme'ðirse) vr act insolently, forget oneself.

desmejorar (desmexo'rar) vt 1 weaken. 2 spoil, impair. **desmejorarse** vr 1 deteriorate. 2 go downhill.

desmembrar (desmem'brar) vt 1 dismember. 2 separate, divide.

desmentir (i) (desmen'tir) vt 1 refute, deny. 2 belie.

desmenuzar (desmenu'θar) vt break into small pieces.

desmesurado (desmesu'raðo) adj 1 disproportionate, excessive. 2 discourteous, insolent. nm discourteous, insolent person.

desmontar (desmon'tar) vt 1 clear, level (land, etc.). 2 dismantle. vi dismount.

desmoralizar (desmorali'θar) vt demoralize.

desmoronar (desmoro'nar) vt destroy little by little. **desmoronarse** vr crumble into pieces.

desnatar (desna'tar) vt 1 skim (milk). 2 take the choicest part of.

desnivel (desni'βel) nm 1 unevenness. 2 difference of level, drop.

desnudar (desnu'ðar) vt strip, lay bare. **desnudarse** vr undress. **desnudamente** adv clearly, plainly. **desnudez** nf nakedness. **desnudo** adj 1 naked. 2 destitute.

desobedecer* (desoβeðe'θer) vt,vi disobey. **desobediencia** nf disobedience, rebellion. **desobediente** adj disobedient.

desocupar (desoku'par) vt vacate. **desocuparse** vr give up a business or occupation. **desocupación** nf 1 leisure. 2 unemployment. **desocupado** adj 1 unoccupied. 2 unemployed.

desodorante (desoðo'rante) nm deodorant.

desolar (deso'lar) vt lay waste, destroy. **desolarse** vr grieve. **desolación** nf desolation. **desolador** adj grieving.

desorden (de'sorðen) nm disorder. **desordenado** adj disordered.

desorganizar (desorgani'θar) vt disorganize. **desorganización** nf disorganization.

desorientar (desorjen'tar) vt lead astray, confuse.

despabilado (despaβi'laðo) adj wide awake.

despacio (des'paθjo) adv slowly, gently.

despachar (despa'tʃar) vt 1 attend to, settle. 2 get done promptly.

despacho (des'patʃo) nm 1 comm office, shop. 2 promptness. 3 message, dispatch. 4 resourcefulness.

despachurrar (despatʃur'rar) vt 1 burst, crush, squash. 2 make a mess of (a report, an account, a story one is telling).

desparpajo (despar'paxo) nm ease of manner, self-confidence.

desparramar (desparra'mar) vt 1 scatter. 2 squander.

despavorido (despaβo'riðo) adj terrified.

despectivo (despek'tiβo) adj scornful, derogatory.

despechar (despe'tʃar) vt cause to despair. **despecharse** vr despair. **despecho** nm despair. **a despecho de** in spite of.

despedazar (despeða'θar) vt 1 tear to pieces. 2 (of the heart) break.

despedir (i) (despe'ðir) vt 1 see off, show out. 2 dismiss (an employee). **despedirse** vr 1 say goodbye. 2 leave one's work. **despedida** nf 1 farewell, leave-taking. 2 dismissal from a job.

despegar (despe'gar) vt unstick, unglue. **despegarse** vr become detached. **despegarse con** not to go well with. **despegado** adj 1 detached. 2 indifferent, cold.

despeinar (despei'nar) vt ruffle (the hair).

despejar (despe'xar) vt free from obstructions. **despejarse** vr 1 clear up. 2 acquire assurance. **despejado** adj 1 clear, open. 2 wide awake. 3 intelligent. **despejo** nm 1 brightness. 2 self-assurance.

despellejar (despeʎe'xar) vt 1 skin, flay. 2 criticize harshly.

despensa (des'pensa) nf 1 pantry, food store. 2 stock of food.

despeñadero (despeɲa'ðero) adj 1 cliff. 2 inf risky business.

desperdiciar (desperði'θjar) vt waste, throw away.

desperezarse (despere'θarse) vr stretch one's limbs.

despertar (ie) (desper'tar) vt awaken. **despertarse** vr wake up. **despertador** nm 1 alarm clock. 2 warning. **despertamiento** nm awakening. **despierto** adj 1 awake. 2 alert.

despiadado (despja'ðaðo) adj cruel, inhuman.

despilfarrar (despilfar'rar) vt squander.

despintar (despin'tar) vt 1 remove paint from. 2 change, distort.

despistar (despis'tar) vt 1 throw off the scent. 2 mislead, confuse. **despistado** adj 1 absent-minded. 2 confused, muddled.

desplazar (despla'θar) vt 1 (of water) displace. 2 take the place of, replace. vr travel. **desplazamiento** nm 1 naut displacement (of water). 2 journey.

desplegar (ie) (desple'gar) vt 1 unfold, spread. 2 deploy.

desplomarse (desplo'marse) vr collapse.

despojar (despo'xar) vt 1 deprive, take away. 2 dispossess. **despojarse** vr undress. **despojo** nm 1 plundering. 2 dispossession. 3 plunder. 4 pl leftovers, scrap, waste.

desposado (despo'saðo) adj newly wed.

desposeer (despose'er) vt dispossess. **desposeerse** vr give up possession of something.

déspota ('despota) nm despot. **despótico** adj tyrannical, lawless. **despotismo** nm despotism.

despreciar (despre'θjar) vt 1 look down on. 2 underestimate. 3 reject. **despreciarse de** not deign to. **despreciable** adj worthless. **desprecio** nm scorn, contempt.

desprender (despren'der) vt detach, separate.

desprestigiar (desprestixi'ar) vt discredit.

desprevenido (despreβe'niðo) adj unprepared.

desproporción (despropor'θjon) nf disproportion.

desprovisto (despro'βisto) adj lacking.

después (des'pwes) adv 1 after, later, afterwards. 2 since, since then. **después (de) que** conj after.

desquiciar (deski'θjar) vt 1 unhinge. 2 disturb, upset.

desquite (des'kite) nm 1 compensation. 2 revenge.

destacar (desta'kar) vt 1 mil detail, detach. 2 Art make stand out.

destajo (des'taxo) nm piecework.

destapar (desta'par) vt 1 uncover, open. **destaparse** vr show one's true character.

destartalado (destarta'laðo) adj 1 (of a house, etc.) rambling. 2 disorderly.

destello (des'teʎo) nm sparkling.

destemplar (destem'plar) vt 1 disturb the harmony of. 2 put out of tune. **destemplarse** vr 1 get out of tune. 2 lose one's temper. **destemplado** adj 1 out of tune. 2 disagreeable.

des·eñi· (deste'ɲir) vt discolour. vi fade.

desterrar (ie) (deste'rrar) vt 1 exile, banish. 2 dismiss. **desterrarse** vr go into exile. **destierro** nm 1 exile. 2 place of exile.

destilar (desti'lar) vi drip, ooze. vt 1 distil. 2 exude. **destilería** nf distillery.

destinar (desti'nar) vt 1 destine. 2 designate. **destino** nm 1 fate. 2 destination. 3 position, job. **dar destino a** find a use for. **destinario** nm addressee.

destituir (destitu'ir) vt 1 deprive of. 2 remove from office. **destitución** nf 1 dismissal. 2 removal.

destornillar (destorni'ʎar) vt unscrew. **destornillarse** vr 1 behave in a wild manner. 2 inf go crazy. **destornillado** adj 1 unscrewed. 2 inf crazy. **destornillador** nm screwdriver.

destreza (des'treθa) nf skill, ability.

destronar (destro'nar) vt 1 dethrone. 2 overthrow from power.

destrozar (destro'θar) vt break, smash. **destrozo** nm destruction. **causar destrozos en** create havoc in.

destruir (destru'ir) vt destroy. **destruirse** vr math cancel each other out. **destructor** adj destructive. nm naut destroyer.

desunir (desu'nir) vt 1 separate, detach. 2 cause a rift between.

desuso (de'suso) nm disuse.

desvalido (desβa'liðo) adj destitute, helpless.

desvalijar (desβali'xar) vt 1 steal the contents of. 2 rob, burgle.

desván (des'βan) nm attic.

desvanecer· (desβane'θer) vt make disappear. **desvanecerse** vr 1 vanish. 2 evaporate. **desvanecimiento** nm disappearance.

desvarío (desβa'rio) nm 1 raving, delirium. 2 whim.

desvelar (desβe'lar) vt keep awake. **desvelarse** vr 1 stay awake. 2 be watchful. **desvelo** nm 1 lack of sleep. 2 watchfulness. **gracias a sus desvelos** thanks to his efforts.

desventaja (desβen'taxa) nf disadvantage. **desventajoso** adj disadvantageous.

desventura (desβen'tura) nf unhappiness, misfortune. **desventurado** adj unfortunate. nm wretched person.

desvergonzado (desβergon'θaðo) adj shameless. **desvergüenza** nf shamelessness.

desviar (des'βjar) vt turn aside, divert. **desviarse** vr turn away, leave, branch off. **desvío** nm 1 deviation, turning away. 2 detour.

desvirtuar (desβir'twar) vt detract from, impair.

desvivirse (desβi'βirse) vr long for, be crazy about.

detallar (deta'ʎar) vt 1 list in detail. 2 comm sell retail. **detalle** nm 1 detail, item. 2 gesture. **al detalle** 1 in detail. 2 comm retail. **detalladamente** adv in detail. **detallista** nm, f retailer.

detective (detek'tiβe) nm, f detective.

detener (ie) (dete'ner) vt detain. **detenerse** vr linger, delay. **detención** nf 1 delay. 2 detention, arrest. **detenido** adj 1 thorough. 2 under arrest. **detenimiento** nm thoroughness.

detergente (deter'xente) adj, nm detergent.

deteriorar (deterjo'rar) vt damage, spoil. vi deteriorate.

determinar (determi'nar) vt determine. **determinarse** vr make up one's mind. **determinación** nf 1 decision. 2 determination.

detestar (detes'tar) vt detest, hate.

detonar (deto'nar) vi detonate.

detractar (detrak'tar) vt defame. **detracción** nf slander, defamation.

detraer· (detra'er) vt 1 take away, separate. 2 denigrate.

detrás (de'tras) adv behind, at the back. **detrás de** prep behind. **por detrás de uno** behind someone's back.

detrimento (detri'mento) nm damage, harm. **en detrimento de** to the detriment of.

deuda ('deuða) nf 1 debt. 2 fault, offence. **deudor** adj indebted. n debtor.

deudo ('deuðo) nm relative.

devanar (deβa'nar) vt wind, spin.

devastar (deβas'tar) vt lay waste. **devastación** nf devastation.

devengar (deβen'gar) vt earn (wages or interest).

devenir· (deβe'nir) vi become. **devenir en** change into. ~nm process of development, change.

devoción (deβo'θjon) nf devotion.

devolver (ue) (deβol'βer) vt return. **devolución** nf return, repayment.

devorar (deβo'rar) vt devour.

devoto (de'βoto) adj 1 devoted. 2 devout.

di (di) v see **dar**.

día ('dia) nm day. **¡buenos días!** good morning. **de día en día** from day to day. **todos los días** every day.

diablo ('djaβlo) nm devil. **diabólico** adj diabolical.

diafragma (dja'fragma) nm diaphragm.

diagnosticar (djagnosti'kar) vt diagnose. **diagnóstico** adj diagnostic. nm diagnosis.

diagrama (dja'grama) nm diagram.

dialecto (dja'lekto) nm dialect. **dialectal** also **dialéctico** adj dialect(al).

diálogo ('djalogo) nm dialogue.

diamante (dja'mante) nm diamond.

diámetro ('djametro) nm diameter.

diario ('djarjo) adj daily. nm 1 newspaper, daily. 2 diary. **diario dominical** Sunday paper. **de diario** for everyday use.

diarrea (djar'rea) nf diarrhoea.

dibujar (dibu'xar) vt draw, sketch. **dibujarse** vr be outlined. **dibujante** nm,f 1 draughtsman. 2 cartoonist. **dibujo** nm drawing. **dibujos animados** animated cartoon.

dicción (dik'θjon) nf 1 word. 2 diction.

diccionario (dikθjo'narjo) nm dictionary.

dice ('diθe) v see **decir.**

diciembre (di'θjembre) nm December.

dictado (dik'taðo) nm 1 title of honour. 2 dictation. 3 pl dictates. **escribir al dictado** take dictation.

dictador (dikta'ðor) n dictator. **dictadura** nf dictatorship.

dictamen (dik'tamen) nm judgment, opinion. **dictamen facultativo** medical report. **dictaminar** vi give an opinion, pass judgment.

dictar (dik'tar) vt 1 dictate. 2 pass (a judgment or decree).

dicha ('ditʃa) nf 1 happiness. 2 good luck. **dichoso** adj happy.

dicho ('ditʃo) v see **decir.** nm 1 statement. 2 saying, proverb. adj above-mentioned. **dicho y hecho** no sooner said than done.

diecinueve (dieθi'inweβe) adj,nm nineteen.

dieciocho (dieθi'otʃo) adj,nm eighteen.

dieciséis (dieθi'seis) adj,nm sixteen.

diecisiete (dieθi'sjete) adj,nm seventeen.

diente ('djente) nm tooth.

diestra ('djestra) nf right hand.

diestro ('djestro) nm bullfighter. adj right, right-hand. **diestramente** adv 1 skilfully. 2 cunningly.

dieta ('djeta) nf diet.

diez ('dieθ) adj,nm ten.

diezmar (dieθ'mar) vt decimate.

difamar (difa'mar) vt slander, libel. **difamación** nf slander.

diferenciar (diferen'θjar) vt differentiate. vi differ. **diferenciarse** vr be different. **diferencia** nf difference. **a diferencia de** unlike. **diferente** adj different.

diferir (ie) (dife'rir) vt 1 defer. 2 extend, prolong.

difícil (di'fiθil) adj difficult. **dificultad** nf difficulty. **dificultar** vt make difficult.

difidencia (difi'ðenθja) nf lack of faith, distrust. **difidente** adj distrustful.

difundir (difun'dir) vt 1 diffuse. 2 spread, divulge (news).

difunto (di'funto) adj deceased. nm 1 deceased person. 2 corpse.

difusión (difu'sjon) nf 1 diffusion. 2 diffuseness. 3 spreading. **difuso** adj 1 diffuse. 2 wordy.

digerir (ie) (dixe'rir) vt digest. **digerible** adj digestible. **digestión** nf digestion.

dignarse (dig'narse) vr condescend, deign.

dignidad (digni'ðað) nf 1 dignity. 2 rank, office. **dignatario** nm dignitary. **digno** adj worthy.

digo ('digo) v see **decir.**

digresión (digre'sjon) nf digression.

dije ('dixe) v see **decir.**

dilación (dila'θjon) nf delay.

dilatar (dila'tar) vt 1 dilate, expand. 2 prolong, delay. **dilatarse** vr dilate.

diligencia (dili'xenθja) nf 1 diligence. 2 job, errand.

dilucidar (diluθi'ðar) vt clear up, explain.

diluir (dilu'ir) vt dilute.

diluvio (di'luβjo) nm deluge, flood.

dimanar (dima'nar) vi arise from.

dimensión (dimen'sjon) nf dimension.

diminutivo (diminu'tiβo) adj diminutive. **diminuto** adj 1 tiny. 2 defective.

dimitir (dimi'tir) vt give up office, resign. **dimisión** nf resignation (from office).

Dinamarca (dina'marka) nf Denmark. **dinamarqués** adj Danish. nm 1 Dane. 2 Danish (language).

dinamita (dina'mita) nf dynamite.

dinamo ('dinamo) nf dynamo.

dinastía (dinas'tia) nf dynasty.

dineral (dine'ral) nm large amount of money, fortune.

dinero (di'nero) nm money. **dinero suelto** small change.

dintel (din'tel) nm lintel.

dio ('dio) v see **dar.**

diócesi(s) (di'oθesi) nf, pl **diócesis** diocese.

dios (di'os) nm god. **diosa** nf goddess.

diploma (di'ploma) nf diploma.

diplomacia (diplo'maθja) nf diplomacy. **diplomático** adj diplomatic. nm diplomat.

diputado (dipu'taðo) nm representative, delegate.

dique ('dike) nm 1 dam. 2 dike.

dirección (direk'θjon) nf 1 direction. 2 guidance. 3 address.

directo (di'rekto) adj direct.

director (direk'tor) nm 1 director. 2 manager. 3 headmaster. 4 mus conductor. adj managing, controlling.

dirigir* (diri'xir) vt 1 direct. 2 mus conduct. **dirigirse** vr go to, head for.

discernir (ie) (disθer'nir) vt discern, distinguish.

disciplina (disθi'plina) nf discipline.

discípulo (dis'θipulo) nm student.

disco ('disko) nm 1 disk, disc. 2 gramophone record.

disconformidad (diskonformi'ðað) nf disagreement.

discontinuo (diskon'tinwo) adj discontinuous.

discordia (dis'korðja) nf discord, disagreement. **discordante** adj also **discorde** discordant.

discoteca (disko'teka) nf 1 record library. 2 discothèque.

discreción (diskre'θjon) nf discretion. **a discreción** optional, discretionary.

discrepancia (diskre'panθja) nf discrepancy.

discreto (dis'kreto) adj 1 discreet. 2 reasonable.

disculpar (diskul'par) vt excuse. **disculparse** vr apologize. **disculpa** nf excuse, apology.

discurrir (diskur'rir) vt invent, think up. vi 1 roam about. 2 flow.

discurso (dis'kurso) nm 1 discourse. 2 use of reason, mental powers. 3 passage (of time).

discusión (disku'sjon) nf 1 discussion. 2 argument.

discutir (disku'tir) vt 1 discuss. 2 debate. vi dispute, argue. **discutible** adj debatable.

disecar (dise'kar) vt 1 dissect. 2 stuff, mount (dead animals). **disección** nf dissection.

diseminar (disemi'nar) vt scatter.

disensión (disen'sjon) nf dissension.

disentería (disente'ria) nf dysentery.

diseñar (dise'nar) vt 1 sketch. 2 design. **diseñador** nm designer. **diseño** nm 1 sketch. 2 design.

disfrazar (disfra'θar) vt disguise. **disfraz** nm fancy dress, disguise.

disfrutar (disfru'tar) vt have the benefit of. vi enjoy oneself. **disfrute** nm enjoyment, use.

disgregar (disgre'gar) vt disintegrate, separate.

disgustar (disgus'tar) vt displease, annoy. **disgustarse** vr be displeased. **disgusto** nm 1

unpleasantness, trouble. 2 displeasure, annoyance. **a disgusto** unwillingly.

disimular (disimu'lar) vt 1 hide, disguise. 2 excuse, overlook. **disimulable** adj excusable. **disimulo** nm 1 dissimulation. 2 tolerance. **con disimulo** slyly.

disipar (disi'par) vt dissipate. **disiparse** vr disappear. **disipación** nf dissipation. **disipado** adj dissipated.

dislocar (dislo'kar) vt dislocate.

disminuir (dismi'nu'ir) vt, vi diminish, decrease. **disminución** nf decrease.

disolución (disolu'θjon) nf dissolution.

disolver (ue) (disol'βer) vt dissolve.

disonar (ue) (diso'nar) vi 1 be discordant. 2 disagree. **dísono** adj discordant. **disonancia** nf dissonance. **disonante** adj dissonant, discordant.

disparar (dispa'rar) vt, vi shoot, fire, discharge. **dispararse** vr 1 rush off. 2 (of firearms) go off. **disparador** nm trigger.

disparatado (dispara'taðo) adj absurd. **disparate** nm absurdity.

disparidad (dispari'ðað) nf disparity.

dispensar (dispen'sar) vt 1 dispense. 2 excuse, pardon. **dispensa** nf dispensation, exemption. **¡dispénseme Usted!** I beg your pardon!

dispersar (disper'sar) vt disperse.

disponer* (dispo'ner) vt 1 dispose, arrange. 2 prepare. vi **disponer de** have. **disponerse a** get ready to, be about to. **disponibilidedes** nf pl money on hand, resources. **disponible** adj available, on hand.

disposición (disposi'θjon) nf disposition. **última disposición** last will and testament.

dispuesto (dis'pwesto) adj arranged, disposed.

disputar (dispu'tar) vt dispute, contest. vi argue. **disputa** nf dispute. **sin disputa** beyond dispute. **disputable** adj debatable.

distancia (dis'tanθja) nf distance.

distinción (distin'θjon) nf distinction.

distinguir (distin'gir) vt distinguish.

distinto (dis'tinto) adj 1 different. 2 distinct.

distraer* (distra'er) vt 1 entertain, amuse. 2 distract. **distraerse** vr 1 amuse oneself. 2 be inattentive. **distracción** nf 1 amusement. 2 absent-mindedness. **distraído** adj 1 inattentive. 2 absent-minded.

distribuir* (distribu'ir) vt 1 distribute. 2 (of post) sort, deliver. **distribución** nf distribution. **distribuidor** nm 1 distributor. 2 dealer, agent. **distribuidor automático** vending machine.

distrito (dis'trito) nm district.

disturbio (dis'turβjo) nm disturbance.

disuadir (diswa'ðir) vt dissuade.

diurno (di'urno) adj day.

divagar (diβa'ɣar) vi 1 digress. 2 wander.

divergir (diβer'xir) vi 1 diverge. 2 differ, disagree. **divergencia** nf divergence. **divergente** adj divergent, opposed.

diversidad (diβersi'ðað) nf diversity. **diverso** adj 1 diverse. 2 different. 3 pl various.

diversión (diβersi'on) nf amusement.

divertir (ie) (diβer'tir) vt 1 entertain, amuse. 2 turn away, divert. **divertirse** vr have a good time. **divertido** adj amusing. **divertimiento** nm amusement.

dividir (diβi'ðir) vt divide.

divinidad (diβini'ðað) nf divinity. **divino** adj divine.

divisa (di'βisa) nf 1 badge, emblem. 2 pl comm foreign exchange. **control de divisas** nm exchange control.

divisar (diβi'sar) vt see at a distance, make out.

división (diβi'sjon) nf division.

divorciar (diβor'θjar) vt divorce. **divorciarse** vr get divorced. **divorcio** nm 1 divorce. 2 division.

divulgar (diβul'ɣar) vt spread, circulate. **divulgarse** vr be spread about. **divulgación** nf disclosure.

doblar (do'βlar) vt 1 double. 2 fold, turn.

doble (do'βle) adj 1 double. 2 insincere. nm double amount. **el doble** twice as much.

doce (do'θe) adj,nm twelve.

docena (do'θena) nm dozen.

docente (do'θente) adj educational. **personal docente** nm teaching staff.

dócil (do'θil) adj obedient, gentle. **docilidad** nf obedience.

doctor (dok'tor) nm doctor. **docto** adj learned. **doctorado** nm doctorate. **doctoral** adj doctoral.

doctrina (dok'trina) nf doctrine. **doctrinal** adj doctrinal.

documentar (dokumen'tar) vt document. **documentación** nf 1 documentation. 2 identification papers. **documento** nm document.

dogal (do'ɣal) nm halter.

dogma ('doɣma) nm dogma. **dogmático** adj dogmatic. **dogmatismo** nm dogmatism.

doler (ue) (do'ler) vt,vi 1 hurt. 2 grieve. **dolerse de** vr feel pity or sorrow for. **dolencia** nf ailment.

dolor (do'lor) nm 1 pain. 2 grief.

domar (do'mar) vt tame. **doma** nf taming. **domable** adj tamable. **domador** nm tamer.

doméstico (do'mestiko) adj,nm domestic.

domiciliar (domiθi'ljar) vt house. **domiciliarse** vr establish oneself. **domicilio** nm home.

dominar (domi'nar) vt,vi dominate.

domingo (do'mingo) nm Sunday. **hacer domingo** take a day off.

dominio (do'minjo) nm dominion. **dominio público** public property.

dominó (domi'no) nm domino.

don[1] (don) nm courteous title equivalent to Mr, used before the Christian name.

don[2] (don) nm 1 present, gift. 2 aptitude, talent.

donación (dona'θjon) nf donation.

donaire (do'naire) nm 1 cleverness, wit. 2 elegance, grace.

donde ('donde) adv where.

doña ('doɲa) nf courteous title, used before a woman's Christian name.

dorar (do'rar) vt 1 gild, cover with gold. 2 cul brown lightly.

dormir (ue) (dor'mir) vi 1 sleep. 2 rest. vt put to sleep. **dormirse** vr go to sleep. **dormilón** nm one who sleeps a lot. **dormitorio** nm 1 bedroom. 2 dormitory.

dorso ('dorso) nm back. **dorsal** adj dorsal.

dos (dos) adj,nm two. **dos veces** twice. **las dos** two o'clock. **los dos** both.

dosis ('dosis) nf invar dose.

dotar (do'tar) vt endow. **dotación** nf 1 endowment. 2 personnel, staff. **dotado** adj gifted. **dote** nm,f 1 dowry. 2 pl endowments, talents.

doy ('doi) v see **dar.**

draga ('draɣa) nf dredge.

dragón (dra'ɣon) nm dragon.

drama ('drama) nm drama. **dramática** nf dramatic art or literature. **dramático** adj dramatic. nm 1 dramatist. 2 dramatic actor.

drenaje (dre'naxe) nm drainage.

droga ('droɣa) nf 1 drug. 2 chemical substance. **drogar** vt drug.

dromedario (drome'ðarjo) nm dromedary.

dual (dwal) adj dual.

ducado (du'kaðo) nm duchy.

dúctil ('duktil) adj ductile, malleable.

ducha ('dutʃa) nf shower (bath).

dudar (du'ðar) vt,vi doubt. **duda** nf doubt. **sin duda** doubtless. **dudoso** adj 1 doubtful, dubious. 2 hesitant.

duelo[1] ('dwelo) nm 1 sorrow. 2 mourning. **sin duelo** unrestrainedly.

duelo² ('dwelo) *nm* duel.

duende ('dwende) *nm* imp, elf.

dueño ('dweɲo) *nm* proprietor. **mi dueño** my love.

duermo (du'ermo) *v* see **dormir**.

dulce ('dulθe) *adj* 1 sweet. 2 (of water) fresh. *adv* 1 sweetly. 2 softly. *nm* sweet.

dulzura (dul'θura) *nf* 1 sweetness. 2 mildness.

duodécimo (duo'ðeθimo) *adj* twelfth.

duplicar (dupli'kar) *vt* duplicate. **duplicado** *adj,nm* duplicate.

duque ('duke) *nm* duke. **duquesa** *nf* duchess.

durar (du'rar) *vi* 1 endure, last. 2 (of clothes, etc.) wear well. **durabilidad** *nf* durability. **durable** *adj* durable. **duración** *nf* duration, period of time.

dureza (du'reθa) *nf* hardness. **dureza de oído** hardness of hearing.

durmiente (dur'mjente) *adj* sleeping.

durmió (dur'mjo) *v* see **dormir**.

duro ('duro) *adj* 1 hard. 2 tough. **duro de mollera** pigheaded. ~*nm* coin worth five pesetas.

E

e (e) *conj* (variant of **y** before words beginning with **i** or **hi**) and.

ebanista (eβa'nista) *nm* cabinet-maker.

ébano ('eβano) *nm* ebony.

ebrio ('eβrjo) *adj* drunk.

eclesiástico (ekle'sjastiko) *adj* ecclesiastical. *nm* priest.

eco ('eko) *nm* echo.

economía (ekono'mia) *nf* economy, economics. **hacer economías** economize. **económico** *adj* economic, financial, economical. **economista** *nm,f* economist. **economizar** *vt* save, economize on. *vi* save money, economize.

ecuador (ekwa'ðor) *nm* equator.

ecuestre (e'kwestre) *adj* equestrian.

echar (e'tʃar) *vt* 1 throw, cast, fling. 2 throw out, eject. 3 send forth, emit. 4 pour out. **echar a** start to. **echar cartas** deal cards. **echar hojas** sprout leaves. **echar la llave** turn the key. **echar una carta** post a letter. **echar de menos** miss someone or something. **echarse** *vr* lie down.

edad (e'ðað) *nf* age. **Edad media** Middle Ages.

edición (eði'θjon) *nf* edition, issue.

edicto (e'ðikto) *nm* edict.

edificar (eðifi'kar) *vt* 1 build, construct. 2 edify. **edificio** *nm* building.

editar (eði'tar) *vt* 1 publish. 2 edit. **editor** *nm* 1 publisher. 2 editor. **casa editorial** publishing house.

edredón (eðre'ðon) *nm* eiderdown.

educar (eðu'kar) *vt* 1 educate. 2 bring up. 3 train. **educación** *nf* 1 education. 2 good manners. **educacional** *adj* educational. **educado** *adj* well-mannered, polite.

efectivo (efek'tiβo) *adj* 1 effective. 2 actual, real. **en efectivo** in cash. **efecto** *nm* 1 effect. 2 result. 3 purpose, end. 4 *pl* effects, goods, assets. **efectos en cartera** holdings, shares.

efectuar (efek'twar) *vt* put into effect, carry out.

efervescencia (eferβes'θenθja) *nf* effervescence. **efervescente** *adj* effervescent, fizzy.

eficacia (efi'kaθja) *nf* 1 efficiency. 2 efficacy. **eficaz** *adj* 1 efficient. 2 effective.

eficiente (efi'θjente) *adj* efficient. **eficiencia** *nf* efficiency.

efigie (e'fixje) *nf* effigy.

efímero (e'fimero) *adj* ephemeral, fleeting.

efusión (efu'sjon) *nf* 1 effusion. 2 shedding (esp. of blood).

Egipto (e'xipto) *nm* Egypt. **egipcio** *adj,n* Egyptian.

egoísmo (ego'ismo) *nm* selfishness, egoism. **egoísta** *adj* selfish, egoistical. *nm* selfish person, egoist.

egregio (e'grexjo) *adj* distinguished, eminent.

eje ('exe) *nm* 1 axle. 2 axis. 3 central part, main idea.

ejecutar (exeku'tar) *vt* 1 execute, fulfil. 2 perform (music). **ejecución** *nf* execution, performance. **ejecutivo** *adj,nm* executive.

ejemplar (exem'plar) *adj* model. *nm* copy (of a book, etc.), specimen. **sin ejemplar** without precedent. **ejemplo** *nm* example. **dar ejemplo** set an example.

ejercer (exer'θer) *vt* 1 exercise, apply (influence). 2 practise. **ejercicio** *nm* 1 exercise. 2 practice.

ejército (e'xerθito) *nm* army.

el (el) *def art* m the.

él (el) *pron 3rd pers* s he, it.

elaborar (elaβo'rar) *vt* manufacture, produce. **elaboración** *nf* manufacture, production.

elástico (e'lastiko) *adj,nm* elastic. **elasticidad** *nf* 1 elasticity, springiness. 2 resilience.

elección (elek'θjon) *nf* 1 election. 2 choice,

option. **elector** n elector. **electorado** nm electorate. **electoral** adj electoral.

electricidad (elektriθi'ðað) nf electricity.

eléctrico (e'lektriko) adj electric, electrical.

electrizar (elektri'θar) vt electrify.

electrocutar (elektroku'tar) vt electrocute.

electrodo (elek'troðo) nm electrode.

electrónico (elek'troniko) adj electronic.

elefante (ele'fante) nm elephant.

elegancia (ele'ganθja) nf elegance, smartness. **elegante** adj smart, fashionable.

elegir (i) (ele'xir) vt choose, select, elect.

elemental (elemen'tal) adj elementary. **elemento** nm element.

elevar (ele'ßar) vt 1 raise, elevate. 2 promote. **elevarse** vr rise, ascend.

eliminar (elimi'nar) vt eliminate.

elocución (eloku ujon) nf elocution.

elocuencia (elo'kwenθja) nf eloquence. **elocuente** adj eloquent.

elogiar (elo'xjar) vt praise. **elogio** nm praise. **elogioso** adj very favourable.

elucidar (eluθi'ðar) vt elucidate.

eludir (elu'ðir) vt elude. **elusivo** adj evasive.

ella ('eʎa) pron 3rd pers s she, it.

ello ('eʎo) pron s it. **ello es que** the fact is that. **ello dirá** time will tell.

emanar (ema'nar) vi emanate, originate from. **emanación** nf emanation.

emancipar (emanθi'par) emancipate. **emancipación** nf emancipation.

embajada (emba'xaða) nf 1 embassy. 2 errand. **embajador** n ambassador.

embalar (emba'lar) vt pack, make a parcel of, wrap.

embarazar (embara'θar) vt 1 make someone pregnant. 2 hinder, get in the way. **embarazada** adj pregnant. **embarazo** nm 1 pregnancy. 2 obstruction, obstacle. **embarazoso** adj cumbersome, awkward.

embarcar (embar'kar) vt put on board, ship. **embarcarse** vr embark, set sail. **embarco** nm embarkation.

embargar (embar'gar) vt 1 law seize, impound. 2 hinder, impede. 3 (of the senses) confuse, paralyse. **embargo** nm seizure, embargo.

embarque (em'barke) nm shipment, loading.

embarrar (embar'rar) vt 1 smear. 2 cover with mud.

embeber (embe'ßer) vt 1 soak up, absorb. 2 insert. 3 (sewing) gather, take in. **embeberse** vr be absorbed or engrossed in.

embellecer* (embeʎe'θer) vt embellish.

embestir (i) (embes'tir) vt 1 assault. 2 charge, rush against. **embestida** nf 1 onslaught. 2 charge (of a wild animal).

emblema (em'blema) nm emblem.

embocar (embo'kar) vt put into the mouth. **embocadura** nf 1 narrows (of a river, etc.). 2 mouth (of a river). 3 taste, flavour (of wine).

embolsar (embol'sar) vt put into one's pocket.

emborrachar (emborra'tʃar) vt make drunk, intoxicate. **emborracharse** vr get drunk.

emboscar (embos'kar) vt ambush. **emboscarse** vr lie in ambush. **emboscada** nf ambush.

embotar (embo'tar) vt 1 tin (food). 2 blunt, take the edge off.

embotellar (embote'ʎar) vt bottle. **embotellamiento** nm traffic jam. **embotellarse** vr mot get into a jam.

embozar (embo'θar) vt muffle, wrap up. **embozo** nm muffler.

embragar (embra'gar) vi mot let the clutch in. **embrague** nm mot clutch.

embriagarse (embrja'garse) vr get drunk.

embrollar (embro'ʎar) vt 1 complicate. 2 confuse. **embrollo** nm entanglement, tangle. **embrollarse** vr get into a muddle.

embrujar (embru'xar) vt bewitch.

embrutecer (embrute'θer) vt brutalize. **embrutecerse** vr become brutalized or depraved.

embudo (em'buðo) nm funnel.

embuste (em'buste) nm lie, fib. **embustería** nf 1 lying. 2 trickery. **embustero** nm 1 liar. 2 trickster. adj deceitful.

embutir (embu'tir) vt stuff, cram. **embutirse** stuff oneself (with food). **embutido** nm sausage.

emergencia (emer'xenθja) nf 1 emergence. 2 emergency.

emigrar (emi'grar) vi 1 emigrate. 2 migrate. **emigración** nf emigration. **emigrante** adj,n emigrant.

eminencia (emi'nenθja) nf 1 height, eminence. 2 prominence. **eminente** adj high, elevated, eminent.

emisario (emi'sarjo) nm emissary.

emitir (emi'tir) vt 1 emit, give off. 2 broadcast, transmit. **emisión** nf 1 programme, broadcast. 2 transmission. **emisor** nm transmitter. **emisora** nf radio station.

emoción (emo'θjon) nf 1 emotion. 2 excitement, thrill. **emocionante** adj exciting, thrilling.

empachar (empa'tʃar) vt 1 clog. 2 impede. 3 give indigestion to. med get indigestion.

empacho nm 1 obstacle. 2 embarrassment. 3 indigestion. **empachaso** adj (of food) indigestible.

empadronar (empaðro'nar) vt make a list of, register. **empadronamiento** nm census.

empalagar (empala'gar) vt 1 bore. 2 weary. vi pall. **empalagarse** become surfeited. **empalagoso** adj sickly, cloying.

empalizada (empali'θaða) nf 1 fence. 2 stockade.

empalmar (empal'mar) vt join, connect. **empalme** nm 1 joint. 2 junction (of railway lines, etc.).

empañar (empa'ɲar) vt blur, tarnish. **empañarse** vr get misty, cloud over. **empañado** adj blurred, misty.

empapelar (empape'lar) vt 1 wrap in paper. 2 to paper (walls, etc.)

empaquetar (empake'tar) vt pack, package.

emparejar (empare'xar) vt 1 match, pair off. 2 smooth, level. vi draw abreast with, catch up.

empastar (empas'tar) vt paste. **empaste** nm (dental) filling.

empatar (empa'tar) vi tie, draw (in games, etc.). **empate** nm draw, tie.

empedernir (empeðer'nir) vt harden. **empedernirse** vr grow hard, become obdurate.

empedrar (empe'ðrar) vt pave.

empeine (em'peine) nm 1 groin. 2 instep.

empeñar (empe'ɲar) vt pawn, pledge. **empeñarse en** insist on. **empeñado** adj 1 pawned. 2 determined.

empeorar (empeo'rar) vt make worse, impair. vi get worse, worsen. **empeorarse** vr worsen.

empequeñecer* (empekeɲe'θer) vt 1 belittle. 2 dwarf.

emperador (empera'ðor) nm emperor.

empezar (ie) (empe'θar) vt,vi begin.

empinar (empi'nar) vt 1 lift, raise. 2 inf drink a lot. **empinarse** vr stand on tip-toe.

empírico (em'piriko) adj empirical.

emplazar (empla'θar) vt 1 summon. 2 place, locate.

emplear (emple'ar) vt use, employ. **empleado** nm employee. **empleo** nm 1 use. 2 employment. 3 job.

empobrecer* (empoβre'θer) vt impoverish. **empobrecerse** vr become poor.

empollar (empo'ʎar) vt 1 hatch. 2 inf study hard.

emponzoñar (emponθo'ɲar) vt poison.

emporcar (ue) (empor'kar) vt make dirty, soil.

empotrar (empo'trar) vt embed.

emprender (empren'der) vt undertake, embark on. **emprendedor** adj enterprising.

empresa (em'presa) nf 1 enterprise. 2 comm company. 3 management.

empréstito (em'prestito) nm loan.

empujar (empu'xar) vt push, shove. **empuje** nm 1 thrust, push. 2 initiative, drive. **empujón** nm violent push.

empuñar (empu'ɲar) vt clasp, grasp. **empuñadura** nf hilt, handle.

emular (emu'lar) vt emulate.

emulsión (emul'sjon) nf emulsion.

en (en) prep 1 on. 2 in. 3 into. 4 onto. **en casa** at home. **en avión/tren** by aeroplane/train.

enaguas (e'nagwas) nf pl petticoat.

enajenar (enaxe'nar) vt 1 transfer (property). 2 alienate. 3 madden. **enajenarse** vr 1 deprive oneself. 2 be enraptured. 3 (of friends) become estranged.

enamorar (enamo'rar) vt 1 cause to fall in love. 2 win the love of. **enamorarse** vr fall in love. **enamorado** adj in love.

enano (e'nano) nm dwarf, midget.

enarbolar (enarβo'lar) vt 1 hoist (a flag, a sail). 2 flourish

enardecer* (enarðe'θer) vt inflame. **enardecerse** vr become impassioned.

encabestrar (enkaβes'trar) vt 1 lead by the reins. 2 dominate

encabezar (enkaβe'θar) vt 1 head (an organization, etc.). 2 put a title to. **encabezamiento** nm heading, title.

encadenar (enkaðe'nar) vt chain, shackle. **encadenamiento** nm 1 chaining. 2 linking, connection.

encajar (enka'xar) vt, vi fit together. **encaje** nm 1 fitting. 2 socket. 3 lace, lacework.

encallar (enka'ʎar) vi 1 run aground. 2 get bogged down. **encalladero** nm sandbank.

encaminar (enkami'nar) vt 1 set off (on a journey). 2 direct, give directions to. **encaminarse** vr set out for.

encandilar (enkandi'lar) vt dazzle **encandilarse** vr (of the eyes) sparkle brightly.

encantar (enkan'tar) vt bewitch, enchant. **¡encantado!** pleased to meet you! **encantador** adj charming, delightful. **encanto** nm 1 spell, enchantment. 2 delight.

encapotar (enkapo'tar) vt muffle, cloak. **encapotarse** vr 1 cloak oneself. 2 become cloudy.

encapricharse (enkapri'tfarse) vr follow one's whims, be obstinate. **encapricharse por** become infatuated with.

encarar (enka'rar) vt 1 aim, point. 2 face. **encararse** vr face, face up to.

encarcelar (enkarθe'lar) vt put in jail, imprison.

encarecer* (enkare'θer) vt 1 raise the price of. 2 praise. **encarecidamente** adv strongly, earnestly. **encarecimiento** nm 1 price rise. 2 exaggeration.

encargar (enkar'gar) vt 1 comm order, commission. 2 entrust. **encargarse** vr take responsibility, to undertake. **encargado** adj charged with, responsible for. nm agent, representative. **encargo** nm 1 commission, assignment. 2 order.

encarnar (enkar'nar) vt 1 personify. 2 play (a rôle in theatre etc.). **encarnado** adj 1 incarnate. 2 blood-red.

encarnizar (enkarni'θar) vt infuriate. **encarnizarse** vr 1 feed on. 2 become infuriated. **encarnizado** adj 1 inflamed, bloodshot. 2 fierce.

encasillar (enkasi'ʎar) vt file, classify.

encauzar (enkau'θar) vt channel, direct.

encender (ie) (enθen'der) vt light, set alight. **encenderse** vr catch fire. **encendedor** nm lighter. **encendido** adj burning, alight.

encerrar (ie) (enθe'rar) vt 1 shut up, enclose. 2 include, contain. **encerrarse** vr shut oneself up, go into seclusion.

encía (en'θia) nf anat gum.

encierro (en'θjerro) nm 1 penning in. 2 enclosure. 3 place of confinement.

encima (en'θima) adv above, overhead. **por encima** overhead. **encima de** on top of, upon, over.

encina (en'θina) nf ilex, evergreen oak.

encinta (en'θinta) adj pregnant.

enclavar (enkla'βar) vt nail, pierce. **enclave** nm enclave.

enclenque (en'klenke) adj weak, feeble.

encoger (enko'xer) vt shrink. **encogerse** vr shrink. **encogerse de hombros** shrug one's shoulders. **encogido** adj 1 shrunken. 2 timid. **encogimiento** nm 1 shrinking. 2 shyness.

encolar (enko'lar) vt glue.

encomendar (enkomen'der) vt entrust. **encomendarse** vr commend oneself. **encomienda** nf 1 commission. 2 tribute. 3 concession (of land).

enconar (enko'nar) vt 1 inflame. 2 provoke. **enconarse** vr become more irritable. **enconado** adj 1 inflamed. 2 angry.

encontrar (ue) (enkon'trar) vt 1 find. 2 meet.

encontrarse vr 1 meet, encounter. 2 be situated.

encopetado (enkope'taðo) adj 1 of noble birth, aristocratic. 2 conceited.

encorvar (enkor'βar) vt curve. **encorvarse** vr stoop, bend over. **encorvado** adj 1 curved. 2 stooping. **encorvadura** nf curve, bend.

encrespar (enkres'par) vt 1 ruffle, ripple. 2 curl. 3 irritate. **encresparse** vr 1 ripple, curl up 2 get angry.

encrucijada (enkruθi'xaða) nf crossroads.

encuadernar (enkwaðer'nar) vt bind (a book). **encuadernación** nf bookbinding, cover.

encuadrar (enkwa'ðrar) vt frame. **encuadre** nm frame.

encubrir* (enku'βrir) vt conceal. **encubrimiento** nm concealment.

encuentro (en'kwentro) nm 1 encounter, meeting. 2 mot collision.

encumbrar (enkum'brar) vt elevate, extol. **encumbrarse** vr 1 soar, be lofty. 2 be haughty. **encumbrado** adj lofty, elevated.

enchufar (entʃu'far) vt 1 connect, join. 2 plug in. **enchufe** nm 1 electric plug. 2 inf personal contact, connection. **enchufismo** nm use of personal contacts to get favours. **enchufado** adj well connected.

endeble (en'deβle) adj frail.

endémico (en'demiko) adj endemic

enderezar (endere'θar) vt 1 straighten. 2 put right. **enderezarse** vr stand upright. **enderezado** adj appropriate.

endeudarse (endeu'ðarse) vr contract debts.

endiablado (endja'βlaðo) adj wicked, devilish. **endiablar** vt bedevil.

endiosar (endjo'sar) vt deify. **endiosarse** vr be conceited. **endiosado** adj conceited.

endosar (endo'sar) vt also **endorsar** endorse. **endoso** nm also **endorso** endorsement.

endulzar (endul'θar) vt sweeten.

endurecer* (endure'θer) vt harden. **endurecido** adj hardened. **endurecimiento** nm hardening.

enemigo (ene'migo) nm enemy, foe. adj hostile, inimical. **enemistar** vt set at odds, alienate.

energía (ener'xia) nf energy.

enérgico (en'erxiko) adj 1 energetic. 2 forthright. 3 drastic (measures, etc.).

enero (e'nero) nm January.

enfadar (enfa'ðar) vt anger. **enfadarse** vr become angry. **enfado** nm anger. **enfadoso** adj annoying.

énfasis ('enfasis) nm,f 1 emphasis. 2 pomposity. **enfático** adj 1 emphatic. 2 pompous.

enfermar (enfer'mar) vt make ill. vi fall ill. **enfermedad** nf illness. **enfermera** nf nurse. **enfermizo** adj sickly. **enfermo** adj ill, sick.

enfilar (enfi'lar) vt line up.

enfocar (enfo'kar) vt 1 focus. 2 approach (a question, etc.). **enfoque** nm 1 focus. 2 approach.

enfrascar (enfras'kar) vt put in bottles, bottle. **enfrascarse** vr become absorbed (in a problem, etc.).

enfrentar (enfren'tar) vt confront. **enfrentarse** face up to, face. **enfrente** adv opposite. **enfrente de** prep opposite, facing.

enfriar (enfri'ar) vt cool. **enfriarse** vr cool down.

enfurecer* (enfure'θer) vt enrage. **enfurecerse** vr rage, get into a rage.

enganchar (engan'tʃar) vt 1 hook, hitch on. 2 harness (a horse). **enganche** nm 1 coupling. 2 hitching-up.

engañar (enga'ɲar) vt deceive. **engaño** nm deceit, fraud. **engañoso** adj deceitful.

engatusar (engatu'sar) vt coax, persuade.

engendrar (enxen'drar) vt engender, breed. **engendro** nm 1 foetus. 2 monstrosity. 3 fantastic plan.

englobar (englo'βar) vt include, lump together.

engordar (engor'ðar) vt fatten. vi gain weight.

engorro (en'gorro) nm nuisance.

engranar (engra'nar) vt mesh, put in gear. vi interlock. **engranaje** nm mot gears.

engrandecer* (engrande'θer) vt magnify, extol. **engrandecimiento** nm 1 enlargement. 2 exaggeration.

engrasar (engra'sar) vt grease. **engrase** nm greasing.

engreído (engre'iðo) adj conceited. **engreimiento** nm vanity, conceit.

engrosar (engro'sar) vt increase, thicken. **engrosarse** vr expand.

engullir (engu'ʎir) vt bolt (food), gobble.

enhestar (enes'tar) vt erect. **enhestarse** vr straighten. **enhiesto** adj 1 erect. 2 lofty.

enhorabuena (enora'βwena) nf congratulations. ¡**enhorabuena**! well done! congratulations! ¡**enhoramala**! bad luck! unluckily!

enigma (e'nigma) nm enigma. **enigmático** adj enigmatic.

enjabonar (enxaβo'nar) vt soap.

enjambre (en'xambre) nm swarm.

enjaular (enxau'lar) vt cage.

enjuagar (enxwa'gar) vt rinse. **enjuague** nm 1 rinse, rinsing. 2 intrigue.

enjugar (enxu'gar) vt wipe, dry.

enjuiciar (enxwi'θjar) vt 1 judge. 2 law try. **enjuiciamiento** nm judgment, trial.

enlace (en'laθe) nm 1 link, connection, liaison. 2 marriage. **enlazar** vt 1 link, tie up. 2 marry. **enlazarse** vr be linked, connected.

enloquecer* (enloke'θer) vt madden, drive insane. **enloquecerse** vr go mad. **enloquecido** adj mad.

enlosar (enlo'sar) vt pave. **enlosado** nm flagstone.

enlucir* (enlu'θir) vt 1 plaster. 2 polish. **enlucido** nm plaster.

enlutar (enlu'tar) vt dress in mourning clothes.

enmascarar (enmaska'rar) vt mask. **enmascararse** vr put on a mask, disguise.

enmendar (ie) (enmen'dar) vt 1 correct, amend. 2 reform. **enmendarse** vr reform oneself. **enmienda** nf correction, amendment.

enmohecerse* (enmoe'θerse) vr become rusty or mouldy. **enmohecido** adj 1 rusty. 2 mouldy.

enmudecer* (enmuðe'θer) vt silence. **enmudecerse** vr fall silent.

enojar (eno'xar) vt anger. **enojarse** vr get angry. **enojado** adj angry. **enojo** nm annoyance, vexation.

enorgullecer* (enorgule'θer) vt make proud. **enorgullecerse** vr grow proud. **enorgullecerse de** pride oneself on.

enorme (e'norme) adj enormous. **enormidad** nf enormity, hugeness.

enrarecer* (enrare'θer) vt make rare or scarce. vi (of air) become thin.

enredar (enre'ðar) vt 1 catch, entangle. 2 complicate. 3 involve (someone in an affair, etc.). **enredarse** vr become involved, get entangled. **enredo** nm entanglement, awkward affair.

enrevesado (enreβe'saðo) adj 1 complicated, involved. 2 (of a person) noisy, ill-disciplined.

enriquecer* (enrike'θer) vt enrich.

enrojecer* (enroxe'θer) vt redden, make red. **enrojecerse** vr blush.

enrollar (enro'ʎar) vt coil up.

enronquecer* (enronke'θer) vt make hoarse. **enronquecerse** vr become hoarse.

enroscar (enros'kar) vt curl, coil, twist. **enroscarse** coil, curl. **enroscado** adj coiled, curled.

ensalada (ensa'laða) nf salad.

ensalmar (ensal'mar) vt 1 set (a bone). 2 cure (by magic).

ensalzar (ensal'θar) vt extol, praise highly. **ensalzamiento** nm praise.

ensamblar (ensam'blar) vt put together, assemble. **ensamblador** n fitter.

ensanchar (ensan't∫ar) vt grow broader, expand. **ensancharse** vr spread, extend. **ensanche** nm 1 extension, enlargement. 2 new suburb (of a town).

ensañar (ensa'ɲar) vt enrage. **ensañarse** become enraged, grow furious.

ensayar (ensa'jar) vt 1 try out, test. 2 rehearse. **ensayarse** vr rehearse, practise. **ensayo** nm 1 test, attempt. 2 essay. 3 rehearsal. **ensayo general** dress rehearsal.

enseñar (ense'ɲar) vt 1 show. 2 teach. **enseñanza** nf education.

enseres (en'seres) nm pl goods and chattels.

ensillar (ensi'ʎar) vt saddle.

ensimismarse (ensimis'marse) vr become absorbed in thought. **ensimismamiento** nm reverie, daydream.

ensordecer* (ensorðe'θer) vt deafen. **ensordecedor** adj deafening.

ensuciar (ensu'θjar) vt dirty, soil. **ensuciarse** vr become dirty.

ensueño (en'sweɲo) nm dream, fantasy.

entablar (enta'βlar) vt 1 cover with planks, board up. 2 set up (games, etc.). 3 table (a motion). 4 strike up a conversation. **entablado** nm planking.

entallar (enta'ʎar) vt 1 carve. 2 tailor. vi fit well.

ente ('ente) nm entity.

entender (ie) (enten'der) vt,vi understand. **entender de** know about (a subject), be versed in. **entenderse** vr 1 be understood. 2 understand one another, be on good terms. **entendido** adj 1 agreed. 2 knowledgeable. nm connoisseur.

enterar (ente'rar) vt inform, advise. **enterado** adj well-informed. **enterarse** vr find out about.

entero (en'tero) adj 1 entire, whole. 2 honest, upright.

enterrar (ie) (enter'rar) vt bury. **enterrador** nm gravedigger.

entidad (enti'ðað) nf 1 entity. 2 board, commission.

entierro (en'tjerro) nm burial, funeral.

entonar (ento'nar) vt 1 intone. 2 sing in tune. 3 tone up (muscles, etc.). vi be in tune, harmonize.

entonces (en'tonθes) adv 1 then, at that time. 2 in that case, and so, then.

entornar (entor'nar) vt half-close (the eyes, door, etc.). **entornado** adj half-closed, ajar.

entorpecer* (entorpe'θer) vt 1 stupefy. 2 hinder. **entorpecimiento** nm lethargy, torpor.

entrada (en'traða) nf 1 entrance, doorway. 2 entry, admission. 3 ticket. 4 sport gate. 5 income, takings.

entrambos (en'trambos) adj pl both.

entraña (en'traɲa) nf 1 core, essential part. 2 pl entrails, bowels. 3 pl feelings, heart. **entrañable** adj 1 intimate. 2 beloved.

entrar (en'trar) vt 1 introduce, bring in. 2 mil attack, invade. 3 influence. vi enter. **el año que entra** the coming year.

entre ('entre) prep among, between. **entre que** while.

entreabierto (entrea'βjerto) adj half-open, ajar.

entrecejo (entre'θexo) nm frown.

entregar (entre'gar) vt 1 hand over, deliver. 2 surrender, give up. **entregarse** surrender, give oneself up. **entrega** nf 1 delivery, handing over. 2 instalment, part (of a novel, journal, etc.).

entrelazar (entrela'θar) vt entwine.

entremés (entre'mes) nm 1 Th short farce. 2 interlude. 3 cul side dish, hors d'oeuvre.

entremeter (entreme'ter) vt insert, introduce. **entremeterse** vr also **entrometerse** interfere. **entremetido** adj also **entrometido** interfering.

entrenar (entre'nar) vt sport train, coach. **entrenarse** vr train oneself. **entrenador** n trainer. **entrenamiento** nm training.

entresacar (entresa'kar) vt select.

entresuelo (entre'swelo) nm mezzanine, ground floor.

entretanto (entre'tanto) adv meanwhile.

entretejer (entrete'xer) vt interweave.

entretener* (entrete'ner) 1 entertain. 2 delay. **entretenerse** vr 1 amuse oneself. 2 linger. **entretenido** adj entertaining. **entretenimiento** nm entertainment.

entrever* (entre'βer) vt 1 glimpse. 2 suspect.

entrevista (entre'βista) nf interview. **entrevistar** vt interview. **entrevistarse** vr have an interview.

entristecer* (entriste'θer) vt sadden. **entristecerse** vr grow sad.

entumecer* (entume'θer) vt numb. **entumecimiento** nm numbness.

enturbiar (entur'βjar) vt 1 make cloudy. 2

muddy. **enturbiarse** vr grow cloudy or confused.

entusiasmar (entusjas'mar) vt fill with enthusiasm. **entusiasmarse** vr grow enthusiastic. **entusiasmo** nm enthusiasm. **entusiasta** adj enthusiastic. nm,f enthusiast, fan. **entusiástico** adj enthusiastic.

enumerar (enume'rar) vt enumerate. **enumeración** nf enumeration.

envainar (enβai'nar) vt sheathe.

envanecer* (enβane'θer) vt make conceited.

envasar (enβa'sar) vt 1 pack, wrap. 2 bottle. **envase** nm 1 act of packing. 2 bottle, container.

envejecer* (enβexe'θer) vt make aged, age. **envejecerse** vr grow old. **envejecido** adj aged, old-looking.

envenenar (enβene'nar) vt poison.

envergadura (enβerga'ðura) nf 1 extent, span. 2 scope.

enviar (en'βjar) vt send.

envidiar (enβi'ðjar) vt envy. **envidia** nf envy. **envidioso** adj envious.

envilecer* (enβile'θer) vt debase, degrade. **envilecerse** vr degrade, abase oneself.

envío (en'βio) nm dispatch, consignment, shipment.

envoltura (enβol'tura) nf 1 cover, wrapping. 2 envelope.

envolver (ue) (enβol'βer) vt 1 wrap, tie up. 2 involve, implicate.

enzarzar (enθar'θar) vt embroil. **enzarzarse** vr get involved.

épico ('epiko) adj epic.

epidemia (epi'ðemja) nf epidemic. **epidémico** adj epidemic.

epígrafe (e'pigrafe) nm epigraph, inscription.

epílogo (e'pilogo) nm epilogue.

episcopado (episko'paðo) nm 1 bishopric, episcopate. 2 episcopacy.

episodio (epi'soðjo) nm episode.

epitafio (epi'tafjo) nm epitaph.

época ('epoka) nf epoch, period.

equidad (eki'ðað) nf equity, fairness.

equilibrar (ekili'βrar) vt balance. **equilibrarse** vr balance, poise. **equilibrio** nm balance, equilibrium.

equinoccio (eki'nokθjo) nm equinox.

equipaje (eki'paxe) nm 1 luggage. 2 equipment. 3 naut crew.

equipar (eki'par) vt equip, furnish.

equipo (e'kipo) nm 1 team. 2 equipment, gear.

equitación (ekita'θjon) nf 1 riding. 2 horsemanship.

equitativo (ekita'tiβo) adj equitable, fair.

equivalencia (ekiβa'lenθja) nf equivalence. **equivalente** adj equivalent. **equivaler** vi be equivalent.

equivocar (ekiβo'kar) vt mistake. **equivocarse** vr be wrong, make a mistake. **equivocación** nf mistake. **equivocado** adj mistaken.

equívoco (e'kiβoko) nm pun, word play. adj equivocal.

era ('era) nf era, age.

eremita (ere'mita) nm also **ermitaño** hermit. nf hermitage.

era ('era) v see **ser.**

eres ('eres) v see **ser.**

erguir (er'gir) vt 1 raise. 2 straighten. **erguirse** vr 1 straighten. 2 (of buildings, mountains, etc.) soar. **erguido** adj 1 upright, straight. 2 proud.

erigir (eri'xir) vt erect.

erizarse (eri'θarse) vr bristle. **erizado** adj bristly.

erradicar (errañi'kar) vt eradicate.

errar* (er'rar) vi wander, roam. vt miss (a shot, one's way). **errarse** vr err. **errado** adj mistaken.

error (er'ror) nm error. **erróneo** adj mistaken, false, erroneous.

eructar (eruk'tar) vi belch.

erudición (eruði'θjon) nf erudition. **erudito** nm scholar. adj erudite.

es (es) v see **ser.**

esbelto (es'βelto) adj slim, slight. **esbeltez** nf slimness.

esbozar (esβo'θar) vt sketch. **esbozo** nm sketch.

escabechar (eskaβe't∫ar) vt 1 cul pickle. 2 dye (hair). **escabeche** nm vinegar sauce.

escabroso (eska'βroso) adj 1 rough, uneven. 2 complex. 3 risqué.

escabullirse (eskaβu'λirse) vr slip or run away.

escala (es'kala) nf 1 ladder. 2 scale. 3 naut port of call. **en gran escala** large scale. **hacer escala** call in, stop at. **escalar** vt 1 climb, scale. 2 escalate **escalamiento** nm escalation.

escaldar (eskal'ðar) vt 1 scald. 2 chafe. 3 make red hot. **escaldado** adj 1 scalded. 2 wary.

escalera (eska'lera) nf stairs.

escalfar (eskal'far) vt cul poach.

escalofrío (eskalo'frio) nm 1 shiver. 2 med fever, chill.

escalón (eska'lon) nm 1 rung (of ladder). 2

tread, step (of stair). **3** stage (of progress, etc.). **escalonar** vt space, set at intervals, stagger.

escalpelo (eskal'pelo) nm scalpel.

escama (es'kama) nf **1** scale (of fish, lizard). **2** flake (of soap).

escamot(e)ar (eskamo'tar) vt **1** whisk away. **2** make vanish. **3** shirk. **escamoteo** nm inf swindle, trick. **escamoteador** nm **1** conjurer. **2** swindler.

escampar (eskam'par) vt clear out. vi (of weather) grow clear, improve.

escándalo (es'kandalo) nm **1** scandal. **2** row. **escandalizar** vt scandalize. vi **1** fuss. **2** cause a scandal. **escandaloso** adj **1** scandalous. **2** uproarious. **3** outrageous.

Escandinavia (eskandi'naβja) nf Scandinavia. **escandinavo** adj,n Scandinavian.

escaño (es'kaɲo) nm **1** bench. **2** seat in parliament.

escapar (eska'par) vi escape, flee. **escaparse** vr **1** escape. **2** leak. **escape** nm **1** escape. **2** leak. **3** mot exhaust. **tubo de escape** exhaust pipe.

escaparate (eskapa'rate) nm shop window.

escarabajo (eskara'βaxo) nm beetle.

escaramuza (eskara'muθa) nf skirmish, quarrel.

escarbar (eskar'βar) vt **1** scratch. **2** poke. **3** investigate.

escarcha (es'kartʃa) nf frost.

escarlata (eskar'lata) adj scarlet.

escarmentar (ie) (eskarmen'tar) vt punish. vi learn by experience. **escarmiento** nm **1** punishment. **2** warning, example.

escarnecer* (eskarne'θer) vt scoff, sneer. **escarnecedor** adj scoffing. **escarnio** nm taunt.

escarola (eska'rola) nf endive.

escarpa (es'karpa) nf slope.

escasear (eskase'ar) vt skimp. vi be scarce. **escasez** nf **1** shortage, lack. **2** meanness. **escaso** adj scarce.

escena (es'θena) nf **1** scene. **2** Th stage. **escenario** nm Th stage, scenery. **escénico** adj scenic.

escéptico (es'θeptiko) adj sceptical. nm,f sceptic. **escepticismo** nm scepticism.

esclarecer* (esklare'θer) vt **1** illuminate. **2** enlighten. vi dawn. **esclarecimiento** nm **1** illumination. **2** enlightenment.

esclavitud (esklaβi'tuð) nf slavery. **esclavizar** vt enslave. **esclavo** nm slave.

esclusa (es'klusa) nf floodgate, lock.

escoba (es'koβa) nf broom, brush. **escobar** vt sweep.

escocer (ue) (esko'θer) vt annoy. vi sting, smart. **escocerse** vr chafe.

Escocia (es'koθja) nf Scotland. **escocés** adj Scots, Scottish. n Scot.

escoger (esko'xer) vt choose. **escogido** adj selected. **escogimiento** nm choosing, choice.

escolar (esko'lar) adj scholastic. nm schoolboy.

escolta (es'kolta) nf escort. **escoltar** vt escort.

escollo (es'koʎo) nm **1** reef, rock. **2** trap, pitfall. **escollera** nf jetty, breakwater.

escombro (es'kombro) nm **1** rubbish. **2** pl dust, litter.

esconder (eskon'der) vt hide. **esconderse** vr conceal oneself.

escopeta (esko'peta) nf shotgun.

escoplo (es'koplo) nm chisel. **escoplear** vt chisel.

escoria (es'korja) nf **1** metal slag, dross. **2** scum.

escorpión (eskor'pjon) nm scorpion.

escotilla (esko'tiʎa) nf naut hatch.

escribir* (eskri'βir) vt,vi write. **escribir a máquina** type. **escribirse** vr correspond with one another.

escrito (es'krito) v see **escribir.** adj written. nm document, manuscript. **escritor** nm writer. **escritorio** nm **1** desk. **2** office.

escrúpulo (es'krupulo) nm **1** scruple, hesitation. **2** scrupulousness. **escrupuloso** adj scrupulous.

escrutinio (eskru'tinjo) nm scrutiny.

escuadra (es'kwaðra) nf **1** carpenter's square. **2** squad. **3** naut squadron. **escuadrar** vt make square.

escuálido (es'kwaliðo) adj **1** weak. **2** emaciated, skinny. **3** squalid. **escualidez** nf **1** weakness. **2** skinniness. **3** squalor.

escuchar (esku'tʃar) vt listen to. vi listen. **escucha** nf listening.

escudero (esku'ðero) nm squire or page (of a knight). **escudo** nm shield.

escudriñar (eskuðri'ɲar) vt scrutinize.

escuela (es'kwela) nf school.

escueto (es'kweto) adj unadorned, plain.

esculpir (eskul'pir) vt sculpture, engrave. **escultor** nm sculptor. **escultura** nf sculpture.

escupir (esku'pir) vt,vi spit.

escurrir (eskur'rir) vt **1** wring, squeeze dry. **2** drain. vi ooze, slide. **escurrirse** vr **1** drip, ooze. **2** slip out.

ese [1] ('ese) adj also **esa** that.

ese [2] ('ese) nf the letter S.

ése ('ese) pron also **ésa** 1 that one. 2 the former.

esencia (e'senθja) nf essence. **esencial** adj essential.

esfera (es'fera) nf sphere, globe. **esférico** adj spherical.

esfinge (es'finxe) nf sphinx.

esforzar (ue) (esfor'θar) vt invigorate, strengthen. **esforzarse** vr make an effort.

esfuerzo (es'fwerθo) nm effort.

esgrimir (esgri'mir) vt brandish. vi sport fence. **esgrima** nf fencing.

eslabón (esla'βon) nm link, join. **eslabonar** vt link, connect.

esmaltar (esmal'tar) vt 1 enamel. 2 varnish (fingernails). **esmalte** nm enamel.

esmerado (esme'raðo) adj painstaking, careful. **esmerar** vt polish. **esmerarse** vr take pains.

esmeralda (esme'ralða) nf emerald.

eso ('eso) pron that thing, that. **en eso** at that moment. **eso es** 1 that is to say. 2 that's right. **nada de eso** not a bit. **por eso** because of that.

esos ('esos) adj pl also **esas** those.

ésos ('esos), **ésas** pron 1 those. 2 the former. **ni por ésas** not at all.

espabilar (espaβi'lar) vt snuff (a candle). **espabilarse** vr 1 wake up. 2 look lively.

espaciar (espa'θjar) vt space out, spread. **espaciarse** vr 1 expatiate. 2 relax. **espacio** nm space. **espacioso** adj spacious. **espacial** adj spatial, space. **viajes espaciales** nm pl space travel.

espada (es'paða) nf sword. nm swordsman.

espalda (es'palda) nf 1 shoulder, back. a **espaldas** behind someone's back. **volverse de espaldas** turn one's back.

espantapájaros (espanta'paxaros) nm invar scarecrow.

espantar (espan'tar) vt scare, frighten off. **espanto** nm fright. **espantoso** adj terrifying.

España (es'paɲa) nf Spain. **español** adj Spanish. nm 1 Spaniard. 2 Spanish (language).

esparcir* (espar'θir) vt 1 scatter, spread. 2 sow. 3 amuse.

espárrago (es'parrago) nm asparagus.

espasmo (es'pasmo) nm spasm.

especia (es'peθja) nf spice.

especial (espe'θjal) adj special, especial. **en especial** especially. **especialidad** nf special-

ity. **especialista** nm specialist. **especializarse** vr specialize.

especie (es'peθje) nf 1 species. 2 kind, type.

específico (espe'θifiko) adj specific. **especificar** vt specify.

espectáculo (espek'takulo) nm 1 spectacle. 2 Th performance. **espectacular** adj spectacular. **espectador** nm spectator.

espejo (es'pexo) nm mirror.

esperar (espe'rar) vt,vi 1 hope. 2 await, wait. 3 expect. **espera** nf 1 wait, waiting. 2 expectation. **sala de espera** nf waiting room. **esperanza** nf hope. **esperanzador** adj encouraging.

esperpento (esper'pento) nm 1 ugly sight. 2 absurdity.

espesar (espe'sar) vt thicken. **espeso** adj thick.

espía (es'pia) nm spy. **espiar** vt spy on.

espiga (es'piga) nf spike, ear of corn. **espigar** vt glean, pick up grains.

espina (es'pina) nf 1 thorn. 2 spine.

espinaca (espi'naka) nf spinach.

espionaje (espjo'naxe) nm espionage.

espiral (espi'ral) adj,nf spiral.

espíritu (es'piritu) nm 1 spirit. 2 mind. **espiritual** adj spiritual.

espléndido (es'plendiðo) adj splendid, lavish. **esplendidez** nf splendour.

espliego (es'pljego) nm lavender.

espolear (espole'ar) vt spur, spur on.

esponja (es'ponxa) nf sponge. **esponjar** vt make fluffy, fluff up. **esponjoso** adj 1 spongy, porous. 2 fluffy.

esponsales (espon'sales) nm pl betrothal.

espontáneo (espon'taneo) adj spontaneous. nm spectator who rushes into the bullring to fight the bull. **espontaneidad** nf spontaneity.

esporádico (espo'raðiko) adj sporadic.

esposa (es'posa) nf 1 wife. 2 pl handcuffs. **esposo** nm husband. **esposar** vt handcuff.

espuela (es'pwela) nf spur.

espuma (es'puma) nf foam, froth, lather.

esquela (es'kela) nf 1 note, short letter. 2 obituary.

esqueleto (eske'leto) nm skeleton.

esquema (es'kema) nm scheme, sketch, diagram.

esquí (es'ki) nm, pl **esquís** ski. **esquiar** vi ski.

esquilar (eski'lar) vt clip, shear.

esquimal (eski'mal) nm Eskimo.

esquina (es'kina) nf (outside) corner **esquinar** vt form a corner with.

esquirol (eski'rol) *nm* strike-breaker, blackleg.

esquivar (eski'βar) *vt* avoid, shun. **esquivo** *adj* shy, unsociable, withdrawn.

estabilidad (estaβili'ðað) *nf* stability. **estable** *adj* stable.

establecer* (estaβle'θer) *vt* establish. **establecerse** *vr* set oneself up, establish oneself. **establecimiento** *nm* establishment.

establo (es'taβlo) *nm* cowshed.

estaca (es'taka) *nf* post, stake. **estacada** *nf* fence.

estación (esta'θjon) *nf* 1 station. 2 season.

estacionar (estaθjo'nar) *vt* park (a car). **estacionamiento** *nm* parking.

estadio (es'taðjo) *nm* 1 stadium. 2 *med* phase.

estado (es'taðo) *nm* 1 state. 2 status. **estar en estado** be pregnant. **estado mayor general** *mil* general staff.

Estados Unidos (es'taðos u'niðos) *nm pl* United States. **estadounidense** *adj* American.

estafa (es'tafa) *nf* swindle. **estafador** *nm* swindler. **estafar** *vt* swindle.

estafeta (esta'feta) *nf* 1 district post office. 2 mail.

estallar (esta'ʎar) *vi* burst, erupt. **estallido** *nm* 1 explosion. 2 outbreak.

estampar (estam'par) *vt* print, imprint. **estampa** *nf* 1 print, footprint. 2 engraving. 3 appearance.

estampida (estam'piða) *nf* stampede. **estampido** *nm* explosion.

estancar (estan'kar) *vt* block, delay. **estancarse** *vr* stagnate. **estancado** *adj* 1 stagnant. 2 at a standstill.

estanco (es'tanko) *nm* 1 state tobacco shop. 2 monopoly.

estandarte (estan'darte) *nm* banner.

estanque (es'tanke) *nm* pond.

estante (es'tante) *nm* 1 shelf. 2 bookcase.

estaño (es'taɲo) *nm* tin.

estar* (es'tar) *vi* be (in a place, temporarily, etc.). **no está** he or she is not at home. **¿estamos?** do we agree? **¡ya está!** that's it! **¿a cuántos estamos?** what's the date? **estar para** 1 be in the mood for. 2 be about to.

estático (es'tatiko) *adj* static.

estatua (es'tatwa) *nf* statue.

estatura (esta'tura) *nf* stature, height.

este[1] ('este) *adj* also **esta** this.

este[2] ('este) *adj,nm* east.

éste ('este) *pron* also **ésta** 1 this one. 2 the latter.

estela (es'tela) *nf* 1 *naut* wake. 2 trail.

estepa (es'tepa) *nf* steppe.

estera (es'tera) *nf* matting, mat.

estereofónico (estereo'foniko) *adj* stereophonic.

estereotipo (estereo'tipo) *nm* stereotype.

estéril (es'teril) *adj* 1 sterile. 2 useless. **esterilizar** *vt* sterilize.

esterlina (ester'lina) *adj* sterling.

estético (es'tetiko) *adj* aesthetic. **estética** *nf* aesthetics.

estetoscopio (estetos'kopjo) *nm* stethoscope.

estiércol (es'tjerkol) *nm* dung, manure.

estigma (es'tigma) *nm* stigma.

estilar (esti'lar) *vt* 1 wear. 2 be in the habit of using. **estilarse** *vr* be in fashion. **estilo** *nm* style.

estimar (esti'mar) *vt* 1 estimate. 2 esteem. **estima** *nf* esteem. **estimable** *adj* esteemed. **estimación** *nf* 1 estimation. 2 esteem.

estimular (estimu'lar) *vt* stimulate. **estimulante** *adj* stimulant. **estímulo** *nm* 1 stimulus. 2 stimulation.

estío (es'tio) *nm* lit summer.

estipular (estipu'lar) *vt* stipulate.

estirar (esti'rar) *vt* stretch, pull out. **estirado** *adj* taut, stretched tight. **estirón** *nm* pull, jerk.

estirpe (es'tirpe) *nf* lineage, stock.

estofa (es'tofa) *nf* 1 quilted material. 2 (of a person) quality, class.

estofar (esto'far) *vt* 1 stew. 2 quilt. **estofado** *nm* stew.

estoico (es'toiko) *adj* stoic. **estoicismo** *nm* stoicism.

estómago (es'tomago) *nm* stomach. **estomagar** *vt* 1 give indigestion to. 2 annoy.

estorbar (estor'βar) *vt* hinder. *vi* be in the way. **estorbo** *nm* hindrance, obstacle.

estornudar (estornu'ðar) *vi* sneeze. **estornudo** *nm* sneeze.

estos ('estos) *adj pl* also **estas** these.

éstos ('estos) *pron pl* also **éstas** 1 these. 2 the latter.

estoy (es'toi) *v* see **estar**.

estrafalario (estrafa'larjo) *adj* outlandish, eccentric.

estragar (estra'gar) *vt* 1 lay waste. 2 pervert. **estrago** *nm* ruin, havoc. **hacer estragos** wreak havoc.

estrangular (estrangu'lar) vt strangle. **estrangulador** nm 1 strangler. 2 mot choke.

estratagema (estrata'xema) nf stratagem. **estrategia** nf strategy. **estratégico** adj strategic.

estrechar (estre't∫ar) vt 1 make narrower, reduce. 2 tighten. 3 embrace, shake (hand). **estrecharse** vr get narrow. **estrechez** nf 1 narrowness. 2 stringency. 3 intimacy. **estrecho** adj 1 narrow, cramped, tight. 2 austere. 3 narrow-minded. nm straits, channel.

estrella (es'treʎa) nf star. **estrellar** vt smash, shatter. **estrellado** adj starry.

estremecer* (estreme'θer) vt shake. **estremecerse** vr tremble, shudder, shiver. **estremecimiento** nm tremor, trembling.

estrenar (estre'nar) vt 1 try on, wear for the first time. 2 Th perform for the first time. **estrenarse** vr make a début. **estreno** nm 1 début. 2 première. 3 first appearance.

estreñido (estre'niðo) adj constipated. **estreñimiento** nm constipation. **estreñirse** vr become constipated.

estrépito (es'trepito) nm noise, din, fuss. **estrepitoso** adj boisterous, noisy.

estribo (es'triβo) nm 1 stirrup. 2 running board. **perder los estribos** lose one's head, go crazy.

estribor (estri'βor) nm naut starboard.

estricto (es'trikto) adj strict, severe.

estridente (estri'ðente) adj strident.

estropajo (estro'paxo) nm 1 scourer. 2 rubbish. **estropajoso** adj 1 gristly. 2 slovenly. 3 (of speech) slurred, indistinct.

estropear (estrope'ar) vt 1 spoil. 2 maim.

estructura (estruk'tura) nf structure, framework.

estruendo (estru'endo) nm noise, din turmoil. **estruendoso** adj noisy, uproarious.

estrujar (estru'xar) vt 1 squeeze. 2 drain. **estrujón** nm squeeze, crush.

estuario (es'twarjo) nm estuary.

estuche (es'tut∫e) nm 1 box. 2 sheath.

estudiar (estu'ðjar) vt,vi study. **estudiante** nm,f student. **estudio** nm 1 study 2 research. 3 studio. **estudioso** adj studious.

estufa (es'tufa) nf 1 stove. 2 hot house.

estupefacto (estupe'fakto) adj astonished. **estupefaciente** nm drug, narcotic.

estupendo (estu'pendo) adj stupendous, marvellous.

estúpido (es'tupiðo) adj stupid. **estupidez** nf stupidity.

estuve (es'tuβe) v see **estar**.

etapa (e'tapa) nf 1 stage (of a journey, etc.). 2 phase. **por etapas** by stages.

éter ('eter) nm ether.

etéreo (e'tereo) adj ethereal.

eternidad (eterni'ðað) nf eternity. **eterno** adj eternal. **eternizar** vt make eternal, perpetuate.

ética ('etika) nf ethics. **ético** adj ethical.

Etiopía (Etjo'pia) nf Ethiopia. **etíope** adj,n Ethiopian.

etiqueta (eti'keta) nf 1 etiquette. 2 label. **etiquetero** adj formal, ceremonious.

eufemismo (eufe'mismo) nm euphemism. **eufemístico** adj euphemistic.

eunuco (eu'nuko) nm eunuch.

Europa (eu'ropa) nf Europe. **europeísmo** nm pro-European attitudes. **europeizar** vt Europeanize. **europeo** adj,n European.

eutanasia (euta'nasja) nf euthanasia.

evacuar (eβa'kwar) vt 1 evacuate. 2 undertake. **evacuación** nf evacuation.

evadir (eβa'ðir) vt evade. **evadirse** vr escape. **evadido** n fugitive.

evangélico (eβan'xeliko) adj evangelical. **evangelio** nm gospel. **evangelista** nm evangelist.

evaporar (eβapo'rar) vt,vi evaporate. **evaporación** nf evaporation.

evasión (eβa'sjon) nf escape, flight. **evasiva** nf loophole, evasion. **evasivo** adj evasive.

evento (e'βento) nm eventuality, unforeseen event.

eventual (eβen'twal) adj 1 conditional, possible. 2 temporary. **eventualmente** adv 1 by chance. 2 circumstantially.

evidencia (eβi'ðenθja) nf 1. evidence. 2 clarity. **evidenciar** vt prove, make evident. **evidente** adj evident, obvious.

evitar (eβi'tar) vt avoid. **evitable** adj avoidable.

evocar (eβo'kar) vt evoke, invoke. **evocación** nf evocation, invocation. **evocador** adj evocative.

evolución (eβolu'θjon) nf evolution. **evolucionar** vi evolve. **evolutivo** adj evolutionary.

exacerbar (eksaθer'βar) vt exacerbate, provoke.

exactitud (eksakti'tuð) nf exactness. **exacto** adj exact, precise, correct.

exagerar (eksaxe'rar) vt exaggerate. **exagerado** adj 1 exaggerated. 2 excessive. **exageración** nf exaggeration.

exaltar (eksal'tar) vt 1 raise. 2 praise. **exaltarse** vr become excited.

examen (ek'samen) nm 1 educ examination. 2

investigation. **examen de conductor** driving test. **examinador** *nm* examiner.

examinar (eksami'nar) *vt* 1 examine, inspect closely. 2 test, question. **examinarse** *vr* take an examination.

exangüe (ek'sangwe) *adj* 1 bloodless, anaemic. 2 worn-out, weak.

exánime (ek'sanime) *adj* 1 lifeless. 2 unconscious. **caer exánime** fall in a faint.

exasperar (eksaspe'rar) *vt* 1 exasperate, annoy. 2 make worse. **exasperarse** *vr* become angry.

excavar (ekska'βar) *vt* 1 excavate. 2 hollow out.

exceder (eksθe'ðer) *vt* exceed, surpass. **excederse** *vr* 1 surpass oneself. 2 go too far, overreach oneself.

excelencia (eksθe'lenθja) *nf* excellence, virtue. **su Excelencia** his Excellency. **excelente** *adj* outstanding, excellent.

excéntrico (eks'θentriko) *adj,nm* eccentric. **excentricidad** *nf* eccentricity.

excepción (eksθep'θjon) *nf* exception. **a excepción de** with the exception of. **hacer una excepción de** make an exception of. **excepcional** *adj* exceptional.

excepto (eks'θepto) *prep* with the exception of.

excesivo (eksθe'siβo) *adj* excessive. **exceso** *nm* 1 excess. 2 abuse.

excitar (eksθi'tar) *vt* excite, stimulate. **excitarse** *vr* become excited.

exclamar (ekskla'mar) *vi* exclaim. **exclamarse contra** protest against.

excluir (eksklu'ir) *vt* exclude, rule out. **exclusión** *nf* exclusion. **exclusivo** *adj* exclusive, sole.

excomulgar (ekskomul'gar) *vt* excommunicate.

excursión (ekskur'sjon) *nf* excursion, outing. **excursión a pie** ramble. **ir de excursión** go on an outing.

excusar (eksku'sar) *vt* 1 forgive. 2 avoid. **excusarse** *vr* apologise. **excusa** *nf* excuse, pretext. **excusado** *adj* 1 unnecessary. 2 private.

exentar (eksen'tar) *vt* exempt (from). **exención** *nf* exemption. **exento** *adj* 1 exempt (from). 2 unobstructed.

exequias (ek'sekjas) *nf pl* funeral ceremony.

exhalar (eksa'lar) *vt* 1 breathe out. 2 give off (fumes, etc.). 3 utter (sigh, etc.).

exhausto (ek'sausto) *adj* exhausted.

exhibir (eksi'βir) *vt* exhibit, show, display. **exhibirse** *vr* show oneself. **exhibición** *nf* exhibition, show. **exhibicionismo** *nm* exhibitionism.

exhortar (eksor'tar) *vt* exhort.

exigir (eksi'xir) *vt* demand, insist on. **exigente** *adj* demanding.

exiguo (ek'sigwo) *adj* small, scanty.

eximir (eksi'mir) *vt* exempt from, relieve of.

existir (eksis'tir) *vi* exist, be. **existe la posibilidad que** it is just possible that. **existencia** *nf* 1 existence. 2 *comm* stocks, supplies. **existencialismo** *nm* existentialism.

éxito ('eksito) *nm* 1 result. 2 success. **éxito de taquilla** box-office success.

éxodo ('eksoðo) *nm* exodus, departure.

exonerar (eksone'rar) *vt* 1 exonerate. 2 free (from responsibility, weight, etc.).

exorbitante (eksorβi'tante) *adj* excessive.

exorcizar (eksorθi'θar) *vt* exorcise. **exorcismo** *nm* exorcism.

expansión (ekspan'sjon) *nf* 1 expansion. 2 relief, relaxation. 3 warmth of feeling. **expansivo** *adj* expansive, affectionate.

expatriar (ekspatri'ar) *vt* exile. **expatriarse** *vr* leave one's country.

expectación (ekspekta'θjon) *nf* expectation. **expectante** *adj* expectant.

expedición (ekspeði'θjon) *nf* 1 expedition. 2 *comm* shipment. 3 speed.

expedir* (ekspe'ðir) *vt* send, dispatch, issue. **expediente** *nm* 1 means device. 2 *law* proceedings. 3 file, record. **expediente académico** academic or school record.

expendedor (ekspende'ðor) *nm,f* dealer, agent. *adj* spending. **expendedor de billetes** booking clerk.

experiencia (ekspe'rjenθja) *nf* experience, skill.

experimentar (eksperimen'tar) *vt* 1 experience (emotion, etc.). 2 experiment (with). **experimental** *adj* experimental. **experimento** *nm* experiment.

experto (eks'perto) *adj,nm* expert.

expiar (eks'pjar) *vt* make atonement for.

expirar (ekspi'rar) *vi* 1 expire. 2 die.

explanar (ekspla'nar) *vt* 1 level, flatten. 2 explain.

explicar (ekspli'kar) *vt* 1 explain. 2 put forward (theory). 3 teach. **explicarse** *vr* 1 express oneself. 2 understand. **explicación** *nf* explanation. **explicativo** *adj* explanatory.

explícito (eks'pliθito) *adj* explicit, clear.

explorar (eksplo'rar) *vt* explore, investigate.

explosión (eksplo'sjon) *nf* explosion. **explosivo** *adj,nm* explosive.

explotar (eksplo'tar) vt 1 run (a business), work (a mine), etc. 2 exploit. vt,vi explode. **explotación** nf 1 operation (of a business, factory, etc.). 2 exploitation.

exponer* (ekspo'ner) vt 1 expose, lay bare. 2 display. 3 explain. 4 phot expose. **exponerse** vr lay oneself open (to danger, etc.). **exponente** nm,f 1 one who explains, interpreter (of art, music). 2 illustration, example. adj explaining, explanatory.

exportar (ekspor'tar) vt export. **exportación** nf exportation, export. **exportador** adj exporting. nm exporter.

exposición (eksposi'θjon) nf 1 exhibition (art, etc.), showing. 2 phot exposure. 3 narrative. 4 position, location.

exprés (eks'pres) nm 1 express (train). 2 cul espresso (coffee).

expresar (ekspre'sar) vt express, state, quote, voice (opinion). **expresarse** vr 1 express oneself. 2 be stated. **expresión** nf 1 expression. 2 pl (kind) regards. **expresivo** adj affectionate.

exprimir (ekspri'mir) vt squeeze or wring (out).

expuesto (eks'pwesto) adj 1 dangerous, risky. 2 exposed.

expulsar (ekspul'sar) vt expel, banish, throw out.

exquisito (ekski'sito) adj exquisite, delicious.

éxtasis (ekstasis) nm invar ecstasy.

extender (ie) (eksten'der) vt 1 extend, lengthen. 2 prolong. 3 unfold, spread out. **extenderse** vr 1 stretch oneself out. 2 talk at length. **extenderse a** or **hasta** run to, amount to.

extenso (eks'tenso) adj 1 wide, spread out, vast. 2 spacious. 3 extended. **por extenso** in great detail. **extensión** nf 1 extension, length. 2 expanse. 3 extent. **extensivo** adj extensive. **extensivo a** applicable to.

extenuar (ekste'nwar) weaken.

exterior (ekste'rjor) adj 1 outer, external. 2 foreign. nm 1 (outward) appearance. 2 foreign countries. **al** or **por el exterior** outwardly. **del exterior** from abroad.

exterminar (ekstermi'nar) vt destroy, wipe out.

externo (eks'terno) adj external. nm day pupil.

extinguir* (ekstin'gir) vt 1 extinguish, put out. 2 wipe out. **extinción** nf extinction. **extinto** adj extinct. **extintor** nm fire extinguisher.

extirpar (ekstir'par) vt 1 stamp out, wipe out. 2 med remove.

extra ('ekstra) adj invar extra. nm bonus, extra

item. nm,nf (film) extra. **extra de** in addition to.

extraer* (ekstra'er) vt 1 extract, remove. 2 release. **extracción** nf 1 extraction. 2 origin, birth. **extracto** nm 1 extract. 2 abstract (of text).

extranjero (ekstran'xero) adj foreign. nm 1 foreigner. 2 stranger. 3 foreign country. **en el extranjero** abroad. **ir al extranjero** go abroad.

extrañar (ekstra'nar) vt 1 find strange or surprising. 2 exile. 3 estrange. **es de extrañar que** it is surprising that. **extrañarse** vr be surprised.

extraordinario (ekstraorði'narjo) adj 1 uncommon. 2 strange, odd. 3 outstanding. nm special number (newspaper, etc.).

extravagancia (ekstraβa'ganθja) nf 1 extravagance. 2 strangeness. **extravagante** adj 1 extravagant. 2 odd.

extraviar (ekstra'βjar) vt 1 lose, mislay (object). 2 mislead (person). **extraviarse** vr 1 get lost. 2 stray (animal). 3 inf fall into bad habits.

extremar (ekstre'mar) vt carry to extremes, overdo. **extremarse en** make every effort to.

extremidad (ekstremi'ðað) nf 1 tip, edge, extremity. 2 pl furthest limits. **extremo** adj 1 extreme, farthest, end. 2 last. 3 desperate. **en caso extremo** as a last resort. nm 1 extreme, end. 2 great care. **al extremo de** to the point of. **de un extremo a otro** from one extreme to the other. **Extremo Oriente** Far East.

extrínseco (eks'trinseko) adj extrinsic, not inherent in.

exuberancia (eksuβe'ranθja) nf 1 exuberance, high spirits. 2 lushness. **exuberante** adj 1 abundant, lush. 2 well-rounded (figure).

exultar (eksul'tar) vi exult, triumph.

F

fábrica ('faβrika) nf 1 factory. 2 manufacture, production. **fabricar** vt 1 manufacture. 2 arch build. **fabricación** nf manufacture. **fabricante** nm manufacturer. **fabricación en serie** mass production.

fábula ('faβula) nf 1 fable, tale. 2 plot, action. 3 gossip, rumour.

fabuloso (faβu'loso) adj 1 fabulous, imaginary. 2 inf wonderful.

facción (fak'θjon) nf 1 faction, party, side. 2 anat pl features.

faceta (fa'θeta) *nf* facet.

fácil ('faθil) *adj* 1 easy, simple. 2 fluent, glib. 3 docile. **facilidad** *nf* facility, ease.

facilitar (faθili'tar) *vt* 1 facilitate. 2 supply, provide.

facsímil (fak'θimil) *adj,nm* facsimile.

factible (fak'tiβle) *adj* feasible.

factor (fak'tor) *nm* 1 factor, element. 2 agent.

facturar (faktu'rar) *vt* 1 invoice. 2 *mot* register (baggage). **factura** *nf* bill, invoice.

facultad (fakul'tað) *nf* 1 power, authority. 2 ability, faculty. 3 *educ* faculty, school (in a university).

facultativo (faculta'tivo) *adj* 1 optional. 2 professional. 3 *med* medical. *nm* doctor.

facha ('fatʃa) *nf inf* appearance, look.

fachada (fa'tʃaða) *nf* façade.

faena (fa'ena) *nf* 1 task, duty. 2 *inf* tough job. **estar de faena** be at work.

faisán (fai'san) *nm* pheasant.

faja ('faxa) *nf* 1 strip of cloth, bandage. 2 belt, zone. 3 girdle.

falaz (fa'laθ) 1 deceitful, treacherous. 2 deceptive, fallacious.

falda ('falda) *nf* 1 skirt. 2 lower slope of a hill. 3 lap.

falsear (false'ar) *vt* 1 falsify. 2 counterfeit. 3 *tech* bevel. *vi* give way, sag.

falsificar (falsifi'kar) *vt* 1 falsify. 2 forge. **falsificación** *nf* 1 falsification. 2 forgery.

falso ('falso) *adj* 1 false. 2 bogus, sham. **en falso** falsely. **falsedad** *nf* falsity.

falta ('falta) *nf* 1 want, need. 2 fault, failure, shortcoming. 3 *sport* foul, fault.

faltar (fal'tar) *vi* 1 be lacking. 2 be absent or missing. **faltar a la verdad** lie.

falto ('falto) *adj* 1 deficient, short. 2 incomplete.

fallar (fa'ʎar) *vt* 1 *law* judge, pronounce sentence on. 2 *game* trump. *vi* fail, go wrong. **falla** *nf* failure, defect.

fallecer* (faʎe'θer) *vi* 1 die. 2 run out, end. **fallecimiento** *nm* decease, demise.

fallir (fa'ʎir) *vi* 1 fail. 2 run out, expire.

fallo ('faʎo) *nm* 1 failure, breakdown. 2 *law* decision, verdict.

fama ('fama) *nf* reputation, fame.

familia (fa'milja) *nf* 1 family. 2 household. **familiar** *adj* 1 of the family. 2 familiar. 3 ordinary, informal. *nm,f* 1 intimate friend. 2 relative. **familiaridad** *nf* familiarity.

familiarizar (familjari'θar) *vt* familiarize.

famoso (fa'moso) *adj* 1 famous. 2 *inf* great (friend).

fanático (fa'natiko) *adj* fanatical. *nm* 1 fanatic. 2 *inf* supporter, enthusiast, fan.

fanfarrón (fanfar'ron) *nm* 1 bully. 2 braggart. *adj* boastful.

fango ('fango) *nm* mud, mire. **fangal** *nm* muddy place, bog. **fangoso** *adj* muddy.

fantasía (fanta'sia) *nf* 1 fantasy. 2 whim, fancy. **joyas de fantasía** *nf pl* imitation jewellery

fantasma (fan'tasma) *nm* ghost.

fantástico (fan'tastiko) *adj* 1 fantastic. 2 imaginary, unreal.

fantoche (fan'totʃe) *nm* 1 puppet. 2 *inf* non-entity, man of straw.

fardo ('farðo) *nm* 1 bundle, pack. 2 load, burden.

fariseo (fari'seo) *nm* hypocrite, Pharisee.

farmacia (far'maθja) *nf* 1 chemist's shop, pharmacy. **farmacia de guardia** all-night chemist's. **farmacéutico** *nm* chemist, pharmacist. *adj* pharmaceutical.

faro ('faro) *nm* 1 lighthouse. 2 beacon. 3 *mot* headlamp.

farol (fa'rol) *nm* 1 lantern. 2 *inf* swank. **farol público** street lamp.

farsa ('farsa) *nf* 1 *Th* farce. 2 humbug. **farsante** *inf* fake, fraud.

fascinar (fasθi'nar) *vt,vi* fascinate. **fascinación** *nf* fascination. **fascinador** *adj* fascinating.

fascismo (fas'θismo) *nm* fascism. **fascista** *adj, n* fascist.

fase ('fase) *nf* phase, stage.

fastidiar (fasti'ðjar) *vt* 1 annoy. 2 bore. 3 disgust. **¡no fastidies!** you're joking! 2 do not bother me! **fastidiarse** *vr* 1 become annoyed. 2 become bored. **fastidio** *nm* 1 annoyance. 2 boredom. **fastidioso** *adj* 1 annoying. 2 boring.

fastuoso (fas'twoso) *adj* 1 magnificent, splendid. 2 pompous.

fatal (fa'tal) *adj* 1 deadly. 2 cursed, ill fated. 3 inescapable. 4 *inf* horrible, awful. **fatalidad** *nf* 1 fate, fatality. 2 misfortune. **fatalista** *adj invar* fatalistic. *nm,f* fatalist. **fatalismo** *nm* fatalism.

fatigar (fati'gar) *vt* 1 tire. 2 annoy. **fatigarse** *vr* become tired or weary. **fatiga** *nf* 1 tiredness. 2 *tech* fatigue. 3 *pl* troubles, worries. **fatigoso** *adj* 1 trying, tiresome. 2 tiring. 3 difficult.

fatuidad (fatwi'ðað) *nf* 1 frivolity, silliness. 2 vanity. **fatuo** *adj* 1 idle, foolish, inane. 2 vain.

fausto ('fausto) *adj* succesful, fortunate. *nm* glory, splendour.

favor (fa'βor) *nm* 1 favour, kindness. 2 help. 3 gift. **a favor de** 1 in favour of. 2 on behalf of. **de favor** complimentary (tickets, etc). **favorable** *adj* favourable. **favorecer*** *vt* 1 favour, prefer. 2 help. **favorito** *adj,nm* favourite.

faz (faθ) *nf* 1 face. 2 front.

fe (fe) *nf* 1 faith, belief. 2 trust. 3 witness, testimony. 4 certificate. **a fe** in truth. **dar fe en** put trust in. **tener fe en** believe in.

fealdad (feal'ðað) *nf* ugliness.

febrero (fe'βrero) *nm* February.

febril (fe'βril) *adj* 1 feverish. 2 agitated.

fecundar (fekun'dar) *vt* fertilize. **fecundidad** *nf* fertility, fruitfulness. **fecundizar*** *vt* fertilize. **fecundo** *auj* 1 fertile, fruitful. 2 abundant, productive. **fecundo en** rich in, full of.

fecha ('fetʃa) *nf* date. **hasta la fecha** to date, up to the present.

federación (feðera'θjon) *nf* federation.

fehaciente (fea'θjente) *adj law* authentic, reliable.

felicidad (feliθi'ðað) *nf* 1 joy, happiness. 2 success, good fortune. **¡felicidades!** congratulations!

felicitar (feliθi'tar) *vt* congratulate.

feligrés (feli'gres) *nm* parishioner.

feliz (fe'liθ) *adj* 1 happy. 2 fortunate. **feliz año nuevo** happy New Year. **feliz cumpleaños** happy birthday.

felpa ('felpa) *nf* 1 plush, towelling. 2 *inf* beating, hiding. **felpudo** *adj* plushy. *nm* doormat.

femenino (feme'nino) *adj* feminine, female.

fenecer* (fene'θer) *vt* 1 cease, end. 2 die, perish.

fenómeno (fe'nomeno) *nm* 1 phenomenon. 2 oddity, freak. 3 person of extraordinary qualities, genius.

feo ('feo) *adj* 1 ugly, plain, unsightly. 2 nasty, foul. 3 unfair, cheating. **más feo que Picio** as ugly as sin. ~*nm* insult.

féretro ('feretro) *nm* coffin.

feria ('ferja) *nf* 1 fair. 2 festival, carnival. **feria de muestras** trade fair.

fermentar (fermen'tar) *vi* ferment.

ferocidad (feroθi'ðað) *nf* ferocity, savageness. **feroz** *adj* fierce, wild, savage.

férreo ('ferreo) *adj* 1 iron. 2 *sci* ferrous. 3 severe, firm.

ferretería (ferrete'ria) *nf* 1 hardware. 2 ironmonger's shop, hardware shop.

ferrocarril (ferrokar'ril) *nm* railway. **por ferrocarril** by rail.

ferroviario (ferro'βjarjo) *adj* railway, rail. *nm* railway worker.

fértil ('fertil) *adj* fertile, productive, abundant. **fertilidad** *nf* fertility, fruitfulness. **fertilizante** *nm* fertilizer. **fertilizar** *vt* fertilize.

ferviente (fer'βjente) *adj* intense, ardent. **fervor** *nm* 1 passion, ardour. 2 enthusiasm, zeal. **fervoroso** *adj* 1 ardent. 2 eager, enthusiastic.

festejar (feste'xar) *vt* 1 feast, celebrate. 2 woo. **festejo** *nm* 1 feast. 2 courtship. **festín** *nm* feast, banquet. **festividad** *nf* 1 festivity. 2 holiday. **festivo** *adj* 1 festive, merry. 2 witty. **día festivo** *nm* holiday.

fétido ('fetiðo) *adj* stinking, rotting.

feto ('feto) *nm* embryo, unborn child.

feudal (feu'ðal) *adj* feudal. **feudalismo** *nm* feudal system. **feudo** *nm* manor, feudal territory.

fiado ('fjaðo) *nm* trust. **combrar al fiado** buy on credit. **en fiado** on bail. **fiador** *nm* 1 sponsor. 2 fastener, catch. 3 trigger (of a gun).

fiambre ('fjambre) *nm* 1 cold cooked meat, cold dish. 2 *inf* dead body. 3 *inf* corny joke.

fiar ('fjar) *vt* 1 *comm* guarantee. 2 give credit to. 3 bail. *vi* confide. **fiarse de** trust in, depend on. **fianza** *nf* 1 *comm* security. 2 bail.

fibra ('fiβra) *nf* 1 fibre, filament. 2 energy, vigour. 3 *min* vein. 4 *pl* sinews, muscles.

ficción (fik'θjon) *nf* 1 fiction. 2 tall story, invention. **ficticio** *adj* imaginary, invented.

ficha ('fitʃa) *nf* 1 counter, token, disc. 2 *game* piece. 3 card, index card.

fidedigno (fiðe'ðigno) *adj* trustworthy. **fidelidad** *nf* loyalty, fidelity. **de alta fidelidad** hi-fi.

fideos (fi'ðeos) *nm pl* noodles.

fiebre ('fjeβre) *nf* fever. **tener fiebre** be feverish, have fever.

fiel (fjel) *adj* 1 loyal, trustworthy. 2 accurate, exact. 3 reliable. 4 honourable. **fiel a** true to. ~*nm* 1 good Christian. 2 needle (of scales, compass, etc.). 3 inspector of weights and measures. 4 *pl* **rel** the faithful.

fieltro ('fjeltro) *nm* 1 felt (material). 2 felt hat.

fiera ('fjera) *nf* 1 wild beast. 2 brute (of a person). **estar hecho una fiera** be beside oneself, be furious.

fiero ('fjero) *adj* wild.

fiesta ('fjesta) nf 1 rel feast day, saint's day. 2 holiday. 3 party. **estar en fiestas** be in high spirits.

figurar (figu'rar) vt 1 form, shape. 2 represent. vi figure in, appear in (book, play, etc.). **figurarse** vr imagine, believe, seem. **figura** nf 1 figure, shape. 2 face. 3 appearance. 4 gram figure, symbol. 5 inf unpleasant person. **figurado** adj 1 figurative. 2 imaginary.

fijar (fi'xar) vt 1 fix, fasten. 2 decide, settle. 3 fix one's attention on. **fijarse en** 1 resolve to. 2 pay attention to. **¡fijamos en esto!** that's settled! **fija** nf 1 hinge. 2 trowel. **fijamente** adv steadily, intently. **fijeza** nf firmness. **fijo** adj 1 decided, settled. 2 steady. 3 immovable, invariable. **fijamente** adv certainly.

fila ('fila) nf 1 row, line. 2 mil file, column. **fila india** single file.

filantropía (filantro'pia) nf philanthropy.

filete (fi'lete) nm 1 cul fillet, steak. 2 (screw) thread. 3 hem, border. 4 arch type of moulding.

filiación (filja'θjon) nf 1 affiliation, association. 2 relationship. 3 personal characteristics. **filial** adj filial. nf affiliated company, subsidiary.

filigrana (fili'grana) nf 1 filigree work. 2 watermark. 3 daintiness.

filo ('filo) nm 1 blade, cutting edge. 2 dividing line. **por filo** exactly. **tirarse un filo con** argue with, pick a quarrel with.

filón (fi'lon) nm 1 min seam, vein. 2 inf bargain, windfall.

filosofía (filoso'fia) nf philosophy. **filósofo** nm philosopher.

filtrar (fil'trar) vt filter, purify, strain. vi seep into, penetrate. **filtración** nf leakage, seepage. **filtrador** adj filtering. nm filter. **filtro** nm 1 filter, strainer. 2 lit love philtre.

fin (fin) nm 1 end, conclusion. 2 death. 3 objective, aim. **a fin de** in order to. **al fin y al cabo** when all is said and done. **en fin** at last. **por fin** at last.

final (fi'nal) adj final, last. nm end, outcome. **al final de** at the end of. **finalidad** nf aim, purpose. **finalizar** vt,vi end, finish. **finalmente** finally.

financiar (finan'θjar) vt finance. **financiero** adj financial. nm financier. **finanzas** nf pl finances.

finca ('finka) nf 1 property. 2 estate, farm land.

fineza (fi'neθa) nf 1 refinement, grace. 2 kindness. 3 gift.

fingir (fin'xir) vt 1 pretend. 2 deceive. 3 fake, appear to. **fingirse** vr pretend to be.

Finlandia (fin'landja) nf Finland. **finlandés** adj Finnish. nm 1 Finn. 2 Finnish (language).

fino ('fino) adj 1 fine, slender, delicate. 2 pure, refined. 3 precious (stone, metal, etc.). 4 sharp (point). 5 shrewd, acute, subtle.

firmar (fir'mar) vt sign. **firma** nf 1 signature. 2 business, firm.

firme ('firme) adj 1 firm, solid, hard. 2 resolute, steady. adv firmly. nm road surface. **de firme** steadily. **en lo firme** in the right. **¡firmes!** mil attention! **firmeza** nf firmness, stability.

fiscal (fis'kal) adj financial. nm 1 law treasurer. 2 law counsel for the prosecution. **fiscalizar** vt 1 supervise. 2 criticise. 3 inf interfere, pry. **fisco** nm exchequer, treasury.

física ('fisika) nf physics.

físico ('fisiko) adj physical, material. nm 1 physicist. 2 physique, body.

fisiología (fisjolo'xia) nf physiology.

fisionomía (fisjono'mia) nf 1 physiognomy. 2 outward appearance.

flaco ('flako) adj 1 skinny. 2 weak. nm weakness, defect.

flagrante (fla'grante) adj blatant, undisguised. **en flagrante** in the act.

flamante (fla'mante) adj 1 blazing. 2 brand new.

flamenco (fla'menko) adj 1 Flemish. 2 gypsy (especially Andalusian). 3 cocky, swaggering. nm 1 flamenco. 2 flamingo.

flanco ('flanko) nm side, flank. **coger por el flanco** catch unawares.

flaquear (flake'ar) vi 1 grow weak. 2 worsen (health). 3 become downhearted. **flaqueza** nf 1 thinness. 2 frailty. 3 failing, lacking.

flauta ('flauta) nf flute. **flautiste** nm,f flautist.

fleco ('fleko) nm tassel, fringe.

flecha ('fletʃa) nf arrow, dart. **flecha de dirección** traffic indicator. **flecha de mar** zool squid. **flechar** vt 1 shoot with an arrow, wound. 2 inf make a conquest. **flechazo** nm 1 arrow shot. 2 wound. 3 sudden realization. 4 love at first sight. **flechero** nm 1 archer. 2 quiver.

fletar (fle'tar) vt charter (plane, etc.). **fletamento** nm comm charter.

flexibilidad (fleksiβili'ðað) nf flexibility, adaptability. **flexible** adj flexible, supple. nm flex, wire. **flexión** nf 1 bending, flexing. 2 gram inflection.

flojo ('floxo) adj 1 loose, slack. 2 weak. 3 inf lazy.

flor (flor) nf 1 flower. 2 ornament. 3 compliment. 4 peak, best part. 5 freshness. **a flor de** on the surface. **echar flores** flatter. **en flor** 1 in flower. 2 in one's prime. **flor de lis** lily. **floral** adj floral. **florar** vi flower.

florecer* (flore'θer) vi 1 flower. 2 flourish, prosper. **florecerse** vr go mouldy. **floreciente** adj 1 flowering. 2 prospering. **florecimiento** nm flowering. **florido** adj 1 flowering. 2 ornate. 3 gram rhetorical.

flotar (flo'tar) vi 1 float. 2 flap, hang loose. **flota** nf fleet. **flotante** adj floating. **a flote** afloat.

fluctuar (fluk'twar) vi 1 fluctuate, vary. 2 hesitate.

fluidez (flui'δeθ) nf 1 fluidity. 2 fluency. **fluido** adj fluent, flowing. **flúido** adj fluid. nm electric current.

fluir* (flu'ir) vi flow, run. **fluente** adj flowing. **flujo** nm 1 stream, surge, flow. 2 rising tide. **flujo de vientre** diarrhoea. **flujo y reflujo** ebb and flow.

fluorescencia (fluores'θenθja) nf fluorescence. **fluorescente** adj fluorescent.

fluoruro (flwo'ruro) nm fluoride.

foca ('foka) nf zool seal.

foco ('foko) nm 1 focus. 2 centre, core. 3 origin, source.

fogata (fo'gata) nf bonfire, blaze.

fogón (fo'gon) nm 1 stove. 2 hearth. 3 fire (of guns). 4 naut galley.

fogoso (fo'goso) adj fiery, high-spirited, impetuous.

follaje (fo'ʎaxe) nm 1 foliage, greenery. 2 excessive decoration.

folletín (foʎe'tin) nm newspaper article or serial. **folleto** nm pamphlet, leaflet.

follón (fo'ʎon) adj 1 idle. 2 cowardly. 3 vain, proud. nm 1 good-for-nothing, lout. 2 commotion.

fomentar (fomen'tar) vt 1 encourage, provoke. 2 promote (business, etc.). **fomento** nm 1 encouragement, provocation. 2 comm productivity, development. 3 med fomentation.

fonda ('fonda) nf inn.

fondear (fonde'ar) vt 1 sound (depth of water). 2 test, examine. **fondear** (a ship). vi anchor.

fondo ('fondo) nm 1 bottom (of box, etc.). 2 depth. 3 sea or river bed. 4 background. 5 pl capital, funds. **a fondo** thoroughly. **en el fondo** at heart. **estar en fondos** be well off.

fontanero (fonta'nero) nm plumber.

forajido (fora'xiδo) nm outlaw, fugitive.

forastero (foras'tero) adj strange. n stranger, alien, visitor.

forcejear (forθexe'ar) vi struggle, strive. **forcejeo** nm struggle, great effort.

forense (fo'rense) adj legal, forensic.

forjar (for'xar) vt 1 forge, beat into shape. 2 create, invent. **forja** nf 1 forge, furnace. 2 forging.

formal (for'mal) adj 1 serious. 2 courteous, correct. 3 reliable. 4 conventional. 5 well behaved. **formalidad** nf 1 formality. 2 convention. 3 seriousness.

formar (for'mar) vt 1 form, shape, make. 2 educate, train. **formarse** vr 1 develop, grow up. 2 be trained. **forma** nf 1 form, shape. 2 method, way. 3 tech mould. **de forma que** so that. **de todas formas** anyway.

formidable (formi'δaβle) adj 1 fearful. 2 tremendous. 3 inf marvellous.

fórmula ('formula) nf 1 formula. 2 med prescription.

fornicar (forni'kar) vi fornicate.

fornido (for'niδo) adj robust.

foro ('foro) nm 1 forum. 2 law court. 3 Th back of the stage.

forraje (for'raxe) nm 1 fodder. 2 plunder, forage.

forrar (for'rar) vt 1 put a cover on. 2 line, pad (clothes). **forrarse** vr 1 inf make lots of money. 2 inf gorge oneself. **forro** nm 1 cover, sheath, coat. 2 lining, padding. **ni por el forro** not the foggiest idea.

fortalecer* (fortale'θer) vt 1 strengthen. 2 encourage. 3 mil fortify. **fortaleza** nf 1 strength. 2 courage, fortitude. 3 mil fortress.

fortuito (for'twito) adj 1 accidental. 2 random.

fortuna (for'tuna) nf 1 fate, chance. 2 good luck. 3 happiness. 4 fortune, wealth. **por fortuna** luckily. **probar fortuna** take a chance, try one's luck.

forzar (ue) (for'θar) vt 1 oblige, compel. 2 rape. 3 break into, force. 4 mil storm.

fosa ('fosa) nf 1 grave. 2 anat cavity.

fosfato (fos'fato) nm phosphate.

fósforo ('fosforo) nm 1 sci phosphorus. 2 match.

fósil ('fosil) adj fossilized. nm fossil.

foso ('foso) nm 1 hole, pit, ditch. 2 Th pit. 3 mil trench.

fotogénico (foto'xeniko) adj photogenic.

fotografía (fotogra'fia) nf 1 photography. 2

photograph. **fotografiar** vt photograph. **fotógrafo** nm photographer.

frac (frak) nm dress coat, tails.

fracasar (fraka'sar) vi fail, come to grief. **fracaso** nm failure, disaster.

fracción (frak'θjon) nf 1 part, portion, fragment. 2 a breaking into parts, sharing out. 3 math fraction.

fractura (frak'tura) nf med fracture.

fragancia (fra'ganθja) nf fragrance, perfume.

frágil ('fraxil) adj fragile, breakable.

fragmento (frag'mento) nm part, fragment.

fragor (fra'gor) nm row, uproar.

fraguar (fra'gwar) vt 1 forge (metal). 2 plan, plot. vi harden (cement, etc.). **fragua** nf forge.

fraile ('fraile) nm friar, monk.

frambuesa (tram'bwesa) nf raspberry.

Francia ('franθja) nf France. **francés** adj French. nm 1 Frenchman. 2 French (language).

franco ('franko) adj 1 open, sincere. 2 generous, free. nm franc (coinage).

franela (fra'nela) nf flannel.

franja ('franxa) nf 1 fringe, border. 2 strip, narrow piece.

franquear (franke'ar) vt 1 release, free. 2 frank (parcel, etc.). 3 clear (path, etc.). 4 get round (obstacle). **franquearse** vr 1 reveal one's thoughts. 2 fall in with someone's wishes. **franqueo** nm 1 franking. 2 postage.

franqueza (fran'keθa) nf 1 frankness, sincerity. 2 generosity. **con franqueza** frankly.

frasco ('frasko) nm flask, small bottle.

frase ('frase) nf 1 gram sentence, phrase, expression. **frase hecha** 1 proverb. 2 cliché.

fraternal (frater'nal) adj brotherly.

fraude ('frauðe) nm 1 fraud. 2 dishonesty. **fraudulencia** nf dishonesty. **fraudulento** adj dishonest, false.

fray (frej) nm rel Friar, Brother.

frecuencia (fre'kwenθja) nf frequency. **con frequencia** often. **frecuentar** vt frequent, visit often. **frecuente** adj 1 frequent. 2 usual, common.

fregar (ie) (fre'gar) vt 1 rub, scrub. 2 wash up. **fregado** nm 1 scrubbing. 2 washing up. 3 inf mess. **fregadero** nm sink. **fregador** nm 1 mop. 2 dish-mop. **fregona** nf inf (kitchen) maid.

freír* (fre'ir) vt 1 fry. 2 inf bore.

frenar (fre'nar) vt 1 mot brake. 2 restrain, check. **freno** nm 1 mot brake. 2 horse's bit, bridle. 3 restraint, check. **freno de mano**

handbrake. **poner el freno** apply the brake. **soltar el freno** release the brake.

frenesí (frene'si) nm frenzy.

frente ('frente) nm 1 front, face. 2 façade. 3 min face. nf forehead, face. **en frente** opposite.

fresa ('fresa) nf 1 strawberry. 2 strawberry plant. 3 tech drill, cutting tool.

fresco ('fresko) adj 1 cool. 2 fresh, new. 3 calm. 4 inf insolent, forward. 5 strong (wind, etc.). **ponerse fresco con** inf get fresh with. **frescura** nf 1 coolness. 2 calmness. 3 inf insolence, cheek. 4 cheeky comment.

fresno ('fresno) nm bot ash.

frialdad (frjal'ðað) nf 1 coldness. 2 indifference. 3 impotence.

fricción (frik'θjon) nf 1 friction. 2 med massage. 3 ill feeling.

frigidez (frixi'ðeθ) nf frigidity, rigidity.

frijol (fri'xol) nm French bean.

frío ('frio) adj 1 cold, cool. 2 indifferent. nm 1 coldness. 2 indifference. **hacer frío** be cold (weather). **tener frío** feel cold.

friolera (frjo'lera) nf triviality, trifle.

frisar (fri'sar) vt frizz, curl. **frisar en** be about, border on (a certain age).

frito ('frito) v see **freír**. adj 1 fried. 2 inf worn out. nm fried food. **estar frito** inf be exhausted. **traer frito a** worry (someone).

frívolo ('friβolo) adj frivolous, superficial.

frondoso (fron'doso) adj 1 leafy. 2 lush.

frontera (fron'tera) nf frontier, border.

frotar (fro'tar) vt 1 rub. 2 strike (match). **frotación** nf rubbing. **frote** nm rub.

fructífero (fruk'tifero) adj 1 bot fruit-bearing. 2 productive.

frugal (fru'gal) adj frugal, sparing.

fruncir (frun'θir) vt 1 wrinkle, ruffle. 2 pleat, gather (sewing). **fruncir las cejas** frown.

frustrar (frus'trar) vt frustrate. **frustrarse** vr 1 be frustrated. 2 fail.

fruta ('fruta) nf 1 fruit. 2 result, consequence. **frutero** adj fruit or fruit-bearing. nm 1 fruit bowl. 2 fruiterer. **fruto** nm 1 fruit. 2 product, result. **sacar fruto de** benefit from.

fue[1] ('fue) v see **ir**.

fue[2] ('fue) v see **ser**.

fuego ('fwego) nm 1 fire, blaze. 2 cul flame, heat. 3 med rash. 4 passion. 5 mil fire. 6 hearth. **apagar el fuego** put out the fire. **fuegos artificiales** fireworks. **pegar fuego a** set fire to.

fuelle ('fweʎe) nm 1 bellows. 2 inf gossip. 3 mot folding hood.

fuente ('fwente) nf 1 fountain, spring. 2 source, origin. 3 cul large dish.

fuera ('fwera) adv outside, out. **desde fuera** from outside. **estar fuera** be away (from home). **ir fuera** go outside. **por fuera** on the outside. **fuera de** prep 1 outside. 2 in addition to. **fuera de alcance** out of reach.

fuero ('fwero) nm 1 law. 2 charter. 3 privilege. 4 pl inf airs and graces.

fuerte ('fwerte) adj 1 strong. 2 energetic. 3 tough, hard. 4 loud. 5 concentrated. 6 heavy. nm 1 strong point. 2 mil fortress. **fuerza** nf 1 strength. 2 loudness. 3 energy. 4 effort. 5 intensity. 6 electric current. 7 violence. 8 pl armed forces.

fugarse (fu'garse) vr 1 run away, escape. 2 leak. **fuga** nf 1 escape. 2 elopement. 3 leak (gas, etc.). 4 mus fugue. **fugaz** adj brief, fleeting. **fugitivo** adj fugitive.

fulano (fu'lano) nm 1 what's-his-name. 2 nobody. **fulano de tal** Mr so-and-so.

fulcro ('fulkro) nm fulcrum.

fulgor (ful'gor) nm 1 glow, brilliant light. 2 brilliance (quality).

fulminante (fulmi'nante) adj 1 med grave, mortal (illness). 2 thundering, explosive.

fumar (fu'mar) vt,vi smoke. **prohibido fumar** no smoking. **fumarse** vr inf squander, fritter away.

fumigar (fumi'gar) vt fumigate. **fumigarse** vr inf get lost.

función (funk'θjon) nf 1 function, operation. 2 performance, show. 3 pl duties, responsibilities.

funcionar (funkθjo'nar) vt function, operate, work, go (machine, etc.).

funda ('funda) nf cover, case.

fundar (fun'dar) vt 1 found, establish. 2 base (theory). **fundarse (en)** vr be founded (on). **fundado** adj justified. **fundamental** adj essential. **fundamento** nm 1 arch foundation. 2 good reason, grounds 3 reliability.

fundir (fun'dir) vt 1 fuse, join together. 2 melt. 3 tech smelt. **fundición** nf 1 foundry. 2 fusing. 3 melting. 4 tech smelting.

fúnebre ('funeβre) adj 1 funerary. 2 gloomy.

funesto (fu'nesto) adj ill fated, gloomy, disastrous.

furgón (fur'gon) nm 1 wagon. 2 truck. **furgoneta** nf van.

furia ('furja) nf 1 fury. 2 frenzy. 3 speed.

furioso adj 1 furious. 2 mad. 3 violent. **ponerse furioso** become furious.

furor (fu'ror) nm 1 fury, rage. 2 madness. 3 passion. 4 violence. **con furor** furiously. **hacer furor** be fashionable.

furtivo (fur'tiβo) adj secretive, sly.

fusible (fu'siβle) nm fuse.

fusil (fu'sil) nm rifle.

fusión (fu'sjon) nf fusion, union.

fuste ('fuste) nm 1 wood. 2 wooden shaft (of spear, column, etc.). 3 wooden saddle. **de poco fuste** of little importance.

fútbol ('futβol) nm football.

fútil ('futil) adj frivolous, trivial.

futuro (fu'turo) adj,nm future.

G

gabán (ga'βan) nm overcoat.

gabardina (gaβar'ðina) nf 1 raincoat. 2 gabardine.

gabinete (gaβi'nete) nm 1 study, studio, laboratory. 2 pol cabinet.

gacela (ga'θela) nf gazelle.

gaceta (ga'θeta) nf gazette.

gachas (ga'tʃas) nf pl porridge.

gacho ('gatʃo) adj drooping.

gafas ('gafas) nf pl spectacles. **gafas de sol** sunglasses.

gajo ('gaxo) nm 1 twig. 2 clump (of herbs). 3 slice (of orange).

gala ('gala) nf 1 formal dress. 2 pomp, elegance. **estar de gala** be in formal dress. **hacer gala de** show off, display. **tener a gala** be proud of.

galán (ga'lan) nm Th leading man.

galante (ga'lante) adj polite, charming. **galantear** vi flirt.

galardón (galar'ðon) nm reward, prize. **galardonar** vt award prize to.

galeón (gale'on) nm galleon.

galera (ga'lera) nf galley, prison.

galería (gale'ria) nf 1 gallery. 2 tunnel, corridor. 3 veranda.

Gales ('gales) nm Wales. **galés** adj,n Welsh. nm Welsh (language).

galgo ('galgo) nm greyhound.

galón¹ (ga'lon) nm 1 silk band. 2 mil stripe. **quitar los galones a** demote.

galón² (ga'lon) nm gallon.

galopar (galo'par) vi gallop. **galope** nm gallop. **a medio galope** at a canter.

galvanizar (galβani'θar) vt galvanize.

gallardo (ga'ʎarðo) adj 1 graceful. 2 dashing.

galleta (ga'ʎeta) nf biscuit.

gallina (ga'ʎina) nf hen. **gallo** nm cock.

gamuza (ga'muθa) nf chamois (leather).

gana ('gana) nf 1 wish. 2 appetite. **de buena/ mala gana** willingly/unwillingly. **tener ganas de** want to.

ganadería (ganaðe'ria) nf 1 cattle-farming. 2 ranch, cattle farm. 3 livestock. **ganadero** nm cattle-farmer. adj of cattle. **ganado** nm cattle, livestock.

ganar (ga'nar) vt 1 win, get, gain. 2 earn. vi 1 win. 2 do well. **ganancia** nf earnings, profit. **ganancioso** adj profitable.

gancho ('gantʃo) nm hook.

gansada (gan'saða) nf stupid behaviour. **ganso** nm goose.

garaje (ga'raxe) nm garage.

garantizar (garanti'θar) vt guarantee. **garantía** nf guarantee, warranty. **bajo garantía** under guarantee.

garbanzo (gar'βanθo) nm chickpea.

garbo ('garβo) nm 1 jauntiness. 2 refinement, gracefulness.

garganta (gar'ganta) nf throat.

gárgara ('gargara) nf gargle.

gárgola ('gargola) nf gargoyle.

garita (ga'rita) nf 1 cab (of a lorry). 2 hut.

garra ('garra) nf claw.

garrafa (gar'rafa) nf decanter.

garrote (gar'rote) nm 1 bar, stick. 2 garrotte. **dar garrote** a execute.

garza ('garθa) nf heron.

gas (gas) nm gas.

gasa ('gasa) nf gauze.

gaseosa (gase'osa) nf carbonated water.

gasolina (gaso'lina) nf petrol.

gastar (gas'tar) vt 1 spend, consume. 2 waste, wear out. **gasto** nm expenditure.

gatillo (ga'tiʎo) nm 1 trigger. 2 dentist's forceps.

gato ('gato) nm 1 cat. 2 mot jack. **gatear** vi crawl on all fours. **a gatas** on all fours. **buscarle tres patas al gato** look for trouble.

gavilán (gaβi'lan) nm hawk.

gavilla (ga'βiʎa) nf sheaf.

gaviota (ga'βjota) nf seagull.

gazapo (ga'θapo) nm 1 small rabbit. 2 slip of the tongue.

gelatina (xela'tina) nf gelatine.

gelignita (xelig'nita) nf gelignite.

gemelo (xe'melo) adj twin. nm twin. 2 pl cufflinks. 3 pl opera glasses. **los Gemelos** Gemini.

gemir (xe'mir) vi groan. **gemido** nm groan.

genealogía (xenealo'xia) nf genealogy.

generación (xenera'θjon) nf generation.

generalizar (xenerali'θar) vt,vi generalize, make general. **general** adj general. nm mil general. **generalidad** nf majority. **generalización** nf generalization. **por lo general** in general.

genérico (xe'neriko) adj generic. **género** nm 1 kind. 2 gram gender. 3 genre. 4 material (cloth). 5 pl general groceries, goods.

generosidad (xenerosi'ðað) nf generosity. **generoso** adj generous.

genética (xe'netika) nf genetics.

genial (xe'njal) adj 1 brilliant. 2 inf nice.

genio ('xenjo) nm 1 temper. 2 genius. **estar de mal genio** be in a bad temper.

gente ('xente) nf people. **gente baja** lower classes.

gentil (xen'til) adj 1 charming, courteous. 2 rel pagan, gentile. **gentileza** nf politeness, kindness.

gentío (xen'tio) nm crowd.

genuino (xe'nwino) adj genuine.

geografía (xeogra'fia) nf geography. **geográfico** adj geographical. **geógrafo** nm geographer.

geología (xeolo'xia) nf geology. **geológico** adj geological. **geólogo** nm geologist.

geometría (xeome'tria) nf geometry. **geométrico** adj geometrical.

geranio (xe'ranjo) nm geranium.

gerencia (xe'renθja) nf management. **gerente** nm manager.

germinar (xermi'nar) vi germinate. **germen** nm 1 germ. 2 seed.

gesticular (xestiku'lar) vi gesticulate. **gesticulación** nf gesture.

gestión (xes'tjon) nf negotiation, business.

gesto ('xesto) nm 1 face. 2 gesture. **hacer un gesto** make a face or gesture.

gigante (xi'gante) nm giant.

gimnasia (xim'nasja) nf gymnastics. **gimnasta** nm,f gymnast. **gimnasio** nm gymnasium.

ginebra (xi'neβra) nf gin.

gira ('xira) nf tour.

giralda (xi'ralda) nf weathercock.

girar (xi'rar) vt 1 turn. 2 comm draw, issue. vi 1 turn, rotate. 2 swing. 3 comm do business. **girar un cheque** send a cheque. **giro** nm 1 turn, rotation. 2 comm draft. 3 tendency.

gitano (xi'tano) *adj,n* gypsy.

glacial (gla'θjal) *adj* freezing.

glándula ('glandula) *nf* gland.

glicerina (gliθe'rina) *nf* glycerine.

global (glo'βal) *adj* global.

gloriarse (glo'rjarse) *vr* boast. **gloria** *nf* 1 glory. 2 puff-pastry cake.

glosar (glo'sar) *vt* annotate. **glosa** *nf* annotation. **glosario** *nm* glossary.

glotón (glo'ton) *adj* greedy.

gobernar (**ie**) (goβer'nar) *vt* govern, control. **gobernación** *nf* government. **gobierno** *nm* 1 government. 2 control.

goce ('goθe) *nm* enjoyment.

golfo ('golfo) *nm* 1 gulf, bay. 2 lout.

golondrina (golon'drina) *nf zool* swallow.

golosina (golo'sina) *nf* sweet. **goloso** *adj* fond of sweets.

golpear (golpe'ar) *vt* strike. **golpe** *nm* blow. **golpe de estado** coup d'état. **golpe de gracia** coup de grâce.

goma ('goma) *nf* 1 rubber. 2 (rubber) tyre. **goma pegante** glue.

gordo ('gorðo) *adj* fat. *nm* fat (of meat). **gordura** *nf* fatness.

gorila (go'rila) *nf* gorilla.

gorjear (gorxe'ar) *vi* chirp, trill. **gorjeo** *nm* chirping.

gorra ('gorra) *nf* 1 peaked cap. 2 *inf* sponger.

gorrión (gor'rjon) *nm* sparrow.

gorro ('gorro) *nm* cap.

gotear (gote'ar) *vi* drip. **gota** *nf* drop. **gotera** *nf* 1 leak. 2 gutter. 3 dripping.

gótico ('gotiko) *adj* Gothic.

gozar (go'θar) *vt* enjoy, have. *vi* enjoy oneself. **gozo** *nm* joy.

gozne (goθne) *nm* hinge.

grabar (gra'βar) *vt* 1 engrave. 2 record. 3 imprint. **grabado** *nm* engraving, print. **grabadora** *nf* tape-recorder.

gracia (gra'θja) *nf* 1 grace. 2 humour. **gracias** thank you. **me hace gracia** it amuses me. **tener gracia** be amusing. **gracioso** *adj* humorous.

grada ('graða) *nf* 1 step. 2 tier of seats.

grado ('graðo) *nm* 1 grade. 2 degree.

gradual (gra'ðwal) *adj* gradual.

grajo ('graxo) *nm* rook.

gramática (gra'matika) *nf* grammar.

gramo ('gramo) *nm* gramme.

gramófono (gra'mofono) *nm* gramophone.

gran (gran) *adj* see **grande**.

Gran Bretaña (gran bre'taɲa) *nf* Great Britain.

grana[1] ('grana) *nf* 1 small seed. 2 seeding time.

grana[2] ('grana) *n* scarlet.

granada (gra'naða) *nf* 1 pomegranate. 2 grenade, shell. **granado** *nm* pomegranate tree.

grande ('grande) *adj* big, great. **grandeza** *nf* size, greatness.

grandioso (gran'djoso) *adj* grandiose, grand.

granel (gra'nel) *nm* heap.

granero (gra'nero) *nm* granary.

granito (gra'nito) *nm* granite.

granizar (grani'θar) *vi* hail. **granizo** *nm* hail.

granja ('granxa) *nf* farm. **granjero** *nm* farmer.

grano ('grano) *nm* 1 grain, corn. 2 pimple.

grapa ('grapa) *nf* staple, clamp.

grasa ('grasa) *nf* grease, fat. **grasiento** *adj* greasy, dirty.

gratificar (gratifi'kar) *vt* gratify, reward. **gratificación** *nf* bonus, prize.

gratis ('gratis) *adv* free of charge.

gratitud (grati'tuð) *nf* gratitude. **grato** *adj* pleasing.

gratuito (gra'twito) *adj* 1 free of charge. 2 gratuitous.

gravamen (gra'βamen) *nm* 1 tax. 2 obligation. **gravar** *vt* impose a burden on. **gravar impuestos a** or **sobre** impose taxes on.

grave ('graβe) *adj* grave, serious. **gravedad** *nf* gravity.

gravitar (graβi'tar) *vi* gravitate.

graznar (graθ'nar) *vi* croak. **graznido** *nm* croak, squawk.

Grecia ('greθja) *nf* Greece. **griego** *adj,n* Greek. *nm* 1 Greek (language). 2 *inf* gibberish, incomprehensible speech.

greda ('greða) *nf* clay. **gredoso** *adj* clayey.

gremio ('gremjo) *nm* 1 guild. 2 *pol* union. **gremio obrero** trade union.

greña ('greɲa) *nf* tangle (esp. of hair). **greñudo** *adj* dishevelled.

grey (grej) *nf* congregation.

grieta ('grjeta) *nf* crack.

grifo ('grifo) *nm* tap. **al grifo** on draught.

grillo ('griʎo) *nm* 1 cricket. 2 *pl* fetters.

gris (gris) *adj* grey.

gritar (gri'tar) *vi* shout. **grito** *nm* shout, cry.

Groenlandia (groen'landja) *nf* Greenland. **groenlandés** *adj* Greenland. *nm* Greenlander.

grosella (gro'seʎa) *nf* currant. **grosella espinosa** gooseberry.

grosería (grose'ria) *nf* vulgarity. **grosero** *adj* vulgar.

grotesco (gro'tesko) *adj* grotesque.

grúa ('grua) nf tech crane.

grueso (gru'eso) adj thick, heavy. nm thickness.

grulla ('gruʎa) nf zool crane.

grumete (gru'mete) nm cabin boy.

gruñir (gru'ɲir) vi growl. **gruñido** nm growl.

grupo ('grupo) nm group, unit.

gruta ('gruta) nf grotto.

guadaña (gwa'ðaɲa) nf scythe.

guante ('gwante) nm glove.

guapo ('gwapo) adj handsome.

guardar (gwar'ðar) vt guard, keep. **guarda** nm guard, keeper. nf guard, custody. **guardarropa** nm cloakroom. nm,f cloakroom attendant.

guardia ('gwarðja) nf guard, police force. nm policeman. **Guardia Civil** nf Civil Guard.

guardián (gwar'ðjan) nm guardian.

guardilla (gwar'ðiʎa) nf attic.

guarida (gwa'riða) nf den, lair.

guarnecer (gwarne'θer) vt 1 equip, adorn. 2 cul garnish. **guarnición** nf 1 mil garrison. 2 garnish. 3 pl fittings.

guasa ('gwasa) nf joke.

gubernamental (guβernamen'tal) adj governmental.

guerra ('gerra) nf war. **guerrear** vi fight. **guerrero** nm warrior. adj warlike. **guerrilla** nf guerrilla war. **guerrillero** nm guerrilla.

guía ('gia) nf guide (book). nm guide (person). **guía sonora** soundtrack.

guiar (gi'ar) vt guide.

guija ('gixa) nf pebble.

guiñar (gi'ɲar) vi wink.

guión (gi'on) nm 1 hyphen. 2 film or radio script. 3 subtitles. 4 summary.

guisa ('gisa) nf way, manner. **a guisa de** like.

guisado (gi'saðo) nm stew. **guisar** vt cook, prepare. **guiso** nm stewed dish.

guisante (gi'sante) nm pea.

guitarra (gi'tarra) nf guitar.

gula ('gula) nf greed.

gusano (gu'sano) nm worm.

gustar (gus'tar) vi please. **gusto** nm 1 pleasure. 2 taste. **de buen/mal gusto** in good/bad taste. **¡mucho gusto!** how do you do?

gutural (gutu'ral) adj guttural.

H

ha (a) v see **haber**.

haba ('aβa) nf broad bean.

habeis (a'βeis) v see **haber**.

haber (a'βer) have. **haber de** have to.

habichuela (aβi'tʃwela) nf kidney bean.

hábil ('aβil) adj capable, skilful, able. **habilidad** nf ability.

habilitar (aβili'tar) vt enable. **habilitación** nf 1 qualification. 2 financing.

habitar (aβi'tar) vi live, dwell. **habitación** nf room. **habitante** nm inhabitant.

hábito ('aβito) nm habit.

habitual (aβi'twal) adj habitual.

hablar (a'βlar) vt,vi speak. **habla** nf speech. **hablador** nm speaker. adj talkative.

hablilla (a'βliʎa) nf 1 rumour, gossip. 2 gossip. **habladuría** nf gossip, idle talk.

hacedero (aθe'ðero) adj practicable.

hacendado (aθen'daðo) nm landowner.

hacer (a'θer) vt do, make. **hacer calor/frío** (of weather) be hot/cold. **hace mucho tiempo que** it is a long time since. **hacerse** vr become.

hacia ('aθja) prep (of time) towards, about.

hacienda (a'θjenda) nf estate.

hacina (a'θina) nf 1 pile. 2 haystack.

hacha ('atʃa) nf axe.

hada ('aða) nm fairy.

hado ('aðo) nm fate.

hago ('ago) v see **hacer**.

halagar (ala'gar) vt flatter. **halago** nm flattery. **halagüeño** adj flattering.

halcón (al'kon) nm falcon.

hálito ('alito) nm breath.

hallar (a'ʎar) vt find. **hallarse** vr be situated. **hallazgo** nm find, discovery.

hamaca (a'maka) nf hammock.

hambre ('ambre) nf hunger. **tener hambre** be hungry. **hambriento** adj hungry.

han (an) v see **haber**.

haragán (ara'gan) adj lazy. **haraganear** vi laze.

harapiento (ara'pjento) adj ragged. **harapo** nm rag.

harina (a'rina) nf flour.

hartar (ar'tar) vt bore, exasperate. **hartarse** vr 1 be exasperated. 2 sl stuff oneself (with food). **harto** adj 1 bored, exasperated. 2 satiated.

has (as) v see **haber**.

hasta ('asta) prep up to, until. adv even.

hastío (as'tio) nm disgust, weariness.

hato ('ato) nm 1 sheep-pen. 2 flock. 3 pack.

hay ('aj) v imp there is. hay que one must.

haya ('aja) nf beech.

haz¹ (aθ) nm bundle, sheaf.

haz² (aθ) nf face.

hazmerreír (aθmerre'ir) nm laughing-stock.

he (e) v see haber.

hebilla (e'βiʎa) nf buckle.

hebra ('eβra) nf 1 thread. 2 grain (wood).

hebreo (e'βreo) adj,n Hebrew. nm Hebrew (language).

hechicero (etʃi'θero) nm wizard. hechicería nf sorcery. hechizar vt bewitch. hechizo nm magic spell.

hecho ('etʃo) v see hacer. adj 1 ready-made. 2 well-cooked. nm fact. hechura nf making, handiwork. de hecho law de facto.

hediondo (e'ðjondo) adj 1 stinking. 2 repugnant. hedor nm stink, stench.

helar (ie) (e'lar) vt freeze. helado nm ice-cream.

helecho (e'letʃo) nm fern.

hélice ('eliθe) nf 1 helix. 2 propeller.

helicóptero (eli'koptero) nm helicopter.

hembra ('embra) nf 1 female. 2 nut (of a screw).

hemorragia (emor'raxja) nf haemorrhage.

hemorroides (emor'rojðes) nf pl piles.

hemos ('emos) v see haber.

henchirse* (en'tʃirse) vr swell up.

hender (ie) (en'der) vt split. hendedura nf split.

heno ('eno) nm hay.

herbaje (er'βaxe) nm pasture. herbicida nm herbicide. herbívoro adj herbivorous.

heredar (ere'ðar) vt inherit. heredero nm heir. hereditario adj hereditary.

hereje (e'rexe) nm heretic. herejía nf heresy.

herencia (e'renθja) nf inheritance.

herir (ie) (e'rir) vt wound. herida nf wound. herido nm casualty.

hermano (er'mano) nm brother. hermana nf sister. hermandad nf brotherhood.

hermético (er'metiko) adj hermetic.

hermoso (er'moso) adj beautiful, handsome. hermosura nf beauty, splendour.

héroe ('eroe) nm hero. heroico adj heroic. heroísmo nm heroism.

heroína¹ (e'roina) nf heroine.

heroína² (ero'ina) nf heroin.

herramienta (erra'mjenta) nf tool.

herrar (ie) (er'rar) vt shoe (a horse). herradura nf horseshoe.

herrería (erre'ria) nf forge. herrero nm blacksmith.

herrumbre (er'rumbre) nf rust.

hervir (ie) (er'βir) vt,vi boil. hervor nm 1 boiling. 2 fervour. hervidero nm inf crowd.

hez (eθ) nf,pl heces dregs.

híbrido ('iβriðo) adj hybrid.

hice ('iθe) v see hacer.

hidalgo (i'ðalgo) nm nobleman. hidalguía nf nobility.

hidráulico (i'ðrauliko) adj hydraulic.

hidroala (iðro'ala) nf hovercraft.

hidroavión (iðroa'βjon) nm seaplane.

hidroeléctrico (iðroe'lektriko) adj hydroelectric.

hidrógeno (i'ðroxeno) nm hydrogen.

hiedra ('jeðra) nf ivy.

hielo ('jelo) nm ice.

hiena ('jena) nf hyena.

hierba ('jerβa) nf 1 grass. 2 herb.

hierro ('jerro) nm iron. hierro colado cast iron.

hígado ('igaðo) nm liver.

higiene (i'xjene) nf hygiene. higiénico adj hygienic.

higo ('igo) nm fig. higuera nf fig-tree.

hijo ('ixo) nm 1 son. 2 pl children. hija nf daughter. hijastro nm stepson.

hilar (i'lar) vt spin. hilandera nf spinner. hilandería nf 1 spinning. 2 spinning mill.

hilera (i'lera) nf rank, row.

himno ('imno) nm hymn. himno nacional national anthem.

hincapié (inka'pje) nm foothold. hacer hincapié stand firm.

hincar (in'kar) vt drive in.

hinchar (in'tʃar) vt inflate. hincharse vr 1 swell up. 2 put on airs. 3 inf stuff oneself (with food). hinchazón nm 1 med swelling. 2 inf conceit, arrogance.

hinojo (i'noxo) nm fennel.

hipnosis (ip'nosis) nm hypnosis. hipnótico adj hypnotic.

hipo ('ipo) nm hiccups.

hipocondria (ipokon'dria) nf hypochondria.

hipocresía (ipokre'sia) nf hypocrisy.

hipócrita (i'pokrita) adj invar hypocritical. nm,f invar hypocrite.

hipopótamo (ipo'potamo) nm hippopotamus.

hipotecar (ipote'kar) vt mortgage. hipoteca nf mortgage.

hipótesis (i'potesis) nf hypothesis. hipotético adj hypothetical.

hirsuto (ir'suto) *adj* hairy.

hispánico (is'paniko) *adj* Hispanic.

hispanoamericano (ispanoameri'kano) *adj,n* Spanish American.

histerectomía (isterekto'mia) *nf* hysterectomy.

histeria (i'sterja) *nf* hysteria. **histérico** *adj* hysterical.

historia (is'torja) *nf* **1** history. **2** story. **historiador** *nm* historian. **histórico** *adj* historical.

hizo (i'θo) *v* see **hacer.**

hogar (o'gar) *nm* hearth, home.

hogaza (o'gaθa) *nf* loaf (of bread).

hoja ('oxa) *nf* **1** leaf. **2** sheet (of metal, etc.). **3** form, questionnaire. **hoja de afeitar** razor blade.

hojear (oxe'ar) *vt* leaf through.

Holanda (o'landa) *nf* Holland. **holandés** *adj* Dutch. *nm* **1** Dutchman. **2** Dutch (language).

holgar (ue) (ol'gar) *vi* **1** be idle. **2** be unnecessary. **3** strike, quit work. **holgazán** *adj* idle. **holgura** *nf* comfort, ease.

hollar (ue) (o'ʎar) *vt* leave footprints on.

hollín (o'ʎin) *nm* soot.

hombre ('ombre) *nm* man. **¡sí, hombre!** of course!

hombro ('ombro) *nm* shoulder.

homenaje (ome'naxe) *nm* homage.

homicida (omi'θiðja) *nm* murderer. **homicidio** *nm* murder.

homogéneo (omo'xeneo) *adj* homogeneous.

homólogo (o'mologo) *adj* corresponding, alike.

honda ('onda) *nf* sling, catapult.

hondo ('ondo) *adj* deep. **hondonada** *nf* ravine. **hondura** *nf* depth.

honestidad (onesti'ðað) *nf* honour. **honesto** *adj* honourable.

hongo ('ongo) *nm* **1** mushroom. **2** bowler hat.

honor (o'nor) *nm* honour. **honorífico** *adj* honorific. **honorario** *nm* fee, honorarium.

honrar (on'rar) *vt* honour. **honra** *nf* honour.

hora ('ora) *nf* hour. **¿qué hora es?** what is the time?

horario (o'rarjo) *nm* **1** timetable. **2** hours of work.

horca ('orka) *nf* **1** gallows. **2** pitchfork.

horda ('orða) *nf* horde.

horizonte (ori'θonte) *nm* horizon.

hormiga (or'miga) *nf* **1** ant. **2** *pl* pins and needles.

hormigón (ormi'gon) *nm* concrete.

hormiguear (ormige'ar) *vi* itch. **hormigueo** *nm* itching.

hormona (or'mona) *nf* hormone.

horno ('orno) *nm* oven. **hornillo** *nm* ring (on a cooker).

horóscopo (o'roskopo) *nm* horoscope.

horquilla (or'kiʎa) *nf* hairpin.

horrendo (or'rendo) *adj* fearful.

horrible (or'riβle) *adj* horrible.

horror (or'ror) *nm* horror. **horrozizar** *vt* horrify.

hortaliza (orta'liθa) *nf* green vegetable.

horticultura (ortikul'tura) *nf* horticulture.

hosco ('osko) *adj* grim.

hospedar (ospe'ðar) *vt* give a room to, put up. **hospedarse** *vr* lodge. **hospedaje** *nm* lodging. **hospedería** *nf* inn.

hospicio (os'piθjo) *nm* orphanage, workhouse.

hospital (ospi'tal) *nm* hospital.

hospitalidad (ospitali'ðað) *nf* hospitality.

hostelero (oste'lero) *nm* hosteller. **hostelería** *nf* hotel business. **hostería** *nf* inn.

hostia ('ostja) *nf rel* host.

hostigar (osti'gar) *vt* punish, beat.

hostil (os'til) *adj* hostile. **hostilidad** *nf* hostility.

hoy ('oi) *adv* today. **hoy (en) día** the present day. **de hoy en mañana** any day now. **de hoy en ocho días** a week today.

hoyo ('ojo) *nm* pit.

hoyuelo (oj'welo) *nm* dimple.

hoz (oθ) *nf* sickle.

hubo ('uβo) *v* see **haber.**

hueco ('weko) *adj* empty. *nm* hole, space.

huelga ('welga) *nf* strike (industrial). **huelguista** *nm* striker.

huelgo ('welgo) *nm* **1** breath. **2** space, room. **3** *tech* play, tolerance.

huelo ('welo) *v* see **oler.**

huella ('weʎa) *nf* footprint. **huella digital** fingerprint.

huérfano ('werfano) *nm* orphan.

huerta ('werta) *nf* **1** vegetable garden. **2** irrigated land. **huerto** *nm* **1** small vegetable garden. **2** orchard.

hueso ('weso) *nm* bone. **huesudo** *adj* bony.

huésped ('wespeð) *nm* **1** guest. **2** host.

hueva ('weβa) *nf* **1** roe (of fish). **2** *pl* spawn.

huevo ('weβo) *nm* egg.

huida ('wiða) *nf* flight, escape.

huir (wir) *vi* flee.

hule[1] ('ule) *nm* **1** oilskin. **2** rubber.

hule[2] ('ule) *nm* goring (bullfight).

hulla ('uʎa) *nf* coal.

humanidad (umani'ðað) *nf* **1** humanity. **2** *pl cap educ* Arts. **humano** *adj* human. **humanismo** *nm* humanism.

humear (ume'ar) *vi* smoke. **humareda** *nf* pall of smoke.
humedad (ume'ðað) *nf* humidity, moisture. **humedecer** *vt* moisten, wet. **húmedo** *adj* humid.
humildad (umil'ðað) *nf* humility. **humilde** *adj* humble.
humillar (umi'ʎar) *vt* humiliate.
humo ('umo) *nm* smoke.
humor (u'mor) *nm* humour. **humorada** *nf* witticism.
hundir (un'dir) *vt* sink.
Hungría (un'gria) *nf* Hungary. **húngaro** *adj,n* Hungarian. *nm* Hungarian (language).
huracán (ura'kan) *nm* hurricane.
hurgar (ur'gar) *vt* poke.
hurón (u'ron) *nm* ferret.
hurtadillas (urta'ðiʎas) **a hurtadillas** *adv* secretively, stealthily.
hurtar (ur'tar) *vt* steal. **hurto** *nm* **1** theft. **2** stolen object.
husmear (usme'ar) *vt* scent, track.
huso ('uso) *nm* spindle.
huyente (u'jente) *adj* fugitive.
huyó (u'jo) *v* see **huir**.

I

ibérico (i'βeriko) *adj* Iberian. **ibero** *adj,n* Iberian.
ictericia (ikte'riθja) *nf* jaundice.
ida ('iða) *nf* **1** journey. **2** departure.
idea (i'ðea) *nf* idea.
ideal (iðe'al) *adj,nm* **1** ideal. **2** abstract, imaginary. **idealismo** *nm* idealism. **idealista** *nm,f* idealist. *adj invar* idealistic.
idealizar (ideali'θar) *vt* idealize.
idéntico (i'ðentiko) *adj* identical. **identidad** *nf* identity.
identificar (iðentifi'kar) *vt* identify. **identificación** *nf* identification.
ideología (ideolo'xia) *nf* ideology. **ideológico** *adj* ideological.
idilio (i'ðiljo) *nm* idyll. **idílico** *adj* idyllic.
idioma (i'ðjoma) *nm* language. **idiomático** *adj* idiomatic.
idiosincrasia (iðjosin'krasja) *nf* idiosyncrasy.
idiota (i'ðjota) *nm,f* idiot. **idiotez** *nf* idiocy.
idólatra (i'ðolatra) *nm* idolater. *adj* idolatrous, heathen. **idolatrar** *vt* worship. **idolatría** *nf* idolatry.
ídolo ('iðolo) *nm* idol.

idóneo (i'ðoneo) *adj* apt, appropriate.
iglesia (i'glesja) *nf* church.
ignominia (igno'minja) *nf* ignominy. **ignominioso** *adj* ignominious.
ignorancia (igno'ranθja) *nf* ignorance. **ignorante** *adj* ignorant.
ignorar (igno'rar) *vt* be unaware of.
igual (i'gwal) *adj* same, equal. **igualar** *vt* equalize. **igualación** *nf* equalization. **igualdad** *nf* equality.
íjada (i'xaða) *nf* flank, side.
ilegal (ile'gal) *adj* illegal.
ileso (i'leso) *adj* unharmed.
ilógico (i'loxiko) *adj* illogical.
iluminar (ilumi'nar) *vt* illuminate. **iluminación** *nf* illumination.
ilusión (ilu'sjon) *nf* illusion, dream.
ilusionarse (ilusjo'narse) *vr* delude oneself. **ilusionismo** *nm* conjuring trick. **ilusionista** *nm,f* conjurer.
ilustrar (ilus'trar) *vt* illustrate. **ilustración** *nf* **1** illustration. **2** enlightenment, learning.
ilustre (i'lustre) *adj* illustrious.
imagen (i'maxen) *nf* image.
imaginar (imaxi'nar) *vt,vi* imagine. **imaginación** *nf* imagination. **imaginativo** *adj* imaginary.
imán (i'man) *nm* magnet.
imbécil (im'beθil) *adj* imbecile. **imbecilidad** *nf* imbecility.
imborrable (imbor'raβle) *adj* unforgettable.
imbuir (imbu'ir) *vt* imbue.
imitar (imi'tar) *vt* copy. **imitación** *nf* copy.
impaciencia (impa'θjenθja) *nf* impatience. **impaciente** *adj* impatient.
impacto (im'pakto) *nm* impact.
impalpable (impal'paβle) *adj* impalpable, intangible.
impar (im'par) *adj math* odd.
imparcial (impar'θjal) *adj* impartial.
impartir (impar'tir) *vt* **1** impart (a teaching). **2** give (orders).
impasibilidad (impasiβili'ðað) *nf* impassivity. **impasible** *adj* impassive.
impávido (im'paβiðo) *adj* fearless. **impavidez** *nf* fearlessness.
impecable (impe'kaβle) *adj* perfect.
impedir (i) (impe'ðir) *vt* impede. **impedimento** *nm* impediment.
impeler (impe'ler) *vt* drive.
impenitente (impeni'tente) *adj* impenitent.
imperar (impe'rar) *vt* rule.

imperativo (impera'tiβo) *adj* imperative. *nm gram* imperative.

imperceptible (imperθep'tiβle) *adj* imperceptible.

imperdible (imper'ðiβle) *nm* safety pin.

imperdonable (imperðo'naβle) *adj* unforgivable.

imperfección (imperfek'θjon) *nf* imperfection. **imperfecto** *adj* imperfect. *nm gram* imperfect.

imperial (impe'rjal) *adj* imperial. **imperialismo** *nm* imperialism. **imperialista** *adj, nm,f* imperialist.

imperio (im'perjo) *nm* empire.

impermeable (imperme'aβle) *adj* waterproof, impermeable. *nm* mackintosh.

impersonal (imperso'nal) *adj* impersonal.

impertinencia (imperti'nenθja) *nf* 1 impudence. 2 inappropriateness. **impertinente** *adj* 1 impudent. 2 inappropriate.

imperturbable (impertur'βaβle) *adj* imperturbable.

ímpetu ('impetu) *nm* impetus. **impetuoso** *adj* impetuous.

impío (im'pio) *adj* irreligious, godless.

implacable (impla'kaβle) *adj* implacable.

implantar (implan'tar) *vt* implant.

implicar (impli'kar) *vt* imply.

implícito (im'pliθito) *adj* implicit.

implorar (implo'rar) *vt* beg.

imponer (impo'ner) *vt* impose. **imponente** *adj* 1 imposing. 2 *inf* smashing.

impopular (impopu'lar) *adj* unpopular.

importancia (impor'tanθja) *nf* importance. **importante** *adj* important.

importar (impor'tar) *vt* 1 import. 2 *comm* amount to. *vi* be important. **importación** *nf* import. **importe** *nm* amount.

importunar (importu'nar) *vt* annoy. **importuno** *adj* impertinent.

imposible (impo'siβle) *adj* impossible. **imposibilidad** *nf* impossibility. **imposibilitar** *vt* 1 make impossible. 2 make incapable.

imposición (imposi'θjon) *nf* 1 tax. 2 *comm* deposit.

impostor (impos'tor) *nm* impostor. **impostura** *nf* fraud.

impotencia (impo'tenθja) *nf* impotence. **impotente** *adj* impotent.

impracticable (imprakti'kaβle) *adj* impracticable.

imprecar (impre'kar) *vt* curse.

impregnar (impreg'nar) *vt* impregnate.

imprenta (im'prenta) *nf* 1 press. 2 printing.

imprescindible (impresθin'diβle) *adj* indispensable.

impresión (impre'sjon) *nf* impression. **impresionar** *vt* impress. **impresionismo** *nf* Art impressionism.

impreso (im'preso) *v see* **imprimir.** *adj* printed.

imprevisto (impre'βisto) *adj* unexpected.

imprimir (impri'mir) *vt* print.

improbabilidad (improβaβili'ðað) *nf* improbability. **improbable** *adj* improbable.

ímprobo ('improβo) *adj* wicked.

improcedente (improθe'ðente) *adj* law inadmissible.

improductivo (improðuk'tiβo) *adj* unproductive.

impropicio (impro'piθjo) *adj* unpropitious.

impropiedad (impropje'ðað) *nf* impropriety. **improprio** *adj* improper, inappropriate.

improvisar (improβi'sar) *vt* improvise.

improvisto (impro'βisto) *adj* unforeseen.

imprudencia (impru'ðenθja) *nf* imprudence. **imprudente** *adj* imprudent.

impúdico (im'puðiko) *adj* shameless, immodest. **impudor** *nm* 1 shamelessness. 2 cynicism.

impuesto (im'pwesto) *nm* 1 tax. 2 duty.

impugnar (impug'nar) *vt* 1 oppose. 2 confute. 3 impugn.

impulsar (impul'sar) *vt* drive, impel. **impulsión** *nf* 1 impulse. 2 impetus. **impulso** *nm* 1 impulse, urge. 2 pressure, force.

impune (im'pune) *adj* unpunished.

impureza (impu'reθa) *nf* 1 impurity, foulness. 2 dishonesty. 3 obscenity.

imputar (impu'tar) *vt* impute, ascribe. **imputación** *nf* imputation, accusation.

inacabable (inaka'βaβle) *adj* endless, interminable.

inaccesible (inakθe'siβle) *adj* inaccessible.

inacción (inak'θjon) *nf* inaction, rest.

inaceptable (inakθep'taβle) *adj* unacceptable.

inactividad (inaktiβi'ðað) *nf* inactivity. **inactivo** *adj* inactive.

inadaptable (inaðap'taβle) *adj* unadaptable.

inadecuado (inaðe'kwaðo) *adj* inadequate.

inadmisible (inaðmi'siβle) *adj* inadmissible.

inadvertencia (inaðβer'tenθja) *nf* inadvertence, carelessness.

inagotable (inago'taβle) *adj* inexhaustible.

inaguantable (inagwan'taβle) *adj* unbearable, intolerable.

inajenable (inaxe'naβle) *adj* inalienable.

inalterable (inalte'raβle) *adj* unchangeable.

inanición (inaniˈθjon) nf 1 med exhaustion, weakness. 2 starvation.

inanimado (inaniˈmaðo) adj inanimate.

inaplicable (inapliˈkaβle) adj inapplicable.

inapreciable (inapreˈθjaβle) adj priceless, invaluable.

inapto (inˈapto) adj unsuited.

inasequible (inaseˈkiβle) adj unattainable.

inaudible (inauˈðiβle) adj inaudible.

inaudito (inauˈðito) adj unheard-of, extraordinary, outrageous.

inaugurar (inauguˈrar) vt inaugurate. **inauguración** nf inauguration.

incalculable (inkalkuˈlaβle) adj incalculable.

incandescencia (inkandesˈθenθja) nf incandescence. **incandescente** adj incandescent.

incansable (inkanˈsaβle) adj indefatigable.

incapacidad (inkapaθiˈðað) nf incapacity.

incapacitar (inkapaθiˈtar) vt incapacitate, disable, disqualify.

incapaz (inkaˈpaθ) adj incapable, unfit.

incautarse (inkauˈtarse) vr law confiscate (property).

incauto (inˈkauto) adj incautious, careless.

incendiar (inθenˈdjar) vt set on fire. **incendiario** adj incendiary. **incendio** nm fire.

incentivo (inθenˈtiβo) nm incentive.

incertidumbre (inθertiˈðumbre) nf uncertainty.

incesante (inθeˈsante) adj incessant, uninterrupted.

incesto (inˈθesto) nm incest. **incestuoso** adj incestuous.

incidencia (inθiˈðenθja) nf incidence.

incidental (inθiðenˈtal) adj incidental, accidental.

incidente (inθiˈðente) adj incidental, chance. nm incident, happening.

incienso (inˈθjenso) nm incense.

incierto (inˈθjerto) adj uncertain.

incinerar (inθineˈrar) vt 1 cremate. 2 incinerate.

incipiente (inθiˈpjente) adj incipient.

incisión (inθiˈsjon) nf incision, cut.

incisivo (inθiˈsiβo) adj incisive, sharp.

incitar (inθiˈtar) vt instigate. **incitación** nf instigation.

incivil (inθiˈβil) adj impolite. **incivilidad** nf impoliteness.

inclemencia (inkleˈmenθja) nf inclemency. **inclemente** adj inclement.

inclinar (inkliˈnar) vt incline. **inclinarse** vr be inclined to. **inclinación** nf inclination.

incluir* (inkluˈir) vt include. **inclusión** nf inclu-

sion. **inclusive** prep including. adv even. **incluso** adv even.

incógnito (inˈkognito) adj unknown.

incoherencia (inkoeˈrenθja) nf incoherence. **incoherente** adj incoherent.

incoloro (inkoˈloro) adj colourless.

incomodar (inkomoˈðar) vt annoy, molest. **incómodo** adj 1 annoying. 2 uncomfortable.

incompatibilidad (inkompatiβiliˈðað) nf incompatibility. adj incompatible.

incompetente (inkompeˈtente) adj incompetent. **incompetencia** nf incompetence.

incompleto (inkomˈpleto) adj incomplete.

incomprensible (inkomprenˈsiβle) adj incomprehensible.

incomunicado (inkomuniˈkaðo) adj isolated.

inconcebible (inkonθeˈβiβle) adj inconceivable.

inconcluso (inkonˈkluso) adj unfinished, inconclusive.

incondicional (inkondiθjoˈnal) adj unconditional.

inconfundible (inkonfunˈdiβle) adj unmistakeable.

incongruente (inkongruˈente) adj incongruous. **incongruencia** nf incongruity.

inconmensurable (inkonmensuˈraβle) adj immeasurable.

inconmovible (inkonmoˈβiβle) adj immovable.

inconsciencia (inkonsˈθjenθja) nf med unconsciousness. **inconsciente** adj 1 unconscious. 2 irresponsible.

inconsecuencia (inkonseˈkwenθja) nf inconsequence. **inconsecuente** adj inconsequential.

inconsiderado (inkonsiðeˈraðo) adj ill-considered.

inconstancia (inkonˈstanθja) nf inconstancy. **inconstante** adj inconstant.

incontestable (inkontesˈtaβle) adj indisputable.

incontinencia (inkontiˈnenθja) nf incontinence. **incontinente** adj incontinent.

inconveniencia (inkonβeˈnjenθja) nf inconvenience. **inconveniente** adj inconvenient. nm objection, impediment.

incorporar (inkorpoˈrar) vt incorporate. **incorporarse** vr sit up. **incorporarse** a become a member of.

incorrección (inkorrekˈθjon) nf inexactitude. **incorrecto** adj incorrect.

incorregible (inkorreˈxiβle) adj incorrigible.

incorruptible (inkorrupˈtiβle) adj incorruptible. **incorrupto** adj incorrupt.

incredulidad (inkreðuli'ðað) *nf* incredulity. **incrédulo** *adj* sceptical.

increíble (inkre'iβle) *adj* incredible.

incremento (inkre'mento) *nm* increase.

increpar (inkre'par) *vt* reproach.

incriminar (inkrimi'nar) *vt* inculpate.

incrustar (inkrus'tar) *vt* encrust.

incubar (inku'βar) *vt* incubate.

inculcar (inkul'kar) *vt* inculcate.

inculto (in'kulto) *adj* uneducated, uncouth.

incumbencia (inkum'benθja) *nf* duty, obligation.

incurable (inku'raβle) *adj* incurable.

incurrir (inkur'rir) *vi* 1 commit. 2 become liable to. 3 incur.

indagar (inda'gar) *vt* investigate. **indagación** *nf* investigation.

indebido (inde'βiðo) *adj* 1 unjust. 2 improper.

indecente (inde'θente) *adj* indecent.

indecible (inde'θiβle) *adj* indescribable.

indecisión (indeθi'sjon) *nf* indecision. **indeciso** *adj* indecisive.

indecoroso (indeko'roso) *adj* indecorous.

indefectible (indefek'tiβle) *adj* inevitable, infallible.

indefenso (inde'fenso) *adj* defenceless.

indefinible (indefi'niβle) *adj* indefinable. **indefinido** *adj* indefinite.

indeleble (inde'leβle) *adj* indelible.

indemne (in'demne) *adj* unharmed. **indemnidad** *nf* indemnity. **indemnizar** *vt* indemnify, compensate.

independencia (independen'denθja) *nf* independence. **independiente** *adj* independent.

indescriptible (indeskrip'tiβle) *adj* indescribable.

indeseable (indese'aβle) *adj* undesirable.

indeterminado (indetermi'naðo) *adj* 1 indeterminate. 2 undetermined.

India ('indja) *nf* India. **indio** *adj,n* Indian.

indiano (indi'ano) *adj,n* South American. *nm* Spaniard who has become rich in South America.

indicar (indi'kar) *vt* indicate. **indicación** *nf* indication. **indicado** *adj* suitable. **indicador** *nm* indicator. **indicativo** *adj,n* indicative. **indicativo de nacionalidad** *mot* nationality plate.

índice ('indiθe) *nm* 1 index. 2 hand (of a clock, etc.). 3 index finger.

indicio (in'diθjo) *nm* 1 sign. 2 *pl law* evidence.

indiferencia (indife'renθja) *nf* indifference. **indiferente** *adj* indifferent.

indígena (in'dixena) *adj,n* native.

indigestión (indixes'tjon) *nf* indigestion. **indigestible** *adj* indigestible.

indignar (indig'nar) *vt* annoy, anger.

indirecta (indi'rekta) *nf* indirect suggestion. **indirecto** *adj* indirect.

indiscreción (indiskre'θjon) *nf* indiscretion. **indiscreto** *adj* indiscreet.

indiscutible (indisku'tiβle) *adj* unquestionable.

indisoluble (indiso'luβle) *adj* indissoluble.

indispensable (indispen'saβle) *adj* indispensable.

indisponer* (indispo'ner) *vt* upset. **indisponerse** *vr med* 1 feel unwell. 2 fall ill.

indistinto (indis'tinto) *adj* indistinct.

individual (indiβi'ðwal) *adj* individual, private. **individualidad** *nf* individuality. **individuo** *nm* individual.

indivisible (indiβi'siβle) *adj* indivisible. **indiviso** *adj* undivided.

índole ('indole) *nm* nature, inclination.

indolencia (indo'lenθja) *nf* sloth, apathy. **indolente** *adj* apathetic, slothful.

indómito (in'domito) *adj* untamed.

indubitable (induβi'taβle) *adj* indubitable.

inducir* (indu'θir) *vt* 1 persuade. 2 *phil* infer. 3 *tech,sci* induce. **inducción** *nf* 1 induction. 2 inducement.

indudable (indu'ðaβle) *adj* unquestionable.

indulgencia (indul'xenθja) *nf* indulgence. **indulgente** *adj* indulgent.

indultar (indul'tar) *vt* pardon. **indulto** *nm law* pardon.

indumentaria (indumen'tarja) *nf* dress, costume.

industria (in'dustrja) *nf* industry.

inédito (i'neðito) *adj* unpublished.

inefable (ine'faβle) *adj* ineffable.

ineficacia (inefi'kaθja) *nf* ineffectiveness. **ineficaz** *adj* inefficient.

ineludible (inelu'ðiβle) *adj* inevitable.

ineptitud (inepti'tuð) *nf* ineptitude. **inepto** *adj* inept.

inequívoco (ine'kiβoko) *adj* unmistakeable.

inercia (i'nerθja) *nf* 1 laziness. 2 *sci* inertia. **inerme** (i'nerme) *adj* unarmed.

inerte (in'erte) *adj* 1 *sci* inert. 2 *inf* sluggish, slow.

inesperado (inespe'raðo) *adj* unexpected.

inestable (ines'taβle) *adj* unsteady.

inevitable (ineβi'taβle) *adj* inevitable.

inexactitud (ineksakti'tuð) *nf* inaccuracy. **inexacto** *adj* inaccurate.

inexperto (ineks'perto) adj inexperienced.

inexplicable (inekspli'kaβle) adj inexplicable.

infalibilidad (infaliβili'ðað) nf infallibility. **infalible** adj infallible.

infamar (infa'mar) vt dishonour. **infame** adj 1 infamous. 2 dishonourable. **infamia** nf 1 infamy. 2 dishonour.

infancia (in'fanθja) nf infancy. **infante** adj infant. nm prince.

infatigable (infati'gaβle) adj indefatigable.

infausto (in'fausto) adj ill-omened.

infectar (infek'tar) vt infect. **infección** nf infection. **infeccioso** adj infectious.

infeliz (infe'liθ) adj unhappy.

inferior (infe'rjor) adj 1 lower. 2 inferior.

inferir (ie) (infe'rir) vt 1 infer. 2 inflict (a wound, etc.).

infernal (infer'nal) adj infernal.

infestar (infes'tar) vt infest.

infiel (infi'el) adj 1 unfaithful. 2 inaccurate.

infierno (in'fjerno) nm hell.

ínfimo ('infimo) adj lowest.

infinidad (infini'ðað) nf infinity. **infinito** adj infinite.

inflación (infla'θjon) nf inflation.

inflamar (infla'mar) vt 1 inflame. 2 set alight. **inflamarse** vr become inflamed. **inflamación** nf 1 inflammation. 2 combustion.

inflar (in'flar) vt inflate.

inflexible (inflek'siβle) adj inflexible.

infligir (infli'xir) vt inflict.

influencia (influ'enθja) nf influence.

influir* (influ'ir) vt influence, affect. **influencia** nf influence. **influyente** adj influential.

influjo (in'fluxo) nm 1 influence. 2 flood (tide).

información (informa'θjon) nf 1 information. 2 character reference.

informal (infor'mal) adj 1 informal. 2 unreliable. **informalidad** nf 1 informality. 2 unreliability.

informar (infor'mar) vt inform. vi law plead. **informe** nm 1 announcement. 2 item of information.

infortunio (infor'tunjo) nm misfortune.

infracción (infrak'θjon) nf offence, breach.

infranqueable (infranke'aβle) adj 1 inaccessible. 2 unsurmountable.

infringir (infrin'xir) vt infringe, break (one's word, oath, etc.).

infructuoso (infruk'twoso) adj fruitless.

infundado (infun'daðo) adj unfounded.

infundir (infun'dir) vt instil.

ingeniería (inxenje'ria) nf engineering. **ingeniero** nm engineer.

ingenio (in'xenjo) nm 1 talent, wit, intuition. 2 device.

ingenuo (in'xenwo) adj 1 frank. 2 simple, credulous.

ingerir (ie) (inxe'rir) vt consume (food).

Inglaterra (ingla'terra) nf England. **inglés** adj English. nm 1 Englishman. 2 English (language).

ingratitud (ingrati'tuð) nf ingratitude. **ingrato** adj 1 ungrateful. 2 unpleasant. 3 unrewarding.

ingrediente (ingre'ðjente) nm ingredient.

ingresar (ingre'sar) vi 1 enter, join. 2 be admitted (to hospital). vt deposit (money). **ingreso** nm 1 entry. 2 comm deposit. 3 pl revenue, income.

inhábil (i'naβil) adj unfit, incapable. **día inhábil** non-working day.

inhabilitar (inaβili'tar) vt 1 disqualify, declare unfit. 2 disable. **inhabilitación** nf 1 declaration of unfitness. 2 endorsement (licence).

inhabitable (inaβi'taβle) adj uninhabitable. **inhabitado** adj uninhabited.

inhalar (ina'lar) vt inhale. **inhalación** nf inhalation.

inherente (ine'rente) adj inherent, innate.

inhibir (ini'βir) vt 1 inhibit. 2 law impede, stay. **inhibirse** vr abstain.

inhospitalario (inospita'larjo) adj inhospitable.

inhumano (inu'mano) adj inhuman.

inhumar (inu'mar) vt bury.

inicial (ini'θjal) adj,nf initial.

iniciar (ini'θjar) vt initiate (into a society, etc.).

inicuo (i'nikwo) adj evil, wicked. **iniquidad** nf iniquity, evil.

injerir (ie) (inxe'rir) vt insert.

injertar (inxer'tar) vt med,bot graft. **injerto** nm graft, grafting.

injuriar (inxuri'ar) vt 1 insult. 2 injure. **injuria** nf 1 insult, outrage. 2 injury. **injurioso** adj 1 insulting. 2 harmful.

injusticia (inxus'tiθja) nf injustice. **injusto** adj unjust.

inmediato (inme'ðjato) adj immediate.

inmejorable (inmexo'raβle) adj unsurpassable.

inmemorial (inmemo'rjal) adj immemorial.

inmenso (in'menso) adj immense.

inmerecido (inmere'θiðo) adj undeserved.

inmigrar (inmi'grar) vi immigrate. **inmigración** nf immigration. **inmigrante** nm immigrant.

inminente (inmi'nente) adj imminent. **inminencia** nf imminence.

inmiscuir* (inmisku'ir) vt mix. **inmiscuirse** vr interfere.

81

inmoderado (inmoðe'raðo) adj excessive.

inmodestia (inmo'ðestja) nf immodesty. **inmodesto** adj immodest.

inmoral (inmo'ral) adj immoral. **inmoralidad** nf immorality.

inmortal (inmor'tal) adj,n immortal. **inmortalidad** nf immortality. **inmortalizar** vt immortalize.

inmóvil (in'moßil) adj 1 immobile. 2 immovable. **inmovilizar** vt immobilize.

inmueble (in'mweßle) nm 1 property. 2 pl real estate.

inmundo (in'munðo) adj dirty, foul.

inmunidad (inmuni'ðað) nf immunity. **inmunizar** vt immunize.

inmutar (inmu'tar) vt alter. **inmutarse** vr change countenance.

innato (in'nato) adj innate.

innecesario (inneθe'sarjo) adj unnecessary.

innegable (inne'gaßle) adj undeniable.

innoble (in'noßle) adj ignoble.

innocuo (in'nokwo) adj also **inocuo** innocuous.

innovar (in'noßar) vt renovate.

innumerable (innume'raßle) adj innumerable.

inobediente (inoße'ðjente) adj disobedient.

inocencia (ino'θenθja) nf innocence. **inocente** adj innocent.

inocular (inoku'lar) vt 1 inoculate. 2 pervert, infect.

inofensivo (inofen'sißo) adj harmless.

inolvidable (inolßi'ðaßle) adj unforgettable.

inopinado (inopi'naðo) adj unexpected, surprising.

inoportuno (inopor'tuno) adj inopportune.

inoxidable (inoksi'ðaßle) adj stainless (steel).

inquebrantable (inkeßran'taßle) adj unbreakable.

inquietar (inkje'tar) vt disquiet, disturb. **inquieto** adj restless. **inquietud** nf restlessness, disquiet.

inquilino (inki'lino) nm 1 lodger, tenant. 2 parasite. **inquilinato** nm 1 rent. 2 lease.

inquirir* (inki'rir) vt examine, scrutinize.

inquisición (inkisi'θjon) nf 1 inquisition, tribunal. 2 enquiry, investigation. **inquisidor** nm inquisitor.

insaciable (insa'θjaßle) adj insatiable.

insalubre (insa'lußre) adj unhealthy.

insano (in'sano) adj 1 mad. 2 unhealthy.

inscribir (inskri'ßir) vt 1 inscribe. 2 enroll. **inscripción** nf 1 inscription. 2 enrolment. **inscrito** adj 1 inscribed. 2 enrolled.

insecto (in'sekto) nm insect.

inseguridad (inseguri'ðað) nf insecurity. **inseguro** adj insecure, unsafe.

insensatez (insensa'teθ) nf stupidity, foolishness. **insensato** adj stupid, foolish.

insensible (insen'sißle) adj 1 insensitive. 2 impassive. 3 imperceptible.

insepulto (inse'pulto) adj unburied.

insertar (inser'tar) vt 1 insert. 2 graft.

inservible (inser'ßißle) adj useless.

insidioso (insi'ðjoso) adj insidious.

insigne (in'signe) adj distinguished.

insignia (in'signia) nf also **insignias** insignia.

insignificancia (insignifi'kanθja) nf insignificance. **insignificante** adj insignificant.

insincero (insin'θero) adj insincere.

insinuar (insi'nwar) vt insinuate. **insinuarse** vr ingratiate oneself.

insípido (in'sipiðo) adj tasteless, insipid.

insistir (insis'tir) vt insist. **insistencia** nf insistence.

insociable (inso'θjaßle) adj unsociable.

insolación (insola'θjon) nf sunstroke.

insolencia (inso'lenθja) nf insolence. **insolente** adj insolent, arrogant.

insólito (in'solito) adj unusual.

insoluble (inso'lußle) adj 1 insoluble. 2 indissoluble.

insolvencia (insol'ßenθja) nf insolvency. **insolvente** adj insolvent, penniless.

insomne (in'somne) adj,n insomniac. **insomnio** nm insomnia.

insondable (inson'daßle) adj unfathomable.

insoportable (insopor'taßle) adj insufferable.

inspección (inspek'θjon) nf inspection. **inspeccionar** vt inspect. **inspector** nm inspector.

inspirar (inspi'rar) vt 1 breathe in. 2 inspire. **inspiración** nf inspiration.

instalar (insta'lar) vt instal, establish. **instalación** nf installation.

instancia (ins'tanθja) nf petition, application.

instante (ins'tante) nm instant. **instantáneo** adj instantaneous. **por instantes** continually.

instaurar (instau'rar) vt restore, re-establish.

instigar (insti'gar) vt incite.

instintivo (instin'tißo) adj instinctive. **instinto** nm instinct.

instituir (institu'ir) vt institute. **Institución** nf institution. **instituto** nm 1 institute. 2 grammar school.

instruir* (instru'ir) vt instruct. **instrucción** nf 1 instruction. 2 education. **instructivo** adj instructive. **instructor** nm instructor.

instrumento (instru'mento) *nm* instrument.

insubordinar (insuβorði'nar) *vt* make rebellious. **insubordinable** *adj also* **insubordinado** rebellious. **insubordinación** *nf* insubordination.

insuficiencia (insufi'θjenθja) *nf* 1 insufficiency. 2 incapability. **insuficiente** *adj* 1 insufficient. 2 incapable.

insufrible (insu'friβle) *adj* unbearable.

insulso (in'sulso) *adj* dull.

insular (insu'lar) *adj* insular.

insultar (insul'tar) *vt* insult, provoke. **insulto** *nm* insult.

insuperable (insupe'raβle) *adj* insuperable.

insurgente (insur'xente) *adj* rebellious. *nm,f* rebel.

insurrección (insurrek'θjon) *nf* rebellion. **insurreccionar** *vt* incite to rebel. **insurreccionarse** *vr* rebel.

intacto (in'takto) *adj* intact.

intachable (inta't∫aβle) *adj* irreproachable.

integrar (inte'grar) *vt* 1 integrate, complete. 2 construct, form. **integración** *nf* integration. **integral** *adj also* **integrante** integral.

íntegro ('integro) *adj* entire. **integridad** *nf* 1 integrity, chastity. 2 entirety.

intelecto (inte'lekto) *nm* intellect. **intelectual** *adj,n* intellectual. **intelectualidad** *nf* intelligentsia.

inteligencia (inteli'xenθja) *nf* 1 intelligence. 2 meaning (of word). 3 relationship, agreement. **inteligente** *adj* intelligent. **inteligible** *adj* intelligible.

intemperie (intem'perje) *nf* bad weather.

intempestivo (intempes'tiβo) *adj* inopportune.

intención (inten'θjon) *nf* intention, meaning.

intenso (in'tenso) *adj* intense.

intentar (inten'tar) *vt* 1 attempt, try. 2 intend. **intento** *nm* 1 intent, design. 2 attempt.

intercalar (interka'lar) *vt* insert.

intercambio (inter'kambjo) *nm* interchange.

interceder (interθe'ðer) *vi* intercede. **intercesión** *nf* intercession.

interceptor (interθep'tor) *nm* interceptor.

interdicción (interðik'θjon) *nf, also* **interdicto** *nm* prohibition.

interés (inte'res) *nm* 1 interest, concern. 2 import, advantage. 3 *comm* interest.

interesar (intere'sar) *vt* interest. **interesado** *adj* self-seeking. *n* person concerned. **interesante** *adj* interesting. **interesarse por** *or* **en** be interested in.

interferencia (interfe'renθja) *nf* interference.

ínterin ('interin) *nm* interim. **interino** *adj* provisional, interim.

interior (inte'rjor) *adj* interior, inner, internal.

interjección (interxek'θjon) *nf* interjection.

intermediario (interme'ðjario) *adj,nm* intermediary. **intermedio** *adj* intermediate. *n* Th interval.

interminable (intermi'naβle) *adj* interminable.

intermisión (intermi'sjon) *nf* intermission.

intermitente (intermi'tente) *adj* intermittent.

internacional (internaθjo'nal) *adj* international.

internar (inter'nar) *vt* intern, confine. **internarse** *vr* penetrate. **interno** *adj* boarding. *nm* 1 boarder. 2 *med* houseman. **escuela interna** boarding school.

interpelar (interpe'lar) *vt* 1 appeal for help to. 2 buttonhole, demand an answer. **interpelación** *nf* plea, appeal.

interponer* (interpo'ner) *vt* 1 interpose. 2 lodge (a complaint, etc.).

interpretar (interpre'tar) *vt* interpret. **interpretación** *nf* interpretation. **intérprete** *nm,f* interpreter.

interrogar (interro'gar) *vt* question. **interrogación** *nf* 1 question. 2 question mark. **interrogativo** *adj* interrogative. **interrogatorio** *nm* questionnaire.

interrumpir (interrum'pir) *vt* interrupt. **interrupción** *nf* interruption. **interruptor** *nm tech* switch.

intervalo (inter'βalo) *nm* interval, distance.

intervenir* (interβe'nir) *vt,vi* 1 take part in. 2 intervene. 3 *med* operate on. 4 *comm* audit. **intervención** *nf* 1 *pol* intervention. 2 audit. 3 *med* operation. **interventor** *nm* 1 auditor. 2 supervisor (of a train).

intestado (intes'taðo) *adj* intestate.

intestino (intes'tino) *adj* internal. *nm* intestine. **intestinal** *adj* intestinal.

intimar (inti'mar) *vt* intimate, declare, notify. **intimarse** *vr* become intimate. **intimación** *nf* declaration. **intimidad** *nf* intimacy. **íntimo** *adj* intimate.

intimidar (intimi'ðar) *vt* intimidate.

intolerable (intole'raβle) *adj* intolerable. **intolerancia** *nf* intolerance. **intolerante** *adj* intolerant.

intoxicar (intoksi'kar) *vt* poison. **intoxicación** *nf* intoxication, poisoning.

intraducible (intraðu'θiβle) *adj* untranslatable.

intranquilidad (intrankili'ðað) *nf* restlessness, disquiet. **intranquilo** *adj* restless, worried.

intransigencia (intransi'xenθja) nf intransigence. **intransigente** adj intransigent.

intransitable (intransi'taβle) adj impassable.

intransitivo (intransi'tiβo) adj gram intransitive.

intratable (intra'taβle) adj 1 unmanageable. 2 unsociable.

intrepidez (intrepi'ðeθ) nf valour. **intrépido** adj intrepid, brave, fearless.

intrigar (intri'gar) vi,vt intrigue.

intrincado (intrin'kaðo) adj 1 intricate. 2 confused.

intrínseco (in'trinseko) adj intrinsic.

introducir (introðu'θir) vt introduce. **introducción** nf introduction.

intrusión (intru'sjon) nf intrusion. **intruso** adj intrusive. nm intruder.

intuición (intwi'θjon) nf intuition.

inundar (inun'dar) vt flood. **inundación** nf flood.

inusitado (inusi'taðo) adj obsolete, rare.

inútil (i'nutil) adj useless. **inutilidad** nf uselessness. **inutilizar** vt render useless.

invadir (inβa'ðir) vt invade.

invalidar (inβali'ðar) vt invalidate, abolish.

inválido (in'βaliðo) adj,n invalid.

invariable (inβa'rjaβle) adj invariable.

invasión (inβa'sjon) nf invasion. **invasor** adj invading. nm invader.

invencible (inβen'θiβle) adj invincible, unconquerable.

inventar (inβen'tar) vt invent. **invención** nf invention. **inventivo** adj inventive. **invento** nm invention. **inventor** nm inventor.

inventario (inβen'tarjo) nm inventory.

invernáculo (inβer'nakulo) nm also **invernadero** hot-house.

invernar (ie) (inβer'nar) vt pass the winter, hibernate. **invernada** nf 1 winter. 2 hibernation. **invernal** adj wintry.

inverosímil (inβero'simil) adj improbable.

invertir (ie) (inβer'tir) vt 1 invert. 2 comm invest. **inversión** nf 1 inversion. 2 comm investment.

investigar (inβesti'gar) vt investigate. **investigación** nf investigation. **investigador** nm researcher.

investir (inβes'tir) vt 1 invest. 2 confer upon. **investidura** nf investiture.

inveterado (inβete'raðo) adj confirmed, rooted.

invicto (in'βikto) adj undefeated.

invierno (in'βjerno) nm winter.

inviolable (inβjo'laβle) adj inviolable.

invitar (inβi'tar) vt 1 invite. 2 treat (to drinks). **invitación** nf invitation.

invocar (inβo'kar) vt invoke. **invocación** nf invocation.

involuntario (inβolun'tarjo) adj 1 automatic. 2 unintended.

inyección (injek'θjon) nf injection.

inyectar (injek'tar) vt inject. **inyectable** nm injectable. **inyector** nm nozzle.

iodo ('joðo) nm iodine.

ir (ir) vi 1 go. 2 walk. **irse** vr go away.

ira ('ira) nf anger. **iracundo** adj 1 furious. 2 irascible.

Irak (i'rak) nm Iraq. **iraquí** adj,n Iraqui.

Irán (i'ran) nm Iran. **iraní** adj,n Iranian.

irguió (irgi'o) v see **erguir.**

iris ('iris) nm iris (of the eye). **arco iris** nm rainbow.

Irlanda (ir'landa) nf Ireland. **irlandés** adj,n Irishman. nm Irish (language).

ironía (iro'nia) nf irony. **irónico** adj ironic.

irracional (irraθjo'nal) adj irrational.

irradiar (irra'ðjar) vt radiate. **irradiación** nf irradiation.

irrazonable (irraθo'naβle) adj unreasonable.

irreal (irre'al) adj unreal.

irreconciliable (irrekonθi'ljaβle) adj irreconcilable.

irreflexión (irreflek'sjon) nf hastiness. **irreflexivo** adj hasty.

irrefrenable (irrefre'naβle) adj uncontrollable.

irregular (irregu'lar) adj irregular, anomalous. **irregularidad** nf irregularity.

irreligioso (irreli'xjoso) adj impious.

irremediable (irreme'ðjaβle) adj 1 irreparable. 2 incurable.

irresoluto (irreso'luto) adj 1 indecisive. 2 perplexed.

irrespetuoso (irrespe'twoso) adj irreverent.

irresponsable (irrespon'saβle) adj irresponsible.

irrigar (irri'gar) vt irrigate. **irrigación** nf irrigation. **irrigador** nm sprinkler.

irritabilidad (irritaβili'ðað) nf irascibility. **irritable** adj irascible.

isla ('isla) nf island.

Islandia (is'landja) nf Iceland. **islandés** adj Icelandic. nm 1 Icelander. 2 Icelandic (language).

isleño (is'leɲo) adj island. nm islander.

Israel (is'rael) nm Israel. **israelí** adj,n Israeli. **israelita** adj,n Israelite.

istmo ('istmo) nm isthmus.

Italia (i'talja) *nf* Italy. **italiano** *adj,n* Italian. *nm* Italian (language).

itinerario (itine'rarjo) *nm* itinerary.

izar (i'θar) *vt* hoist.

izquierdo (iθ'kjerðo) *adj* left. **a la izquierda** on or to the left. **la izquierda** *also* **los izquierdistas** *pol* the left wing.

J

jabalí (xaβa'li) *nm* boar.

jabalina (xaβa'lina) *nf* javelin.

jabón (xa'βon) *nm* soap. **jabonar** *vt* soap, wash. **jabonoso** *adj* soapy.

jaca ('xaka) *nf* pony.

jacinto (xa'θinto) *nm* hyacinth.

jactarse (xak'tarse) *vr* boast, brag. **jactancia** *nf* boasting. **jactancioso** *adj* boastful.

jadear (xaðe'ar) *vt* pant, gasp. **jadeante** *adj* panting.

jalear (xale'ar) *vt* 1 urge on (dogs in hunting). 2 clap, stamp in time to a song, dance, etc. **jaleo** *nm* 1 audience participation (in flamenco, etc.). 2 row. **armar un jaleo** or **estar de jaleo** kick up a row.

jamás (xa'mas) *adv* never. **nunca jamás** never ever.

jamón (xa'mon) *nm* ham.

Japón (xa'pon) *nm* Japan. **japonés** *adj,n* Japanese. *nm* Japanese (language).

jaque ('xake) *nm* check (in chess).

jaqueca (xa'keka) *nf* migraine.

jarabe (xa'rabe) *nm* syrup.

jarana (xa'rana) *nf* drinking bout, spree.

jardín (xar'ðin) *nm* garden. **jardinería** *nf* gardening. **jardinero** *nm* gardener.

jarra ('xarra) *nf* deep earthenware jar. **jarro** *nm* earthenware jug. **jarrón** *nm* vase.

jaula ('xaula) *nf* cage.

jazmín (xaθ'min) *nm* jasmine.

jefatura (xefa'tura) *nf* headquarters. **jefe** *nm* 1 chief, head. 2 manager, boss.

jengibre (xen'xiβre) *nm* ginger.

jerarquía (xerar'kia) *nf* hierarchy. **jerárquico** *adj* hierarchical.

jerez (xe'reθ) *nm* sherry.

jerga ('xerga) *nf also* **jerigonza** jargon.

jeringa (xe'ringa) *nf* syringe.

jeroglífico (xero'glifiko) *adj,nm* hieroglyph.

jersey (xer'sei) *nm* jersey.

Jerusalén (xerusa'len) *nm* Jerusalem.

jesuita (xesu'ita) *adj,n* Jesuit.

jeta ('xeta) *nf* 1 protruding mouth, snout. 2 *fam* face. **poner jeta** pout.

jilguero (xil'gero) *nm* goldfinch.

jinete (xi'nete) *nm* rider.

jirafa (xi'rafa) *nf* giraffe.

jocosidad (xokosi'ðað) *nf* joviality, cheer. **jocoso** *adj* cheerful, humorous.

jofaina (xo'faina) *nf* washbowl.

jornada (xor'naða) *nf* 1 journey, day's journey. 2 day's work. 3 *Th* act. **jornal** *nm* wage, day's wage. **jornalero** *nm* day-labourer.

joroba (xo'roβa) *nf* 1 hump. 2 bother. **jorobado** *adj,n* hunchback (person).

jota ('xota) *nf* 1 the letter *j*. 2 folk dance.

joven ('xoβen) *adj* young. *nm,f, pl* **jóvenes** youth, young person.

joya ('xoja) *nf* jewel. **joyería** *nf* jewellery. **joyero** *nm* jeweller.

jubilar (xuβi'lar) *vt* pension off, superannuate, retire. **jubilación** *nf* 1 pension. 2 retirement. **jubilado** *nm* pensioner.

jubileo (xuβi'leo) *nm* jubilee.

júbilo ('xuβilo) *nm* rejoicing.

judaísmo (xuða'ismo) *nm* Judaism.

judía (xu'ðia) *nf* 1 string bean. 2 (kidney) bean.

judiada (xu'ðjaða) *nf* 1 cruelty, cruel action. 2 *comm* extortion.

judicial (xuði'θjal) *adj* judicial.

judío (xu'ðio) *adj* Jewish. *nm* Jew.

juego ('xwego) *nm* 1 game, play. 2 gaming, gambling. 3 set, assembly.

juerga ('xwerga) *nf sl* party, spree.

jueves ('xweβes) *nm* Thursday.

juez (xweθ) *nm* judge.

jugar (ue) (xu'gar) *vi,vt* play. **jugarse** *vr* gamble. **jugada** *nf game* go, move. **jugador** *nm* player.

juglar (xu'glar) *nm* minstrel.

jugo ('xugo) *nm* juice. **jugoso** *adj* juicy.

juguetear (xugete'ar) *vi* frolic. **juguete** *nm* toy, plaything.

juicio ('xwiθjo) *nm* judgment. **juicioso** *adj* 1 good. 2 sensible.

julio ('xuljo) *nm* July.

jumento (xu'mento) *nm* donkey, ass.

junco ('xunko) *nm* reed.

jungla ('xungla) *nf* jungle.

junio ('xunjo) *nm* June.

junquillo (xun'kiʎo) *nm* garden reed, bullrush.

juntar (xun'tar) *vt* join, assemble. **junta** *nf* 1 assembly. 2 *tech* joint, washer. 3 junta. **la junta directiva** the board of directors. **junto** *adj,adv* together, joint. **junto a** *prep* near.

juramentar (xuramen'tar) *vt* swear in. **juramento** *nm* 1 oath. 2 swearword.

jurar (xu'rar) *vi,vt* swear. **jurado** *nm* jury, juror.

jurídico (xu'riðiko) *adj* juridical.

jurisconsulto (xuriskon'sulto) *nm* legal expert. **jurisdicción** *nf* jurisdiction. **jurisprudencia** *nf* jurisprudence. **jurista** *nm* jurist.

justa ('xusta) *nf* joust, competition.

justicia (xus'tiθja) *nf* 1 justice. 2 tribunal.

justificar (xustifi'kar) *vt* justify. **justificación** *nf* justification.

justo ('xusto) *adj* just, correct.

juvenil (xuβe'nil) *adj* youthful.

juventud (xuβen'tuð) *nf* youth.

juzgar (xuθ'gar) *vt* judge. **juzgado** *nm* court.

K

kilo ('kilo) *nm* kilo.

kilogramo (kilo'gramo) *nm* kilogramme.

kilolitro (kilo'litro) *nm* kilolitre.

kilómetro (ki'lometro) *nm* kilometre. **kilométrico** *adj* kilometric.

kilovatio (kilo'βatjo) *nm* kilowatt.

kiosco ('kjosko) *nm* kiosk.

L

la (la) *def art f* the. *pron 3rd pers s* 1 her, it. 2 *fml* you. 3 that, that one.

laberinto (laβe'rinto) *nm* labyrinth, maze.

labio ('laβjo) *nm* lip. **labial** *adj,n* labial.

labor (la'βor) *nf* 1 work, handiwork. 2 knitting.

laborar (laβo'rar) *vt* work, till. **laborioso** *adj* 1 industrious. 2 laborious. **laborista** *adj* Labour (Party).

labrar (la'βrar) *vt* 1 till, cultivate. 2 work, fashion. **labrador** *nm* ploughman, farmer. **labranza** *nf* farming. 2 farmland. **labriego** *adj, nm* peasant.

laca ('laka) *nf* lacquer, varnish.

lacayo (la'kajo) *nm* lackey.

lacerar (laθe'rar) *vt* 1 wound. 2 damage (fruit). **laceración** *nf* laceration, damage.

lacio ('laθjo) *adj* limp, creased, lank.

lacrar¹ (la'krar) *vt* infect. **lacra** *nf* blemish, scar.

lacrar² (la'krar) *vt* seal. **lacre** *nm* sealing wax.

lacrimoso (lakri'moso) *adj* tearful.

lácteo ('lakteo) *adj* milky. **vía láctea** *nf* Milky Way.

ladear (laðe'ar) *vt* overturn, tip, tilt.

ladera (la'ðera) *nf* slope.

lado ('laðo) *nm* side. **al lado de** beside.

ladrar (la'ðrar) *vi* bark. **ladride** *nm* barking.

ladrillo (la'ðriλo) *nm* brick, tile.

ladrón (la'ðron) *nm* thief.

lagarto (la'garto) *nm* lizard.

lago ('lago) *nm* lake.

lágrima ('lagrima) *nf* tear, drop.

laguna (la'guna) *nf* 1 pond, lagoon. 2 gap.

laico ('laiko) *adj* secular.

lamentar (lamen'tar) *vt* 1 lament. 2 regret. **lamentación** *nf* lamentation. **lamento** *nm* lament.

lamer (la'mer) *vt* lick.

lámina ('lamina) *nf* 1 sheet (of metal). 2 plate (of a book). **laminar** *vt* laminate.

lámpara ('lampara) *nf* lamp.

lana ('lana) *nf* wool.

lance ('lanθe) *nm* 1 throw. 2 occasion, opportunity.

lanceta (lan'θeta) *nf* lancet.

lancha ('lantʃa) *nf* launch.

langosta (lan'gosta) *nf* 1 lobster. 2 locust.

languidecer* (langiðe'θer) *vi* languish. **languidez** *nf* languor. **lánguido** *adj* languid.

lanudo (la'nuðo) *adj* woolly.

lanza ('lanθa) *nf* spear.

lanzar (lan'θar) *vt* 1 throw, fling. 2 evict. **lanzarse** *vr* rush, jump. **lanzamiento** *nm* ejection.

lapicero (lapi'θero) *nm* pencil-holder.

lápida ('lapiða) *nf* slab (of stone).

lápiz ('lapiθ) *nm* pencil.

lapso ('lapso) *nm* lapse.

largar (lar'gar) *vt* free, loosen. **largarse** *vr* run away.

largo ('largo) *adj* long. *nm* length. **a lo largo de** along, the length of. **dar largas** a delay.

laringe (la'ringe) *nf* larynx.

larva ('larβa) *nf* larva.

lascivo (las'θiβo) *adj* lascivious. **lascivia** *nf* lasciviousness.

lástima ('lastima) *nf* pity. **¡qué lástima!** what a pity! **lastimar** *vt* hurt.

lastre ('lastre) *nm* ballast.

lata ('lata) *nf* 1 tin, can. 2 *inf* nuisance.

latente (la'tente) *adj* latent.

lateral (late'ral) *adj* lateral.

látigo ('latigo) *nm* whip. **latigazo** *nm* whiplash.

latín (la'tin) *nm* Latin.

latir (la'tir) *vi* (of the heart) beat. **latido** *nm* heartbeat.

latitud (lati'tuð) nf 1 breadth. 2 geog latitude.

latón (la'ton) nm brass.

latoso (la'toso) adj inf annoying.

latrocinio (latro'θinjo) nm theft.

laúd (la'uð) nm lute.

laudable (lau'ðaβle) adj praiseworthy.

laurel (lau'rel) nm 1 bay tree. 2 bayleaf. 3 laurel, chaplet.

lava ('laβa) nf lava.

lavabo (la'βaβo) nm 1 washbasin. 2 toilet.

lavar (la'βar) vt wash, clean. **lavadero** nm laundry (place). **lavadora** nf washing machine.

laxante (lak'sante) nm laxative.

lazo ('laθo) nm 1 loop, lasso. 2 bootlace.

leal (le'al) adj loyal. **lealdad** nf loyalty.

lebrel (le'βrel) nm greyhound.

lección (lek'θjon) nf lesson.

lector (lek'tor) nm 1 reader. 2 lecturer. **lectura** nf reading matter.

leche ('letʃe) nf milk. **lechería** nf dairy. **lechero** nm milkman.

lecho ('letʃo) nm bed.

lechón (le'tʃon) nm suckling pig.

lechuga (le'tʃuɣa) nf lettuce.

lechuza (le'tʃuθa) nf owl.

leer* (le'er) vt read.

legación (lega'θjon) nf legation. **legado** nm delegate.

legal (le'gal) adj lawful. **legalizar** vt legalize, authenticate. **legalización** nf legalization, authentication.

legar (le'gar) vt bequeath. **legado** nm bequest, legacy.

legendario (lexen'darjo) adj legendary.

legión (le'xjon) nf legion.

legislar (lexis'lar) vi legislate. **legislación** nf legislation.

legitimar (lexiti'mar) vt 1 prove, justify. 2 legitimize. **legítimo** adj legitimate, real.

lego ('lego) adj lay. nm layman.

legua ('legwa) nf league.

legumbre (le'gumbre) nf vegetable.

lejanía (lexa'nia) nf distance, far-away place. **lejano** adj far-away.

lejía (le'xia) nf bleach.

lejos ('lexos) adv far away.

lema ('lema) nm motto.

lengua ('lengwa) nf 1 tongue. 2 language. **soltar la lengua** inf be indiscreet.

lenguado (len'gwaðo) nm sole (fish).

lenguaje (len'gwaxe) nm language.

lengüeta (len'gweta) nf tongue of a shoe, tab.

lenidad (leni'ðað) nf lenience, mildness.

lente ('lente) nm lens. **lentes de contacto** contact lenses.

lenteja (len'texa) nf lentil.

lentitud (lenti'tuð) nf slowness. **lento** adj sluggish.

leña ('leɲa) nf firewood. **leñador** nm woodcutter.

león (le'on) nm lion.

lepra ('lepra) nf leprosy. **leproso** adj leprous. nm leper.

lesión (le'sjon) nf injury. **lesionar** vt injure.

letanía (leta'nia) nf 1 litany. 2 sl interminable list.

letargo (le'targo) nm lethargy.

letra ('letra) nf 1 letter of the alphabet. 2 handwriting, script. 3 lyrics. 4 comm draft. 5 pl cap literature, Arts. **letras de molde** block letters.

leva ('leβa) nf tech spoke.

levadizo (leβa'ðiθo) adj able to be raised. **puente levadizo** nm drawbridge.

levadura (leβa'ðura) nf yeast.

levantar (leβan'tar) vt raise, set up. **levantarse** vr 1 stand up, get up. 2 rebel. **levantamiento** nm revolt.

leve ('leβe) adj slight.

léxico ('leksiko) adj lexical. nm 1 vocabulary. 2 lexicon, dictionary.

ley (lej) nf law.

leyó (le'jo) v see **leer**.

leyenda (le'jenda) nf legend.

liar (ljar) vt bind, tie up.

libélula (li'βelula) nf dragonfly.

liberal (liβe'ral) adj generous. adj, n liberal. **liberalidad** nf generosity. **liberalismo** nm liberalism. **liberalizar** vt liberalize.

libertar (liβer'tar) vt liberate, free. **libertad** nf liberty, freedom. **libertador** nm liberator.

libertinaje (liβerti'naxe) nm licentiousness. **libertino** nm libertine.

libra ('libra) nf pound. **libra esterlina** pound sterling.

librar (li'βrar) vt 1 free, exempt. 2 expedite, draw (letters of exchange, etc.). **libranza** nf draft, bill of exchange.

libre ('libre) adj free.

librería (liβre'ria) nf 1 bookshop. 2 bookshelf. **librero** nm bookseller.

libreta (li'βreta) nf 1 notebook. 2 cashbook.

libro ('liβro) nm book.

licenciar (liθen'θjar) vt license. **licenciarse** vr

graduate. **licencia** *nf* 1 licence. 2 *mil* leave. **licenciado** *adj, nm* graduate.

licencioso (liθen'θjoso) *adj* dissolute.

lícito ('liθito) *adj* authorized.

licor (li'kor) *nm* 1 liquor. 2 liqueur.

líder ('liðer) *nm* leader.

lidiar (li'ðjar) *vi* fight (bulls). **lidia** *nf* bullfight. **lidiador** *nm* bullfighter.

liebre ('ljeβre) *nf* hare.

lienzo ('ljenθo) *nm* linen, canvas.

liga ('liga) *nf* 1 garter. 2 alloy. 3 league.

ligamento (liga'mento) *nm* ligament.

ligar (li'gar) *vt,vi* unite, bind together. **ligadura** *nf* bond. **ligazón** *nm* bond, tie-beam.

ligereza (lixe'reθa) *nf* 1 lightness, agility. 2 flippant remark. **ligero** *adj* 1 light, agile. 2 slight, unimportant.

lija ('lixa) *nf* sandpaper.

lila ('lila) *nf* lilac.

limar (li'mar) *vt* file, sand. **lima** *nf* 1 file. 2 polishing, filing.

limitar (limi'tar) *vt* limit. **limitación** *nf* limitation. **límite** *nm* limit, boundary.

limón (li'mon) *nm* lemon. **limonada** *nf* lemonade. **limonero** *nm* lemon tree.

limosna (li'mosna) *nf* alms.

limpiabotas (limpja'βotas) *nm invar* bootblack.

limpiar (lim'pjar) *vt* clean. **limpieza** *nf* 1 cleaning. 2 cleanness. **limpio** *adj* clean.

linaje (li'naxe) *nm* lineage.

linaza (li'naθa) *nf* linseed.

lince ('linθe) *nm* lynx.

lindar (lin'dar) *vi* adjoin. **lindero** *adj* adjoining. *nm* boundary.

lindo ('lindo) *adj* pretty. **lindeza** *nf* prettiness.

línea ('linea) *nf* line. **lineal** *adj* linear.

lingüista (lin'gwista) *nm* linguist. **lingüística** *nf* linguistics.

lino ('lino) *nm* linen.

linóleo (li'noleo) *nm* linoleum.

linterna (lin'terna) *nf* torch.

lío ('lio) *nm* 1 parcel. 2 fuss, trouble.

liquidar (liki'ðar) *vt* 1 *comm* liquidate, settle up. 2 *sci* liquify. **liquidación** *nf* 1 liquidation. 2 clearance sale.

líquido ('likido) *nm* liquid. **líquido imponible** net taxable amount. ~*adj* 1 liquid. 2 *comm* net. **liquidez** *nf* fluidity.

lira ('lira) *nf* 1 lyre. 2 *lit* type of verse, stanza.

lírica ('lirika) *nf* lyric poetry. **lírico** *adj* lyric. *nm* lyric poet.

lirio ('lirjo) *nm* iris.

liso ('liso) *adj* smooth.

lisonjear (lisonxe'ar) *vt* flatter. **lisonja** *nf* flattery. **lisonjero** *adj* flattering.

lista ('lista) *nf* list.

listo ('listo) *adj* 1 ready. 2 *inf* clever.

litera (li'tera) *nf* 1 berth. 2 bunk, litter.

literato (lite'rato) *adj* well-read. *nm* man of letters. **literatura** *nf* literature.

litigar (liti'gar) *vt,vi* dispute (in law), litigate. **litigio** *nm* lawsuit.

litografía (litogra'fia) *nf* lithograph.

litoral (lito'ral) *adj* coastal. *nm* coast.

litro ('litro) *nm* litre.

liturgia (litur'xia) *nf* liturgy.

liviano (li'βjano) *adj* 1 slight, trivial. 2 lewd. **liviandad** *nf* triviality, frivolity.

lo (lo) *def art* the. *pron 3rd pers s* 1 him, it. 2 that, what.

loable (lo'aβle) *adj* praiseworthy.

lobo ('loβo) *nm* wolf.

lóbrego ('loβrego) *adj* gloomy.

lóbulo ('loβulo) *nm* lobe.

local (lo'kal) *adj* local. *nm* place, locale.

localizar (lokali'θar) *vt* locate.

loción (lo'θjon) *nf* lotion.

loco ('loko) *adj* mad. *nm* madman.

locomoción (lokomo'θjon) *nf* locomotion. **locomotora** *nf* locomotive.

locuaz (lo'kwaθ) *adj* talkative.

locura (lo'kura) *nf* madness.

locutor (lo'kutor) *nm* 1 radio announcer, commentator. 2 news reader.

lodo ('loðo) *nm* mud.

lógica ('loxika) *nf* logic. **lógico** *adj* logical.

lograr (lo'grar) *vt* 1 obtain. 2 perfect, achieve. **logro** *nm* 1 success, achievement. 2 gain, usury.

loma ('loma) *nf* hill.

lombriz (lom'briθ) *nf* earthworm.

lomo ('lomo) *nm* 1 back (of an animal). 2 loin (of meat).

lona ('lona) *nf* canvas, sailcloth.

Londres ('londres) *nm* London.

longaniza (longa'niθa) *nf* pork sausage.

longitud (lonxi'tuð) *nf* longitude. **longitud de onda** wavelength.

lonja ('lonxa) *nf* 1 slice (of food). 2 *comm* market.

loro ('loro) *nm* parrot.

lote ('lote) *nm comm* lot. **lotería** *nf* lottery. **lotero** *nm* lottery-ticket seller.

loza ('loθa) *nf* crockery.

lozano (lo'θano) *adj* 1 radiant, healthy. 2 (of greenery) lush. 3 proud.

lubrificar (luβrifiˈkar) vt lubricate. **lubrificante** adj, nm lubricant.

lucidez (luθiˈðeθ) nf lucidity, brightness. **lúcido** adj lucid, clear, shining.

luciérnaga (luˈθjernaɣa) nf glow-worm.

lucir (luˈθir) vi shine, be distinguished. vt show off.

lucro (ˈlukro) nm profit.

luchar (luˈtʃar) vi struggle. **lucha** nf struggle.

luego (ˈlweɣo) adv then, later. **luego que** conj as soon as. **desde luego** of course. **hasta luego** goodbye.

lugar (luˈɣar) nm 1 place. 2 occasion, opportunity.

lúgubre (ˈluɣuβre) adj lugubrious.

lujo (ˈluxo) nm luxury. **lujoso** adj luxurious.

lujuria (luˈxurja) nf lust. **lujurioso** adj lecherous.

lumbre (ˈlumbre) nf light, flame. **lumbrera** nf 1 luminary. 2 tech vent. 3 skylight. 4 bright and learned person.

luminoso (lumiˈnoso) adj bright.

luna (ˈluna) nf moon. **luna de miel** honeymoon.

lunes (ˈlunes) nm Monday.

lupa (ˈlupa) nf magnifying glass.

lustrar (lusˈtrar) vt polish. **lustre** nm 1 polish. 2 lustre.

luto (ˈluto) nm mourning.

Luxemburgo (luxemˈburɣo) nm Luxemburg.

luz (luθ) nf light. **a todas luces** at any rate.

LL

llaga (ˈʎaɣa) nf ulcer.

llama (ˈʎama) nf flame.

llamar (ʎaˈmar) vt 1 call. 2 name. **llamar la atención** attract the attention. **llamarse** vr be called, be named. **llamada** nf call, telephone call.

llamear (ʎameˈar) vi flame, blaze.

llana (ˈʎana) nf trowel.

llano (ˈʎano) adj 1 flat. 2 plain. nm plain.

llanta (ˈʎanta) nf tyre.

llanto (ˈʎanto) nm lament, weeping.

llanura (ʎaˈnura) nf plain.

llave (ˈʎaβe) nf 1 key. 2 spanner.

llegar (ʎeˈɣar) vi arrive, reach. **llegar a** end up at.

llenar (ʎeˈnar) vt fill up. **lleno** adj full.

llevar (ʎeˈβar) vt 1 take. 2 wear, bear. 3 spend, pass (time, life, etc.) **llevarse** vr take away. **llevarse bien** get on well together.

llorar (ʎoˈrar) vi weep, cry. vt mourn. **llorón** adj weeping. nm cry-baby.

llover (ʎoˈβer) vi rain.

lloviznar (ʎoβiθˈnar) vi drizzle. **llovizna** nf drizzle.

lluvia (ˈʎuβja) nf 1 rain. 2 shower. **lluvioso** adj rainy, wet.

M

macabro (maˈkaβro) adj macabre.

macarrón (makarˈron) nm 1 macaroon. 2 pl macaroni.

maceta (maˈθeta) nf flowerpot.

macilento (maθiˈlento) adj 1 faded. 2 lean, gaunt.

macis (maˈθis) nf invar cul mace.

macizo (maˈθiθo) adj massive, solid, stout. nm 1 mass, clump. 2 flowerbed.

machacar (matʃaˈkar) vt crush, pound, grind. vi harp on a matter, go on about something.

machete (maˈtʃete) nm 1 cutlass. 2 large knife.

macho (ˈmatʃo) adj 1 male, masculine. 2 strong. nm 1 male. 2 inf he-man. 3 mule. 4 sledgehammer.

madeja (maˈðexa) nf 1 skein, hank. 2 mop of hair.

madera[1] (maˈðera) nm Madeira wine.

madera[2] (maˈðera) nf 1 wood, timber. 2 disposition, aptitude. **maderaje** nm wood(work). **maderero** nm 1 timber merchant. 2 carpenter. **madero** nm beam, log.

madrastra (maˈðrastra) nf stepmother.

madre (maðre) nf mother. **madre adoptiva** foster mother. **madre política** mother-in-law.

madreselva (maðresˈelβa) nf honeysuckle.

Madrid (maˈðrið) nm Madrid. **madrileño** adj of Madrid. nm native or inhabitant of Madrid.

madriguera (maðriˈɣera) nf den, burrow.

madrina (maˈðrina) nf 1 godmother. 2 protectress. **madrina de boda** bridesmaid.

madrugar (maðruˈɣar) vi get up early. **madrugada** nf early morning, dawn.

madurar (maðuˈrar) vt,vi ripen, mature. **madurez** nf ripeness, maturity. **maduro** adj ripe, mature, mellow.

maestría (maesˈtria) nf mastery, skill. **maestro** adj 1 masterly, skilled. 2 main, master. nm master, teacher. **magistral** adj masterly.

magia (ˈmaxia) nf magic. **mágico** adj magic(al). nm magician.

magistrado (maxisˈtraðo) nm magistrate.

magnánimo (mag'nanimo) adj magnanimous.

magnético (mag'netiko) adj magnetic.

magnetofón (magneto'fon) nm also **magnetófono** tape recorder.

magnífico (mag'nifiko) adj magnificent.

magnitud (magni'tuð) nf size, magnitude.

mago ('mago) nm magician, wizard.

magro ('magro) adj 1 thin, lean. 2 (of land) poor.

magullar (magu'ʎar) vt bruise, damage, mangle. **magulladura** nf bruise.

maíz (ma'iθ) nm maize.

majadero (maxa'ðero) adj silly, boring. nm 1 bore. 2 pestle.

majar (ma'xar) vt 1 pound, crush. 2 bother.

majestad (maxes'taθ) nf majesty. **majestuoso** adj majestic, stately.

majo ('maxo) adj smart, dashing. nm 1 dandy, fop. **maja** nf belle.

mal (mal) adj see **malo**. adv badly, wrongly, poorly. nm 1 evil, wrong. 2 illness, harm, misfortune. **de mal en peor** from bad to worse. **echar a mal** 1 despise. 2 waste. **llevar a mal** take offence at. **mal que bien** rightly or wrongly, anyhow. **menos mal que** luckily, a good job that.

malaconsejado (malakonse'xaðo) adj unwise, ill-advised.

malbaratar (malbara'tar) vt 1 sell off cheaply. 2 squander.

malcontento (malkon'tento) adj discontented, hard to please. nm malcontent.

malcriado (malkri'aðo) adj bad-mannered, ill-bred.

maldad (mal'daθ) nf evil, act of wickedness.

maldecir* (malde'θir) vt curse. vi slander. **maldición** nf curse. **maldito** adj damned, accursed.

maleficio (male'fiθjo) nm curse, spell.

maleta (ma'leta) nf 1 (suit)case. 2 boot of a car. **hacer la maleta** pack.

malévolo (ma'leβolo) adj 1 malicious, spiteful. 2 malignant. **malevolencia** nf malevolence, ill-will, spite.

maleza (ma'leθa) nf scrub, thicket.

malgastar (malgas'tar) vt waste, squander. **malgastador** nm, adj spendthrift.

malhechor (male'tʃor) nm wrongdoer, criminal. **malhecho** nm misdeed.

malhumorado (malumo'raðo) adj ill-tempered, cross, surly.

malicia (ma'liθja) nf malice, naughtiness, wickedness. **malicioso** adj spiteful, mischievous, wicked.

malignidad (maligni'ðað) nf evil, malice, malignancy. **maligno** adj evil, harmful.

malintencionado (malintenθjo'naðo) adj hostile, ill-disposed.

malo ('malo) adj also **mal** 1 bad, evil. 2 obnoxious. 3 cunning. **estar malo** be ill.

malograr (malo'grar) vt spoil, waste. **malograrse** vr fail, come to naught. **malogrado** adj unlucky. **malogro** nm failure, untimely end.

malsano (mal'sano) adj 1 unhealthy. 2 sick. 3 insanitary.

malta ('malta) nf malt.

Malta ('malta) nf Malta. **maltés,** adj,n Maltese. nm Maltese (language).

maltratar (maltra'tar) vt ill-treat, abuse, damage. **maltrato** nm ill-treatment, abuse.

malva ('malβa) nf 1 mallow. 2 marshmallow.

malvado (mal'βaðo) adj wicked, evil. nm villain.

malla ('maʎa) nf 1 mesh, net(work). 2 coat of mail. **hacer malla** knit.

Mallorca (ma'ʎorka) nf Majorca. **mallorquín** adj,n Majorcan.

mamá (ma'ma) nf also **mama** mummy, mother.

mamar (ma'mar) vt 1 suck. 2 absorb, acquire. 3 achieve. **mamarse** vr inf get drunk.

mamífero (ma'mifero) adj,nm mammal.

mampostería (mamposte'ria) nf masonry.

manada (ma'naða) nf 1 herd, flock, pack. 2 crowd. 3 handful.

manantial (manan'tial) nm spring, fountain, source, origin.

manar (ma'nar) vi run, flow, abound in.

mancebo (man'θeβo) nm 1 youth. 2 bachelor. 3 shop assistant.

manco ('manko) adj 1 one-armed, one-handed. 2 armless. 3 maimed. nm cripple, one-armed person.

mancomunar (mankomu'nar) vt unite, combine. **mancomunidad** nf union, association, commonwealth.

manchar (man'tʃar) vt stain, make dirty, mark. **mancha** nf spot, mark, blemish, bruise.

mandar (man'dar) vt 1 order, command. 2 send. vi give orders. **mandamiento** nm 1 order, warrant. 2 rel commandment.

mandatario (manda'tarjo) nm 1 agent. 2 attorney. 3 leader. **mandato** nm order, mandate, writ. **mandato internacional** international money order.

mandíbula (man'diβula) nf jaw.

mando ('mando) nm 1 command. 2 authority.

manejar (mane'xar) vt handle, operate, manage. **manejarse** vr manage. **manejable** adj manageable. **manejo** (man'exo) nm 1 handling, operation. 2 shrewdness. 3 intrigue.

manera (ma'nera) nf 1 way, manner, mode. 2 kind, type. 3 fashion, style. **de ninguna manera** by no means, certainly not. **de todas maneras** at any rate.

manga ('manga) nf 1 sleeve. 2 hose, spout. **tener manga ancha** be easygoing.

mango[1] ('mango) nm mango (tree).

mango[2] ('mango) nm handle, shaft, stick.

manguera (man'gera) nf hose, tube.

manía (ma'nia) nf 1 mania, rage. 2 whim, fad, oddity.

maníaco (ma'niako) adj maniac(al). nm maniac.

maniatar (manja'tar) vt handcuff, manacle.

manicomio (mani'komjo) nm lunatic asylum.

manifestar (ie) (manifes'tar) vt 1 show, demonstrate. 2 declare. 3 expose.

manifiesto (mani'fjesto) adj manifest, obvious. nm pol manifesto.

maniobrar (manio'βrar) vt handle, operate. vt,vi manoeuvre. **maniobra** nf handling, manoeuvre, move.

manipular (manipu'lar) vt manipulate.

maniquí (mani'ki) nm 1 mannequin, model. 2 puppet.

manivela (mani'βela) nf mot crank.

mano ('mano) nf 1 hand. 2 paw. 3 game hand, round, turn. **a mano** by hand. **a (la) mano** at hand, handy. **de segunda mano** second hand. **coger con las manos en la masa** catch red-handed. **darse las manos** to shake hands.

manojo (ma'noxo) nm handful, bunch.

manosear (manose'ar) vt 1 handle. 2 paw. 3 fondle.

mansión (mansi'on) nf mansion.

manso ('manso) adj 1 gentle, meek, mild. 2 tame. **mansedumbre** nf 1 gentleness. 2 tameness.

manta ('manta) nf 1 blanket. 2 shawl. 3 rug.

manteca (man'teka) nf 1 lard. 2 fat. 3 butter.

mantecado (mante'kaðo) nm 1 ice-cream. 2 shortbread, type of biscuit.

mantel ('mantel) nm tablecloth.

mantener* (mante'ner) vt 1 hold. 2 maintain. 3 defend. **mantenimiento** nm maintenance, upkeep.

mantequera (mante'kera) nf 1 churn. 2 butter dish. **mantequilla** nf butter.

mantilla (man'tiʎa) nf mantilla, shawl.

manto ('manto) nm cloak. **mantón** nm shawl.

manual (manu'al) adj manual. nm manual, handbook.

manubrio (ma'nubrio) nm 1 handle, crank, winch. 2 barrel organ.

manufactura (manufak'tura) nf 1 manufacture. 2 factory. **manufacturar** vt manufacture.

manuscrito (manus'krito) nm manuscript.

manzana (man'θana) nf 1 apple. 2 block of flats. **manzano** nm apple tree. **manzanilla** nf 1 camomile (tea). 2 type of dry sherry.

maña ('maɲa) nf 1 skill. 2 ingenuity. 3 trick, ruse, vice.

mañana (ma'ɲana) nf morning. adv tomorrow. **mañana por la mañana** tomorrow morning. **pasado mañana** the day after tomorrow

mañoso (ma'ɲoso) adj clever, skilful, crafty.

mapa ('mapa) nm 1 map. 2 chart.

máquina ('makina) nf 1 machine. 2 locomotive. 3 edifice. 4 scheme. **máquina de escribir** typewriter. **máquina de fotografiar** camera.

maquinación (makina'θjon) nf machination, scheme, plotting. **maquinal** adj automatic. **maquinar** vt,vi plot.

mar (mar) nm,f sea, ocean.

maraña (ma'raɲa) nf 1 thicket, tangle. 2 mess.

maravillar (maraβi'ʎar) vt wonder, marvel. **maravilla** nf 1 wonder, marvel. 2 marigold. **maravilloso** adj wonderful, marvellous.

marcar (mar'kar) vt 1 mark, show. 2 dial. vt,vi sport score. **marca** nf mark, make, brand.

marcial (marθi'al) adj 1 martial. 2 military.

marco ('marko) nm 1 frame, framework. 2 setting. 3 mark (German coin).

marchar (mar'tʃar) vi 1 go, move. 2 work, function. 3 march. **marcharse** vr go away, leave. **marcha** nf 1 march, progress, course. 2 mot gear. **marcha atrás** reverse gear. **poner en marcha** mot start.

marchitar (martʃi'tar) vt,vi wither, fade, shrivel. **marchito** adj faded, shrunken.

marea (ma'rea) nf tide.

marearse (mare'arse) vr 1 feel (sea) sick. 2 be sick. **mareado** adj (sea) sick, dizzy. **mareo** nm 1 sickness, nausea. 2 bore, nuisance.

marfil (mar'fil) nm ivory.

margarina (marga'rina) nf margarine.

margarita (marga'rita) nf 1 daisy. 2 pearl.

margen ('marxen) nm 1 border, edge, margin. 2 space. 3 occasion, motive. 4 comm profit. 5 bank (of a river).

marica (ma'rika) *nf* magpie. *nm inf* sissy. **maricón** *nm sl* homosexual.

marido (ma'riðo) *nm* husband.

marina (ma'rina) *nf* 1 navy. 2 seamanship. 3 coast. **marinero** *adj* seafaring, seaworthy, seamanlike. *nm* sailor, mariner. **marino** *adj* marine. *nm* sailor, seaman.

mariposa (mari'posa) *nf* butterfly. **mariposa nocturna** moth.

mariscal (maris'kal) *nm* 1 marshal. 2 major general.

mariscos (ma'riskos) *nm pl* shellfish, seafood.

marítimo (ma'ritimo) *adj* maritime.

marmita (mar'mita) *nf* stew-pot, casserole.

mármol ('marmol) *nm* marble.

marmóreo (mar'moreo) *adj* 1 marble. 2 stony.

marqués (mar'kes) *nm* marquis. **marquesa** *nf* marchioness.

marrano (mar'rano) *adj* filthy, dirty. *nm* pig, boar.

marrón (mar'ron) *adj* chestnut brown, maroon. *nm* 1 chestnut (colour). 2 marron glacé.

Marruecos (marru'ekos) *nm* Morocco. **marroquí** *adj,n* Moroccan.

martes ('martes) *nm invar* Tuesday. **martes de carnaval** Shrove Tuesday.

martillar (marti'ʎar) *vt* hammer **martillo** *nm* hammer.

martín (mar'tin) *nm* **martín pescador** kingfisher.

martinete (marti'nete) *nm* 1 drop-hammer. 2 pile-driver.

mártir ('martir) *nm,f* martyr. **martirio** *nm* martyrdom.

marzo ('marθo) *nm* March.

mas (mas) *conj* but.

más (mas) *adj invar* more. *adv* 1 more. 2 most. 3 besides. *conj* and, plus.

masa ('masa) *nf* 1 dough. 2 mortar. 3 mass, volume.

masaje (ma'saxe) *nm* massage. **masajista** *nm,f* masseur, masseuse.

mascar (mas'kar) *vt,vi* 1 chew. 2 *inf* mumble.

máscara ('maskara) *nf* mask, disguise.

mascarada (maska'raða) *nf* 1 masquerade. 2 charade.

masculino (masku'lino) *adj* masculine, manly, male. *nm gram* masculine.

masón (ma'son) *nm* freemason. **masonería** *nf* freemasonry.

masticar (masti'kar) *vt* masticate, chew.

mástil ('mastil) *nm* 1 mast. 2 pole.

mastín (mas'tin) *nm* 1 mastiff. 2 bulldog.

mata ('mata) *nf* 1 bush, shrub. 2 *pl* thicket, grove. **mata de pelo** head or mop of hair.

matar (ma'tar) *vt,vi* 1 kill, slay, slaughter. 2 put out (light). 3 *game* mate. **matadero** *nm* slaughterhouse. **matador** *nm* bullfighter **matanza** *nf* slaughter, killing.

mate¹ ('mate) *nm* (check)mate.

mate² ('mate) *adj* dull, unpolished.

matemáticas (mate'matikas) *nf pl* mathematics. **matemático** *adj* mathematical. *nm* mathematician.

materia (ma'terja) *nf* 1 matter. 2 subject. **materia prima** raw material. **material** *adj* material. **materialismo** *nm* materialism.

maternal (mater'nal) *adj* maternal. **maternidad** *nf* motherhood, maternity. **materno** *adj* maternal.

matinal (mati'nal) *adj* morning.

matiz (ma'tiθ) *nm* shade, hue, tint, hint. **matizar** *vt* blend.

matorral (mator'ral) *nm* 1 thicket. 2 shrub.

matricular (matriku'lar) *vt,vi* register, enrol, license. **matrícula** *nf* 1 register. 2 registration, matriculation. 3 licence plate.

matrimonio (matri'monjo) *nm* 1 matrimony, marriage. 2 married couple. **cama matrimonial** or **de matrimonio** *nf* double bed.

matriz (ma'triθ) *nf* 1 womb. 2 mould, die. 3 matrix.

matrona (ma'trona) *nf* 1 matron. 2 midwife.

matutino (matu'tino) *adj* (early) morning.

matute (ma'tute) *nm* smuggling, contraband.

maullar (mau'ʎar) *vi* mew. **maullido** *nm* mewing.

máxima ('maksima) *nf* maxim.

máxime ('maksime) *adv* especially, all the more so.

máximo ('maksimo) *adj,nm* maximum.

maya¹ ('maja) *adj,n* Mayan. *nm* Mayan (language).

maya² ('maja) *nf* daisy.

mayo ('majo) *nm* May.

mayonesa (majo'nesa) *nf* mayonnaise.

mayor (ma'jor) *adj* 1 older, elder. 2 major, main. 3 larger. 4 adult. *nm* 1 chief, boss, elder. 2 *pl* elders (and betters). 3 *pl* ancestors. **al por mayor** wholesale. **mayoral** *nm* foreman, manager of a farm.

mayorazgo (majo'raθgo) *nm* 1 primogeniture. 2 entailed estate. 3 first born.

mayordomo (major'ðomo) *nm* butler, steward.

mayoría (majo'ria) *nf* 1 majority, greater part. 2 adult status.

mayorista (majo'rista) *nm,f* wholesaler.

mayúscula (ma'juskula) *nf* capital letter.

maza ('maθa) *nf* 1 mace, club. 2 hammer. 3 bat, stick.

mazapán (maθa'pan) *nm* marzipan.

mazmorra (maθ'morra) *nf* dungeon.

me (me) *pron 1st pers* s me, myself.

mear (me'ar) *vt,vi* urinate. **mearse** *vr* wet oneself.

mecánica (me'kanika) *nf* mechanics. **mecánico** *adj* mechanical. *nm* mechanic, fitter.

mecanógrafa (meka'nografa) *nf* typist. **mecanografía** *nf* typing.

mecer* (me'θer) *vt* swing, rock, sway. **mecedora** *nf* rocking chair.

mecha ('metʃa) *nf* wick, fuse. **mechero** *nm* 1 cigarette-lighter. 2 burner, jet.

medalla (me'daʎa) *nf* medal.

media ('meðja) *nf* 1 stocking. 2 *math* mean.

mediados (me'ðjaðos) *prep* **a mediados de** in the middle of.

mediano (me'ðjano) *adj* middling, average, mediocre.

medianoche (meðja'notʃe) *nf* midnight.

mediante (me'ðjante) *prep* by means of, through.

mediar (me'ðjar) *vi* 1 mediate, intervene. 2 be in the middle, lie between.

medicina (meði'θina) *nf* medicine.

médico ('meðiko) *adj* medical. *nm* doctor, physician.

medida (me'ðiða) *nf* 1 measure(ment). 2 step, move. 3 moderation. **a medida que** according as, in step with.

medio ('meðjo) *adj* 1 half. 2 middle. 3 medium, average. *adv* half, partly. *nm* 1 middle. 2 medium, mean. 3 way, method. 4 *pl* resources. 5 *pl* circumstances. **a medias** by halves, partly. **de por medio** in between, in the way. **por medio de** by means or way of.

mediocre (me'ðjokre) *adj* mediocre. **mediocridad** *nf* mediocrity.

mediodía (meðjo'ðia) *nm* 1 midday, noon. 2 south.

medir (i) (me'ðir) *vt,vi* 1 measure. 2 *lit* scan.

meditar (meði'tar) *vt* ponder, meditate on. *vi* think, meditate, muse. **meditabundo** *adj* pensive.

mediterráneo (meðiter'raneo) *adj* Mediterranean. **mar mediterráneo** *nm* Mediterranean Sea.

medrar (me'ðrar) *vi* thrive, prosper, grow. **medra** *nf* growth, prosperity.

medroso (me'ðroso) *adj* timid, fearful.

médula ('meðula) *nf* 1 *anat* marrow. 2 essence, substance.

medusa (me'ðusa) *nf* jellyfish.

Méjico ('mexiko) *nm* Mexico. **mejicano** *adj,n* Mexican.

mejilla (me'xiʎa) *nf* cheek.

mejor (me'xor) *adj* better, best. *adv* 1 better, best. 2 rather. **a lo mejor** probably, most likely, rather.

mejorar (mexo'rar) *vt* improve, better. **mejora** *nf* improvement.

melancolía (melanko'lia) *nf* melancholy. **melancólico** *adj* melancholy, sad, gloomy.

melena (me'lena) *nf* mane, long hair.

melindroso (melin'droso) *adj* squeamish, finicky.

melocotón (meloko'ton) *nm* peach.

melodía (melo'ðia) *nf* melody, tune. **melódico** *adj* melodic.

melón (me'lon) *nm* melon.

meloso (me'loso) *adj* 1 honeyed, sweet. 2 sickly.

mella ('meʎa) *nf* notch, dent.

mellizo (me'ʎiθo) *adj,n* twin.

membrana (mem'brana) *nf* membrane.

membrillo (mem'briʎo) *nm* quince.

memorable (memo'rable) *adj* memorable.

memoria (me'morja) *nf* 1 memory, remembrance. 2 report, record.

mencionar (menθjo'nar) *vt* mention, name.

mendigar (mendi'gar) *vt,vi* beg. **mendigo** *nm* beggar.

menear (mene'ar) *vt* 1 move, shake, wag, wave. 2 conduct (business).

menester (menes'ter) *nm* 1 duty. 2 occupation. 3 need, want. **ser menester** be necessary.

menguar (men'gwar) *vt,vi* lessen, decrease. **mengua** *nf* 1 decrease, decline. 2 loss. 3 discredit.

menguado (men'gwaðo) *adj* 1 decreased. 2 cowardly, wretched, miserable. *nm* coward, wretch.

menopausia (meno'pausja) *nf* menopause.

menor (me'nor) *adj* 1 minor. 2 younger. 3 lesser, least. *nm* minor. **al por menor** retail.

Menorca (me'norka) *nf* Minorca.

menos ('menos) *adj* less, fewer. *adv* except, minus, less. **al, a lo,** or **por lo menos** at least. **echar de menos** miss.

menoscabar (menoska'βar) *vt* 1 reduce. 2 impair. 3 discredit. **menoscabo** *nm* 1 reduction. 2 detriment.

menospreciar (menospre'θjar) vt 1 scorn, despise. 2 underrate. **menospreciable** adj contemptible. **menosprecio** nm 1 scorn. 2 undervaluation. 3 disrespect.

mensaje (men'saxe) nm message. **mensajero** nm messenger.

mensual (mensu'al) adj monthly.

menta ('menta) nf peppermint.

mental (men'tal) adj mental, intellectual. **mentalidad** nf mentality, mind.

mente ('mente) nf mind, intelligence.

mentecato (mente'kato) adj silly, stupid. nm fool.

mentir (ie) (men'tir) vi tell lies. **mentira** nf 1 lie. 2 deceitfulness.

menudear (menuðe'ar) vt repeat frequently. vi happen often.

menudencia (menu'ðenθia) nf 1 trifle, small thing. 2 pl odds and ends, minute detail. 3 pl offal.

menudo (me'nuðo) adj small, tiny, minute, petty. nm 1 small change. 2 pl offal, giblets. **a menudo** often.

meñique (me'ɲike) adj tiny. nm little finger.

meollo (me'oʎo) nm 1 anat marrow. 2 brains. 3 essence, core, gist.

mercado (mer'kaðo) nm market. **Mercado Común** Common Market. **mercader** nm merchant. **mercadería** nf merchandise, goods.

merced (mer'θed) nf 1 favour. 2 mercy.

mercurio (mer'kurjo) nm mercury.

merecer* (mere'θer) vt,vi deserve, be worthy of. **merecimiento** nm deserts, merit.

merendar (ie) (meren'dar) vt have for lunch. vi have lunch, a snack, a picnic.

merengue (me'renge) nm meringue.

meridiano (meri'ðjano) nm meridian. **meridional** adj southern.

merienda (me'rjenda) nf 1 afternoon tea. 2 snack. 3 picnic.

mérito ('merito) nm merit, worth, value.

merluza (mer'luθa) nf 1 hake. 2 sl drunkenness.

mermar (mer'mar) vt reduce, decrease. vi decrease. **merma** nf reduction, wastage, loss.

mermelada (merme'laða) nf jam, marmalade.

mero ('mero) adj mere, pure, simple.

merodear (meroðe'ar) vi maraud, pillage.

mes (mes) nm month.

mesa ('mesa) nf table, desk.

meseta (me'seta) nf 1 plateau. 2 arch landing.

mesón (me'son) nm inn, hostelry. **mesonero** nm innkeeper, landlord.

mestizo (mes'tiθo) adj,nm half-caste.

mesura (me'sura) nf 1 moderation. 2 gravity, dignity. 3 courtesy.

meta ('meta) nf 1 goal, aim. 2 sport goal. **guardameta** nm goalkeeper.

metafísica (meta'fisika) nf metaphysics.

metáfora (me'tafora) nf metaphor.

metal (me'tal) nm 1 metal. 2 mus brass. 3 timbre. **metálico** adj metallic, metal. nm coin, cash.

metalurgia (meta'lurxia) nf metallurgy.

meteoro (mete'oro) nm meteor. **meteórico** adj meteoric.

meter (me'ter) vt 1 put in, insert, introduce. 2 wager. **meterse** vr interfere in, meddle in. **meterse con** 1 quarrel with. 2 accost.

meticuloso (metiku'loso) adj meticulous.

método ('metoðo) nm method, manner. **metódico** adj methodical.

métrico ('metriko) adj metric(al).

metro ('metro) nm 1 metre. 2 ruler, tape. 3 underground railway.

metrópoli (me'tropoli) nf metropolis.

mezclar (meθ'klar) vt 1 mix, blend. 2 shuffle. **mezcla** nf mixture, blend.

mezcolanza (meθko'lanθa) nf jumble, hotchpotch.

mezquindad (meθkin'dað) nf meanness, pettiness. **mezquino** adj mean.

mezquita (meθ'kita) nf mosque.

mi (mi) poss pron 1st pers s my.

mí (mi) pron 1st pers s me, myself.

miaja ('mjaxa) nf crumb, bit.

mico ('miko) nm monkey.

micrófono (mi'krofono) nm 1 microphone. 2 mouthpiece.

microscopio (mikro'skopjo) nm microscope.

miedo (mi'eðo) nm fear. **tener miedo** be afraid. **miedoso** adj fearful, timid.

miel (mi'el) nf honey.

miembro (mi'embro) nm 1 limb. 2 member.

mientes (mientes) nf pl **¡ni por mientes!** not on your life! **parar mientes en** consider carefully.

mientras (mi'entras) conj while, as long as, whereas. adv meanwhile, meantime. **mientras tanto** meanwhile.

miércoles (mi'erkoles) nm Wednesday. **miércoles de ceniza** Ash Wednesday.

mies (mjes) nf 1 ripe corn. 2 pl cornfields.

miga ('miga) nf 1 crumb. 2 substance. **hacer buenas migas con** get on well with.

mil (mil) adj,nm thousand. **milésimo** adj thousandth. **miles de** masses of. **mil gracias** many thanks.

milagro (mi'lagro) nm miracle, wonder, marvel. **milagroso** adj miraculous.

milicia (mi'liθja) nf 1 militia. 2 military service.

militar (mili'tar) adj 1 military. 2 warlike. nm soldier. vi 1 serve as a soldier. 2 militate.

milla ('miʎa) nf mile.

millar (mi'ʎar) nm thousand. **a millares** in thousands.

millón (mi'ʎon) nm million. **millonésimo** adj millionth. **millonario** nm millionaire.

mimar (mi'mar) vt spoil, pamper. **mimo** nm 1 petting. 2 mime.

mimbre ('mimbre) nm,f wicker.

minar (mi'nar) vt mine. **mina** nf mine, deposit, store.

mineral (mine'ral) adj,nm mineral. **minero** nm miner.

mínimo ('minimo) adj, nm minimum.

ministerio (minis'terjo) nm ministry, office.

ministro (mi'nistro) nm minister. **primer ministro** prime minister.

minoría (mino'ria) nf minority.

minucioso (minu'θjoso) adj 1 meticulous. 2 minute.

minúscula (mi'nuskula) nf small letter.

minuta (mi'nuta) nf 1 agenda, list. 2 menu.

mío ('mio) poss pron 1st pers s my, mine.

miope (mi'ope) adj shortsighted. **miopía** nf myopia.

mirar (mi'rar) vt 1 look. 2 consider. **mira** nf 1 sight. 2 intention. **con miras a** with a view to. **mirada** nf look, glance. **mirador** nm 1 viewpoint. 2 balcony. **miramiento** nm 1 courtesy. 2 caution.

mirlo ('mirlo) nm blackbird.

mirra ('mirra) nf myrrh.

misa ('misa) nf rel mass. **misa mayor** high mass.

miserable (mise'raβle) adj wretched, miserable. **miseria** nf poverty, wretchedness.

misericordia (miseri'korðja) nf pity, compassion, mercy.

misión (mi'sjon) nf mission.

mismo ('mismo) adj 1 same. 2 very. 3 self. **por lo mismo** for this reason. **aquí mismo** right here.

misterio (mis'terjo) nm 1 mystery, secret. 2 mystery play. **misterioso** adj mysterious.

místico ('mistiko) adj mystic(al). **misticismo** nm mysticism.

mitad (mi'taθ) nf 1 half. 2 middle.

mítico ('mitiko) adj mythical.

mitigar (miti'gar) vt mitigate, reduce.

mitin ('mitin) nm pol meeting.

mito ('mito) nm myth. **mitología** nf mythology.

mixto ('miksto) adj mixed.

mobiliario (moβi'ljarjo) nm furniture.

mocedad (moθe'ðað) nf 1 youth. 2 youthful prank.

moción (mo'θjon) nf 1 motion. 2 proposal.

moco ('moko) nm 1 mucus. 2 inf brat. **mocoso** adj snivelling.

mochila (mo'tʃila) nf rucksack, pack.

moda ('moða) nf fashion, style. **de moda** fashionable. **pasado de moda** out-dated.

modales (mo'ðales) nm pl manners.

modelo (mo'ðelo) nm model, pattern. nf fashion model.

moderar (moðe'rar) vt moderate, control. **moderado** adj moderate.

moderno (mo'ðerno) adj modern.

modestia (mo'ðestja) nf modesty. **modesto** adj modest.

módico ('moðiko) adj moderate, reasonable (price).

modificar (moðifi'kar) vt modify.

modismo (mo'ðismo) nm idiom, phrase.

modista (mo'ðista) nf dressmaker.

modo ('moðo) nm 1 way, manner, method. 2 mood. 3 mus mode. **de modo que** so that. **de todos modos** in any case.

modorra (mo'ðorra) nf drowsiness.

modular (moðu'lar) vt modulate.

mofar (mo'far) vi mock, jeer. **mofarse** vr mock, sneer at. **mofa** nf mockery.

mohín (mo'in) nm grimace, pout. **mohino** adj gloomy, sulky, peevish.

moho ('moo) nm 1 rust. 2 mould, mildew. **mohoso** adj rusty, mouldy.

mojar (mo'xar) vt wet, moisten, drench.

mojigato (moxi'gato) adj hypocritical, prudish.

mojón (mo'xon) nm landmark.

moldar (mol'dar) vt mould. **molde** nm mould.

molécula (mo'lekula) nf molecule.

moler (ue) (mo'ler) vt 1 grind, crush, pound. 2 weary, bore.

molestar (moles'tar) vt annoy, upset. **molestarse** vr put oneself out. **molestia** nf trouble, bother. **molesto** adj 1 annoying. 2 upset.

molinero (moli'nero) nm miller. **molino** nm mill, grinder.

molusco

molusco (mo'lusko) *nm* mollusc.
mollera (mo'ʎera) *nf* 1 crown of the head. 2 *inf* brains. **cerrado de mollera** dim-witted, dense.
momentáneo (momen'taneo) *adj* momentary.
momento (mo'mento) *nm* 1 moment, instant. 2 momentum. 3 importance.
momia ('momja) *nf* mummy (corpse).
monarca (mo'narka) *nm* monarch. **monarquía** *nf* monarchy. **monárquico** *adj* monarchic(al), royalist.
monasterio (monas'terjo) *nm* monastery.
mondar (mon'dar) *vt* prune, trim, peel, clean.
moneda (mo'neða) *nf* 1 coin. 2 currency, money. **monedero** *nm* purse, wallet.
monitor (moni'tor) *nm* 1 monitor. 2 assistant (teacher). **monitorio** *adj* admonitory.
monja ('monxa) *nf* nun, sister. **monje** *nm* monk, friar.
mono¹ ('mono) *nm* monkey, ape.
mono² ('mono) *adj* pretty, lovely.
monólogo (mo'nologo) *nm* monologue.
monopolizar (monopoli'θar) *vt* monopolize. **monopolio** *nm* monopoly.
monosílabo (mono'silaβo) *adj* monosyllabic. *nm* monosyllable.
monstruo ('monstruo) *nm* monster. **monstruoso** *adj* monstrous.
monta ('monta) *nf* 1 mounting. 2 amount, value. **montacargas** *nm invar* service lift.
montaña (mon'taɲa) *nf* mountain. **montañés** *adj* mountain, highland. *nm* highlander. **montañismo** *nm* mountaineering. **montañoso** *adj* mountainous.
montar (mon'tar) *vt* 1 mount, ride. 2 set up, assemble. *vi* mount, ride.
monte ('monte) *nm* 1 mountain, hill. 2 woodland, scrub.
montera (mon'tera) *nf* 1 bullfighter's hat. 2 cloth cap. **montero** *nm* huntsman.
montón (mon'ton) *nm* heap, pile, mass.
monumento (monu'mento) *nm* monument, memorial.
moño ('moɲo) *nm* bun, topknot.
mora¹ ('mora) *nf* 1 blackberry. 2 mulberry.
mora² ('mora) *nf* 1 delay. 2 default.
morada (mo'raða) *nf* 1 dwelling, abode. 2 period of residence.
morado (mo'raðo) *adj* purple, violet. *nm* bruise.
moral (mo'ral) *adj* moral. *nf* morality. **moraleja** *nf* moral. **moralidad** *nf* morality.
morar (mo'rar) *vi* reside, dwell, stay.
mórbido ('morβiðo) *adj* 1 morbid. 2 diseased.

morboso (mor'βoso) *adj* morbid, unhealthy.
morcilla (mor'θiʎa) *nf* blood sausage, black pudding.
mordaz (mor'ðaθ) *adj* sarcastic, scathing.
mordaza (mor'ðaθa) *nf* gag, muzzle.
morder (ue) (mor'ðer) *vt,vi* bite, gnaw, eat away. **mordisco** *nm* bite.
moreno (mo'reno) *adj* 1 brown, swarthy. 2 dark-haired.
morera (mo'rera) *nf* mulberry tree.
morfina (mor'fina) *nf* morphine.
moribundo (mori'βundo) *adj* moribund.
morir* (mo'rir) *vi* 1 die. 2 fade. **morir de hambre** starve to death. **morirse por** be dying to, be keen on.
moro ('moro) *adj* Moorish. *nm* Moor.
moroso (mo'roso) *adj* slow, sluggish, tardy.
morral (mor'ral) *nm* 1 haversack. 2 game-bag.
morriña (mor'riɲa) *nf* homesickness.
mortaja (mor'taxa) *nf* shroud.
mortal (mor'tal) *adj* mortal. **mortalidad** *nf* mortality.
mortandad (mortan'dað) *nf* massacre, carnage.
mortero (mor'tero) *nm* mortar.
mortífero (mor'tifero) *adj* deadly, lethal.
mortificar (mortifi'kar) *vt* mortify.
mosca ('moska) *nf* fly.
moscardón (moskar'ðon) *nm* 1 blowfly. 2 hornet.
mosquete (mos'kete) *nm* musket. **mosquetero** *nm* musketeer.
mosquito (mos'kito) *nm* mosquito, gnat.
mostaza (mos'taθa) *nf* mustard.
mostrar (ue) (mos'trar) *vt* 1 show, point out, explain. 2 prove. **mostrador** *nm* counter, bar.
mote ('mote) *nm* nickname.
motín (mo'tin) *nm* revolt, uprising.
motivar (moti'βar) *vt* cause, give rise to. **motivo** *nm* motive, reason, cause. **con motivo de** owing to.
motor (mo'tor) *nm* motor, engine. **motorista** *nm* motorcyclist. **motorizado** *adj* motorized.
mover (ue) (mo'βer) *vt,vi* move. **moverse** *vr* stir, get a move on.
móvil ('moβil) *adj* mobile. *nm* motive.
movilizar (moβili'θar) *vt* mobilize. **movilización** *nf* mobilization.
movimiento (moβi'mjento) *nm* movement, motion, activity.
moza ('moθa) *nf* 1 girl. 2 servant, maid. **mozo** *nm* 1 youth. 2 waiter. 3 porter.
mucosidad (mukosi'ðað) *nf* mucus. **mucoso** *adj* mucous.

muchacha (mu'tʃatʃa) nf 1 girl. 2 maid, servant. **muchacho** nm boy, lad.

muchedumbre (mutʃe'ðumbre) nf crowd, mass.

mucho ('mutʃo) adj much, a lot, great. adv much, a lot, a great deal. **con mucho** by far, easily.

mudar (mu'ðar) vt,vi change, alter. **mudarse** vr 1 move house. 2 change one's clothes. **mudanza** nf 1 change. 2 removal.

mudo ('muðo) adj dumb, mute. **mudez** nf dumbness.

mueble ('mweβle) nm piece of furniture.

mueca ('mweka) nf grimace.

muela ('mwela) nf molar, tooth.

muelle ('mweʎe) nm 1 tech spring, watch spring. 2 wharf, dock, pier, quay.

muérdago ('mwerðago) nm mistletoe.

muerte ('mwerte) nf 1 death. 2 murder. **estar a la muerte** be at death's door.

muerto ('mwerto) v see **morir**. adj dead, lifeless. nm corpse.

muestra ('mwestra) nf 1 sign, proof. 2 example, sample, pattern.

muevo ('mwevo) v see **mover**.

mugir (mu'xir) vi moo, bellow, roar. **mugido** nm roar, howl.

mujer (mu'xer) nf woman, wife.

mulo ('mulo) nm mule.

muleta (mu'leta) nf 1 crutch. 2 bullfighter's cape or its supporting stick.

multar (mul'tar) vt fine, penalize. **multa** nf fine, penalty.

múltiple ('multiple) adj 1 math complex, multiple. 2 pl numerous.

multiplicar (multipli'kar) vt multiply, increase.

multitud (multi'tuð) nf crowd, multitude.

mullir (mu'ʎir) vt fluff up, soften, loosen.

mundo ('mundo) nm world, earth. **todo el mundo** everybody. **mundial** adj world-wide, universal.

munición (muni'θjon) nf 1 ammunition. 2 stores, provisions.

municipal (muniθi'pal) adj municipal. **municipio** nm town, town council.

muñeca (mu'ɲeka) nf 1 doll, puppet. 2 wrist.

muralla (mu'raʎa) nf wall, rampart.

murciélago (mur'θjelago) nm zool bat.

murmullo (mur'muʎo) nm murmur, whispering, rustling.

murmurar (murmu'rar) vi 1 murmur, whisper. 2 gossip. 3 grumble. **murmuración** nf backbiting, gossip.

muro ('muro) nm external wall.

músculo ('muskulo) nm muscle. **muscular** adj muscular.

museo (mu'seo) nm museum, gallery.

musgo ('musgo) nm moss.

música ('musika) nf music. **musical** adj musical. **músico** nm musician, player.

muslo ('muslo) nm thigh.

mustio ('mustjo) adj 1 faded. 2 tired.

mutación (muta'θjon) nf change, mutation.

mutilar (muti'lar) vt 1 mutilate. 2 cripple. 3 spoil. **mutilado** nm disabled person.

mutual (mu'twal) adj mutual. **mutuo** adj mutual, joint.

muy ('muj) adv very, greatly, highly, most.

N

nabo ('nabo) nm turnip.

nácar ('nakar) nm mother-of-pearl, nacre.

nacer (na'θer) vi 1 be born. 2 begin, originate. **nacido** adj born. **naciente** adj rising, growing. **nacimiento** nm birth, nativity.

nación (na'θjon) nf nation. **nacional** adj 1 national. 2 native, domestic. nm native. **nacionalidad** nf nationality.

nada ('naða) nf nothing. adv not at all. **por nada** by no means.

nadar (na'ðar) vi swim. **nadador** nm swimmer.

nadie ('naðje) pron nobody, no one, none.

naipe ('naipe) nm playing card.

nalga ('nalga) nf buttock.

naranja (na'ranxa) nf orange.

narciso (nar'θiso) nm narcissus.

narcótico (nar'kotiko) adj narcotic. nm 1 narcotic, sleeping pill. 2 pl narcotic drugs. **narcotizar** vt drug.

nariz (na'riθ) nf, pl **narices** nose. **narizudo** adj big-nosed.

narrar (nar'rar) vt narrate, tell. **narración** nf narration.

nata ('nata) nf cream, curd.

natación (nata'θjon) nf swimming.

natal (na'tal) adj 1 natal. 2 native. **natalicio** adj,nm birthday. **natalidad** nf birth rate.

nativo (na'tiβo) adj,nm native. **natividad** nf nativity. **nato** adj 1 born. 2 natural.

natural (natu'ral) adj natural. nm,f 1 native. 2 inhabitant. **naturaleza** nf 1 nature. 2 naturalization.

naufragar (naufra'gar) vi be shipwrecked. **nau-**

fragio nm shipwreck. **náufrago** adj shipwrecked. nm a shipwrecked person.

náusea ('nausea) nf nausea.

náutico ('nautiko) adj nautical.

naval (na'βal) adj naval.

nave ('naβe) nf 1 ship. 2 arch nave.

navegar (naβe'gar) vt sail, navigate. **navegación** nf navigation, sailing. **navegador** nm also **navegante** navigator, voyager.

navío (na'βjo) nm ship.

neblina (ne'βlina) nf mist, fog.

necesario (neθe'sarjo) adj necessary. **necesidad** nf 1 necessity. 2 need, poverty. 3 pl hardships.

necesitar (neθesi'tar) vt need, require.

necio ('neθjo) adj 1 foolish. 2 stupid. 3 imprudent. **necedad** nf 1 foolishness. 2 stupidity. 3 nonsense.

nefasto (ne'fasto) adj unlucky, ill-fated.

negar (ie) (ne'gar) vt deny, refuse. **negación** nf 1 negation. 2 denial. **negativa** nf 1 negation. 2 denial, refusal. **negativo** adj 1 negative. 2 math minus. adj,nm phot negative.

negligencia (negli'xenθja) nf negligence. **negligente** adj negligent.

negociar (nego'θjar) vt negotiate, trade. **negociante** nm businessman. **negocio** nm business, transaction.

negro ('negro) adj 1 black. 2 Negro. nm Negro. **negroide** adj negroid. **negrura** nf blackness.

nene ('nene) nm baby.

nenúfar (ne'nufar) nm waterlily.

nervio ('nerβjo) nm 1 nerve. 2 anat tendon. **tener los nervios en punta** be on edge. **tener nervio** be brave. **nerviosidad** nf nervousness. **nervioso** adj nervous, edgy. **crisis nerviosa** nf nervous breakdown.

neto ('neto) adj 1 clear, neat. 2 comm net.

neumático (neu'matiko) adj pneumatic. nm tyre.

neurótico (neu'rotiko) adj,nm neurotic.

neutro ('neutro) adj 1 neutral. 2 neuter.

nevar (ie) (ne'βar) vi snow. **nevada** nf snowfall. **nevado** adj snow-covered.

nevera (ne'βera) nf refrigerator.

ni (ni) conj neither, nor.

nicho ('nitʃo) nm niche.

nido ('niðo) nm nest.

niebla ('njeβla) nf fog.

nieto ('njeto) nm 1 grandson. 2 pl grandchildren.

nieve (njeβe) nf snow.

nilón (ni'lon) nm nylon.

ninguno (nin'guno) adj, pron also **ningún** no, no-one, not any.

niña ('nina) nf 1 girl. 2 anat pupil. **niñez** nf childhood. **niño** adj 1 young. 2 childish. nm boy, child.

níquel ('nikel) nm nickel.

nítido ('nitiðo) adj bright, clear.

nitrógeno (ni'troxeno) nm nitrogen.

nivelar (niβe'lar) vt make level. **nivel** nm level.

no (no) adv no, not.

noble ('noβle) adj noble. nm nobleman. **nobleza** nf nobility.

noción (no'θjon) nf 1 notion, idea. 2 pl rudiments.

nocivo (no'θiβo) adj harmful.

nocturno (nok'turno) adj night, nocturnal. nm mus nocturne.

noche ('notʃe) nf night. **Nochebuena** nf Christmas Eve. **Nochevieja** nf New Year's Eve.

nogal (no'gal) nm walnut tree.

nómada ('nomaða) adj nomadic. nm,f nomad.

nombrar (nom'brar) vt 1 name. 2 nominate. 3 mention. **nombramiento** nm nomination, appointment. **nombre** nm 1 name. 2 noun. **nombre artístico** pseudonym. **nombre de pila** Christian name.

nómina ('nomina) nf 1 list. 2 comm payroll.

non (non) adj math odd. nm odd number.

nonagésimo (nona'xesimo) adj ninetieth.

nordeste (nor'ðeste) adj northeast. nm 1 northeast. 2 northeaster (wind).

noria ('norja) nf waterwheel.

norma ('norma) nf norm, rule. **normal** adj normal, regular. **normalidad** nf normality.

noroeste (noro'este) adj northwest. nm 1 northwest. 2 northwester (wind).

norte ('norte) adj,nm north.

Noruega (no'rwega) nf Norway. **noruego** adj 1 Norwegian. 2 Norse. nm 1 Norwegian (man). 2 Norseman. 3 Norwegian (language).

nos (nos) pron 1st pers pl us, ourselves.

nosotros (no'sotros) pron 1st pers pl 1 we. 2 us, ourselves.

nostalgia (nos'talxja) nf nostalgia. **nostálgico** adj 1 homesick. 2 nostalgic.

notar (no'tar) vt 1 note, notice, perceive. 2 note down. **nota** nf 1 note, memo. 2 comm account. 3 educ grade, marks. 4 mus note. **notable** adj notable.

notario (no'tarjo) nm notary. **notaría** nf notary's office.

noticiar (noti'θjar) vt notify. **noticiero** adj

containing news. *nm* newspaper. **noticia(s)** *nf (pl)* news, information.

notificar (notifi'kar) *vt* notify, inform.

notorio (no'torjo) *adj* notorious, well-known.

novato (no'βato) *adj* inexperienced. *nm* novice.

novedad (noβe'ðað) *nf* 1 newness. 2 novelty. 3 latest news or fashion.

novela (no'βela) *nf* novel. **novelesco** *adj* 1 fictional. 2 fantastic, unbelievable. **novelista** *nm,f* novelist.

noveno (no'βeno) *adj* ninth.

noventa (no'βenta) *adj* ninety.

novia ('noβja) *nf* 1 girlfriend, fiancée. 2 bride. **noviazgo** *nm* engagement, betrothal.

novicio (no'βiθjo) *nm* 1 beginner, novice. 2 *rel* novice.

noviembre (no'βjembre) *nm* November.

novilla (no'βiʎa) *nf* heifer. **novillada** *nf* bullfight for novice bullfighters and young bulls. **novillero** *nm* novice bullfighter. **novillo** *nm* bullock. **hacer novillos** play truant.

nube ('nuβe) *nf* cloud. **por las nubes** 1 astronomical (prices, figures, etc.). 2 (praise, etc.) to the skies. **estar en las nubes** be daydreaming.

nublado (nu'βlaðo) *adj* cloudy, overcast.

núcleo ('nukleo) *nm* 1 nucleus. 2 core. 3 *bot* kernel, stone.

nudillo (nu'ðiʎo) *nm* knuckle.

nudo ('nxðo) *nm* knot.

nuera ('nwera) *nf* daughter-in-law.

nuestro ('nwestro) *poss adj* our.

nueva ('nweβa) *nf* piece of news.

Nueva Zelanda ('nweβa θe'landa) *nf* New Zealand.

nueve ('nweβe) *adj,nm* nine.

nuez (nweθ) *nf bot* nut, walnut. **nuez de la garganta** Adam's Apple.

nulidad (nuli'ðað) *nf* nullity. **nulo** *adj* null, nil.

numerar (nume'rar) *vt* number. **numeral** *adj,nm* numeral.

número ('numero) *nm* 1 number. 2 quantity. 3 size. **numérico** *adj* numerical. **numeroso** *adj* numerous.

nunca ('nunka) *adv* 1 never. 2 ever. **¡nunca jamás!** not on your life! never! **más que nunca** more than ever.

nuncio ('nunθjo) *nm* nuncio.

nupcial (nup'θjal) *adj* nuptial. **nupcias** *nf pl* wedding.

nutria ('nutrja) *nf* otter.

nutrir (nu'trir) *vt* feed, nourish. **nutritivo** *adj* nutritious.

Ñ

ñaque ('nake) *nm* junk.

ñoño ('nono) *adj* 1 doddery. 2 characterless. 3 timid. **ñoñería** *nf also* **ñoñez** 1 senility. 2 lack of character. 3 shyness.

O

o (o) *conj* or. **o...o** either...or.

oasis (o'asis) *nm* oasis.

obcecar (oβθe'kar) *vt* blind, deceive. **obcecación** *nf* blindness, stubbornness.

obedecer* (oβeðe'θer) *vt,vi* obey.

obediencia (oβe'ðjenθja) *nf* obedience. **obediente** *adj* obedient.

obertura (oβer'tura) *nf* overture.

obesidad (oβesi'ðað) *nf* obesity. **obeso** *adj* obese.

obispo (o'βispo) *nm* bishop. **obispado** *nm* bishopric.

objetar (oβxe'tar) *vt,vi* object (to). **objeción** *nf* objection. **objetividad** *nf* objectivity. **objetivo** *adj, nm* objective. **objeto** *nm* object. **objetor** *nm* objector.

oblicuo (o'βlikwo) *adj* oblique.

obligar (oβli'gar) *vt* oblige, compel, force. **obligarse** *vr* agree, promise to do something. **obligación** *nf* obligation.

obrar (o'βrar) *vt* 1 work, operate. 2 make, construct, build. 3 put into practice. *vi* 1 work. 2 behave, act. **obra** *nf* work. **obra maestra** masterpiece. **obrero** *adj* working. *nm* workman.

obsceno (oβs'θeno) *adj* obscene. **obscenidad** *nf* obscenity.

obscurecer* (oβskure'θer) *vt also* **oscurecer** obscure, darken. *vi* grow dark. **obscuridad** *nf* obscurity, darkness. **obscuro** *adj* obscure, dark.

obsequiar (oβseki'ar) *vt* 1 shower with gifts. 2 give a present to. **obsequio** *nm* 1 gift. 2 courtesy. **obsequioso** *adj* attentive.

observar (oβser'βar) *vt* observe. **observación** *nf* observation. **observador** *nm* observer. **observancia** *nf* observance. **observante** *adj* observant, observing. **observatorio** *nm* observatory.

obsesión (oβse'sjon) *nf* obsession. **obsesionante** *adj* obsessive. **obseso** *adj* obsessed.

obstáculo (oβs'takulo) *nm* obstacle.

obstante (oβs'tante) *prep* in spite of. **no obstante** nevertheless, however.

obstar (oβs'tar) *vi* oppose, obstruct.

obstetricia (obste'triθja) *nf* obstetrics.

obstinarse (oβsti'narse) *vr* be obstinate, stand firm. **obstinación** *nf* obstinacy. **obstinado** *adj* obstinate.

obstruir (oβstru'ir) *vt* 1 obstruct. 2 seal up, stop up. **obstrucción** *nf* obstruction. **obstructivo** *adj* obstructive. **obstructor** *adj* obstructing.

obtener (oβte'ner) *vt* obtain.

obturar (oβtu'rar) *vt* plug, stop up. **obturador** *nm* 1 stopper. 2 *mot* choke.

obtuso (oβ'tuso) *adj* obtuse.

obvio ('oββjo) *adj* obvious.

oca ('oka) *nf* goose.

ocasión (oka'sjon) *nf* 1 occasion. 2 opportunity, chance. **ocasional** *adj* accidental.

ocasionar (okasjo'nar) *vt* 1 cause. 1 stir up, excite. 2 endanger.

ocaso (o'kaso) *nm* 1 sunset. 2 west. 3 decline.

occidental (okθiðen'tal) *adj* western, occidental. **occidente** *nm* west, occident.

océano (o'θeano) *nm* ocean.

ocio ('oθjo) *nm* 1 idleness. 2 leisure. **ociosidad** *nf* idleness. **ocioso** *adj* idle. *nm* idler.

ocre ('okre) *nm* ochre.

octágono (ok'tagono) *adj* octagonal. *nm* octagon.

octava (ok'taβa) *nf* octave.

octavo (ok'taβo) *adj* eighth.

octogésimo (okto'xesimo) *adj* eightieth.

octubre (ok'tuβre) *nm* October.

ocular (oku'lar) *adj* ocular. *nm* 1 lens. 2 eyepiece. **oculista** *nm,f* oculist.

ocultar (okul'tar) *vt* conceal. **ocultación** *nf* concealment. **ocultista** *adj,nm,f* occultist. **oculto** *adj* hidden, unknown.

ocupar (oku'par) *vt* occupy. **ocuparse con** be engaged in. **ocupación** *nf* occupation. **ocupado** *adj* occupied, busy. **ocupante** *adj* occupying. *nm* occupant.

ocurrir (okur'rir) *vi* occur. **ocurrencia** *nf* 1 occurrence. 2 witticism. 3 bright idea. **ocurrente** *adj* witty, clever.

ochenta (o'tʃenta) *adj,nm* eighty.

ocho ('otʃo) *adj,nm* eight.

odiar (o'ðjar) *vt* hate. **odio** *nm* hate. **odiosidad** *nf* odiousness. **odioso** *adj* odious, hateful. *nm* detestable person.

odorífero (oðo'rifero) *adj* odoriferous, fragrant.

oeste (o'este) *nm* 1 west. 2 westerly wind.

ofender (ofen'der) *vt* offend.

ofensa (o'fensa) *nf* offence, insult. **ofensiva** *nf* *mil* offensive. **ofensivo** *adj* offensive. **ofensor** *adj* offending. *nm* offender.

oferta (o'ferta) *nf* 1 offer. 2 *comm* supply.

oficial (ofi'θjal) *adj* official. *nm* officer, official.

oficina (ofi'θina) *nf* office.

oficio (o'fiθjo) *nm* job, work, duty.

oficioso (ofi'θjoso) *adj* 1 unofficial, informal. 2 helpful, attentive. 3 officious, intrusive.

ofrecer (ofre'θer) *vt* offer. **ofrecerse** *vr* volunteer, offer one's services. **¿qué se le ofrece?** what would you like? **ofrecimiento** *nm* offer.

ofrendar (ofren'dar) *vt* give, contribute. **ofrenda** *nf* offering, gift.

ofuscar (ofus'kar) *vt* blind, dazzle.

oída (o'iða) *nf* hearing. **oíble** *adj* audible. **oído** *nm* 1 ear. 2 hearing.

oigo (o'igo) *v* see **oír**.

oír (o'ir) *vt* hear.

ojal (o'xal) *nm* buttonhole.

ojalá (oxa'la) *interj* let's hope so! if only it would! *conj* if only, I hope.

ojear[1] (oxe'ar) *vt* eye, examine. **ojeada** *nf* glance.

ojear[2] (oxe'ar) *vt* 1 drive, chase away. 2 beat (in hunting).

ojo ('oxo) *nm* 1 eye. 2 span (of a bridge). **¡ojo!** *interj* look out! **ojo de la llave** keyhole.

ola ('ola) *nf* wave.

olé (o'le) *interj* bravo!

óleo ('oleo) *nm* Art, rel oil. **oleoducto** *nm* pipeline. **oleosidad** *nf* oiliness.

oler (ue) (o'ler) *vt,vi* smell.

olfatear (olfate'ar) *vt* sniff, smell at.

oliva (o'liba) *nf* olive.

olmo ('olmo) *nf* elm tree.

olor (o'lor) *nm* smell. **oloroso** *adj* fragrant.

olvidar (olβi'ðar) *vt* forget. **olvidadizo** *adj* forgetful. **olvido** *nm* 1 forgetfulness. 2 oblivion.

olla ('oʎa) *nf* 1 *cul* pan, pot. 2 *cul* meat and vegetable stew. 3 eddy, whirlpool. **olla exprés** pressure cooker.

ombligo (om'bligo) *nm* 1 navel. 2 umbilical cord.

ominoso (omi'noso) *adj* ominous.

omisión (omi'sjon) *nf* 1 omission. 2 neglect. **omiso** *adj* careless.

omitir (omi'tir) *vt* omit.

ómnibus ('omniβus) *nm* omnibus.

omnipotencia (omnipo'tenθja) *nf* omnipotence. **ommipotente** *adj* omnipotent.

once ('onθe) *adj, nm* eleven.

onda ('onda) *nf* wave. **ondear** *vt* wave. *vi* wave, undulate. **ondearse** *vr* swing.

ondular (ondu'lar) *vt* wave. *vi* undulate. **ondulado** *adj* undulating. *nm* wave (of hair).

oneroso (one'roso) *adj* onerous.

onza ('onθa) *nf* ounce.

opaco (o'pako) *adj* 1 opaque. 2 dull.

opción (op'θjon) *nf* option.

ópera ('opera) *nf* opera.

operar (ope'rar) *vt, vi* operate. **operable** *adj* operable. **operación** *nf* operation. **operario** *nm* operator, worker. **operativo** *adj* operative.

opinar (opi'nar) *vi* judge, give an opinion. **opinión** *nf* opinion.

opio ('opjo) *nm* opium.

oponer (opo'ner) *vt* 1 oppose, resist. 2 hinder. 3 contradict, dispute. **oponerse a** compete for.

oportunidad (oportuni'ðað) *nf* opportunity. **oportunista** *nm, f* opportunist. **oportuno** *adj* opportune.

oposición (oposi'θjon) *nf* 1 opposition. 2 *pl* competition for a post.

opresión (opre'sjon) *nf* oppression. **opresivo** *adj* oppressive. **opresor** *nm* oppressor.

oprimir (opri'mir) *vt* 1 oppress. 2 depress, press down.

optar (op'tar) *vt, vi* opt, choose. **optante** *nm* chooser. **optativo** *adj* optional. *nm, gram* optative.

óptico ('optiko) *adj* optic, optical. *nm* optician.

optimismo (opti'mismo) *nm* optimism. **optimista** *adj* optimistic. *nm* optimist.

óptimo ('optimo) *adj* optimum, best.

opuesto (o'pwesto) *adj* opposed, opposite.

opulencia (opu'lenθja) *nf* opulence. **opulento** *adj* opulent.

oquedad (oke'ðað) *nf* 1 hollow, cavity. 2 hollowness (of words, etc).

oráculo (o'rakulo) *nm* oracle.

orador (ora'ðor) *nm* orator, public speaker.

orar (o'rar) *vi* 1 pray. 2 harangue. *vt* beg, plead. **oración** *nf* 1 prayer. 2 oration, speech. 3 *gram* sentence. **oracional** *nm* prayer book.

orbe ('orβe) *nm* orb, sphere.

órbita ('orβita) *nf* orbit. **orbitar** *vt* orbit.

orden ('orðen) *nm* order, sequence. *nf* order, command.

ordenar (orðe'nar) *vt* 1 order, command. 2 put in order, tidy. 3 ordain. **ordenación** *nf* 1 arrangement, order, array. 2 ordinance. **ordenanza** *nf* 1 order, method. 2 statute, law. 3 command. *nm mil* orderly.

ordeñar (orðe'ɲar) *vt* milk.

ordinal (orði'nal) *adj, nm* ordinal.

ordinario (orði'narjo) *adj* ordinary. **ordinariez** *nf* vulgarity.

oreja (o'rexa) *nf* 1 ear. 2 flap of shoe.

orfebre (or'feβre) *nm* goldsmith, silversmith. **orfebrería** *nf* gold or silver work.

orfeón (orfe'on) *nm* choral society.

orgánico (or'ganiko) *adj* organic.

organismo (orga'nismo) *nm* organism.

organizar (organi'θar) *vt* organize. **organización** *nf* organization. **organizado** *adj* 1 well-organized. 2 *sci* organic. **organizador** *adj* organizing.

órgano ('organo) *nm* organ. **organista** *nf* organist.

orgía (or'xia) *nf also* **orgia** orgy.

orgullo (or'guʎo) *nm* pride. **orgulloso** *adj* proud.

orientarse (orjen'tarse) *vr* find one's bearings. **orientación** *nf* orientation.

oriente (o'rjente) *nm* orient. **oriental** *adj* oriental, eastern.

orificio (ori'fiθjo) *nm* orifice, hole.

origen (o'rixen) *nm* origin.

original (orixi'nal) *adj, nm* original. **originador** *nm* originator. **originalidad** *nf* originality. **originar** *vt, vi* originate.

orilla (o'riʎa) *nf* edge, border.

oriundo (o'rjundo) *adj* native of, originating from.

orlar (or'lar) *vt* border, edge. **orla** *nf* border, trimming.

ornamentar (ornamen'tar) *vt* adorn, decorate. **ornamentación** *nf* ornamentation. **ornamento** *nm* ornament.

ornato (or'nato) *nm* ornament, adornment.

ornitología (ornitolo'xia) *nf* ornithology.

oro ('oro) *nm* gold. **oro batido** gold leaf. **oropel** *nm* tinsel.

orquesta (or'kesta) *nf also* **orquestra** orchestra. **orquestación** *nf* orchestration. **orquestar** *vt* orchestrate.

orquídea (or'kiðea) *nf* orchid.

ortiga (or'tiga) *nf* nettle.

ortodoxo (orto'ðokso) *adj* orthodox. **ortodoxia** *nf* orthodoxy.

ortografía (ortogra'fia) *nf* orthography, spelling.

oruga (o'ruga) *nf* caterpillar.

101

os (os) *pron* 2nd pers *pl* you.

osa ('osa) *nf* she-bear. **Osa Mayor** Ursa Major.

osadía (osa'ðia) *nf* daring, boldness. **osado** *adj* daring, bold. **osar** *vi* dare.

oscilar (osθi'lar) *vi* oscillate, swing. **oscilación** *nf* oscillation.

oscuro (os'kuro) *adj* dark, obscure, dull.

ostensible (osten'siβle) *adj* ostensible, apparent. **ostentación** *nf* ostentation, show. **ostentativo** *adj also* **ostentoso** ostentatious.

ostentar (osten'tar) *vt* show, display.

ostra ('ostra) *nf* oyster.

otear (ote'ar) *vt* make out, perceive.

otoño (o'toɲo) *nm* autumn.

otorgar (otor'gar) *vt* grant, confer.

otro ('otro) *adj,pron* 1 s another. 2 *pl* other.

ovación (oβa'θjon) *nf* ovation. **ovacionar** *vt* applaud.

óvalo ('oβalo) *nm* oval.

ovario (o'βarjo) *nm* ovary.

oveja (o'βexa) *nf* sheep, ewe. *nm* ram. **ovejuno** *adj* sheep.

ovillo (o'βiʎo) *nm* 1 ball (of wool, etc.). 2 tangle.

oxidar (oksi'ðar) *vt* rust.

óxido ('oksiðo) *nm* oxide.

oxígeno (ok'sixeno) *nm* oxygen.

oye ('oje) *v see* **oír**.

oyente (o'jente) *nm,f* 1 listener. 2 *educ* unregistered student. *adj* hearing.

P

pabellón (paβe'ʎon) *nm* 1 pavilion. 2 bell tent. 3 flag. 4 ward, hospital wing.

pacer (pa'θer) *vt,vi* graze, pasture.

paciencia (pa'θjenθja) *nf* patience. **paciente** *adj,n* patient. **pacienzudo** *adj* patient, long-suffering.

pacificar (paθifi'kar) *vt* pacify, calm. **pacificación** *nf* pacification. **pacificador** *adj* pacifying, peace-making.

pacífico (pa'θifiko) *adj* pacific, peaceful. **el Océano Pacífico** the Pacific Ocean. **pacifismo** *nm* pacifism.

pacotilla (pako'tiʎa) *nf* inferior merchandise, junk. **de pacotilla** of poor quality, shoddy.

pactar (pak'tar) *vt,vi* agree, make a pact. **pacto** *nm* pact, agreement, covenant.

padecer* (paðe'θer) *vt,vi* suffer. **padecimiento** *nm* suffering.

padrastro (pa'ðrastro) *nm* stepfather.

padre ('paðre) *nm* 1 father. 2 *pl* parents. **padrenuestro** *nm* Lord's prayer. **padrino** *nm* 1 godfather. 2 best man. 3 patron. 4 *pl* godparents. **padrinazgo** *nm* 1 act of being a godfather, best man, sponsor, etc. 2 patronage, sponsorship.

padrón (pa'ðron) *nm* 1 poll, census. 2 *tech* pattern. 3 blot, disgrace. 4 *inf* indulgent father.

paga ('paga) *nf* payment, pay. **pagadero** *adj* payable, due. **pagado** *adj* 1 paid. 2 self satisfied. **pago** *adj* paid, paid up. *nm* payment.

pagano (pa'gano) *adj,nm* pagan.

pagar (pa'gar) *vt,vi* 1 pay. 2 atone for. **pagarse** *vr* 1 be content with. 2 be conceited about.

página ('paxina) *nf* page.

país (pa'is) *nm* 1 country. 2 region.

paisaje (pai'saxe) *nm* countryside, scenery.

paisano (pai'sano) *adj* of the same country. *nm* fellow countryman. **vestido de paisano** in civilian clothes, in mufti.

paja ('paxa) *nf* straw.

pájaro ('paxaro) *nm* bird.

paje ('paxe) *nm* pageboy.

Pakistán (pakis'tan) *nm* Pakistan. **Pakistaní** *adj,n* Pakistani.

pala ('pala) *nf* shovel, scoop.

palabra (pa'labra) *nf* word.

palacio (pa'laθjo) *nm* 1 palace. 2 mansion.

paladar (pala'ðar) *nm* palate.

paladear (palaðe'ar) *vt* taste, savour.

palanca (pa'lanka) *nf* 1 lever, crowbar. 2 *inf* influence.

palangana (palan'gana) *nf* washbasin.

palco ('palko) *nm* Th box.

Palestina (pales'tina) *nf* Palestine.

paleta (pa'leta) *nf* 1 shovel, trowel. 2 *Art* palette. 3 *tech* blade, vane. 4 *anat* shoulder blade.

paliar (pali'ar) *vt* alleviate.

palidecer* (paliðe'θer) *vi* become pale. **palidez** *nf* paleness.

pálido ('paliðo) *adj* pale, pallid.

palillo (pa'liʎo) *nm* 1 toothpick. 2 small stick.

paliza (pa'liθa) *nf* beating.

palma ('palma) *nf* 1 *anat* palm. 2 palm tree. **palmada** *nf* light blow, slap. **dar palmas** clap, applaud.

palmatoria (palma'torja) *nf* 1 candlestick. 2 cane.

palmo ('palmo) *nm* measure of approx. 21

cms. **palmo a palmo** inch by inch, little by little.

paloma (pa'loma) *nf* 1 dove. 2 pigeon. **palomar** *nm* dovecote.

palpable (pal'paβle) *adj* palpable, tangible.

palpar (pal'par) *vt* touch, feel.

palpitar (palpi'tar) *vi* palpitate, throb. **palpitación** *nf* throb, palpitation.

paludismo (palu'ðismo) *nm* malaria.

palurdo (pa'lurðo) *adj, nm* rustic.

palustre[1] (pa'lustre) *adj* marshy.

palustre[2] (pa'lustre) *nm* trowel.

pan (pan) *nm* 1 bread. 2 loaf.

pana ('pana) *nf* 1 velveteen. 2 corduroy.

panal (pa'nal) *nm* honeycomb.

Panamá (pana'ma) *nm* Panama.

pancarta (pan'karta) *nf* placard.

pandereta (pande'reta) *nf* tambourine.

pandilla (pan'diλa) *nf* group, gang.

pánico ('paniko) *adj, nm* panic.

pantalón (panta'lon) *nm also* **pantalones** trousers.

pantalla (pan'taλa) *nf* 1 screen. 2 lampshade.

pantano (pan'tano) *nm* 1 marsh, bog. 2 reservoir, lake. **pantanal** *nm* marshland. **pantanoso** *adj* marshy.

pantera (pan'tera) *nf* panther.

pantorrilla (pantor'riλa) *nf anat* calf.

panza ('panθa) *nf* belly.

pañal (pa'ñal) *nm* nappy.

pañería (pañe'ria) *nf* drapery. **pañero** *nm* draper. **pañete** *nm* light cloth. **paño** *nm* cloth.

pañuelo (pa'ñwelo) *nm* 1 headscarf. 2 handkerchief.

papa[1] ('papa) *nm* pope.

papa[2] ('papa) *nf* potato.

papá (pa'pa) *nm inf* dad, daddy.

papada (pa'paða) *nf* double chin.

papagayo (papa'gajo) *nm* parrot.

papamoscas (papa'moskas) *nm invar* 1 *zool* fly catcher. 2 simpleton.

papel (pa'pel) *nm* paper. **papeleo** *nm* 1 paper work. 2 *inf* red tape. **papelera** *nf* 1 wastepaper basket. 2 desk. **papelería** *nf* 1 stationery. 2 stationer's shop.

papera (pa'pera) *nf* 1 goitre. 2 *pl* mumps.

paquete (pa'kete) *nm* packet.

par (par) *adj* equal, even. *nm* pair. **pares y nones** odds or evens.

para ('para) *prep* for, to. **¿para qué?** why? what for?

parabrisas (para'βrisas) *nm invar* windscreen.

paracaídas (parake'iðas) *nm invar* parachute. **paracaidista** *nm* parachutist.

parachoques (para'tʃokes) *nm invar* 1 *mot* bumper. 2 shock absorber.

parada (pa'raða) *nf* 1 stop, stopping place. 2 stoppage, shutdown. 3 *mil* parade. **paradero** *nm* 1 stopping place. 2 lodgings. 3 whereabouts. **parado** *adj* 1 motionless, stopped. 2 unemployed.

paradoja (para'ðoxa) *nf* paradox. **paradójico** *adj* paradoxical.

parador (para'ðor) *nm* tourist hotel.

parafina (para'fina) *nf* paraffin wax.

paráfrasis (pa'rafrasis) *nf invar* paraphrase.

paraguas (pa'ragwas) *nm invar* umbrella.

paraíso (para'iso) *nm* 1 paradise. 2 *Th* gallery, the gods.

paralela (para'lela) *nf* parallel. **paralelo** *adj, nm* parallel.

parálisis (pa'ralisis) *nf* paralysis. **paralítico** *adj, nm* paralytic. **paralizar** *vt* paralyse.

páramo ('paramo) *nm* wilderness, waste land, moor.

parangón (paran'gon) *nm* 1 comparison. 2 paragon, model.

parapeto (para'peto) *nm* 1 parapet. 2 barricade.

parar (pa'rar) *vt, vi* stop, halt. **parar en mal** come to a bad end.

pararrayos (parar'rajos) *nm invar* lightning conductor.

parásito (pa'rasito) *adj* parasitic. *nm* parasite.

parasol (para'sol) *nm* parasol.

parcela (par'θela) *nf* plot of land.

parcial (par'θjal) *adj* partial. **parcialidad** *nf* 1 partiality, bias. 2 group, faction.

parco ('parko) *adj* frugal, sparing.

pardo ('parðo) *adj* brown, dark.

parecer* (pare'θer) *vi* appear, seem. **parecerse** *vr* resemble. ~*nm* opinion. **parecido** *adj* similar, like. *nm* resemblance.

pared (pa'red) *nf* (interior) wall.

pareja (pa'rexa) *nf* 1 pair, couple. 2 partner.

parentela (paren'tela) *nf* 1 relations. 2 parentage. **parentesco** *nm* kinship, relationship.

paréntesis (pa'rentesis) *nm invar* parenthesis, bracket.

paridad (pari'ðað) *nf* 1 parity, equality. 2 comparison.

pariente (pa'rjente) *nm* relative.

parir (pa'rir) *vt, vi* bear, give birth.

París (pa'ris) *nm* Paris.

parla ('parla) *nf* chatter, gossip.

parlamentar (parlamen'tar) *vi* 1 converse. 2

103

perley. **parlamentario** adj parliamentary. nm member of parliament. **parlamento** nm parliament.

parlanchín (parlan'tʃin) adj gossipy, indiscreet. nm talkative person, gossip.

parlar (par'lar) vi chatter.

paro ('paro) nm 1 stoppage, standstill. 2 unemployment.

parpadear (parpaðe'ar) vi 1 blink, wink (the eye). 2 flicker, twinkle. **parpadeo** nm wink, blink.

párpado ('parpaðo) nm eyelid.

parque ('parke) nm park.

párrafo ('parrafo) nm paragraph.

parricida (parri'θiða) nm,f parricide (person). **parricidio** nm parricide (act).

parrilla (par'riʎa) nf gridiron, cooking grill.

párroco ('parroko) nm parish priest.

parroquia (par'rokja) nf 1 parish. 2 clientele. **parroquial** adj parochial, parish. **parroquiano** nm 1 parishioner. 2 client.

parsimonia (parsi'monja) nf 1 parsimony, frugality. 2 deliberateness.

parte ('parte) nf 1 part. 2 place. 3 law party. 4 Th role. 5 report.

partición (parti'θjon) nf division, partition.

participar (partiθi'par) vt notify, inform. vi participate. **participación** nf 1 participation. 2 notice, notification. 3 comm share. **participante** nm,f participant.

partícipe (par'tiθipe) nm,f participant.

participio (parti'θipjo) nm participle.

partícula (par'tikula) nf particle.

particular (partiku'lar) adj 1 particular. 2 private. nm 1 particular, detail. 2 private individual.

particularizar (partikulari'θar) vt 1 specify, itemize. 2 single out (a person). **particularizarse** vr be characterized, distinguished. **particularidad** nf 1 particularity, characteristic. 2 intimacy.

partida (par'tiða) nf 1 departure. 2 certificate. 3 comm entry, item. 4 game (of cards, chess, etc.).

partidario (parti'ðarjo) adj partisan. nm supporter.

partido (par'tiðo) adj divided. nf 1 pol party. 2 sport game, match. **tomar partido** take sides. **sacar partido** benefit from.

partir (par'tir) vt divide, cut up. vi leave, depart. **a partir de ahora** from now on.

partitura (parti'tura) nf mus score.

parto ('parto) nm childbirth, delivery.

parvo ('parβo) adj small, little.

párvulo ('parβulo) adj 1 small. 2 humble. nm child, infant.

pasa ('pasa) nf raisin.

pasada (pa'saða) nf passage. **mala pasada** dirty trick, bad turn. **pasadero** adj tolerable, passable.

pasado (pa'saðo) adj, nm past. **la semana pasada** last week. **pasado mañana** day after tomorrow.

pasador (pasa'ðor) nm 1 fastener, pin, bolt. 2 filter. 3 pl shoelaces, cufflinks.

pasaje (pa'saxe) nm 1 passage, voyage. 2 fare. 3 passageway. **pasajero** adj transient, passing. nm passenger.

pasamano (pasa'mano) nm handrail, bannister.

pasaporte (pasa'porte) nm passport.

pasar (pa'sar) vt 1 pass, give. 2 cross. 3 pierce, penetrate. 4 spend (time). **pasarlo bien/mal** have a good/bad time. vi 1 pass, go. 2 happen, occur. **pasar por alto** overlook. **pasar de la raya** be too much, be the last straw.

pasatiempo (pasa'tjempo) nm hobby, pastime.

pascua ('paskwa) nf rel feast. **Pascua de Navidad** Christmas. **Pascua de Resurrección** Easter. **¡felices pascuas!** Merry Christmas.

pase ('pase) nm pass.

pasear (pase'ar) vt 1 take for a walk. 2 parade, exhibit. vi go for a walk or ride. **paseo** nm 1 stroll. 2 outing. 3 walk, promenade.

pasillo (pa'siʎo) nm passage, corridor.

pasión (pa'sjon) nf passion.

pasividad (pasiβi'ðað) nf passivity. **pasivo** adj passive, inactive. nm comm liabilities, debit.

pasmar (pas'mar) vt 1 astound, amaze. 2 chill (to the marrow). **pasmado** adj 1 amazed. 2 chilled. 3 idiotic. **pasmo** nm 1 astonishment. 2 chill.

paso ('paso) nm 1 step, pace. 2 geog pass. **paso a nivel** level crossing. **paso a paso** step by step.

pasta ('pasta) nf 1 paste. 2 dough, pastry. 3 pasta.

pastar (pas'tar) vt,vi graze.

pastel (pas'tel) nm 1 cake. 2 art pastel. **pastelería** nf 1 pastry shop. 2 pastry-making. 3 pastry. **pastelero** nm pastry cook.

pastilla (pas'tiʎa) nf tablet, pill.

pasto ('pasto) nm grass, fodder.

pastor (pas'tor) nm 1 shepherd. 2 clergyman.

pastorear (pastore'ar) vt 1 pasture. 2 tend (a flock).

pata ('pata) nf zool paw, leg. **meter la pata** inf put one's foot in it.

patada (pa'taða) nf 1 kick. 2 stamp.

patalear (patale'ar) vi 1 stamp. 2 kick about.

patán (pa'tan) nm yokel, oaf.

patata (pa'tata) nf potato.

patear (pate'ar) vt,vi 1 kick. 2 stamp.

patente (pa'tente) adj obvious. nm comm patent.

paternal (pater'nal) adj paternal. **paternidad** nf paternity. **paterno** adj paternal.

patético (pa'tetiko) adj 1 pathetic. 2 poignant.

patíbulo (pa'tiβulo) nm gallows.

patillas (pa'tiʎas) nf pl whiskers, sideboards.

patín (pa'tin) nm skate. **patinar** vi 1 skate. 2 skid. **patinadero** nm skating rink. **patinazo** nm 1 skid. 2 mistake.

patio ('patjo) nm courtyard, patio.

pato ('pato) nm duck.

patología (patolo'xia) nf pathology. **patológico** adj pathological. **patólogo** nm pathologist.

patraña (pa'traɲa) nf 1 tall story. 2 fib.

patria ('patrja) nf native land.

patriarca (pa'trjarka) nm patriarch.

patricio (pa'triθjo) adj,nm patrician.

patrimonio (patri'monjo) nf 1 inheritance. 2 heritage.

patriota (pa'trjota) nm,f patriot. **patriótico** adj patriotic. **patriotismo** nm patriotism.

patrocinar (patroθi'nar) vt sponsor. **patrocinador** nm sponsor. **patrocinio** nm sponsorship.

patrón (pa'tron) nm 1 patron. 2 owner. 3 pattern, model. **patronato** nm 1 patronage. 2 comm employer's association. 3 board of trustees.

patrulla (pa'truʎa) nf patrol.

paulatinamente (paulatina'mente) adv gradually.

pausa ('pausa) nf 1 pause. 2 mus rest. **pausado** adj slow, deliberate.

pauta ('pauta) nf 1 lines, guide lines. 2 ruler.

pávido ('paβiðo) adj timid, fearful.

pavimentar (paβimen'tar) vt pave, surface. **pavimento** nm pavement.

pavo ('paβo) nm turkey. **pavo real** peacock.

pavor (pa'βor) nm terror. **pavoroso** adj awesome, dreadful, terrifying.

payaso (pa'jaso) nm clown, buffoon.

paz (paθ) nf peace. **hacer las paces** make peace.

peaje (pe'axe) nm toll.

peca ('peka) nf spot, freckle.

pecar (pe'kar) vi sin. **pecado** nm sin.

pécora ('pekora) nf 1 sheep, head of sheep. 2 inf cunning or crafty woman.

peculiar (peku'ljar) adj 1 peculiar. 2 characteristic. **peculiaridad** nf 1 peculiarity. 2 characteristic.

pechera (pe'tʃera) nf front of a dress or shirt.

pecho ('petʃo) nm 1 chest, bosom. 2 courage, heart. **tomar a pecho** take to heart.

pechuga (pe'tʃuga) nf cul breast (of chickens, etc.).

pedagogía (peðaɡo'xia) nf pedagogy. **pedagogo** nm 1 schoolmaster. 2 mentor.

pedal (pe'ðal) nm pedal.

pedante (pe'ðante) adj pedantic. nm pedant. **pedantería** nf pedantry.

pedazo (pe'ðaθo) nm piece, fragment.

pedernal (peðer'nal) nm flint.

pedestal (peðes'tal) nm pedestal.

pedestre (pe'ðestre) adj pedestrian.

pediatría (peðja'tria) nf paediatrics.

pedicuro (peði'kuro) nm chiropodist.

pedir (i) (pe'ðir) vt ask for, request. **pedido** nm comm order. **pedigüeño** adj importunate, insistent. **pedimento** nf 1 petition. 2 law claim.

pedregal (peðre'ɡal) nm stony ground. **pedregoso** adj stony, rocky.

pedrería (peðre'ria) nf jewels.

pedrisco (pe'ðrisko) nm hailstorm.

pegar (pe'ɡar) vt 1 hit, strike. 2 fasten, stick, glue. 3 med infect. vi 1 stick. 2 take effect. **pegar fuego** set fire to. **pegar un tiro** shoot. **pega** nf 1 heating. 2 trick, joke. 3 problem, difficulty. **pegajoso** adj 1 sticky. 2 med infectious.

peinar (pei'nar) vt comb. **peinado** nm coiffure. **peinador** nm 1 hairdresser. 2 dressing-gown. **peine** nm comb.

pelado (pe'laðo) adj bare, barren.

pelar (pe'lar) vt 1 peel, skin. 2 shear.

peldaño (pel'daɲo) nm step, stair.

pelear (pele'ar) vi fight, brawl, row. **pelea** nf fight, brawl. **peleador** adj quarrelsome, belligerent.

peliagudo (pelja'ɡuðo) adj tricky, difficult.

pelícano (pe'likano) nm pelican.

película (pe'likula) nf film.

peligrar (peli'ɡrar) vi be in danger. **peligro** nm danger. **peligroso** adj dangerous.

pelmazo (pel'maθo) nm also **pelma** 1 dull person. 2 crushed mass.

pelo ('pelo) nm hair.

pelota (pe'lota) nf ball. **en pelota** naked.

pelotón

pelotón (pelo'ton) *nm mil* platoon, squad.

peltre ('peltre) *nm* pewter.

peluca (pe'luka) *nf* wig.

pelusa (pe'lusa) *nf* 1 down, fine hair. 2 *inf* jealousy.

pelleja (pe'ʎexa) *nf also* **pellejo** *nm* skin, hide.

pellizcar (peʎiθ'kar) *vt* pinch, nip. **pellizco** *nm* pinch, nip.

pena ('pena) *nf* 1 grief, sorrow. 2 penalty, punishment. 3 pain.

penal (pe'nal) *adj* penal. *nm* prison. **penalidad** *nf* 1 hardship. 2 *law* penalty.

penar (pe'nar) *vt* punish, penalize. *vi* suffer, grieve.

pender (pen'der) *vi* 1 hang. 2 *law* be pending. **pendiente** *adj* 1 hanging. 2 pending. *nm* earring. *nf* hill, slope.

pene ('pene) *nm* penis.

penetrar (pene'trar) *vt* penetrate, pierce. **penetrable** *adj* penetrable. **penetración** *nf* penetration. **penetrante** *adj* penetrating.

penicilina (peniθi'lina) *nf* penicillin.

península (pe'ninsula) *nf* peninsula.

penitencia (peni'tenθja) *nf* penitence, penance. **penitencial** *adj* penitential. **penitente** *adj,n* penitent.

penoso (pe'noso) *adj* 1 painful, distressing. 2 difficult.

pensar (ie) (pen'sar) *vi* think. **pensar en** think about. **pensamiento** *nm* thought.

pensión (pen'sjon) *nf* 1 pension, allowance. 2 pension, boarding house.

penúltimo (pe'nultimo) *adj* penultimate.

penumbra (pe'numbra) *nf* half-light, dimness.

penuria (pe'nurja) *nf* penury, scarcity.

peña ('peɲa) *nf* 1 cliff. 2 mountain top. 3 group (of friends).

peón (pe'on) *nm* 1 labourer. 2 foot-soldier. 3 pedestrian. 4 *game* pawn.

peor (pe'or) *adj,adv* 1 worse. 2 worst.

pepino (pe'pino) *nm* cucumber.

pepita (pe'pita) *nf* pip.

pequeño (pe'keɲo) *adj* small.

pera ('pera) *nf* 1 pear. 2 light switch. **peral** *nm* pear tree.

percance (per'kanθe) *nm* mishap.

percatarse (perka'tarse) *vr* notice.

percibir (perθi'βir) *vt* 1 perceive. 2 *comm* earn, receive (salary). **percepción** *nf* 1 perception. 2 idea. 3 *comm* collection. **perceptible** *adj* 1 perceptible. 2 *comm* receivable. **perceptivo** *adj* perceptive.

percusión (perku'sjon) *nf* percussion.

percha ('pertʃa) *nf* 1 pole, support. 2 coat rack or hanger.

perder (ie) (per'ðer) *vt* lose. **pérdida** *nf* loss, waste. **perdido** *adj* lost.

perdiz (per'ðiθ) *nf* partridge.

perdonar (perðo'nar) *vt* pardon, excuse. **perdón** *nm* pardon.

perdurar (perðu'rar) *vi* last, endure.

perecer* (pere'θer) *vi* perish. **perecedero** *adj* perishable.

peregrinar (peregri'nar) *vi* 1 travel, voyage. 2 *rel* go on a pilgrimage. **peregrino** *adj* 1 wandering, travelling. 2 migratory. *nm* pilgrim.

perejil (pere'xil) *nm bot* parsley.

perenne (pe'renne) *adj* perennial, everlasting.

perentorio (peren'torjo) *adj* 1 peremptory. 2 urgent. 3 decisive.

pereza (pe'reθa) *nf* laziness, idleness. **perezoso** *adj* lazy, idle.

perfección (perfek'θjon) *nf* perfection. **perfeccionamiento** *nm* perfection, improvement. **perfecto** *adj* perfect.

perfidia (per'fiðja) *nf* perfidy, treachery. **pérfido** ('perfiðo) *adj* perfidious, treacherous.

perfilar (perfi'lar) *vt* outline. **perfil** *nm* 1 profile. 2 outline.

perforar (perfo'rar) *vt* 1 perforate. 2 drill. **perforación** *nf* 1 perforation. 2 drilling. **perforadora** *nf* 1 punch. 2 drill.

perfumar (perfu'mar) *vt* perfume, scent. **perfume** *nm* perfume, scent. **perfumería** *nf* perfume shop.

pericia (pe'riθja) *nf* skill, expertise.

periferia (peri'ferja) *nf* periphery.

perímetro (pe'rimetro) *nm* perimeter.

periódico (pe'rjoðiko) *adj* periodic. *nm* 1 newspaper. 2 periodical.

periodismo (perjo'ðismo) *nm* journalism. **periodista** *nm,f* journalist. **periodístico** *adj* journalistic.

período (pe'rioðo) *nm* 1 period. 2 *gram* sentence.

peripecia (peri'peθja) *nf* 1 incident. 2 *pl* adventures.

perjudicar (perxuði'kar) *vt* 1 harm. 2 prejudice.

perjuicio (per'xwiθjo) *nm* harm, damage, detriment.

perjurar (perxu'rar) *vi* 1 perjure oneself. 2 swear, curse.

perla ('perla) *nf* pearl.

permanecer* (permane'θer) *vi* remain, stay.

permanencia (perma'nenθja) *nf* 1 permanence.

2 stay. **permanente** adj permanent. nf perm (hairdressing).

permiso (per'miso) nm **1** permission. **2** permit, licence. **3** leave. **con permiso** excuse me, if I may. **permisible** adj permissible. **permisivo** adj permissive.

permitir (permi'tir) vt permit, allow. **ne permite?** may I?

permutar (permu'tar) vt **1** math permute. **2** exchange. **permuta** nf barter, exchange. **permutación** nf permutation.

pernicioso (perni'θjoso) adj pernicious, injurious.

pernoctar (pernok'tar) vi stay overnight.

pero ('pero) conj but, yet.

perogrullada (perogru'ʎaða) nf platitude.

perorar (pero'rar) vi make a speech.

perpendicular (perpenðiku'lar) adj,nf perpendicular.

perpetrar (perpe'trar) vt perpetrate. **perpetración** nf perpetration.

perpetuar (perpe'twar) vt perpetuate. **perpetuidad** nf perpetuity. **perpetuo** adj perpetual.

perplejidad (perplexi'ðað) nf **1** perplexity. **2** hesitation. **perplejo** adj bewildered, perplexed.

perro ('perro) nm dog.

persecución (perseku'θjon) nf **1** pursuit, chase, hunt. **2** persecution.

perseguir (i) (perse'gir) vt **1** pursue, chase, hunt down. **2** persecute.

perseverar (perseβe'rar) vi persevere. **perseverancia** nf perseverance, persistence. **perseverante** adj persevering, persistent.

persiana (per'sjana) nf **1** Venetian blind. **2** shutter.

persistir (persis'tir) vi persist. **persistencia** nf persistence. **persistente** adj persistent.

persona (per'sona) nf person. **personaje** nm **1** personage, celebrity. **2** Th character. **personal** adj personal. nm personnel. **personalidad** nf personality.

personarse (perso'narse) vr appear in person.

personificar (personifi'kar) vt personify, embody.

perspectiva (perspek'tiβa) nf **1** perspective. **2** view, scene. **3** outlook, prospect.

perspicacia (perspi'kaθja) nf perspicacity, shrewdness. **perspicaz** adj perspicacious, shrewd.

persuadir (perswa'ðir) vt persuade. **persuasión** nf **1** persuasion. **2** conviction. **persuasivo** adj persuasive.

pertenecer (pertene'θer) vi **1** belong to. **2** pertain to. **perteneciente** adj **1** belonging, member. **2** relevant. **pertenencia** nf **1** ownership. **2** pl possessions, property.

pértiga ('pertiga) nf pole.

pertinacia (perti'naθja) nf persistence, pertinacity. **pertinaz** adj persistent, pertinacious. **pertinencia** nf relevance, pertinence. **pertinente** adj pertinent.

pertrechar (pertre't∫ar) vt supply, equip.

perturbar (pertur'βar) vt disturb, perturb. **perturbación** nf disturbance.

Perú (pe'ru) nm Peru. **peruano** adj,n Peruvian.

pervertir (ie) (perβer'tir) vt pervert, corrupt. **perversión** (perβer'sjon) nf **1** perversion. **2** wickedness. **perverso** adj perverse. **pervertido** adj perverted. nm pervert.

pesa ('pesa) nf weight. **pesadez** nf **1** weight, heaviness. **2** slowness. **3** drowsiness.

pesadilla (pesa'ðiʎa) nf nightmare.

pesado (pe'saðo) adj **1** heavy. **2** slow. **3** boring. nm boring person. **pesadumbre** nf grief, sorrow.

pésame ('pesame) nm condolence, sympathy. **mi sentido pésame** my deepest regrets or sympathy.

pesar (pe'sar) vt weigh.

pescar (pes'kar) vt **1** fish. **2** catch. **pesca** nf **1** fishing. **2** catch of fish. **pescadería** nf fish shop. **pescadero** nm fishmonger. **pescado** nm fish. **pescador** nm fisherman. **pesquería** nf fishery.

pescuezo (pes'kweθo) nm neck.

pesebre (pe'seβre) nm manger, crib.

pesimismo (pesi'mismo) nm pessimism. **pesimista** adj pessimistic. nm,f pessimist.

pésimo ('pesimo) adj terrible, extremely bad.

peso ('peso) nm **1** weight. **2** scales. **3** comm peso (currency).

pesquisa (pes'kisa) nf investigation, search.

pestañear (pestaɲe'ar) vi blink. **pestaña** nf **1** eyelash. **2** anat,bot fringe. **pestañeo** nm blink.

peste ('peste) nf plague, epidemic. **echar pestes** curse, fume. **pesticida** nm pesticide. **pestífero** adj **1** pestiferous. **2** foul.

pestilencia (pesti'lenθja) nf **1** pestilence, plague. **2** stink, stench. **pestilente** adj **1** pestilent. **2** foul-smelling.

pestillo (pes'tiʎo) nm latch, bolt.

petaca (pe'taka) nf cigarette case.

pétalo ('petalo) nm petal.

petardo (pe'tarðo) nm firework.

petición (peti'θjon) *nf* 1 plea, request. 2 petition.

petirrojo (petir'roxo) *nm* robin.

peto ('peto) *nm* 1 bodice. 2 breastplate.

pétreo ('petreo) *adj* stony.

petrificar (petrifi'kar) *vt* petrify.

petróleo (pe'troleo) *nm min* oil. **petrolero** *nm* 1 *naut* tanker. 2 oilman. *adj* oil.

petulancia (petu'lanθja) *nf* 1 petulance. 2 vanity. **petulante** *adj* 1 petulant. 2 vain.

peyorativo (pejora'tiβo) *adj* pejorative.

pez (peθ) *nm* fish. *nf* pitch, tar.

pezón (pe'θon) *nm* 1 *anat* teat, nipple. 2 *bot* stalk.

pezuña (pe'θuɲa) *nf* hoof.

piadoso (pja'ðoso) *adj* pious, devout.

piano ('pjano) *nm* piano. **pianista** *nm,f* pianist.

piar (pjar) *vi* cheep, chirp.

piara ('pjara) *nf* herd, drove (esp. of pigs).

picadillo (pika'ðiλo) *nm* minced meat.

picante (pi'kante) *adj* 1 *cul* hot, highly-seasoned. 2 sharp, piquant.

picaporte (pika'porte) *nm* 1 doorlatch. 2 door knocker.

picar (pi'kar) *vt* 1 prick, sting. 2 chop (meat). **picarse** *vr* 1 go rotten. 2 be piqued or annoyed. **picado** *adj* 1 minced, chopped. 2 perforated. 3 bitten, stung. 4 offended. **picador** *nm* picador (bullfight). **picadura** *nf* 1 prick. 2 bite, sting.

picardía (pikar'ðia) *nf* mischief, roguery.

pícaro ('pikaro) *nm* scoundrel. *adj inf* naughty. **picaresco** *adj lit* picaresque.

pico ('piko) *nm* 1 beak, spout. 2 peak. 3 pickaxe.

picotear (pikote'ar) *vt* peck. *vi inf* chatter. **picotero** *adj, n* chatterbox.

pichón (pi'tʃon) *nm* pigeon.

pie (pje) *nm* 1 foot. 2 bottom. **al pie de la letra** literally, word for word. **dar pie a/para** give cause to/for. **en pie de** on the basis of.

piedad (pje'ðað) *nf* 1 piety. 2 pity.

piedra ('pjeðra) *nf* stone.

piel (pjel) *nf* skin.

pienso ('pjenso) *nm* fodder.

pierna ('pjerna) *nf* leg.

pieza ('pjeθa) *nf* 1 piece, part. 2 roll (of material). **quedarse de una sola pieza** be flabbergasted.

pigmento (pig'mento) *nm* pigment.

pijama (pi'xama) *nm* pyjamas.

pila[1] ('pila) *nf* 1 heap, pile. 2 battery.

pila[2] ('pila) *nf* 1 sink. 2 fountain. 3 font. **nombre de pila** Christian name.

pilar (pi'lar) *nm* pillar.

píldora ('pildora) *nf* pill.

pilón (pi'lon) *nm* pillar.

piloto (pi'loto) *nm* pilot.

piltrafa (pil'trafa) *nf* piece of offal, scrap.

pillar (pi'λar) *vt inf* catch. **pillaje** *nm* pillage, sack.

pillo ('piλo) *adj* 1 villainous. 2 naughty. *nm* 1 villain. 2 scamp. **pillastre** *nm also* **pilluelo** rascal (child).

pimienta (pi'mjenta) *nf* pepper. **pimiento** *nm* pepper (vegetable). **pimentón** *nm* 1 red pepper. 2 paprika.

pimpollo (pim'poλo) *nm* 1 sapling. 2 beauty (young person or child).

pináculo (pi'nakulo) *nm* pinnacle.

pinar (pi'nar) *nm* pine forest.

pincel (pin'θel) *nm* paintbrush. **pincelada** *nf* brush-stroke.

pinchar (pin'tʃar) *vt* puncture. **pincharse** *vr mot* have a puncture. **pinchazo** *nm* 1 *mot* puncture. 2 *med* injection. **pincho** *nm* 1 spike, skewer. 2 *pl cul* snacks.

pingo ('pingo) *nm* 1 shred, rag. 2 *inf* prostitute. 3 *pl* odds and ends.

pino ('pino) *nm* pine tree. **pinocha** *nf* pine needle.

pintar (pin'tar) *vt* paint. **pintarse** *vr* make oneself up. **pinta** *nf* 1 spot. 2 appearance. **pintura** *nf* 1 painting. 2 paint.

pinzas ('pinθas) *nf pl* tweezers, pincers.

pinzón (pin'θon) *nm* finch.

piña ('piɲa) *nf* 1 pineapple. 2 pine cone.

piñón (pi'ɲon) *nm* pinion.

pío[1] ('pio) *nm* chirp, chirping.

pío[2] ('pio) *adj* 1 pious. 2 merciful.

piojo ('pjoxo) *nm* louse.

pipa ('pipa) *nf* pipe.

pique ('pike) *nm* pique, resentment.

piqueta (pi'keta) *nf* pickaxe.

piquete (pi'kete) *nm* 1 prick, cut. 2 hole. 3 picket (of strikers).

piragua (pi'ragwa) *nf* canoe.

pirámide (pi'ramiðe) *nf* pyramid.

pirata (pi'rata) *nm* pirate. **piratería** *nf* piracy.

Pirineos (piri'neos) *nm pl* Pyrenees.

piropear (pirope'ar) *vt* pay compliments to, flatter. **piropo** *nm* compliment, flattery.

pirotecnia (piro'teknja) *nf* fireworks.

pirueta (pi'rweta) *nf* pirouette.

poder

pisar (pi'sar) vt tread, trample. vi tread. **pisada** nf step, footprint.

piscina (pis'θina) nf swimming pool.

piscolabis (pisko'laβis) nm invar inf snack.

piso ('piso) nm 1 floor, storey. 2 flat, apartment.

pisotear (pisote'ar) vt 1 trample. 2 inf abuse.

pista ('pista) nf track. **pista de baile** dance floor.

pistola (pis'tola) nf 1 pistol. 2 tech spray. **pistolero** nm gunman.

pistón (pis'ton) nm piston.

pitar (pi'tar) vi whistle. **pito** nm whistle.

pitón (pi'ton) nm python.

pizarra (pi'θarra) nf slate, blackboard.

pizca ('piθka) nf 1 crumb. 2 pinch.

placa ('plaka) nf plate, sheet (metal, photographic, etc.).

placer (pla'θer) vt please. nm pleasure. **placentero** adj pleasant.

plácido ('plaθiðo) adj placid.

plagar (pla'gar) vt plague. **plaga** nf plague, pest.

plagiar (pla'xjar) vt plagiarize. **plagio** nm plagiarism, copy.

plan (plan) nm 1 plan. 2 basis.

plana ('plana) nf 1 page. 2 trowel. **en primera plana** 1 on the front page. 2 important.

plancton ('plankton) nm plankton.

planchar (plan'tʃar) vt iron (clothes). **plancha** nf 1 iron. 2 plate (printing). 3 slab (concrete).

planear (plane'ar) vt plan. vi glide. **planeador** nm glider.

planeta (pla'neta) nm planet.

planicie (pla'niθje) nf level, flat surface.

planificar (planifi'kar) vt plan. **planificación** nf planning. **planificación familiar** family planning.

plano ('plano) adj flat, level. nm 1 plane, dimension. 2 plan, diagram. 3 phot shot, angle. **primer plano** foreground (picture).

plantar (plan'tar) vt plant, set up. **plantarse** vr establish oneself. **planta** nf 1 plant. 2 ground plan. 3 anat sole. 4 tech plant. **plantación** nf plantation. **plante** nm programme. **plantío** nm 1 planting. 2 land planted or ready to be planted. **plantón** nm 1 bot seedling. 2 mil sentry.

plantear (plante'ar) vt put, pose (question, etc.).

plantel (plan'tel) nm bot nursery.

plantilla (plan'tiʎa) nf 1 sole (of shoe). 2 template.

plasma ('plasma) nm plasma.

plástico ('plastiko) adj,nm plastic.

plata ('plata) nf silver.

plataforma (plata'forma) nf 1 platform. 2 oil rig. 3 Th stage.

plátano ('platano) nm 1 banana. 2 plane tree.

platea (pla'tea) nf Th orchestra pit.

platear (plate'ar) vt silverplate. **platero** nm silversmith.

plática ('platika) nf talk, chat.

platillo (pla'tiʎo) nm saucer.

platino (pla'tino) nm platinum.

plato ('plato) nm 1 plate. 2 cul course. **un plato típico** a local delicacy.

platónico (pla'toniko) adj platonic.

playa ('plaja) nf 1 beach. 2 seaside.

plaza ('plaθa) nf 1 town square. 2 place, seat.

plazo ('plaθo) nm 1 time limit. 2 comm instalment. **comprar a plazos** buy on hire-purchase.

pleamar (plea'mar) nf high tide.

plebe ('pleβe) nf proletariat. **plebeyo** adj proletarian.

plegar (ie) (ple'gar) vt fold. **plegable** adj pliable, folding. ·

pleitear (pleite'ar) vi start legal proceedings. **pleito** nm lawsuit.

plenitud (pleni'tuð) nf fullness. **pleno** adj complete.

pliego ('pljego) nm 1 sheaf of papers. 2 folder.

pliegue ('pljege) nm 1 crease. 2 pleat, tuck.

plomo ('plomo) nm 1 lead, plumb. 2 tech fuse-wire.

pluma ('pluma) nf 1 feather. 2 pen. **plumaje** nm plumage.

plural (plu'ral) adj,nm plural.

pluscuamperfecto (pluskwamper'fekto) nm pluperfect.

poblar (ue) (po'βlar) vt populate, inhabit. **población** 1 population. 2 village. **poblado** nm built-up area.

pobre ('poβre) adj poor. nm pauper. **pobreza** nf poverty.

pocilga (po'θilga) nf pigsty.

poción (po'θjon) nf potion.

poco ('poko) adj 1 little (quantity). 2 pl few. **poco** or **un poco** adv a little, not much. **poco a poco** gradually. **poco interesante** not very interesting. **por poco** nearly.

podar (po'ðar) vt prune. **podadera** nf pruning shears.

poder (ue) (po'ðer) vi 1 can, be able. 2 be possible. **poder** nm power. **poderío** nm authority. **poderoso** adj powerful. **no puedo**

109

más I can do no more. **no puedo menos** í can't help it. **puede ser** maybe.

poema (po'ema) *nm* poem. **poesía** *nf* 1 poetry. 2 poem. **poeta** *nm* poet. **poética** *nf* art of poetry, poetics. **poético** *adj* poetic.

polaco (po'lako) *adj* Polish. *nm* 1 Pole. 2 Polish (language).

polaridad (polari'ðað) *nf* polarity.

polea (po'lea) *nf* pulley.

polémica (po'lemika) *nf* polemic, argument.

polen ('polen) *nm* pollen.

policía (poli'θia) *nm* policeman. *nf* police force. **policiaco** *adj also* **policial** police. **novela policíaca** *nf* detective novel.

polígono (po'ligono) *nm* 1 building site. 2 housing estate. 3 *math* polygon.

polilla (po'liʎa) *nf* moth.

pólipo ('polipo) *nm* polyp.

política (po'litika) *nf* 1 politics. 2 political manifesto. 3 political policy. **político** *adj* political, *nm* politician.

póliza ('poliθa) *nf* 1 fiscal stamp, certificate. 2 policy. **póliza de seguro** insurance policy.

polizón (poli'θon) *nm* 1 stowaway. 2 vagrant.

polo ('polo) *nm* 1 pole. 2 *tech* terminal. 3 *sport* polo. 4 polo-neck sweater.

Polonia (po'lonja) *nf* Poland.

poltrona (pol'trona) *nf* easy chair.

polvareda *nf* 1 cloud of dust. 2 altercation. **pólvora** *nf* gunpowder. **polvoriento** *adj* dusty.

polvo ('polbo) *nm* 1 dust. 2 *pl* powder.

polla ('poʎa) *nf* pullet. **pollo** *nm* chicken.

pómez ('pomeθ) *nf* pumice.

pomo ('pomo) *nm* 1 doorknob. 2 pommel. 3 fruit.

pompa ('pompa) *nf* 1 pomp. 2 *pl* bubbles.

pómulo ('pomulo) *nm* cheekbone.

ponche ('pontʃe) *nm* punch.

poncho ('pontʃo) *nm* poncho.

ponderar (ponde'rar) *vt* 1 ponder. 2 estimate. 3 esteem. **ponderación** *nf* consideration, esteem.

ponente (po'nente) *nm* 1 proposer (of motion, etc.). 2 spokesman.

poner (po'ner) *vt* put (down, up, on, etc.). **ponerse** *vr* 1 put on (clothes). 2 set (sun). **poner con** connect (telephone). **poner la radio** turn on the radio. **ponerse bravo** get angry. **ponerse rojo** turn red.

pongo ('pongo) *v see* **poner.**

pontificado (pontifi'kaðo) *nm* papacy. **pontifical** *adj* papal. **pontífice** *nm* pope.

pontón (pon'ton) *nm* pontoon.

ponzoña (pon'θoɲa) *nf* poison. **ponzoñoso** *adj* poisonous.

popa ('popa) *nf* poop, stern.

populacho (popu'latʃo) *nm* mob.

popular (popu'lar) *adj* popular. **popularidad** *nf* popularity. **popularizar** *vt* popularize.

poquedad (poke'ðað) *nf* 1 paucity. 2 timidity.

poquito (po'kito) *adj* very little. *nm* a little bit.

por (por) *prep* 1 for. 2 to. 3 from. 4 by. 5 through, about (place). 6 in exchange for. **por ciento** percent. **por la noche** at or in the night. **¿por qué?** why?

porcelana (porθe'lana) *nf* porcelain.

porcentaje (porθen'taxe) *nm* percentage.

porción (por'θjon) *nf* portion.

porche ('portʃe) *nm* 1 porch. 2 arcade.

porfiar (por'fjar) *vi* insist. **porfía** *nf* insistence, persistence.

pormenor (porme'nor) *nm* detail.

pornografía (pornogra'fia) *nf* pornography.

poro ('poro) *nm* pore. **poroso** *adj* porous.

porque ('porke) *conj* because.

porquería (porke'ria) *nf sl* rubbish, trash.

porra ('porra) *nf* truncheon. **porrazo** *nm* blow, beating.

porrón (por'ron) *adj* dull, stupid.

portador (porta'ðor) *nm comm* bearer.

portal (por'tal) *nm* portal, entrance.

portamonedas (portamo'neðas) *nm invar* wallet.

portarse (por'tarse) *vr* behave.

portátil (por'tatil) *adj* portable.

portazgo (por'taɣgo) *nm* toll, road-tax.

portazo (por'taθo) *nm* bang. **dar un portazo** slam the door.

porte ('porte) *nm* 1 postage, transport costs. 2 behaviour. 3 bearing (of a person). **franco de porte** postage paid.

portento (por'tento) *nm* prodigy. **portentoso** *adj* prodigious.

portería (porte'ria) *nf* porter's lodge. **portero** *nm* doorman, porter.

portezuela (porte'θwela) *nf* door (of car).

pórtico ('portiko) *nm* portico.

portilla (por'tiʎa) *nf* porthole.

Portugal (portu'gal) *nm* Portugal. **portugués** *adj,nm* Portuguese. *nm* Portuguese (language).

porvenir (porβe'nir) *nm* future.

pos (pos) *prep* **en pos de** behind, after.

posada (po'saða) *nf* 1 lodging. 2 inn. 3 dwelling, home.

posar (po'sar) vt place, put down. posarse vr settle. pose nm pose, posture. poso nm sediment.

poseer* (pose'er) vt possess. posesión nf possession.

posibilitar (posiβili'tar) vt facilitate.

posible (po'siβle) adj possible. posibilidad possibility, opportunity.

posición (posi'θjon) nf position.

positivo (posi'tiβo) adj positive. nm tech,phot positive.

posponer* (pospo'ner) vt 1 postpone. 2 put below. 3 think less of.

postal (pos'tal) adj postal. nf postcard.

poste ('poste) nm pole, post.

postergar (poster'gar) vt pass over, put aside.

posteridad (posteri'ðað) nf posterity. posterior adj 1 later. 2 latter. 3 rear.

postizo (pos'tiθo) adj artificial.

postrar (pos'trar) vt prostrate.

postre ('postre) nm dessert.

postular (postu'lar) vt postulate, demand.

póstumo ('postumo) adj posthumous.

postura (pos'tura) nf 1 posture. 2 stand.

potable (po'taβle) adj drinkable.

potaje (po'taxe) nm stew.

potasio (po'tasjo) nm potassium.

pote ('pote) nm pot, jar.

potencia (po'tenθja) nf capability, potential. potencia en caballos horsepower. potencial adj potential. potentado nm potentate. potente adj powerful.

potestad (potes'tað) nf authority.

potro ('potro) nm 1 colt. 2 rack (torture). potrero nm paddock.

pozo ('poθo) nm well.

práctica ('praktika) nf practice, exercise. practicable adj usable. practicar vt practise. práctico adj 1 practical. 2 practised, expert.

pradera (pra'ðera) nf 1 meadow. 2 prairie. prado nm meadow, field.

preámbulo (pre'ambulo) nm preamble.

precario (pre'karjo) adj precarious.

precaución (prekau'θjon) nf 1 precaution. 2 caution.

preceder (preθe'ðer) vt,vi precede.

precepto (pre'θepto) nm precept.

preciarse (pre'θjarse) vr boast. precio nm price, value.

precioso (pre'θjoso) adj 1 valuable. 2 beautiful.

precipicio (preθi'piθjo) nm precipice.

precipitar (preθipi'tar) vt hasten, precipitate.

precipitarse vr throw oneself headlong. precipitoso adj rash.

precisar (preθi'sar) vt,vi 1 need, be necessary. 2 clarify. preciso adj 1 necessary. 2 precise. precisión nf precision.

preconizar (prekoni'θar) vt praise.

precoz (pre'koθ) adj precocious. precosidad nf precocity.

precursor (prekur'sor) nm forerunner.

predecesor (preðeθe'sor) nm predecessor.

predecir* (preðe'θir) vt foretell. predicción nf prediction.

predestinar (preðesti'nar) vt predestine.

prédica ('preðika) nf sermon. predicar vt,vi preach.

predilección (preðilek'θjon) nf predilection.

predisponer* (preðispo'ner) vt predispose. predisposición nf predisposition.

predominar (preðomi'nar) vi predominate. vt dominate. predominante adj predominant. predominio nm predominance.

preeminencia (preemi'nenθja) nf pre-eminence. preeminente adj pre-eminent.

prefacio (pre'faθjo) nm preface.

prefecto (pre'fekto) nm prefect. prefectura nf prefecture.

preferir (ie) (prefe'rir) vt prefer. preferencia nf preference.

prefijo (pre'fixo) nm prefix.

pregonar (prego'nar) vt announce. pregón nm announcement. pregonero nm street-crier.

preguntar (pregun'tar) vt 1 ask. 2 question. vi inquire. pregunta nf question.

prejuicio (pre'xwiθjo) nm prejudice.

prejuzgar (prexuθ'gar) vt prejudge.

prelado (pre'laðo) nm prelate.

preliminar (prelimi'nar) adj,nm preliminary.

preludio (pre'luðjo) nm prelude.

prematuro (prema'turo) adj premature.

premeditar (premeði'tar) vt premeditate. premeditación nf premeditation.

premiar (pre'mjar) vt reward. premio nm 1 prize. 2 comm premium.

premisa (pre'misa) nf proposition, premise.

premura (pre'mura) nf urgency.

prenda ('prenda) nf 1 pledge. 2 garment. prendero nm second-hand dealer, pawnbroker. dejar en prenda pawn.

prender (pren'der) vt take, catch. vi catch, get caught. prendimiento nm capture, arrest.

prensa ('prensa) nf press. prensar vt press.

preñado (pre'ñaðo) adj 1 bulging. 2 pregnant. preñar vt make pregnant.

preocupar (preoku'par) vt worry. **preocupación** nf worry.

preparar (prepa'rar) vt prepare. **preparación** nf preparation.

preponderar (preponde'rar) vi be in the majority. **preponderancia** nf preponderance.

prerrogativa (prerroga'tiβa) nf prerogative.

presa[1] ('presa) nf 1 prey, victim. 2 claw. 3 hold, clutch.

presa[2] ('presa) nf 1 dam. 2 ditch.

presagiar (presa'xjar) vt presage. **presagio** nm omen.

présbita ('presβita) adj invar long-sighted.

presbítero (pres'βitero) nm priest.

prescindir (presθin'dir) vi dispense with. **prescindible** adj dispensable.

prescribir (preskri'βir) vt prescribe. **prescripción** nf prescription.

presenciar (presen'θjar) vt attend, witness. **presencia** nf presence.

presentar (presen'tar) vt 1 present. 2 introduce (a person).

presente (pre'sente) adj,nm present.

presentir (ie) (presen'tir) vt have forebodings of. **presentimiento** nm foreboding.

preservar (preser'βar) vt protect. **preservación** nf protection.

presidencia (presi'ðenθja) nf presidency. **presidente** nm president.

presidiario (presi'ðjarjo) nm convict. **presidio** nm 1 prison. 2 penal sentence. 3 pol praesidium.

presidir (presi'ðir) vt preside over. vi preside.

presilla (pre'siʎa) nf loop, fastener.

presión (pre'sjon) nf pressure.

preso ('preso) adj under arrest. nm prisoner.

préstamo ('prestamo) nm loan.

prestar (pres'tar) vt lend. **prestador** nm lender. **prestamista** nm money-lender. **prestatario** nm borrower.

presteza (pres'teθa) nf promptness.

prestidigitador (prestiðixita'ðor) nm conjurer.

prestigio (pres'tixjo) nm prestige. **prestigioso** adj prestigious.

presto ('presto) adj prompt. adv at once.

presumir (presu'mir) vi 1 presume. 2 be presumptuous. **presumido** adj presumptuous.

presunción (presun'θjon) nf presumption. **presunto** adj presumed. **presuntuoso** adj conceited.

presuponer* (presupo'ner) vt presuppose.

presupuesto (presu'pwesto) nm budget.

presura (pre'sura) nf haste. **presuroso** adj hasty.

pretender (preten'der) vt 1 claim. 2 aspire to. 3 allege. **pretendiente** nm 1 claimant. 2 suitor.

pretensión (preten'sjon) nf 1 claim. 2 pretension.

pretexto (pre'teksto) nm pretext.

prevalecer* (preβale'θer) vi prevail.

prevaricar (preβari'kar) vi prevaricate.

prevención (preβen'θjon) nf 1 preparation, precaution. 2 police station. **preventivo** adj preventive.

prevenir (preβe'nir) vt 1 prepare. 2 prevent, foresee. 3 warn.

prever (pre'βer) vt foresee.

previo ('preβjo) adj previous. nm playback (film).

previsión (preβi'sjon) nf foresight. **previsión social** social security.

prieto ('prjeto) adj 1 dark (colour). 2 tight, packed.

prima ('prima) nf premium, bonus.

primario (pri'marjo) adj primary. **primacía** nf primacy.

primavera (prima'βera) nf 1 spring, springtime. 2 primrose. **primaveral** adj 1 spring. 2 fresh, virginal.

primero (pri'mero) adj 1 first. 2 foremost. adv first.

primitivo (primi'tiβo) adj original, primitive.

primo ('primo) nm cousin.

primogénito (primo'xenito) adj first-born.

primor (pri'mor) nm beauty. **primoroso** adj beautiful.

princesa (prin'θesa) nf princess.

principal (prinθi'pal) adj,nm 1 principal. 2 comm capital.

príncipe ('prinθipe) nm prince.

principiar (prinθi'pjar) vt begin. **principio** nm 1 beginning. 2 principle.

pringar (prin'gar) vt 1 baste. 2 soil (with grease). **pringoso** adj greasy.

prior (pri'or) nm prior. **prioridad** nf priority.

prisa ('prisa) nf hurry.

prisión (pri'sjon) nm imprisonment. **prisionero** nm prisoner.

prisma ('prisma) nm prism. **prismático** adj prismatic.

privar[1] (pri'βar) vt deprive. **privarse** vr forgo. **privado** adj private.

privar[2] (pri'βar) vi be favourite. **privado** nm favourite. **privanza** nf favour, period of favour.

privilegiar (priβile'xjar) *vt* favour, grant privilege to. **privilegio** *nm* 1 privilege. 2 concession.

pro (pro) *prep* **en pro de** on behalf of.

proa ('proa) *nf* 1 *naut* bows, prow. 2 *aviat* nose.

probable (pro'βaβle) *adj* probable. **probabilidad** *nf* probability.

probar (ue) (pro'βar) *vt,vi* test, try. 2 taste. 3 prove. **probador** *nm* fitting-room. **probatorio** *adj* serving as evidence. **probeta** *nf* 1 test tube. 2 cylinder.

problema (pro'βlema) *nm* problem.

proceder (proθe'ðer) *vi* 1 procede. 2 originate. 3 be appropriate. **proceder** *nm* also **procedimiento** 1 procedure. 2 *law* proceedings. **procedencia** *nf* origin. **procedente** *adj* 1 originating from. 2 appropriate.

procesar (proθe'sar) *vt law* try, prosecute. **procesado** *nm* accused, defendant. **procesal** *adj law* legal. **proceso** *nm* 1 process. 2 trial, prosecution.

proclamar (prokla'mar) *vt* proclaim. **proclama** *nf* also **proclamación** proclamation.

procrear (prokre'ar) *vt,vi* procreate.

procurar (proku'rar) *vt* 1 attempt, try. 2 obtain, succeed. **procuración** *nf law* proxy. **procurador** *nm law* attorney.

prodigar (proði'gar) *vt* lavish, squander. **prodigarse** *vr* be prodigal.

prodigio (pro'ðixjo) *nm* prodigy. **prodigioso** *adj* prodigious.

pródigo ('proðigo) *adj* prodigal, lavish.

producir (proðu'θir) *vt* produce. **producirse** *vr* come about, take place. **producción** *nf* production. **productividad** *nf* productivity. **productivo** *adj* productive. **producto** *nm* 1 product. 2 produce. 3 profit. **productor** *adj* producing. *nm* producer.

proeza (pro'eθa) *nf* deed.

profanar (profa'nar) *vt* profane. **profano** *adj* profane.

profecía (profe'θia) *nf* prophecy.

proferir (ie) (profe'rir) *vt* utter.

profesar (profe'sar) *vt* profess. **profesión** *nf* profession. **profesional** *adj* professional. **profesor** *nm* teacher, professor.

profeta (pro'feta) *nm* prophet.

prófugo ('profugo) *nm* fugitive.

profundidad (profundi'ðað) *nf* depth. **profundo** *adj* deep, profound.

profundizar (profundi'θar) *vt* deepen.

profusión (profu'sjon) *nf* profusión. **profuso** *adj* profuse.

programa (pro'grama) *nm* programme.

progresar (progre'sar) *vi* progress. **progresivo** *adj* progressive. **progreso** *nm* progress.

prohibir (proi'βir) *vt* prohibit. **prohibición** *nf* prohibition.

prohijar (proi'xar) *vt* adopt.

prójimo ('proximo) *nm* 1 fellow man. 2 neighbour.

prole ('prole) *nf* offspring.

proletario (prole'tarjo) *adj,nm* proletarian.

prolífico (pro'lifiko) *adj* prolific.

prolijo (pro'lixo) *adj* longwinded.

prólogo ('prologo) *nm* prologue.

prolongar (prolon'gar) *vt* prolong.

promediar (prome'ðjar) *vt* 1 bisect. 2 *math* average. *vi* be midway. **promedio** *nm* average.

promesa (pro'mesa) *nf* promise.

prometer (prome'ter) *vt,vi* promise. **prometerse** *vr* expect.

prominencia (promi'nenθja) *nf* bump, hillock. **prominente** *adj* prominent.

promiscuo (pro'miskwo) *adj* 1 motley. 2 ambiguous.

promontorio (promon'torjo) *nm* promontory.

promover (ue) (promo'βer) *vt* promote. **promoción** *nf* promotion. **promotor** *nm* promoter.

promulgar (promul'gar) *vt* promulgate.

pronombre (pro'nombre) *nm* pronoun.

pronosticar (pronosti'kar) *vt* predict, forecast. **pronóstico** (pro'nostiko) *nm* prediction, forecast.

prontitud (pronti'tuð) *nf* promptness, quickness. **pronto** *adj* quick, prompt. *adv* quickly, at once.

pronunciar (pronun'θjar) *vt* pronounce. **pronunciación** *nf* pronunciation.

propagar (propa'gar) *vt* propagate. **propaganda** *nf* 1 advertisement. 2 propaganda.

propalar (propa'lar) *vt* make public.

propenso (pro'penso) *adj* inclined, prone.

propicio (pro'piθjo) *adj* propitious.

propiedad (propje'ðað) *nf* 1 property. 2 *comm* copyright. **propietario** *nm* owner.

propina (pro'pina) *nf* tip (money).

propio ('propjo) *adj* 1 own, particular. 2 proper.

proponer (propo'ner) *vt* propose.

proporción (propor'θjon) *nf* proportion. **proporcionar** *vt* provide.

proposición (proposi'θjon) *nf* proposition.

propósito (pro'posito) *nm* purpose. **a propó-**

propuesta

sito on purpose. **a propósito de** with regard to.

propuesta (pro'pwesta) *nf* proposal.

propulsar (propul'sar) *vt tech* drive. **propulsión** *nf* propulsion.

prorrata (pror'rata) *nf* quota. **a prorrata** *adv* pro rata.

prórroga ('prorroga) *nf* 1 respite. 2 extension.

prorrogar (prorro'gar) *vt* 1 adjourn. 2 defer

prorrumpir (prorrum'pir) *vi* break out.

prosa ('prosa) *nf* prose. **prosaico** *adj* prosaic.

proscribir (proskri'βir) *vt* outlaw, ban.

prosecución (proseku'θjon) *nf* continuation.

proseguir (i) (prose'gir) *vt,vi* continue.

prospecto (pros'pekto) *nm* prospectus.

prosperar (prospe'rar) *vi* prosper. **prosperidad** *nf* prosperity. **próspero** *adj* prosperous.

prostituir* (prostitu'ir) *vt* prostitute. **prostitución** *nf* prostitution. **prostituta** *nf* prostitute.

protagonista (protago'nista) *nm,f Th* protagonist, hero

protección (protek'θjon) *nf* protection. **protector** *adj* protective. *nm* protector.

proteger (prote'xer) *vt* protect. **protegido** *nm* protégé.

proteína (prote'ina) *nf* protein.

protestar (protes'tar) *vi* protest. *vt* bounce (a cheque) **protesta** *nf* protest. **protestación** *nf* protestation. **protestante** *nm,f* Protestant.

protocolo (proto'kolo) *nm* protocol, formalities.

prototipo (proto'tipo) *nm* prototype.

protuberancia (protuβe'ranθja) *nf* protuberance

provecho (pro'βetʃo) *nm* advantage, profit. **provechoso** *adj* advantageous, profitable.

proveer (proβe'er) *vt* 1 provide. 2 deal with. **proveedor** *nm* 1 supplier. 2 dealer.

provenir* (proβe'nir) *vi* originate.

proverbio (pro'βerβjo) *nm* proverb.

providencia (proβi'ðenθja) *nf* 1 providence, forethought. 2 *law* ruling.

provincia (pro'βinθja) *nf* province. **provincial** *adj* provincial. **provinciano** *nm* 1 provincial 2 *inf* boor

provisión (proβi'sjon) *nf* provision. **provisional** *adj* provisional.

provocar (proβo'kar) *vt* provoke. **provocación** *nf* provocation. **provocador** *adj also* **provocativo** provocative.

próximo ('proksimo) *adj* next, nearest.

proyectar (projek'tar) *vt* 1 project, throw (out). 2 plan, design. **proyectil** *nm* projectile.

proyecto *nm* plan, project. **proyector** *nm* 1 *phot* projector. 2 spotlight.

prudencia (pru'ðenθja) *nf* prudence. **prudencial** *adj* (of an action) wise. **prudente** *adj* (of a person) wise.

prueba ('prweβa) *nf* 1 proof. 2 test. **a prueba de** proof against.

prurito (pru'rito) *nm* 1 *med* itch. 2 urge.

psicoanálisis (psikoa'nalisis) *nm* psychoanalysis.

psicología (psikolo'xia) *nf* psychology. **psicológico** *adj* psychological. **psicólogo** *nm* psychologist.

psiquiatría (psikia'tria) *nf* psychiatry. **psiquiatra** *nm* psychiatrist. **psiquiátrico** *adj* psychiatric.

púa ('pua) *nf* 1 spine. 2 tooth. 3 needle.

pubertad (puβer'tað) *nf* puberty.

publicar (puβli'kar) *vt* publish. **publicación** *nf* publication. **publicidad** *nf* publicity, advertising.

público ('puβliko) *adj,nm* public.

pude ('puðe) *v see* **poder.**

púdico ('puðiko) *adj* chaste, modest.

pudiente (pu'ðjente) *adj* rich.

pudor (pu'ðor) *nm* modesty. **pudoroso** *adj* chaste, modest.

pudrir* (pu'ðrir) *vt* rot.

pueblo ('pweβlo) *nm* 1 *pol* people. 2 provincial town.

puente ('pwente) *nm* bridge.

puerco ('pwerko) *nm* pig.

pueril (pwe'ril) *adj* childish.

puerro ('pwerro) *nm* leek.

puerta ('pwerta) *nf* 1 door. 2 gate. **puerto** *nm* 1 port. 2 mountain pass.

pues (pwes) *adv* 1 then, so. 2 *inf* well. *conj* for, since.

puesta ('pwesta) *nf* 1 setting (of sun). 2 *game* stake. **puesta en escena** stage management.

puesto ('pwesto) *v see* **poner.** *nm* place, post. **puesto que** *conj* since, given that.

pugnar (pug'nar) *vi* fight. **pugnaz** *adj* pugnacious.

pujar (pu'xar) *vi* strain. **pujante** *adj* 1 straining. 2 powerful

pulcritud (pulkri'tuð) *nf* neatness. **pulcro** *adj* neat.

pulga ('pulga) *nf* flea.

pulgada (pul'gaða) *nf* inch. **pulgar** *nm* thumb.

pulir (pu'lir) *vt* polish. **pulimiento** *nm* polish.

pulmón (pul'mon) *nm* lung.

pulmonía (pulmo'nia) *nf* pneumonia.

114

pulpa ('pulpa) nf pulp.

púlpito ('pulpito) nm pulpit.

pulsar (pul'sar) vi pulsate. **pulso** nm 1 pulse. 2 wrist. 3 steadiness (of the hand).

pulsera (pul'sera) nf bracelet.

pulverizar (pulβeri'θar) vt pulverize.

pulla ('puʎa) nf 1 obscenity. 2 taunt.

punción (pun'θjon) nf med puncture.

punición (puni'θjon) nf punishment. **punible** adj punishable. **punitivo** adj punitive.

punta ('punta) nf point, tip.

puntapié (puntapi'e) nm kick.

puntear (punte'ar) vt 1 tick (off). 2 perforate, stitch.

puntería (punte'ria) nf aim.

puntilla (pun'tiʎa) nf 1 tack, nib. 2 lace.

punto ('punto) nm 1 point, spot. 2 full stop. 3 stitch.

puntual (pun'twal) adj 1 reliable. 2 punctual. **puntualidad** nf 1 reliability. 2 punctuality.

puntualizar (puntwali'θar) vt 1 clarify. 2 work out in detail.

punzar (pun'θar) vt pierce. **punzada** nf puncture, prick.

puñado (pu'ɲaðo) nm handful. **puñada** nf also **puñetazo** nm punch, blow. **puño** nm 1 fist. 2 handle, knob.

puñal (pu'ɲal) nm dagger. **puñalada** nf stab.

pupila (pu'pila) nf pupil (eye).

pupilaje (pupi'laxe) nm boarding (house). **pupilo** nm law ward.

pupitre (pu'pitre) nm desk.

puré (pu're) nm purée.

pureza (pu'reθa) nf purity.

purgar (pur'gar) vt purge, purify. **purgarse** vr med take a purge. **purgante** adj also **purgativo** purgative.

purgatorio (purga'torjo) nm purgatory.

purificar (purifi'kar) vt purify. **purificación** nf purification.

puritano (puri'tano) adj,n puritan.

puro ('puro) adj pure, simple. nm cigar.

púrpura ('purpura) nf purple.

puse ('puse) v see **poner.**

pusilánime (pusi'lanime) adj cowardly.

pústula ('pustula) nf med pustule, pimple.

puta ('puta) nf inf prostitute.

putrefacción (putrefak'θjon) nf rot, decay.

pútrido ('putriðo) adj putrid.

puya ('puja) nf goad.

Q

que (ke) pron who, that, which. conj that, than.

qué (ke) pron, adj what? ¡qué raro! how extraordinary!

quebrantar (keβran'tar) vt shatter. **quebranto** nm exhaustion.

quebrar (ie) (ke'βrar) vt break. vi go bankrupt. **quebrado** adj 1 broken, rough. 2 weakened. 3 bankrupt. **quebradura** nf crack, break.

quedar (ke ðar) vi 1 stay, remain. 2 be, lie (in a place). **quedarse** vr 1 stay behind. 2 grow calm (sea). **quedar bien** give a good impression. **quedar en nada** come to nothing.

quedo ('keðo) adj quiet. adv quietly. **queda** nf curfew.

quehacer (kea'θer) nm chore.

quejarse (ke'xarse) vr complain. **queja** nf complaint. **quejido** nm moan.

quemar (ke'mar) vt burn. vi be scalding. **quemadura** nf burn. **quemazón** nf burning, smarting.

quepo ('kepo) v see **caber.**

querella (ke'reʎa) nf 1 quarrel. 2 law complaint. nm plaintiff. **querellar** vt reprimand. **querellarse** vr law make a complaint.

querer (ie) (ke'rer) vt,vi 1 want. 2 love, like. nm affection. **querido** adj dear.

queso ('keso) nm cheese.

quiá (ki'a) interj never!

quicio ('kiθjo) nm hinge.

quiebra ('kjeβra) nf 1 fissure, break. 2 bankruptcy. **quiebro** nm mus trill.

quien (kjen) pron 1 who. 2 whom. 3 whoever.

quieto ('kjeto) adj still. **quietud** nf stillness.

quijote (ki'xote) nm quixotic person.

quilate (ki'late) nm carat.

quilla ('kiʎa) nf keel.

quimera (ki'mera) nf 1 false notion, hallucination. 2 unjustified suspicion. 3 quarrel.

química (ki'mika) nf chemistry. **químico** adj chemical. nm chemist.

quincalla (kin'θaʎa) nf 1 hardware. 2 small wares. 3 ironmongery. **quincallero** nm 1 dealer in hardware or small wares. 2 ironmonger.

quince ('kinθe) adj, nm fifteen.

quincena (kin'θena) nf fortnight.

quincuagésimo (kinkwa'xesimo) adj fiftieth.

quinta ('kinta) nf 1 country estate. 2 mil call-up.

quintal (kin'tal) nm hundredweight.

quinteto (kin'teto) *nm* quintet.

quinto ('kinto) *adj* fifth.

quiosco ('kjosko) *nm* kiosk.

quirúrgico (ki'rurxiko) *adj* surgical.

quise ('kise) *v* see **querer.**

quisquilla (kis'kiʎa) *nf* 1 quibble. 2 *zool* shrimp. **quisquilloso** *adj* quibbling.

quiste ('kiste) *nm* cyst.

quitar (ki'tar) *vt* remove, take away. **quitarse** *vr* 1 withdraw. 2 get rid of, take off, undress. **quitamanchas** *nm invar* stain-remover.

quitasol (kita'sol) *nm* parasol.

quizá(s) (ki'θa) *adv* perhaps.

R

rábano ('raβano) *nm* radish.

rabiar (raβi'ar) *vi* rage, rave. **rabia** *nf* 1 rage, fury. 2 *med* rabies. **rabioso** *adj* 1 *med* rabid. 2 raging, furious.

rabo ('raβo) *nm* tail.

racial (ra'θjal) *adj* racial.

racimo (ra'θimo) *nm* bunch of grapes, bunch.

raciocinar (raθjoθi'nar) *vi* reason, consider rationally. **raciocinio** *nm* reason.

ración (ra'θjon) *nf* 1 ration, portion. 2 *math* ratio.

racional (raθjo'nal) *adj* reasonable.

racionar (raθjo'nar) *vt* share, ration. **racionamiento** *nm* rationing.

racha ('ratʃa) *nf* 1 gust (of wind). 2 stroke of luck.

radiactivo (raðjak'tivo) *adj* also **radioactivo** radioactive. **radiactividad** *nf* radioactivity.

radiar (ra'ðjar) *vt* radiate. **radiación** *nf* radiation. **radiador** *nm* radiator. **radiante** *adj* radiant.

radicar (raði'kar) *vi* take or have roots. **radical** *adj* radical.

radio[1] ('raðjo) *nf* radio. **radiodifusión** *nf* broadcasting. **radiografía** *nf* 1 X-ray. 2 radiography. **radiología** *nf* radiology. **radiólogo** *nm* radiologist. **radioyente** *nm,f* listener (to the radio).

radio[2] ('raðjo) *nm* 1 radius. 2 spoke (wheel).

radiogente (raðjo'jente) *nm,f* listener (to the radio).

raer (ra'er) *vt* scrape.

raíz (ra'iθ) *nf* root.

rajar (ra'xar) *vt* crack, split. **raja** *nf* also **rajadura** 1 split, crack. 2 slice, sliver.

ralea (ra'lea) *nf* sort, kind.

rallar (ra'ʎar) *vt* grate (cheese, etc.). **rallador** *nm* grater.

rama ('rama) *nf* branch. **ramada** *nf* also **ramaje** *nm* foliage. **ramal** *nm* 1 *mot* branch, sideroad. 2 halter.

rambla ('rambla) *nf* 1 riverbed. 2 avenue.

ramificarse (ramifi'karse) *vr* ramify, branch off. **ramificación** *nf* ramification.

ramillete (rami'ʎete) *nm* bouquet of flowers.

ramo ('ramo) *nm* 1 *comm* branch, department. 2 branch (of a tree).

rampa ('rampa) *nf* ramp.

ramplón (ram'plon) *adj* vulgar.

rana ('rana) *nf* frog.

rancio ('ranθjo) *adj* 1 rancid. 2 ancient. 3 old-fashioned. **rancidez** *nf* 1 age, antiquity. 2 mustiness, rancidness.

rancho ('rantʃo) *nm* 1 farmhouse. 2 hut. 3 *mil* communal meal.

rango ('rango) *nm* rank.

ranura (ra'nura) *nf* slot.

rapaz (ra'paθ) *adj* rapacious. **rapacidad** *nf* rapacity.

rapido (ra'piðo) *adj* swift. *adv* quickly. **rapidez** *nf* rapidity.

rapiña (ra'piɲa) *nf* robbery.

raptar (rap'tar) *vt* abduct. **rapto** *nm* abduction.

raqueta (ra'keta) *nf* racquet.

rareza (ra'reθa) *nf* 1 rarity. 2 oddity. **raro** *adj* 1 odd. 2 rare, remarkable.

ras (ras) *nm* 1 ground level. 2 level. **a ras de** level with.

rascacielos (raska'θjelos) *nm invar* skyscraper.

rascar (ras'kar) *vt* scrape, scratch.

rasgar (ras'gar) *vt* tear, rip. **rasgón** *nm* tear. **rasguño** *nm* 1 scratch. 2 *Art* sketch.

rasgo ('rasgo) *nm* 1 stroke, flourish. 2 feature, characteristic.

raso ('raso) *adj* 1 smooth. 2 level. 3 (of the sky) clear.

raspar (ras'par) *vt* scrape, file down. **raspa** *nf* 1 ear of corn. 2 fishbone.

rastra ('rastra) *nf* 1 string of garlic, dry fruit, etc. 2 harrow. 3 sledge. 4 trawling dredge.

rastrear (rastre'ar) *vt* 1 drag, dredge, harrow. 2 track, hunt.

rastrillar (rastri'ʎar) *vt* rake up. **rastrillo** *nm* rake.

rastro ('rastro) *nm* 1 track, trace. 2 rake.

rastrojo (ras'troxo) *nm* stubble.

rasurar (rasu'rar) *vt* shave.

rata ('rata) *nf* rat.

ratería (rate'ria) *nf* petty thieving. **ratero** *nm* petty thief.

ratificar (ratifi'kar) *vt* ratify.

rato ('rato) *nm* while, period of time.

ratón (ra'ton) *nm* mouse. **ratonera** *nf* mousetrap.

rayar (ra'jar) *vt* 1 stripe. 2 cross out. 3 scratch (furniture, etc.). **rayar en** border on. **raya** *nf* 1 stripe, line. 2 trouser crease. 3 boundary. 4 parting (of hair).

rayo ('rajo) *nm* 1 ray, beam. 2 lightning.

raza ('raθa) *nf* race, breed.

razón (ra'θon) *nf* 1 reason. 2 rationale. **tener razón** be right.

razonar (raθo'nar) *vt* argue out, justify. **razonable** *adj* reasonable.

reacción (reak'θjon) *nf* reaction. **reaccionar** *vi* react. **reaccionario** *adj,n* reactionary. **reactivo** *nm* reagent. **reactor** *nm* 1 reactor. 2 *aviat* jet.

reacio (re'aθjo) *adj* stubborn.

real [1] (re'al) *adj* real.

real [2] (re'al) *adj* royal.

realce (re'alθe) *nm* 1 highlight. 2 importance.

realizar (reali'θar) *vt* 1 fulfil. 2 *comm* realize.

realzar (real'θar) *vt* 1 highlight. 2 *art* emboss.

reanimar (reani'mar) *vt* revive.

reanudar (reanu'ðar) *vt* renew.

rebajar (reβa'xar) *vt* 1 lower. 2 *comm* reduce, discount. 3 weaken (a drink). **rebaja** *nf* 1 discount, reduction. 2 *pl comm* sale.

rebanada (reβa'naða) *nf* slice.

rebaño (re'βaɲo) *nm* flock.

rebasar (reβa'sar) *vt* exceed.

rebatir (reβa'tir) *vt* repel, refute. **rebato** *nm* 1 call to arms. 2 surprise attack.

rebeca (re'βeka) *nf* cardigan.

rebelarse (reβe'larse) *vr* rebel. **rebelde** *adj* rebellious. *nm,f* rebel. **rebelión** *nf* rebellion.

rebosar (reβo'sar) *vi* overflow.

rebotar (reβo'tar) *vt,vi* bounce, turn back. **rebote** *nm* 1 bounce, rebound. 2 ricochet.

rebozar (reβo'θar) *vt* wrap up. **rebozo** *nm* muffler.

rebuscar (reβus'kar) *vt* search out. **rebuscado** *adj* elaborate.

rebuznar (reβuθ'nar) *vi* bray. **rebuzno** *nm* bray.

recado (re'kaðo) *nm* 1 message. 2 gift.

recaer* (reka'er) *vi* relapse. **recaída** *nf* relapse.

recalcar (rekal'kar) *vt* 1 emphasize. 2 press, squeeze.

recalcitrante (rekalθi'trante) *adj* recalcitrant.

recalentar (ie) (rekalen'tar) *vt* reheat. **recalentarse** *vr* overheat.

recambio (re'kambjo) *nm* 1 spare part. 2 replacement, refill.

recargar (rekar'gar) *vt* 1 overload. 2 *tech* recharge. **recargo** *nm* comm surcharge.

recatarse (reka'tarse) *vr* 1 act modestly. 2 be cautious. **recato** *nm* 1 modesty. 2 caution.

recaudar (rekau'ðar) *vt* comm, pol collect (debts, taxes). **recaudo** *nm* 1 comm collection (tax). 2 safekeeeping.

recelar (reθe'lar) *vt,vi* suspect. **recelo** *nm* suspicion. **receloso** *adj* suspicious.

recepción (reθep'θjon) *nf* reception. **recepcionista** *nf* receptionist.

receptáculo (reθep'takulo) *nm* receptacle.

receptor (reθep'tor) *nm* receiver.

recesión (reθe'sjon) *nf* comm,pol recession.

receta (re'θeta) *nf* 1 recipe. 2 prescription.

recibir (reθi'βir) *vt* 1 receive. 2 welcome. **recibo** *nm* receipt.

recién (re'θjen) *adv* recently, just. **reciente** *adj* recent, new.

recinto (re'θinto) *nm* precinct.

recio ('reθjo) *adj* tough.

recipiente (reθi'pjente) *nm* 1 receptacle. 2 recipient.

reciprocar (reθipro'kar) *vt* reciprocate. **recíproco** *adj* reciprocal.

recitar (reθi'tar) *vt* recite. *nm* recital.

reclamar (rekla'mar) *vt* claim. *vi* law appeal. **reclamación** *nf* 1 claim. 2 complaint. **reclamo** *nm* 1 advertisement. 2 lure (for birds).

reclinar (rekli'nar) *vt* lean.

reclusión (reklu'sjon) *nf* 1 seclusion. 2 imprisonment. **recluso** *adj,n* 1 recluse. 2 convict.

recluta (re'kluta) *nf* recruitment. *nm* recruit.

recobrar (reko'βrar) *vt* 1 recover. 2 reclaim.

recoger (reko'xer) *vt* 1 collect, gather. **recogerse** *vr* withdraw, retire.

recolección (rekolek'θjon) *nf* 1 harvest. 2 recollection. 3 compilation.

recomendar (ie) (rekomen'dar) *vt* 1 recommend. 2 praise. **recomendación** *nf* recommendation.

recompensar (rekompen'sar) *vt* 1 compensate. 2 reward. **recompensa** *nf* 1 compensation. 2 reward.

reconciliarse (rekonθi'ljarse) *vr* reconcile oneself. **reconciliación** *nf* reconciliation.

recóndito (re'kondito) *adj* obscure.

reconocer* (rekono'θer) *vt* 1 recognize. 2

117

acknowledge. 3 inspect. **reconocible** adj recognizable. **reconocimiento** nm 1 recognition. 2 acknowledgement. 3 inspection.

reconquista (rekon'kista) nf reconquest.

reconstituir (rekonstitu'ir) vt reconstitute.

reconstruir* (rekonstru'ir) vt reconstruct.

reconvenir* (rekonβe'nir) vt reprimand.

recopilar (rekopi'lar) vt 1 compile. 2 law codify. **recopilación** nf 1 summary. 2 law code.

recordar (rekor'ðar) vt,vi 1 remember. 2 remind. 3 recall.

recorrer (rekor'rer) vt 1 travel about. 2 look over, survey. 3 overhaul. **recorrido** nm route, stretch of journey.

recortar (rekor'tar) vt trim, cut back. **recortarse** vr stand out, show up. **recorte** nm 1 cutout. 2 cutting.

recoveco (reko'βeko) nm 1 street-corner. 2 nook.

recrearse (rekre'arse) vr entertain oneself. **recreo** nm recreation.

recriminar (rekrimi'nar) vt reproach.

recrudecer* (rekruðe'θer) vt make worse.

rectángulo (rek'tangulo) nm rectangle. adj rectangular, right-angled. **rectangular** adj rectangular.

rectificar (rektifi'kar) vt rectify, correct.

rectitud (rekti'tuð) nf rectitude. **recto** adj 1 straight. 2 upright, honest.

rector (rek'tor) nm head (of a school or university).

recua ('rekwa) nf mule train.

recuento (re'kwento) nm count, reckoning.

recuerdo (re'kwerðo) nm 1 memory. 2 souvenir. 3 pl regards, best wishes.

recular (reku'lar) vi recoil.

recuperar (rekupe'rar) vt recuperate, retrieve.

recurrir (reku'rir) vi 1 resort. 2 revert. **recurrir a** have recourse to.

recurso (re'kurso) nm 1 recourse. 2 pl comm funds, resources.

recusar (reku'sar) vt refuse.

rechazar (retʃa'θar) vt 1 repel. 2 reject. **rechazo** nm rebuff.

rechinar (retʃi'nar) vi creak.

rechoncho (re'tʃontʃo) adj thickset.

red (reð) nf 1 net. 2 network.

redactar (reðak'tar) vt 1 edit. 2 draft. **redacción** nf 1 editing. 2 editorial office or staff. **redactor** nm editor.

redención (reden'θjon) nf redemption. **redentor** nm redeemer.

redimir (reði'mir) vt redeem.

rédito ('reðito) nm comm interest, return.

redoblar (reðo'βlar) vt 1 fold, bend. 2 redouble. 3 beat (a drum). **redoble** nm drum roll.

redondear (reðonde'ar) vt round off. **redondo** adj round.

reducir* (reðu'θir) vt reduce. **reducción** nf reduction.

redundar (reðun'dar) vi redound. **redundancia** nf redundancy.

reduzco (re'ðuθko) v see **reducir.**

reembolsar (reembol'sar) vt reimburse. **reembolsable** adj refundable. **reembolso** nm refund.

reemplazar (reempla'θar) vt replace. **reemplazable** adj replaceable. **reemplazo** nm replacement.

referencia (refe'renθja) nf reference.

referéndum (refe'rendum) nm referendum.

referir (ie) (refe'rir) vt 1 relate, retell. 2 refer. **referirse a** refer to.

refinar (refi'nar) vt refine. **refinadura** nf process of refining. **refinamiento** nm refinement. **refinería** nf refinery.

reflector (reflek'tor) nm reflector.

reflejar (refle'xar) vt,vi reflect. **reflejo** nm 1 reflection. 2 reflex. adj reflex, reflected.

reflexionar (refleksjo'nar) vt,vi reflect on, consider.

reflexivo (reflek'siβo) adj,nm reflexive.

reflujo (re'fluxo) nm ebb.

reformar (refor'mar) vt 1 reform. 2 alter. **reforma** nf reform, reformation. **reformación** nf reform, reformation. **reformador** nm reformer. **reformatorio** nm reformatory.

reforzar (ue) (refor'θar) vt reinforce.

refractario (refrak'tarjo) adj 1 ovenproof. 2 obstinate.

refrán (re'fran) nm proverb.

refregar (ie) (refre'gar) vt scrub.

refrenar (refre'nar) vt hold back, curb.

refrescar (refres'kar) vt refresh. vi cool. **refrescante** adj cooling. **refresco** nm refreshment, long drink.

refrigerar (refrixe'rar) vt 1 cool. 2 refrigerate. **refrigeración** nf cooling system. **refrigerador** nm refrigerator.

refuerzo (re'fwerθo) nm reinforcement.

refugiarse (refu'xjarse) vr take refuge, flee. **refugiado** nm refugee. **refugio** nm refuge, shelter.

refulgir (reful'xir) vi shine brightly. **refulgencia** nf brilliance.

refundir (refun'dir) vt 1 recast. 2 reconstruct.

refunfuñar (refunfu'ɲar) vi 1 growl. 2 grumble.

refutar (refu'tar) vt refute.

regadera (rega'ðera) nf watering-can. **regadío** adj also **regadizo** irrigable.

regalar (rega'lar) vt 1 give (a present). 2 pamper, indulge. **regalo** nm present.

regaliz (rega'liθ) nm liquorice.

regañar (rega'ɲar) vt 1 reprimand. 2 inf nag. vi 1 grumble. 2 quarrel.

regar (ie) (re'gar) vt irrigate, water.

regatear (regate'ar) vt haggle over. vi haggle, bargain. **regateo** nm haggling.

regazo (re'gaθo) nm anat lap.

regencia (re'xenθja) nf regency.

regenerar (rexene'rar) vt regenerate. **regeneración** nf regeneration.

regentar (rexen'tar) vt occupy temporarily. **regente** nm 1 regent. 2 head man.

régimen ('reximen) nm 1 regime. 2 diet.

regimiento (rexi'mjento) nm 1 regiment. 2 government.

región (re'xjon) nf region. **regional** adj regional. **regionalismo** nm regionalism.

regir (i) (re'xir) vt govern.

registrar (rexis'trar) vt 1 register, record. 2 search, inspect. **registro** nm 1 registration. 2 register. 3 register office. 4 search, inspection.

reglar (re'glar) vt 1 rule (with lines). 2 regulate, adjust. **regla** nf rule, ruler.

regocijar (regoθi'xar) vt cheer, delight. **regocijo** nm rejoicing.

regresar (regre'sar) vi return. **regreso** nm return.

regular (regu'lar) vt regulate. adj regular, ordinary. **regulación** nf regulation, control. **regulador** nm control, regulator. **regularidad** nf regularity.

regularizar (regulari'θar) vt standardize.

rehabilitar (reaβili'tar) vt rehabilitate.

rehacer (rea'θer) vt 1 remake. 2 do again. **rehacerse** vr 1 rally, gain strength again. 2 get well.

rehén (re'en) nm hostage.

rehuir (reu'ir) vt avoid, shrink from.

rehusar (reu'sar) vt refuse.

reimprimir (reimpri'mir) vt reprint. **reimpresión** nf reprint.

reina ('reina) nf queen.

reinar (rei'nar) vi reign, rule. **reino** nm kingdom.

reincidir (reinθi'ðir) vi fall back, relapse.

reintegrar (reinte'grar) vt 1 reintegrate. 2 comm reimburse. **reintegro** nm 1 reimbursement, refund. 2 withdrawal (from a bank account).

reír* (re'ir) vi laugh. vt mock. **reírse de** have a laugh at.

reiterar (reite'rar) vt repeat.

reivindicar (reiβindi'kar) vt 1 vindicate. 2 claim. **reivindicación** nf 1 vindication 2 claim.

reja ('rexa) nf 1 grating, grille. 2 ploughshare. **rejilla** nf 1 small grating. 2 luggage rack.

rejuvenecer* (rexuβene'θer) vt rejuvenate.

relación (rela'θjon) nf 1 relation. 2 ratio. 3 account, telling (of a story). 4 pl relations, connections. 5 pl intercourse.

relacionar (relaθjo'nar) vt relate.

relajar (rela'xar) vt 1 relax. 2 slacken.

relámpago (re'lampago) nm lightning. **relampaguear** vi flash with lightning.

relatar (rela'tar) vt relate, narrate. **relato** nm account, story.

relatividad (relatiβi'ðað) nf relativity. **relativo** adj,nm relative.

relevar (rele'βar) vt 1 relieve. 2 Art carve in relief. **relevo** nm relief, change (of guard, etc.).

relicario (reli'karjo) nm 1 locket. 2 reliquary.

relieve (re'ljeβe) nm 1 art relief, embossing. 2 prominence, eminence.

religión (reli'xjon) nf religion. **religiosidad** nf religiosity. **religioso** adj religious. nm member of a religious order.

reliquia (re'likja) nf relic.

reloj (re'lox) nm clock.

relucir* (relu'θir) vi gleam. **reluciente** adj shining, gleaming.

relumbrar (relum'brar) vi 1 be dazzling. 2 shine.

rellenar (reʎe'nar) vt refill, stuff. **relleno** adj stuffed. nm stuffing, filling.

remachar (rema'tʃar) vt hammer in, rivet. **remache** nm rivet.

remanente (rema'nente) adj surplus.

remanso (re'manso) nm backwater.

remar (re'mar) vi row.

rematar (rema'tar) vt 1 put an end to, finish or kill off. 2 comm sell off. vi finish off. **remate** nm finishing touch.

remediar (reme'ðjar) vt remedy. **remedio** nm remedy.

remendar (ie) (remen'dar) vt mend, repair. **remendón** nm cobbler.

remesa (re'mesa) nf 1 remittance. 2 shipment.

remiendo (re'mjendo) nm repair, patch.

119

remilgado (remil'gaðo) *adj* prudish. **remilgo** *nm* prudery.

remirado (remi'raðo) *adj* overcautious.

remisión (remi'sjon) *nf* 1 remission. 2 *comm* consignment. **remiso** *adj* remiss.

remitir (remi'tir) *vt* 1 remit. 2 refer, entrust.

remo ('remo) *nm* oar.

remojar (remo'xar) *vt* soak.

remolacha (remo'latʃa) *nf* beetroot.

remolcar (remol'kar) *vt* tow. **remolque** *nm* 1 towing. 2 towrope. 3 trailer.

remolino (remo'lino) *nm* 1 eddy, whirl. 2 throng.

remontar (remon'tar) *vt* 1 climb, surmount. 2 remount. **remontarse** *vr* rise. **remontarse a** amount to, reach.

remordimiento (remorði'mjento) *nm* remorse.

remoto (re'moto) *adj* remote.

remover (ue) (remo'βer) *vt* 1 remove. 2 stir.

remunerar (remune'rar) *vt* remunerate. **remuneración** *nf* remuneration.

renacer (rena'θer) *vi* 1 be reborn. 2 revive. **renacentista** *adj* Renaissance. **renacimiento** *nm* Renaissance.

renacuajo (rena'kwaxo) *nm* tadpole.

rencilla (ren'θiʎa) *nf* 1 feud. 2 grudge.

rencor (ren'kor) *nm* bitterness. **rencoroso** *adj* bitter.

rendir (i) (rèn'dir) *vt* 1 yield, give. 2 reduce, defeat. **rendirse** *vr* 1 surrender. 2 exhaust oneself.

renegar (ie) (rene'gar) *vt* 1 deny. 2 detest. *vi* 1 renounce, turn renegade 2 grumble. **renegado** *adj,n* renegade. **reniego** *nm* 1 oath, curse. 2 complaint. 3 blasphemy.

renglón (ren'glon) *nm* 1 line (of printing). 2 *comm* entry (in accounts).

reno ('reno) *nm* reindeer.

renombrado (renom'braðo) *adj* renowned. **renombre** *nm* renown.

renovar (ue) (reno'βar) *vt* renew, renovate. **renovación** *nf* renewal, renovation.

rentar (ren'tar) *vt* *comm* yield. **renta** *nf* 1 *comm* yield. 2 income.

renunciar (renun'θjar) *vt* renounce. *vi* resign. **renuncia** *nf* resignation.

reñir (i) (re'ɲir) *vt* scold. *vi* quarrel.

reo ('reo) *nm* 1 accused. 2 culprit.

reojo (re'oxo) *adv* **de reojo** sideways, out of the corner of the eyes.

reorganizar (reorgani'θar) *vt* reorganize.

reparar[1] (repa'rar) *vt* 1 repair. 2 make amends.

reparación *nf* 1 repair. 2 amends. **reparo** *nm* repair.

reparar[2] (repa'rar) *vi* stay, stop. **reparar en** notice, take notice of. **reparo** *nm* 1 hesitation, doubt. 2 criticism.

repartir (repar'tir) *vt* 1 share out. 2 *comm* deliver **reparto** *nm* 1 sharing out, distribution. 2 *comm* delivery.

repasar (repa'sar) *vt* go over, check. **repaso** *nm* revision, check.

repatriar (repatri'ar) *vt* repatriate.

repeler (repe'ler) *vt* 1 repel. 2 reject. **repelente** *adj* 1 repellent. 2 resistant.

repente (re'pente) **de repente** *adv* suddenly. **repentino** *adj* sudden.

repercutir (reperku'tir) *vi* rebound. **repercusión** *nf* repercussion.

repertorio (reper'torjo) *nm* 1 handbook, list. 2 repertory.

repetir (i) (repe'tir) *vt* repeat. **repetirse** *vr* recur. **repetición** *nf* repetition.

repisa (re'pisa) *nf* 1 shelf. 2 mantelpiece.

replegar (ie) (reple'gar) *vt* fold back.

repleto (re'pleto) *adj* full.

réplica ('replika) *nf* 1 retort. 2 *law* answer (to charge). 2 copy.

replicar (repli'kar) *vt* argue.

repliegue (repli'ege) *nm* crease.

repoblación (repoβla'θjon) *nf* repopulation.

repollo (re'poʎo) *nm* cabbage.

reponer (repo'ner) *vt* replace, restore. **reponerse** *vr med* recover.

reportar (repor'tar) *vt* bring, carry. **reportarse** *vr* regain one's composure. **reportaje** *nm* newspaper report. **repórter** *nm also* **reportero** reporter.

reposar (repo'sar) *vi* rest. **reposo** *nm* repose.

repostería (reposte'ria) *nf* confectionery, confectioner's. **repostero** *nm* confectioner.

reprender (repren'der) *vt* scold, reprehend. **reprensible** *adj* reprehensible. **reprensión** *nf* reprimand.

represalia (repre'salja) *nf* reprisal.

representar (represen'tar) *vt* 1 represent. 2 *Th* play, act. **representación** *nf* 1 representation. 2 *Th* production. **representante** *nm,f* 1 *pol* representative. 2 *Th* actor. **representativo** *adj* representative.

represión (repre'sjon) *nf* suppression.

reprimenda (repri'menda) *nf* reprimand.

reprimir (repri'mir) *vt* suppress.

reprobar (ue) (repro'βar) *vt* condemn.

réprobo ('reproβo) *adj* reprobate.

reprochar (repro'tʃar) vt reproach. **reproche** nm reproach.

reproducir* (reproðu'θir) vt reproduce. **reproducción** nf reproduction.

reptil (rep'til) adj,nm reptile.

república (re'puβlika) nf republic. **republicano** adj,nm republican.

repudiar (repu'ðjar) vt repudiate. **repudio** nm repudiation.

repuesto (re'pwesto) 1 replacement, spare part. 2 store, larder. 3 sideboard.

repugnar (repug'nar) vt 1 nauseate. 2 hate. **repugnancia** nf repugnance. **repugnante** adj repugnant.

repulsivo (repul'siβo) adj repulsive. **repulsión** nf repulsion.

reputar (repu'tar) vt 1 esteem. 2 prize. **reputación** nf reputation.

requebrar (ie) (reke'βrar) vt flatter.

requemar (reke'mar) vt scorch.

requerir (ie) (reke'rir) vt require.

requesón (reke'son) nm 1 cottage cheese. 2 curd.

requisar (reki'sar) vt requisition.

res (res) nf head of cattle.

resabio (re'saβjo) nm aftertaste.

resaca (re'saka) nf 1 undercurrent, undertow. 2 inf hangover.

resaltar (resal'tar) vi stick out.

resarcir (resar'θir) vt repay, compensate.

resbalar (resβa'lar) vi slip. **resbaladizo** adj slippery. **resbalón** nm slip, skid.

rescatar (reska'tar) vt rescue, recover, redeem. **rescate** nm 1 rescue, recovery. 2 ransom.

rescindir (resθin'dir) vt 1 repeal. 2 cancel. **rescisión** nf 1 repeal. 2 cancellation.

rescoldo (res'koldo) nm cinders, embers.

resecar (rese'kar) vt parch. **reseco** adj lean, parched.

resentirse (ie) (resen'tirse) vr resent, take offence. **resentirse de** suffer from, feel the effects of. **resentido** adj resentful. **resentimiento** nm resentment.

reseñar (rese'nar) vt review, report on. **reseña** nf review, report.

reservar (reser'βar) vt reserve. **reservarse** vr save one's strength. **reserva** nf 1 reservation, doubt. 2 reserve, stock. 3 geog reserve. 4 discretion. 5 reservation, booking.

resfriar (resfri'ar) vi turn cold. **resfriarse** vr catch cold.

resguardar (resgwar'ðar) vt safeguard. **res-**

guardo nm 1 safeguard. 2 comm guarantee, security.

residencia (resi'ðenθja) nf 1 residence. 2 educ hostel. **residente** adj,n resident.

residir (resi'ðir) vi reside.

residuo (re'siðwo) nm residue.

resignar (resig'nar) vt resign. **resignación** nf resignation.

resina (re'sina) nf resin.

resistir (resis'tir) vt,vi 1 resist. 2 put up with, endure. **resistirse** vr 1 resist. 2 refuse. **resistencia** nf 1 resistance. 2 endurance. **resistente** adj 1 durable. 2 resistant.

resolución (resolu'θjon) nf 1 resolution. 2 decision.

resolver (ue) (resol'βer) vt resolve, settle, decide.

resollar (ue) (reso'ʎar) vi pant, puff.

resonar (ue) (reso'nar) vi resound. **resonancia** nf resonance. **resonante** adj resonant.

resoplar (reso'plar) vi breathe heavily. **resoplido** nm snort, puff.

resorte (re'sorte) nm 1 means, resort. 2 sl strings, influence. 3 spring, elasticity.

respaldar (respal'ðar) vt back, support. **respaldarse** lean back. **respaldo** nm 1 back (of a chair, etc.), support. 2 wall.

respecto (res'pekto) prep **respecto a** or **de** with respect to.

respetar (respe'tar) vt respect. **respeto** nm respect. **respetuoso** adj respectful.

respirar (respi'rar) vt,vi breathe. **respiración** nf respiration, breath. **respiro** nm 1 breathing. 2 reprieve.

resplandecer* (resplande'θer) vi glitter. **resplandeciente** adj glittering. **resplandor** nm glitter, glint.

responder (respon'der) vi reply, respond. **responder de** or **por** be answerable for.

responsable (respon'saβle) adj responsible. **responsabilidad** nf responsibility.

respuesta (res'pwesta) nf response.

resquebrajar (ie) (reskeβra'xar) vt split, crack.

resquemar (reske'mar) vt scald. **resquemor** nm 1 burn. 2 heartburn. 3 resentment.

resquicio (res'kiθjo) nm chink.

restablecer* (restaβle'θer) vt re-establish. **restablecimiento** nm 1 re-establishment. 2 med recovery.

restallar (resta'ʎar) vi crackle.

restante (res'tante) adj remaining.

restar (res'tar) vt subtract. vi remain.

restaurante (restau'rante) nm restaurant.

restaurar (restau'rar) vt restore. **restauración** nf restoration.

restituir (restitu'ir) vt restore, give back. **restitución** nf restitution.

resto ('resto) nm remainder, rest.

restregar (ie) (restre'gar) vt rub, scrub.

restricción (restrik'θjon) nf restriction. **restrictivo** adj restrictive.

restringir (restrin'xir) vt restrict.

resucitar (resuθi'tar) vt,vi resuscitate.

resuello (re'sweλo) nm breath, breathing.

resuelto (re'swelto) adj resolved, determined.

resultar (resul'tar) vi result, turn out. **resultado** nm result.

resumir (resu'mir) vt summarize. **resumen** nm summary.

retablo (re'taβlo) nm altarpiece.

retaguardia (reta'gwarðja) nf rearguard.

retal (re'tal) nm remnant.

retama (re'tama) nf bot broom.

retardar (retar'ðar) vt retard, delay. **retardo** nm delay.

retén (re'ten) nm 1 catch, reserve. 2 mil reserve.

retener (rete'ner) vt retain. **retención** nf retention.

retina (re'tina) nf retina.

retintín (retin'tin) nm jingle.

retirar (reti'rar) vt withdraw. **retiro** nm 1 seclusion, retreat. 2 withdrawal.

reto ('reto) nm challenge.

retocar (reto'kar) vt retouch. **retoque** nm retouching.

retorcer (ue) (retor'θer) vt twist. **retorcido** adj 1 involved. 2 devious.

retórica (re'torika) nf rhetoric.

retornar (retor'nar) vt,vi return. **retorno** nm return.

retractar (retrak'tar) vt retract. **retracción** nf retraction. **retractable** adj also **retráctil** retractable.

retraer (retra'er) vt withdraw. **retraído** adj shy.

retrasar (retra'sar) vt delay. **retrasarse** vr be late. **retraso** nm delay.

retratar (retra'tar) vt portray. **retrato** nm portrait.

retrete (re'trete) nm lavatory.

retribuir (retriβu'ir) vt repay. **retribución** nf repayment.

retroceder (retroθe'ðer) vi retreat. **retroceso** nm 1 retreat. 2 comm slump.

retruécano (retru'ekano) nm pun.

retumbar (retum'bar) vi resound.

reuma ('reuma) nm rheumatism. **reumático** adj rheumatic.

reunir (reu'nir) vt 1 unite. 2 collect. **reunirse** vr meet, assemble. **reunión** nf 1 meeting. 2 party.

revalidar (reβali'ðar) vt confirm, ratify.

revancha (re'βantʃa) nf revenge.

revelar (re'βelar) vt 1 reveal. 2 phot develop. **revelación** nf revelation. **revelado** nm phot developing.

revendedor (reβende'ðor) nm retailer.

reventar (ie) (reβen'tar) vt,vi burst. **reventarse** vr blow up. **reventón** nm 1 bursting. 2 mot puncture.

reverberar (reβerβe'rar) vi 1 shimmer. 2 reverberate. **reverbero** or **reverberación** nm 1 reverberation. 2 reflector.

reverdecer (reβerðe'θer) vi 1 grow green. 2 grow young.

reverenciar (reβeren'θjar) vt revere. **reverencia** nf 1 reverence. 2 bow. **reverendo** adj 1 revered. 2 Reverend.

reversión (reβer'sjon) nf reversion. **reversible** adj reversible.

revés (re'βes) nm 1 reverse, back. 2 setback. **al revés** the wrong way round.

revisar (reβi'sar) vt revise, review. **revisión** nf 1 revision, review. 2 comm audit. **revista** nf 1 review. 2 journal, magazine.

revivir (reβi'βir) vt revive.

revocar (reβo'kar) vt revoke. **revocación** nf revocation.

revolcar (ue) (reβol'kar) vt knock over. **revolcarse** vr wallow.

revoltillo (reβoltiλo) nm confusion, mess.

revoltoso (reβol'toso) adj unruly.

revolución (reβolu'θjon) nf revolution. **revolucionario** adj revolutionary.

revolver (ue) (reβol'βer) vt 1 turn over. 2 disturb. **revolverse** vr turn around.

revólver (re'βolβer) nm revolver.

revoque (re'βoke) nm stucco, plaster.

revuelta (re'βwelta) nf 1 turn, bend. 2 disturbance.

revuelto (re'βwelto) adj disturbed, disorderly.

rey (rej) nm king.

reyerta (re'jerta) nf brawl, fight.

rezagar (reθa'gar) vt 1 overtake. 2 leave behind. **rezagarse** vr leave behind, straggle. **rezago** nm remainders, stragglers.

rezar (re'θar) vt pray for. vi pray. **rezo** nm prayers, praying.

rezumarse (reθu'marse) vr ooze, leak out.

nachuelo (rja'tʃwelo) nm stream.

ribera (ri'βera) nf river-bank.

ribete (ri'βete) nm border, trimmings (clothes, etc.).

ricino (ri'θino) nm castor-oil plant. **aceite de ricino** nm castor oil.

rico ('riko) adj 1 rich. 2 delicious.

ridiculizar (riðikuli'θar) vt ridicule. **ridículo** adj ridiculous. nm ridicule. **ridiculez** nf ridiculousness, absurdity.

riego ('rjego) nm irrigation.

riel (rjel) nm rail, track.

rienda ('rjenda) nf rein.

riesgo ('rjesgo) nm risk.

rifar (ri'far) vt raffle. **rifa** nf 1 raffle. 2 argument, quarrel.

rifle ('rifle) nm rifle.

rígido ('rixiðo) adj 1 rigid. 2 stern. **rigidez** nf rigidity.

rigor (ri'gor) nm 1 strictness, severity. 2 rigour. **riguroso** adj rigorous, severe.

rimar (ri'mar) vt,vi rhyme. **rima** nf rhyme.

rimbombante (rimbom'bante) adj bombastic.

rincón (rin'kon) nm corner, nook.

rinoceronte (rinoθe'ronte) nm rhinoceros.

riña ('riɲa) nf 1 quarrel. 2 fight.

riñón (ri'ɲon) nm kidney.

río [1] ('rio) nm river.

río [2] ('rio) v see **reír**.

ripio ('ripjo) nm 1 rubble. 2 waste.

riqueza (ri'keθa) nf wealth.

risa ('risa) nf 1 laugh. 2 laughter. **risueño** adj 1 smiling. 2 cheerful.

ristre ('ristre) nm **en ristre** all set, ready.

ritmo ('ritmo) nm rhythm. **rítmico** adj rhythmic.

rito ('rito) nm rite. **ritual** adj,nm ritual.

rival (ri'βal) adj,n rival.

rivalizar (riβali'θar) vi rival, compete. **rivalidad** nf rivalry.

rizar (ri'θar) vt 1 curl. 2 ripple. **rizado** adj curly. **rizo** nm 1 curl. 2 ripple.

robar (ro'βar) vt 1 steal. 2 rob. **robo** nm robbery.

roble ('roβle) nm oak.

robustecer* (roβuste'θer) vt strengthen. **robusto** nm robust.

roca ('roka) nf min rock.

roce ('roθe) nm graze, rub.

rociar (ro'θjar) vt sprinkle. **rocío** nm dew.

rocín (ro'θin) nm nag, old horse.

rodapié (roða'pje) nm skirting board.

rodar (ue) (ro'ðar) vi,vt roll. **rodaja** nf 1 roller.

2 slice. **rodaje** nm 1 wheels. 2 shooting (of a film). 3 mot running-in.

rodear (roðe'ar) vt encircle, surround. vi go round. **rodeo** nm 1 evasive remark. 2 rodeo.

rodezno (ro'ðeθno) nm 1 waterwheel. 2 cogwheel.

rodilla (ro'ðiʎa) nf knee.

rodillo (ro'ðiʎo) nm 1 roller. 2 rolling pin.

roer (ro'er) vt 1 gnaw. 2 corrode.

rogar (ue) (ro'gar) vi,vt beg. **rogación** nf petition.

rojo ('roxo) adj red. nm 1 red. 2 rouge.

rollizo (ro'ʎiθo) adj plump, round.

rollo ('roʎo) nm 1 roll. 2 phot film.

romance (ro'manθe) nm ballad. adj,nm lit Romance. **romancero** nm ballad collection.

romántico (ro'mantiko) adj romantic. **romanticismo** nm lit Romanticism.

romería (rome'ria) nf pilgrimage. **romero** nm 1 pilgrim. 2 bot rosemary.

romo ('romo) adj 1 snub-nosed. 2 obtuse (person).

rompecabezas (rompeka'βeθas) nm invar 1 puzzle, brain-teaser. 2 jigsaw puzzle.

rompeolas (rompe'olas) nm invar breakwater.

romper (rom'per) vt,vi break. **rompimiento** nm 1 breaking. 2 break.

ron (ron) nm rum.

roncar (ron'kar) vi 1 snore. 2 roar.

ronco ('ronko) adj hoarse.

rondar (ron'dar) vt,vi 1 haunt, frequent. 2 patrol. 3 prowl. **ronda** nf 1 night watch, patrol. 2 round (drinks, cards, etc.).

ronquedad (ronke'ðað) nf also **ronquera** huskiness, hoarseness.

ronquido (ron'kiðo) nm snore.

ronronear (ronrone'ar) vi purr.

ronzal (ron'θal) nm halter.

roña ('roɲa) nf 1 scab. 2 mange. 3 grime. 4 mean person. **roñoso** adj 1 mangy. 2 grimy. 3 mean. **roñería** nf meanness.

ropa ('ropa) nf clothing. **ropero** nm wardrobe. **ropa interior** underclothes.

roque ('roke) nm rook (chess).

rosa ('rosa) nf rose. **rosado** adj pink. **rosal** nm 1 rosebush. 2 rose garden.

rosario (ro'sarjo) nm rosary.

rosca ('roska) nf 1 ring. 2 coil. 3 thread (of a screw). **hacer la rosca** flatter.

rostro ('rostro) nm 1 face. 2 rostrum.

rotación (rota'θjon) nf rotation.

roto ('roto) adj broken. nm break, hole. **rotura** nf rupture, break.

rotular (rotu'lar) vt label. **rótulo** nm 1 label. 2 poster.

rotundo (ro'tundo) adj 1 round. 2 peremptory.

roturar (rotu'rar) vt plough up (ground).

rozar (ro'θar) vt,vi rub, graze. **rozarse** vr 1 get worn, chafed. 2 be in close contact. **rozadura** nf graze, chafe.

rubí (ru'βi) nm, pl **rubíes** ruby.

rubio ('ruβjo) adj blond.

rubor (ru'βor) nm blush.

rúbrica ('ruβrika) nf 1 rubric, heading. 2 flourish (of a signature).

rudeza (ru'ðeθa) nf roughness. **rudo** adj rough, plain.

rudimento (ruði'mento) nm rudiment.

rueca ('rweka) nf distaff, spinning wheel.

rueda ('rweða) nf 1 wheel. 2 circle.

ruedo ('rweðo) nm 1 turn, revolution. 2 hem. 3 bullring.

ruego ('rwego) nm request.

rugir (ru'xir) vi roar. **rugido** nm roar, bellow.

rugoso (ru'goso) adj wrinkled.

ruibarbo (rui'βarβo) nm rhubarb.

ruido ('ruiðo) nm noise. **ruidoso** adj noisy.

ruin (ru'in) adj mean, contemptible. **ruindad** nf meanness.

ruina ('ruina) nf 1 ruin. 2 ruins, remains. **ruinoso** adj ruinous.

ruiseñor (ruise'ɲor) nm nightingale.

rumbo ('rumbo) nm 1 direction, course. 2 inf pomp, ostentation. **rumboso** adj 1 splendid, lavish. 2 generous.

rumiar (ru'mjar) vt digest, ruminate. **rumiante** adj,n ruminant.

rumor (ru'mor) nm 1 rumour. 2 murmur. **rumoroso** adj murmuring (of a stream, etc.).

ruptura (rup'tura) nf rupture.

rural (ru'ral) adj rural.

Rusia ('rusja) nf Russia. **ruso** adj,n Russian. nm Russian (language).

rústico ('rustiko) adj rustic.

ruta ('ruta) nf route, way.

rutina (ru'tina) nf routine. **rutinario** adj routine, everyday.

S

sábado ('saβaðo) nm Saturday.

sabana (sa'βana) nf savannah.

sábana ('saβana) nf sheet.

sabañón (saβa'ɲon) nm chilblain.

saber* (sa'βer) vt 1 know. 2 know how. vi

taste. **saber a** taste of. **saber de** know about. **sabio** adj wise. nm learned man. **sabiduría** nf wisdom.

sabor (sa'βor) nm 1 taste. 2 flavour.

saborear (saβore'ar) vt savour, relish. **saborearse** vr 1 anticipate. 2 relish the thought of.

sabotear (saβote'ar) vt sabotage. **sabotaje** nm sabotage.

sabroso (sa'βroso) adj 1 tasty, delicious. 2 racy, daring.

sacabocados (sakaβo'kaðos) nm invar tech punch.

sacacorchos (saka'kortʃos) nm,pl **sacacorchos** corkscrew.

sacar (sa'kar) vt 1 take out. 2 buy (tickets). 3 sport serve. 4 bring out, publish.

sacerdote (saθer'ðote) nm priest.

saciar (sa'θjar) vt satisfy, appease. **saciedad** nf satiety.

saco ('sako) nm 1 bag, sack. 2 plunder. **entrar a saco** sack, plunder.

sacramento (sakra'mento) nm sacrament.

sacrificar (sakrifi'kar) vt sacrifice. **sacrificio** nm 1 sacrifice. 2 slaughter.

sacrilegio (sakri'lexjo) nm sacrilege.

sacro ('sakro) adj sacred.

sacudir (saku'ðir) vt shake, jolt. **sacudida** nf shake, jolt.

sádico ('saðiko) adj sadistic. **sadismo** nm sadism. **sadista** nm,f sadist.

saeta (sa'eta) nf 1 arrow. 2 dart. 3 hand (of a watch). 4 brief religious song.

sagacidad (sagaθi'ðað) nf shrewdness. **sagaz** adj shrewd, wise.

sagrado (sa'graðo) adj sacred, holy. nm sanctuary.

sajón (sa'xon) adj Saxon.

sal (sal) nf 1 salt. 2 wit, charm.

sala ('sala) nf 1 drawing room. 2 hall (of theatre, etc.). **sala de espera** waiting room.

salar (sa'lar) vt salt. **salado** adj 1 salty. 2 witty.

salario (sa'larjo) nm salary, pay.

salchicha (sal'tʃitʃa) nf sausage.

saldar (sal'dar) vt settle, pay off. **saldo** nm 1 payment. 2 clearance sale. 3 comm balance.

salero (sa'lero) nm 1 salt cellar. 2 wit. 3 charm.

salgo ('salgo) v see **salir**.

salida (sa'liða) nf 1 departure. 2 exit. 3 rising (of sun, moon). 4 Th appearance, entry. 5 outcome.

saliente (sa'ljente) nm 1 projection. 2 salient. adj overhanging, jutting out.

salir* (sa'lir) vi 1 emerge, come out. 2 depart,

leave. **3** rise (sun, moon, etc.). **4** *Th* make an entry. **5** happen, turn out. **salirse** *vr* **1** get away from the point. **2** leak.

salmón (sal'mon) *nm* salmon.

salmuera (sal'mwera) *nf* brine, pickling fluid.

salón (sa'lon) *nm* **1** large hall. **2** drawing room.

salpicar (salpi'kar) *vt* **1** splash, spatter. **2** sprinkle. **salpicadura** *nf* splash, sprinkle.

salsa ('salsa) *nf cul* sauce, gravy.

saltamontes (salta'montes) *nm invar* grasshopper.

saltar (sal'tar) *vt* **1** jump. **2** miss out, skip. **3** blow up (with explosives). *vi* **1** jump, leap. **2** blow up, explode.

saltear (salte'ar) *vt* **1** rob, hold up. **2** attack by surprise, assail. **salteador** *nm* robber.

salto ('salto) *nm* **1** leap, jump. **2** hop. **salto de altura** high diving. **salto mortal** somersault. **salto de agua** waterfall.

salubre (sa'luβre) *adj* healthy. **salubridad** *nf* healthiness.

salud (sa'luð) *nf* **1** health. **¡salud!** *interj* **1** cheers, good health. **2** cheerio, goodbye.

saludar (salu'ðar) *vt* **1** greet. **2** salute. **le saluda atentamente** yours faithfully. **saludo** *nm* **1** greeting. **2** *pl* regards, best wishes.

salvaje (sal'βaxe) *adj* **1** *bot, zool* wild. **2** savage. *nm* savage.

salvar (sal'βar) *vt* **1** rescue, save. **2** except. **3** cross, clear (an obstacle). **salvador** *nm* saviour. **salvamento** *nm* rescue, salvage. **bote de salvamento** *nm* lifeboat.

salvedad (salβe'ðað) *nf* proviso, qualification. **con la salvedad de que** with the proviso that.

salvia ('salβja) *nf bot* sage.

salvo ('salβo) *adv* except, saving. **a salvo** safe, out of danger. **poner a salvo** rescue. **salvo que** unless. ~*adj* safe. **sano y salvo** safe and sound.

salvoconducto (salβokon'dukto) *nf* safe conduct.

san (san) *adj* see **santo**.

sanar (sa'nar) *vt* heal, cure. *vi* get better, regain one's health. **sanatorio** *nm* sanatorium.

sandalia (san'dalja) *nf* sandal.

sandía (san'dia) *nf* watermelon.

sanear (sane'ar) *vt* **1** drain. **2** repair (damage). **3** insure. **saneamiento** *nm* **1** drainage. **2** cleaning-up. **3** *law* security, insurance.

sangrar (san'grar) *vt* **1** *med* bleed. **2** drain off. *vi* bleed. **sangre** *nf* blood.

sangría (san'gria) *nf* **1** *cul* a drink of red wine

and fruit. **2** *med* bleeding, blood-letting. **sangriento** *adj* bloody, bloodstained.

sanguijuela (sangi'xwela) *nf* leech.

sanguíneo (san'gineo) *adj* **1** of or like blood. **2** sanguine.

sanidad (sani'ðað) *nf* health, healthiness. **sanitario** *adj* sanitary. **sano** *adj* **1** healthy, wholesome. **2** intact, unbroken.

santa ('santa) *nf* saint. See also **santo**.

santiamén (santja'men) *nm* **en un santiamén** in a flash.

santificar (santifi'kar) *vt* sanctify, consecrate, hallow. **santificación** *nf* sanctification.

santiguar (santi'gwar) *vt* bless. **santiguarse** *vr* cross oneself.

santo ('santo) *adj* **1** sacred, holy. **2** saintly. **santo y bueno** all well and good. ~*nm* **1** saint. **2** *mil* password. **3** saint's day.

santuario (san'twarjo) *nm* sanctuary, shrine.

saña ('saɲa) *nf* fury, rage. **sañudo** *adj* **1** furious, enraged. **2** vicious.

sapo ('sapo) *nm* toad.

saquear (sake'ar) *vt* loot, plunder. **saqueo** *nm* plunder. **saqueador** *nm* looter.

sarampión (saram'pjon) *nm* measles.

sarcasmo (sar'kasmo) *nm* sarcasm. **sarcástico** *adj* sarcastic.

sardina (sar'ðina) *nf* sardine.

sargento (sar'xento) *nm* sergeant.

sarna ('sarna) *nf* scabies. **sarnoso** *adj* **1** mangy. **2** itchy.

sartén (sar'ten) *nf* frying pan.

sastre ('sastre) *nm* tailor. **sastrería** *nf* **1** tailoring. **2** tailor's shop.

satélite (sa'telite) *nm* satellite.

sátira ('satira) *nf* satire. **satírico** *adj* satirical. **satirizar** *vt* satirize.

satisfacer (satisfa'θer) *vt* satisfy. **satisfacerse** *vr* content oneself. **satisfacción** *nf* satisfaction. **satisfactorio** *adj* satisfactory. **satisfecho** *adj* satisfied.

saturar (satu'rar) *vt* saturate. **saturación** *nf* saturation.

sauce ('sauθe) *nm bot* willow.

savia ('saβja) *nf bot* sap.

saya ('saja) *nf* skirt, petticoat. **sayo** *nm* smock.

sazonar (saθo'nar) *vt* **1** ripen, mature. **2** *cul* season. **sazón** *nf* **1** time. **2** *cul* flavour. **a la sazón** then, at that moment. **en sazón** ripe. **sazonado** *adj* **1** ripe. **2** *cul* seasoned.

se[1] (se) *pron* **1** himself, herself, itself, themselves. **2** each other. **3** oneself.

se[2] (se) *v* see **saber**.

sebo ('seβo) nm grease, fat. **seboso** adj greasy, fatty.

secar (se'kar) vt dry. **secador** nm drying place, drier. **secadora** nf drier. **secano** nm dry barren land. **secante** adj drying. nm blotting paper.

sección (sek'θjon) nf section.

seco ('seko) adj 1 dry, withered. 2 brusque, cold. 3 (of sound) dull. **a secas** curtly, abruptly.

secretario (sekre'tarjo) nm secretary. **secretaría** nf secretariat. 2 secretary's office.

secreto (se'kreto) nm 1 secret. 2 secrecy. adj secret, confidential. **secretear** vi whisper, exchange confidences.

secta ('sekta) nf sect.

secuaz (se'kwaθ) nm follower, supporter.

secuestrar (sekwes'trar) vt 1 kidnap. 2 hijack. **secuestrador** nm 1 kidnapper. 2 hijacker. **secuestro** nm 1 kidnap. 2 hijack.

secundar (sekun'dar) vt second, support.

sed (seð) nf thirst. **tener sed** be thirsty.

seda ('seða) nf silk.

sedante (se'ðante) nm sedative. adj calming, sedative.

sede ('seðe) nf seat (of government, etc.). **Santa Sede** Holy See.

sedería (seðe'ria) nf silk goods.

sedición (seði'θjon) nf sedition. **sedicioso** nm rebel, adj seditious.

sediento (se'ðjento) adj thirsty.

sedimento (seði'mento) nm sediment. **sedimentar** vt deposit.

seducir* (seðu'θir) vt 1 seduce. 2 charm, captivate. **seducción** nf seduction. **seductor** nm seducer. adj seductive.

segar (ie) (se'gar) vt mow, reap. **segadora** nf mower, mowing machine. 2 reaper.

seglar (se'glar) nm layman. adj secular.

segregar (segre'gar) vt 1 segregate. 2 anat secrete. **segregación** nf 1 segregation. 2 secretion.

seguida (se'giða) nf continuation. **coger la seguida** get into the swing. **en seguida** straight away. **seguidamente** adv immediately after.

seguido (se'giðo) adj continuous, unbroken. **todo seguido** straight ahead.

seguir (i) (se'gir) vt 1 follow. 2 pursue. 3 continue. **seguidor** nm follower.

según (se'gun) prep according to. adv it all depends.

segundo (se'gundo) adj,nm second.

segundón (segun'don) nm second son.

seguridad (seguri'ðað) nf 1 security, safety. 2 certainty. **seguro** adj 1 safe. 2 sure. nm 1 safety catch. 2 insurance.

seis ('seis) adj,nm six.

selección (selek'θjon) nf selection. **selecto** adj select, choice.

selva ('selβa) nf 1 forest. 2 jungle. **selvoso** adj wooded, forested.

sello ('seʎo) nm 1 postage stamp. 2 seal. 3 hallmark. **sellado** adj sealed. nm sealing, stamping.

semáforo (se'maforo) nm 1 semaphore. 2 traffic lights.

semana (se'mana) nf week.

semblante (sem'blante) nm 1 face. 2 appearance.

sembrar (ie) (sem'brar) vt 1 sow. 2 scatter.

semejar (seme'xar) vi be like, resemble. **semejante** adj similar. nm equal, like. **semejanza** nf similarity.

semestre (se'mestre) nm semester. **semestral** adj half-yearly.

semilla (se'miʎa) nf seed. **semillero** nm 1 seedbed, nursery. 2 hotbed.

seminario (semi'narjo) nm 1 seminar. 2 eccl seminary. 3 seedbed, nursery.

senado (se'naðo) nm senate. **senador** nm senator.

sencillez (senθi'ʎeθ) nf 1 simplicity. 2 simple-mindedness. **sencillo** adj 1 easy. 2 simple, unsophisticated.

senda ('senda) nf path. **sendero** nm path.

sendos ('sendos) adj pl 1 each. 2 both.

senectud (senek'tuð) nf old age.

senil (se'nil) adj senile.

seno ('seno) nm 1 bosom, breast. 2 haven, refuge.

sensación (sensa'θjon) nf sensation. **sensacional** adj sensational.

sensatez (sensa'teθ) nf good sense. **sensato** adj sensible.

sensibilidad (sensiβili'ðað) nf 1 sensibility. 2 sensitivity. **sensible** adj 1 sensitive, responsive. 2 perceptible. 3 regrettable.

sensiblería (sensiβle'ria) nf sentimentality. **sensiblero** adj sentimental.

sensitivo (sensi'tiβo) adj 1 relating to the sense. 2 sensitive.

sensual (sen'swal) adj sensual. **sensualidad** nf sensuality.

sentar (ie) (sen'tar) vt 1 place, locate. 2

establish. 3 suit, agree with. **sentarse** vr 1 sit down. 2 settle. **sentada** nf sit-in.

sentencia (sen'tenθja) nf 1 law sentence. 2 ruling: **sentenciar** law vt sentence. vi lay down ruling. **sentencioso** adj 1 pithy. 2 sententious.

sentido (sen'tiðo) nm 1 sense. 2 meaning. 3 direction. ·adj 1 susceptible, touchy. 2 offended.

sentimiento (senti'mjento) nm 1 feeling, emotion. 2 sentiment. 3 grief, regret. **sentimental** adj 1 sentimental. 2 emotional.

sentir (ie) (sen'tir) vt 1 feel. 2 hear. 3 regret. **lo siento mucho** I am very sorry. **sentirse** vr feel. **sentirse enfermo** feel ill.

seña ('sena) nf 1 mark. 2 sign. 3 pl name and address.

señal (se'nal) nf 1 signal. 2 sign. 3 mark.

señalar (sena'lar) vt 1 point out, point to. 2 denote. 3 mark. **señalarse** vr make one's mark. **señalado** adj 1 marked out, singled out. 2 distinguished.

señor (se'nor) nm 1 gentleman. 2 mister. **señora** nf 1 lady. 2 wife. 3 madam. **señorita** nf Miss.

separar (sepa'rar) vt separate. **separarse** vr 1 separate, come free. 2 cut oneself off. **separación** nf separation. **separado** adj separate. **separatismo** nm separatism.

septentrional (septentrijo'nal) adj northern.

séptico ('septiko) adj septic.

septiembre (sep'tjembre) nm September.

séptimo ('septimo) adj seventh.

septuagésimo (septwa'xesimo) adj seventieth.

sepulcro (se'pulkro) nm tomb, grave.

sepultar (sepul'tar) vt bury. **sepultura** nf 1 burial. 2 grave. **sepulturero** nm gravedigger.

sequedad (seke'ðað) nf 1 dryness. 2 brusqueness.

sequía (se'kia) nf drought.

séquito ('sekito) nm entourage, followers.

ser* (ser) vi be. **siendo así que** since. **a no ser por** but for. **sea lo que sea** come what may. ~nm being.

serenar (sere'nar) vt calm, quieten. **sereno** adj 1 serene, calm. 2 (of weather) settled, calm. nm 1 night watchman. 2 night dew. **serenidad** nf calmness.

serie ('serje) nf series.

seriedad (serje'ðað) nf seriousness. **serio** adj 1 grave, solemn. 2 serious, responsible. **tomar en serio** take seriously.

sermón (ser'mon) nm sermon.

serpentear (serpente'ar) vi 1 wriggle. 2 meander. **serpenteo** nm wriggling, twisting.

serpiente (ser'pjente) nf snake.

serrano (ser'rano) adj of the mountains. nm highlander.

serrar (ie) (ser'rar) vt saw. **serrín** nm sawdust.

servicio (ser'viθjo) nm 1 service. 2 pl toilet, lavatory. **estar de servicio** be on duty. **servicial** adj helpful.

servidor (serβi'ðor) nm servant. **servidumbre** nf servitude. **servil** adj servile.

servilleta (serβi'ʎeta) nf napkin.

servir (i)* (ser'βir) vt serve.

sesenta (se'senta) adj sixty.

sesgar (ses'gar) vt slant, twist to one side. **sesgo** nm slant, twist. adj sloped, biased.

sesión (sesi'on) nf 1 session. 2 Th performance.

seso ('seso) nm brain.

seta ('seta) nf mushroom.

setenta (se'tenta) adj seventy.

seto ('seto) nm fence.

seudónimo (seu'ðonimo) nm pseudonym.

severidad (seβeri'ðað) nf severity. **severo** adj 1 severe. 2 strict, harsh.

sexagésimo (seksa'xesimo) adj sixtieth.

sexo ('sekso) nm sex. **sexual** adj sexual.

sexto ('seksto) adj sixth.

si (si) conj 1 if. 2 whether.

sí[1] (si) adv 1 yes. 2 certainly. **sí que es** of course it is.

sí[2] (si) pron 3rd pers s himself, herself, itself. **sí mismo** himself. **entre sí** among themselves. **de por sí** in itself.

siderurgia (siðe'rurxja) nf iron and steel industry.

sidra ('siðra) nf cider.

siega ('sjega) nf reaping, harvesting.

siembra ('sjembra) nf sowing.

siempre ('sjempre) adv always. **siempre que 1** whenever. 2 provided that.

sien (sjen) nf anat temple.

siento ('sjento) v see **sentir**.

sierra ('sjerra) nf 1 saw. 2 sierra, mountain range.

siervo ('sjerβo) nm 1 slave. 2 servant.

siesta ('sjesta) nf siesta.

siete ('sjete) adj,nm seven.

sífilis ('sifilis) nm syphilis.

sifón (si'fon) nm 1 soda water. 2 syphon.

sigilo (si'xilo) nm secrecy. **sigiloso** adj 1 secret. 2 discreet.

siglo ('siglo) nm century.

signar (sig'nar) vt sign, seal.

significar (signifi'kar) *vt* 1 mean, signify. 2 express. **significarse** *vr* become famous or notorious. **significado** *adj* well-known. *nm* meaning, significance.

signo ('signo) *nm* sign.

siguiente (si'gjente) *adv* following.

sílaba ('silaβa) *nf* syllable.

silbar (sil'βar) *vt* 1 whistle. 2 hiss. **silbido** *nm* 1 whistle. 2 hiss.

silencio (si'lenθjo) *nm* silence. **silenciar** *vt* silence. **silencioso** *adj* silent.

silueta (si'lweta) *nf* silhouette, outline.

silvestre (sil'βestre) *adj* bot wild.

silla ('siʎa) *nf* 1 chair, seat. 2 saddle. **sillon** *nm* armchair.

sima ('sima) *nf* abyss.

símbolo ('simbolo) *nm* symbol. **simbólico** *adj* symbolic. **simbolizar** *vt* symbolize.

simetría (sime'tria) *nf* symmetry. **simétrico** *adj* symmetrical.

simiente (si'mjente) *nf* seed.

símil ('simil) *adj* similar. *nm* 1 comparison. 2 simile.

similar (simi'lar) *adj* similar.

simpatía (simpa'tia) *nf* 1 affection. 2 friendliness, likeableness. 3 mutual support, sympathy.

simpático (sim'patiko) *adj* nice, pleasant.

simpatizar (simpati'θar) *vi* get on well, become friends.

simple ('simple) *adj* 1 simple. 2 simple-minded. **simplemente** *adv* merely.

simplificar (simplifi'kar) *vt* simplify. **simplificación** *nf* simplification.

simulacro (simu'lakro) *nm* 1 image. 2 semblance.

simular (simu'lar) *vt* simulate. **simulado** *adj* simulated, sham.

simultáneo (simul'taneo) *adj* simultaneous.

sin (sin) *prep* without. **sin que** *conj* without.

sinagoga (sina'goga) *nf* synagogue.

sincero (sin'θero) *adj* sincere. **sinceridad** *nf* sincerity.

sindicato (sindi'kato) *nm* 1 syndicate. 2 trade union. **sindical** *adj* trade-union.

sinfín (sin'fin) *nm* **un sinfín de** a large number of, a great many.

sinfonía (sinfo'nia) *nf* symphony. **sinfónico** *adj* symphonic.

singular (singu'lar) *adj* 1 singular. 2 exceptional. **singularizar** *vt* single out. **singularizarse** *vr* excel.

siniestro (si'njestro) *adj* 1 left (opposite of right). 2 sinister. *nm* catastrophe. **siniestrado** *nm* victim (of an accident).

sino ('sino) *nm* fate, destiny. *conj* but, except.

sinrazón (sinra'θon) *nf* injustice.

sinsabor (sinsa'βor) *nm* trouble, worry.

sintaxis (sin'taksis) *nf* syntax. **sintáctico** *adj* syntactic.

síntesis ('sintesis) *nf invar* synthesis. **sintético** *adj* synthetic.

sintió (sin'tjo) *v* see **sentir.**

síntoma ('sintoma) *nm* symptom. **sintomático** *adj* symptomatic.

sintonizar (sintoni'θar) *vt tech* tune.

siquiera (si'kjera) *adv* 1 even if, even though. 2 at least. **ni siquiera** not even.

sirena (si'rena) *nf* 1 siren, mermaid. 2 siren, foghorn.

sirviente (sir'βjente) *nm* servant.

sisar (si'sar) *vt* 1 pilfer. 2 cheat. **sisa** *nf* theft, pilfering.

sistema (sis'tema) *nm* system, method.

sitiar (si'tjar) *vt* 1 besiege. 2 surround.

sitio ('sitjo) *nm* 1 place. 2 room, space. 3 siege.

situar (si'twar) *vt* situate. **situación** *nf* situation. **situado** *adj* situated.

so (so) *prep* under.

sobaco (so'βako) *nm* armpit.

sobado (so'βaðo) *adj* shabby, well-worn.

sobar (so'βar) *vt* 1 crumple. 2 knead. 3 fondle.

soberanía (soβera'nia) *nf* sovereignty. **soberano** *adj,nm* sovereign.

soberbia (so'βerβja) *nf* 1 pride. 2 magnificence, pomp. **soberbio** *adj* 1 proud. 2 superb.

sobornar (soβor'nar) *vt* bribe. **soborno** *nm* 1 bribe. 2 bribery.

sobrar (so'βrar) *vt* exceed. *vi* remain, be left over. **de sobra** more than enough. **sobradamente** *adv* amply, only too well. **sobrado** *adj* superfluous. **sobrante** *adj* spare, surplus. *nm* surplus.

sobre ('soβre) *prep* on, upon, over.

sobrecama (soβre'kama) *nm* bedspread.

sobrecargar (soβrekar'gar) *vt* overload.

sobrecejo (soβre'θexo) *nm* frown.

sobrecoger (soβreko'xer) *vt* scare, startle. **sobrecogerse** *vr* 1 be scared. 2 be overcome.

sobremanera (soβrema'nera) *adv* exceedingly.

sobremesa (soβre'mesa) *nf* 1 dessert. 2 table cover. 3 period after dinner (for conversation, etc.).

sobrenatural (soβrenatu'ral) *adj* supernatural.

sobrepasar (soβrepa'sar) *vt* surpass.

sobreponer (soβrepo'ner) *vt* 1 superimpose. 2

put before. **sobreponerse** *vr* 1 win through, overcome. 2 master oneself.

sobresalir* (soβresa'lir) *vi* 1 jut out, project. 2 be outstanding, excel.

sobresaltar (soβresal'tar) *vt* startle. **sobresalto** *nm* scare, shock. **de sobresalto** suddenly.

sobretodo (soβre'toðo) *nm* overcoat.

sobrevenir* (soβreβe'nir) *vi* happen suddenly.

sobrevivir (soβreβi'βir) *vi* survive. **sobreviviente** *nm* survivor.

sobriedad (soβrje'ðað) *nf* sobriety. **sobrio** *adj* sober, moderate.

sobrino (so'βrino) *nm* nephew. **sobrina** *nf* niece.

socarrón (sokar'ron) *adj* sarcastic.

socavar (soka'βar) *vt* undermine. **socavón** *nm* 1 cavity. 2 subsidence.

sociable (so'θjaβle) *adj* sociable.

socialismo (soθja'lismo) *nm* socialism. **socialista** *nm* socialist.

sociedad (soθje'ðað) *nf* 1 society. 2 *comm* company. **socio** *nm* member (of club, etc.).

sociología (soθjolo'xia) *nf* sociology. **sociólogo** *nm* sociologist.

socorrer (sokor'rer) *vt* help. **socorrido** *adj* 1 useful, helpful. 2 trite, hackneyed. 3 well-provided. **socorro** *nm* help, assistance.

soez (so'eθ) *adj* obscene, vulgar.

sofocar (sofo'kar) *vt* 1 suffocate, stifle, smother. 2 embarrass, make blush. **sofoco** *nm* 1 suffocation. 2 embarrassment.

soga ('soga) *nf* rope, cord.

sois (sojs) *v* see **ser**.

soja ('soxa) *nf* soya.

sojuzgar (soxuθ'gar) *vt* subdue.

sol (sol) *nm* sun.

solapa (so'lapa) *nf* 1 flap. 2 lapel. 3 slyness. **solapado** *adj* sly. **solapar** *vt* overlap.

solar (so'lar) *nm* 1 piece of ground, site. 2 ancestral home. *adj* solar.

solaz (so'laθ) *nm* relaxation, solace. **solazar** *vt* distract, amuse.

soldado (sol'daðo) *nm* soldier.

soldar (ue) (sol'dar) *vt* solder, weld. **soldador** *nm* soldering iron. **soldadura** *nf* welding.

soledad (sole'ðað) *nf* loneliness, solitude.

solemne (so'lemne) *adj* solemn. **solemnidad** *nf* solemnity.

soler (ue) (so'ler) *vi* be in the habit of, be accustomed to.

solera (so'lera) *nf* 1 prop, support. 2 typical character. 3 vintage.

solicitar (soliθi'tar) *vt* 1 request. 2 apply for. 3 canvass. **solicitante** *nm,f* applicant.

solícito (so'liθito) *adj* solicitous, careful, concerned about.

solicitud (soliθi'tuð) *nf* 1 solicitude. 2 application. 3 petition.

solidaridad (soliðari'ðað) *nf* solidarity. **solidarizarse** *vr* side with, declare support for.

sólido ('soliðo) *adj* solid, firm, sound. **solidez** *nf* 1 hardness. 2 solidity.

solitario (soli'tarjo) *adj* lonely, solitary. *nm* recluse, hermit.

solo ('solo) *adj* 1 alone. 2 single, unique. 3 *mus* solo. **a solas** by oneself.

sólo ('solo) *adv* only, merely.

soltar (ue) (sol'tar) *vt* let go, release, untie. **soltarse** *vr* begin, start to be fluent.

soltero (sol'tero) *nm* bachelor. *adj* single, unmarried. **soltera** *nf* spinster. **solterona** *nf* old maid.

soltura (sol'tura) *nf* looseness, ease of movement. **hablar con soltura** speak fluently.

soluble (so'luβle) *adj* soluble. **solubilidad** *nf* solubility. **solución** *nf* solution. **solucionar** *vt* solve.

solvencia (sol'βenθja) *nf* *comm* solvency. **solvente** *adj* solvent.

sollozar (soʎo'θar) *vi* sob. **sollozo** *nm* sob.

sombra ('sombra) *nf* shadow, shade.

sombrero (som'brero) *nm* hat.

sombrilla (som'briʎa) *nf* parasol.

sombrío (som'brio) *adj* 1 shady, dark. 2 sombre, gloomy.

somero (so'mero) *adj* superficial.

someter (some'ter) *vt* 1 conquer, overwhelm. 2 subordinate. 3 submit (to trial, etc.).

somnífero (som'nifero) *nm* sleeping pill.

somnolencia (somno'lenθja) *nf* sleepiness.

somos ('somos) *v* see **ser**.

son[1] (son) *nm* 1 sound. 2 rumour.

son[2] (son) *v* see **ser**.

sonar (ue) (so'nar) *vt,vi* 1 ring. 2 sound. **sonarse** *vr* blow one's nose. **sonado** *adj* sensational, talked-about.

sondear (sonde'ar) *vt* 1 *naut* sound, take soundings of. 2 bore, drill. 3 sound out (opinion, etc.). **sondeo** *nm* 1 *tech* boring, drilling. 2 inquiry, investigation.

soneto (so'neto) *nm* sonnet.

sonido (so'niðo) *nm* sound.

sonoro (so'noro) *adj* 1 sonorous. 2 sound.

sonreír (sonre'ir) *vi* smile. **sonriente** *adj* smiling. **sonrisa** *nf* smile.

sonrojar (sonro'xar) vt make blush, embarrass. **sonrojarse** vr blush, flush. **sonrojo** nm 1 blush. 2 insult.

soñar (ue) (so'ɲar) vt,vi dream. **soñar con** dream of. **soñar despierto** to daydream. **soñador** adj dreamy. nm dreamer.

soñoliento (soɲo'ljento) adj drowsy, sleepy.

sopa ('sopa) nf 1 soup. 2 sl hangover. **sopa juliana** vegetable soup. **hecho una sopa** soaked to the skin.

sopapo (so'papo) nm blow, punch.

soplar (so'plar) vt 1 blow away. 2 blow out, inflate. 3 whisper. 4 Th prompt. **soplarse** vr gobble (food). **soplado** adj smartly dressed. **soplo** nm 1 gust. 2 puff of breath.

sopor (so'por) nm drowsiness.

soportar (sopor'tar) vt 1 carry. 2 withstand, endure. **soportable** adj bearable. **soporte** nm support.

sorber (sor'ßer) vt 1 sip, suck. 2 soak up, absorb. **sorbo** nm 1 sip. 2 gulp.

sordera (sor'ðera) nf deafness.

sórdido ('sorðiðo) adj squalid. **sordidez** nf squalor.

sordo ('sorðo) adj 1 deaf. 2 muffled.

sordomudo (sorðo'muðo) adj deaf and dumb.

sorprender (sorpren'der) vt surprise. **sorprendente** adj surprising. **sorpresa** nf surprise.

sortear (sorte'ar) vt 1 draw lots for, raffle. 2 avoid, swerve round. **sorteo** nm 1 raffle, draw. 2 sport toss.

sortija (sor'tixa) nf 1 ring. 2 curl (of hair).

sortilegio (sorti'lexjo) nm 1 sorcery. 2 charm.

sosegar (ie) (sose'gar) vt calm, quieten. **sosiego** nm calm, quiet.

soslayar (sosla'jar) vt 1 lay obliquely. 2 avoid, get round. **al soslayo** aslant, obliquely. **de soslayo** sidelong, from the side.

soso ('soso) adj 1 tasteless. 2 dull, insipid.

sospechar (sospe'tʃar) vt suspect. **sospecha** nf suspicion. **sospechoso** adj suspicious, suspect.

sostener* (soste'ner) vt 1 prop up, support. 2 sustain, nourish. 3 maintain. 4 defend. **sostenerse** vr 1 support oneself upright. 2 continue unchanged. 3 support oneself, keep going. **sostén** nm 1 support, prop. 2 brassière. 3 sustenance. **sostenido** adj sustained, continuous. **sostenimiento** nm support, maintenance.

sota ('sota) nf game jack.

sotana (so'tana) nf rel cassock.

sótano ('sotano) nm basement, cellar.

soto ('soto) nm thicket, copse.

soviet (so'ßjet) nm, pl **soviets** Soviet. **soviético** adj Soviet.

soy (soj) v see **ser**.

su (su) poss adj 1 his, her, its. 2 your. 3 their.

suave ('swaße) adj 1 smooth. 2 gentle, mild. **suavidad** nf 1 smoothness. 2 mildness.

suavizar (swaßi'θar) vt 1 smooth. 2 calm down, soothe.

subarrendar (ie) (sußarren'dar) vt sublet. **subarriendo** nm sublet.

subasta (su'ßasta) nf auction. **subastar** vt auction.

subconsciencia (sußkons'θjenθja) nf subconscious. **subconsciente** adj subconscious.

subdesarrollado (sußðesarro'ʎaðo) adj underdeveloped. **subdesarrollo** nm underdevelopment.

súbdito ('sußðito) nm pol subject, citizen.

subdividir (sußðiβi'ðir) vt subdivide. **subdivisión** nf subdivision.

subir (su'ßir) vt 1 raise, lift. 2 ascend, go up. 3 promote. vi rise, go up. **subir al coche** get into the car. **subirse** vr 1 rise, climb. 2 become proud or conceited. **subida** nf 1 climb, ascent. 2 rise. **subido** adj (of colour) bright, strong.

súbito ('sußito) adj sudden. adv suddenly.

sublevar (sußle'ßar) vt rouse, stir up. **sublevarse** vr revolt, rebel. **sublevación** nf rebellion.

sublime (su'ßlime) adj sublime, lofty.

submarino (subma'rino) adj underwater. nm submarine.

subordinado (sußorði'naðo) adj subordinate.

subrayar (sußra'jar) vt 1 underline, underscore. 2 emphasize. **subrayado** nm 1 underlining. 2 emphasis.

subsanar (sußsa'nar) vt 1 repair. 2 excuse (fault, etc.). 3 overcome (problem). **subsanable** adj 1 excusable. 2 easily remedied.

subscribir (sußskri'ßir) vt 1 subscribe to. 2 ratify, endorse.

subsidio (sub'siðjo) nm subsidy, grant, allowance.

subsistir (sußsis'tir) vi subsist, survive. **subsistencia** nf subsistence. **subsistente** adj 1 enduring. 2 surviving.

substancia (su'stanθja) nf substance. **substancial** adj substantial. **substancioso** adj substantial, solid.

substituir* (sustitu'ir) vt,vi substitute. **substi-

tución nf substitution. **substitutivo** adj substitute. **substituto** nm substitute.

substraer* (sustra'er) vt **1** remove, steal. **2** subtract. **substraerse** vr withdraw, retire. **substracción 1** removal, theft. **2** subtraction.

subterfugio (suβter'fuxjo) nm subterfuge.

subterráneo (suβter'raneo) adj subterranean.

subtítulo (suβ'titulo) nm subtitle.

suburbio (su'βurβjo) nm **1** slum. **2** shanty town. **3** outskirts.

subvención (suββen'θjon) nf subsidy. **subvencionar** vt subsidize.

subyugar (suβju'gar) vt subjugate.

suceder (suθe'ðer) vi **1** succeed. **2** inherit. **sucederse** follow one another, be consecutive. **suceso** nm **1** event. **2** news item. **3** outcome, result.

sucesión (suθe'sjon) nf **1** succession. **2** inheritance. **sucesivo** adj consecutive, following.

suciedad (suθje'ðað) nf dirt, dirtiness. **sucio** adj **1** dirty. **2** vile, mean.

sucumbir (sukum'bir) vi succumb.

sucursal (sukur'sal) nm branch (of office, bank, etc.).

sud (suð) adj,nm south.

sudamericano (suðameri'kano) adj,n South American.

sudar (su'ðar) vt,vi sweat.

sudeste (su'ðeste) adj,nm south-east.

sudoeste (suðo'este) adj,nm south-west.

sudor (su'ðor) nm sweat. **sudoroso** adj also **sudoriento** sweaty.

Suecia ('sweθja) nf Sweden. **sueco** adj Swedish. nm **1** Swede. **2** Swedish (language).

suegro ('swegro) nm father-in-law.

suela ('swela) nf sole (of shoe).

sueldo ('_.weldo) nm salary, pay.

suelo ('swelo) nm **1** soil. **2** ground. **3** floor.

suelto ('swelto) adj **1** free, untied, loose. **2** separate. **3** flowing, fluent. nm loose change.

sueño ('sweɲo) nm **1** dream. **2** sleep. **tener sueño** be sleepy.

suero ('swero) nm **1** buttermilk, whey. **2** serum.

suerte ('swerte) nf **1** luck, chance. **2** fate, lot. **3** sort, kind. **echar suertes** draw lots.

suéter ('sweter) nm sweater.

suficiencia (sufi'θjenθja) nf **1** sufficiency, adequacy. **2** conceit, smugness. **suficiente** adj **1** sufficient. **2** smug, conceited.

sufragar (sufra'gar) vt **1** comm defray. **2** support, aid. **sufragio** nm **1** vote. **2** suffrage. **3** aid.

sufrir (su'frir) vt,vi **1** suffer. **2** tolerate, with-

stand. **sufrido** adj **1** long-suffering. **2** durable, long-lasting. **sufrimiento** nm **1** suffering. **2** long-suffering, patience.

sugerir (ie) (suxe'rir) vt **1** suggest. **2** hint. **sugerencia** nf suggestion.

sugestión (suxes'tjon) nf **1** suggestion. **2** hint. **sugestionar** vt hypnotize. **sugestionable** adj gullible, suggestible.

suicidarse (swiθi'ðarse) vr commit suicide. **suicida** adj suicidal. nm suicidal case. **suicidio** nm suicide.

Suiza ('swiθa) nf Switzerland. **suizo** adj,n Swiss.

sujetar (suxe'tar) vt **1** grasp, clamp, fasten. **2** conquer, subdue. **sujetarse** vr **1** abide by. **2** subject oneself to.

sujeto (su'xeto) nm **1** individual, person. **2** gram subject. adj **1** secured, locked. **2** tight.

sumar (su'mar) vt **1** add. **2** summarize. **3** amount to. **sumarse** vr join, enlist. **suma** nf **1** addition. **2** sum. **sumamente** adv highly, extremely.

sumergir (sumer'xir) vt **1** submerge. **2** plunge. **sumersión** nf submersion.

suministrar (suminis'trar) vt provide, supply. **suministros** nm pl supplies, provisions.

sumir (su'mir) vt submerge, sink.

sumisión (sumi'sjon) nf **1** submission. **2** submissiveness. **sumiso** adj submissive, docile.

sumo ('sumo) adj extreme, great.

suntuoso (sun'twoso) adj sumptuous. **suntuosidad** nf sumptuousness.

supe ('supe) v see **saber.**

supeditar (supeði'tar) vt **1** subdue. **2** subordinate.

superar (supe'rar) vt **1** surpass, excel. **2** overcome (difficulty, etc.). **superarse** vr excel, stand out.

superávit (supe'raβit) nm surplus.

superchería (supertʃe'ria) nf swindle, fraud.

superficial (superfi'θjal) adj superficial. **superficie** nf **1** surface. **2** area.

superfluo (su'perfluo) adj superfluous. **superfluidad** nf superfluity.

superior (supe'rjor) adj **1** superior. **2** upper(most). nm superior, better.

supermercado (supermer'kaðo) nm supermarket.

superstición (supersti'θjon) nf superstition. **supersticioso** adj superstitious.

supervivencia (superβi'βenθja) nf survival. **superviviente** adj surviving. nm,f survivor.

suplantar (suplan'tar) vt supplant.

suplemento (suple'mento) nm supplement. **suplementario** adj supplementary, extra. **horas suplementarias** nf pl overtime.

suplente (su'plente) adj,n substitute.

súplica ('suplika) nf petition. 2 request. **suplicar** vt 1 beg for, petition for. 2 implore. 3 law appeal.

suplicio (su'pliθjo) nm torture.

suplir (su'plir) vt make up for, substitute.

suponer' (supo'ner) vt 1 suppose. 2 involve, require, entail.

suposición (suposi'θjon) nf supposition.

supremo (su'premo) adj supreme.

suprimir (supri'mir) vt suppress. **supresión** nf suppression, elimination.

supuesto (su'pwesto) adj supposed, self-styled. **nombre supuesto** nm assumed name. ~nm assumption, hypothesis. **¡por supuesto!** of course.

sur (sur) adj southern. nm south.

surcar (sur'kar) vt score, furrow. **surco** nm furrow, rut.

surgir (sur'xir) vi 1 arise, emerge. 2 spout or soar up.

surtido (sur'tiðo) adj mixed, assorted. **bien surtido** well-stocked, well-supplied. ~nm assortment, choice.

surtidor (surti'ðor) nm fountain, spout. **surtidor de gasolina** petrol pump.

surtir (sur'tir) vt supply, provide. vi spout, gush.

susceptibilidad (susθeptiβili'ðað) nf susceptibility. **susceptible** adj susceptible.

suscitar (susθi'tar) vt agitate, stir up. **suscitar interés** arouse interest.

suscribir (suskri'βir) vt 1 sign (a contract, etc.). 2 agree to, endorse.

susodicho (suso'ðitʃo) adj aforementioned.

suspender (suspen'der) vt 1 suspend, hang up. 2 adjourn. 3 suspend from duty. 4 fail. 5 astound. **suspense** nm suspense. **suspensión** nf 1 suspension. 2 adjournment. 3 astonishment. **suspenso** adj 1 failed. 2 suspended.

suspicacia (suspi'kaθja) nf 1 suspicion. 2 misgiving. **suspicaz** adj suspicious.

suspirar (suspi'rar) vi sigh. **suspirado** adj desired, longed-for. **suspiro** nm sigh.

sustancia (sus'tanθja) nf see **substancia.**

sustentar (susten'tar) vt 1 support. 2 maintain. 3 nourish. **sustento** nm 1 support. 2 sustenance.

sustituir' (sustitu'ir) vt,vi see **substituir.**

susto ('susto) nm fright. **dar susto** frighten, scare.

susurrar (susur'rar) vi 1 whisper. 2 rustle. 3 hum. **susurro** nm 1 whispering. 2 humming.

sutil (su'til) adj 1 subtle. 2 fine, light. **sutileza** nf fineness, subtlety.

sutura (su'tura) nf med suture.

suyo ('sujo) poss pron 3rd pers s 1 his, hers, its. 2 theirs. 3 yours. **de suyo** in itself. **ir a lo suyo** go one's own way.

T

tabaco (ta'βako) nm tobacco.

taberna (ta'βerna) nf tavern, public house.

tabique (ta'βike) nm partition, dividing wall.

tabla ('taβla) nf 1 plank, board. 2 pl Th the stage. 3 pl game stalemate. **hacer** or **quedar (en) tablas** reach a stalemate. **tabla de planchar** ironing board.

tabular (taβu'lar) vt tabulate. adj tabular.

taburete (taβu'rete) nm stool.

tacaño (ta'kaɲo) adj mean, stingy. **tacañería** nf meanness.

tácito ('taθito) adj tacit.

taco ('tako) nm 1 stopper. 2 oath, swearword. 3 billiard cue. 4 inf mess.

tacón (ta'kon) nm heel. **taconazo** nm blow or tap with the heel.

taconear (takone'ar) vi tap the ground with the heels. **taconeo** nm flamenco tap-dancing.

tacto ('takto) nm 1 touch. 2 sense of touch. 3 tact.

tachar (ta'tʃar) vt 1 cross out, erase. 2 criticize. 3 denounce. **tachadura** nf erasure.

tahona (ta'ona) nf bakery.

taimado (tai'maðo) adj crafty, sly.

tajar (ta'xar) vt slice, cut. **tajada** nf 1 cul chunk. 2 cut, share (of money, etc.). **tajadera** nf chopper. **tajante** adj cutting, biting. **tajo** nm 1 cut, slash. 2 cliff, cleft.

tal (tal) adj such, such a. pron such a one, such a person. **con tal de que** provided that. **¿qué tal?** 1 how are you? 2 how is it? **tal como** such as. **tal cual** such-and-such. adv so, in such a way.

taladrar (tala'ðrar) vt bore, drill. **taladro** nm bore, drill.

talante (ta'lante) nm 1 mood. 2 appearance, look. **estar de buen talante** be well disposed.

talar (ta'lar) vt cut down, fell.

talco ('talko) nm talcum powder.

talega (ta'lega) nf 1 (money) bag. 2 nappy.

talento (ta'lento) nm talent. **talentoso** adj also **talentudo** talented.

talón (ta'lon) nm heel.

talonario (talo'narjo) nm 1 wad (of tickets, etc.) 2 book (of cheques, tickets).

talud (ta'luð) nm slope.

tallar (ta'ʎar) vt 1 carve, shape. 2 game deal. **talla** nf 1 carving, sculpture. 2 height, stature. 3 size (of clothes, etc.) 4 reward.

talle ('taʎe) anat 1 waist. 2 figure, frame.

taller (ta'ʎer) nm 1 workshop. 2 factory.

tallo ('taʎo) nm bot shoot, stem.

tamaño (ta'maɲo) nm size. adj so big, such a big.

tambalearse (tambale'arse) vr stagger. **tambaleante** adj 1 staggering. 2 swaying.

también (tam'bjen) adv also, too.

tambor (tam'bor) nm drum.

Támesis ('tamesis) nm Thames.

tamiz (ta'miθ) nm sieve.

tampoco (tam'poko) adv neither.

tan (tan) adv so.

tanda ('tanda) nf 1 batch. 2 shift (at work, etc.)

tangible (tan'xiβle) adj tangible.

tanque ('tanke) nm tank.

tantear (tante'ar) vt 1 guess, estimate roughly. 2 weigh up, consider. 3 test. 4 sport keep the score of. **tanteo** nm 1 reckoning, rough guess. 2 trial, test. 3 sport score, scoring.

tanto ('tanto) adj,adv 1 so or as much. 2 so long. **hasta tanto que** until. **no es para tanto** it's not that bad. ~nm 1 comm amount. 2 sport point. **estar al tanto** be up to date, be informed. **un tanto** rather, somewhat. **veinte y tantos** twenty and a bit more.

tañer (ta'ɲer) vt mus play.

tapar (ta'par) vt 1 cover. 2 stop, plug. **tapa** nf 1 cover. 2 plug. 3 cul snack, tit-bits. **tapete** nm table cover. **estar sobre el tapete** be under discussion.

tapia ('tapja) nf (garden) wall.

tapicería (tapiθe'ria) nf 1 tapestry. 2 upholstery.

tapizar (tapi'θar) vt 1 upholster. 2 carpet. **tapiz** nm 1 tapestry. 2 carpet.

tapón (ta'pon) nm 1 plug, bung. 2 stopper. **taponar** vt 1 plug. 2 stopper.

taquigrafía (takigra'fia) nf shorthand. **taquígrafo** nm shorthand writer.

taquilla (ta'kiʎa) nf 1 booking office, box office. 2 Th takings.

tararear (tarare'ar) vt,vi hum.

tardar (tar'ðar) vi 1 take a long time. 2 be late. **tardanza** nf slowness.

tarde ('tarðe) nf 1 afternoon. 2 evening. adv late.

tarea (ta'rea) nf task.

tarifa (ta'rifa) nf 1 tariff. 2 rate.

tarima (ta'rima) nf stand, low platform.

tarjeta (tar'xeta) nf card.

tarro ('tarro) nm jar.

tarta ('tarta) nf cul tart, cake.

tartamudear (tartamuðe'ar) vt,vi stutter, stammer. **tartamudeo** nm stammer, stutter.

tasar (ta'sar) vt 1 fix (price). 2 value, estimate. **tasa** nf 1 estimate, valuation. 2 fixed price, official rate. **tasa de cambio** rate of exchange.

tatarabuelo (tatara'βwelo) nm great-great-grandfather.

tatuaje (ta'twaxe) nm tattoo. **tatuar** vt tattoo.

tauromaquia (tauro'makja) nf art of bullfighting.

taxi ('taksi) nm taxi. **taxímetro** nm taximeter. **taxista** nm taxi-driver.

taza ('taθa) nf cup.

te (te) pron 2nd pers s fam you, to you.

té (te) nm tea.

teatro (te'atro) nm theatre. **teatral** adj theatrical.

tecla ('tekla) nf key. **teclado** nm keyboard. **teclear** vt mus strum.

técnica ('teknika) nf technique. **técnico** adj technical. nm technician. **tecnológico** adj technological.

techado (te'tʃaðo) nm also **techo, techumbre** roof.

tedio ('teðjo) nm tedium.

teja ('texa) nf tile. **tejado** nm tiled roof.

tejer (te'xer) vt 1 weave. 2 fashion. 3 spin. **tejido** nm 1 weave, woven material. 2 anat tissue.

tejón (te'xon) nm badger.

tela ('tela) nf 1 fabric, cloth. 2 film, skin. 3 matter, material, subject.

telar (te'lar) nm loom.

telaraña (tela'raɲa) nf cobweb.

telefonear (telefone'ar) vt telephone. **teléfono** nm telephone.

telegrafiar (telegra'fjar) vt telegraph. **telegrafía** nf telegraphy. **telégrafo** nm telegraph.

telegrama (tele'grama) nm telegram.

telepatía (telepa'tia) nf telepathy. **telepático** adj telepathic.

telescopio (teles'kopjo) nm telescope. **telescópico** adj telescopic.

televisión (teleβi'sjon) nf television. **televi-**

sado adj televised. **televisor** nm television set.

telón (te'lon) nm Th curtain. **telón de acero** Iron Curtain.

tema ('tema) nm theme.

temblar (tem'blar) vi tremble, shake. **temblor** nm shiver, shudder. **temblor de tierra** earthquake. **tembloroso** adj trembling, shaking.

temer (te'mer) vt,vi fear, be afraid. **temerario** adj rash. **temeridad** nf temerity, rashness. **temor** nm fear, dread.

temperamento (tempera'mento) nm temperament, nature.

temperatura (tempera'tura) nf temperature.

tempestad (tempes'taδ) nf storm. **tempestuoso** adj stormy.

templar (tem'plar) vt 1 temper, moderate. 2 warm up (temperature, liquid). 3 mus tune up.

temple ('temple) nm 1 temper (of steel, etc.). 2 mood. 3 state of the weather.

templo ('templo) nm 1 temple. 2 church.

temporada (tempo'raδa) nf 1 season. 2 period.

temporal (tempo'ral) adj 1 temporary. 2 secular, worldly. nm rough weather.

temprano (tem'prano) adv,adj early.

tenacidad (tenaθi'δaδ) nf tenacity.

tenaz (te'naθ) adj 1 tenacious. 2 tough. **tenazas** nf pl 1 pincers. 2 pliers.

tendedero (tende'δero) nm 1 clothes-line. 2 place for hanging clothes.

tendencia (ten'denθja) nf tendency, trend.

tender (ie) (ten'der) vt 1 stretch, spread out. 2 hang out (washing). vi incline, tend, have a tendency. **tenderse** vr stretch out, lie down.

tendero (ten'δero) nm shopkeeper.

tendón (ten'don) nm tendon, sinew.

tenebroso (tene'βroso) adj dark, gloomy.

tenedor (tene'δor) nm 1 fork. 2 holder, keeper. **tenedor de libros** bookkeeper.

teneduría (teneδu'ria) nf bookkeeping.

tenencia (te'nenθja) nf tenancy, tenure.

tener* (te'ner) vt 1 have, possess. 2 keep. 3 hold. **tener veinte años** be twenty years old. **tener hambre/sed/calor/frío** be hungry/thirsty/hot/cold. **tener que** have to. **tenerse** vr stand, stand up. **tenerse en mucho** have a high opinion of oneself.

tengo ('tengo) v see **tener.**

teniente (te'njente) nm lieutenant. **teniente coronel** lieutenant-colonel.

tenis ('tenis) nm tennis.

tenor¹ (te'nor) nm mus tenor.

tenor² (te'nor) nm meaning, sense.

tensión (ten'sjon) nf tension. **tensión arterial** blood pressure. **tenso** adj tense, taut.

tentación (tenta'θjon) nf temptation.

tentáculo (ten'takulo) nm tentacle.

tentar (ie) (ten'tar) vt 1 touch, feel. 2 grope, feel one's way. 3 try, attempt. 4 tempt. **tentativa** nf attempt. **tentativo** adj tentative.

tentempié (tentem'pje) nm inf snack.

tenue ('tenwe) adj 1 tenuous. 2 thin, slight. **tenuidad** nf tenuousness.

teñir* (te'ɲir) vt dye, colour.

teología (teolo'xia) nf theology. **teológico** adj theological. **teólogo** nm theologian.

teoría (teo'ria) nf theory. **teórico** adj theoretical.

tercero (ter'θero) adj,n third.

terciar (ter'θjar) vt 1 divide into three. 2 place diagonally. vi mediate.

tercio ('terθjo) nm 1 third. 2 mil regiment.

terciopelo (terθjo'pelo) nm velvet.

terco ('terko) adj 1 stubborn, obstinate. 2 hard material.

tergiversar (terxiβer'sar) vt distort, twist, misrepresent.

terminar (termi'nar) vt end, finish, complete.

término ('termino) nm end. **dar término a** bring to an end.

termo ('termo) nm Thermos bottle.

termodinámica (termoδi'namika) nf thermodynamics.

termómetro (ter'mometro) nm thermometer.

termonuclear (termonukle'ar) adj thermonuclear.

termostato (termos'tato) nm thermostat.

ternera (ter'nera) nf 1 female calf. 2 veal. **ternero** nm male calf.

terneza (ter'neθa) nf also **ternura** nf 1 tenderness. 2 fondness. 3 pl endearing words.

terquedad (terke'δaδ) nf 1 stubbornness. 2 toughness.

terraplén (terra'plen) nm 1 embankment. 2 terrace. 3 slope.

terraza (ter'raθa) nf 1 terrace. 2 flat roof. 3 balcony. 4 outdoor cafe.

terremoto (terre'moto) nm earthquake.

terreno (ter'reno) adj earthly, terrestrial. nm 1 land, soil. 2 plot. 3 area. **ceder/perder/ganar terreno** give/lose/gain ground.

terrestre (ter'restre) adj terrestrial.

terrible (ter'riβle) adj terrible, awful.

territorial (territo'rjal) adj territorial. **territorio** nm territory.

terrón (ter'ron) *nm* 1 lump (of sugar, salt, etc.). 2 clod.

terror (ter'ror) *nm* terror. **terrorismo** *nm* terrorism. **terrorista** *nm,f* terrorist.

terso ('terso) *adj* 1 smooth, polished. 2 terse.

tertulia (ter'tulja) *nf* 1 social gathering. 2 group.

tesis ('tesis) *nf invar* thesis.

tesón (te'son) *nm* tenacity, firmness, persistence.

tesoro (te'soro) *nm* treasure. **tesorería** *nf* 1 treasury. 2 treasurership. **tesorero** *nm* treasurer.

testa ('testa) *nf* head.

testar (tes'tar) *vi* make a will. **testamento** *nm* will, testament.

testarudo (testa'ruðo) *adj* stubborn, obstinate.

testificar (testifi'kar) *vt* attest, testify. **testigo** *nm* witness, one who testifies.

teta ('teta) *nf* 1 teat, nipple. 2 breast, udder.

tetera (te'tera) *nf* teapot.

tétrico ('tetriko) *adj* 1 gloomy. 2 sullen.

textil (teks'til) *adj, nm* textile.

texto ('teksto) *nm* 1 text. 2 textbook.

textura (teks'tura) *nf* texture.

tez (teθ) *nf* complexion, skin.

ti (ti) *pron* 2nd pers *s fam* you, yourself.

tía ('tia) *nf* aunt.

tibio ('tiβjo) *adj* lukewarm.

tiburón (tiβu'ron) *nm* shark.

tiempo ('tjempo) *nm* 1 time. 2 weather.

tienda ('tjenda) *nf* 1 shop, store. 2 tent.

tienta ('tjenta) *nf* 1 *med* probe. 2 shrewdness, cleverness. 3 (in bullfighting) test of bullocks for fierceness. **a tientas** gropingly, haphazardly.

tiento ('tjento) *nm* 1 touch, feel. 2 tact. **a tiento** by touch, gropingly.

tierno ('tjerno) *adj* 1 tender. 2 fresh.

tierra ('tjerra) *nf* 1 earth, world. 2 land, soil, ground. 3 country, homeland. **tierra natal** native land.

tieso ('tjeso) *adj* 1 stiff, rigid. 2 strong, firm. *adv* 1 stiffly. 2 firmly.

tiesto ('tjesto) *nm* 1 piece of pottery. 2 flowerpot.

tifo ('tifo) *nm also* **tifus** typhus. **tifo asiático** cholera.

tifón (ti'fon) *nm* 1 typhoon. 2 waterspout.

tigre ('tigre) *nm* tiger.

tijeras (ti'xeras) *nf pl* 1 scissors. 2 shears.

tilín (ti'lin) *nm* sound of bell.

tilo ('tilo) *nm* linden tree.

timar (ti'mar) *vt* cheat. **timador** *nm* swindler, cheat.

timbrar (tim'brar) *vt* stamp. **timbre** *nm* 1 seal. 2 stamp-duty. 3 bell. 4 *mus* timbre.

tímido ('timiðo) *adj* timid. **timidez** *nf* timidity.

timo ('timo) *nm* 1 hoax. 2 swindle.

tímpano ('timpano) *nm* 1 eardrum. 2 kettledrum.

tina ('tina) *nf* tub.

tinglado (tin'glaðo) *nm* 1 shed. 2 roof. 3 machination, intrigue.

tiniebla(s) (ti'njeβla) *nf (pl)* darkness, obscurity.

tino ('tino) *nm* 1 good judgment, tact. 2 skill, knack. 3 aim.

tinta ('tinta) *nf* 1 ink. 2 hue, tint.

tinte ('tinte) *nm* 1 dyeing. 2 paint, dye. **tintero** *nm* inkwell.

tintín (tin'tin) *nm* tinkle, clinking.

tinto ('tinto) *adj* dyed. **vino tinto** *nm* red wine.

tintorería (tintore'ria) *nf* dry-cleaner's, dyer's. **tintorero** *nm* dry-cleaner, dyer. **tintura** *nf* dye.

tío ('tio) *nm* uncle.

tiovivo (tjo'βiβo) *nm* merry-go-round.

típico ('tipiko) *adj* 1 typical. 2 native.

tiple ('tiple) *nm* treble. *nf* 1 soprano. 2 chorus girl.

tipo ('tipo) *nm* 1 type, model. 2 *sl* fellow, guy.

tira ('tira) *nf* long strip.

tirada (ti'raða) *nf* 1 throw. 2 stretch (of time). 3 edition.

tirado (ti'raðo) *adj comm* very cheap.

tirador (tira'ðor) *nm* 1 marksman. 2 handle, knob.

tiranía (tira'nia) *nf* tyranny. **tirano** *nm* tyrant. *adj* tyrannical.

tirante (ti'rante) *nm* 1 *arch* brace. 2 strap. 3 *pl* braces. *adj* taut.

tirar (ti'rar) *vt,vi* 1 throw, cast. 2 pull, draw.

tiritar (tiri'tar) *vi* shiver.

tiro ('tiro) *nm* 1 throw. 2 shot.

tirón (ti'ron) *nm* tug, jerk, pull.

tiroteo (tiro'teo) *nm* firing, gunshots.

tisis ('tisis) *nf* tuberculosis.

titubear (tituβe'ar) *vi* 1 hesitate. 2 totter. 3 stammer.

titular (titu'lar) *adj* titular. *nm,f* holder of an office. *nm* newspaper headline. *vt* 1 name. 2 entitle.

título ('titulo) *nm* 1 title. 2 diploma, degree.

tiza ('tiθa) *nf* chalk.

tiznar (tiθ'nar) *vt* stain, smear. **tiznado** *adj* grimy.

toalla (to'aʎa) *nf* towel.

tobillo (to'βiʎo) *nm* ankle.

tocadiscos (toka'ðiskos) *nm invar* record-player.

tocado (to'kaðo) *adj* touched, crazy. **tocado de la cabeza** touched in the head.

tocador (toka'ðor) *nm* 1 dressing table. 2 powder room. 3 *mus* player.

tocante (to'kante) *adj* touching. **tocante a** concerning.

tocar (to'kar) *vt* 1 touch, feel. 2 touch upon (a subject). 3 *mus* play. *vi* be one's turn. **en lo que toca a** with regard to.

tocino (to'θino) *nm* bacon, salt pork.

todavía (toða'βia) *adv* yet, still.

todo ('toðo) *adj* all, every, whole. *nm* entirety. **todos** *pron* everybody. **con todo** nevertheless, all the same.

toldo ('toldo) *nm* 1 awning. 2 sunshade.

tolerar (tole'rar) *vt* tolerate. **tolerancia** *nf* tolerance. **tolerante** *adj* tolerant.

tomar (to'mar) *vt* 1 take, seize. 2 receive. 3 eat, drink. **toma** *nf* 1 taking, seizure. 2 portion. 3 *med* dose. 4 take (in films).

tomate (to'mate) *nm* tomato.

tomillo (to'miʎo) *nm* thyme.

tomo ('tomo) *nm* 1 bulk. 2 volume, tome. 3 importance.

ton (ton) *nm* motive, reason.

tonel (to'nel) *nm* barrel.

tonelada (tone'laða) *nf* ton. **tonelaje** *nm* tonnage.

tónico ('toniko) *nm,adj* tonic.

tono ('tono) *nm* 1 pitch, tone. 2 manner.

tontería (tonte'ria) *nf* foolishness. **tonto** *adj* foolish, stupid, ignorant.

topacio (to'paθjo) *nm* topaz.

topar (to'par) *vi* 1 collide. 2 encounter, meet.

tope ('tope) *nm* 1 top, end. 2 summit.

tópico ('topiko) *nm* topic. *adj* topical.

topo ('topo) *nm* mole.

topografía (topogra'fia) *nf* topography.

toque ('toke) *nm* 1 touch, tap. 2 peal of bells.

torbellino (torβe'ʎino) *nm* whirlwind.

torcer (ue) (tor'θer) *vt* twist, bend, turn. **torcerse** *vr* 1 turn sour. 2 be dislocated. **torcido** *adj* twisted, bent.

tordo ('torðo) *nm* *zool* thrush.

torear (tore'ar) *vi* fight a bull. **toreo** *nm* bull-fighting. **torero** *nm* bull-fighter.

tormenta (tor'menta) *nf* storm. **tormentoso** *adj* stormy.

tormentar (tormen'tar) *vt* torment. **tormento** *nm* torment, anguish, pain.

tornar (tor'nar) *vt,vi* 1 return. 2 change. **tornarse** *vr* 1 become. 2 change.

tornasol (torna'sol) *nm* 1 sunflower. 2 litmus.

torneo (tor'neo) *nm* tournament.

tornillo (tor'niʎo) *nm* 1 screw. 2 *mech* vice. **torniquete** *nm* tourniquet. **torno** *nm* lathe. **en torno a** round, about.

toro ('toro) *nm* 1 bull. 2 *pl* bullfight.

toronja (to'ronxa) *nf* grapefruit.

torpe ('torpe) *adj* 1 stupid. 2 slow, torpid. **torpeza** *nf* 1 torpor. 2 clumsiness. 3 impurity, obscenity.

torre ('torre) *nf* tower.

torrente (tor'rente) *nm* torrent. **torrencial** *adj* torrential.

tórrido ('torriðo) *adj* torrid.

torta ('torta) *nf* 1 round cake or bread. 2 *inf* slap.

tortilla (tor'tiʎa) *nf* omelette.

tortuga (tor'tuga) *nf* 1 turtle. 2 tortoise.

tortura (tor'tura) *nf* torture. **tortuoso** *adj* tortuous.

tos (tos) *nf* cough.

tosco ('tosko) *adj* 1 coarse. 2 rude, uncouth.

toser (to'ser) *vi* cough.

tostar (ue) (tos'tar) *vt* toast. **tostada** *nf* toasted bread. **tostado** *adj* 1 tanned. 2 toasted.

total (to'tal) *nm* total.

tóxico ('toksiko) *nm* poison. *adj* poisonous.

tozudo (to'θuðo) *adj* stubborn.

traba ('traβa) *nf* 1 obstacle. 2 brace, clasp.

trabajar (traβa'xar) *vt* 1 work. 2 till. 3 form, shape. **trabajador** *nm* worker, labourer. *adj* hard-working. **trabajo** *nm* work.

trabalenguas (traβa'lengwas) *nm invar* tongue-twister.

trabar (tra'βar) *vt* 1 fasten, clasp, grasp, join. 2 engage in. **trabazón** *nf* union, juncture. **trabe** *nf* *arch* beam.

tracción (trak'θjon) *nf* traction.

tractor (trak'tor) *nm* tractor.

tradición (traði'θjon) *nf* tradition.

traducir (traðu'θir) *vt* 1 translate. 2 interpret. **traducción** *nf* translation. **traducible** *adj* translatable. **traductor** *nm* translator.

traer (tra'er) *vt* 1 bring, carry, fetch. 2 lead. 3 occasion, bring about.

traficar (trafi'kar) *vi* 1 deal, trade. 2 journey, go,

keep on the move. **traficante** nm dealer, trader. **tráfico** nm traffic.

tragaluz (traga'luθ) nf skylight.

tragar (tra'gar) vt swallow. **tragarse** vr accept, believe. **trago** nm 1 drink. 2 swig.

tragedia (tra'xeðja) nf tragedy. **trágico** adj tragic.

traicionar (traiθjo'nar) vt betray. **traición** nf treason, disloyalty. **traicionero** adj treacherous. **traidor** nm traitor.

traje[1] ('traxe) nm 1 suit. 2 dress. 3 costume. **traje de baño** swimming costume.

traje[2] ('traxe) v see **traer**.

trajín (tra'xin) nm 1 carriage. 2 coming and going. **trajinar** vt cart (goods). vi travel back and forth.

tramar (tra'mar) vt 1 weave. 2 plan, plot.

tramitar (trami'tar) vt transact, proceed with. **trámite** nm 1 transaction. 2 procedure. 3 law proceedings.

tramo ('tramo) nm piece, section, area (of ground).

trampear (trampe'ar) vt cheat, swindle, trick. **trampa** nf 1 trap. 2 fraud. **tramposo** nm 1 swindler. 2 a person who does not pay his debts.

trampolín (trampo'lin) nm trampoline, springboard.

trancar (tran'kar) vt bar (window, door). **tranca** nf bar (across window, door).

tranco ('tranko) nm stride.

trance ('tranθe) nm emergency, difficult situation.

tranquilizar (trankili'θar) vt calm. **tranquilidad** nf tranquillity. **tranquilo** adj tranquil.

transacción (transak'θjon) nf transaction.

transatlántico (transat'lantiko) adj transatlantic. nm naut liner.

transbordar (transβor'ðar) vt transfer, change (trains, etc.). **transbordador** nm ferry. **transbordo** nm transfer.

transcribir (transkri'βir) vt transcribe.

transcurrir (transku'rir) vi pass, elapse. **transcurso** nm lapse of time.

transeúnte (transe'unte) adj transitory, transient. nm passer-by.

transferir (ie) (transfe'rir) vt transfer. **transferible** adj transferable.

transformar (transfor'mar) vt transform. **transformación** nf transformation.

tránsfuga ('transfuga) nm deserter.

transgredir (transgre'ðir) vt transgress, violate.

transgresión nf transgression. **transgresor** nm transgressor.

transido (tran'siðo) adj overwhelmed.

transigir (transi'xir) vi 1 compromise. 2 yield. 3 tolerate.

transitar (transi'tar) vi 1 pass by, pass along. 2 travel along the road.

tránsito ('transito) nm 1 transit. 2 traffic.

transitorio (transi'torjo) adj transitory.

transmitir (transmi'tir) vt transmit. **transmisión** nf transmission. **transmisora** nf 1 transmitter. 2 radio station.

transparencia (transpa'renθja) nf transparency. **transparente** adj transparent.

transpirar (transpi'rar) vi 1 perspire. 2 transpire.

transponer* (transpo'ner) vt 1 transpose, exchange. 2 transplant. **transponerse** vr (of the sun) set.

transportar (transpor'tar) vt transport. **transportación** nf transportation. **transporte** nm transport, conveyance.

tranvía (tran'βia) nm 1 tram. 2 tramway.

trapaza (tra'paθa) nf swindle, trick.

trapecio (tra'peθjo) nm trapeze.

trapo ('trapo) nm 1 rag. 2 pl old clothes.

traquetear (trakete'ar) vt,vi agitate, shake. vi make a loud noise, crack. **traqueteo** nm 1 shaking. 2 cracking. 3 clatter.

tras (tras) prep after, behind.

trascender (ie) (trasθen'ðer) 1 go beyond. 2 smell. **trascender a** 1 be suggestive of, reek of. 2 have effect upon. **trascendencia** nf 1 significance, importance. 2 transcendence. **trascendental** adj 1 important. 2 transcendental.

trasegar (ie) (trase'gar) vt 1 move about. 2 turn upside down, upset (things). **trasiego** nm 1 upset. 2 change, switch.

trasero (tra'sero) adj back, hind, rear. nm 1 rump. 2 behind, buttocks. 3 pl predecessors.

trasladar (trasla'ðar) vt move, transfer to another place. **traslado** nm 1 transfer. 2 copy.

traslucirse* (traslu'θirse) vr 1 be translucent. 2 be revealed, become clear.

trasnochar (trasno'tʃar) vi be up all or most of the night.

traspasar (traspa'sar) vt 1 pierce, go through. 2 pass, cross over. 3 trespass. 4 sell (business premises, etc.). **traspaso** nm transfer, sale.

trasplantar (trasplan'tar) vt transplant. **trasplantarse** vr migrate. **trasplante** nm transplant.

trasquilar (traski'lar) *vt* shear, clip.

traste ('traste) *nm mus* fret.

trasto ('trasto) *nm* **1** piece of furniture. **2** rubbish. **3** *pl* utensils, tools.

trastornar (trastor'nar) *vt* **1** upset, disarrange. **2** trouble, disturb. **3** drive insane. **trastorno** *nm* **1** upheaval, disturbance. **2** mental disorder.

trasunto (tra'sunto) *nm* **1** copy. **2** likeness.

tratar (tra'tar) **1** treat, handle (a subject, etc.). **2** deal with, trade. **3** call, accuse. *vi* try. **tratarse** *vr* **1** have dealings with. **2** be on speaking terms.

través (tra'βes) *nm* **1** *arch* crossbeam. **2** reversal, calamity. **al través** across.

travesero (traβe'sero) *adj* transverse.

travesura (traβe'sura) *nf* prank.

traviesa (tra'βjesa) *nf* **1** (railway) sleeper. **2** *arch* rafter.

travieso (tra'βjeso) *adj* **1** lively, mischievous. **2** transverse.

trayecto (tra'jekto) *nm* **1** journey. **2** distance. **trayectoria** *nf* trajectory.

trazar (tra'θar) *vt* trace, plot, delineate. **trazo** *nm* sketch, plan.

trébol ('treβol) *nm* clover.

trece ('treθe) *adj,nm* thirteen.

trecho ('tretʃo) *nm* space, distance, stretch.

tregua ('tregwa) *nf* **1** truce. **2** rest, respite.

treinta ('treinta) *adj* thirty.

tremendo (tre'mendo) *adj* tremendous.

trémulo ('tremulo) *adj* tremulous.

tren (tren) *nm* train.

trenzar (tren'θar) *vt* braid. **trenza** *nf* plait, braid.

trepar (tre'par) *vi* climb. **trepa** *nf* climbing. **trepador** *nm* climber.

trepidar (trepi'ðar) *vi* quiver, tremble.

tres (tres) *adj, nm* three.

triángulo ('trjangulo) *nm* triangle.

tribu ('triβu) *nm,f* tribe.

tribuna (tri'βuna) *nf* **1** tribune. **2** stage, platform.

tributar (triβu'tar) *vt* pay. **tributo** *nm* tribute, tax. **tributario** *nm, adj* tributary.

trigo ('trigo) *nm* wheat. **trigal** *nm* wheat-field.

trigésimo (tri'xesimo) *adj* thirtieth.

trillar (tri'ʎar) *vt* **1** thresh, beat. **2** mash. **trillado** *adj* threshed. **trillador** *nm* thresher.

trimestre (tri'mestre) *nm educ* three-month term.

trinar (tri'nar) *vi* trill, warble.

trincar (trin'kar) *vt* **1** tie up. **2** lash. **3** break, chop. *vt,vi* drink.

trinchar (trin'tʃar) *vt* slice. **trinchador** *nm* carving knife. **trinchera** *nf* **1** trench. **2** trench coat.

trineo (tri'neo) *nm* sledge, sleigh.

trinidad (trini'ðað) *nf* trinity.

tripa ('tripa) *nf* **1** *anat* intestine. **2** *inf* tummy.

triple ('triple) *adj* triple.

trípode ('tripoðe) *nm* tripod.

tripulación (tripula'θjon) *nf* crew of a ship or aircraft.

triscar (tris'kar) *vt* mingle. *vi* (of lambs) frisk.

triste ('triste) *adj* sad, gloomy. **tristeza** *nf* sadness.

triturar (tritu'rar) *vt* grind, crush.

triunfar (trjun'far) *vi* triumph. **triunfal** *adj* triumphal. **triunfante** *adj* triumphant. **triunfo** *nm* **1** triumph, victory. **2** *game* trumps.

trivial (tri'βjal) *adj* trivial. **trivialidad** *nf* triviality.

triza ('triθa) *nf* shred, fragment.

trocar (ue) (tro'kar) *vt* exchange. **trocarse** *vr* change into.

trochemoche (trotʃe'motʃe) *adv* **a trochemoche** helter-skelter.

trofeo (tro'feo) *nm* trophy.

trole ('trole) *nm* trolley.

tromba ('tromba) *nf* whirlwind. **tromba de agua** heavy rainfall, downpour.

trombón (trom'bon) *nm* trombone.

trompa ('trompa) *nf* **1** horn. **2** humming top. **3** (of an elephant) trunk.

trompeta (trom'peta) *nf* trumpet.

tronar (ue) (tro'nar) *vi* thunder, roar. **tronada** *nf* thunderstorm.

tronco ('tronko) *nm* **1** tree trunk. **2** stem.

trono ('trono) *nm* throne.

tropa ('tropa) *nf* troop.

tropel (tro'pel) *nm* crowd. **en tropel** in a mad rush.

tropezar (ie) (trope'θar) *vi* stumble, trip. **tropezar con** run across, run into.

trópico ('tropiko) *nm* tropic. **tropical** *adj* tropical.

trotar (tro'tar) *vi* trot. **trote** *nm* trot.

trozo ('troθo) *nm* piece, bit.

truco ('truko) *nm* trick.

trucha ('trutʃa) *nf* trout.

trueno ('trweno) *nm* thunder.

trueque ('trweke) *nm* exchange, barter.

trufa ('trufa) *nf* truffle.

truncar (trun'kar) *vt* shorten, truncate.

tu (tu) *poss adj* 2nd pers s fam your.

tú (tu) *pron* 2nd pers s fam you.

tubo ('tuβo) *nm* tube, pipe.

tuerca ('twerka) *nf* nut.

tuerto ('twerto) *adj* one-eyed. *nm* wrong.

tuétano ('twetano) *nm anat* marrow.

tufo ('tufo) *nm* 1 vapour, fume. 2 stink.

tul (tul) *nm* tulle.

tulipán (tuli'pan) *nm* tulip.

tumba[1] ('tumba) *nf* tomb.

tumba[2] ('tumba) *nf* tumble.

tumbar (tum'bar) *vt* knock over. *vi* fall over. **tumbarse** *vr* lie down, sprawl. **tumbo** *nm* 1 tumble. 2 jolt.

tumido (tu'miðo) *adj* swollen.

tumor (tu'mor) *nm* tumour.

tumulto (tu'multo) *nm* turmoil, tumult. **tumultuoso** *adj* tumultuous.

tunante (tu'nante) *nm* rogue, crook.

túnel ('tunel) *nm* tunnel.

túnica ('tunika) *nf* tunic.

tuno ('tuno) *nm* rascal.

tupé (tu'pe) *nm* toupee.

tupido (tu'piðo) *adj* matted, entangled.

turba ('turba) *nf* crowd.

turbar (tur'βar) *vt* disturb, alarm. **turbarse** *vr* 1 become disturbed. 2 be embarrassed. **turbado** *adj* 1 upset. 2 embarrassed.

turbina (tur'βina) *nf* turbine.

turbulento (turβu'lento) *adj* turbulent, unruly. **turbulencia** *nf* turbulence.

turco *adj* Turkish. *nm* Turk.

turismo (tu'rismo) *nm* 1 tourism. 2 passenger car.

turnar (tur'nar) *vi* take turns. **turno** *nm* shift, turn.

turquesa (tur'kesa) *nf* turquoise.

Turquía (tur'kia) *nf* Turkey. **turquesco** *adj* Turkish. *nm* Turkish (language).

turrón (tur'ron) *nm cul* almond sweet, nougat.

tutear (tute'ar) *vt* address familiarly by using tú. **tutearse** *vr* be on familiar terms, call one another tú.

tutela (tu'tela) *nf* guardianship, tutelage.

tutor (tu'tor) *nm* 1 tutor. 2 guardian.

tuve ('tuβe) *v* see **tener**.

tuyo ('tujo) *poss pron* 2nd pers s *fam* yours.

U

u (u) *conj* (before o or ho) or.

ubicar (ubi'kar) *vi* lie, be situated.

ubicuidad (uβikui'ðað) *nf* ubiquity.

ubre ('uβre) *nf* udder.

ufanarse (ufa'narse) *vr* boast. **ufano** *adj* proud, vain. **ufanía** *nf* pride, conceit.

ujier (u'xjer) *nm* usher.

úlcera ('ulθera) *nf* ulcer. **ulceroso** *adj* ulcerous.

ulterior (ulte'rjor) *adj* further, farther. **ulteriormente** *adv* later.

ultimar (ulti'mar) *vt* conclude, bring to an end. **ultimación** *nf* conclusion.

último ('ultimo) *adj* last, most recent. **por último** finally.

ultrajar (ultra'xar) *vt* outrage, abuse. **ultraje** *nm* outrage. **ultrajoso** *adj* offensive, abusive.

ultramarino (ultrama'rino) *adj* overseas.

ultranza (ul'tranθa) **a ultranza** *adv* at all costs, to the last, out-and-out.

umbral (um'bral) *nm* threshold.

umbrío (um'brio) *adj also* **umbroso** shaded, shady.

un (un) *indef art m also* **una** f a, an. *adj,n* one.

unánime (u'nanime) *adj* unanimous. **unanimidad** *nf* unanimity.

unción (un'θjon) *nf* anointing, unction. **extremaunción** *nf rel* extreme unction.

uncir (un'θir) *vt* yoke.

undécimo (un'deθimo) *adj* eleventh.

undoso (un'doso) *adj also* **ondoso** wavy, rippling.

undular (undu'lar) *vi also* **ondular** undulate, be wavy.

ungir (un'xir) *vt* anoint, rub with oil.

ungüento (un'gwento) *nm* ointment.

único ('uniko) *adj* 1 only, single. 2 unique. **hijo único** *nm* only child.

unidad (uni'ðað) *nf* 1 unity. 2 unit.

unificar (unifi'kar) *vt* unify.

uniformar (unifor'mar) *vt* make uniform or standard. **uniforme** *adj,nm* uniform. **uniformidad** *nf* uniformity, evenness.

unión (u'njon) *nf* union.

Unión Soviética (u'njon so'βjetika) *nf* Soviet Union.

unir (u'nir) *vt* 1 unite, join. 2 *cul* mix.

unísono (u'nisono) *adj* on the same tone. **al unísono** in unison, unanimous.

universidad (uniβersi'ðað) *nf* university. **universitario** *adj* of or belonging to a university.

universo (uni'βerso) *nm* universe. **universal** *adj* universal. **universalidad** *nf* universality.

uno ('uno) *adj* 1 one. 2 sole, only. *pron* 1 one. 2 someone.

unos ('unos) *pron pl* some, a few.

untar (un'tar) *vt* 1 smear. 2 oil. **untadura** *nf* 1 ointment. 2 anointing.

uña ('uɲa) nf anat 1 nail. 2 claw. 3 hoof.

uranio (u'ranjo) nm uranium.

urbanidad (urβani'ðað) nf courtesy. **urbano** adj 1 urban. 2 polite. 3 urbane.

urbanizar (urβani'θar) vt build on, develop. **urbanización** nf urban development scheme. **urbanizado** adj built-up.

urdir (ur'ðir) vt 1 warp. 2 contrive, scheme.

urgencia (ur'xenθja) nf 1 urgency. 2 emergency. **urgente** adj urgent.

urgir (ur'xir) vt 1 be urgent. 2 be urgently needed.

urna ('urna) nf 1 urn. 2 ballot box.

urraca (ur'raka) nf magpie.

usanza (usan'θa) nf usage, custom.

usar (u'sar) vt 1 use. 2 wear (clothes). vi be accustomed. **uso** nm 1 use. 2 practice. 3 usage, custom. **al uso** according to custom.

usted (us'ted) pron 2nd pers s fml,pl **ustedes** you.

usual (u'swal) adj usual.

usufructo (usu'frukto) nm use, enjoyment.

usura (u'sura) nf usury. **usurero** nm usurer.

usurpar (usur'par) vt usurp. **usurpación** nf usurpation.

utensilio (uten'siljo) nm 1 utensil. 2 pl tools.

útero ('utero) nm uterus.

útil ('util) adj useful. **utilidad** nf utility, usefulness.

utilizar (utili'θar) vt utilize, use.

uva ('uβa) nf grape.

V

va (ba) v see **ir.**

vaca ('baka) nf 1 cow. 2 cul beef.

vacación (baka'θjon) nf 1 vacation. 2 pl holidays.

vacante (ba'kante) adj vacant. nf vacancy.

vaciar (ba'θjar) vt 1 empty, drain. 2 pour out.

vacilar (baθi'lar) vi hesitate. **vacilante** adj unsteady, wobbly. **vacilación** nf vacillation, hesitancy.

vacío (ba'θio) adj empty. nm 1 emptiness, void. 2 vacuum.

vacunar (baku'nar) vt vaccinate.

vacuo ('bakwo) adj 1 empty. 2 vacuous, empty-headed.

vadear (baðe'ar) vt 1 ford. 2 wade across. 3 overcome (problems, etc.). **vado** nm ford.

vagar (ba'gar) vi wander, roam. nm 1 free time, leisure. 2 ease.

vago ('bago) adj 1 vague. 2 lazy. nm tramp, idler. **vaguedad** nf vagueness.

vagón (ba'gon) nm 1 railway carriage. 2 wagon.

vagoneta (bago'neta) nm mot pick-up, light truck.

vahear (bae'ar) vi steam. **vaho** nm vapour.

vahido (ba'iðo) nm dizzy spell, dizziness.

vaina ('baina) nf 1 sheath, scabbard. 2 pl green beans.

vainilla (bai'niʎa) nf vanilla.

vaivén (bai'βen) nm 1 fluctuation, oscillation. 2 swinging movement.

vajilla (ba'xiʎa) nf crockery, dishes.

vale ('bale) nm comm promissory note, voucher.

valedero (bale'ðero) adj valid.

valentía (balen'tia) nf 1 bravery, courage. 2 bold or courageous act.

valer* (ba'ler) vt 1 be worth, cost. 2 be worthy. 3 be all right. 4 equal.

valeroso (bale'roso) adj brave.

valgo ('balgo) v see **valer.**

valía (ba'lia) nf worth, value.

validar (bali'ðar) vt validate, ratify. **validación** nf 1 validation. 2 ratification.

válido ('baliðo) adj valid. **validez** nf validity.

valiente (ba'ljente) adj 1 brave, courageous. 2 strong, powerful.

valija (ba'lixa) nf 1 case, valise. 2 mail bag.

valimiento (bali'mjento) nm 1 value. 2 goodwill, favour.

valioso (ba'ljoso) adj valuable, useful.

valor (ba'lor) nm 1 value, price. 2 valour. 3 pl comm bonds, assets.

valorar (balo'rar) vt value, assess. **valoración** nf assessment, valuation.

valsar (bal'sar) vi waltz. **vals** nm waltz.

valuar (ba'lwar) vt value, assess.

válvula ('balβula) nf valve.

vallar (ba'ʎar) vt enclose, fence in. **valla** nf fence.

valle ('baʎe) nm valley.

vampiro (bam'piro) nm vampire.

vanagloriarse (banaglo'rjarse) vr boast. **vanagloria** nf boasting, vainglory.

vándalo ('bandalo) nm vandal.

vanguardia (ban'gwarðja) nf 1 vanguard. 2 avant-garde.

vano ('bano) adj 1 useless. 2 imaginary, groundless. 3 conceited, vain. **en vano** in vain. **vanidad** nf 1 vanity. 2 futility, uselessness. **vanidoso** adj vain, conceited.

vapor (ba'por) nm 1 steam. 2 vapour, mist. 3 steamship. 4 med faintness. **vaporizar** vt vaporize. **vaporización** nf vaporization. **vaporoso** adj 1 steamy. 2 filmy, tenuous.

vaquero (ba'kero) nm cowboy.

vaqueta (ba'keta) nf cowhide.

vara ('bara) nf 1 stick, pole. 2 wand. 3 baton (of office). 4 lance.

varar (ba'rar) vt launch. **vararse** vr naut run aground. **varado** adj stranded, aground. **varadura** nf 1 launching. 2 running aground.

variar (ba'rjar) vt,vi vary, change. **variación** nf variation, change. **variado** adj mixed, assorted.

varilla (ba'riʎa) nf 1 bot twig, wand. 2 rib (of an umbrella, fan).

vario ('barjo) adj 1 varied, assorted. 2 pl several.

varón (ba'ron) adj,nm male. **varonil** adj 1 manly, virile. 2 male.

vasco ('basko) adj also **vascongado** Basque. nm 1 Basque. 2 Basque (language).

vasija (ba'sixa) nf container, vessel.

vaso ('baso) nm 1 cul glass. 2 glassful. 3 anat,naut vessel.

vástago ('bastago) nm 1 bot shoot, sprout. 2 offspring.

vasto ('basto) adj vast. **vastedad** nf vastness.

vaticinar (batiθi'nar) vt predict, prophesy. **vaticinador** nm prophet. **vaticinio** nm prophecy.

vatio ('batjo) nm watt.

vecinal (beθi'nal) adj local. **vecindad** nf neighbourhood. **vecino** nm 1 neighbour. 2 resident. adj neighbouring.

vedar (be'ðar) vt prohibit. **veda** nf 1 prohibition. 2 sport close season. **vedado** nm reserve, restricted area.

vega ('bega) nf plain, fertile lowland.

vegetación (begeta'θjon) nf vegetation. **vegetal** adj vegetable. **vegetar** vi 1 vegetate. 2 grow.

vehemencia (bee'menθja) nf vehemence. **vehemente** adj vehement.

vehículo (be'ikulo) nm vehicle.

veinte ('beinte) adj twenty.

vejar (be'xar) vt annoy, vex. **vejación** nf vexation.

vejez (be'xeθ) nf old age.

vejiga (be'xiga) nf 1 anat bladder. 2 med blister.

vela ('bela) nf naut sail.

velar (be'lar) vt keep watch over. vi stay awake. **vela** nf 1 vigil. 2 candle.

veleidad (belei'ðað) nf 1 whim, fancy. 2 capriciousness.

velero (be'lero) nm 1 sailing ship. 2 glider.

velo ('belo) nm veil.

velocidad (beloθi'ðað) nf speed, velocity. **velocímetro** nm speedometer. **veloz** adj fast.

vello ('beʎo) nm fluff, down. **velloso** adj downy.

vena ('bena) nf 1 anat vein. 2 streak, trait. 3 min vein, seam.

venado (be'naðo) nm 1 deer. 2 cul venison.

venal (be'nal) adj 1 corrupt, venal. 2 comm marketable.

vencer (ben'θer) vt conquer, defeat. vi 1 triumph, succeed. 2 comm expire. **vencedor** adj victorious. nm conqueror. **vencimiento** nm 1 giving way, collapse. 2 comm expiry.

vendar (ben'dar) vt bandage. **venda** nf also **vendaje** nm bandage.

vendaval (benda'βal) nm gale.

vender (ben'der) vt sell. **vendedor** nm seller, salesman.

vendimia (ben'dimja) nf grape harvest. **vendimiar** vt harvest (grapes).

veneno (be'neno) nm poison. **venenoso** adj poisonous.

venerar (bene'rar) vt venerate. **veneración** nf veneration.

venero (be'nero) nm 1 water spring. 2 source, origin.

vengar (ben'gar) vt avenge. **vengarse** vr take revenge. **vengador** adj avenging. nm avenger. **venganza** nf revenge. **vengativo** adj vindictive.

vengo ('bengo) v see **venir**.

venia ('benja) nf 1 pardon. 2 permission, leave.

venida (be'niða) nf 1 coming, arrival. 2 return. **venidero** adj future.

venir* (be'nir) vi come. **venir bien** suit, be convenient.

venta ('benta) nf 1 comm sale. 2 rural inn. **venta a plazos** hire purchase.

ventaja (ben'taxa) nf advantage. **ventajoso** adj advantageous.

ventana (ben'tana) nf window.

ventilar (benti'lar) vt ventilate. **ventilación** nf ventilation. **ventilador** nm ventilator, fan.

ventosa (ben'tosa) nf vent.

ventoso (ben'toso) adj windy.

ventrílocuo (ben'trilokwo) nm ventriloquist.

ventura (ben'tura) nf joy, happiness.

ver* (ber) vt see. nm 1 view, opinion. 2 looks, appearance.

vera ('bera) nf verge, edge.

veracidad (beraθi'ðað) nf truth.

verano (be'rano) nm summer.

veras ('beras) *nf pl* truth. **de veras** in truth, really, for real.

veraz (be'raθ) *adj* truthful.

verbo ('berβo) *nm* verb.

verdad (ber'ðað) *nf* truth. **verdadero** *adj* 1 true. 2 real, genuine. 3 trustworthy, truthful.

verde ('berðe) *adj* 1 green. 2 immature, young. 3 obscene.

verdugo (ber'ðugo) *nm* hangman, executioner.

verdulero (berðu'lero) *nm* greengrocer.

veredicto (bere'ðikto) *nm* verdict.

vergonzoso (bergon'θoso) *adj* 1 timid, shy. 2 shameful.

vergüenza (ber'gwenθa) *nf* 1 timidity. 2 shame, disgrace.

verídico (be'riðiko) *adj* truthful.

verificar (berifi'kar) *vt* 1 check, inspect. 2 verify. **verificarse** *vr* prove true, be realized.

verosímil (bero'simil) *adj* likely, probable. **verosimilitud** *nf* likeliness, probability.

verruga (ber'ruga) *nf* wart.

versado (ber'saðo) *adj* versed, skilful.

versar (ber'sar) *vi* spin, revolve. **versar sobre** deal with.

versátil (ber'satil) *adj* 1 adaptable, versatile. 2 fickle.

versículo (ber'sikulo) *nm* verse (of Bible).

versificar (bersifi'kar) *vt,vi* versify.

versión (ber'sjon) *nf* version.

verso ('berso) *nm* 1 verse. 2 line of poetry.

vértebra ('berteβra) *nf* vertebra.

verter (ie) (ber'ter) *vt* 1 pour, spill. 2 translate.

vertical (berti'kal) *adj* vertical.

vértice ('bertiθe) *nm* apex.

vértigo ('bertigo) *nm* vertigo, dizziness. **vertiginoso** *adj* giddy, dizzy.

vesícula (be'sikula) *nf* blister, vesicle.

vestíbulo (bes'tiβulo) *nm* 1 entrance hall. 2 *Th* lobby, foyer.

vestido (bes'tiðo) *nm* dress.

vestigio (bes'tixjo) *nm* vestige, trace.

vestir (i) (bes'tir) *vt* clothe, dress, put on.

veta ('beta) *nf* 1 vein, streak. 2 grain of wood.

veterano (bete'rano) *adj,nm* veteran.

veterinaria (beteri'narja) *nf* veterinary science. **veterinario** *nm* vet.

veto ('beto) *nm* veto.

vez (beθ) *nf* 1 time. 2 one's turn in a queue. **a veces** sometimes. **de una vez** once and for all. **de vez en cuando** from time to time. **en vez de** instead of. **muchas veces** often. **tal vez** perhaps. **una vez** once.

vía ('bia) *nf* 1 road, route. 2 track (railway). **vía aérea** air mail. **en vías de** in the process of.

viable ('bjaβle) *adj* viable, feasible.

viajar (bja'xar) *vi* travel. **viaje** *nm* journey. **viajero** *nm* 1 traveller. 2 passenger.

víbora ('biβora) *nf* zool viper.

vibrar (bi'βrar) *vi,vt* vibrate, shake. **vibración** *nf* vibration.

viciar (bi'θjar) *vt* 1 corrupt. 2 adulterate. **viciado** *adj* corrupt, foul. **vicio** *nm* 1 vice. 2 blemish. **vicioso** *adj* 1 vicious, depraved. 2 blemished, faulty.

vicisitud (biθisi'tuð) *nf* mishap.

víctima ('biktima) *nf* victim.

victoria (bik'torja) *nf* victory.

vid (bið) *nf* vine.

vida ('biða) *nf* life.

vidriar (bi'ðrjar) *vt* glaze. **vidriera** *nf* stained glass. **vidrio** *nm* glass. **vidrioso** *adj* glassy.

viejo ('bjexo) *adj* old. *nm* old man.

viento ('bjento) *nm* wind.

vientre ('bjentre) *nm* 1 belly. 2 bowels.

viernes ('bjernes) *nm* Friday.

viga ('biga) *nf* timber, beam.

vigencia (bi'xenθja) *nf* 1 validity, effectiveness. 2 social norm, convention. **en vigencia** in effect, effective. **vigente** *adj* valid, in force.

vigésimo (bi'xesimo) *adj* twentieth.

vigilar (bixi'lar) *vt* watch over. **vigilia** *nf* 1 watchfulness. 2 vigil.

vigor (bi'gor) *nm* vigour. **vigoroso** *adj* vigorous.

vil (bil) *adj* despicable, vile. **vileza** *nf* vileness.

vilo ('bilo) *adv* **en vilo** 1 in the air, aloft, suspended. 2 in suspense, up in the air.

villa ('biʎa) *nf* 1 villa. 2 town.

villancico (biʎan'θiko) *nm* Christmas carol.

villanía (biʎa'nia) *nf* 1 low birth. 2 villainy. 3 obscene remark. **villano** *adj* 1 low, coarse. 2 villainous. *nm* base person, cad.

vinagre (bi'nagre) *nm* vinegar.

vínculo ('binkulo) *nm* link, tie.

vindicar (bindi'kar) *vt* vindicate.

vino[1] ('bino) *nm* wine. **vinícola** *adj* relating to wine or wine-growing. **vino tinto** red wine. **vino de solera** vintage wine.

vino[2] ('bino) *v* see **venir**.

viña ('biɲa) *nf* vineyard.

viñeta (bi'ɲeta) *nf* vignette.

violar (bjo'lar) *vt* 1 violate. 2 rape. **violación** *nf* 1 violation. 2 rape.

violencia (bjo'lenθja) *nf* 1 violence. 2 embarrassment. **violento** adj 1 violent. 2 embarrassing, awkward.

violentar (bjolen'tar) vt 1 force. 2 twist (words). 3 break in. 4 do violence to.

violeta (bjo'leta) adj,nf violet.

violín (bjo'lin) nm violin.

violón (bjo'lon) nm double bass.

virar (bi'rar) vi 1 change direction. 2 swerve. 3 naut tack.

virgen ('birxen) adj,nf virgin.

viril (bi'ril) adj virile. **virilidad** nf virility.

virtual (bir'twal) adj 1 virtual. 2 potential.

virtud (bir'tuð) nf virtue. **virtuoso** adj virtuous.

viruela (bi'rwela) nf smallpox.

virulencia (biru'lenθja) nf virulence. **virulento** adj virulent.

visado (bi'saðo) nm visa.

visaje (bi'saxe) nm grimace, wry face.

viscoso (bis'koso) adj viscous. **viscosidad** nf viscosity.

visera (bi'sera) nf 1 peak of cap. 2 eyeshade.

visible (bi'sible) adj visible. **visibilidad** nf visibility.

visión (bi'sjon) nf 1 eyesight. 2 vision, fantasy. 3 view.

visitar (bisi'tar) vt 1 visit. 2 inspect. **visita** nf 1 visit. 2 visitor.

vislumbrar (bislum'brar) vt glimpse. **vislumbre** nf glimpse, glimmer.

viso ('biso) nm 1 appearance. 2 glint.

visón (bi'son) nm mink.

víspera ('bispera) nf eve.

vista ('bista) nf 1 eyesight. 2 look, gaze. **a primera vista** at first sight. **con vistas de** with a view to. **tener vista** be far-sighted.

visto ('bisto) v see **ver.** adj 1 seen. 2 evident. **por lo visto** apparently. **muy visto** out of date. **visto que** seeing that.

vistoso (bis'toso) adj gaudy, showy.

visual (bi'swal) adj visual.

vital (bi'tal) adj vital. **vitalidad** nf vitality.

vitamina (bita'mina) nf vitamin.

vitorear (bitore'ar) vt acclaim, cheer. **vítor** nm cheer.

vítreo ('bitreo) adj vitreous.

vituperar (bitupe'rar) vt condemn. **vituperio** nm 1 condemnation. 2 pl abuse. **vituperioso** adj abusive, insulting.

viuda ('bjuða) nf widow. **viudo** adj widowed. nm widower. **viudez** nf widowhood.

vivacidad (biβaθi'ðað) nf sprightliness, liveliness. **vivaz** adj 1 long-lived. 2 sprightly, sharp-witted.

víveres ('biβeres) nm pl provisions.

vivero (bi'βero) nm bot nursery.

viveza (bi'βeθa) nf liveliness.

vivienda (bi'βjenda) nf 1 housing. 2 residence, dwelling.

vivificar (biβifi'kar) vt bring to life.

vivir (bi'βir) vt,vi live. **¿quién vive?** who goes there? ~nm way of life.

vivo ('biβo) adj 1 living, alive. 2 vivid, sharp.

vizconde (biθ'konde) nm viscount.

vocablo (bo'kaβlo) nm word. **vocabulario** nm vocabulary.

vocación (boka'θjon) nf vocation.

vocal (bo'kal) adj vocal. nm member of a committee, board, etc. nf vowel.

vocear (boθe'ar) vt 1 shout to. 2 acclaim. 3 advertise by shouting. vi boast. **voceador** adj loud-mouthed. nm town crier.

vociferar (boθife'rar) vt,vi shout, scream.

vocinglero (boθin'glero) adj loud-mouthed, talkative. **vocinglería** nf uproar.

volante (bo'lante) adj flying. nm 1 steering wheel. 2 shuttlecock. 3 sport winger.

volar (ue) (bo'lar) vt blow up, demolish. vi fly. **volarse** vr fly away.

volátil (bo'latil) adj volatile. **volatilidad** nf volatility.

volcán (bol'kan) nm volcano. **volcánico** adj volcanic.

volcar (ue) (bol'kar) vt upset, knock over. vi turn over. **volcarse** vr tip over, overturn.

volición (boli'θjon) nf volition.

voltaje (bol'taxe) nm voltage.

voltear (bolte'ar) vt 1 turn over, roll over. 2 throw up in the air, toss. 3 peal (bells). vi roll over. **voltereta** nf somersault.

voltio ('boltjo) nm volt.

volubilidad (boluβili'ðað) nf fickleness. **voluble** adj 1 fickle. 2 bot climbing, twining.

volumen (bo'lumen) nm volume. **voluminoso** adj voluminous.

voluntad (bolun'tað) nf 1 will. 2 intention. 3 desire.

voluntario (bolun'tarjo) adj voluntary. nm volunteer.

voluptuoso (bolup'twoso) adj voluptuous.

volver (ue) (bol'βer) vt 1 turn round, turn, return. 2 turn inside out. vi return. **volver en sí** regain consciousness. **volverse** vr 1 turn round. 2 become, turn into.

vomitar (bomi'tar) vt,vi vomit, cough up. **vómito** nm vomit.

voracidad (boraθi'ðað) *nf* voraciousness. **voraz** *adj* voracious.

vórtice ('bortiθe) *nm* whirlpool.

vosotros (bo'sotros) *pron* 2nd pers *pl fam* you.

votar (bo'tar) *vt,vi* vote. **voto** *nm* 1 vote. 2 vow. 3 *pl* wishes. **mejores votos** best wishes.

voy (boj) *v* see **ir.**

voz (boθ) *nf* 1 voice. 2 rumour. 3 vote, say. 4 word. **hacer** or **dar voces** shout.

vuelco ('bwelko) *nm* tumble, spill.

vuelo ('bwelo) *nm* 1 flight. 2 fullness (clothes). **vuelo fletado** charter flight.

vuelta ('bwelta) *nf* 1 turn. 2 revolution (of a wheel). 3 rotation. 4 change, reversal. 5 return. 6 walk, stroll. 7 *also pl* change (of money).

vuelto ('bwelto) *v* see **volver.**

vuestro ('bwestro) *poss adj* 2nd pers *s* your. *poss pron* 2nd pers *s* yours.

vulcanizar (bulkani'θar) *vt* vulcanize.

vulgar (bul'gar) *adj* 1 vulgar. 2 commonplace, trivial. **vulgaridad** *nf* 1 vulgarity. 2 triviality. **vulgarizar** *vt* popularize. **vulgarmente** *adv* commonly, ordinarily. **vulgo** *nm* common people.

vulnerar (bulne'rar) *vt* damage, harm. **vulnerable** *adj* vulnerable. **vulnerabilidad** *nf* vulnerability.

X

xilófono (ksi'lofono) *nm* xylophone.

Y

y (i) *conj* and.

ya (ja) *adv* 1 already. 2 now, finally. *interj* of course! **ya que** since, seeing that. **ya no** no longer.

yacimiento (jaθi'mjento) *nm geol* bed, deposit.

yangui ('janki) *adj* Yankee, North American.

yarda ('jarða) *nf* yard.

yate ('jate) *nm* yacht.

yedra ('jeðra) *nf* ivy.

yegua ('jegwa) *nf* mare.

yelmo ('jelmo) *nm* helmet.

yema ('jema) *nf* 1 egg yolk. 2 fingertip. 3 *bot* bud, shoot.

yerba ('jerβa) *nf* 1 grass. 2 herb.

yergo ('jergo) *v* see **erguir.**

yermo ('jermo) *adj* barren, waste.

yerno ('jerno) *nm* son-in-law.

yerro ('jerro) *v* see **errar.** *nm* error, lapse.

yeso ('jeso) *nm* 1 plaster. 2 gypsum.

ye-yé (je'je) *inf adj* trendy. *nm,f* trendy member of the modern generation.

yo (jo) *pron* 1st pers *s* I.

yodo ('joðo) *nm* iodine.

yogur (jo'gur) *nm* yoghurt.

yugo ('jugo) *nm* yoke.

Yugo(e)slavia (jugoes'laβja) *nf* Yugoslavia. **yugo(e)slavo** *adj,nm* Yugoslav.

yunque ('junke) *nm* anvil.

yunta ('junta) *nf* team of oxen.

yute ('jute) *nm* jute.

yuxtaponer (jukstapo'ner) *vt* juxtapose. **yuxtaposición** *nf* juxtaposition.

Z

zafar (θa'far) *vt* make lighter. **zafarse** *vr* run or slip away.

zafio ('θafjo) *adj* uncouth.

zafiro (θa'firo) *nm* sapphire.

zaga ('θaga) *nf* rear. **ir a la zaga** lag behind.

zaguán (θa'gwan) *nm* hallway, entry.

zaherir (ie) (θae'rir) *vt* 1 reproach. 2 wound, mortify. **zaherimiento** *nm* 1 blame, criticism. 2 mortification.

zalamería (θalame'ria) *nf* flattery. **zalamero** *adj* flattering.

zamarra (θa'marra) *nf* sheepskin jacket.

zambo ('θambo) *adj* knock-kneed.

zambullir (θambu'ʎir) *vt* plunge, dip. **zambullirse** *vr* dive. **zambullida** *nf* dive.

zampar ('θampar) *vt* 1 hide (an object) away hurriedly. 2 eat greedily. **zampabollos** *nm invar* glutton.

zanahoria (θana'orja) *nf* carrot.

zancada (θan'kaða) *nf* stride.

zanco ('θanko) *nm* stilt.

zancudo (θan'kuðo) *adj* long-legged.

zángano ('θangano) *nm* 1 drone (bee). 2 idler, sponger.

zangolotear (θangolote'ar) *vt* fiddle with. **zangolotearse** *vr* rattle, clatter.

zanja ('θanxa) *nf* trench, ditch.

zapa ('θapa) *nf* spade.

zapatear (θapate'ar) *vt* kick with the shoe. *vi* 1 tap. 2 tap-dance.

zapatería (θapate'ria) *nf* 1 shoemaking. 2 shoemaker's shop. **zapatero** *nm* shoemaker.

zapatilla (θapa'tiλa) nf slipper.

zapato (θa'pato) nm shoe.

zar (θar) nm tsar.

zarandear (θarande'ar) vt shake about.

zaraza (θa'raθa) nf chintz.

zarcillo (θar'θiλo) nm earring.

zarco ('θarko) adj pale blue.

zarpa ('θarpa) nf paw, claw.

zarpar (θar'par) vi naut set sail.

zarza ('θarθa) nf bramble. **zarzamora** nf black-berry.

zarzuela (θar'θwela) nf light opera, musical comedy.

zigzaguear (θigθage'ar) vi zig-zag.

zinc (θink) nm zinc.

zócalo ('θokalo) nm 1 arch plinth. 2 skirting board.

zona ('θona) nf zone.

zoología (θoolo'xia) nf zoology. **zoológico** adj zoological. **zoólogo** nm zoologist.

zoquete (θo'kete) nm 1 block of wood. 2 chunk of bread. 3 blockhead.

zorro ('θorro) nm fox. adj cunning. **zorra** nf 1 vixen. 2 cheap woman, tart.

zozobrar (θoθo'βrar) vi 1 naut capsize. 2 collapse, be ruined. 3 worry.

zueco ('θweko) nm clog.

zumbar ('θumbar) vi buzz. vt tease, annoy. **zumbido** nm buzzing noise.

zumbón (θum'bon) adj bantering, joking. nm joker, teaser.

zumo ('θumo) nm juice.

zurcir (θur'θir) vt darn, patch. **zurcido** nm darning, mending.

zurdo ('θurðo) adj left-handed.

zurrar (θur'rar) vt 1 tech tan (leather). 2 inf give a beating to. 3 inf criticize harshly, defeat in an argument. **zurriago** nm whip.

zurrón (θur'ron) nm pouch, small bag.

zutano (θu'tano) nm so-and-so.

A

a, an (ə, ən; *stressed* ei, æn) *indef art* un *ms.* una *fs.*

aback (ə'bæk) *adv* atrás. **taken aback** desconcertado, perplejo.

abandon (ə'bændən) *vt* abandonar, dejar. **abandonment** *n* abandono *m.*

abate (ə'beit) *vt,vi* bajar, disminuir, aminorar. **abatement** *n* disminución *f.* abatimiento *m.*

abbess ('æbis) *n* abadesa *f.*

abbey ('æbi) *n* abadía *f.*

abbot ('æbət) *n* abad *m.*

abbreviate (ə'bri:vieit) *vt* abreviar. **abbreviation** *n* abreviación *f.*

abdicate ('æbdikeit) *vt,vi* abdicar, renunciar. **abdication** *n* abdicación *f.* renuncia *f.*

abdomen ('æbdəmən) *n* abdomen *m.* vientre *m.* **abdominal** *adj* abdominal.

abduct (æb'dʌkt) *vt* secuestrar, raptar. **abduction** *n* secuestro, rapto *m.* **abductor** *n* secuestrador, raptor *m.*

abet (ə'bet) *vt* instigar, inducir, patrocinar.

abhor (əb'hɔ:) *vt* aborrecer, detestar, odiar, despreciar. **abhorrence** *n* odio, horror *m.* aversión *f.* **abhorrent** *adj* aborrecible, detestable.

abide' (ə'baid) *vi* permanecer, continuar. *vt* aguantar, aceptar. **abide by** atenerse a, cumplir con.

ability (ə'biliti) *n* **1** habilidad, capacidad *f.* **2** talento *m.* **3** alcance *m.*

abject ('æbdʒekt) *adj* abyecto, vil, despreciable, bajo. **abjection** *n* **1** abyección *f.* **2** servilismo *m.*

ablative ('æblətiv) *n* ablativo *m.*

ablaze (ə'bleiz) *adj* en llamas, ardiente.

able ('eibəl) *adj* hábil, inteligente, fuerte, capaz. **be able** poder, ser capaz. **able-bodied** *adj* robusto, sano.

abnormal (æb'nɔ:məl) *adj* **1** anormal. **2** excepcional. **abnormality** *n* anormalidad *f.* **abnormally** *adv* excepcionalmente.

aboard (ə'bɔ:d) *adv* a bordo.

abode¹ (ə'boud) *n* domicilio *m.*

abode² (ə'boud) *v see* **abide.**

abolish (ə'bɔliʃ) *vt* **1** abolir. **2** revocar, anular. **abolition** *n* abolición *f.*

abominable (ə'bɔminəbəl) *adj* abominable.

Aborigine (æbə'ridʒini) *n* aborigen *m.*

abort (ə'bɔ:t) *vt,vi* **1** abortar. **2** frustrar. **abortion** *n* aborto *m.* **abortive** *adj* abortivo, frustrado, malogrado.

abound (ə'baund) *vi* abundar.

about (ə'baut) *prep* alrededor de, cerca de, hacia, acerca de, sobre. *adv* alrededor, más o menos.

above (ə'bʌv) *prep* por encima de, sobre, superior a. *adv* arriba, encima. **aboveboard** *adv* abiertamente.

abrasion (ə'breiʒən) *n* **1** raspadura *f.* **2** rasguño *m.* **3** *tech* abrasión *f.* **abrasive** *adj* **1** raspante. **2** *tech* abrasivo.

abreast (ə'brest) *adv* de frente. **abreast of** *or* **with** al corriente de.

abridge (ə'bridʒ) *vt* abreviar.

abroad (ə'brɔ:d) *adv* **1** en el extranjero. **2** fuera.

abrupt (ə'brʌpt) *adj* abrupto, brusco. **abruptly** *adv* precipitadamente, bruscamente. **abruptness** *n* precipitación, aspereza, brusquedad *f.*

abscess ('æbses) *n* absceso *m.*

abscond (əb'skɔnd) *vi* fugarse.

absent (*adj* 'æbsənt; *v* ab'sent) *adj* ausente. *vr* ausentarse. **absent-minded** *adj* absorto, distraído, despistado. **absent-mindedness** *n* distracción *f.* despiste *m.* **absence** *n* ausencia *f.* **absentee** *n* ausente *m,f.* absentista *m,f.* **absenteeism** *n* absentismo *m.*

absolute ('æbsəlu:t) *adj* absoluto, total.

absolve (əb'zɔlv) *vt* absolver. **absolution** *n* absolución *f.*

absorb (əb'zɔ:b) *vt* **1** absorber, empapar, chupar. **2** preocupar. **absorbent** *adj* absorbente. **absorption** *n* absorción *f.*

abstain (əb'stein) *vi* abstenerse. **abstention** *n*

abstención f. **abstinence** n abstinencia, sobriedad f.

abstract (adj,n 'æbstrækt; v əb'strækt) adj abstracto. n resumen, sumario m. vt abstraer, resumir. **abstract art** n arte abstracto m.

absurd (əb'sə:d) adj absurdo, disparatado. **absurdity** n absurdo, disparate m.

abundance (ə'bʌndəns) n abundancia f. **abundant** adj abundante, suficiente.

abuse (v ə'bju:z; n ə'bju:s) vt 1 abusar. 2 injuriar. n 1 abuso m. 2 injurias f pl. **abusive** adj 1 abusivo. 2 injurioso.

abyss (ə'bis) n abismo m. sima f. **abysmal** adj abismal, profundo.

academy (ə'kædəmi) n academia f. **academic** adj,n académico.

accelerate (ək'seləreit) vt acelerar, apresurar. vi acelerarse, apresurarse. **acceleration** n aceleración f. apresuramiento m. **accelerator** n acelerador m.

accent (n 'æksənt; v æk'sent) n acento m. vt acentuar. **accentuate** vt acentuar.

accept (ək'sept) vt aceptar, acoger. **acceptance** n 1 aceptación f. 2 acogida favorable f.

access ('ækses) n acceso m.

accessory (ək'sesəri) adj accesorio, adicional. n 1 accesorio m. 2 law cómplice m,f.

accident ('æksidənt) n 1 accidente m. 2 casualidad f. **by accident** por casualidad, sin querer. **accidental** adj accidental, casual, fortuito.

acclaim (ə'kleim) vt aclamar, vitorear, celebrar. n aclamación f. ovación f. aplauso m.

acclimatize (ə'klaimətaiz) vt aclimatar.

accommodate (ə'kɔmədeit) vt 1 acomodar, complacer. 2 alojar. **accommodating** adj complaciente. **accommodation** n 1 acomodación, adaptación f. facilidades f pl. 2 alojamiento m.

accompany (ə'kʌmpəni) vt acompañar. **accompaniment** n acompañamiento m.

accomplice (ə'kʌmplis) n cómplice m,f.

accomplish (ə'kʌmpliʃ) vt cumplir, realizar, completar, lograr. **accomplishment** n cumplimiento, logro, éxito m. realización f.

accord (ə'kɔ:d) vt,vi 1 conceder, otorgar. 2 concordar. **accord with** concordar con. ~n acuerdo, convenio m. **of one's own accord** espontáneamente. **accordance** n acuerdo m. **in accordance with** de acuerdo con, conforme a. **according to** según, conforme a. **accordingly** adv en consecuencia, en conformidad.

accordion (ə'kɔ:diən) n acordeón m.

accost (ə'kɔst) vt abordar.

account (ə'kaunt) n 1 cuenta f. relato m. 2 importancia f. **of no account** de poca importancia. **on account of** a causa de. **on no account** de ninguna manera. **take into account** tener en cuenta. ~vi dar cuenta de, justificar. **account for** responder de, dar una explicación de. **accountant** n contable m,f. contador m.

accumulate (ə'kju:mjuleit) vt acumular. **accumulation** n acumulación f. montón m.

accurate ('ækjurət) adj exacto, preciso. **accuracy** n exactitud, precisión f. **accurately** adv con exactitud, con precisión.

accuse (ə'kju:z) vt acusar, delatar. **accusation** n acusación f.

accustom (ə'kʌstəm) vt acostumbrar, habituar. vi soler.

ace (eis) n as m. **within an ace of** a dos dedos de.

ache (eik) n dolor m. **headache** dolor de cabeza. **toothache** dolor de muelas. ~vi doler.

achieve (ə'tʃi:v) vt acabar, realizar, lograr, alcanzar. **achievement** n realización, hazaña f. logro m.

acid ('æsid) adj ácido, agrio. n ácido m. **acidity** n acidez f.

acknowledge (ək'nɔlidʒ) vt 1 reconocer, aceptar. 2 comm acusar recibo. **acknowledgment** n 1 reconocimiento m. gratitud f. 2 comm acuso de recibo m.

acne ('ækni) n acné m.

acorn ('eikɔ:n) n bellota f.

acoustic (ə'ku:stik) adj acústico. **acoustics** n acústica f.

acquaint (ə'kweint) vt enterar, dar a conocer, familiarizar. **acquaintance** n 1 conocimiento m. 2 conocido m.

acquiesce (ækwi'es) vi consentir, someterse. **acquiescence** n aquiescencia f. consentimiento m. **acquiescent** adj conforme, aquiescente.

acquire (ə'kwaiə) vt adquirir. **acquisition** n adquisición f. **acquisitive** adj adquisitivo.

acquit (ə'kwit) vt 1 absolver, exculpar. 2 cumplir, desempeñar. **acquittal** absolución f. descargo m.

acre ('eikə) n acre m. terrenos m pl.

acrimony ('ækriməni) n acrimonia f. **acrimonious** adj áspero, mordaz.

acrobat

acrobat ('ækrəbæt) n acróbata m,f. **acrobatic** adj acrobático.

across (ə'krɔs) prep a través, al través de, contra. adv al través, de través.

acrylic (ə'krilik) adj acrílico.

act (ækt) vt,vi actuar, obrar, representar, fingir. n 1 acto, m. 2 law acta f. decreto m. 3 Th acto m. jornada f. **catch in the act** coger con las manos en la masa.

action ('ækʃən) n 1 acto m. acción f. 2 law demanda f. proces m. 3 mil batalla f. **put out of action** inutilizar.

active ('æktiv) adj 1 activo. 2 vigoroso. **activate** vt activar. **activist** n activista m,f. **activity** n actividad f.

actor ('æktə) n actor m. protagonista m,f.

actress ('æktris) n actriz f.

actual ('æktʃuəl) adj 1 actual. 2 real, efectivo.

acupuncture ('ækjupʌŋktʃə) n acupuntura f.

acute (ə'kju:t) adj agudo, penetrante.

adamant ('ædəmənt) adj firme, seguro, inflexible.

Adam's apple ('ædəmz) n nuez de la garganta f.

adapt (ə'dæpt) vt 1 adaptar, ajustar. 2 arreglar. **adaptability** n adaptabilidad f. **adaptable** adj adaptable.

add (æd) vt,vi añadir, aumentar. **add up** sumar. **adding machine** n máquina sumadora f. **addition** n adición, suma f. aumento m. **in addition to** además de. **additional** adj adicional, suplementario. **additive** n aditivo m.

addendum (ə'dendəm) n, pl **addenda** apéndice, suplemento m. adición f.

adder ('ædə) n víbora f.

addict (n 'ædikt; v ə'dikt) n adicto, partidario m. **be addicted to** 1 ser adicto a, ser aficionado a. 2 estar enviciado con. **drug-addict** toxicómano m. **addiction** n 1 afición f. 2 toxicomanía f.

addled ('ædld) adj huero.

address (ə'dres) vt 1 (a letter) dirigir. 2 (a meeting) pronunciar un discurso ante. 3 (oneself) dirigirse. n 1 dirección f. señas f pl. 2 discurso m. 3 destreza f. **address book** n cuaderno de direcciones m.

adenoids ('ædinɔidz) n vegetaciones adenoideas, glándulas adenoideas f pl.

adept ('ædept) n experto m. adj versado, hábil, consumado.

adequate ('ædikwət) adj suficiente, adecuado. **adequacy** n suficiencia f.

adhere (əd'hiə) vi 1 adherirse. 2 observar, cumplir. **adherent** adj adherente, adhesivo. n adherente, m,f. partidario m. **adhesion** n adhesión f.

adhesive (əd'hi:siv) adj adhesivo, engomado. n adhesivo m.

adjacent (ə'dʒeisənt) adj adyacente, contiguo.

adjective ('ædʒiktiv) n adjetivo m.

adjourn (ə'dʒə:n) vt aplazar, levantar la sesión. **adjournment** n suspensión f.

adjudicate (ə'dʒu:dikeit) vt adjudicar. **adjudication** n juicio m.

adjust (ə'dʒʌst) vt ajustar. **adjustable** adj ajustable.

ad-lib (æd'lib) adv a voluntad. vt,vi improvisar.

administer (əd'ministə) vt administrar. **administration** n administración f. **administrative** adj administrativo. **administrator** n administrador m.

admiral ('ædmərəl) n almirante m. **admiralty** n almirantazgo m.

admire (əd'maiə) vt admirar, contemplar. **admirable** adj admirable. **admiration** n admiración f. **admirer** n admirador m.

admit (əd'mit) vt admitir, dar entrada. **admission** n admisión f. entrada f. **admittance** n admisión f.

ado (ə'du:) n trabajo m. dificultad f.

adolescence (ædə'lesəns) n adolescencia f. **adolescent** adj,n adolescente.

adopt (ə'dɔpt) vt adoptar, escoger, aceptar. **adoption** n adopción f. **adoptive** adj adoptivo.

adore (ə'dɔ:) vt adorar. **adorable** adj adorable. **adoration** n adoración f. **adorer** n adorador m. **adoringly** adv apasionadamente.

adorn (ə'dɔ:n) vt adornar.

adrenaline (ə'drenəlin) n adrenalina f.

Adriatic (eidri'ætik) n Adriático m. **Adriatic (Sea)** n (Mar) Adriático m.

adrift (ə'drift) adv a la deriva.

adroit (ə'drɔit) adj hábil, diestro.

adulation (ædju'leiʃən) n adulación f. **adulator** n adulador m. **adulatory** adj adulador.

adult ('ædʌlt) adj,n adulto.

adulterate (ə'dʌltəreit) vt adulterar. **adulteration** n adulteración f.

adultery (ə'dʌltəri) n adulterio m. corrupción f. **adulterer** n adúltero m. **adulterous** adj adúltero.

advance (əd'va:ns) vt,vi avanzar, adelantar. n avance, adelanto, progreso m. **in advance** de antemano. **advancement** n promoción f.

advantage (əd'va:ntidʒ) n ventaja, superioridad

f. **take advantage of** aprovechar(se) de. **have the advantage of** llevar ventaja a. **advantageous** *adj* ventajoso.

advent ('ædvent) *n* advenimiento *m.*

adventure (əd'ventʃə) *n* aventura *f.* **adventurer** *n* aventurero *m.* **adventurous** *adj* audaz.

adverb ('ædvə:b) *n* adverbio *m.*

adverse ('ædvə:s) *adj* adverso, hostil. **adversity** *n* adversidad, desgracia *f.*

advertise ('ædvətaiz) *vt* anunciar, advertir. **advertisement** *n* anuncio, aviso *m.* **advertising** *n* publicidad *f. adj* publicitario.

advise (əd'vaiz) *vt* aconsejar, avisar. **advice** *n* consejo, aviso *m.* **advisable** *adj* aconsejable, conveniente. **adviser** *n* consejero, asesor *m.* **advisory** *adj* consultivo.

advocate (*n* 'ædvəkət; *v* 'ædvəkeit) *n* abogado, defensor *m. vt* abogar por, propugnar, defender.

Aegean (i'dʒi:ən) *adj* Egeo. **Aegean (Sea)** *n* (Mar) Egeo *m.*

aerate ('εəreit) *vt* ventilar, airear.

aerial ('εəriəl) *adj* aéreo. *n* antena *f.*

aerodynamics (εəroudai'næmiks) *n* aerodinámica *f.*

aeronautics (εərə'nɔ:tiks) *n* aeronáutica *f.* **aeronautical** *adj* aeronáutico.

aeroplane ('εərəplein) *n* avión, aeroplano *m.*

aesthetic (is'θetik) *adj* estético.

afar (ə'fɑ:) *adv* lejos.

affable ('æfəbəl) *adj* afable. **affability** *n* afabilidad *f.*

affair (ə'fεə) *n* **1** asunto, negocio *m.* **2** amorío *m.*

affect[1] (ə'fekt) *vt* afectar, conmover, impresionar, influir, atacar. **affected** *adj* conmovido, afectado.

affect[2] (ə'fekt) *vt* **1** aparentar, fingir. **2** *inf* dárselas de. **affected** *adj* amanerado, cursi. **affectation** *n* afectación *f.* cursilería *f.*

affection (ə'fekʃən) *n* **1** afecto, cariño *m.* **2** *med* afección *f.* **affectionate** *adj* afectuoso, cariñoso.

affiliate (ə'filieit) *vi* **affiliate to** *or* **with** afiliarse a. **affiliation** *n* afiliación *f.*

affinity (ə'finiti) *n* afinidad *f.*

affirm (ə'fə:m) *vt* afirmar, declarar, asegurar. *vr* afirmarse. **affirmation** *n* afirmación, aseveración *f.* **affirmative** *adj* afirmativo.

affix (*v* ə'fiks; *n* 'æfiks) *vt* fijar, pegar, añadir. *n gram* afijo *m.*

afflict (ə'flikt) *vt* afligir, aquejar. **affliction** *n* aflicción *f.* dolor *m.*

affluent ('æfluənt) *adj* opulento, acaudalado, rico. **affluence** *n* afluencia, opulencia *f.* **the affluent society** *n* la sociedad opulenta *f.*

afford (ə'fɔ:d) *vt* **1** dar, proporcionar. **2** costear, darse el lujo.

affront (ə'frʌnt) *n* afrenta, injuria *f.* insulto *m.*

Afghanistan (æf'gænistɑ:n, -stæn) *n* Afganistán *m.* **Afghan** *adj,n* afgano.

afloat (ə'flout) *adv* a flote, a nado, en el mar.

afoot (ə'fut) *adv* **1** a pie. **2** en proyecto.

aforesaid (ə'fɔ:sed) *adj* susodicho.

afraid (ə'freid) *adj* temeroso. **be afraid** temer, tener miedo.

Africa ('æfrikə) *n* África *f.* **African** *adj,n* africano.

aft (ɑ:ft) *adv* a popa, en popa.

after ('ɑ:ftə) *prep* **1** después de. **2** detrás. **3** según. **time after time** repetidas veces. ~*adv* **1** después. **2** detrás. *adj* posterior, ulterior. **after-effect** *n* efecto secundario *m.* consecuencias *f pl.* **aftermath** *n* consecuencias *f pl.* **afternoon** *n* tarde *f.* **good afternoon** buenas tardes. **afterthought** *n* ocurrencia tardía *f.* reparo *m.* **afterwards** *adv* después, más tarde.

again (ə'gen) *adv* otra vez, de nuevo, nuevamente.

against (ə'genst) *prep* **1** contra, junto a. **2** en contra de. **be against** oponerse. **over against** enfrente de.

age (eidʒ) *n* **1** edad *f.* **2** época *f.* siglo *m.* **3** vejez *f.* **of age** mayor de edad. **under age** menor de edad. ~*vt,vi* envejecer. **aged** *adj* viejo, anciano, envejecido.

agency ('eidʒənsi) *n* agencia, mediación *f.*

agenda (ə'dʒendə) *n* agenda *f.*

agent ('eidʒənt) *n* agente, representante *m,f.*

aggravate ('ægrəveit) *vt* **1** agravar, empeorar. **2** *inf* exasperar, molestar.

aggregate (*adj,n* 'ægrigit; *v* 'ægrigeit) *adj,nm* agregado. *vt* agregar, juntar.

aggression (ə'greʃən) *n* agresión *f.* **aggressive** *adj* **1** agresivo. **2** emprendedor.

aggrieved (ə'gri:vd) *adj* agraviado, ofendido.

aghast (ə'gɑ:st) *adj* **1** horrorizado. **2** pasmado.

agile ('ædʒail) *adj* ágil. **agility** *n* agilidad *f.*

agitate ('ædʒiteit) *vt* agitar, alborotar. **agitation** *n* agitación *f.* alboroto *m.* **agitator** *n* agitador, instigador *m.*

aglow (ə'glou) *adj* encendido.

agnostic (æg'nɔstik) adj,n agnóstico.

ago (ə'gou) adv hace. **long ago** hace mucho tiempo.

agog (ə'gɔg) adj ansioso, ávido.

agony ('ægəni) n agonía f. **agonize** vi agonizar.

agree (ə'gri:) vi concordar, estar de acuerdo. **agreeable** adj 1 agradable. 2 dispuesto. **agreement** n acuerdo m.

agriculture ('ægrikʌltʃə) n agricultura f. **agricultural** adj agrícola.

aground (ə'graund) adv varado, encallado.

ahead (ə'hed) adv delante, adelante. **be ahead** ir delante. **get ahead** adelantarse. **go ahead!** ¡adelante! **straight ahead** todo seguido.

aid (eid) vt ayudar. n ayuda f. ayudante m,f. **first aid** primeros auxilios m pl. **in aid of** a beneficio de.

ailment ('eilmənt) n dolencia f. achaque m. **ailing** adj enfermizo, achacoso.

aim (eim) vt,vi 1 apuntar. 2 aspirar, pretender. n. 1 puntería f. 2 meta f.

air (ɛə) n 1 aire m. 2 aspecto, porte m. **by air** por avión. **on the air** en la radio. ~vt airear, ventilar.

airbed n colchón neumático m.

airborne ('ɛəbɔ:n) adj 1 en el aire. 2 aerotransportado.

air-conditioning n aire acondicionado m.

aircraft ('ɛəkra:ft) n avión m.

aircraft carrier n port(a)aviones m invar.

airfield ('ɛəfi:ld) n campo de aviación m.

airforce ('ɛəfɔ:s) n aviación f.

air-hostess n azafata f.

air lift n puente aéreo m.

airline ('ɛəlain) n línea aérea f.

airmail ('ɛəmeil) n correo aéreo m.

airman ('ɛəmən) n aviador m.

airport ('ɛəpɔ:t) n aeropuerto m.

air-raid n bombardeo aéreo m.

airtight ('ɛətait) adj hermético.

airy ('ɛəri) adj 1 airoso. 2 bien ventilado.

aisle (ail) n nave lateral f. pasillo m.

ajar (ə'dʒɑ:) adj entreabierto, entornado.

alabaster ('æləbɑ:stə) n alabastro m.

alarm (ə'lɑ:m) n alarma f. vt alarmar. **alarm clock** n despertador m.

alas (ə'læs) interj ¡ay!

Albania (æl'beiniə) n Albania f. **Albanian** adj,n albanés.

albatross ('ælbətrɔs) n albatros m.

albeit (ɔ:l'bi:it) conj aunque, bien que.

album ('ælbəm) n álbum m.

alchemy ('ælkəmi) n alquimia f. **alchemist** n alquimista m.

alcohol ('ælkəhɔl) n alcohol m. **alcoholic** adj,n alcohólico.

alcove ('ælkouv) n alcoba f.

alderman ('ɔ:ldəmən) n 1 teniente de alcalde m. 2 regidor m.

ale (eil) n cerveza f.

alert (ə'lə:t) adj,nm alerta.

algebra ('ældʒibrə) n álgebra f.

Algeria (æl'dʒiəriə) n Argelia f. **Algerian** adj,n argelino.

alias ('eiliəs) adv,nm alias.

alibi ('ælibai) n coartada f.

alien ('eiliən) adj ajeno, extranjero. n extranjero m. **alienate** vt enajenar, alienar. **alienation** n enajenación, alienación f.

alight[1] (ə'lait) adj encendido, iluminado.

alight[2] (ə'lait) vi 1 bajar, apearse. 2 posarse. 3 descargar.

align (ə'lain) vt alinear.

alike (ə'laik) adj semejante, parecido.

alimentary (æli'mentəri) adj alimenticio.

alimony ('æliməni) n mantenimiento de divorcio m.

alive (ə'laiv) adj 1 vivo, viviente. 2 activo, vivaz. 3 sensible. **alive with** rebosante de.

alkali ('ælkəlai) n álcali m.

all (ɔ:l) adj todo. **all day** todo el día. ~pron todo ms. todos mpl. toda fs. todas fpl. n todo m. totalidad f. adv todo, enteramente. **all but** casi, menos. **all right** ¡está bien! **at all** en lo más mínimo. **not at all** en absoluto, de ninguna manera.

allay (ə'lei) vt apaciguar, calmar.

allege (ə'ledʒ) vt alegar.

allegiance (ə'li:dʒəns) n lealtad f.

allegory ('æligəri) n alegoría f. **allegorical** adj alegórico.

allergy ('ælədʒi) n alergia f. **allergic** adj alérgico.

alleviate (ə'li:vieit) vt aliviar. **alleviation** n alivio m.

alley ('æli) n 1 paseo m. 2 callejón m. **alleyway** n callejón, pasadizo m. **blind alley** callejón sin salida m.

alliance (ə'laiəns) n alianza f.

allied (ə'laid, 'ælaid) adj aliado.

alligator ('æligeitə) n caimán m.

alliteration (əlitə'reiʃən) n aliteración f.

allocate ('æləkeit) vt asignar, repartir. **allocation** n asignación f. reparto m.

allot (ə'lɔt) vt asignar. **allotment** n lote m. asignación, parcela f.

allow (ə'lau) vt permitir, admitir, conceder. **allow for** tener en cuenta. **allowance** n 1 concesión f. 2 dieta f. 3 subsidio m. pensión f.

alloy ('ælɔi) n aleación f. vt alear, mezclar.

allude (ə'lu:d) vi aludir. **allusion** n alusión f. **allusive** adj alusivo.

allure (ə'ljuə) n atractivo m. fascinación f. vt atraer, seducir, tentar. **alluring** adj atractivo, tentador.

ally (v ə'lai; n 'ælai) vr aliarse, unirse, emparentar. n aliado m.

almanac ('ɔ:lmənæk) n almanaque m.

almond ('ɑːmənd) n almendra f. **almond tree** n almendro m.

almost ('ɔːlmoust) adv casi.

alms (ɑːmz) n limosna f.

aloft (ə'lɔft) adv 1 arriba, en lo alto. 2 naut en la arboladura.

alone (ə'loun) adj solo. adv solamente, sólo.

along (ə'lɔŋ) adv a lo largo, adelante. prep a lo largo de, a lo largo por. **alongside** adv al lado. prep junto a, al lado de.

aloof (ə'lu:f) adv distante.

aloud (ə'laud) adv en voz alta.

alphabet ('ælfəbet) n alfabeto m. **alphabetical** adj alfabético.

alpine ('ælpain) adj alpino, alpestre.

Alps (ælps) n Alpes mpl.

already (ɔ:l'redi) adv ya, previamente.

also ('ɔ:lsou) adv también, además.

altar ('ɔ:ltə) n altar m.

alter ('ɔ:ltə) vt alterar, cambiar. **alteration** n alteración, reforma f. cambio m.

alternate (v 'ɔ:ltəneit; adj ɔ:l'tɜ:nit) vt,vi alternar, variar. adj alterno, alternativo. **alternative** n alternativa f. adj alternativo.

although (ɔ:l'ðou) conj aunque.

altitude ('æltitju:d) n altitud, altura f.

alto ('æltou) adj,n alto, contralto f.

altogether (ɔ:ltə'geðə) adv 1 en total, en conjunto. 2 enteramente, del todo.

aluminium (ælju'miniəm) n aluminio m.

always ('ɔ:lweiz) adv siempre.

am (əm; stressed æm) v see **be**.

amalgamate (ə'mælgəmeit) vt amalgamar, unir. vi amalgamarse.

amass (ə'mæs) vt acumular, amontonar.

amateur ('æmətə) n aficionado m.

amaze (ə'meiz) vt asombrar, dejar atónito. **amazement** n asombro m.

ambassador (æm'bæsədə) n embajador m.

amber ('æmbə) n ámbar m.

ambidextrous (æmbi'dekstrəs) adj ambidextro.

ambiguous (æm'bigjuəs) adj ambiguo. **ambiguity** n ambigüedad f.

ambition (æm'biʃən) n ambición f. anhelo m. **ambitious** adj ambicioso.

ambivalent (æm'bivələnt) adj ambivalente.

amble ('æmbəl) vi 1 andar despacio. 2 amblar. n paso de andadura m.

ambulance ('æmbjuləns) n ambulancia f.

ambush ('æmbuʃ) n emboscada f. vt emboscar.

amenable (ə'mi:nəbəl) adj 1 dócil, tratable. 2 law responsable.

amend (ə'mend) vt enmendar, rectificar. **amendment** n enmienda f. **amends** n reparación, compensación f. **make amends** indemnizar, dar satisfacción.

amenity (ə'mi:niti) n amenidad f.

America (ə'merikə) n America f. **American** adj,n Americano.

amethyst ('æmiθist) n amatista f.

amiable ('eimiəbəl) adj afable, amistoso.

amicable ('æmikəbəl) adj amigable, amistoso.

amid (ə'mid) also **amidst** prep entre, en medio de.

amiss (ə'mis) adv mal, fuera de lugar, impropiamente. **take amiss** llevar a mal.

ammonia (ə'mouniə) n amoníaco m.

ammunition (æmju'niʃən) n municiones f pl.

amnesty ('æmnəsti) n amnistía f.

amoeba (ə'mi:bə) n ameba f.

among (ə'mʌŋ) prep entre, en medio de.

amorous ('æmərəs) adj amoroso, enamoradizo.

amorphous (ə'mɔ:fəs) adj amorfo.

amount (ə'maunt) n 1 cantidad f. 2 importe m. vi 1 sumar, ascender a. 2 equivaler.

ampere ('æmpɛə) n amperio m.

amphetamine (æm'fetəmi:n) n anfetamina f.

amphibian (æm'fibiən) adj,n anfibio m. **amphibious** adj anfibio.

amphitheatre ('æmfiθiətə) n anfiteatro m.

ample ('æmpəl) adj 1 amplio. 2 abundante. 3 bastante.

amplify ('æmplifai) vt amplificar, ampliar. **amplifier** n amplificador m.

amputate ('æmpjuteit) vt amputar. **amputation** n amputación f.

amuse (ə'mju:z) vt divertir, entretener, distraer. **amusement** 1 diversión f. 2 pasatiempo, recreo m. **amusing** adj gracioso, divertido.

an (ən; stressed æn) indef art see **a**.

anachronism (ə'nækrənizəm) n anacronismo m. **anachronistic** adj anacrónico.

anaemia (ə'ni:miə) n anemia f.

anaesthetic (ænis'θetik) n,adj anestésico. **anaesthetist** n anestesista m,f. **anaesthetize** vt anestesiar.

anagram ('ænəgræm) n anagrama m.

anal ('einl) adj anal.

analogy (ə'nælədʒi) n analogía f. **analogous** adj análogo.

analysis (ə'nælisis) n, pl **analyses** análisis m. **analyse** vt analizar. **analytic** or **analytical** adj analítico.

anarchy ('ænəki) n anarquía f. **anarchist** n anarquista m,f.

anatomy (ə'nætəmi) n anatomía f.

ancestor ('ænsestə) n antepasado m. **ancestral** adj ancestral. **ancestry** n linaje m.

anchor ('æŋkə) n ancla, áncora f. vt,vi anclar, fijar.

anchovy ('æntʃəvi) n anchoa f.

ancient ('einʃənt) adj antiguo.

ancillary ('ænsiləri) adj auxiliar.

and (ən, ənd; stressed ænd) conj y, e.

Andalusia n Andalucía f. **Andalusian** n,adj andaluz.

Andorra (æn'dɔːrə) n Andorra f.

anecdote ('ænikdout) n anécdota f.

anemone (ə'neməni) n anémona f.

anew (ə'nju:) adv de nuevo, otra vez.

angel ('eindʒəl) n ángel m. **angelic** adj angélico.

anger ('æŋgə) n cólera, ira f. vt enojar, enfadar, encolerizar.

angle[1] ('æŋgəl) n **1** ángulo m. **2** punto de vista m.

angle[2] ('æŋgəl) vi pescar con caña. **angle for** inf ir a la caza de. **angler** n pescador de caña m.

Anglican ('æŋglikən) adj,n anglicano.

angry ('æŋgri) adj enojado, enfadado, encolerizado. **get angry** enojarse, montar en cólera.

anguish ('æŋgwiʃ) n angustia f.

angular ('æŋgjulə) adj angular, anguloso.

animal ('æniməl) n animal m. bestia f. adj animal.

animate (adj 'ænimət; v 'ænimeit) vt animar. adj animado.

aniseed ('ænisi:d) n anís m.

ankle ('æŋkəl) n tobillo m.

annals ('ænlz) n anales m pl.

annex (ə'neks) vt **1** anexar, agregar. **2** adjuntar. **annexe** n anexo m.

annihilate (ə'naiəleit) vt aniquilar. **annihilation** n aniquilación f.

anniversary (æni'vɜːsəri) n aniversario m.

annotate ('ænəteit) vt,vi anotar, glosar.

announce (ə'nauns) vt anunciar, proclamar. **announcement** n anuncio, aviso m.

annoy (ə'nɔi) vt molestar, fastidiar. **annoyed** adj enojado. **annoying** adj molesto.

annual ('ænjuəl) adj anual.

annul (ə'nʌl) vt **1** anular. **2** law abrogar. **annulment** n anulación f.

anode ('ænoud) n ánodo m.

anoint (ə'nɔint) vt ungir, consagrar.

anomaly (ə'nɔməli) n anomalía f. **anomalous** n anómalo m.

anonymous (ə'nɔniməs) adj anónimo. **anonymity** n anonimato m.

another (ə'nʌðə) adj otro. pron otro m. otra f.

answer ('ɑːnsə) vt,vi contestar, responder, replicar. **answer for** responder de. n respuesta f.

ant (ænt) n hormiga f.

antagonize (æn'tægənaiz) vt antagonizar. **antagonism** n antagonismo m. **antagonist** n antagonista m,f. **antagonistic** adj antagónico.

Antarctic (æn'tɑːktik) adj antártico.

antelope ('æntiloup) n antílope m.

antenna (æn'tenə) n, pl **-ae** or **-as** antena f.

anthem ('ænθəm) n motete m. **national anthem** himno nacional m.

anthology (æn'θɔlədʒi) n antología f.

anthropology (ænθrə'pɔlədʒi) n antropología f.

anti-aircraft adj antiaéreo.

antibiotic (æntibai'ɔtik) n antibiótico m.

antibody ('æntibɔdi) n anticuerpo m.

anticipate (æn'tisipeit) vt **1** anticiparse a. **2** prever. **3** esperar. **anticipation** n **1** anticipación f. **2** expectación f.

anticlimax (ænti'klaimæks) n anticlímax m. decepción f.

anticlockwise (ænti'klɔkwaiz) adj en dirección contraria a las agujas del reloj.

antics ('æntiks) n payasadas f pl.

anticyclone (ænti'saikloun) n anticiclón m.

antidote ('æntidout) n antídoto m.

antifreeze ('æntifriːz) n anticongelante m. adj anticuado.

antique (æn'tiːk) adj antiguo. n antigüedad f. **antique dealer** n anticuario m. **antiquated** adj anticuado. **antiquity** n antigüedad f.

anti-Semitic adj antisemítico. **anti-Semitism** n antisemitismo.

antiseptic (ænti'septik) adj,n antiséptico m.

antithesis (æn'tiθəsis) n antítesis f.

antler ('æntlə) n asta f. cuerno m.

anus ('einəs) n ano m.

anvil ('ænvil) n yunque m.

anxious ('æŋkʃəs) adj ansioso, inquieto, deseoso. **be anxious** inquietarse. **anxiety** n ansiedad f.

any ('eni) adj algún, cualquier invar. ningún. pron alguno ms. alguna fs. algunos m pl. algunas f pl. cualquiera invar. ninguno ms. ninguna fs. adv algo. **anybody** pron alguien, cualquiera, nadie. **anyhow** adv 1 de todos modos. 2 de cualquier modo. **anyone** pron see anybody. **anything** pron algo, cualquier cosa, nada. **anyway** see anyhow. **anywhere** adv en cualquier parte, en todas partes, en ninguna parte.

apart (ə'pɑːt) adv aparte.

apartment (ə'pɑːtmənt) n 1 apartamento m. habitación f. 2 piso m.

apathy ('æpəθi) n apatía f. **apathetic** adj apático.

ape (eip) n 1 mono m. 2 imitador m. vt imitar.

aperitive (ə'peritiv) n aperitivo m.

aperture ('æpətʃə) n abertura f.

apex ('eipeks) n ápice m. cúspide f.

apiece (ə'piːs) adv por persona, cada uno.

apology (ə'pɔlədʒi) n 1 disculpa f. 2 apología f. **apologetic** adj lleno de disculpas. **apologize** vi disculparse, pedir perdón.

apostle (ə'pɔsəl) n apóstol m.

apostrophe (ə'pɔstrəfi) n apóstrofo m. apóstrofe m,f.

appal (ə'pɔːl) vt horrorizar, pasmar, consternar. **appalling** adj espantoso.

apparatus (æpə'reitəs) n aparato m.

apparent (ə'pærənt) adj 1 aparente. 2 evidente, manifiesto, claro.

appeal (ə'piːl) vi 1 law apelar. 2 interesar, atraer. n. 1 law apelación f. 2 llamamiento m. 3 atractivo m.

appear (ə'piə) vi 1 aparecer. 2 parecer. 3 law comparecer. **appearance** n 1 aparición f. 2 apariencia f. 3 law comparecencia f. **put in an appearance** hacer acto de presencia.

appease (ə'piːz) vt apaciguar, satisfacer. **appeasement** n apaciguamiento m.

appendix (ə'pendiks) n apéndice m. **appendicitis** n apendicitis f.

appetite ('æpitait) n apetito m.

applaud (ə'plɔːd) vt,vi aplaudir. **applause** n aplauso m.

apple ('æpəl) n manzana f. **apple tree** n manzano m.

apply (ə'plai) vt 1 aplicar. 2 referir. 3 solicitar. vi aplicarse, referirse. **appliance** n aparato, dis-

positivo m. **applicable** adj aplicable. **applicant** n aspirante m,f. candidato m. suplicante m,f. **application** n 1 aplicación f. 2 solicitud f.

appoint (ə'pɔint) vt 1 señalar. 2 nombrar.

appointment (ə'pɔintmənt) n 1 designación f. 2 nombramiento m. 3 cita f. **make an appointment** citarse, pedir hora.

appraise (ə'preiz) vt evaluar, tasar. **appraisal** n valoración f.

appreciate (ə'priːʃieit) vt 1 apreciar. 2 percibir. 3 aumentar de valor. **appreciable** adj apreciable. **appreciation** n 1 apreciación f. aprecio m. 2 percepción f. 3 aumento de valor m.

apprehend (æpri'hend) vt 1 prender, capturar. 2 aprehender, percibir, comprender. 3 temer. **apprehension** n 1 captura f. 2 percepción f. 3 aprensión f. **apprehensive** adj aprensivo, receloso.

apprentice (ə'prentis) n aprendiz m. **apprenticeship** n aprendizaje m.

approach (ə'proutʃ) vi 1 acercarse, aproximarse. 2 abordar, dirigirse. n 1 acercamiento m. 2 aproximación f. 3 acceso m. 4 método m.

appropriate (adj ə'proupriət; v ə'prouprieit) adj apropiado. vt 1 apropiarse. 2 destinar, asignar.

approve (ə'pruːv) vt,vi aprobar. **approval** n aprobación f. **on approval** a prueba.

approximate (adj ə'prɔksimət; v ə'prɔksimeit) adj aproximado. vt,vi aproximar(se). **approximation** n aproximación f.

apricot ('eiprikɔt) n albaricoque m.

April ('eiprəl) n abril m.

apron ('eiprən) n delantal, mandil m.

apse (æps) n ábside m,f.

apt (æpt) adj 1 apto. 2 propenso. **aptitude** ('æptitjuːd) n aptitud f.

aquarium (ə'kwɛəriəm) n acuario m.

Aquarius (ə'kwɛəriəs) n Acuario m.

aquatic (ə'kwætik) adj acuático.

aqueduct ('ækwədʌkt) n acueducto m.

Arabia (ə'reibiə) n Arabia. **Arab** n,adj árabe. **Arabic** adj árabe, arábigo.

arable ('ærəbəl) adj arable.

arbitrary ('ɑːbitrəri) adj arbitrario.

arbitrate ('ɑːbitreit) vt arbitrar. **arbitration** n arbitraje m. **arbitrator** n 1 arbitrador, árbitro m. 2 tercero m.

arc (ɑːk) n arco m.

arcade (ɑː'keid) n 1 arcada f. 2 pasaje, pasadizo m. 3 soportales m pl.

arch (ɑːtʃ) n 1 arch arco m. 2 bóveda f. vt,vi arquear, abovedar. **archway** n arcada f.

archaeology (a:ki'ɔlədʒi) n arqueología f. **archaeologist** n arqueólogo m.

archaic (a:'keiik) adj arcaico.

archbishop (a:tʃ'biʃəp) n arzobispo m.

archduke (a:tʃ'dju:k) n archiduque m.

archery ('a:tʃəri) n tiro con arco m. **archer** n arquero m.

archetype ('a:kitaip) n arquetipo m.

archipelago (a:ki'peləgou) n pl **-os** or **-oes** archipiélago m.

architect ('a:kitekt) n arquitecto m. **architecture** n arquitectura f.

archives ('a:kaivz) n archivo m.

Arctic ('a:ktik) adj ártico. **the Arctic** n el Ártico m.

ardent ('a:dnt) adj ardiente, apasionado, fervoroso.

ardour ('a:də) n ardor m. **arduous** adj arduo.

are (ə; stressed a:) vi see **be**.

area ('εəriə) n 1 área, superficie f. 2 zona f.

arena (ə'ri:nə) n arena f. campo de combate m.

Argentina (a:dʒən'ti:nə) n Argentina f. **Argentinian** adj,n argentino m.

argue ('a:gju:) vt argüir, sostener. vi disputar, discutir. **argument** n 1 argumento m. 2 disputa, discusión f. **argumentative** adj 1 argumentativo. 2 argumentador.

arid ('ærid) adj árido. **aridity** n aridez f.

Aries ('εəri:z) n Aries m.

arise* (ə'raiz) vi surgir, aparecer, alzarse.

aristocracy (æri'stɔkrəsi) n aristocracia f. **aristocrat** n aristócrata m,f. **aristocratic** adj aristocrático.

arithmetic (ə'riθmətik) n aritmética f.

arm[1] (a:m) n 1 brazo m. 2 rama f. **arm in arm** de bracete. **at arm's length** a distancia. **within arm's reach** al alcance de la mano. **armchair** n sillón m. **armful** n brazada f. **armpit** n axila f.

arm[2] (a:m) n arma f. vt armar. vr armarse. **arms** n pl 1 armas f. armamentos m. 2 escudo, blasón m.

armour ('a:mə) n armadura f.

army ('a:mi) n ejército m.

arose (ə'rouz) v see **arise.**

around (ə'raund) adv alrededor, por todos lados. prep alrededor de, en torno de.

arouse (ə'rauz) vt despertar, excitar.

arrange (ə'reindʒ) vt arreglar, ajustar, disponer, concertar. **arrangement** n arreglo, convenio m.

array (ə'rei) n 1 formación f. 2 hilera f. 3 despliegue m. vt desplegar.

arrears (ə'riəz) n pl atrasos, pagos atrasados m pl.

arrest (ə'rest) vt 1 arrestar. 2 parar. 3 prorrogar. 4 llamar. n arresto m. detención f. **under arrest** preso, detenido. **arresting** adj impresionante.

arrive (ə'raiv) vi llegar. **arrival** n 1 llegada f. 2 advenimiento m.

arrogant ('ærəgənt) adj arrogante. **arrogance** n arrogancia f.

arrow ('ærou) n flecha, saeta f. **arrowroot** n arrurruz m.

arsenic ('a:snik) n arsénico m.

arson ('a:sən) n incendio premeditado m.

art (a:t) n arte m. **fine arts** bellas artes f pl. **art gallery** museo de arte m. **artful** adj 1 artero, astuto. 2 ingenioso.

artery ('a:təri) n arteria f. **arterial** adj 1 arterial. 2 principal.

arthritis (a:'θraitis) n artritis f.

artichoke ('a:titʃouk) n alcachofa f.

article ('a:tikəl) n artículo, objeto m. cosa f. vt contratar(se). poner(se) de aprendiz.

articulate (v a:'tikjuleit; adj a:'tikjulət) adj 1 articulado. 2 claro, distinto. 3 capaz de hablar bien. vt articular.

artificial (a:ti'fiʃəl) adj artificial. **artificial respiration** respiración artificial f.

artillery (a:'tiləri) n artillería f.

artist ('a:tist) n artista m,f. **artistic** adj artístico.

as (əz; stressed æz) conj 1 como, ya que. 2 cuando, mientras, a medida que. **as for, as to** en cuanto a. **as from** a partir de. **as good as** tan bueno como. **as it were** por decirlo así. **as well** también. **as well as** así como.

asbestos (æs'bestəs) n asbesto m.

ascend (ə'send) vt,vi ascender. **ascension** n ascensión f.

ascertain (æsə'tein) vt averiguar, determinar.

ash[1] (æʃ) n ceniza f. **ashtray** n cenicero m.

ash[2] (æʃ) n fresno m.

ashamed (ə'ʃeimd) adj avergonzado. **be ashamed** avergonzarse.

ashore (ə'ʃɔ:) adv a tierra, en tierra. **go ashore** desembarcar. **run ashore** encallar.

Ash Wednesday n Miércoles de Ceniza m.

Asia ('eiʃə) n Asia f. **Asian** adj,n asiático.

aside (ə'said) adv aparte, a un lado. n aparte m.

ask (a:sk) vt,vi 1 preguntar. 2 pedir. 3 invitar. **ask a question** hacer una pregunta. **ask for trouble, ask for it** inf buscársela. **for the asking** sin más que pedirlo.

askew (ə'skju:) adv ladeado.

asleep (ə'sli:p) adj dormido. **fall asleep** dormirse.

asparagus (ə'spærəgəs) n espárrago m.

aspect ('æspekt) n aspecto m.

asphalt ('æsfælt) n asfalto m.

aspire (ə'spaiə) vi aspirar.

aspirin ('æsprin) n aspirina f.

ass (æs) n asno, burro m.

assassinate (ə'sæsineit) vt asesinar. **assassin** n asesino m.

assault (ə'sɔ:lt) n 1 mil asalto m. 2 agresión f. vt asaltar, agredir.

assemble (ə'sembəl) vt 1 reunir, juntar. 2 tech montar 3 mil formar. vi reunirse. **assembly** n 1 asamblea f. 2 tech montaje m. **assembly hall** sala de actos f. **assembly line** cadena de montaje f.

assent (ə'sent) n asentimiento m. vi asentir.

assert (ə'sɔ:t) vt 1 afirmar, aseverar, declarar. 2 hacer valer. **assertion** n afirmación, aserción f.

assess (ə'ses) vt evaluar, tasar, asesorar. **assessment** n valoración f.

asset ('æset) n 1 posesión f. 2 inf ventaja f. **assets** n pl comm activo m.

assign (ə'sain) vt 1 asignar, consignar. 2 law traspasar. **assignment** n asignación f.

assimilate (ə'simileit) vt asimilar.

assist (ə'sist) vt,vi ayudar, auxiliar, asistir. **assistance** n ayuda, asistencia f. **assistant** n ayudante auxiliar m,f.

assizes (ə'saiziz) n pl sesión de un tribunal jurídico f.

associate (ə'souʃieit) vt asociar, juntar. vi asociarse, juntarse. n 1 socio m. 2 compañero m. 3 cómplice m,f. **association** n asociación f.

assort (ə'sɔ:t) vi convenir, concordar. **assortment** n 1 surtido m. 2 colección, variedad f.

assume (ə'sju:m) vt 1 asumir. 2 suponer. **assumption** n 1 asunción f. 2 suposición f.

assure (ə'ʃuə) vt asegurar, garantizar. **assurance** n 1 seguridad f. 2 garantía f. 3 desenvoltura f. ♦ comm seguro m.

asterisk ('æstərisk) n asterisco m.

asthma ('æsmə) n asma f.

astonish (ə'stɔniʃ) vt asombrar. **astonishment** n asombro m.

astound (ə'staund) vt pasmar, aturdir.

astray (ə'strei) adv extraviado, descarriado. **go astray** extraviarse.

astride (ə'straid) adv a horcajadas.

astrology (ə'strɔlədʒi) n astrología f.

astronaut ('æstrənɔ:t) n astronauta m,f.

astronomy (ə'strɔnəmi) n astronomía f. **astronomer** n astrónomo m. **astronomical** adj astronómico.

astute (ə'stju:t) adj astuto.

asunder (ə'sʌndə) adv separadamente, en dos, a pedazos.

asylum (ə'sailəm) n 1 asilo m. 2 manicomio m.

at (ət; stressed æt) prep en, a. **at last** por último. **at least** por lo menos. **at work** trabajando.

ate (eit, et) v see eat.

atheism ('eiθiizəm) n ateísmo m. **atheist** n ateo m.

Athens ('æθinz) n Atenas. **Athenian** adj,n ateniense.

athlete ('æθli:t) n atleta m,f. **athletic** adj atlético. **athletics** n atletismo m.

Atlantic (ət'læntik) n Atlántico m. adj atlántico.

atlas ('ætləs) n atlas m.

atmosphere ('ætməsfiə) n atmósfera f.

atom ('ætəm) n átomo m. **atomic** adj atómico.

atone (ə'toun) vi expiar, reparar.

atrocious (ə'trouʃəs) adj atroz. **atrocity** n atrocidad f.

attach (ə'tætʃ) vt 1 atar, pegar, adherir. 2 atribuir, conceder. 3 comm adjuntar.

attaché (ə'tæʃei) n agregado m.

attack (ə'tæk) vt atacar. n ataque m.

attain (ə'tein) vt alcanzar, lograr. **attainable** adj asequible. **attainment** n logro m. consecución f.

attempt (ə'tempt) vt intentar. n intento m. tentativa f.

attend (ə'tend) vt,vi atender, asistir. **attendance** n asistencia f. **attendant** adj 1 concomitante. 2 acompañante. n 1 criado, ordenanza m. 2 acomodador m. **attention** n atención f. **attentive** adj atento.

attic ('ætik) n desván m.

attire (ə'taiə) n atavío, adorno m. vt ataviar, vestir.

attitude ('ætitju:d) n actitud f.

attorney (ə'tɔ:ni) n 1 apoderado m. 2 abogado m. **power of attorney** poder m.

attract (ə'trækt) vt atraer, llamar. **attraction** n atracción f. atractivo m. **attractive** adj atrayente, atractivo.

attribute (v ə'tribju:t; n 'ætribju:t) vt atribuir, imputar, achacar. n atributo m.

atypical (ei'tipikəl) adj atípico.

aubergine ('oubəʒi:n) n berenjena f.

auburn ('ɔ:bən) adj castaño rojizo.

auction

auction (ˈɔːkʃən) vt subastar. n subasta f.
audacious (ɔːˈdeiʃəs) adj audaz, atrevido.
audible (ˈɔːdibəl) adj audible.
audience (ˈɔːdiəns) n 1 auditorio, público m. 2 audiencia f.
audiovisual (ɔːdiouˈviʒuəl) adj audiovisual.
audit (ˈɔːdit) vt intervenir, examinar. n intervención f. exámen oficial de cuentas m. **auditor** n revisor de cuentas m.
audition (ɔːˈdiʃən) n audición f.
auditorium (ɔːdiˈtɔːriəm) n auditorio m.
August (ˈɔːgəst) n agosto m.
aunt (ɑːnt) n tia f.
au pair (ou ˈpɛə) n ayudante doméstica a cambio de alojamiento y manutención f.
aura (ˈɔːrə) n aura f. aureola f.
austere (ɔːˈstiə) adj austero.
Australia (ɔˈstreiliə) n Australia f. **Australian** adj,n australiano.
Austria (ˈɔstriə) n Austria f. **Austrian** adj,n austríaco.
authentic (ɔːˈθentik) adj auténtico.
author (ˈɔːθə) n autor m.
authority (ɔːˈθɔriti) n autoridad f. **on the best authority** de beuna tinta. **authoritarian** adj autoritario. **authoritative** adj 1 autorizado. 2 autoritario. **authorize** vt autorizar.
autistic (ɔːˈtistik) adj autístico.
autobiography (ɔːtəbaiˈɔgrafi) n autobiografía f. **autobiographical** adj autobiográfico.
autograph (ˈɔːtəgrɑːf) n autógrafo m. vt firmar, dedicar.
automatic (ɔːtəˈmætik) adj automático.
automation (ɔːtəˈmeiʃən) n automatización f.
autonomous (ɔːˈtɔnəməs) adj autónomo. **autonomy** n autonomía f.
autumn (ˈɔːtəm) n otoño m.
auxiliary (ɔːgˈziliəri) adj auxiliar.
available (əˈveiləbəl) adj disponible.
avalanche (ˈævəlɑːnʃ) n avalancha f. alud m.
avenge (əˈvendʒ) vt vengar, vindicar.
avenue (ˈævənjuː) n avenida f.
average (ˈævridʒ) n promedio m. **on average** por regla general. ~adj medio. vt calcular el término medio, resultar por término medio.
aversion (əˈvəːʃən) n aversión f.
aviary (ˈeiviəri) n pajarera f.
aviation (eiviˈeiʃən) n aviación f.
avid (ˈævid) adj ávido. **avidity** n avidez f.
avocado (ævəˈkɑːdou) n aguacate m
avoid (əˈvɔid) vt evitar, eludir. **avoidable** adj evitable, eludible.
await (əˈweit) vt esperar, aguardar.

156

awake (əˈweik) vt despertar. vi despertarse. adj despierto, alerta. **awaken** vt,vi 1 despertar. 2 poner al corriente. 3 darse cuenta.
award (əˈwɔːd) vt 1 conceder, otorgar. 2 law adjudicar, sentenciar. n 1 premio m. 2 adjudicación f. 3 law sentencia f. 4 mil condecoración f.
aware (əˈwɛə) adj consciente, enterado. **become aware of** enterarse de, darse cuenta de. **awareness** n conciencia f. conocimiento m.
away (əˈwei) adv ausente, en otro lugar, fuera.
awe (ɔː) n 1 temor, espanto m. 2 veneración, reverencia f. **awe-inspiring** adj imponente, temible. **awe-struck** adj atemorizado, asustado, aterrado.
awful (ˈɔːfəl) adj tremendo, espantoso. **awfully** adv inf muy, excesivamente.
awkward (ˈɔːkwəd) adj 1 torpe, desmañado. 2 embarazoso, difícil, peliagudo.
awoke (əˈwouk) v see **awake.**
axe (æks) n hacha f. vt inf reducir, cortar.
axis (ˈæksis) n, pl **axes** eje m.
axle (ˈæksəl) n tech eje m.
azalea (əˈzeiliə) n azalea f.

B

babble (ˈbæbəl) vi 1 balbucear. 2 murmurar. n 1 balbuceo m. 2 murmullo m.
baboon (bəˈbuːn) n mandril m.
baby (ˈbeibi) n niño, nene, bebé m. adj infantil. **babyhood** n niñez, infancia f. **baby-sitter** n cuidaniños m,f invar.
bachelor (ˈbætʃələ) n 1 soltero m. 2 educ licenciado m.
back (bæk) n 1 anat espalda f. 2 dorso m. 3 final m. 4 sport defensa m. adj trasero, posterior, de atrás. adv 1 atrás. 2 de vuelta. vt apoyar, respaldar. vi retroceder. **back out** echarse atrás, desdecirse.
backache (ˈbækeik) n dolor de espaldas.
backbone (ˈbækboun) n 1 espinazo m. 2 firmeza f.
backdate (ˈbækdeit) vt poner fecha atrasada.
backfire (ˈbækfaiə) n mot petardeo m. vi 1 petardear. 2 inf salir el tiro por la culata.
backgammon (ˈbækgæmən) n chaquete m.
background (ˈbækgraund) n 1 fondo m. 2 antecedentes m pl. 3 educación f.
backhand (ˈbækhænd) n revés m. **backhanded** adj 1 de revés. 2 irónico.

backing ('bækiŋ) n **1** apoyo m. garantía f. **2** refuerzo, forro m. **3** contrafuerte m.

backlash ('bæklæʃ) n reacción f.

backlog ('bækloɡ) n **1** atrasos m pl. **2** comm pedidos pendientes m pl.

backstage (bæk'steidʒ) adv entre bastidores.

backward ('bækwəd) adj **1** vuelto hacia atrás. **2** atrasado. **backwards** adv hacia atrás.

backwater ('bækwɔːtə) n **1** remanso m. **2** lugar atrasado m.

bacon ('beikən) n tocino, bacón m.

bacteria (bæk'tiəriə) n pl bacteria f.

bad (bæd) adj **1** malo. **2** dañoso, nocivo. **bad-tempered** adj **1** de mal genio. **2** malhumorado.

bade (beid) v see **bid**.

badge (bædʒ) n **1** insignia, divisa f. **2** distintivo m.

badger ('bædʒə) n tejón m. vt molestar.

badminton ('bædmintən) n volante m.

baffle ('bæfəl) vt **1** frustrar. **2** confundir, desconcertar.

bag (bæɡ) n **1** bolsa f. **2** saco m. **3** valija f. vt ensacar. **baggy** adj holgado. **baggage** n equipaje m. **bagpipes** n pl gaita f.

bail (beil) n fianza, caución f. vt poner bajo fianza, caucionar.

bailiff ('beilif) n alguacil m.

bait (beit) n **1** cebo, señuelo m. vt **1** poner cebo en. **2** azuzar.

bake (beik) vt **1** cocer al horno. **2** endurecer, calcinar. **baker** n panadero m. **bakery** n panadería f. **baking powder** n levadura en polvo f.

balance ('bæləns) n **1** equilibrio m. **2** comm balance m. **3** balanza f. vt,vi **1** equilibrar. **2** comm saldar.

balcony ('bælkəni) n **1** balcón m. **2** anfiteatro m.

bald (bɔːld) adj calvo. **baldness** n calvicie f.

bale[1] (beil) n **1** fardo m. **2** bala f. vt embalar.

bale[2] (beil) vt naut ahicar, baldear. **bale out** aviat lanzarse en paracaídas.

ball[1] (bɔːl) n **1** bola, esfera f. **2** sport pelota f. balón m. **ball-bearing** n cojinete de bolas m. **ball-point pen** n bolígrafo m. **play ball** inf cooperar.

ball[2] (bɔːl) n baile m. **fancy-dress ball** baile de disfraces. **ballroom** n salón de baile m.

ballad ('bæləd) n romance m. balada f.

ballast ('bæləst) n lastre m. vt lastrar.

ballet ('bælei) n **1** ballet m. **2** danza f.

ballistic (bə'listik) adj balístico. **ballistics** n balística f.

balloon (bə'luːn) n globo m. vi subir en globo. **balloonist** n ascensionista m.

ballot ('bælət) n **1** votación f. **2** sufragio m. **3** papeleta de votación f. vi votar. **ballot-box** n urna electoral f.

Baltic ('bɔːltik) adj báltico. **Baltic Sea** n Mar Báltico m.

bamboo (bæm'buː) n bambú m.

ban (bæn) n **1** prohibición f. **2** bando, edicto m. **3** excomunión f. destierro m. vt prohibir, proscribir, excomulgar.

banal (bə'naːl) adj trivial, vulgar. **banality** n trivialidad f.

banana (bə'naːnə) n plátano m.

band[1] (bænd) n grupo m. banda f. **2** mus orquesta, banda f. vi agruparse, asociarse.

band[2] (bænd) n faja, tira, banda f. **bandage** n venda f. vendaje m. vt vendar.

bandit ('bændit) n bandido m.

bandy ('bændi) vt intercambiar. **bandy about** divulgar, esparcir.

bang (bæŋ) n **1** detonación f. estallido m. **2** golpe m. vt,vi golpear, cerrar con estrépito. **be bang on** sl dar en el clavo. —interj ¡pum!

bangle ('bæŋɡəl) n ajorca f. brazalete m.

banish ('bæniʃ) vt desterrar. **banishment** n destierro m.

banister ('bænistə) n barandilla f. pasamano m.

bank[1] (bæŋk) n **1** ribera, orilla f. **2** loma i. terraplén m. vt estancar, amontonar.

bank[2] (bæŋk) n banco m. **savings bank** caja de ahorros f. **bank account** n cuenta bancaria f. **bank holiday** n día festivo m. **banknote** n billete de banco m. ~vt depositar dinero. **bank on** inf contar con. **banker** n banquero m.

bankrupt ('bæŋkrʌpt) adj insolvente, quebrado. **become bankrupt** quebrar. **bankruptcy** n quiebra, bancarrota f.

banner ('bænə) n bandera f. estandarte m.

banquet ('bæŋkwit) n banquete m. vt,vi banquetear.

baptize (bæp'taiz) vt bautizar. **baptism** n **1** bautismo m. **2** bautizo m.

bar (baː) n **1** barra f. **2** bar m. **3** mus compás m. **4** impedimento m. vt **1** atrancar. **2** impedir, obstruir. **3** excluir. **barmaid** n camarera f. **barman** n mozo de bar m.

barbarian (baː'bɛəriən) adj,n bárbaro m. **barbaric** adj barbárico. **barbarity** n barbaridad f. **barbarous** adj bárbaro.

barbecue ('ba:bikju:) n parrillada, barbacoa f. asedo a la parrilla m.

barber ('ba:bə) n barbero, peluquero m. **barber's shop** barbería f.

barbiturate (ba:'bitjurət) n barbitúrico m.

Barcelona (ba:si'lounə) n Barcelona f.

bare (bɛə) adj desnudo, desprovisto, descubierto, escaso. vt desnudar, descubrir. **barefaced** adj descarado. **barefoot** adj descalzo. **barely** adv apenas.

bargain ('ba:gin) n 1 pacto, convenio m. 2 ganga f. vi regatear, negociar.

barge (ba:dʒ) n gabarra, barcaza f. v **barge in** inf irrumpir. **barge into** inf entrometerse.

baritone ('bæritoun) n barítono m.

bark[1] (ba:k) n ladrido m. vi ladrar.

bark[2] (ba:k) n bot corteza f.

barley ('ba:li) n cebada f.

barn (ba:n) n granero m.

barometer (bə'rɔmitə) n barómetro m.

baron ('bærən) n 1 barón m. 2 potentado m. **baroness** n baronesa f. **baronet** n baronet m.

barracks ('bærəks) n cuartel m.

barrage ('bæra:ʒ) n 1 presa f. 2 mil cortina de fuego f.

barrel ('bærəl) n 1 tonel, barril m. cuba f. 2 tech cilindro, tambor m. 3 cañón m.

barren ('bærən) adj estéril, árido.

barricade ('bærikeid) n barricada f. vt barrear, parapetarse.

barrier ('bæriə) n barrera f.

barrister ('bæristə) n abogado m.

barrow ('bærou) n carretilla f.

barter ('ba:tə) vt,vi trocar, permutar. n trueque, intercambio m.

base[1] (beis) n base f. vt basar.

base[2] (beis) adj bajo, vil. **baseness** n bajeza, vileza f.

baseball ('beisbɔ:l) n béisbol m.

basement ('beismənt) n sótano m.

bash (bæʃ) vt 1 golpear, apalear. 2 hacer añicos.

bashful ('bæʃfəl) adj tímido, vergonzoso.

basic ('beisik) adj básico, fundamental.

basil ('bæzəl) n albahaca f.

basin ('beisən) n 1 jofaina. f. 2 lavabo m. 3 escudilla f. tazón m. 4 geog cuenca f.

basis ('beisis) n, pl **bases** base f. fundamento m.

bask (ba:sk) vi tomar el sol, tostarse.

basket ('ba:skit) n cesta, canasta f. cesto m. **basketball** n baloncesto m.

bass[1] (beis) n 1 mus bajo m. 2 contrabajo m.

bass[2] (bæs) n zool róbalo m.

bassoon (bə'su:n) n bajón m.

bastard ('ba:stəd) n bastardo m.

baste ('beist) vt untar, rociar con grasa.

bat[1] (bæt) n maza f. palo m. **off one's own bat** sin ayuda. vt,vi 1 golpear, pegar. 2 pestañear.

bat[2] (bæt) n zool murciélago m.

batch (bætʃ) n 1 hornada f. 2 remesa, tanda f.

bath (ba:θ) n 1 baño m. 2 bañera f. **have a bath** tomar un baño. vt bañar. **bathrobe** n albornoz m. **bathroom** n cuarto de baño m.

bathe (beið) vt,vi bañar. **bathing costume** n traje de baño, bañador m. **bathing trunks** n pl pantalones de baño m pl.

baton ('bætən) n 1 mus batuta f. 2 mil bastón de mando m.

battalion (bə'tæliən) n batallón m.

batter[1] ('bætə) vt 1 apalear, magullar. 2 mil cañonear. **battering** n paliza f. castigo m.

batter[2] ('bætə) n cul pasta f. batido m.

battery ('bætəri) n batería, pila f. **storage battery** acumulador m.

battle ('bætl) n batalla f. combate m. **pitched battle** batalla campal. ~vi batallar, combatir, luchar. **battlefield** n campo de batalla m. **battleship** n acorazado m.

bawl (bɔ:l) vt,vi vocear, desgañitarse.

bay[1] (bei) n geog bahía f. golfo m.

bay[2] (bei) n arch galería, nave, crujía f. **bay window** mirador m.

bay[3] (bei) n bot laurel m.

bay[4] (bei) vi aullar, ladrar. n aullido, ladrido m. **at bay** acorralado. **keep at bay** mantener a raya.

bayonet ('beiənit) n bayoneta f. vt pasar a la bayoneta.

be[*] (bi:) vi 1 ser, existir. 2 estar, encontrarse, haber. **be off** marcharse.

beach (bi:tʃ) n playa f. vt varar. **beachcomber** n raquero m.

beacon ('bi:kən) n 1 faro, fanal m. atalaya f. 2 guía f. 3 semáforo intermitente m.

bead (bi:d) n cuenta, perla f. abalorio m. vt 1 ensartar. 2 perlar.

beak (bi:k) n 1 pico m. 2 nariz f. **beaked** adj picudo.

beaker ('bi:kə) n vaso alto m.

beam (bi:m) n 1 arch viga f. 2 rayo luminoso m. vt,vi 1 emitir rayos luminosos, irradiar. 2 vi sonreír radiantemente.

bean (bi:n) n judía, alubia f. **broad bean** haba f.

bear[1] (bɛə) vt **1** soportar, aguantar, sufrir. **2** llevar. **3** producir, rendir. **4** parir, dar a luz. **bear in mind** tener presente. **bearing** n **1** porte, aspecto m. **2** relación f. **3** pl situación, orientación f. **lose one's bearings** desorientarse. **take one's bearings** orientarse.

bear[2] (bɛə) n oso m. **teddy-bear** n osito de felpa m.

beard (biəd) n barba f. vt desafiar. **bearded** adj barbudo. **beardless** adj imberbe, lampiño.

beast (bi:st) n bestia f. **beastly** adj **1** bestial. **2** inf molesto, desagradable.

beat[*] (bi:t) vt **1** batir. **2** apalear, dar una paliza **3** vencer, superar. vi pulsar, latir. n **1** med latido m. **2** mus compás, ritmo m.

beauty (ˈbju:ti) n belleza, hermosura, f. **beautiful** adj hermoso, bello. **beautify** vt embellecer.

beaver (ˈbi:və) n castor m.

became (biˈkeim) v see **become.**

because (biˈkɔ:z) conj porque. **because of** a causa de.

beckon (ˈbekən) vt,vi llamar con señas, hacer señas, atraer.

become[*] (biˈkʌm) vi **1** hacerse, volverse, ponerse, convertirse en. **2** vt sentar bien, favorecer. **becoming** adj **1** decoroso, correcto. **2** que sienta bien, favorecedor.

bed (bed) n **1** cama f. lecho m. **2** tech base f. apoyo m. capa f. **bedding** n **1** ropa de cama f. **2** colchón m. **bedridden** adj encamado. **bedroom** n dormitorio m. **bed-sitter** n salón con cama m. **bedspread** n colcha f. cubrecama m. **flower bed** macizo de flores m. **river bed** cauce m. **go to bed** acostarse. **take to one's bed** encamarse.

bedbug (ˈbedbʌg) n chinche m.

bedraggled (biˈdrægəld) adj enlodado, salpicado de barro.

bee (bi:) n abeja f. **bee line** n línea recta f. **beehive** n colmena f.

beech (bi:tʃ) n haya f.

beef (bi:f) n carne de vaca f. **beefy** adj **1** que sabe a carne. **2** inf fornido.

been (bi:n) v see **be.**

beer (biə) n cerveza f.

beet (bi:t) n remolacha f.

beetle (ˈbi:tl) n **1** zool escarabajo m. **2** tech pisón m.

befall (biˈfɔ:l) vt,vi acontecer, acaecer, suceder.

before (biˈfɔ:) adv **1** delante. **2** antes. conj antes (de) que. prep delante de, ante, antes de. **beforehand** adv de antemano.

befriend (biˈfrend) vt,vi amistarse, favorecer, patrocinar.

beg (beg) vt,vi **1** suplicar, rogar. **2** mendigar, pordiosear. **I beg your pardon?** ¿cómo dice? **beg the question** ser una petición de principio. **beggar** n mendigo, pordiosero m. **beggarly** adj indigente.

begin[*] (biˈgin) vt,vi empezar, comenzar, iniciar. **to begin with** en primer lugar. **beginner** n principiante m,f. **beginning** n principio, comienzo m.

begrudge (biˈgrʌdʒ) vt **1** conceder de mala gana, escatimar. **2** envidiar.

behalf (biˈhɑ:f) n **on behalf of** en nombre de.

behave (biˈheiv) vi **1** comportarse, portarse. **2** funcionar. vr portarse bien. **behaviour** n **1** comportamiento m. conducta f. **2** funcionamiento m.

behind (biˈhaind) adv detrás, atrás. **be behind** ir con retraso. **fall behind** retrasarse. ~prep detrás de, tras. **behindhand** adv retrasado, con retraso.

behold (biˈhould) vt **1** contemplar. **2** advertir. interj ¡mira(d)! ¡aquí está!

beige (beiʒ) adj beige.

being (ˈbi:iŋ) n **1** ser m. **2** existencia f. **wellbeing** n bienestar m.

belch (beltʃ) vt arrojar, echar. vi eructar. n eructo m.

belfry (ˈbelfri) n campanario m.

Belgium (ˈbeldʒəm) n Bélgica f. **Belgian** adj,n belga m,f.

believe (biˈli:v) vt,vi **1** creer, pensar. **2** opinar. **3** dar crédito a. **make-believe** n ficción, simulación f. simulacro m. **belief** n **1** creencia f. **2** fe f. **3** opinión f.

bell (bel) n campana, campanilla f. **electric bell** timbre m. **bellringer** n campanero m.

belligerent (bəˈlidʒərənt) adj beligerante.

bellow (ˈbelou) vi bramar, rugir. n bramido m.

bellows (ˈbelouz) n pl fuelle m.

belly (ˈbeli) n vientre m. barriga, panza f. **bellyful** n hartazgo, hartón m.

belong (biˈlɔŋ) vi **1** pertenecer. **2** corresponder. **belongings** n pl **1** posesiones, cosas f pl. **2** inf bártulos m.

below (biˈlou) adv debajo, abajo. prep (por) debajo de.

belt (belt) n **1** cinturón m. **2** tech correa f. **3** zona f. vt **1** ceñir. **2** azotar con una correa.

bench (bentʃ) n **1** banco m. **2** tribunal m.

bend* (bend) n 1 curva f. recodo m. 2 naut gaza f. **go round the bend** volverse loco. ~vt,vi 1 doblar, torcer. 2 inclinar, encorvarse.

beneath (bi'ni:θ) adv debajo, abajo. prep (por) debajo de.

benefit ('benifit) vt,vi beneficiar, sacar provecho. n 1 beneficio m. 2 subsidio m. **beneficial** adj beneficioso, provechoso. **beneficiary** n beneficiario m.

benevolent (bi'nevələnt) adj benévolo, caritativo.

bent (bent) v see **bend.**

bereave* (bi'ri:v) vt 1 despojar, arrebatar. 2 afligir. **bereavement** n 1 aflicción f. duelo m. 2 fallecimiento m.

beret ('berei) n boina f.

berry ('beri) n baya f.

berth (bə:θ) n 1 naut fondeadero m. amarradero m. 2 naut camarote m. 3 litera f.

beside (bi'said) prep 1 junto a, cerca de. 2 comparado con. **beside oneself** fuera de sí. **besides** adv además, también. prep 1 además de. 2 excepto.

besiege (bi'si:dʒ) vt asediar, sitiar.

best (best) adj mejor, óptimo. adv mejor. **at best** a lo más. ~n lo mejor neu. **for the best** con la mejor intención. **make the best of it** sacar el mejor partido posible. **best man** n padrino de boda m. **best-seller** n éxito de librería m.

bestow (bi'stou) vt conferir, otorgar.

bet* (bet) n apuesta f. vt apostar. **better** n apostador m. **betting shop** n establecimiento de apuestas m.

betray (bi'trei) vt traicionar, delatar. **betrayal** n 1 traición f. 2 revelación f.

better ('betə) adj mejor, superior. **get better** mejorar(se). ~adv mejor. **better off** en mejor posición. **so much the better** tanto mejor. ~vt,vi mejorar(se), progresar.

between (bi'twi:n) prep entre. **in between** en medio.

beverage ('bevridʒ) n bebida f.

beware (bi'wɛə) vi precaverse, guardarse. interj ¡cuidado!

bewilder (bi'wildə) vt aturdir, aturrullar, desconcertar. **bewilderment** n aturdimiento m. perplejidad f.

beyond (bi'jɔnd) adv más allá, más lejos. prep 1 más allá de, fuera de, superior a. 2 además de. ~n más allá m.

biannual (bai'aenjuəl) adj bianual.

bias ('baiəs) n 1 sesgo m. diagonal f. 2 propen-

sión, predisposición f. prejuicio m. vt 1 sesgar. 2 torcer(se), influir en. **biased** adj parcial, predispuesto.

bib (bib) n babero m.

Bible ('baibəl) n Biblia f. **biblical** adj bíblico.

bibliography (bibli'ɔgrəfi) n bibliografía f.

biceps ('baiseps) n bíceps m.

bicker ('bikə) vi altercar, reñir.

bicycle ('baisikəl) n bicicleta f.

bid* (bid) vt,vi 1 ordenar, mandar. 2 pujar. n 1 oferta, postura f. 2 tentativa f. **no bid** game paso. **bidder** n postor m. **bidding** n 1 orden f. 2 postura f.

biennial (bai'eniəl) adj bienal.

big (big) adj 1 grande. 2 grueso. 3 abultado. 4 importante.

bigamy ('bigəmi) n bigamia f. **bigamist** n bígamo m. **bigamous** adj bígamo.

bigot ('bigət) n fanático m. **bigotry** n fanatismo m. intolerancia f.

bikini (bi'ki:ni) n bikini m.

bile (bail) n med bilis f. **bilious** adj bilioso.

bilingual (bai'lingwəl) adj bilingüe.

bill[1] (bil) n 1 comm cuenta, factura f. letra de cambio f. 2 law proyecto de ley m. 3 anuncio, programa m. **bill of sale** escritura de venta f. ~vt 1 enviar una cuenta a. 2 Th anunciar.

bill[2] (bil) n zool pico m.

billiards ('biliədz) n pl billar m.

billion ('biliən) n 1 billón m. 2 US mil millones m pl.

bin (bin) n cubo m. papelera f.

binary ('bainəri) adj binario.

bind* (baind) vt,vi 1 atar, ligar. 2 vendar. 3 encuadernar. 4 aglutinar. 5 obligar. n mus ligadura f. **binding** adj obligatorio. n 1 ligadura f. 2 encuadernación f. 3 aglutinante m.

binoculars (bi'nɔkjuləz) n pl gemelos m pl.

biography (bai'ɔgrəfi) n biografía f. **biographer** n biógrafo m. **biographical** adj biográfico.

biology (bai'ɔlədʒi) n biología f. **biological** adj biológico. **biologist** n biólogo m.

birch (bə:tʃ) n 1 bot abedul m. 2 vara f. vt varear.

bird (bə:d) n 1 ave f. pájaro m. 2 sl chica f. **bird of prey** ave de rapiña. **bird's eye view** a vista de pájaro. **birdcage** n jaula f.

birth (bə:θ) n 1 nacimiento m. 2 med parto m. 3 linaje m. 4 origen, comienzo m. **give birth to** 1 dar a luz. 2 med parir. **birth certificate** n partida de nacimiento f. **birth control** n control de la natalidad m. **birthday** n cumpleaños m pl.

biscuit ('biskit) n galleta f. bizcocho m.

bishop ('biʃəp) n obispo m. **bishopric** n obispado m.

bit[1] (bit) n 1 trozo m. trocito m. pedacito m. 2 bocado m. 3 inf moneda f. **not a bit** ni pizca. adv (un) poco. **bit by bit** poco a poco.

bit[2] (bit) n freno m.

bitch (bitʃ) n 1 perra f. 2 inf zorra f.

bite (bait) n 1 mordedura f. mordisco m. 2 picadura f. 3 bocado m. 4 mordacidad f. vt,vi 1 morder. 2 picar. **biting** adj mordaz, penetrante.

bitter ('bitə) adj amargo, áspero. n cerveza clara f. **bitterness** n amargura, aspereza f.

bizarre (bi'zɑː) adj raro, grotesco.

black (blæk) adj 1 negro. 2 aciago, funesto. n negro m. **blacken** vt,vi 1 ennegrecer. 2 denigrar.

blackberry ('blækbəri) n zarzamora f.

blackbird ('blækbɔːd) n mirlo m.

blackboard ('blækbɔːd) n pizarra f. encerado m.

blackcurrant (blæk'kʌrənt) n grosella negra f. casis m.

blackleg ('blækleg) n esquirol m.

blackmail ('blækmeil) n chantaje m. vt hacer chantaje. **blackmailer** n chantajista m,f.

black market n mercado negro m.

blackout ('blækaut) n 1 apagón m. 2 desmayo m. amnesia temporal. f. vi desmayarse.

black pudding n morcilla f.

blacksmith ('blæksmiθ) n herrero m.

bladder ('blædə) n vejiga f.

blade (bleid) n 1 hoja f. filo m. 2 pala, paleta f.

blame (bleim) vt culpar. n culpa f. **blameless** adj 1 intachable. 2 inocente.

blancmange (blə'mɔnʒ) n natillas de leche f pl.

blank (blæŋk) adj 1 en blanco, vacío. 2 desconcertado. **blank verse** verso libre. ~n 1 blanco, hueco m. 2 vacío m.

blanket ('blæŋkit) n manta f. **wet blanket** aguafiestas. m,f. ~vt 1 mantear. 2 encubrir. adj general, comprensivo.

blare (blɛə) vi sonar muy fuerte. vt vociferar. n 1 trompetazo m. 2 estrépito m.

blaspheme (blæs'fiːm) vi blasfemar. **blasphemous** adj blasfemo. **blasphemy** n blasfemia f.

blast (blɑːst) n 1 ráfaga f. soplo m. 2 explosión, sacudida f. 3 carga de explosivos f. 4 trompetazo m. **blast furnace** alto horno. ~vt 1 volar, destruir. 2 marchitar.

blatant ('bleitnt) adj 1 descarado. 2 vocinglero.

blaze (bleiz) n 1 hoguera f. 2 llamarada f. vi 1 arder, encenderse, inflamarse. 2 enardecer. **blazer** n chaqueta deportiva f.

bleach (bliːtʃ) vt,vi blanquear, descolorar. n lejía f.

bleak (bliːk) adj 1 desierto, pelado. 2 crudo.

bleat (bliːt) n balido m. vi balar.

bleed[*] (bliːd) vi sangrar, desangrar.

blemish ('blemiʃ) n defecto m. mancha f. vt manchar, mancillar.

blend (blend) vt,vi mezclar, combinar. n mezcla, combinación f.

bless (bles) vt 1 bendecir. 2 favorecer. **blessing** n bendición f.

blew (bluː) v see **blow**[1].

blind (blaind) adj ciego. n 1 persiana f. 2 pretexto m. vt cegar. **blindfold** n venda f. vt vendar los ojos de. **blindness** n ceguera f.

blink (bliŋk) n 1 parpadeo, guiño m. 2 destello m. vi parpadear, guiñar. **blinkers** n pl anteojeras f pl.

bliss (blis) n bienaventuranza f. embeleso m. **blissful** adj bienaventurado, dichoso.

blister ('blistə) n ampolla f. vt hacer ampollas en.

blizzard ('blizəd) n ventisca f.

bloat (blout) vt,vi hinchar.

blob (blɔb) n 1 gota. 2 borrón m.

bloc (blɔk) n bloque m.

block (blɔk) n 1 bloque m. 2 tajo m. 3 arch manzana f. 4 obstáculo m. vt bloquear, tapar.

blond (blɔnd) adj rubio. **blonde** n rubia f.

blood (blʌd) n 1 sangre f. 2 parentesco m. **bloodless** adj 1 exangüe. 2 incruento. **blood pressure** n presión arterial f. **bloodshed** n matanza f. **bloodstream** n corriente sanguínea f. **bloodthirsty** adj sanguinario. **bloody** adj 1 sangriento. 2 sl maldito. adv sl muy.

bloom (bluːm) n 1 flor f. 2 florecimiento m. 3 lozanía f. vi florecer, lozanear. **blooming** adj floreciente.

blossom ('blɔsəm) n flor f. vi florecer.

blot (blɔt) n borrón m. tachadura f. vt 1 manchar, tachar. 2 empañar. 3 secar. **blotting paper** n papel secante m. **blotch** n 1 mancha f. 2 med erupción f.

blouse (blauz) n blusa f.

blow[*1] (blou) vi 1 soplar. 2 sonar. 3 inflar.

blow over pasar. **blow up** estallar, reventar. ~n soplo m.

blow[2] (blou) n golpe m. bofetada f.

blubber ('blʌbə) n llanto m. vi gimotear.

blue (blu:) adj,n azul m. **bluish** adj azulado. **the blues** melancolía, murria f.

bluebell ('blu:bel) n jacinto silvestre m.

blueprint ('blu:print) n bosquejo, proyecto m.

bluff (blʌf) vt,vi fanfarronear, embaucar. n fanfarronada f.

blunder ('blʌndə) vi desatinar. n desatino m.

blunt (blʌnt) adj 1 desafilado, embotado. 2 despuntado. 3 franco, brusco. vt embotar, despuntar, desafilar. **bluntness** n 1 embotamiento m. 2 franqueza, brusquedad f.

blur (blə:) vt,vi emborronar, manchar. vi empañar, hacer borroso. n 1 borrón m. 2 contorno borroso m. **blurred** adj borroso.

blush (blʌʃ) vi ruborizarse, sonrojarse. n rubor, sonrojo m.

boar (bɔ:) n verraco m. **wild boar** jabalí m.

board (bɔ:d) n 1 tabla f. 2 tablero m. 3 comm junta f. **go by the board** tirar por la borda. **on board** naut a bordo. ~vt 1 entablar. 2 naut abordar. 3 hospedar. **boarding house** n pensión f. casa de huéspedes f.

boast (boust) vi jactarse, presumir. n baladronada, ostentación f. alarde m. **boaster** n fanfarrón, pavero m. **boastful** adj jactancioso.

boat (bout) n 1 barca, lancha f. bote m. 2 barco, buque m. vi navegar, ir en bote. **boatsman** n barquero m.

bob (bɔb) vi bambolear. vt menear. n 1 balanceo m. 2 sacudida f.

bodice ('bɔdis) n corpiño m.

body ('bɔdi) n 1 cuerpo m. 2 cadáver m. 3 mot carrocería f. 4 tech armazón f. **able-bodied** robusto, sano. **busybody** n entrometido m. **bodily** adj corporal, corpóreo. **bodyguard** n guardaespaldas m invar.

bog (bɔg) n pantano m. ciénaga f.

bohemian (bə'hi:miən) adj bohemio.

boil[1] (bɔil) vt,vi hervir. **boil over** irse, sobrarse un líquido. ~n hervor m. **boiler** n caldera f. **boiling point** n punto de ebullición m.

boil[2] (bɔil) n furúnculo, divieso m.

boisterous ('bɔistərəs) adj 1 bullicioso, borrascoso, tormentoso. **boisterousness** n tumulto, bullicio m.

bold (bould) adj 1 atrevido, audaz. 2 claro, vigoroso. **boldness** n atrevimiento m. audacia f.

Bolivia (bə'liviə) n Bolivia f. **Bolivian** adj,n boliviano m.

bolster ('boulstə) n 1 travesaño m. 2 almohada f. vt 1 apoyar, sostener. 2 alentar.

bolt (boult) n 1 cerrojo, pestillo m. 2 tech perno m. 3 rayo m. 4 saeta f. 5 salida repentina f. vt 1 pasar el cerrojo. 2 tech empernar. 3 engullir. vi desbocarse.

bomb (bɔm) n bomba f. vt,vi bombardear. **bombard** vt bombardear. **bombardment** n bombardeo m. **bomber** n bombardero m.

bond (bɔnd) n 1 lazo, vínculo m. 2 comm obligación f. bono m. 3 comm fianza f. vt comm 1 obligar por fianza. 2 poner en depósito. **bondage** n esclavitud f.

bone (boun) n hueso m. **make no bones about** inf no andarse con rodeos. **bony** adj huesudo.

bonfire ('bɔnfaiə) n hoguera, fogata, falla f.

bonnet ('bɔnit) n 1 gorra f. 2 mot capó m.

bonus ('bounəs) n extra m. prima f.

booby trap ('bu:bi) n trampa explosiva f.

book (buk) n libro m. **bookcase** n librería f. estante para libros m. **booking office** n taquilla f. despacho de billetes m. **bookkeeping** n teneduría de libros f. **booklet** n folleto, opúsculo m. **bookmaker** n corredor profesional de apuestas m. **bookseller** n librero m. **bookshop** n librería f. **bookstall** n puesto de libros m. **bookworm** n polilla f. 2 ratón de biblioteca m. ~vt 1 asentar, anotar, apuntar. 2 reservar.

boom (bu:m) n 1 comm auge repentino m. 2 estampido m. vi 1 prosperar, estar en bonanza. 2 retumbar.

boost (bu:st) vt 1 inf empujar. 2 fomentar, animar. 3 tech recargar. n inf empujón m.

boot (bu:t) n 1 bota f. 2 mot maleta f. **get the boot** ser despedido. **to boot** también. ~vt patear.

booth (bu:θ) n cabina f.

booze (bu:z) vi inf emborracharse. n 1 bebida alcohólica f. 2 sl morapio m. 3 borrachera f.

border ('bɔ:də) n 1 borde m. 2 frontera f. 3 orla, cenefa f. vt,vi lindar. 3 ribetear. adj fronterizo. **borderline** adj dudoso, incierto.

bore[1] (bɔ:) vt taladrar. n 1 tech taladro m. sonda f. 2 mil calibre m. alma f.

bore[2] (bɔ:) vt aburrir, dar la lata. n 1 pesado, pelmazo m. 2 inf rollo m. **boredom** n aburrimiento m. **boring** adj aburrido, pesado.

bore[3] (bɔ:) v see **bear**[1].

born (bɔ:n) adj nato, innato. **be born** nacer.

borne (bɔːn) v see **bear**[1].

borough ('bʌrə) n 1 villa f. 2 municipio m.

borrow ('bɔrou) vt pedir prestado. **borrower** n prestatario m.

bosom ('buzəm) n 1 seno m. 2 pecho m.

boss (bɔs) n 1 jefe, patrón m. 2 cacique m. vt dirigir, mandar, dominar.

botany ('bɔtəni) n ·botánica f. **botanical** adj botánico.

both (bouθ) adj,pron ambos, los dos.

bother ('bɔðə) vt molestar. n molestia, lata f.

bottle ('bɔtl) n botella f. frasco m. vt embotellar.

bottom ('bɔtəm) n 1 fondo m. 2 casco m. 3 anat trasero m. adj más bajo. **bottomless** adj 1 sin fondo. 2 insondable.

bough (bau) n rama f.

bought (bɔːt) v see **buy.**

boulder ('bouldə) n canto rodado m.

bounce (bauns) vi rebotar, botar. n rebote m. **bouncing** adj fuerte, vigoroso.

bound[1] (baund) v see **bind.**

bound[2] (baund) n salto, brinco m. vi saltar, brincar, botar.

bound[3] (baund) n límite, lindero m. vt limitar, deslindar. **boundless** adj ilimitado. **boundary** n límite, lindero m.

bound[4] (baund) adj destinado, con rumbo a.

bountiful ('bauntifəl) adj liberal, generoso.

bouquet (bu'kei) n 1 ramillete, ramo m. 2 aroma m.

bourgeois ('buəʒwaː) adj burgués.

bout (baut) n 1 turno m. 2 med ataque m.

bow[1] (bau) vi 1 inclinarse, hacer una reverencia. 2 someterse. n 1 inclinación, reverencia f. saludo m. 2 lazo m.

bow[2] (bau) n proa f.

bow[3] (bou) n arco m.

bowels ('bauəlz) n pl intestinos m pl. entrañas f pl.

bowl[1] (boul) n tazón, bol m. escudilla f.

bowl[2] (boul) n sport bola, bocha f. vi jugar a las bochas. **bowl over** hacer rodar. **bowler** n jugador de bochas. **bowler hat** hongo m.

box[1] (bɔks) n 1 caja f. cajón m. 2 palco m. 3 bot boj m. vt encajonar. **box number** n apartado m. **box office** n taquilla f. **be good box office** ser taquillero.

box[2] (bɔks) vt,vi boxear. n cachete m. **boxer** n boxeador m. **boxing** n boxeo m.

boy (bɔi) n niño, muchacho, chico, joven m. **boyhood** n niñez, juventud f. **boyfriend** n novio m.

boycott ('bɔikɔt) vt boicotear. n boicot m.

brace (breis) n 1 tirante, refuerzo m. 2 tech abrazadera f. 3 corchete m. 4 par, berbiquí m. vt reforzar, trabar. **braces** n pl tirantes m pl. **bracing** adj vigorizador, tónico.

bracelet ('breislət) n pulsera f.

bracket ('brækit) n 1 arch repisa f. 2 tech puntal m. 3 brazo m. 4 corchete, paréntesis m. vt 1 poner entre corchetes. 2 agrupar.

brag (bræg) vi jactarse de, fanfarronear.

braid (breid) n 1 trenza f. 2 trencilla f. galón m. vt 1 trenzar. 2 galonear.

Braille (breil) n alfabeto para ciegos, Braille m.

brain (brein) n 1 med cerebro m. 2 sesos m pl. vt romper la crisma. **brains** n pl talento m. **brainwash** vt lavar el cerebro. **brainy** adj sesudo, talentudo.

braise (breiz) vt estofar, guisar.

brake (breik) n freno m. vt,vi frenar.

branch (braːntʃ) n 1 rama f. 2 sección f. 3 ramal m. 4 comm sucursal f. vi 1 ramificarse, bifurcarse. 2 bot echar ramas.

brand (brænd) n 1 comm marca f. 2 tizón m. 3 hierro de marcar m. vt marcar. **brand-new** adj enteramente nuevo.

brandish ('brændiʃ) vt blandir.

brandy ('brændi) n coñac m.

brash (bræʃ) adj inf insolente, descarado.

brass (braːs) n 1 latón m. 2 mus cobre m. 3 inf pasta f. **brassy** adj 1 de latón. 2 presuntuoso.

brassiere ('bræziə) n also **bra** sostén m.

brave (breiv) adj valiente, bravo. vt desafiar, arrostrar. **bravery** n valentía f. valor m.

brawl (brɔːl) n riña f. alboroto m. vi alborotar, armar camorra.

bray (brei) vi rebuznar. n rebuzno m.

brazen ('breizən) adj 1 de latón. 2 desvergonzado.

Brazil (brə'zil) n Brasil m. **Brazilian** adj,n brasileño m.

breach (briːtʃ) n 1 brecha f. 2 ruptura f. 3 infracción, violación f. vt,vi 1 abrir brecha. 2 romper.

bread (bred) n pan m. **breadcrumb** n migaja f. **breadcrumbs** pan rallado m. **breadwinner** n cabeza de familia m.

breadth (bredθ) n 1 anchura f. ancho m. 2 amplitud, tolerancia f.

break[1] (breik) n 1 ruptura f. 2 abertura, grieta f. 3 pausa, interrupción f. 4 descanso, recreo m. vt romper, quebrantar, quebrar. **break away** desprenderse. **break down** 1 derribar. 2 enfermar. 3 echarse a llorar. 4 tener una avería. **break in** forzar la entrada. **break out**

estallar. **break up 1** desmenuzar. **2** disolver. **breakdown** n **1** colapso m. crisis f. **2** mot avería f. **breakthrough** n avance m.

breakfast ('brekfəst) n desayuno m. vi desayunarse.

breast (brest) n pecho m. **make a clean breast of it** confesarlo todo con franqueza. **breaststroke** n brazada de pecho, braza f.

breath (breθ) n **1** aliento m. respiración f. **2** soplo m. **under one's breath** en voz baja. **waste one's breath** gastar saliva. **breathless** adj sin aliento. **breathtaking** adj **1** vertiginoso. **2** pasmoso.

breathe (bri:ð) vt,vi **1** respirar. **2** exhalar. **3** inspirar.

breed* (bri:d) n raza, casta f. vt,vi **1** criar, reproducirse, engendrar. **2** educar. **breeding** n **1** cría f. **2** crianza, educación f.

breeze (bri:z) n brisa f. **breezy** adj ventilado, oreado.

brew (bru:) vt **1** fabricar (cerveza). **2** infusionar. n poción f. **brewery** n fábrica de cerveza f.

bribe (braib) n soborno m. vt sobornar. **briber** n sobornador m. **bribery** n soborno m.

brick (brik) n ladrillo m. vt cerrar con ladrillos, cegar. **bricklayer** n albañil m.

bride (braid) n novia, desposada f. **bridal** adj nupcial. **bridegroom** n novio, desposado m. **bridesmaid** n dama de honor f.

bridge[1] (bridʒ) n **1** puente m. **drawbridge** puente levadizo. **suspension bridge** puente colgante. ~vt tender un puente.

bridge[2] (bridʒ) n game bridge m.

bridle ('braidl) n brida f. freno m. vt enfrenar, refrenar. vi picarse.

brief (bri:f) adj breve. n **1** resumen, memorial m. **2** law autos jurídicos m pl. **3** breve m. vt dar instrucciones. **briefcase** n cartera f.

brigade (bri'geid) n brigada f. **brigadier** n brigadier m.

bright (brait) adj **1** brillante, claro. **2** alegre, vivo. **3** listo, agudo. **brighten** vt,vi **1** abrillantar. **2** aclarar. **3** mejorar, avivar. **brightness** n **1** brillantez f. **2** viveza f. **3** talento m.

brilliant ('briliant) adj brillante.

brim (brim) n **1** borde m. **2** ala de sombrero f.

bring* (briŋ) vt traer, conducir, llevar. **bring about** ocasionar. **bring down 1** rebajar. **2** mil derribar. **bring forth** producir. **bring forward 1** presentar. **2** adelantar. **bring in 1** introducir. **2** rendir. **bring off** conseguir. **bring on** causar, inducir. **bring out 1** sacar.

revelar. **2** publicar. **3** alentar. **bring together** reunir. **bring up** criar, educar.

brink (briŋk) n borde m. orilla f.

brisk (brisk) adj enérgico, vigoroso, animado.

bristle ('brisəl) n cerda f. vi erizarse.

Britain ('britn) n Gran Bretaña f. **British** adj británico. **Briton** n británico m.

brittle ('britl) adj quebradizo, frágil.

broad (brɔ:d) adj **1** ancho. **2** amplio, extenso. **3** general, aproximado. **broadly** adj **1** en general. **2** plenamente. **broadness** n **1** anchura f. **2** amplitud f. liberalismo m. **broad-minded** adj de miras amplias, liberal, tolerante.

broad bean n haba verde f.

broadcast ('brɔ:dka:st) vt,vi **1** emitir, radiar. **2** diseminar, divulgar. n emisión f. programa radiofónico m. **broadcasting** n radiodifusión f. **broadcasting station** n emisora f.

broaden ('brɔ:dn) vt,vi **1** ensanchar. **2** ampliar.

broccoli ('brɔkəli) n brécoles m pl.

brochure ('brəuʃə) n folleto m.

broke (brouk) v see **break.** adj inf sin blanca.

broken ('broukən) v see **break.**

broker ('broukə) n corredor de bolsa m.

bronchitis (brɔŋ'kaitis) n bronquitis f.

bronze (brɔnz) n bronce m.

brooch (broutʃ) n broche m.

brood (bru:d) n **1** camada, nidada f. **2** progenie, prole f. vi empollar. **brood on** or **over** rumiar, meditar.

brook (bruk) n arroyo m.

broom (bru:m) n **1** escoba f. **2** retama f.

brothel ('brɔðəl) n burdel, prostíbulo m.

brother ('brʌðə) n hermano m. **brotherhood** n fraternidad f. **brotherly** adj fraternal. **brother-in-law** n cuñado, hermano político m.

brought (brɔ:t) v see **bring.**

brow (brau) n **1** ceja f. **2** frente f. **3** cumbre f. **browbeat** vt intimidar verbalmente.

brown (braun) adj pardo, castaño, moreno. vt **1** poner moreno, tostar. **2** dorar. n color pardo, etc. m. **brownish** adj parduzco.

browse (brauz) vi hojear. vt pacer, ramonear.

bruise (bru:z) n contusión, magulladura f. cardenal m. vt magullar, machacar.

brunette (bru:'net) n morena f.

brush (brʌʃ) n **1** cepillo m. **2** brocha f. pincel m. vt **1** cepillar. **2** rozar.

brusque (bru:sk) adj brusco, rudo.

Brussels ('brʌsəlz) n Bruselas f. **Brussels sprout** n col de Bruselas f.

brute (bru:t) n bruto m. bestia m,f. adj bruto.

business

brutal *adj* brutal, salvaje. **brutality** *n* brutalidad *f*. **brutalize** *vt* brutalizar.

bubble ('bʌbəl) *n* burbuja *f*. *vi* burbujear, borbotear.

buck[1] (bʌk) *n* 1 gamo *m*. 2 macho *m*.

buck[2] (bʌk) *vi* corcovear.

bucket ('bʌkit) *n* cubo, balde *m*.

buckle ('bʌkəl) *n* hebilla *f*. *vt* abrochar. *vi* doblegarse.

bud (bʌd) *n* 1 brote *m*. pimpollo *m*. 2 capullo *m*. *vi* 1 brotar. 2 florecer.

Buddhism ('budizəm) *n* budismo *m*. **Buddhist** *adj,n* budista *m,f*.

budget ('bʌdʒit) *n* presupuesto *m*. *vi* presupuestar.

buffalo ('bʌfəlou) *n, pl* **-oes** *or* **-os** búfalo *m*.

buffer ('bʌfə) *n* tope, amortiguador *m*.

buffet[1] ('bufei) *n* buffet *m*.

buffet[2] ('bʌfit) *n* bofetón *m*. bofetada *f*. *vt* abofetear, golpear.

bug (bʌg) *n* 1 chinche *f*. 2 bicho *m*. 3 *inf* microbio, virus *m*.

bugle ('bju:gəl) *n* corneta *f*. **bugler** *n* corneta *m*.

build* (bild) *vt,vi* 1 construir. 2 edificar. 3 establecer, fundar. **builder** *n* constructor, maestro de obras *m*. **building** *n* 1 edificio *m*. 2 construcción *f*. **building site** *n* solar *m*. **building society** *n* cooperativa de la vivienda *f*.

bulb (bʌlb) *n* 1 *bot* bulbo *m*. 2 bombilla *f*. 3 ampolla *f*.

bulge (bʌldʒ) *n* comba, hinchazón *f*. bulto *m*. *vi* combarse, bombearse, abultar.

bulk (bʌlk) *n* 1 bulto, volumen, tamaño *m*. 2 grueso *m*. **in bulk** a granel. **bulkiness** *n* volumen, bulto *m*. **bulky** *adj* voluminoso.

bull (bul) *n* toro *m*. **bullfight** *n* corrida de toros *f*. *vt,vi* torear. **bullfighter** *n* torero *m*. **bullring** *n* plaza de toros *f*. **bull's-eye** *n* centro del blanco *m*.

bulldog ('buldɔg) *n* dogo, perro de presa *m*.

bulldozer ('buldouzə) *n* excavadora *f*. buldozer *m*. **bulldoze** *vt inf* intimidar.

bullet ('bulit) *n* bala *f*. **bullet-proof** *adj* a prueba de bala.

bulletin ('bulətin) *n* boletín *m*. **news bulletin** boletín informativo.

bullion ('buljən) *n* oro en barras *m*. plata en barras *f*.

bully ('buli) *n* matón *m*. *vt* intimidar, amedrantar.

bum (bʌm) *n* 1 *inf* posaderas *f pl*. pompis *m*. 2 *inf* holgazán *m*.

bump (bʌmp) *n* 1 trompazo, topetón *m*. 2 sacudida *f*. 3 comba, giba *f*. 4 protuberancia *f*. 5 chichón *m*. *vt* 1 dar un trompazo a. 2 chocar, topar. **bumper** *n* parachoques *m invar*. *adj* abundante.

bun (bʌn) *n* 1 bollo *m*. 2 moño *m*.

bunch (bʌntʃ) *n* 1 manojo *m*. 2 ranco *m*. 3 racimo *m*. 4 *inf* pandilla *f*. montón *m*.

bundle ('bʌndl) *n* 1 lío, paquete *m*. 2 haz *m*. manojo *m*. *vt* envolver, liar.

bungalow ('bʌngəlou) *n* chalet *m*.

bungle ('bʌngəl) *n* chapucería, torpeza *f*. *vt* chapucear, echar a perder. **bungler** *n* chapucero *m*. **bungling** *adj* chapucero, torpe.

bunk (bʌnk) *n* 1 litera *f*. 2 *inf* palabrería *f*.

bunker ('bʌnkə) *n* 1 refugio, bunker *m*. 2 carbonera *f*. 3 *sport* hoya de arena *f*.

buoy (bɔi) *n* boya *f*. flotador *m*. **buoyant** *adj* boyante. **buoyancy** *n* fluctuación *f*. capacidad de recuperación *f*.

burden ('bə:dn) *n* carga *f*. *vt* cargar, gravar.

bureau ('bjuərou) *n* 1 oficina, agencia *f*. departamento *m*. 2 escritorio *m*.

bureaucracy (bju'rɔkrəsi) *n* burocracia *f*. **bureaucrat** *n* burócrata *m,f*. **bureaucratic** *adj* burocrático.

burglar ('bə:glə) *n* ladrón, escalador *m*. **burglar alarm** *n* alarma contra ladrones *f*. **burglary** *n* robo *m*. **burgle** *vt* robar, escalar.

burn* (bə:n) *vt* 1 quemar, abrasar. 2 requemar, curtir. *vi* arder. *n* quemadura *f*. **burner** *n* quemador *m*. **burning** *adj* ardiente, abrasador.

burrow ('bʌrou) *n* madriguera *f*. *vi* socavar, minar.

burst* (bə:st) *vt* 1 reventar, estallar, romper. 2 irrumpir. 3 rebosar. 4 brotar. *n* 1 reventón *m*. 2 estallido *m*.

bury ('beri) *vt* 1 enterrar, sepultar. 2 ocultar. **burial** *n* entierro *m*. **burial ground** *n* cementerio, camposanto *m*.

bus (bʌs) *n, pl* **-es** *or* **-ses** autobús *m*. **bus-stop** parada de autobús *f*.

bush (buʃ) *n* 1 arbusto *m*. 2 matorral *m*.

bushy ('buʃi:) *adj* 1 espeso. 2 matoso. 3 peludo.

business ('biznis) *n* 1 negocio, comercio *m*. empresa *f*. 2 ocupación *f*. 3 asunto *m*. 4 tarea *f*. **mind one's own business** no meterse donde no le llaman. **businessman** *n* hombre de negocios *m*. **business-like** *adj* metódico, práctico.

165

bust[1] (bʌst) n busto m.

bust[2] (bʌst) n inf 1 reventón m. 2 fracaso m. **go bust** quebrar. vt romper, reventar, estropear.

bustle ('bʌsəl) n bullicio m. animación, bulla f. vi 1 bullir. 2 afanarse. **bustling** adj bullicioso.

busy ('bizi) adj 1 ocupado, atareado. 2 activo. **busybody** entrometido.

but (bət; stressed bʌt) conj pero, sino. prep excepto. adv solamente.

butcher ('butʃə) n carnicero m. vt 1 matar. 2 destrozar, hacer una carnicería con. **butcher's shop** n carnicería f.

butler ('bʌtlə) n mayordomo m.

butt[1] (bʌt) n 1 cabo, mango m. 2 culata f.

butt[2] (bʌt) n 1 blanco m. 2 meta f. objeto m.

butt[3] (bʌt) vt dar cabezadas contra, embestir. **butt in** inf entrometerse, interrumpir.

butter ('bʌtə) n mantequilla f. vt untar con mantequilla. **buttercup** n ranúnculo m. **butterfly** n mariposa f.

buttocks ('bʌtəks) n pl nalgas f pl.

button ('bʌtn) n botón m. vt abotonar.

buttress ('bʌtrəs) n arch contrafuerte m. vt apoyar. reforzar.

buy[*] (bai) vt comprar. n compra f. **buyer** n comprador m.

buzz (bʌz) n zumbido m. vi zumbar. **buzzer** n timbre, silbato m.

by (bai) prep 1 por, a, de. 2 cerca de. adv 1 cerca, al lado. 2 a un lado, aparte. **by the way** a propósito. **by and large** en generales. **by-election** n elecciones complementarias f pl. **bylaw** n estatuto m. ley local f. **bypass** n desviación f. vt 1 desviar. 2 evitar. **by-product** n subproducto m. **bystander** n espectador m. circunstante m,f.

C

cab (kæb) n taxi, coche de alquiler m. **cabman** n cochero m.

cabaret ('kæbərei) n cabaret m.

cabbage ('kæbidʒ) n col f. repollo m.

cabin ('kæbin) n 1 cabaña f. 2 naut camarote m. **cabin cruiser** n motonave f.

cabinet ('kæbinət) n 1 armario m. vitrina f. 2 gabinete m. 3 pol consejo de ministros m. **medicine cabinet** botiquín m.

cable ('keibəl) n cable m. vt,vi cablegrafiar.

cackle ('kækəl) vi cacarear. n cacareo m.

cactus ('kæktəs) n, pl -ti or -tuses cacto m.

cadence ('keidns) n 1 cadencia f. 2 compás m.

cadet (kə'det) n mil cadete m.

cafe ('kæfei) n 1 café m. 2 restaurante m.

cafeteria (kæfi'tiəriə) n cafetería f.

caffeine ('kæfi:n) n cafeína f.

cage (keidʒ) n jaula f. vt enjaular.

cake (keik) n 1 pastel m. 2 (of soap) pastilla f. vi endurecerse.

calamity (kə'læməti) n calamidad f.

calcium ('kælsiəm) n calcio m.

calculate ('kælkjuleit) vt,vi calcular. **calculable** adj calculable. **calculation** n cálculo m. calculación f. **calculator** n calculador m.

calendar ('kælində) n calendario m.

calf[1] (ka:f) n, pl **calves** zool ternero, becerro m.

calf[2] (ka:f) n, pl **calves** anat pantorrilla f.

calibre ('kælibə) n 1 calibre m. 2 talento m.

call (kɔ:l) vt llamar. **call for** pedir, exigir. **call off** cancelar, abandonar. **call on** 1 visitar. 2 invitar. **call up** 1 evocar. 2 convocar. 3 llamar por teléfono. **call upon** visitar. ∼n 1 llamada f. llamamiento m. 2 grito m. 3 visita f.

callbox ('kɔ:lbɔks) n cabina telefónica f.

calling ('kɔ:liŋ) n vocación, profesión f.

callous ('kæləs) adj insensible, duro.

calm (ka:m) n calma, tranquilidad f. sosiego m. adj 1 calmoso. 2 tranquilo, sosegado. vt,vi calmar. 2 tranquilizar.

calorie ('kæləri) n caloría f.

Cambodia (kæm'boudiə) n Camboya f.

came (keim) v see **come**.

camel ('kæməl) n camello m.

camera ('kæmrə) n 1 máquina fotográfica f. 2 cámara f. **cameraman** n cameraman m.

camouflage ('kæməfla:ʒ) n camuflaje m. vt camuflar.

camp[1] (kæmp) n campamento m. vi acampar. **camp-bed** n cama plegable f. **camping site** n camping m.

camp[2] (kæmp) adj inf 1 afeminado. 2 homosexual.

campaign (kæm'pein) n campaña f. **election campaign** campaña electoral. vi hacer campaña.

campus ('kæmpəs) n recinto universitario, campus m.

can[*1] (kæn) vi 1 poder. 2 saber.

can[2] (kæn) n lata f. bote m. vt enlatar. **canned** adj enlatado, en conserva. **canning** n enlatado m.

Canada ('kænədə) n Canadá m. **Canadian** n,adj canadiense m,f.

canal (kə'næl) n canal m.

canary (kə'nɛəri) n canario m.

Canary Islands n pl (Islas) Canarias f pl.

cancel ('kænsəl) vt,vi 1 cancelar. 2 tachar. cancel out destruirse, anularse. cancellation n cancelación, anulación f.

cancer ('kænsə) n cáncer m. cancerous adj canceroso.

candid ('kændid) adj franco, sincero.

candidate ('kændidət) n candidato m.

candle ('kændl) n vela, candela f. candlestick n 1 candelero m. 2 candelabro m.

candour ('kændə) n franqueza f.

cane ('kein) n 1 caña f. 2 bastón m. 3 palmeta f. vt azotar, castigar con la palmeta.

canine ('keinain) n,adj canino m.

cannabis ('kænəbis) n marijuana f.

cannibal ('kænibəl) n caníbal m,f. adj antropófago. cannibalism n canibalismo m.

cannon ('kænən) n 1 cañón m. 2 carambola f. cannonade n cañoneo m. cannonball n bala de cañón f.

cannot ('kænət) v see can¹.

canoe (kə'nu:) n canoa f. vi ir en canoa.

canon¹ ('kænən) n canon m. canon law derecho canónico m. canonize vt canonizar. canonization n canonización f.

canon² ('kænən) n canónigo m.

canopy ('kænəpi) n dosel, baldaquín m.

canteen (kæn'ti:n) n 1 cantina f. 2 cantimplora f.

canter ('kæntə) n medio galope m. vi ir a medio galope.

canton ('kæntɔn) n cantón m.

canvas ('kænvəs) n 1 lona f. 2 cañamazo m. 3 art tela f. lienzo m.

canvass ('kænvəs) vt escrutinar, sondear. vi solicitar apoyo. canvassing n 1 sondeo m. 2 solicitación de apoyo f.

canyon ('kænjən) n desfiladero m. cañada f.

cap (kæp) n 1 gorra f. 2 casquete m. vt coronar, rematar.

capable ('keipəbəl) adj capaz, hábil. capability n capacidad, habilidad f.

capacity (kə'pæsiti) n 1 capacidad f. 2 mot cilindrada f.

cape¹ (keip) n capa f.

cape² (keip) n cabo m.

caper ('keipə) n cul alcaparra f.

capital ('kæpitl) n 1 capital f. 2 mayúscula f. 3 capital m. capitalism n capitalismo m. capitalist n capitalista m,f. capitalistic adj capitalista. capitalize vt capitalizar. capitalization n capitalización f.

capricious (kə'priʃəs) adj caprichoso. caprice or capriciousness n capricho m.

Capricorn ('kæprikɔ:n) n Capricornio m.

capsicum ('kæpsikəm) n pimiento m.

capsize ('kæpsaiz) vt 1 volcar. 2 hacer zozobrar.

capsule ('kæpsju:l) n cápsula f.

captain ('kæptin) n capitán m. vt capitanear.

caption ('kæpʃən) n 1 encabezamiento m. 2 pie, subtítulo m. vt poner subtítulos.

captivate ('kæptiveit) vt cautivar.

captive ('kæptiv) n,adj cautivo m. captivity n cautividad f.

capture ('kæptʃə) vt 1 capturar. 2 tomar. 3 captar. n 1 captura, toma f. 2 presa f.

car (ka:) n 1 coche m. 2 vagón m. car park n aparcamiento m.

caramel ('kærəməl) n azúcar quemado, caramelo m.

carat ('kærət) n quilate m.

caravan ('kærəvæn) n 1 caravana f. 2 mot remolque m.

caraway ('kærəwei) n alcaravea f.

carbohydrate (ka:bou'haidreit) n carbohidrato m. fécula f.

carbon ('ka:bən) n 1 carbono m. 2 carbón m. carbonic adj carbónico. carbonize vt carbonizar(se). carbon dioxide n bióxido de carbono m. carbon paper n papel carbón m.

carburettor (ka:bju'retə) n carburador m.

carcass ('ka:kəs) n 1 res muerta f. 2 cadáver de animal m. 3 armazón f.

card (ka:d) n 1 tarjeta f. 2 ficha f. 3 naipe m. carta f. 4 carnet m. cardboard n cartón m. card index n fichero m.

cardigan ('ka:digən) n rebeca f.

cardinal ('ka:dinl) n cardenal m. adj cardinal.

care (kɛə) n 1 cuidado m. 2 esmero m. 3 cuita f. 4 cargo m. care of 1 en casa de. 2 a manos de. take care of cuidar de. ~vi importar, preocuparse. care for 1 cuidar. 2 querer, desear. 3 gustar. care to tener ganas de. carefree adj despreocupado. careful adj 1 cuidadoso. 2 esmerado. 3 cauteloso. be careful tener cuidado. carefulness n cuidado, esmero m. cautela f. careless adj 1 descuidado, dejado. 2 desatento, desaplicado.

caretaker ('kɛəteikə) n 1 conserje, portero m. 2 custodio m.

career (kə'riə) n carrera, profesión f. vi correr a) carrera tendida.

caress (kə'res) vt acariciar. n caricia f.

cargo ('ka:gou) n, pl cargoes cargamento m. carga f.

Caribbean (kæri'biən) n Caribe m. adj caribe. **Caribbean Sea** n Mar Caribe m.

caricature ('kærikətjuə) n caricatura f. vt caricaturizar. **caricaturist** n caricaturista m,f.

carnal ('ka:nl) adj carnal. **carnality** n carnalidad f.

carnation (ka:'neiʃən) n clavel m.

carnival ('ka:nivəl) n carnaval m.

carnivorous (ka:'nivərəs) adj carnívoro.

carol ('kærəl) n villancico m.

carpenter ('ka:pintə) n carpintero m. **carpentry** n carpintería f.

carpet ('ka:pit) n alfombra f. vt alfombrar.

carriage ('kæridʒ) n 1 carruaje, carro m. 2 vagón m. 3 comm porte m. **carriageway** n carretera, calzada f.

carrier ('kæriə) n 1 portador m. 2 empresa de transportes f. **aircraft carrier** n portaviones m invar. **carrier bag** n bolsa f. **carrier pigeon** n paloma mensajera f.

carrot ('kærət) n zanahoria f.

carry ('kæri) vt 1 llevar, acarrear. 2 sostener. **carry forward** comm pasar. **carry out** realizar, llevar a cabo.

carrycot ('kærikɔt) n cuna portátil f.

cart (ka:t) n carro m. carreta f. vt carretear.

cartilage ('ka:tlidʒ) n cartílago m.

carton ('ka:tn) n cartón, envase m.

cartoon (ka:'tu:n) n 1 caricatura f. chiste m. 2 dibujos animados m pl. película de dibujos f. 3 Art cartón m.

cartridge ('ka:tridʒ) n cartucho m.

carve (ka:v) vt 1 trinchar. 2 tallar, esculpir. **carving** n talla, escultura f.

cascade (kæ'skeid) n cascada f. vi caer en cascada.

case¹ (keis) n 1 caso m. 2 argumento convincente m. **in case** 1 en caso de que. 2 por si acaso. **in any case** 1 en todo caso.

case² (keis) n 1 caja f. 2 estuche m. funda f. 3 vitrina f. 4 bastidor, marco m. vt 1 encajonar. 2 enfundar. **casing** n 1 envoltura, cubierta f. 2 cerco m.

cash (kæʃ) n 1 dinero contante m. 2 pago al contado m. **cash desk** n caja f. **cash in on** inf sacar provecho de, aprovecharse. **cash on delivery** pago contra recibo. **cash register** n caja registradora f. **in cash** en metálico. vt cobrar, hacer efectivo.

cashier¹ (kæ'ʃiə) n cajero m.

cashier² (kæ'ʃiə) vt despedir, destituir.

cashmere (kæʃ'miə) n cachemira f. casimir m.

casket ('ka:skit) n cofrecito, joyero m.

casserole ('kæsəroul) n cacerola f.

cassette (kə'set) n cassette m.

cassock ('kæsək) n sotana f.

cast¹ (ka:st) vt,vi 1 echar, arrojar. 2 desechar. 3 tech fundir, moldear. **cast off** 1 abandonar. 2 naut desamarrar. ~n 1 vaciado m. 2 molde m. 3 reparto m. 4 estampa f. matriz m. **cast iron** n hierro colado m. adj duro, fuerte. **castaway** n náufrago m.

castanets (kæstə'nets) n pl castañuelas f pl.

caste (ka:st) n casta f.

castle ('ka:səl) n 1 castillo m. 2 torre f.

castrate (kæ'streit) vt castrar. **castration** n castración f.

casual ('kæʒuəl) adj 1 casual. 2 indiferente, descuidado. **casualty** n 1 accidente m. 2 víctima f. 3 mil baja f.

cat (kæt) n 1 gato m. **cat's eye** n cimofana f.

catalogue ('kætəlɔg) n catálogo m. vt catalogar.

catamaran (kætəmə'ræn) n catamarán m.

catapult ('kætəpʌlt) n catapulta, honda f.

cataract ('kætərækt) n catarata f.

catarrh (kə'ta:) n catarro m.

catastrophe (kə'tæstrəfi) n catástrofe f. **catastrophic** adj catastrófico.

catch¹ (kætʃ) vt 1 coger, agarrar, atrapar. 2 prender. **catch on** 1 prender. 2 inf caer en la cuenta. **catch out** inf pillar. ~n 1 cogida f. 2 presa, pesca f. 3 pestillo m. 4 trampa f.

catechism ('kætikizəm) n catecismo m. **catechize** vt catequizar.

category ('kætigəri) n categoría f. **categorical** adj categórico. **categorize** vt categorizar.

cater ('keitə) vi 1 proveer. 2 abastecer. **caterer** n 1 proveedor m. 2 hostelero m. **catering** n abastecimiento m.

caterpillar ('kætəpilə) n oruga f.

cathedral (kə'θi:drəl) n catedral f.

cathode ('kæθoud) n cátodo m. **cathode ray** n rayo catódico m.

catholic ('kæθlik) n católico m. adj 1 católico. 2 universal. 3 ortodoxo. **catholicism** n catolicismo m. **catholicity** n catolicidad f.

cattle ('kætl) n ganado m.

caught (kɔ:t) v see **catch**.

cauliflower ('kɔliflauə) n coliflor f.

cause (kɔ:z) n 1 causa f. vt causar. **causal** adj causal. **causality** n causalidad f. **causeless** adj infundado, sin causa.

causeway ('kɔ:zwei) n 1 arrecife m. 2 terraplén m. 3 acera f.

caustic ('kɔ:stik) adj cáustico.

caution n 1 cautela f. 2 advertencia, amonestación f. *vt* advertir, amonestar. **cautionary** *adj* amonestador. **cautious** *adj* cauteloso, precavido.

cavalry ('kævlri) *n* caballería f.

cave (keiv) *n* cueva, caverna f.

caviar ('kævia:) *n* caviar m.

cavity ('kæviti) *n* cavidad f.

cayenne (kei'en) *n* pimentón m.

cease (si:s) *vt,vi* cesar. **cease-fire** *n* cese de hostilidades m. tregua f.

cedar ('si:də) *n* cedro m.

cedilla (si'dilə) *n* cedilla f.

ceiling ('si:liŋ) *n* 1 techo m. 2 límite m. tope f.

celebrate ('seləbreit) *vt,vi* celebrar, festejar. **celebrated** *adj* célebre, celebrado. **celebration** *n* celebración f.

celebrity (si'lebriti) *n* celebridad f.

celery ('seləri) *n* apio m.

celestial (si'lestiəl) *adj* celestial.

celibate ('selibət) *n,adj* célibe. **celibacy** *n* celibato m.

cell (sel) *n* 1 celda f. 2 *med* célula f. 3 celdilla f.

cellar ('selə) *n* 1 sótano m. 2 bodega f.

cello ('tʃelou) *n* violoncelo m. **cellist** *n* violoncelista m,f.

Cellophane ('seləfein) *n Tdmk* celofán m.

Celt (kelt) *n* celta m,f. **Celtic** *adj* céltico, celta. **Celtic** (language) *n* céltico m.

cement (si'ment) *n* cemento m. *vt* cimentar.

cemetery ('semətri) *n* cementerio m.

censor ('sensə) *n* censor m. *vt* censurar. **censorious** *adj* hipercrítico, criticón. **censorship** *n* censura f.

censure ('senʃə) *n* censura f. *vt* censurar. **censurable** *adj* censurable.

census ('sensəs) *n* censo m.

cent (sent) *n* centavo m.

centenary (sen'ti:nəri) *n* centenario m. **centenarian** *n,adj* centenario m. **centennial** *adj* centenario.

centigrade ('sentigreid) *adj* centígrado.

centimetre ('sentimi:tə) *n* centímetro m.

centipede ('sentipi:d) *n* ciempiés m invar.

centre ('sentə) *n* centro m. **centre-forward** *n* delantero centro m. **centre-half** *n* medio centro m. ~*vi* centrar. **central** *adj* central. **central heating** *n* calefacción central f. **centralize** *vi,vt* centralizar. **centralization** *n* centralización f.

century ('sentʃəri) *n* siglo m.

ceramic (si'ræmik) *adj* cerámico. **ceramics** *n pl* cerámica f.

cereal ('siəriəl) *n,adj* cereal m.

ceremony ('serəməni) *n* ceremonia f. **ceremonial** *n,adj* ceremonial m. **ceremonious** *adj* ceremonioso.

certain ('sə:tn) *adj* cierto. **make certain** asegurarse, cerciorarse. **certainty** *n* certeza f.

certify ('sə:tifai) *vt* 1 certificar. 2 garantizar. **certificate** *n* 1 certificado, título m. 2 partida f.

chaffinch ('tʃæfintʃ) *n* pinzón m.

chain (tʃein) *n* cadena f. *vt* encadenar.

chair (tʃɛə) *n* 1 silla f. 2 cátedra f. 3 presidencia f. *vt* presidir. **chairman** *n* presidente m.

chalet ('ʃælei) *n* chalet m.

chalk (tʃɔ:k) *n* 1 yeso m. 2 tiza f. 3 creta f. *vt* 1 marcar con tiza. 2 apuntar. **chalky** *adj* 1 yesoso. 2 cretáceo.

challenge ('tʃæləndʒ) *n* 1 desafío, reto m. 2 *law* recusación f. *vt* desafiar, retar. **challenger** *n* desafiador, retador m.

chamber ('tʃeimbə) *n* 1 cámara f. 2 recámara f. **chambermaid** *n* doncella, camarera f. **chamber music** *n* música de cámara f.

chamberlain ('tʃeimbəlin) *n* chambelán m.

chameleon (kə'mi:liən) *n* camaleón m.

chamois ('ʃæmwa:) *n invar* gamuza f.

champagne (ʃæm'pein) *n* champaña m.

champion ('tʃæmpiən) *n* 1 campeón m. 2 paladín m. *vt* 1 defender. 2 abogar. **championship** *n* campeonato m.

chance (tʃɑ:ns) *n* 1 casualidad, suerte f. azar m. 2 ocasión, oportunidad f. 3 posibilidad f. 4 riesgo m. *adj* casual, fortuito. *vi* acaecer. **chance upon** tropezarse con.

chancellor ('tʃɑ:nsələ) *n* canciller m. **chancellery** *n* cancillería f.

chandelier (ʃændə'liə) *n* araña f.

change (tʃeindʒ) *n* 1 cambio m. 2 muda f. 3 vuelta f. **for a change** por cambiar. ~*vt,vi* 1 cambiar, mudar. 2 hacer transbordo. **changeable** *adj* cambiable, cambiante, inestable.

channel ('tʃænl) *n* 1 canal m. 2 vía f. cauce m. *vt* 1 acanalar. 2 encauzar.

Channel Islands *n pl* Islas Normandas f pl.

chant (tʃɑ:nt) *n* cantilena f. canto m. *vt,vi* entonar.

chaos ('keiɔs) *n* caos m. **chaotic** *adj* caótico.

chap¹ (tʃæp) *vt,vi* agrietar. *n* grieta f.

chap² (tʃæp) *n inf* tipo, sujeto m.

chapel ('tʃæpəl) *n* 1 capilla f. 2 templo m.

chaperon ('ʃæpəroun) *n* 1 acompañanta f. 2 *inf* carabina f. *vt* acompañar.

chaplain ('tʃæplin) *n* capellán m.

169

chapter ('tʃæptə) n 1 capítulo m. 2 rel cabildo m.

char ¹ (tʃɑ:) vt,vi carbonizar.

char ² (tʃɑ:) n inf asistenta, mujer de la limpieza f.

character ('kærɪktə) n 1 carácter m. 2 personaje m. **in character** conforme al tipo. **characterize** vt caracterizar. **characterization** n caracterización f. **characteristic** adj característico.

charcoal ('tʃɑːkoul) n 1 carbón de leña m. 2 carboncillo m.

charge (tʃɑːdʒ) n 1 carga f. 2 cargo m. 3 precio, coste m. **in charge of** encargado de. **take charge of** hacerse cargo de. ~vt 1 cargar. 2 mandar, encomendar. 3 law acusar.

chariot ('tʃærɪət) n carro de combate m.

charisma (kə'rɪzmə) n carisma m.

charity ('tʃærɪti) n 1 caridad f. 2 obra benéfica f. **charitable** adj 1 caritativo. 2 benéfico.

charm (tʃɑːm) n 1 encanto hechizo m. 2 amuleto m. vt encantar, hechizar. **charming** adj encantador.

chart (tʃɑːt) n 1 tabla f. 2 gráfico m. 3 naut carta de navegar f. vt 1 tabular. 2 trazar.

charter (tʃɑːtə) n 1 law carta f. 2 comm flete m. vt 1 estatuir. 2 fletar. 3 alquilar.

chase (tʃeis) vt perseguir, dar caza. n persecución, caza f.

chasm ('kæzəm) n abismo m. sima f.

chassis ('ʃæsi) n invar chasis m. armazón f.

chaste (tʃeist) adj casto, honesto **chastity** n castidad f.

chasten ('tʃeisən) vt 1 corregir. 2 castigar. 3 depurar.

chastise (tʃæ'staiz) vt castigar.

chat (tʃæt) vi charlar. n charla f. **chatty** adj hablador.

chatter ('tʃætə) vi 1 chacharear. 2 refrenar. 3 castañetear. n 1 cháchara f. parloteo m. 2 castañeteo m. **chatterbox** n inf charlatán m.

chauffeur ('ʃoufə) n chófer m.

chauvinism n ('ʃouvinizəm) n chauvinismo m. **chauvinist** n,adj chauvinista m,f.

cheap (tʃiːp) adj 1 barato. 2 de mal gusto. 3 de pacotilla. **cheapen** vt abaratar.

cheat (tʃiːt) vi hacer trampa. vt engañar, estafar. n 1 trampa f. 2 tramposo m.

check (tʃek) vt 1 parar, impedir. 2 refrenar. 3 comprobar. 4 controlar. n 1 parada, súbita f. 2 impedimento m. restricción f. 3 comprobación f. 4 control m. inspección f. **checkpoint** n control m. **check-up** n 1 revisión f. 2 med reconocimiento general m.

checkmate ('ʃekmeit) n jaque mate. vt dar el mate.

cheek (tʃiːk) 1 mejilla f. carrillo m. 2 inf desfachatez f. **cheekbone** n pómulo m. **cheeky** adj descarado, fresco.

cheer (tʃiə) n regocijo, buen humor m. vt 1 alegrar. 2 vitorear. **cheerful** adj alegre, animado, jovial. **cheerfulness** n alegría, jovialidad f. **cheerio** interj inf ¡hasta luego!

cheese (tʃiːz) n queso m. **cheesecake** n pastel de queso m.

cheetah ('tʃiːtə) n leopardo indio m.

chef (ʃef) n jefe de cocina m.

chemical ('kemikəl) adj químico. n sustania química f.

chemist ('kemist) n 1 químico m. 2 farmacéutico m. **chemist's shop** n farmacia f.

chemistry (kemistri) n química f.

cheque (tʃek) n cheque m. **chequebook** n talonario de cheques m. **cheque card** n tarjeta de crédito f.

cherish ('tʃeriʃ) vt 1 querer, apreciar. 2 cuidar. 3 mimar.

cherry ('tʃeri) n cereza f.

cherub ('tʃerəb) n querubín m.

chess (tʃes) n ajedrez m. **chess-board** n tablero de ajedrez m. **chessman** n pieza de ajedrez f. **chess set** n juego de ajedrez m.

chest (tʃest) n 1 anat pecho m. 2 arca f. cofre m. **chest of drawers** n cómoda f.

chestnut ('tʃesnʌt) n castaña f. **chestnut tree** n castaño m.

chew (tʃuː) vt,vi mascar, masticar. **chewing gum** n chicle m.

chick (tʃik) n pollito, polluelo m.

chickpea ('ʃikpiː) n garbanzo m.

chicken ('tʃikən) n pollo m. polla, gallina f. **chicken pox** n varicela f.

chicory ('tʃikəri) n achicoria f.

chief (tʃiːf) adj principal, primero. n jefe m. **chieftain** n jefe, cacique m.

chilblain ('tʃilblein) n sabañón m.

child (tʃaild) n, pl **children** 1 niño m. 2 hijo m. **with child** encinta. **childbirth** n parto m. **childhood** n niñez, infancia f. **childish** adj infantil, pueril. **childlike** adj aniñado.

Chile ('tʃili) n Chile m. **Chilean** n,adj chileno m.

chill (tʃil) vt,vi 1 enfriar. 2 helar. 3 congelar. n 1 escalofrío m. 2 resfriado m. **chilly** adj 1 frío. 2 desapacibile. 3 friolero.

chilli ('tʃili) n chile m.

chime (tʃaim) vi repicar, sonar. n **1** carillón m. **2** repique m.

chimney ('tʃimni) n chimenea f. **chimney-sweep** n limpiachimeneas m invar.

chimpanzee (tʃimpæn'zi:) n chimpancé m.

chin (tʃin) n barbilla f. mentón m. **double chin** papada f.

china ('tʃainə) n **1** porcelana f. **2** loza f.

China ('tʃainə) n China f. **Chinese** n,adj chino m. **Chinese** (language) n chino m.

chink[1] (tʃiŋk) n grieta f. resquicio m.

chink[2] (tʃiŋk) n tintineo m. vi,vt tintinear.

chip (tʃip) n **1** astilla f. **2** lasca f. **3** ficha f. **chips** n pl patatas fritas f pl. ~vt **1** astillar. **2** cincelar. **chip in** inf interrumpir, cortar.

chiropody (ki'rɔpədi) n pedicura f. **chiropodist** n pedicuro m.

chirp (tʃə:p) vi,vt gorjear, piar. n gorjeo, pío m. **chirpy** adj inf alegre.

chisel ('tʃizəl) n cincel m. vt cincelar.

chivalry ('ʃivəlri) n **1** caballería f. **2** caballerosidad f. **chivalrous** adj caballeroso.

chives (tʃaivz) n pl cebollino m.

chlorine ('klɔ:ri:n) n cloro m.

chlorophyll ('klɔrəfil) n clorofila f.

chocolate ('tʃɔklit) n chocolate m.

choice (tʃɔis) n **1** elección f. **2** preferencia f. **3** surtido m. adj selecto, escogido.

choir (kwaiə) n coro m.

choke (tʃouk) vt,vi **1** estrangular, ahogar. **2** atascar. n **1** obturador m. **2** mot aire m.

cholera ('kɔlərə) n cólera m.

choose* (tʃu:z) vt,vi elegir, escoger, optar. **choosy** adj inf delicado, exigente.

chop (tʃɔp) **1** tajo m. **2** cul chuleta f. vt cortar, tajar. **chop off** tronchar. **chop up** trinchar.

chop[2] (tʃɔp) vi (of wind) vivrar. **choppy** adj (of the sea) agitado.

chopstick ('tʃɔpstik) n palillo chino m.

chord (kɔ:d) n **1** cuerda f. **2** mus acorde m.

chore (tʃɔ:) n tarea rutinaria f. **chores** n pl quehaceres domésticos m pl.

choreography (kɔri'ɔgrəfi) n coreografía f. **choreographer** n coreógrafo m.

chorus ('kɔ:rəs) n coro m. **choral** adj coral.

chose (tʃouz) v see **choose.**

chosen ('tʃouzən) v see **choose.**

Christ (kraist) n Cristo m.

christen ('krisən) vt bautizar. **christening** n **1** bautizo m. **2** bautismo m.

Christian ('kristʃən) adj,n cristiano m. **Christian name** n nombre de pila m. **Christianity** n cristiandad f. **christianize** vt cristianizar.

Christmas ('krisməs) n Navidad f. Navidades f pl. **Father Christmas** n Papá Noel m. ~adj navideño. **Christmas Eve** n Nochebuena f. **Christmas tree** n árbol de Navidad m.

chromatic (krə'mætik) adj cromático.

chrome (kroum) n cromo m.

chromium ('kroumiəm) n cromo m.

chromosome ('krouməsoum) n cromosoma m.

chronic ('krɔnik) adj crónico.

chronicle ('krɔnikəl) n crónica f. vt historiar.

chronology (krə'nɔlədʒi) n cronología f. **chronological** adj cronológico.

chrysalis ('krisəlis) n crisálida f.

chrysanthemum (kri'zænθiməm) n crisantemo m.

chubby ('tʃʌbi) adj **1** rollizo. **2** mofletudo.

chuck (tʃʌk) vt tirar, arrojar.

chuckle (tʃʌkəl) vi reirse entre dientes, soltar una risita. n risita f.

chunk (tʃʌŋk) n pedazo, trozo m. **chunky** adj grueso, rechoncho.

church (tʃə:tʃ) n iglesia f. **Church of England** Iglesia anglicana. **churchgoer** n fiel, devoto m. **churchyard** n cementerio, camposanto m.

churn (tʃə:n) n **1** mantequera f. **2** lechera f. vt batir.

chute (ʃu:t) n **1** salto de agua m. **2** rampa de caída f. vertedero m. **3** paracaídas m invar.

chutney ('tʃʌtni) n salsa picante f.

cicada (si'ka:də) n cigarra f.

cider ('saidə) n sidra f.

cigar (si'ga:) n puro m. **cigarette** n cigarrillo, pitillo m. **cigarette lighter** n mechero m.

cinder ('sində) n ceniza f.

cinecamera ('sinikæmrə) n cámara cinematográfica f.

cinema ('sinəmə) n cine m. **cinematographic** adj cinematográfico.

cinnamon ('sinəmən) n canela f.

circle ('sə:kəl) n círculo m. vt circundar, cercar. **circular** adj,n circular f. **circulate** vi circular. vt hacer circular, poner en circulación. **circulation** n circulación f.

circuit ('sə:kit) n circuito m. **circuitous** adj tortuoso, indirecto.

circumcise ('sə:kəmsaiz) vt circuncidar. **circumcision** n circuncisión f.

circumference (sə'kʌmfərəns) n circunferencia f.

circumflex ('sə:kəmfleks) n circunflejo m.

circumscribe ('sə:kəmskraib) vt circunscribir. **circumscription** n circunscripción f.

circumstance ('sə:kəmstæns) n circunstancia

171

f. **under no circumstances** de ninguna manera. **circumstantial** adj 1 circunstancial. 2 circunstanciado, detallado.

circus ('sɔ:kɔs) n 1 circo m. 2 plaza redonda, glorieta f.

cistern ('sistɔn) n 1 tanque, depósito m. 2 cisterna f.

cite (sait) vt 1 citar. 2 mil mencionar. **citation** n 1 citación. 2 mil mención f.

citizen ('sitizɔn) n ciudadano m. **citizenship** n ciudadanía f.

citrus ('sitrɔs) n cidro m. **citrus fruits** n pl agrios m pl.

city ('siti) n ciudad f. adj ciudadano, municipal.

civic ('sivik) adj cívico.

civil ('sivɔl) adj 1 civil. 2 cortés. **civil service** n cuerpo de funcionarios m. **civil servant** n funcionario m. **civil engineering** n ingeniería de caminos m. **civil war** n guerra civil f.

civilian (si'viliɔn) adj civil. n paisano m.

civilize ('sivilaiz) vt civilizar. **civilization** n civilización f.

claim (kleim) n 1 demanda f. 2 petición f. 3 pretensión f. 4 concesión f. vt 1 demandar. 2 reclamar. 3 pretender. **claimant** n 1 law demandante m,f. 2 pretendiente m,f.

clam (klæm) n almeja f.

clamber ('klæmbɔ) vi trepar.

clammy ('klæmi) adj húmedo, pegajoso.

clamour ('klæmɔ) n 1 clamor m. 2 clamoreo m. vi 1 clamar. 2 clamorear, vociferar.

clamp (klæmp) n 1 abrazadera f. 2 tornillo de banco m. 3 montón, amontonamiento m. vt afianzar, sujetar, apretar los tornillos.

clan (klæn) n clan m.

clandestine (klæn'destin) adj clandestine.

clang (klæŋ) n estrépito, estruendo m. vi sonar estrepitosamente. **clanger** n inf plancha f.

clank (klæŋk) n golpeteo metálico m. vi golpetear, resonar.

clap (klæp) n 1 palmada f. 2 palmoteo, aplauso m. vi 1 aplaudir. 2 dar palamadas, batir palmas. **clapper** n badajo m.

claret ('klærɔt) n clarete m.

clarify ('klærifai) vt aclarar. **clarification** n aclaración f. **clarity** n claridad f.

clarinet ('klæri'net) n clarinete m.

clash (klæʃ) n 1 choque, encuentro m. 2 estruendo, fragor m. 3 conflicto m. incompatibilidad f. vi 1 chocar. 2 pelear.

clasp (klɑ:sp) n 1 cierre m. 2 corchete m. 3 apretón m. vt abrochar.

class (klɑ:s) n clase f. vt clasificar. **classify** vt

clasificar. **classification** n clasificación f. **classy** adj inf elegante.

classroom ('klɑ:srum) n aula, clase f.

classic ('klæsik) adj,n clásico m. **classical** adj clásico. **classics** n pl clásicas f pl.

clatter ('klætɔ) n 1 estruendo m. 2 repiqueto m. vi repiquetear, martillear.

clause (klɔ:z) n cláusula f.

claustrophobia (klɔstrɔ'foubiɔ) n claustrofobia f.

claw (klɔ:) n 1 garra f. 2 pinza f. 3 tech garfio, gancho m. vt,vi arañar, desgarrar.

clay (klei) n arcilla f. barro m.

clean (kli:n) adj 1 limpio. 2 nítido, definido. vt limpiar, asear. **cleanliness** n 1 limpieza f. aseo m. 2 esmero m.

cleanse (klenz) vt limpiar, purificar.

clear (kliɔ) adj 1 claro. 2 despejado. 3 evidente. adv claramente, perfectamente. vt,vi 1 aclarar. 2 despejar. 3 law absolver. **clearance** n 1 claro m. 2 acreditación f. 3 tech espacio muerto m. **clearance sale** n liquidación f.

clef (klef) n clave f.

clench (klentʃ) vt apretar, cerrar.

clergy ('klɔ:dʒi) n clero m. **clergyman** n clérigo m.

clerical ('klerikɔl) adj 1 de oficina. 2 clerical. **clerical error** n error de copia m.

clerk (klɑ:k) n 1 empleado, secretario m. oficinista m,f. 2 law escribano m.

clever ('klevɔ) adj 1 listo, inteligente. 2 hábil, diestro. 3 ingenioso. **cleverness** n 1 habilidad f. 2 ingenio m.

cliché ('kliʃei) n cliché m. frase hecha f.

click (klik) n 1 taconeo m. 2 chasquido m. vi,vt 1 taconear. 2 chasquear.

client ('klaiɔnt) n cliente m,f.

cliff (klif) n 1 acantilado m. 2 risco m.

climate ('klaimit) n 1 clima m. 2 ambiente m. **climatic** adj climático.

climax ('klaimæks) n 1 punto culminante, colmo m. 2 apogeo m. 3 climax m.

climb (klaim) vt,vi 1 subir. 2 trepar. 3 escalar. n subida, escalada f. ascenso m. **climber** n escalador m. alpinista m,f.

cling* (kliŋ) vi 1 adherirse, pegarse, agarrarse. 2 abrazarse. **clinging** adj 1 ceñido. 2 pegajoso.

clinic ('klinik) n clínica f. **clinical** adj clínico.

clip¹ (klip) vt 1 cortar. 2 trasquilar. 3 abreviar. n 1 tijeretada f. 2 esquileo m.

clip² (klip) n 1 grapa f. 2 sujetapapeles m invar. vt sujetar, prender.

clitoris ('klitɔris) n clítoris m.

cloak (klouk) n capa f. manto m. vt **1** encapotar. **2** encubrir. **cloakroom** n **1** guardarropa m. **2** lavabos m pl.

clock (klɔk) n reloj m. **alarm clock** n despertador m. ~vt registrar. **clocktower** n campanario m. **clockwise** en la dirección de las agujas del reloj. **clockwork** n aparato de relojería m.

clog (klɔg) n **1** zueco m. **2** traba f. vt **1** atascar. **2** estorbar.

cloister ('klɔistə) n claustro m. vt enclaustrar.

close vt,vi (klouz) **1** cerrar. **2** terminar. n **1** (klouz) final m. conclusión f. **2** (klous) cercado m. adj (klous) **1** cercano, próximo. **2** tupido. **3** detallado, exacto. **4** sofocante. adv (klous) cerca. **close-up** n primer plano m.

closet ('klɔzit) n **1** wáter, lavabo m. **2** armario m.

clot (klɔt) n **1** grumo m. **2** coágulo, cuajarón m. **3** med embolia f. vi cuajarse, coagularse.

cloth (klɔθ) n **1** tela f. paño m. **2** trapo m. **table-cloth** n mantel m.

clothe (klouð) vt **1** vestir. **2** cubrir, revestir. **clothes** n pl ropa f. vestidos m pl. **clothes brush** n cepillo para la ropa m. **clothes line** n cuerda para tender la repa f. **clothes peg** n pinza f.

cloud (klaud) n nube f. nubarrón m. vt,vi nublar. **cloudburst** n chaparrón m. **cloudless** adj sin nubes. **cloudy** adj **1** nebuloso. **2** turbio.

clove (klouv) n clavo de especia m.

clover ('klouvə) n trébol m.

clown (klaun) n payaso m. vi hacer el payaso.

club (klʌb) n **1** porra f. **2** sport palo m. **3** club m. vt aporrear. **club together** asociarse.

clue (klu:) n pista f. indicio m.

clump (klʌmp) n **1** arboleda f. matorral m. **2** grupo m. vi andar pesadamente.

clumsy ('klʌmzi) adj **1** torpe, desmañado. **2** chapucero. **clumsiness** n torpeza, desmaña f.

clung (klʌŋ) v see **cling.**

cluster ('klʌstə) n **1** grupo m. **2** racimo m. vi agruparse, arracimarse.

clutch (klʌtʃ) n **1** apretón m. **2** mot embrague m. **3** midada. vt agarrar(se), apretar.

clutter ('klʌtə) n desorden m. confusión f. vt llenar desordenadamente, atestar.

coach (koutʃ) n **1** coche m. diligencia, carroza f. **2** sport entrenador m. **3** educ instructor, profesor particular m. vt entrenar, enseñar.

coagulate (kou'ægjuleit) vt coagular.

coal (koul) n carbón m. hulla f. **live coal** n brasa f. **coalfield** n yacimiento de carbón m. **coalmine** n mina de carbón f.

coalition (kouə'liʃən) n coalición f.

coarse (kɔ:s) adj basto, tosco, grosero. **coarseness** n tosquedad, grosería f.

coast (koust) n costa f. litoral m. vi costear. **coastguard** n guardacostas m invar. **coastline** n litoral m.

coat (kout) n **1** chaqueta f. abrigo m. **2** pelo m. lana f. vt cubrir. **coat-hanger** n percha f.

coax (kouks) vt engatusar.

cobble ('kɔbəl) n guijarro m. vt **1** empedrar. **2** remendar.

cobbler ('kɔblə) n zapatero m.

cobra ('koubrə) n cobra f.

cobweb ('kɔbweb) n telaraña f.

cock[1] (kɔk) n 'gallo, macho de ave m. **cocky** adj engreído.

cock[2] (kɔk) vt **1** amartillar. **2** aguzar.

cockle ('kɔkəl) n zool berberecho m.

cockpit ('kɔkpit) n **1** aviat cabina f. **2** reñidero de gallos m.

cockroach ('kɔkroutʃ) n cucaracha f.

cocktail ('kɔkteil) n cóctel m.

cocoa ('koukou) n **1** cacao m. **2** chocolate m.

coconut ('koukənʌt) n coco m.

cocoon (kə'ku:n) n capullo m.

cod (kɔd) n bacalao m.

code (koud) n **1** law código m. **2** cifra f. vt cifrar. **highway code** código de la circulación m.

codeine ('koudi:n) n codeína f.

coeducation (kouedju'keiʃən) n coeducación f.

coerce vt forzar, obligar. **coercion** n coerción f.

coexist (kouig'zist) vi coexistir. **coexistence** n coexistencia f.

coffee ('kɔfi) n café m. **black coffee** café solo. **white coffee** café con leche. **coffee bar** n cafetería f. **coffee bean** n grano de café m. **coffee pot** n cafetera f. **coffee table** n mesita de café f.

coffin ('kɔfin) n ataúd m.

cog (kɔg) n diente m. rueda dentada f.

cognac ('kɔnjæk) n coñac m.

cohabit (kou'hæbit) vi cohabitar. **cohabitation** n cohabitación f.

cohere (kou'hiə) vi adherirse, pegarse, enlazarse. **coherent** adj coherente, lógico. **coherence** n coherencia f.

coil (kɔil) n **1** rollo m. **2** tech carrete m. vt arrollar, enrollar.

coin (kɔin) n moneda f. vt acuñar. **coinage** n acuñación f.

coincide (kouin'said) vi coincidir, estar de acuerdo. **coincidence** n coincidencia, casualidad f.

colander ('kʌləndə) n escurridor m.

cold (kould) adj,n frío m. **cold-blooded** adj 1 zool de sangre fría. 2 insensible.

collaborate (kə'læbəreit) vi colaborar. **collaboration** n colaboración f. **collaborator** n colaborador m.

collapse (kə'læps) n 1 colapso m. 2 hundimiento m. vi sufrir colapso.

collar ('kɔlə) n 1 cuello m. 2 zool collar m. vt prender por el cuello. **collarbone** n clavicula f.

colleague ('kɔli:g) n colega m.

collect (kə'lekt) vt reunir, acumular, cobrar, coleccionar. vi reunirse, congregarse. **collection** n 1 colección f. 2 montón m. 3 recaudación f. **collective** adj colectivo. **collector** n coleccionador m.

college ('kɔlidʒ) n 1 colegio m. 2 escuela f. **collegiate** adj colegial, colegiado.

collide (kə'laid) vi chocar. **collision** n choque m. colisión f.

colloquial (kə'loukwiəl) adj familiar, popular. **colloquialism** n expresión familiar m.

Cologne (kə'loun) n Colonia f.

Colombia (kə'lʌmbiə) n Colombia f. **Colombian** adj,n colombiano.

colon ('koulən) n 1 dos puntos m pl. 2 anat colon m.

colonel ('kə:nl) n coronel m.

colony ('kɔləni) n colonia f. **colonial** adj colonial. n colono m. **colonist** n colonizador, colono m. **colonize** vt colonizar. **colonization** n colonización f.

colossal (kə'lɔsəl) adj colosal.

colour ('kʌlə) n color m. **be off colour** estar indispuesto. **colour-bar** n barrera racial f. **colour-blind** adj daltoniano. **colour-blindness** n daltonismo m. **colour film** n película en colores f. **colourful** adj lleno de color. ~v colorear, colorar. vi sonrojarse.

colt (koult) n potro m.

column ('kɔləm) n columna f. **columnist** n periodista, columnista m,f.

coma ('koumə) n coma m.

comb (koum) n peine m. vt peinar.

combat ('kɔmbæt) n combate m. vt combatir, luchar contra. **combatant** n combatiente m.

combine (n 'kɔmbain; v kəm'bain) n monopolio m. vt combinar. ~reunir.

combustion (kəm'bʌstʃən) n combustión f.

come* (kʌm) vi venir. **come across** encontrar, dar con. **come along!** ¡vamos! **come back** volver. **come in** entrar. **comeback** n restablecimiento m. **come off 1** desprenderse. 2 tener lugar. 3 tener éxito.

comedy ('kɔmədi) n comedia f. **musical comedy** 1 opereta f. 2 zarzuela f. **comedian** n cómico m. **comedienne** n cómica f. **comic** adj cómico, divertido, entretenido. n tebeo m. **comical** adj cómico.

comet ('kɔmit) n cometa m.

comfort ('kʌmfət) n consuelo, alivio, confort m. comodidad f. bienestar m. vt consolar, aliviar. **comfortable** adj cómodo, confortable. **comforting** adj consolador.

comma ('kɔmə) n coma f. **inverted commas** comillas f pl.

command (kə'ma:nd) n orden f. mandato, mando m. **be in command** estar al mando. vt mandar, ordenar. **commandant** n comandante m. **commanding** adj imponente, dominante. **commandment** n mandamiento m.

commemorate (kə'neməreit) vt conmemorar. **commemoration** n conmemoración f. **commemorative** adj conmemorativo.

commence (kə'mens) vt comenzar, empezar. **commencement** n comienzo m.

commend (kə'mend) vt encomendar, recomendar, alabar, elogiar. **commendable** adj recomendable. **commendation** n alabanza f. encomio m.

comment ('kɔment) n comentario m. vi comentar, observar. **commentary** n comentario m. **commentator** n comentador m.

commerce ('kɔmə:s) n comercio m. **commercial** adj 1 comercial. 2 mercantil. n emisión publicitaria f. **commercial traveller** n agente comercial, viajante m. **commercialism** n mercantilismo m. **commercialize** vt comercializar.

commission (kə'miʃən) n 1 comisión. 2 mil graduación f. vt nombrar, comisionar. **commissioner** n comisario m.

commit (kə'mit) vt cometer, hacer, entregar. **commitment** n obligación f.

committee (kə'miti) n comité m. comisión f.

commodity (kə'mɔditi) n mercancía f. artículo m.

common ('kɔmən) adj 1 común. 2 público. 3 frecuente. 4 ordinario. n campo común, ejido m. **commoner** n plebeyo m. **commonly** adv generalmente. **Common Market** n Mercado

Común m. **commonplace** adj común, trivial. n cosa común f. **commonsense** adj racional, lógico. n sentido común m. **commonwealth** n república f.

commotion (kə'mouʃən) n tumulto m.

commune[1] (kə'mju:n) vi 1 conversar. 2 meditar. 3 comulgar. **communion** n comunión f.

commune[2] ('kɔmju:n) n comuna f. **communal** adj comunal.

communicant (kə'mju:nikənt) n comulgante m,f.

communicate (kə'mju:nikeit) vt comunicar. **communication** n comunicación f. **communicative** adj comunicativo.

communism ('kɔmjunizəm) n comunismo m. **communist** n comunista m,f.

community (kə'mju:niti) n comunidad, sociedad f. **community centre** n centro social m.

commute (kə'mju:t) vt conmutar. vi viajar a diario.

compact[1] (kəm'pækt) adj compacto, conciso. vt comprimir.

compact[2] ('kɔmpækt) n 1 pacto, convenio m. 2 polvera f.

companion (kəm'pæniən) n compañero m. **companionable** adj sociable. **companionship** n compañerismo m.

company ('kʌmpəni) n 1 compañía f. 2 sociedad, empresa f.

compare (kəm'pɛə) vt comparar. **comparable** adj comparable. **comparative** adj 1 relativo. 2 gram comparativo. **comparison** n comparación f.

compartment (kəm'pɑ:tmənt) n compartimiento, departamento m.

compass ('kʌmpəs) n 1 brújula f. 2 alcance m. vt rodear.

compassion (kəm'pæʃən) n compasión f. **compassionate** adj compasivo.

compatible (kəm'pætibəl) adj compatible. **compatibility** n compatibilidad f.

compel (kəm'pel) vt 1 obligar. 2 imponer.

compensate ('kɔmpənseit) vt 1 compensar. 2 indemnizar. **compensation** n 1 compensación f. 2 indemnización f. 3 recompensa f.

compete (kəm'pi:t) vi competir. **competition** n 1 competencia f. 2 concurso m. **competitive** adj competidor, competitivo. **competitor** n 1 competidor m. 2 opositor m.

competent ('kɔmpitənt) adj competente, capaz, hábil. **competence** n competencia, capacidad f.

compile (kəm'pail) vt compilar, recopilar. **compilation** n compilación f.

complacent (kəm'pleisənt) adj complaciente. **complacence** also **complacency** n satisfacción de sí mismo f.

complain (kəm'plein) vi quejarse. **complaint** n 1 queja f. 2 law querella, demanda f.

complement ('kɔmplimənt) n complemento m. vt complementar. **complementary** adj complementario.

complete (kəm'pli:t) adj completo, entero. vt completar, terminar. **completion** n cumplimiento m. terminación f.

complex ('kɔmpleks) adj complejo, complicado. n complejo m. **complexity** n complejidad f.

complexion (kəm'plekʃən) n 1 tez f. cutis m. 2 aspecto m.

complicate ('kɔmplikeit) vt complicar. **complicated** adj complicado. **complication** n complicación f.

compliment ('kɔmplimənt) n cumplido, piropo m. **compliments** n pl saludos m pl. ~vt felicitar. **complimentary** adj 1 lisonjero. 2 de regalo.

comply (kəm'plai) vi 1 obedecer. 2 conformarse.

component (kəm'pounənt) adj,n componente.

compose (kəm'pouz) vt componer. **be composed of** constar de, componerse de. **composer** n compositor m. **composition** n composición f. **composure** n serenidad, calma f.

composite ('kɔmpəzit) adj compuesto.

compound[1] (adj,n 'kɔmpaund; v kəm'paund) adj,n compuesto m. vt componer.

compound[2] ('kɔmpaund) n recinto m.

comprehend (kɔmpri'hend) vt comprender. **comprehensible** adj comprensible. **comprehension** n comprensión f. **comprehensive** adj extenso, comprensivo. **comprehensive school** n colegio integrado m.

compress (n 'kɔmpres; v kəm'pres) n compresa f. vt comprimir. **compression** n compresión f.

comprise (kəm'praiz) vt comprender, abarcar.

compromise ('kɔmprəmaiz) n compromiso, arreglo m. vt comprometer, arreglar. **compromising** adj comprometedor.

compulsion (kəm'pʌlʃən) n obligación, compulsión f. **compulsive** adj compulsivo. **compulsory** adj obligatorio.

compute (kəm'pju:t) vt computar, calcular. **computer** n computador m. calculadora f.

comrade ('kɔmrəd, -reid) n camarada, compañero m.

concave ('kɔŋkeiv) adj cóncavo. **concavity** n concavidad f.

conceal (kən'siːl) vt ocultar, disimular. **concealed** adj 1 oculto. 2 disimulado. **concealment** n encubrimiento m. disimulación f.

concede (kən'siːd) vt conceder.

conceit (kən'siːt) n presunción f. engreimiento m. **conceited** adj presumido, engreído.

conceive (kən'siːv) vi concebir. vt 1 imaginar. 2 concebir. **conceivable** adj concebible.

concentrate ('kɔnsəntreit) n concentrado m. vt concentrar. **concentration** n concentración f. **concentration camp** n campo de concentración m.

concentric (kən'sentrik) adj concéntrico.

concept ('kɔnsept) n concepto m. **conception** n 1 concepción f. 2 concepto m. idea f.

concern (kən'sɔːn) n 1 asunto, negocio m. 2 interés m. 3 preocupación f. 4 empresa f. vt interesar, concernir. **concerned** adj inquieto, preocupado. **concerning** prep sobre, a cerca de.

concert ('kɔnsət) n concierto m. **concert hall** n sala de conciertos f.

concertina (kɔnsə'tiːnə) n concertina f.

concerto (kən'tʃɛətou) n concierto m.

concession (kən'seʃən) n concesión f.

concise (kən'sais) adj conciso. **concision** n concisión f.

conclude (kən'kluːd) vt terminar, concluir. **concluding** adj final. **conclusion** n conclusión, terminación f. **conclusive** adj conclusivo.

concoct (kən'kɔkt) vt 1 confeccionar. 2 inventar. 3 tramar. **concoction** n 1 confección f. 2 trama f.

concrete ('kɔŋkriːt) adj 1 concreto. 2 tech de hormigón. n tech hormigón m.

concussion (kən'kʌʃən) n conmoción cerebral f.

condemn (kən'dem) vt 1 condenar. 2 censurar. **condemned** adj condenado. **condemnation** n condenación f. **condemnatory** adj condenador.

condense (kən'dens) vt 1 condensar. 2 abreviar. **condensation** n 1 condensación f. 2 compendio m. **condenser** n condensador m.

condescend (kɔndi'send) vi condescender, dignarse. **condescending** adj superior. **condescension** n aire de superioridad m.

condition (kən'diʃən) n 1 condición f. 2 estado m. vt condicionar, determinar. **conditional** adj condicional. **conditionally** adv con reservas.

condolence (kən'douləns) n pésame m.

condone (kən'doun) vt condonar.

conduct (n 'kɔndʌkt; v kən'dʌkt) n conducta f. comportamiento m. vt conducir, dirigir. vi mus llevar la batuta. **conduct oneself** comportarse. **conduction** n conducción f.

conductor (kən'dʌktə) n 1 mus director. 2 mot cobrador m. 3 (of lightning) pararrayos m invar.

cone (koun) n cono m.

confectioner (kən'fekʃənə) n confitero m.

confederate (adj,n kən'fedərət; v kən'fedəreit) adj, n confederado m. vt confederar. **confederacy** n confederación f.

confer (kən'fəː) vt conferir, conceder, otorgar. vi conferir, consultar. **conference** n conferencia f.

confess (kən'fes) vt confesar. **confession** n confesión f. **confessional** n confesionario m.

confetti (kən'feti) n confeti m.

confide (kən'faid) vt confiar. **confidence** n 1 confianza f. 2 confidencia f. **confidence man** n timador m. **confident** adj seguro de si mismo, lleno de confianza. **confidential** adj confidencial. **confidentially** adv en confianza.

confine (kən'fain) n confín, límite m. vt 1 encerrar. 2 limitar. **confined** adj reducido. **confinement** n 1 encierro m. 2 med parto m.

confirm (kən'fəːm) vt confirmar. **confirmation** n confirmación f. **confirmed** adj inveterado.

confiscate ('kɔnfiskeit) vt confiscar. **confiscation** n confiscación f.

conflict (v kən'flikt; n 'kɔnflikt) vi luchar. n conflicto m. **conflicting** adj contradictorio.

conform (kən'fɔːm) vi conformarse. **conformist** adj,n conformista m,f. **conformity** n conformidad f.

confound (kən'faund) vt confundir.

confront (kən'frʌnt) vt hacer frente a, confrontar. **confrontation** n confrontación f.

confuse (kən'fjuːz) vt 1 confundir. 2 desconcertar. **confused** adj confuso, perplejo. **confusing** adj confuso, desconcertante. **confusion** n confusión f.

congeal (kən'dʒiːl) vt congelar, coagular.

congenial (kən'dʒiːniəl) adj congenial, agradable.

congested (kən'dʒestid) adj 1 superpoblado. 2 med congestionado. **congestion** n congestión f.

Congo ('kɔŋgou) n el Congo m.

congratulate (kən'grætjuleit) vt felicitar. **congratulations** n pl felicitaciones f pl. interj ¡enhorabuena!

congregate ('kɔŋgrigeit) *vi* congregarse. **congregation** *n* 1 congregación f. 2 asamblea f. 3 (in church) los fieles *m pl*. **congregational** *adj* congregacionalista.

congress ('kɔŋgres) *n* congreso *m*.

conical ('kɔnikəl) *adj* cónico.

conifer ('kɔnifə) *n* conífera f. **coniferous** *adj* conífero.

conjugal ('kɔndʒugəl) *adj* conyugal.

conjugate ('kɔndʒugeit) *vt* conjugar. **conjugation** *n* conjugación f.

conjunction (kən'dʒʌŋkʃən) *n* conjunción f. **conjunctive** *adj* conjuntivo.

conjure ('kʌndʒə) *vt* conjurar. *vi* hacer juegos de manos. **conjurer** *n* ilusionista *m*. **conjuring trick** *n* juego de manos *m*.

connect (kə'nekt) *vt* 1 juntar, unir. 2 conectar, poner en comunicación. **connection** *n* 1 unión, comunicación f. 2 relación f.

connoisseur (kɔnə'səː) *n* entendido, experto *m*.

connotation (kɔnə'teiʃən) *n* connotación f.

conquer ('kɔŋkə) *vt* vencer. **conqueror** *n* conquistador, vencedor *m*. **conquest** *n* conquista f.

conscience ('kɔnʃəns) *n* conciencia f. **conscientious** *adj* concienzudo.

conscious ('kɔnʃəs) *adj* 1 consciente. 2 intencional. **be conscious** *med* tener conocimiento. **consciousness** *n* consciencia f.

conscript (kən'skript) *n* recluta *m*. *vt* reclutar. **conscription** *n* servicio militar obligatorio *m*.

consecrate ('kɔnsikreit) *vt* consagrar. **consecration** *n* consagración f.

consecutive (kən'sekjutiv) *adj* consecutivo.

consent (kən'sent) *n* consentimiento *m*. *vi* consentir.

consequence ('kɔnsikwəns) *n* consecuencia f. resultado *m*. **consequent** *adj* consiguiente.

conserve (kən'səːv) *n* conserva f. *vt* conservar. **conservation** *n* conservación f. **conservative** *adj,n pol* conservador. *adj* conservativo, moderado. **conservatory** *n* invernadero *m*.

consider (kən'sidə) *vt* considerar, tomar en cuenta. **considerable** *adj* considerable. **consideration** *n* 1 consideración f. 2 retribución f. **considerate** *adj* considerado.

consign (kən'sain) *vt* 1 consignar. 2 enviar. **consignment** *n* consignación f.

consist (kən'sist) *vi* consistir, constar. **consistency** *n* consistencia f. **consistent** *adj* consecuente, lógico. **consistently** *adv* 1 sin excepción, constantemente. 2 consecuentemente.

console (kən'soul) *vt* consolar.

consolidate (kən'sɔlideit) *vt* consolidar.

consonant ('kɔnsənənt) *adj,n* consonante f.

conspicuous (kən'spikjuəs) *adj* visible, evidente.

conspire (kən'spaiə) *vi* conspirar. **conspiracy** *n* conspiración, conjuración f. **conspirator** *n* conspirador *m*.

constable ('kʌnstəbəl) *n* policía, guardia *m*. **constabulary** *n* policía f.

constant ('kɔnstənt) *adj,n* constante f.

constellation (kɔnstə'leiʃən) *n* constelación f.

constipation (kɔnsti'peiʃən) *n* estreñimiento *m*. **constipate** *vt* estreñir.

constitute ('kɔnstitjuːt) *vt* constituir. **constituency** *n* distrito electoral *m*. **constituent** *adj* constitutivo, integrante. *n* 1 constitutivo, componente *m*. 2 elector *m*. **constitution** *n* constitución f. **constitutional** *adj* constitucional. *n* paseo *m*.

constrain (kən'strein) *vt* constreñir, obligar. **constraint** *n* 1 encierro *m*. 2 fuerza f.

constrict (kən'strikt) *vt* estrechar, apretar.

construct (kən'strʌkt) *vt* construir. **construction** *n* 1 construcción f. 2 interpretación f. **constructive** *adj* constructivo. **constructor** *n* constructor *m*.

consul ('kɔnsəl) *n* cónsul *m*. **consular** *adj* consular. **consulate** *n* consulado *m*.

consult (kən'sʌlt) *vt* consultar. **consultation** *n* consulta, consultación f. **consultant** *n* 1 asesor *m*. 2 *med* especialista *m,f*.

consume (kən'sjuːm) *vt* consumir, utilizar. **consumer** *n* consumidor *m*. **consumption** *n* consumición f. 2 *med* tísis f.

contact ('kɔntækt) *n* contacto *m*. *vt* ponerse en contacto con. **contact lenses** *n pl* lentes de contacto, microlentillas f *pl*.

contagious (kən'teidʒəs) *adj* contagioso. **contagion** *n* contagio *m*.

contain (kən'tein) *vt* contener. **container** *n* 1 envase *m*. 2 caja f. 3 recipiente *m*.

contaminate (kən'tæmineit) *vt* contaminar. **contamination** *n* contaminación f.

contemplate ('kɔntəmpleit) *vt* 1 contemplar. 2 pensar. **contemplation** *n* contemplación f. **contemplative** *adj* contemplativo.

contemporary (kən'tempərəri) *adj,n* contemporáneo *m*.

contempt (kən'tempt) *n* desprecio, desdén *m*. **contemptible** *adj* despreciable, vil. **contemptuous** *adj* desdeñoso.

content[1] (ˈkɔntent) n contenido m. **contents** n pl contenido m.

content[2] (kənˈtent) adj contento, satisfecho. n contento m. satisfacción f. vt contentar, satis-·facer. **contentment** n contento m.

contest (n ˈkɔntest; v kənˈtest) n 1 contienda, lucha f. 2 concurso m. vt 1 impugnar, atacar. 2 defender. **contestant** n contendiente m,f.

context (ˈkɔntekst) n contexto m.

continent (ˈkɔntinənt) adj,n continente m. **the Continent** el continente europeo. **continental** adj continental.

contingency (kənˈtindʒənsi) n contingencia f.

continue (kənˈtinjuː) vt,vi continuar, seguir. **continual** adj continuo, incesante. **continually** adv constantemente. **continuation** n continuación f. **continuity** n continuidad f. **continuous** adj continuo.

contour (ˈkɔntuə) n contorno m.

contraband (ˈkɔntrəbænd) n contrabando m.

contraception (kɔntrəˈsepʃən) n anticoncepción m. **contraceptive** adj,n anticonceptivo m. **contraceptive pill** n píldora anticoncep-tiva f.

contract (n ˈkɔntrækt; v kənˈtrækt) n contrato m. vt contraer. **contraction** n contracción f. **contractor** n contratista m.

contradict (kɔntrəˈdikt) vt 1 contradecir. 2 desmentir. **contradiction** n contradicción f. **contradictory** adj contradictorio.

contralto (kənˈtræltou) n contralto m,f.

contraption (kənˈtræpʃən) n ingenio m.

contrary (ˈkɔntrəri) adj,n contrario m.

contrast (v kənˈtrɑːst; n ˈkɔntrɑːst) n contraste m. **in contrast** por contraste. **in contrast to** a diferencia de. ~vt poner en contraste, comparar. **contrasting** adj que hace con-traste.

contravene (kɔntrəˈviːn) vt contravenir. **contravention** n contravención f.

contribute (kənˈtribjuːt) vt,vi contribuir. **contribution** n contribución f. **contributor** n contribuyente m.

contrive (kənˈtraiv) vt inventar, idear. **contrived** adj artificial. **contrivance** n invención f.

control (kənˈtroul) n 1 mando m. 2 inspección f. vt 1 controlar, mandar. 2 dirigir. **controller** n inspector m. **controlling** adj predominante.

controversy (ˈkɔntrəvəsi, kənˈtrɔvəsi) n contro-versia f. **controversial** adj discutible.

convalesce (kɔnvəˈles) vi convalecer. **con-valescence** n convalecencia f.

convenience (kənˈviːniəns) n 1 conveniencia, comodidad f. 2 ventaja f. **convenient** adj 1 cómodo, práctico. 2 oportuno.

convent (ˈkɔnvənt) n convento m.

convention (kənˈvenʃən) n 1 convención f. 2 asamblea f. congreso m. **conventional** adj convencional.

converge (kənˈvəːdʒ) vi convergir. **conver-gence** n convergencia f. **converging** adj convergente.

converse (adj,n ˈkɔnvəːs; v kənˈvəːs) adj contra-rio, inverso. n math inversa f. vi conversar, hablar. **conversation** n conversación f. **con-versational** adj 1 familiar. 2 locuaz. **conver-sationalist** n conversador m.

convert (v kənˈvəːt; n ˈkɔnvəːt) vt convertir, transformar. n converso m,f. **conversely** adv a la inversa. **conversion** n conversión f. **con-version table** n tabla da conversión f.

convex (ˈkɔnveks) adj convexo.

convey (kənˈvei) vt 1 transportar, llevar. 2 comunicar. **conveyance** n 1 transporte m. 2 law escritura de traspaso f.

convict (v kənˈvikt; n ˈkɔnvikt) vt condenar. n presidiario m. **conviction** n 1 convicción f. creencia f. 2 law condena f.

convince (kənˈvins) vt convencer. **convincing** adj convincente.

convoy (ˈkɔnvɔi) n convoy m. vt convoyar.

cook (kuk) n cocinero m. vt,vi cocinar. **cooking** n cocina f. **cooker** n cocina f. **cookery** n arte de cocina m. **cookery book** n libro de cocina m.

cool (kuːl) adj 1 fresco. 2 tranquilo, impertur-bable. 4 frío, indiferente. n fresco m. vt enfriar, refrescar.

coop (kuːp) n gallinero m. **coop up** encerrar.

cooperate (kouˈɔpəreit) vi cooperar, colaborar. **cooperation** n cooperación f. **cooperative** adj cooperativo. **cooperative society** n co-operativa f.

coordinate (n kouˈɔːdnət; v kouˈɔːdineit) n math coordenada f. vt coordinar. **coordination** n coordinación f.

cope[1] (koup) vi arreglarse bien. **cope with** poder con.

cope[2] (koup) n rel capa pluvial f.

Copenhagen (koupənˈheigən) n Copenhague m.

copper[1] (ˈkɔpə) n min cobre m. **copper plate** plancha de cobre f. **coppery** adj cobrizo.

copper[2] (ˈkɔpə) n inf polizonte m.

coupon

copulate ('kɔpjuleit) vi copularse. **copulation** n cópula f.

copy ('kɔpi) n 1 copia f. 2 ejemplar m. **fair copy** n copia en limpio f. **rough copy** n borrador m. ~vt copiar, imitar. **copyright** n derecho de propiedad literaria m.

coral ('kɔrəl) n coral m. adj coralino, decoral.

cord (kɔːd) n 1 cuerda f. 2 med cordón m. 3 pana. vt encordelar.

cordial ('kɔːdiəl) adj cordial. n cordial m. **cordiality** n cordialidad f.

cordon ('kɔːdn) n cordón m. **cordon off** acordonar.

corduroy ('kɔːdərɔi) n pana f.

core (kɔː) n 1 centro, corazón m. 2 esencia f.

cork (kɔːk) n 1 corcho m. 2 tapón m. vt tapar con corcho. **corkscrew** n sacacorchos m invar.

corn[1] (kɔːn) n 1 trigo m. 2 maíz m. **corny** adj inf gastado, trillado. **cornflour** n harina de maíz f. **cornflower** n aciano m.

corn[2] (kɔːn) n med callo m.

corner ('kɔːnə) n 1 esquina f. 2 ángulo m. 3 rincón m. 4 curva f. 5 aprieto m. vt 1 arrinconar. 2 detener, cazar. 3 acaparar.

cornet ('kɔːnit) n mus corneta f.

coronary ('kɔrənəri) adj coronario. **coronary thrombosis** n trombósis coronaria f.

coronation (kɔrə'neiʃən) n coronación f.

corporal[1] ('kɔːprəl) adj corporal.

corporal[2] ('kɔːprəl) n cabo m.

corporation (kɔːpə'reiʃən) n 1 corporación f. 2 sociedad anónima f. **corporate** adj colectivo, corporativo.

corps (kɔː) n invar cuerpo m. **army corps** cuerpo de ejército. **diplomatic corps** cuerpo diplomático.

corpse (kɔːps) n cadáver m.

correct (kə'rekt) adj correcto, exacto, justo. vt corregir, rectificar. **correction** n corrección, rectificación f. **corrective** adj correctivo.

correlate ('kɔrəleit) vt correlacionar. vi tener correlación. **correlation** n correlación f.

correspond (kɔri'spɔnd) vi 1 corresponder. 2 escribirse. **correspondence** n correspondencia f. **correspondent** n 1 correspondiente m,f. 2 (of a newspaper) corresponsal m,f.

corridor ('kɔridɔː) n pasillo, corredor m.

corrode (kə'roud) vt corroer. **corrosion** n corrosión f.

corrupt (kə'rʌpt) adj corrompido. vt corromper. **corruption** n corrupción f.

corset ('kɔːsit) n faja f.

Corsica ('kɔːsikə) n Córcega f.

cosmetic (kɔz'metik) adj,n cosmético m.

cosmopolitan (kɔzmə'pɔlitən) adj, n cosmopolita m,f.

cosmos ('kɔzmɔs) n cosmos m. **cosmic** adj cósmico.

cost[1] (kɔst) n 1 precio m. 2 costo, coste m. costa f. **cost of living** costo de la vida m. **at all costs** a todo trance. ~vt calcular el coste de. vi costar, valer. **costly** adj costoso.

costume ('kɔstjuːm) n traje m.

cosy ('kouzi) adj 1 cómodo, agradable. 2 acogedor, amistoso.

cot (kɔt) n cuna, camita de niño f.

cottage ('kɔtidʒ) n casita de campo f. chalet m. **cottage cheese** n requesón m.

cotton ('kɔtn) n algodón m. **cottonwool** n algodón hidrófilo m.

couch (kautʃ) n sofá m. vt acostar.

cough (kɔf) n tos f. vi toser.

could (kud; unstressed kəd) v see **can**[1].

council ('kaunsəl) n 1 consejo m. junta f. 2 concilio m. 3 ayuntamiento m. **councillor** n concejal m.

counsel ('kaunsəl) n 1 consejo m. 2 law abogado m. vt aconsejar. **counsellor** n consejero m.

count[1] (kaunt) n cuenta f. cálculo m. vt contar, calcular. vi contar. **countdown** n cuenta hacia atrás f.

count[2] (kaunt) n conde m.

counter[1] ('kauntə) n 1 mostrador, contador m. 2 ficha f. **under the counter** sl por la trastienda.

counter[2] ('kauntə) adj contrario. vt contradecir, contrarrestar.

counterattack ('kauntərətæk) n contraataque m. vt contraatacar.

counterfeit ('kauntəfit) adj falso, falsificado. n falsificación f. vt falsificar.

counterfoil ('kauntəfɔil) n talón m.

counterpart ('kauntəpɑːt) n contraparte f.

countess ('kauntis) n condesa f.

country ('kʌntri) n 1 país m. 2 campo m. **countryman** n 1 campesino. 2 compatriota m. **countryside** n campo m.

county ('kaunti) n condado m. **county council** n diputación provincial f.

coup (kuː) n golpe m. **coup d'état** n golpe de estado m.

couple ('kʌpəl) n 1 par m. 2 pareja f. **married couple** n matrimonio m. ~vt juntar, unir.

coupon ('kuːpɔn) n cupón m.

179

courage (ˈkʌridʒ) n valor m. valentía f. **courageous** adj valiente.

courgette (kuəˈʒet) n calabacín m.

courier (ˈkuriə) n 1 estafeta f. 2 agente de turismo m,f.

course (kɔːs) n 1 curso m. dirección f. 2 naut rumbo m. 3 plato m. 4 pista f. campo m. **in due course** a su tiempo. **of course** por supuesto. ~vt cazar.

court (kɔːt) n 1 corte f. 2 tribunal m. 3 sport pista, cancha f. 4 patio m. vt cortejar. vi estar en relaciones, ser novios. **courtier** n cortesano m. **courtly** adj cortés, elegante. **court-martial** n consejo de guerra m. vt someter a un consejo de guerra. **courtship** n noviazgo m. **courtyard** n patio m.

courteous (ˈkɔːtiəs) adj cortés. **courtesy** n cortesía f.

cousin (ˈkʌzən) n primo m. **first cousin** n primo carnal m.

cove (kouv) n cala f.

covenant (ˈkʌvənənt) n pacto, convenio m.

cover (ˈkʌvə) n 1 cubierta, tapa f. 2 cubierto m. vt cubrir, tapar. **cover charge** n precio del cubierto m. **coverage** n alcance m.

cow (kau) n 1 vaca f. 2 hembra f. vt intimidar, acobardar. **cowboy** n vaquero m.

coward (ˈkauəd) n cobarde m.

cower (ˈkauə) vi agacharse, accurrucarse.

coy (kɔi) adj tímido, reservado.

crab (kræb) n cangrejo m. **crab apple** n manzana silvestre f. **crabbed** adj 1 amargado. 2 desapacible. 3 (of writing) indecifrable.

crack (kræk) n 1 grieta, hendedura f. 2 crujido m. 3 chasquido m. 4 chiste m. vt,vi chasquear, crujir.

cracker (ˈkrækə) n petardo m.

crackle (ˈkrækəl) n crujido m. crepitación f. vi crepitar, crujir. **crackling** n 1 crujido m. 2 cul chicharrón m.

cradle (ˈkreidl) n cuna f. vt mecer, acunar.

craft (krɑːft) n 1 oficio, empleo m. 2 destreza f. 3 astucia f. **craftsman** n artesano m. **craftsmanship** n artesanía f. **crafty** adj astuto, socarrón.

cram (kræm) vt 1 embutir, rellenar. 2 cebar. 3 educ inf empollar.

cramp[1] (kræmp) n med calambre m.

cramp[2] (kræmp) tech grapa f. vt engrapar, estorbar.

crane (krein) n 1 zool grulla f. 2 tech grúa f.

crash (kræʃ) n 1 estruendo, estrépito, estallido m. 2 accidente, choque m. 3 comm quiebra f.
vt estrellar. vi 1 caer con estrépito. 2 tener un accidente. 3 fracasar, quebrar. **crash-helmet** n casco protector m.

crate (kreit) n cajón de embalaje m.

crater (ˈkreitə) n cráter m.

crave (kreiv) vt 1 suplicar, implorar. 2 anhelar, ansiar. **craving** n ansia f.

crawl (krɔːl) n 1 arrastramiento m. vi 1 arrastrarse. 2 andar a gatas.

crayfish (ˈkreifiʃ) n ástaco, cangrejo de río m.

crayon (ˈkreiən) n lápiz de tiza m.

craze (kreiz) n 1 manía, locura f. 2 moda f. **crazed** adj enloquecido. **crazy** adj loco, chiflado.

creak (kriːk) n crujido, chirrido m. vi crujir, chirriar.

cream (kriːm) n 1 nata f. 2 crema f. vt 1 desnatar. **creamy** adj cremoso.

crease (kriːs) n 1 pliegue m. 2 arruga f. 3 raya f. vt 1 arrugar. 2 plegar. **crease-resistant** adj inarrugable.

create (kriˈeit) vt crear. **creation** n creación f. **creative** adj creador.

creature (ˈkriːtʃə) n criatura f.

creche (kreʃ) n 1 guardería infantil f. 2 rel belén m.

credentials (kriˈdenʃəlz) n pl credenciales f pl.

credible (ˈkredibəl) adj creíble. **credibility** n credibilidad f.

credit (ˈkredit) n crédito m. **on credit** a crédito. ~vt 1 creer. 2 acreditar. **creditable** adj estimable, honorable. **creditor** n acreedor m. **credit card** n tarjeta de crédito m.

creep* (kriːp) vi 1 arrastrarse. 2 ir cautelosamente. n inf pelotillero m. **creepy** adj horripilante.

cremate (kriˈmeit) vt incinerar. **cremation** n incineración f. **crematorium** n horno crematorio m.

creosote n creosota f.

crept (krept) v see **creep.**

crescent (ˈkresənt) adj creciente. n 1 media luna f. 2 calle en forma de semicírculo f.

cress (kres) n berro, mastuerzo m.

crest (krest) n 1 cresta f. 2 cima, cumbre f. **crested** adj crestado. **crestfallen** adj alicaído.

crevice (ˈkrevis) n grieta, hendedura f.

crew (kruː) n 1 tripulación f. 2 banda, pandilla f.

crib (krib) n 1 pesebre m. 2 educ inf chuleta f. vt plagiar.

cricket[1] (ˈkrikit) n zool grillo m.

cricket[2] (ˈkrikit) n criquet m.

crime (kraim) *n* crimen, delito *m*. **criminal** *adj,n* criminal *m*.

crimson ('krimzən) *adj,n* carmesí *m*.

cringe (krindʒ) *vi* agacharse, encogerse. **cringing** *adj* servil.

crinkle ('kriŋkəl) *n* arruga *f*. *vi* arrugarse.

cripple ('kripəl) *n* lisiado, mutilado *m*. *vt* lisiar, mutilar.

crisis ('kraisis) *n*, *pl* **crises** crisis *f*.

crisp (krisp) *adj* 1 crespo, rizado. 2 crujiente, tostado. **crisps** *n pl* patatas fritas a la inglesa *f pl*.

criterion (krai'tiəriən) *n*, *pl* **criteria** criterio *m*.

criticize ('kritisaiz) *vt* criticar. **critic** *n* crítico *m*. **critical** *adj* crítico. **criticism** *n* crítica *f*.

croak (krouk) *n* graznido *m*. *vi* 1 graznar. 2 croar. 3 gruñir.

crochet ('kroufei) *n* croché, labor de ganchillo *m*.

crockery ('krɔkəri) *n* loza, vajilla *f*.

crocodile ('krɔkədail) *n* cocodrilo *m*.

crocus ('kroukəs) *n bot* azafrán *m*.

crook (kruk) *n* 1 cayado *m*. 2 criminal, ladrón *m*. *vt* encorvar.

crooked ('krukid) *adj* 1 torcido, encorvado. 2 *inf* torcido, avieso.

crop (krɔp) *n* 1 cosecha *f*. cultivo *m*. 2 látigo *m*. *vt* cortar, recortar. **crop up** surgir.

croquet ('kroukei) *n* croquet *m*.

cross (krɔs) *n* cruz *f*. *vt* atravesar, cruzar. *adj* 1 cruzado. 2 malhumorado. 3 transversal, oblicuo. **cross-examination** *n law* repregunta, interrogación *f*. **cross-eyed** *adj* bizco. **crossfire** *n* fuego cruzado *m*. **crossing** *n* cruce *m*. travesía *f*. **level crossing** paso a nivel *m*. **crossroads** *n* cruce *m*. encrucijada *f*. **crossword puzzle** crucigrama *m*.

crotchet ('krɔtʃit) *n* 1 *mus* negra *f*. 2 capricho *m*. excentricidad *f*.

crouch (krautʃ) *vi* agacharse, encogerse.

crow[1] (krou) *n* cuervo *m*. corneja *f*. **as the crow flies** en línea recta.

crow[2] (krou) *n* canto, cacareo *m*. *vi* cantar, cacarear.

crowd (kraud) *n* multitud, muchedumbre *f*. gentío *m*. *vt* amontonar. *vi* congregarse. **crowded** *adj* lleno, atestado.

crown (kraun) *n* 1 corona *f*. 2 copa *f*. 3 cumbre *f*. *vt* coronar. **crowning** *adj* supremo.

crucial ('kru:ʃəl) *adj* decisivo, crítico.

crucify ('kru:sifai) *vt* crucificar. **crucifix** *n* crucifijo *m*.

crude (kru:d) *adj* 1 crudo. 2 tosco. 3 ordinario. **crude oil** *n* aceite crudo *m*.

cruel ('kruəl) *adj* cruel. **cruelty** *n* crueldad *f*.

cruise (kru:z) *n* crucero, viaje por mar *m*. *vi* cruzar, navegar. **cruiser** *n* crucero *m*.

crumb (krʌm) *n* migaja, miga *f*.

crumble ('krʌmbəl) *vt* desmenuzar, desmigajar. *vi* desmoronarse. **crumbly** *adj* desmenuzable.

crumple ('krʌmpəl) *vt* 1 ajar. 2 plegar.

crunch (krʌntʃ) *n* 1 crujido *m*. 2 *inf* punto decisivo *m*. *vt* ronzar, mascar. *vi* crujir. **crunchy** *adj* crujiente.

crusade (kru:'seid) *n* cruzada *f*. *vi* participar en una cruzada.

crush (krʌʃ) *n* 1 agolpamiento *m*. 2 aplastamiento *m*. *vt* 1 aplastar. 2 aniquilar, destruir. **crushing** *adj* aplastante.

crust (krʌst) *n* 1 corteza *f*. 2 mendrugo *m*.

crustacean (krʌs'teiʃən) *n* crustáceo *m*.

crutch (krʌtʃ) *n* muleta *f*.

cry (krai) *n* grito *m*. *vi* 1 gritar. 2 llorar. **crybaby** *n* llorón *m*.

crypt (kript) *n* cripta *f*.

crystal ('kristl) *adj* cristalino. *n* cristal *m*. **crystallize** *vt* cristalizar.

cub (kʌb) *n* cachorro *m*.

cube (kju:b) *n* 1 cubo *m*. 2 terrón *m*. *vt* cubicar. **cubic** *adj* cúbico. **cubicle** *n* 1 cubículo *m*. 2 caseta *f*.

cuckoo ('kuku:) *n* cuco, cuclillo *m*.

cucumber ('kju:kʌmbə) *n* pepino *m*.

cuddle ('kʌdl) *n* abrazo *m*. caricia *f*. *vt* abrazar amorosamente. *vi* abrazarse.

cue[1] (kju:) *n* pie, apunte *m*. entrada *f*.

cue[2] (kju:) *n game* taco *m*.

cuff[1] (kʌf) *n* puño *m*. **cufflinks** *n pl* gemelos *m pl*. **off the cuff** de improviso.

cuff[2] (kʌf) *n* bofetada *f*. *vt* abofetear.

culinary ('kʌlinri) *adj* culinario.

culprit ('kʌlprit) *n* culpado, culpable *m*.

cult (kʌlt) *n* culto *m*.

cultivate ('kʌltiveit) *vt* cultivar. **cultivated** *adj* culto, refinado. **cultivation** *n* cultivo *m*.

culture ('kʌltʃə) *n* 1 cultura *f*. 2 cultivo *m*. **cultural** *adj* cultural. **cultured** *adj* culto.

cumbersome ('kʌmbəsəm) *adj* molesto, incómodo.

cunning ('kʌniŋ) *adj* astuto, taimado. *n* astucia *f*.

cup (kʌp) *n* 1 taza *f*. 2 *rel* cáliz *m*. 3 *sport* copa *f*. **cupful** *n* taza *f*.

cupboard ('kʌbəd) *n* armario *m*.

curate ('kjuəreit) *n* cura *m*.

curator ('kjuˈreitə) *n* director, conservador *m*.

curb (kə:b) *n* freno, estorbo *m*. *vt* refrenar.

curdle ('kə:dl) *vt* cuajar. *vi* cuajarse. **curd** *n* cuajada *f*.

cure (kjuə) *n* cura *f*. *vt* curar.

curfew ('kə:fju:) *n* toque de queda *m*.

curious ('kjuəriəs) *adj* curioso. **curiosity** *n* curiosidad *f*.

curl (kə:l) *n* **1** rizo, bucle *m*. **2** espiral *f*. *vt* **1** rizar. **2** ondular. **3** fruncir. *vi* **1** rizarse. **2** arrollarse. **curler** *n* bigudí *m*. **curly** *adj* rizado.

currant ('kʌrənt) *n* **1** pasa. **2** grosella *f*.

current ('kʌrənt) *adj* corriente, actual. *n* corriente *f*. **current affairs** actualidades *f pl*. **current account** *n* cuenta corriente *f*. **currency** *n* moneda *f*.

curry ('kʌri) *n* cari, curry *m*. *vt* preparar con cari. **curry powder** *n* especias en polvo *f pl*.

curse (kə:s) *n* **1** maldición *f*. **2** palabrota *f*. **3** calamidad *f*. *vt* maldecir. *vi* blasfemar, echar pestes. **cursed** *adj* maldito.

curt (kə:t) *adj* brusco, seco. **curtness** *n* brusquedad *f*.

curtail (kə:'teil) *vt* acortar, reducir. **curtailment** *n* acortamiento *m*. restricción *f*.

curtain ('kə:tn) *n* **1** cortina *f*. **2** telón *m*. **iron curtain** *n* telón de acero *m*.

curtsy ('kə:tsi) *n* reverencia *f*. *vi* hacer una reverencia.

curve (kə:v) *n* curva *f*. *vi* encorvarse, torcerse. **curved** *adj* curvo, encorvado.

cushion ('kuʃən) *n* **1** cojín, almohadón *m*. **2** banda *f*. *vt* amortiguar. **cushy** *adj* inf fácil, agradable.

custard ('kʌstəd) *n* natillas *f pl*.

custody ('kʌstədi) *n* custodia *f*. **be in custody** estar detenido. **custodian** *n* custodio *m*.

custom ('kʌstəm) *n* **1** costumbre *f*. **2** clientela, parroquia *f*. **customs** *n pl* aduana *f*. **customary** *adj* acostumbrado, de costumbre. **customer** *n* **1** cliente *m,f*. **2** inf tío, sujeto *m*.

cut (kʌt) *n* **1** corte *m*. **2** cortadura *f*. **3** tajada, parte *f*. **4** reducción *f*. **short cut** *n* atajo *m*. ~*vt* **1** cortar. **2** reducir. *vi* **1** cortar. **2** cruzarse. **cut across** atajar. *adj* **1** cortado. **2** tallado. **cut-price** *adj* a precio reducido. **cutting** *n* **1** recorte *m*. **2** desmonte *m*. **3** *bot* esqueje *m*. *adj* **1** cortante. **2** mordaz.

cute (kju:t) *adj* inf **1** mono. **2** astuto, listo.

cuticle ('kju:tikəl) *n* cutícula *f*.

cutlery ('kʌtləri) *n* cubiertos *m pl*. cuchillería *f*.

cutlet ('kʌtlit) *n* chuleta *f*.

cycle ('saikəl) *n* **1** ciclo *m*. **2** bicicleta *f*. *vi* ir en bicicleta. **cyclical** *adj* cíclico. **cycling** *n* ciclismo *m*. **cyclist** *n* ciclista *m,f*.

cyclone ('saikloun) *n* ciclón *m*.

cygnet ('signit) *n* pollo de cisne *m*.

cylinder ('silində) *n* cilindro *m*. **cylindrical** *adj* cilíndrico.

cymbal ('simbəl) *n* platillo *m*.

cynic ('sinik) *n* cínico *m*. **cynical** *adj* cínico, escéptico.

cypress ('saiprəs) *n* ciprés *m*.

Cyprus ('saiprəs) *n* Chipre *f*. **Cypriot** *adj,n* chipriota *m,f*.

czar (za:) *n* zar *m*.

Czechoslovakia (tʃekəslə'vækiə) *n* Checoslovaquia *f*. **Czech** *adj,n* checo. **Czech** (language) *n* checo *m*.

D

dab (dæb) *n* **1** pequeña cantidad *f*. **2** gota *f*. *vt* tocar ligeramente.

dabble ('dæbəl) *vt* **1** salpicar, mojar. **2** chapotear. **dabble in** interesarse en por pasatiempo.

dad (dæd) *n* inf papá *m*.

daffodil ('dæfədil) *n* narciso trompón *m*.

daft (da:ft) *adj* estúpido.

dagger ('dægə) *n* daga *f*. puñal *m*.

dahlia ('deiliə) *n* dalia *f*.

daily ('deili) *adj* diario, cotidiano. *adv* a diario, cada día. *n* **1** diario *m*. **2** *dom* asistenta *f*.

dainty ('deinti) *adj* delicado, fino.

dairy ('dɛəri) *n* lechería *f*.

daisy ('deizi) *n* margarita *f*.

dam[1] (dæm) *n* presa *f*. dique *m*. *vt* represar. **dam up** cerrar, tapar.

dam[2] (dæm) *n* zool madre *f*.

damage ('dæmidʒ) *n* **1** daño, perjuicio *m*. **2** avería *f*. **damages** law daños y perjuicios *m pl*. ~*vt* **1** dañar, perjudicar. **2** averiar. **damaging** *adj* perjudicial.

damn (dæm) *vt* **1** condenar. **2** maldecir. **damn it!** ¡maldito sea! **damned** *adj* maldito, condenado. ~*adv* inf muy, terriblemente. **damning** *adj* damnificador. **damnable** *adj* detestable. **damnation** *n* condenación *f*.

damp (dæmp) *adj* **1** húmedo. **2** mojado. *n* humedad *f*. **dampen** *vt* **1** humedecer, mojar. **2** amortiguar. **3** desalentar.

damson ('dæmzən) *n* ciruela damascena *f*.

dance (dɑːns) n baile m. danza f. vi bailar, danzar. **dancer** n bailador, bailarín m.

dandelion ('dændilaiən) n diente de león m.

dandruff ('dændrʌf) n caspa f.

Dane (dein) n danés m. **Danish** adj danés, dinamarqués. **Danish** (language) n danés m.

danger ('deindʒə) n peligro m. **dangerous** adj peligroso, arriesgado.

dangle ('dæŋgəl) vt colgar, dejar colgado.

Danube ('dænjuːb) n Danubio m.

dare (dɛə) vt 1 arriesgar. 2 desafiar. vi atreverse. **daredevil** adj,n temerario m. **daring** adj atrevido, osado.

dark (dɑːk) adj 1 oscuro. 2 moreno. n oscuridad f. tinieblas f pl. **be in the dark** inf no saber nada en absoluto. **darken** vt 1 oscurecer. 2 hacer más oscuro. **darkness** n oscuridad f.

darling ('dɑːliŋ) adj,n querido m.

darn (dɑːn) vt zurcir.

dart (dɑːt) n 1 dardo m. 2 game rehilete m. 3 movimiento rápido m. vi lanzarse, precipitarse. **dartboard** n blanco m.

dash (dæʃ) n 1 pequeña cantidad f. 2 rasgo m. 3 guión m. 4 carrera f. **make a dash for** precipitarse hacia. vt romper, estrellar. vi precipitarse. **dashing** adj brioso, gallardo. **dashboard** n tablero de instrumentos m.

data ('deitə) n pl datos m pl. **data processing** n proceso de datos m.

date[1] (deit) n 1 fecha f. 2 inf cita f. **be up to date** tener ideas modernas. **out of date** anticuado. **to date** hasta la fecha. **date line** n línea de cambio de fecha f. ~vt fechar.

date[2] (deit) n dátil m. **date palm** n palmera datilera f.

daughter ('dɔːtə) n hija f. **daughter-in-law** n nuera, hija política f.

dawdle ('dɔːdl) vi holgazanear, perder el tiempo. **dawdler** n holgazán m.

dawn (dɔːn) n alba f. amanecer m. vi amanecer. **dawn on** caer en la cuenta.

day (dei) n 1 día m. 2 jornada f. **the day after tomorrow** pasado mañana. **from day to day** de día en día. **daybreak** n amanecer m. **daydream** n ensueño m. vi soñar despierto. **daylight** n luz del día f. **in broad daylight** en pleno día.

daze (deiz) n aturdimiento m. vt aturdir. **be in a daze** estar aturdido. **dazed** adj aturdido.

dazzle ('dæzəl) n brillo m. vt deslumbrar. **dazzling** adj deslumbrante, deslumbrador.

dead (ded) adj 1 muerto. 2 desierto. 3 apagado. **deadly** adj 1 mortal. 2 fatal. **deadline** n

fecha tope f. límite, plazo m. **deadlock** n 1 parálisis f. 2 punto muerto m. **deaden** vt 1 amortiguar. 2 aliviar.

deaf (def) adj sordo. **deaf-aid** n aparato del oído m. **deaf-mute** n sordomudo m. **deafen** vt ensordecer. **deafening** adj ensordecedor. **deafness** n sordera f.

deal[1] (diːl) n 1 negocio m. transacción f. 2 pacto, convenio m. 3 reparto m. **a great deal** muchísimo. ~vt 1 dar. 2 descargar. 3 repartir. vi negociar, comerciar. **deal with** tratar de.

dean (diːn) n 1 rel deán m. 2 educ decano m.

dear (diə) adj 1 querido. 2 estimado. 3 caro, costoso. n persona simpática f. **oh dear!** interj ¡caramba!

death (deθ) n 1 muerte f. 2 fallecimiento m. **deathly** adj 1 mortal. 2 profundo.

debase (di'beis) vt 1 degradar. 2 (coins) alterar.

debate (di'beit) n 1 discusión f. 2 debate m. vt,vi discutir, debatir.

debit ('debit) n 1 debe m. 2 cargo m. vt cargar.

debris ('deibri) n escombros m pl.

debt (det) n deuda f. **debtor** n deudor m.

decade ('dekeid) n decenio m.

decadent ('dekədənt) adj decadente. **decadence** n decadencia f.

decant (di'kænt) vt decantar. **decanter** n jarra, garrafa f.

decay (di'kei) n 1 decadencia f. decaimiento m. 2 pudrición, putrefacción. f. 3 caries f. vt deteriorar, pudrir. vi 1 decaer. 2 pudrirse.

decease (di'siːs) n fallecimiento m. vi fallecer. **deceased** adj,n difunto.

deceit (di'siːt) n 1 engaño, fraude m. 2 mentira f. **deceitful** or **deceptive** adj engañoso.

deceive (di'siːv) vt 1 engañar. 2 defraudar.

December (di'sembə) n diciembre m.

decent ('diːsənt) adj 1 decente. 2 simpático, amable. **decency** n 1 decencia f. 2 bondad f.

decibel ('desibel) n decibelio m.

decide (di'said) vt decidir, determinar. vi resolver. **decided** adj decidido, resuelto.

deciduous (di'sidjuəs) adj de hoja caduca.

decimal ('desiməl) adj,n decimal f. **decimal point** coma de decimales f.

decipher (di'saifə) vt descifrar.

decision (di'siʒən) n decisión f. **decisive** adj decisivo, concluyente. **decisively** adv con decisión.

deck (dek) n 1 cubierta f. 2 piso m. 3 game baraja f. **deckchair** n hamaca, tumbona f.

declaration (deklə'reiʃən) n declaración f.

declare (di'klɛə) vt declarar, afirmar. vi pronun-

ciarse. **nothing to declare** nada de declarar.
declared adj abierto, manifiesto.
decline (di'klain) n 1 declinación f. descenso m.
2 baja f. 3 decaimiento m. vt,vi 1 rehusar. 2
gram declinar. **declension** n declinación f.
decorate ('dekəreit) vt decorar, adornar.
interior decorating decoración del hogar
f. **decoration** n 1 adorno m. 2 decoración f.
decorative adj hermoso, elegante. **decorator**
n decorador m.
decoy (n 'di:kɔi; v di'kɔi) n 1 señuelo m. 2
reclamo m. vt atraer con señuelo.
decrease (di'kri:s) n disminución f. vt disminuir,
reducir.
decree (di'kri:) n decreto m. vt decretar.
decrepit (di'krepit) adj decrépito.
dedicate ('dedikeit) vt dedicar. **dedication** n 1
dedicación f. 2 dedicatoria f. 3 devoción f.
deduce (di'dju:s) vt deducir.
deduct (di'dʌkt) vt restar, rebajar, descontar.
deduction n 1 deducción, conclusión f. 2
descuento m. rebaja f.
deed (di:d) n 1 hecho m. acción f. 2 hazaña f. 3
law escritura f.
deep (di:p) adj 1 profundo, hondo. 2 bajo. 3
insondable. **deep-freeze** n congeladora f.
deer (diə) n ciervo m.
deface (di'feis) vt desfigurar, mutilar.
default (di'fɔ:lt) n 1 omisión f. descuido m. 2
falta f. incumplimiento m. vi 1 faltar, delin-
quir. 2 sport dejar de presentarse.
defeat (di'fi:t) n derrota f. vt vencer, derrotar.
defect (n 'di:fekt; v di'fekt) n defecto m. vi
desertar. **defection** n deserción, defección
f. **defective** adj 1 defectuoso. 2 defectivo.
defence (di'fens) n defensa f. **defenceless** adj
indefenso. **defend** vt defender. **defender** n
defensor m. **defensive** adj defensivo.
defer (di'fə:) vt aplazar, diferir. **deference** n
deferencia f. respecto m. **in deference to** por
respeto a. **deferential** adj deferente, cortés,
respetuoso.
defiant (di'faiənt) adj desafiador. **defiance** n
desafío, reto m.
deficient (di'fiʃənt) adj deficiente. **deficiency**
n deficiencia f.
deficit ('defisit) n déficit m. adj deficitario.
define (di'fain) vt 1 definir. 2 caracterizar.
definition n definición f.
definite ('defənit) adj 1 determinado, definido.
2 preciso.
deflate (di'fleit) vt,vi 1 desinflar. 2 comm

reducir la inflación. **deflation** n comm defla-
ción f.
deform (di'fɔ:m) vt deformar, desfigurar.
deformation n deformación f.
defraud (di'frɔ:d) vt defraudar, engañar, estafar.
defrauder n defraudador m.
defrost (di'frɔst) vt deshelar.
deft (deft) adj hábil, mañoso. **deftness** n habilidad, destriza, maña f.
defunct (di'fʌŋkt) adj difunto, muerto.
defy (di'fai) vt 1 desafiar, retar, provocar. 2
contravenir.
degenerate (di'dʒenəreit) adj,n degenerado m.
degrade (di'greid) vt degradar, envilecer.
degree (di'gri:) n 1 grado m. 2 educ título m.
dehydrate (di'haidreit) vt deshidratar.
deity ('deiiti) n 1 deidad f. 2 dios m.
dejected (di'dʒektid) adj desanimado, abatido,
desalentado. **dejection** n abatimiento, desaliento m.
delay (di'lei) n retraso m. tardanza, dilación f. vt
retardar, diferir. vi tardar.
delegate (n 'deligət; v 'deligeit) n 1 delegado
m. 2 substituto. vt delegar, disputar.
delete (di'li:t) vt borrar, tachar. **deletion** n
supresión f.
deliberate (adj di'libərət; v di'libəreit) adj deli-
berado, premeditado. vt deliberar, reflexionar,
pensar. **deliberation** n 1 discusión f. 2 reflexión f.
delicate ('delikət) adj 1 delicado. 2 exquisita. 3
fino. **delicacy** n delicadeza, finura f. 2 exqui-
sitez f.
delicatessen (delikə'tesən) n tienda de fiam-
bres y manjares delicados f.
delicious (di'liʃəs) adj delicioso.
delight (di'lait) n 1 deleite m. 2 delicia f. placer
m. vt deleitar, agradar, recrear. **delightful**
adj delicioso, precioso.
delinquency (di'liŋkwənsi) n delincuencia f.
delinquent adj,n delincuente.
deliver (di'livə) vt 1 liberar, librar, salvar. 2
entregar, transmitir. 3 despachar, servir. 4 dar,
descargar. **delivery** n 1 entrega f. reparto de
correo m. 2 med parto m.
delta ('deltə) n geog delta m.
delude (di'lu:d) vt engañar. **delusion** n
engaño, error m. ilusión f.
delve (delv) vt cavar, ahondar.
demand (di'ma:nd) n 1 demanda, solicitación f.
2 pregunta, reclamación f. vt pedir, exigir,
preguntar. **demanding** adj exigente.
democracy (di'mɔkrəsi) n democracia f. **demo-**

cratic adj democrático. **democrat** n demócrata m,f.

demolish (di'mɔliʃ) vt 1 demoler. 2 arrasar. 3 derruir. **demolition** n demolición f.

demon ('di:mən) n demonio, diablo m.

demonstrate ('demənstreit) vt demostrar, probar, exponer. **demonstration** n demostración f.

demoralize (di'mɔrəlaiz) vt desmoralizar.

demure (di'mjuə) adj 1 grave, serio. 2 modesto.

den (den) n 1 guarida f. cubil m. 2 lugar de retiro, cueva f.

denial (di'naiəl) n negación, contradicción f.

denim ('denim) n dril de algodón m.

Denmark ('denmɑ:k) n Dinamarca.

denomination (dinɔmi'neiʃən) n 1 denominación f. 2 secta f. grupo religioso m. 3 categoría f. **denominator** n denominador m.

denote (di'nout) vt denotar.

denounce (di'nauns) vt denunciar.

dense (dens) adj denso. **density** n densidad f.

dent (dent) n mella, abolladura f.

dental ('dentl) adj dental, dentista. **dentist** n dentista m. **dentistry** n odontología, cirugía dental f. **denture** n dentadura f.

deny (di'nai) vt negar, desmentir.

deodorant (di'oudərənt) n desodorante m.

depart (di'pɑ:t) vi 1 partir, irse. 2 apartarse, salirse. 3 dejar. **departure** n partida, salida f.

department (di'pɑ:tmənt) n departamento m. sección f. **department store** almacenes m pl.

depend (di'pend) vi depender. **dependence** n dependencia f. **dependent** adj dependiente, subordinado.

depict (di'pikt) vt 1 describir. 2 pintar.

deplete (di'pli:t) vt vaciar, agotar. **depletion** n agotamiento f.

deplore (di'plɔ:) vt deplorar, lamentar.

deport (di'pɔ:t) vt deportar. **deportation** n deportación f.

depose (di'pouz) vt deponer.

deposit (di'pɔzit) n 1 depósito m. 2 min yacimiento m.

depot ('depou) n depósito, almacén m.

deprave (di'preiv) vt depravar.

depreciate (di'pri:ʃieit) vt depreciar. vi depreciarse, perder valor.

depress (di'pres) vt deprimir. **depression** n depresión f.

deprive (di'praiv) vt privar, desposeer.

depth (depθ) n 1 profundidad, hondura f. 2 fondo m.

deputize ('depjutaiz) vt diputar. **deputation** n deputación, delegación f. **deputy** n 1 diputado m. 2 sustituto m. adj 1 vice, segundo. 2 suplente.

derail (di'reil) vt hacer descarrilar.

derelict ('derəlikt) adj derelicto, abandonado.

deride (di'raid) vt ridiculizar. **derision** n irrisión f.

derive (di'raiv) vt derivar. vi provenir. **derivation** n derivación f.

derogatory (di'rɔgətri) adj despectivo, rebajante.

descend (di'send) vt,vi descender, bajar. **descendant** adj descendiente.

descent (di'sent) n 1 descenso m. bajada f. 2 descendencia hereditaria f.

describe (di'skraib) vt describir. **description** n 1 descripción f. 2 especie f. tipo m.

desert[1] ('dezət) n desierto m.

desert[2] (di'zə:t) vt abandonar, desertar. **deserter** n desertor m.

deserve (di'zə:v) vt merecer.

design (di'zain) vt 1 diseñar. 2 proyectar. 3 dibujar. n 1 proyecto, plan m. 2 objeto, propósito m. 3 dibujo, modelo m.

designate ('dezigneit) vt 1 nombrar. 2 denominar. 3 señalar. 4 designar.

desire (di'zaiə) n deseo m. vt desear.

desk (desk) n pupitre, escritorio m.

desolate ('desələt) adj desolado, desierto, triste.

despair (di'spɛə) n desesperación, desesperanza f. vi desesperar.

desperate ('despərət) adj desesperado.

despise (di'spaiz) vt despreciar.

despite (di'spait) prep a pesar de.

despondent (di'spɔndənt) adj desanimado, abatido. **despondency** n desaliento, abatimiento m.

dessert (di'zə:t) n postre m. **dessertspoon** n cuchara de postres f.

destine ('destin) vt destinar. **destination** n destinación f. **destiny** n destino, hado m. suerte f.

destitute ('destitju:t) adj indigente, menesteroso.

destroy (di'strɔi) vt destruir, destrozar.

detach (di'tætʃ) vt despegar.

detail ('di:teil) n 1 detalle, pormenor m. 2 mil destacamento m. vt detallar, enumerar.

detain (di'tein) vt 1 detener. 2 retener. **detention** n detención f.

detect (di'tekt) vt 1 detectar. 2 descubrir. **detective** n detective m.

deter (di'tə:) *vt* disuadir. **deterrent** *n* **1** freno *m*. **2** *mil* fuerza disuasiva f. *adj* disuasivo.

detergent (di'tə:dʒənt) *n* detergente *m*.

deteriorate (di'tiəriəreit) *vi* deteriorarse.

determine (di'tə:min) *vt* determinar. **determination** *n* determinación f.

detest (di'test) *vt* detestar, aborrecer, odiar.

detonate ('detəneit) *vi* detonar. *vt* hacer estallar.

detour ('di:tuə) *n* rodeo *m*. vuelta f. *vi* hacer un rodeo, desviarse.

detract (di'trækt) *vi* **detract from** desvirtuar.

devalue (di'vælju:) *vt* devaluar.

devastate ('devəsteit) *vt* devastar.

develop (di'veləp) *vt* **1** desarrollar. **2** explotar. *vi* desarrollarse, evolucionar. **development** *n* desarrollo *m*. evolución f.

deviate ('di:vieit) *vi* desviarse. **devious** *adj* **1** taimado. **2** tortuoso.

device (di'vais) *n* mecanismo, aparato *m*.

devil ('devəl) *n* diablo *m*. **devil's advocate** *n* abogado del diablo *m*. **devilish** *adj* diabólico.

devise (di'vaiz) *vt* idear, planear.

devoid (di'vɔid) *adj* desprovisto, falto.

devote (di'vout) *vt* dedicar. **devotedly** *adv* con fervor, devotamente. **devotee** *n* devoto *m*. **devotion** *n* **1** devoción f. **2** dedicación f.

devour (di'vauə) *vt* devorar.

devout (di'vaut) *adj* devoto, piadoso.

dew (dju:) *n* rocío *m*.

dexterous ('dekstrəs) *adj* **1** diestro, hábil. **2** ágil.

diabetes (daiə'bi:tiz) *n* diabetes f. **diabetic** *adj,n* diabético.

diagnosis (daiəg'nousis) *n, pl* **diagnoses** diagnóstico *m*.

diagonal (dai'agənl) *adj,n* diagonal f.

diagram ('daiəgræm) *n* diagrama, esquema *m*.

dial (dail) *n* **1** esfera del reloj f. **2** cuadrante *m*. **sun dial** reloj de sol *m*. *vt* marcar.

dialect ('daiəlekt) *n* dialecto *m*.

dialogue ('daiələg) *n* diálogo *m*.

diameter (dai'æmitə) *n* diámetro *m*.

diamond ('daiəmənd) *n* diamante *m*.

diaphragm ('daiəfræm) *n* diafragma *m*.

diarrhoea (daiə'riə) *n* diarrea f.

diary ('daiəri) *n* diario *m*.

dice (dais) *n pl* dados *m pl*.

dictate (*v* dik'teit; *n* 'dikteit) *vt* dictar, mandar, imponer. *n* orden f. mandato *m*. **dictation** *n* dictado *m*. **dictator** *n* dictador *m*. **dictatorship** *n* dictadura f.

dictionary ('dikʃənri) *n* diccionario *m*.

did (did) *v* see **do**.

die[1] (dai) *vi* morir, fallecer.

die[2] (dai) *n* **1** *tech* cuño, troquel *m*. matriz f. **2** *game* dado *m*.

diesel ('di:zəl) *n* diesel *m*.

diet ('daiət) *n* dieta f. régimen *m*. *vi* estar a dieta.

differ ('difə) *vi* **1** diferir. **2** discrepar. **difference** *n* diferencia f. **it makes no difference** da lo mismo. **different** *adj* diferente, distinto. **differential** *adj* diferencial. **differentiate** *vt* distinguir.

difficult ('difikəlt) *adj* difícil, arduo. **difficulty** *n* dificultad f.

dig* (dig) *vt* cavar, excavar. *n* **1** excavación f. **2** codazo *m*. **3** alojamiento *m*.

digest (*n* 'daidʒest; *v* dai'dʒest) *n* **1** resumen *m*. **2** *law* digesto *m*. *vt* **1** digerir. **2** resumir. **digestion** *n* digestión f.

digit ('didʒit) *n* dígito *m*. **digital** *adj* digital.

dignity ('digniti) *n* dignidad f. **dignified** *adj* **1** dignificado. **2** digno, solemne.

dilapidated (di'læpideitid) *adj* ruinoso.

dilemma (di'lemə) *n* dilema *m*.

diligent ('dilidʒənt) *adj* diligente.

dilute (dai'lu:t) *vt* diluir, aguar.

dim (dim) *adj* **1** obscuro. **2** débil. **3** apagado. *vt* obscurecer.

dimension (di'menʃən) *n* dimensión f.

diminish (di'miniʃ) *vt* disminuir.

diminutive (di'minjutiv) *adj* diminutivo, diminuto.

dimple ('dimpəl) *n* hoyuelo *m*.

din (din) *n* estruendo, estrépito *m*.

dine (dain) *vi* comer. **dining car** *n* vagón restaurante *m*. **dining room** *n* comedor *m*.

dinghy ('diŋgi) *n naut* bote *m*.

dingy ('dindʒi) *adj* sucio, negruzco.

dinner ('dinə) *n* cena, comida f.

dinosaur ('dainəsɔ:) *n* dinosauro *m*.

diocese ('daiəsis) *n* diócesis f.

dip (dip) *vt* **1** sumergir, zambullir. **2** mojar. *n* **1** zambullida f. **2** pendiente f. declive *m*.

diphthong ('difθɔŋ) *n* diptongo *m*.

diploma (di'ploumə) *n* diploma *m*.

diplomacy (di'plouməsi) *n* diplomacia f. **diplomat** *n* diplomático *m*. **diplomatic** *adj* diplomático.

direct (di'rekt) *adj* directo. *vt* **1** dirigir. **2** mandar. **direct object** *n gram* complemento directo *m*. **direction** *n* **1** dirección f. **2** instrucciones f pl. **director** *n* director *m*. **board of**

directors n consejo de administración m. **directory** n 1 directorio m. 2 guía f.

dirt (də:t) n 1 polvo m. 2 suciedad f. **dirty** adj 1 sucio. 2 malo, bajo.

disability (disə'biliti) n incapacidad f. **disabled** adj incapacitado, mutilado.

disadvantage (disəd'va:ntidʒ) n desventaja f.

disagree (disə'gri:) vi discrepar, no estar de acuerdo.

disappear (disə'piə) vi desaparecer.

disappoint (disə'pɔint) vt defraudar, decepcionar.

disapprove (disə'pru:v) vi desaprobar, censurar.

disarm (dis'a:m) vt desarmar. **disarmament** n desarme m.

disaster (di'za:stə) n desastre m.

disc (disk) n disco m. **disc jockey** n presentador de discos m.

discard (di'ska:d) vt descartar, desechar.

discern (di'sə:n) vt discernir. **discernible** adj perceptible. **discerning** adj perspicaz.

discharge (n 'distʃa:dʒ; v dis'tʃa:dʒ) n 1 descarga f. 2 liberación f. 3 descargo m. 4 pago m. 5 supuración f. vt 1 descargar. 2 exonerar. 3 cumplir.

disciple (di'saipəl) n discípulo m.

discipline ('disəplin) n disciplina f. vt disciplinar.

disclose (dis'klouz) vt revelar.

discomfort (dis'kʌmfət) n molestia f. malestar m. vt incomodar, molestar.

disconnect (diskə'nekt) vt 1 desenchufar, desconectar. 2 disociar, separar.

disconsolate (dis'kɔnsələt) adj desconsolado.

discontinue (diskən'tinju:) vt descontinuar.

discord ('diskɔ:d) n 1 discordia f. 2 mus disonancia f.

discotheque ('diskətek) n discoteca f.

discount ('diskaunt) n descuento m. rebaja f. vt descontar, rebajar.

discourage (dis'kʌridʒ) vt 1 desanimar. 2 disuadir.

discover (dis'kʌvə) vt descubrir. **discovery** n descubrimiento m.

discredit (dis'kredit) n descrédito m. vt desacreditar.

discreet (dis'kri:t) adj 1 discreto. 2 prudente.

discrepancy (dis'krepənsi) n discrepancia f.

discrete (dis'kri:t) adj discreto.

discretion (dis'kreʃən) n 1 discreción f. 2 prudencia f.

discriminate (dis'krimineit) vt distinguir. **discriminate against** discriminar contra.

discuss (dis'kʌs) vt discutir, tratar. **discussion** n discusión f. debate m.

disease (di'zi:z) n enfermedad f.

disembark (disim'ba:k) vt,vi desembarcar. **disembarkation** n desembarque m.

disfigure (dis'figə) vt desfigurar.

disgrace (dis'greis) n 1 desgracia f. vergüenza f. vt deshonrar.

disgruntled (dis'grʌntəld) adj malhumorado.

disguise (dis'gaiz) n disfraz m. vt disfrazar.

disgust (dis'gʌst) n 1 repugnancia f. 2 disgusto m. vt repugnar. **disgusting** adj repugnante.

dish (diʃ) n plato m. fuente f. **dishcloth** n paño de cocina m.

dishearten (dis'ha:tn) vt desanimar.

dishevelled (di'ʃevəld) adj despeinado.

dishonest (dis'ɔnist) adj tramposo, falso.

dishonour (dis'ɔnə) n deshonra f. deshonor m. vt deshonrar.

disillusion (disi'lu:ʒən) n desilusión f. vt desilusionar.

disinfect (disin'fekt) vt desinfectar. **disinfectant** n,adj desinfectante m.

disinherit (disin'herit) vt desheredar.

disintegrate (dis'intigreit) vi desintegrarse, desmoronarse. **disintegration** n disgregación, desintegración f.

disinterested (dis'intrəstid) adj desinteresado.

disjointed (dis'dʒɔintid) adj dislocado, desarticulado.

dislike (dis'laik) n aversión, antipatía f. vt aborrecer, tener aversión a or antipatía a.

dislocate ('disləkeit) vt dislocar. **dislocation** n 1 dislocación f. 2 anat descoyuntamiento m.

dismal ('dizməl) adj 1 triste. 2 sombrío.

dismantle (dis'mæntl) vt desmantelar.

dismay (dis'mei) n 1 consternación f. 2 desaliento m. vt consternar.

dismiss (dis'mis) vt 1 descartar. 2 licenciar, despedir. 3 dar por terminado. **dismissal** n despedida m.

dismount (dis'maunt) vt desmontar.

disobey (disə'bei) vt,vi desobedecer. **disobedient** adj desobediente. **disobedience** n desobediencia f.

disorder (dis'ɔ:də) n 1 desorden, disturbio m. 2 med trastorno m. vt desordenar.

disorganized (dis'ɔ:gənaizd) adj desorganizado.

disown (dis'oun) vt repudiar, rechazar.

disparage (dis'pæridʒ) vt desacreditar, despreciar. **disparagement** n menosprecio, descrédito m.

dispassionate (dis'pæʃənət) adj desapasionado, imparcial.

dispatch (dis'pætʃ) n 1 despacho m. 2 expedición f. 3 comunicación f. vt despachar, expedir.

dispel (dis'pel) vt dispersar.

dispense (dis'pens) vt 1 dispensar. 2 administrar. **dispense with** prescindir de. **dispensary** n dispensario m.

disperse (dis'pə:s) vt dispersar.

displace (dis'pleis) vt 1 desplazar. 2 desalojar. **displacement** n cambio de sitio m.

display (dis'plei) n 1 despliegue m. 2 exhibición f. vt 1 desplegar. 2 exhibir.

displease (dis'pli:z) vt 1 desagradar. 2 ofender, disgustar.

dispose (dis'pouz) vt disponer, arreglar. **disposable** adj disponible. **disposal** n 1 disposición, colocación f. 2 enajenación f. **disposition** n 1 disposición f. 2 tendencia f. 3 humor m.

disprove (dis'pru:v) vt refutar.

dispute (dis'pju:t) n 1 disputa f. 2 litigio m. vt,vi 1 disputar. 2 poner en duda, cuestionar.

disqualify (dis'kwɔlifai) vt descalificar, incapacitar. **disqualification** n 1 descalificación f. 2 inhabilitación f.

disregard (disri'gɑ:d) n 1 descuido m. 2 desprecio m. 3 desconsideración f. vt 1 despreciar. 2 pasar por alto.

disreputable (dis'repjutəbəl) adj 1 de mala fama, despreciable. 2 bajo. **disrepute** n 1 deshonra f. descrédito m.

disrespect (disri'spekt) n 1 falta de respeto f. 2 desacato m. **disrespectful** adj irrespetuoso.

disrupt (dis'rʌpt) vt 1 desorganizar. 2 trastornar. 3 romper. **disruption** n 1 desorganización f. 2 ruptura f.

dissatisfy (di'sætisfai) vt 1 desagradar. 2 no dar satisfacción. **dissatisfaction** n descontento m.

dissect (di'sekt) vt 1 disecar. 2 seccionar. **dissection** n disección f.

dissent (di'sent) n 1 disentimiento m. 2 disidencia f. vt 1 disentir. 2 disidir.

dissimilar (di'similə) adj desigual, disímil. **dissimilarity** n 1 disimilitud f. 2 disparidad f.

dissociate (di'souʃieit) vt disociar.

dissolve (di'zɔlv) vt disolver. vi 1 disolverse. 2 desaparecer.

dissuade (di'sweid) vt disuadir.

distance ('distəns) n distancia f. vt distanciar. **distant** adj distante, lejano.

distaste (dis'teist) n disgusto m. aversión f. **distasteful** adj desagradable, repugnante.

distil (dis'til) vt destilar. **distillation** n destilación f. **distillery** n destilería f.

distinct (dis'tiŋkt) adj distinto, preciso, claro. **distinction** n distinción f. **distinctive** adj distintivo, característico.

distinguish (dis'tiŋgwiʃ) vt distinguir. **distinguished** adj eminente.

distort (dis'tɔ:t) vt torcer, falsear. **distortion** n distorsión f. torcimiento m.

distract (dis'trækt) vt 1 distraer. 2 perturbar, enloquecer. **distraction** n distracción f.

distraught (dis'trɔ:t) adj 1 distraído. 2 enloquecido.

distress (dis'tres) n 1 dolor m. aflicción f. 2 miseria f. infortunio m. vt afligir, apenar.

distribute (dis'tribju:t) vt distribuir, repartir. **distribution** n repartimiento m.

district ('distrikt) n 1 distrito m. 2 región f. 3 sector m.

distrust (dis'trʌst) vt desconfiar. **distrustful** adj desconfiado.

disturb (dis'tə:b) vt 1 molestar, perturbar. 2 desordenar, alterar. 3 inquietar. **disturbance** n 1 perturbación f. 2 desorden, tumulto, disturbio m. 3 trastorno m.

ditch (ditʃ) n 1 zanja f. 2 trinchera f.

ditto ('ditou) n idem, lo mismo.

divan (di'væn) n diván m.

dive (daiv) vi 1 zambullirse. 2 aviat picar. n 1 zambullida f. 2 salto m. **diving board** n trampolín m.

diverge (dai'və:dʒ) vi divergir.

diverse (dai'və:s) adj 1 diverso, diferente. 2 variado. **diversity** n diversidad f.

divert (dai'və:t) vt 1 divertir, entretener. 2 desviar, apartar. **diversion** n 1 diversión, distracción f. 2 desviación f.

divide (di'vaid) vt 1 dividir, partir. vi dividirse, separarse. **divisible** adj divisible. **division** n 1 división f. 2 desunión f.

dividend ('dividend) n dividendo m.

divine (di'vain) adj divino. vt adivinar. **divinity** n 1 divinidad f. 2 teología f.

divorce (di'vɔ:s) n divorcio m. vi divorciarse.

divulge (di'vʌldʒ) vt divulgar.

dizzy ('dizi) adj 1 vertiginoso. 2 aturdido. **dizziness** n 1 vértigo m. 2 desvanecimiento m.

do* (du:) vt hacer. vi hacer, obrar, portarse. **do**

away with eliminar. **do up** atar, arreglar.
how do you do? ¿cómo está Usted?
docile ('dousail) *adj* dócil.
dock[1] (dɔk) *n* 1 dique *m*. 2 muelle *m*. **dockyard** *n* 1 astillero *m*. 2 arsenal *m*.
dock[2] (dɔk) *vt* 1 descolar, recortar. 2 rebajar.
dock[3] (dɔk) *bot n* malva silvestre, ramaza *f*.
doctor ('dɔktə) *n* 1 doctor *m*. 2 médico *m*. *vt* 1 medicinar. 2 *inf* adulterar.
doctrine ('dɔktrin) *n* doctrina *f*.
document ('dɔkjumənt) *n* documento *m*. *vt* documentar. **documentary** *adj,n* documental *m*.
dodge (dɔdʒ) *vt* esquivar, evitar, eludir. *n* regate *m*. maña *f*.
does (dʌz) *v* see **do**.
dog (dɔg) *n* perro *m*. **dog days** *n pl* caniculares *m pl*. **dogged** *adj* tenaz. ~*vt* seguir los pasos de.
dogma ('dɔgmə) *n* dogma *m*. **dogmatic** *adj* dogmático.
dole (doul) *n* 1 limosna *f*. 2 subsidio de paro *m*. **be on the dole** estar parado.
doll (dɔl) *n* muñeca *f*.
dollar ('dɔlə) *n* dólar *m*.
dolphin ('dɔlfin) *n* delfín *m*.
domain (də'mein) *n* dominio *m*. propiedad *f*.
dome (doum) *n* arch cúpula *f*. domo *m*.
domestic (də'mestik) *adj* 1 doméstico. 2 interno. **domesticate** *vt* domesticar.
dominate ('dɔmineit) *vt* dominar. **dominant** *adj* dominante. **domineer** *vt,vi* dominar, tiranizar. **domineering** *adj* dominante.
dominion (də'miniən) *n* dominio *m*.
donate (dou'neit) *vt* donar. **donation** *n* donativo, regalo *m*.
done (dʌn) *v* see **do**.
donkey ('dɔŋki) *n* burro *m*.
donor ('dounə) *n* donador, donante *m*.
doom (du:m) *n* 1 condena *f*. 2 perdición *f*. 3 juicio final *m*. **doomsday** *n* día del juicio final *m*. ~*vt* condenar.
door (dɔ:) *n* puerta *f*. **doorbell** *n* timbre *m*. campanilla *f*. **doorhandle** *n* mano de la puerta, empuñadura *f*. **doorknob** *n* tirador de puerta, botón *m*. **doorknocker** *n* llamador *m*. aldaba *f*. **doormat** *n* felpudo *m*.
dope (doup) *n* 1 *inf* narcótico *m*. droga *f*. 2 grasa lubrificante *f*. *vi* drogarse, narcotizarse.
dormant ('dɔ:mənt) *adj* durmiente, inactivo, latente.
dormitory ('dɔ:mitri) *n* dormitorio *m*.
dormouse ('dɔ:maus) *n zool* lirón *m*.

dose (dous) *n* dosis *f*. *vt* dar una dosis. **dosage** *n* dosificación, dosis *f*.
dot (dɔt) *n* punto *m*. *vt* puntear.
dote (dout) *vi* 1 chochear. 2 idolatrar. **dote on** estar chocho por.
double ('dʌbl) *adj,n* doble *m*. *vt* 1 doblar. 2 redoblar. **double bass** *n mus* contrabajo *m*. **double-cross** *n* traición *f*. *vt* traicionar. **double-decker bus** *n* autobús de dos pisos *m*.
doubt (daut) *n* duda *f*. *vt,vi* dudar. **doubtful** *adj* dudoso, incierto.
dough (dou) *n* masa, pasta *f*. **doughnut** *n* buñuelo *m*.
dove (dʌv) *n* paloma *f*. **dovecote** *n* palomar *f*.
dowdy ('daudi) *adj* poco atractivo.
down[1] (daun) *adv* abajo. **down with...** ¡...abajo! **upside down** al revés.
down[2] (daun) *n* plumón *m*. pelusa *f*.
downcast ('daunka:st) *adj* deprimido, abatido, bajo.
downfall ('daunfɔ:l) *n* 1 caída *f*. 2 ruina *f*. hundimiento *m*.
downhearted (daun'ha:tid) *adj* descorazonado, desalentado.
downhill ('daunhil) *adv* cuesta abajo.
downpour ('daunpɔ:) *n* chaparrón, chubasco *m*.
downright ('daunrait) *adv* 1 en absoluto, categóricamente. 2 francamente. *adj* directo, franco, claro.
downstairs (daun'steəz) *adv* escalera abajo. **go downstairs** bajar la escalera. ~*n* la planta baja *f*.
downstream (daun'stri:m) *adv* río abajo, corriente abajo.
downtrodden ('dauntrɔdn) *adj* oprimido, tiranizado.
downward ('daunwəd) *adj* descendente.
downwards ('daunwədz) *adv* hacia abajo, de arriba abajo.
dowry ('dauəri) *n* dote *f*.
doze (douz) *vi* dormitar. *n* sueño ligero *m*.
dozen ('dʌzən) *n* docena *f*.
drab (dræb) *adj* 1 pardo. 2 monótono.
draft (dra:ft) *n* 1 plan, esquema *m*. 2 *comm* giro *m*. letra de cambio *f*. *vt* 1 redactar. 2 llamar al servicio militar.
drag (dræg) *vt* arrastrar. **drag on** prolongar. *n* 1 estorbo *m*. 2 *inf* lata *f*.
dragon ('drægən) *n* dragón *m*. **dragonfly** *n* libélula *f*.
drain (drein) *n* 1 zanja *f*. 2 desagüe *m*. *vt* vaciar

desaguar. **drainage** n desagüe. **drainpipe** n tubo de desagüe m.

drake (dreik) n pato m.

dram (dræm) n 1 dracma f. 2 trago de bebida m.

drama ('drɑːmə) n drama m. **dramatic** adj dramático. **dramatist** n dramaturgo m. **dramatize** vt dramatizar.

drank (dræŋk) v see **drink**.

drape (dreip) n colgadura f. vt 1 cubrir con ropa. 2 recoger en pliegues.

draper ('dreipə) n pañero m. **drapery** n 1 pañería f. 2 colgaduras f pl.

drastic ('dræstik) adj 1 drástico. 2 enérgico.

draught (drɑːft) n 1 corriente de aire f. 2 trago m. **draughty** adj lleno de corrientes de aire. **draughts** n pl game juego de damas m. **draughtsman** n delineante m.

draw* (drɔː) n 1 sport empate m. 2 rifa f. sorteo m. vt 1 sacar, extraer. 2 arrastrar. 3 sortear. vi 1 tirar arrostrando. 2 atraer. 3 dibujar. 4 desenvainar la espada. 5 game empatar. **drawbridge** n puente levadizo m. **drawer** n 1 cajón m. 2 comm girador m. **drawers** n pl calzoncillos m pl. **drawing** n dibujo m. **drawing board** tablero de dibujo m. **drawing pin** n chincheta f. **drawing room** n salón m.

drawl (drɔːl) n voz lenta f. vt pronunciar lentamente. vi arrastrar las palabras.

dread (dred) n 1 miedo m. 2 terror, pavor m. vt temer. **dreadful** adj 1 terrible. 2 espantoso.

dream* (driːm) n sueño m. vt,vi soñar.

dreary ('driəri) adj 1 triste. 2 lúgubre. 3 monótono.

dredge (dredʒ) n draga m. vt dragar.

dregs (dregz) n pl 1 heces f pl. 2 sedimento m.

drench (drentʃ) vt 1 mojar. 2 empapar. 3 saturar.

dress (dres) n 1 vestido m. 2 ropa f. **evening dress** 1 traje de noche m. 2 traje de etiqueta m. **dressmaker** n costurera, modista f. ~vt 1 vestir. 2 cul aliñar. vi vestirse. **dress up** vestirse de etiqueta. **dress circle** n anfiteatro m. **dress rehearsal** n ensayo general m.

dresser[1] ('dresə) n 1 persona que ayuda a vestir f. 2 él que se viste de manera especial m.

dresser[2] ('dresə) n tocador m.

dressing ('dresiŋ) n 1 acción de vestir f. 2 cul aderezo, condimento m. 3 med vendaje m. **dressing-gown** n bata f. peinador m. **dressing-room** n cuarto de vestir m. **dressing-table** n mueble tocador m.

drew (druː) v see **draw**.

dribble ('dribəl) n 1 goteo m. 2 sport regate m. vi gotear. vt sport regatear.

drift (drift) n 1 naut deriva f. 2 montón m. 3 tendencia f. 4 intención f. vi 1 ir sin rumbo. 2 desviar. 3 amontonar.

drill (dril) n 1 tech taladro, perforador m. 2 mil instrucción f. vt 1 taladrar, perforar. 2 entrenar. 3 enseñar instrucción a.

drink* (driŋk) n 1 bebida f. 2 trago m. vt,vi beber. **drinkable** adj potable. **drinking water** n agua potable m.

drip (drip) n 1 goteo m. 2 gota f. vi gotear, chorrear. **drip-dry** adj de lava y pon.

drive* (draiv) n 1 paseo m. 2 impulso, empuje m. 3 calzada f. vt 1 empujar, mover. 2 conducir, guiar. vi mot conducir. **driver** n mot conductor, chófer m. **driving licence** n permiso de conducir. **driving test** n examen de conducir m.

drivel ('drivəl) n tonterías f pl. vi decir tonterías.

drizzle ('drizəl) vi lloviznar. n llovizna f.

drone[1] (droun) n zángano, abejón m.

drone[2] (droun) vi zumbar.

droop (druːp) vi 1 marchitarse. 2 desanimarse. **drooping** adj bajo, caído.

drop (drɔp) n 1 gota f. 2 descenso m. caída f. 3 pastilla f. vt 1 dejar caer. 2 abandonar. 3 omitir. 4 bajar. vi 1 caer. 2 descender. **drop out** vi 1 desaparecer. 2 quedarse atrás, rezagarse.

drought (draut) n sequía f.

drove (drouv) v see **drive**.

drown (draun) vt 1 ahogar. 2 inundar. vi ahogarse.

drowse (drauz) vi dormitar. **drowsy** adj soñoliento. **be drowsy** tener sueño.

drudge (drʌdʒ) n esclavo m. vi trabajar penosamente. **drudgery** n trabajo penoso m.

drug (drʌg) n 1 droga f. narcótico m. vt drogar, narcotizar.

drum (drʌm) n 1 tambor m. 2 bombo m. 3 barril m. vi mus tocar el tambor. **drummer** n tambor m.

drunk (drʌŋk) v see **drink**. **drunken** adj borracho, bebido m. **drunkenness** n borrachera f.

dry (drai) adj 1 seco. 2 árido. vt secar. **dry-clean** vt lavar en seco.

dual ('djuəl) adj doble. **duality** n dualidad f. **dual carriageway** n pista doble f.

dubious ('djuːbiəs) adj 1 dudoso. 2 ambiguo.

duchess ('dʌtʃis) n duquesa f.

duck[1] (dʌk) n pato m. **duckling** n patito m.

duck[2] (dʌk) vt chapuzar. vi agacharse.

duct (dʌkt) n conducto, canal, tubo m.

dud (dʌd) n 1 fracaso, fracasado m. 2 mil granada fallida f. adj defectuoso, inútil.

due (dju:) adj 1 debido. 2 merecido. 3 conveniente. 4 esperado. n deuda f. merecido m.

duel ('djuəl) n duelo m. vi batirse en duelo. **duellist** n duelista m.

duet (dju'et) n mus dúo m.

dug (dʌg) v see **dig**.

duke (dju:k) n duque m.

dull (dʌl) adj 1 sombrío. 2 deslustrado. 3 sordo. 4 torpe. 5 tonto, estúpido. vt 1 embotar. 2 entristecer.

dumb (dʌm) adj mudo m. **dumbfound** vt 1 confundir. 2 dejar atónito. **dumbfounded** adj confuso, pasmado, atónito.

dummy ('dʌmi) n 1 maniquí, muñeco m. 2 tonto, zoquete m. 3 game muerto m. adj falso.

dump (dʌmp) n 1 depósito de basuras m. 2 montón m. vt 1 vaciar, descargar. 2 dejar.

dunce (dʌns) n tonto, ignorante m.

dune (dju:n) n duna f.

dung (dʌŋ) n estiércol m.

dungeon ('dʌndʒən) n calabozo m. mazmorra f.

duplicate (adj,n 'dju:plikət; v 'dju:plikeit) adj duplicado. n duplicado, doble m. copia f. vt duplicar.

durable ('djuərəbəl) adj durable.

duration (djuə'reiʃən) n duración f.

during ('djuəriŋ) prep durante.

dusk (dʌsk) n crepúsculo, anochecer m. **dusky** adj 1 obscuro. 2 sombrío. 3 pardo.

dust (dʌst) n polvo m. **dusty** adj polvoriento. ~vt quitar el polvo a. **dustbin** n cajón de basura m. **duster** n 1 trapo, paño m. 2 plumero m. 3 guardapolvo m. **dustman** n basurero m. **dustpan** n recogedor de basura m.

Dutch (dʌtʃ) adj,n holandés. **Dutchman** n holandés m.

duty ('dju:ti) n 1 deber m. obligación f. 2 derechos de aduana m pl. impuesto m. **on duty** 1 de servicio. 2 de guardia. **duty-free** adj libre de derechos de aduana. **dutiful** adj obediente.

duvet ('du:vei) n colcha de plumón f.

dwarf (dwɔ:f) n,adj enano m. vt empequeñecer.

dwell* (dwel) vt habitar, morar, vivir. **dwelling** n 1 morada f. 2 residencia f. 3 casa f.

dwindle ('dwindl) vi disminuir, mermar, reducirse.

dye (dai) n tintura f. tinte m. vt teñir, colorar.

dyke (daik) n 1 dique m. presa f. 2 zanja f.

dynamic (dai'næmik) adj dinámico.

dynamite ('dainəmait) n dinamita f. vt volar con dinamita.

dynasty ('dinəsti) n dinastía f. **dynastic** adj dinástico.

dysentery ('disəntri) n med disentería f.

E

each (i:tʃ) adj cada invar. pron cada uno m. cada una f. **each other** (el) uno a(l) otro. ~adv por persona.

eager ('i:gə) adj ansioso, anhelante. **be eager for** ansiar. **be eager to** tener vivos deseos de. **eagerness** n ansia f. anhelo m.

eagle ('i:gəl) n águila f.

ear[1] (iə) n 1 oreja f. 2 oído m. **eardrum** n tímpano m. **earmark** vt 1 reservar. 2 destinar. **earphones** n pl auriculares m pl. **earring** n pendiente m.

ear[2] (iə) n bot espiga f.

earl (ə:l) n conde m.

early ('ə:li) adj 1 temprano, precoz. 2 primero, primitivo. adv 1 temprano, pronto. 2 a principios.

earn (ə:n) vt 1 ganar. 2 devengar. **earnings** n pl 1 ingresos m pl. 2 ganancias f pl.

earnest ('ə:nist) adj 1 serio, formal. 2 fervoroso, ardiente. **in earnest** en serio.

earth (ə:θ) n tierra f. vt tech conectar a tierra. **earthenware** n loza de barro f. **earthly** adj terrenal. **earthquake** n terremoto m. **earthworm** n lombriz de tierra f. **earthy** adj 1 terroso. 2 mundano. 3 grosero, basto.

earwig ('iəwig) n tijereta f.

ease (i:z) n 1 facilidad f. soltura f. 2 desenvoltura f. 3 comodidad f. 4 alivio m. vt aliviar, mitigar.

easel ('i:zəl) n caballete m.

east (i:st) n 1 este, oriente m. adj del este, oriental. adv al este. **easterly** adj este, del este. **eastern** adj del este, oriental. **eastward** adv al este. **eastwards** adv hacia el este.

Easter ('i:stə) n Pascua de Resurrección f.

easy ('i:zi) adj 1 fácil. 2 cómodo, holgado. 3 pausado. **easygoing** adj 1 acomodadizo. 2 indolente, holgazán. 3 sereno.

eat* (i:t) vt,vi comer. **eat away** corroer. **eat into** desgastar, reducir. **eat up** comerse, devorar.

eavesdrop ('i:vzdrɔp) vi fisgonear, escuchar a escondidas. **eavesdropper** n fisgón m.

ebb (eb) n reflujo, menguante m. vi 1 bajar, menguar. 2 decaer.

ebony ('ebəni) n ébano m.

eccentric (ik'sentrik) adj,n excéntrico m. **eccentricity** n excentricidad f.

ecclesiastical (ikli:zi'æstikəl) also **ecclesiastic** adj eclesiástico.

echo ('ekou) n, pl **echoes** eco m. vi resonar, hacer eco.

eclair (ei'klɛə) n bizcocho relleno m.

eclipse (i'klips) n eclipse m. vt eclipsar.

ecology (i:'kɔlədʒi) n ecología f. **ecological** adj ecológico. **ecologist** n ecólogo m.

economy (i'kɔnəmi) n economía f. **economic** adj económico. **economics** n pl economía política f. económicas f pl. **economist** n economista m,f. **economize** vi economizar.

ecstasy ('ekstəsi) n éxtasis m. **ecstatic** adj extático.

Ecuador ('ekwədɔ:) n El Ecuador m. **Ecuadorian** adj,n ecuatoriano.

eczema ('eksimə) n eczema m.

edge (edʒ) n 1 filo m. 2 borde, margen m. 3 canto. 4 extremo m. vt 1 afilar. 2 orlar, ribetear. **edgeways** adj de canto. **edgy** adj inf nervioso.

edible ('edibəl) adj comestible.

edict ('i:dikt) n edicto m.

edit ('edit) vt editar. **editor** n 1 editor m. 2 redactor en jefe m.

edition (i'diʃən) n edición f.

editorial (edi'tɔ:riəl) adj,n editorial f. **editorial staff** redacción f.

educate ('edjukeit) vt 1 educar. 2 instruir. **educated** adj culto. **education** n educación f. **educational** adj educacional.

eel (i:l) n anguila f.

eerie ('iəri) adj misterioso.

effect (i'fekt) n 1 efecto m. 2 impresión f. **side effect** efecto secundario. ~vt efectuar. **effective** adj 1 eficaz. 2 efectivo.

effeminate (i'feminət) adj afeminado.

effervesce (efə'ves) vi estar en efervescencia. **effervescence** n efervescencia f. **effervescent** adj efervescente.

efficient (i'fiʃənt) adj 1 eficiente. 2 eficaz. **efficiency** n 1 eficiencia f. 2 eficacia f.

effigy ('efidʒi) n efigie f.

effort ('efət) n esfuerzo m. **effortless** adj fácil.

effusion n efusión f. **effusive** adj efusivo.

egg (eg) n huevo m. **eggbeater** n cul batidor m.

egg[2] (eg) vt **egg on** azuzar.

ego ('i:gou) n el yo, ego m. **egocentric** adj egocéntrico. **egoism** n egoísmo m. **egoist** n egoísta m,f. **egoistical** adj egoísta. **egotism** n egotismo m.

Egypt ('i:dʒipt) n Egipto m. **Egyptian** adj,n egipcio.

eiderdown ('aidədaun) n edredón m.

eight (eit) adj,n ocho m. **eighth** adj octavo.

eighteen (ei'ti:n) adj dieciocho. **eighteenth** adj decimoctavo.

eighty ('eiti) adj ochenta. **eightieth** adj octogésimo.

either ('aiðə) adj 1 cualquier. 2 ambos. pron cualquiera or ninguno de los dos. conj **either...or** o...o. adv tampoco.

ejaculate (i'dʒækjuleit) vt 1 exclamar. 2 med eyacular. **ejaculation** n 1 exclamación f. 2 med eyaculación f.

eject (i'dʒekt) vt 1 expulsar, echar. 2 law desahuciar. **ejection** n 1 expulsión f. 2 law desahucio m. **ejector** n expulsor m.

elaborate (adj i'læbərit; v i'læbəreit) adj 1 complicado. 2 detallado. vt elaborar. **elaborate on** ampliar. **elaboration** n elaboración f.

elapse (i'læps) vi transcurrir.

elastic (i'læstik) adj,n elástico m. **elasticity** n elasticidad f.

elated (i'leitid) adj 1 jubiloso. 2 exaltado. **elation** n 1 júbilo, regocijo m. 2 exaltación f.

elbow ('elbou) n codo m. vt empujar a codazos.

elder[1] ('eldə) adj mayor. n anciano m. **elderly** adj mayor, de edad.

elder[2] ('eldə) n saúco m. **elderberry** n baya del saúco f.

elect (i'lekt) vt elegir. **elect to** optar por. ~adj electo. **election** n elección f. **elector** n elector m. **electoral** adj electoral. **electorate** n electorado m.

electric (i'lektrik) adj also **electrical** eléctrico.

electrician (ilek'triʃən) n electricista m,f.

electricity (ilek'trisiti) n electricidad f.

electrify (i'lektrifai) vt 1 electrificar. 2 electrizar. **electrification** n electrificación f.

electrocute (i'lektrəkju:t) vt electrocutar.

electrode (i'lektroud) n electrodo m.

electron (i'lektrɔn) n electrón m.

electronic (ilek'trɔnik) adj electrónico. **electronics** n electrónica f.

enclose

elegant ('eligənt) adj elegante. elegance n elegancia f.
element ('eləmənt) n elemento m. elemental adj elemental. elementary adj elemental.
elephant ('elifənt) n elefante m.
elevate ('eliveit) vt elevar. elevation n elevación f.
elevator ('eliveitə) n 1 montacargas m invar. elevador m.
eleven (i'levən) adj,n once m. eleventh adj undécimo.
elf (elf) n, pl elves duende, enanito m.
eligible ('elidʒibəl) adj elegible. eligibility n elegibilidad f.
eliminate (i'limineit) vt eliminar. elimination n eliminación f.
elite (ei'liːt) n minoría selecta, élite f.
ellipse (i'lips) n elipse f. elliptical adj elíptico.
elm (elm) n olmo m.
elocution (eləˈkjuːʃən) n elocución f.
elope (i'loup) vi fugarse. elopement n fuga f.
eloquent ('eləkwənt) adj elocuente. eloquence n elocuencia f.
else (els) adv 1 más. 2 de otra manera. elsewhere adv en or a otra parte.
elucidate (i'luːsideit) vt dilucidar, elucidar. elucidation n elucidación f.
elude (i'luːd) vt eludir. elusive adj difícil de encontrar, esquivo.
emaciated (i'meisieitid) adj demacrado.
emanate ('emaneit) vi emanar. emanation n emanación f.
emancipate (i'mænsipeit) vt emancipar. emancipation n emancipación f.
embalm (im'bɑːm) vt embalsamar.
embankment (im'bæŋkmənt) n 1 terraplén m. 2 dique m.
embargo (im'bɑːgou) n, pl embargoes 1 embargo m. 2 prohibición, suspensión f.
embark (im'bɑːk) vi embarcarse. embarkation n 1 embarco m. 2 embarque m.
embarrass (im'bærəs) vt 1 turbar, azorar. 2 avergonzar. embarrassing adj 1 embarazoso. 2 violento. embarrassment n turbación f.
embassy ('embəsi) n embajada f.
embellish (im'beliʃ) vt embellecer. embellishment n embellecimiento m.
embers ('embəz) n pl rescoldo m. ascua f.
embezzle (im'bezəl) vt malversar. embezzlement n malversación f. embezzler n malversador m.
embitter (im'bitə) vt amargar.
emblem ('embləm) n emblema m.

embody (im'bɔdi) vt encarnar. embodiment n encarnación f.
emboss (im'bɔs) vt estampar en relieve.
embrace (im'breis) vt,vi 1 abrazar. 2 abarcar. n abrazo m.
embroider (im'brɔidə) vt 1 bordar. 2 adornar. embroidery n bordado m.
embryo ('embriou) n embrión m. embryonic adj embrionario.
emerald ('emrəld) n esmeralda f.
emerge (i'məːdʒ) vi emerger. emergence n emergencia f.
emergency (i'məːdʒənsi) n emergencia f.
emigrate ('emigreit) vi emigrar. emigrant n,adj emigrante. emigration n emigración f.
eminent ('eminənt) adj eminente. eminence n eminencia f.
emit (i'mit) vt 1 emitir. 2 arrojar. 3 despedir. emission n emisión f.
emotion (i'mouʃən) n emoción f. emotional adj 1 emocional. 2 emocionante.
empathy ('empəθi) n empatía f.
emperor ('empərə) n emperador m.
emphasis ('emfəsis) n énfasis m. emphasize vt 1 acentuar. 2 subrayar, recalcar. emphatic adj enfático.
empire ('empaiə) n imperio m.
empirical (em'pirikəl) adj empírico. empiricism n empirismo m.
employ (im'plɔi) vt emplear. employee n empleado m. employer n patrono, empresario m. employment n empleo m.
empower (im'pauə) vt 1 autorizar. 2 habilitar.
empress ('emprəs) n emperatriz f.
empty ('empti) adj 1 vacío. 2 vano. vt vaciar. emptiness n vacío m. empty-handed adj con las manos vacías. empty-headed adj tonto.
emu ('iːmjuː) n emú m.
emulate ('emjuleit) vt emular. emulation n emulación f.
emulsion (i'mʌlʃən) n emulsión f.
enable (i'neibəl) vt permitir, poner en condiciones.
enact (i'nækt) vt 1 decretar. 2 law promulgar. 3 representar.
enamel (i'næməl) n esmalte m. vt esmaltar.
enchant (in'tʃɑːnt) vt encantar. enchanting adj encantador.
encircle (in'səːkəl) vt cercar, rodear.
enclose (in'klouz) vt 1 cercar. 2 encerrar. 3 incluir, adjuntar. enclosure n 1 cercado, recinto m. 2 inclusión f

193

encore ('ɔŋkɔ:) *interj* ¡bis! ¡que se repita! *n* repetición *f*.

encounter (in'kauntə) *n* encuentro *m*. *vt* encontrar, tropezar.

encourage (in'kʌridʒ) *vt* 1 animar, alentar. 2 fomentar, estimular. **encouragement** *n* 1 aliento, estímulo *m*. 2 fomento *m*.

encroach (in'krout∫) *vi* 1 invadir. 2 usurpar.

encumber (in'kʌmbə) *vt* 1 gravar, cargar. 2 estorbar.

encyclopedia (insaiklə'pi:diə) *n* enciclopedia *f*.

end (end) *n* 1 fin *m*. 2 final *m*. 3 extremo, cabo *m*. punta *f*. *vt,vi* terminar, acabar. **endless** *adj* interminable. **ending** *n* conclusión *f*. fin *m*.

endanger (in'deindʒə) *vt* poner en peligro.

endeavour (in'devə) *n* esfuerzo, empeño *m*. *vt,vi* esforzar, procurar.

endemic (en'demik) *adj* endémico.

endive ('endaiv) *n* escarola endibia *f*.

endorse (in'dɔ:s) *vt* 1 endosar. **endorsement** *n* 1 endoso *m*. 2 *mot* nota de inhabilitación *f*. **endorser** *n* endosante *m,f*.

endow (in'dau) *vt* dotar. **endowment** *n* 1 dotación *f*. 2 dote *f*.

endure (in'djuə) *vt* 1 aguantar, soportar. 2 resistir. *vi* durar, perdurar. **endurable** *adj* soportable. **endurance** *n* resistencia *f*. aguante *m*.

enemy ('enəmi) *n,adj* enemigo *m*.

energy ('enədʒi) *n* energía *f*. **energetic** *adj* enérgico.

enfold (in'fould) *vt* 1 envolver, abrazar, estrechar.

enforce (in'fɔ:s) *vt* 1 hacer cumplir, imponer. 2 poner en vigor. 3 hacer valer. **enforcement** *n* 1 imposición *f*. 2 ejecución *f*.

engage (in'geidʒ) *vt* 1 alquilar, apalabrar. 2 ocupar. 3 trabar. **be engaged** 1 estar ocupado. 2 estar prometido para casarse. **engagement** *n* 1 compromiso *m*. 2 contrato *m*. **engaging** *adj* simpático, agraciado.

engine ('endʒin) *n* 1 motor *m*. 2 máquina, locomotora *f*. **engine-driver** *n* maquinista *m*.

engineer (endʒi'niə) *n* 1 ingeniero *m*. 2 mecánico *m*. *vt* maquinar, agenciar. **engineering** *n* ingeniería *f*.

England ('iŋglənd) *n* Inglaterra *f*. **English** *adj* inglés. **English** (language) *n* inglés *m*. **Englishman** *n* inglés *m*.

engrave (in'greiv) *vt* grabar. **engraver** *n* grabador *m*. **engraving** *n* grabado *m*.

engross (in'grous) *vt* absorber, acaparar.

engulf (in'gʌlf) *vt* 1 sumergir, hundir. 2 tragar.

enhance (in'ha:ns) *vt* realzar.

enigma (i'nigmə) *n* enigma *m*. **enigmatic** *adj* enigmático.

enjoy (in'dʒɔi) *vt* 1 disfrutar de, gozar de. 2 gustar. **enjoyable** *adj* 1 agradable. 2 divertido. **enjoyment** *n* 1 disfrute, goce *m*. 2 gozo, gusto *m*.

enlarge (in'la:dʒ) *vt,vi* 1 extender, ensanchar. 2 aumentar. 3 ampliar. 4 *med* dilatar. **enlargement** *n* 1 extensión *f*. ensanche *m*. 2 aumento *m*. 3 ampliación *f*. 4 *med* dilatación *f*.

enlighten (in'laitn) *vt* 1 instruir, informar. 2 ilustrar, iluminar. **enlightening** *adj* instructivo, informativo. **enlightenment** *n* ilustración *f*.

enlist (in'list) *vt* 1 alistar. 2 granjear, procurar.

enormous (i'nɔ:məs) *adj* enorme. **enormity** *n* enormidad *f*.

enough (i'nʌf) *adj,adv* bastante.

enquire (in'kwaiə) *vt* 1 averiguar. 2 preguntar. 3 informarse de. **enquirer** *n* 1 el que pregunta *m*. 2 investigador *m*. **enquiring** *adj* 1 curioso, investigador. 2 interrogativo. **enquiry** *n* 1 indagación, pesquisa *f*. 2 pregunta, petición de informes *f*. 3 encuesta *f*.

enrage (in'reidʒ) *vt* enfurecer.

enrich (in'rit∫) *vt* enriquecer. **enrichment** *n* enriquecimiento *m*.

enrol (in'roul) *vt* 1 inscribir. 2 matricular. 3 *mil* alistar. **enrolment** *n* 1 inscripción *f*. 2 matrícula *f*. 3 alistamiento *m*.

ensign ('ensain) *n* 1 insignia *f*. 2 abanderado *m*.

enslave (in'sleiv) *vt* esclavizar. **enslavement** *n* esclavitud *f*.

ensure (in'∫uə) *vt* asegurar.

entail (in'teil) *vt* 1 ocasionar, acarrear. 2 suponer. 3 *law* vincular.

entangle (in'tæŋgəl) *vt* enredar, embrollar. **entanglement** *n* enredo, embrollo *m*.

enter ('entə) *vi,vt* 1 entrar. 2 ingresar. 3 registrar, asentar. 4 inscribir.

enterprise ('entəpraiz) *n* 1 empresa *f*. 2 iniciativa *f*. **enterprising** *adj* emprendedor.

entertain (entə'tein) *vt* 1 entretener. 2 recibir. 3 divertir. **entertainment** *n* 1 entretenimiento *m*. 2 espectáculo *m*.

enthral (in'θrɔ:l) *vt* encantar, embelesar.

enthusiasm (in'θju:ziæzəm) *n* entusiasmo *m*. **enthusiast** *n* entusiasta *m,f*. **enthusiastic** *adj* 1 entusiasta. 2 entusiástico.

entice (in'tais) *vt* tentar, seducir. **enticement** *n* tentación, seducción *f*.

entire (in'taiə) adj entero, completo. **entirety** n totalidad f.

entitle (in'tait|) vt 1 titular. 2 dar derecho a. **be entitled** tener derecho.

entity ('entiti) n entidad f. ente m.

entrails ('entreilz) n pl entrañas f pl.

entrance[1] ('entrəns) n 1 entrada f. 2 ingreso m. **entrance hall** vestíbulo m.

entrance[2] (in'trɑ:ns) vt extasiar, hechizar.

entreat (in'tri:t) vt suplicar, implorar. **entreaty** n súplica, imploración f.

entrench (in'trentʃ) vt atrincherar. **entrenchment** n atrincheramiento m.

entrepreneur (ɔntrəprə'nə:) n 1 empresario m. 2 socio capitalista m.

entrust (in'trʌst) vt confiar.

entry ('entri) n 1 entrada f. 2 ingreso m. 3 comm partida f. 4 artículo m. 5 participante m,f. 6 participación f.

entwine (in'twain) vt entrelazar, entretejer.

enunciate (i'nʌnsieit) vt enunciar. **enunciation** n enunciación f.

envelop (in'veləp) vt envolver. **enveloping** adj envolvente.

envelope ('envəloup) n 1 sobre m. 2 envoltura f.

environment (in'vairənmənt) n medio ambiente m. **environmental** adj ambiental.

envisage (in'vizidʒ) vt 1 prever. 2 concebir.

envoy ('envɔi) n enviado m.

envy ('envi) vt envidiar. n envidia f.

enzyme ('enzaim) n enzima f.

epaulet ('epɔlet) n charretera f.

ephemeral (i'femərəl) adj efímero.

epic ('epik) adj épico. n 1 épica f. 2 epopeya f.

epidemic (epi'demik) adj epidémico. n epidemia f.

epilepsy ('epilepsi) n epilepsia f. **epileptic** adj,n epiléptico m.

epilogue ('epilɔg) n epílogo m.

episcopal (i'piskəpəl) adj episcopal. **episcopate** n episcopado m.

episode ('episoud) n episodio m. **episodic** adj episódico.

epitaph ('epitɑ:f) n epitafio m.

epitome (i'pitəmi) n epítome m. **epitomize** vt epitomar.

epoch ('i:pɔk) n época f.

equable ('ekwəbəl) adj 1 uniforme, igual. 2 ecuánime.

equal ('i:kwəl) adj igual. **be equal to 1** tener fuerzas para. **2** estar a la altura de. ∼n igual

m,f. vt igualar. **equality** n igualdad f. **equalize** vt igualar. vi empatar.

equate (i'kweit) vt 1 igualar, considerar equivalente. 2 poner en ecuación. **equation** n ecuación f.

equator (i'kweitə) n ecuador m. **equatorial** adj ecuatorial.

equestrian (i'kwestriən) adj ecuestre. n jinete m.

equilateral (i:kwi'lætərəl) adj equilátero.

equilibrium (i:kwi'libriəm) n equilibrio m.

equinox ('i:kwinɔks) n equinoccio m.

equip (i'kwip) vt 1 equipar. 2 dotar, proveer. **equipment** n 1 equipo m. 2 material m. 3 dotes f pl.

equity ('ekwiti) n equidad f. **equitable** adj equitativo.

equivalent (i'kwivələnt) adj equivalente. **equivalence** n equivalencia f.

era ('iərə) n era f.

eradicate (i'rædikeit) vt erradicar. **eradication** n erradicación f.

erase (i'reiz) vt borrar. **eraser** n goma de borrar f.

erect (i'rekt) vt erigir. adj erguido. **erection** n erección f.

ermine ('ə:min) n armiño m.

erode (i'roud) vt 1 erosionar, desgastar. 2 corroer. 3 mermar. **erosion** n 1 erosión f. 2 desgaste m.

erotic (i'rɔtik) adj erótico. **eroticism** n erotismo m.

err (ə:) vi 1 errar. 2 pecar.

errand ('erənd) n 1 recado m. 2 misión f. **run an errand** llevar un recado.

erratic (i'rætik) adj 1 desigual. 2 med errático.

error ('erə) n error m. **erroneous** adj erróneo.

erupt (i'rʌpt) vi 1 hacer erupción. 2 estallar. 3 irrumpir. **eruption** n erupción f.

escalate ('eskəleit) vt,vi extender, intensificar. **escalation** n extensión, intensificación f. **escalator** n escalera móvil f.

escalope (i'skæləp) n escalope m.

escape (i'skeip) vt,vi escapar. **escape notice** pasar inadvertido. ∼n 1 escape m. 2 fuga f.

escort ('eskɔ:t) vt 1 acompañar. 2 mil escoltar. n 1 acompañante m,f. 2 mil escolta f.

Eskimo ('eskimou) adj,n esquimal.

esoteric (esə'terik) adj esotérico.

especial (i'speʃəl) adj 1 especial. 2 particular. **especially** adv especialmente, sobre todo.

espionage ('espiənɑ:ʒ) n espionaje m.

esplanade ('espləneid) n paseo m.

195

essay ('esei) n ensayo m. **essayist** n ensayista m,f.

essence ('esəns) n esencia f. **essential** adj 1 esencial. 2 imprescindible.

establish (i'stæbliʃ) vt establecer. **establishment** n establecimiento m. **the Establishment** las clases directoras f pl.

estate (i'steit) n 1 finca, propiedad f. 2 bienes m pl. 3 herencia f. 4 estado m. **estate agent** n corredor de fincas m. **estate car** n rubia f.

esteem (i'sti:m) n estima, estimación f. vt estimar, apreciar.

estimate (n 'estimət; v 'estimeit) n 1 estimación f. 2 cálculo m. 3 tasación f. 4 presupuesto m. vt 1 estimar, calcular. 2 tasar. 3 presupuestar, hacer un presupuesto.

estuary ('estʃuəri) n estuario m.

etching ('etʃiŋ) n aguafuerte, grabado m.

eternal (i'tə:nļ) adj eterno.

eternity (i'tə:niti) n eternidad f.

ether ('i:θə) n éter m.

ethereal (i'θiəriəl) adj etéreo.

ethics ('eθiks) n pl ética f. **ethical** adj ético.

Ethiopia (i:θi'oupiə) n Etiopía f. **Ethiopian** adj,n etíope.

ethnic ('eθnik) adj étnico.

etiquette ('etikit) n 1 etiqueta f. 2 honor profesional f.

etymology (eti'mɔlədʒi) n etimología f. **etymological** adj etimológico.

eucalyptus (ju:kə'liptəs) n eucalipto m.

Eucharist ('ju:kərist) n Eucaristía f.

eunuch ('ju:nək) n eunuco m.

euphemism ('ju:fəmizəm) n eufemismo m. **euphemistic** adj eufemístico.

euphoria (ju:'fɔ:riə) n euforia f.

Europe ('juərəp) n Europa f. **European** adj,n europeo.

European Economic Community n Comunidad Económica Europea f.

euthanasia (ju:θə'neiziə) n eutanasia f.

evacuate (i'vækjueit) vt evacuar. **evacuation** n evacuación f. **evacuee** n evacuado m.

evade (i'veid) vt evadir, eludir. **evasion** n evasión m. **evasive** adj evasivo.

evaluate (i'væljueit) vt evaluar. **evaluation** n evaluación f.

evangelical (i:væn'dʒelikəl) adj evangélico. **evangelist** n evangelizador m.

evaporate (i'væpəreit) vt,vi evaporar. **evaporation** n evaporación f.

evasive (i'veisiv) adj evasivo.

eve (i:v) n víspera f.

even ('i:vən) adj 1 llano, liso. 2 constante, invariable, igual. 3 par. **break even** inf salir sin ganar ni perder. ~adv. 1 hasta, incluso. 2 aun, todavía. **even if** or **though** aunque, aun cuando. **not even** ni siquiera. ~vt allanar, nivelar.

evening ('i:vəniŋ) n 1 atardecer m. 2 noche f. 3 velada f. **good evening!** ¡buenas tardes! ¡buenas noches! ~adj vespertino. **evening class** n clase nocturna f. **evening dress** n traje de etiqueta, traje de noche m.

event (i'vent) n 1 acontecimiento m. 2 caso, evento m. 3 resultado m. **in the event of** en caso de. **eventful** adj accidentado, azaroso. **eventual** adj 1 final. 2 consiguiente. **eventuality** n eventualidad f. **eventually** adv con el tiempo.

ever ('evə) adv 1 siempre. 2 alguna vez. 3 nunca, jamás. **everlasting** adj 1 eterno, perdurable. 2 interminable.

every ('evri) adj 1 cada. 2 todo. **every now and then** de vez en cuando. **every so often** cada cierto tiempo. **everybody** pron todo el mundo. **everyday** adj 1 diario. 2 cotidiano, acostumbrado. 3 corriente, rutinario. **everyone** pron 1 todo el mundo. 2 cada uno. **everything** pron todo. **everywhere** adv 1 en todas partes. 2 dondequiera.

evict (i'vikt) vt desahuciar. **eviction** n desahucio m.

evidence ('evidəns) n 1 evidencia f. 2 prueba f. 3 law testimonio m. declaración f. **give evidence** 1 prestar declaración. 2 dar testimonio. **evident** adj evidente.

evil ('i:vəl) adj 1 malo, pernicioso. 2 malvado. n mal m. maldad f.

evoke (i'vouk) vt evocar.

evolve (i'vɔlv) vt desarrollar. vi evolucionar. **evolution** n 1 evolución f. 2 desarrollo m.

ewe (ju:) n oveja f.

exact (ig'zækt) adj exacto. vt exigir. **exacting** adj 1 exigente. 2 arduo. **exaction** n exacción f. **exactitude** n exactitud f.

exaggerate (ig'zædʒəreit) vt exagerar. **exaggeration** n exageración f.

exalt (ig'zɔ:lt) vt exaltar. **exaltation** n exaltación f.

examine (ig'zæmin) vt 1 examinar. 2 med hacer un reconocimiento. 3 law interrogar. **examination** n 1 examen m. 2 med reconocimiento m. 3 law interrogación f.

example (ig'zɑ:mpəl) n ejemplo m. **make an**

example of castigar de modo ejemplar. **set an example** dar ejemplo.

exasperate (ig'zɑːspəreit) vt exasperar, sacar de quicio. **exasperation** n exasperación f.

excavate ('ekskəveit) vt excavar. **excavation** n excavación f. **excavator** n 1 excavador m. 2 tech excavadora f.

exceed (ik'siːd) vt exceder. **exceedingly** adv sumamente.

excel (ik'sel) vi sobresalir. vt aventajar, superar.

excellent ('eksələnt) adj excelente. **excellence** n excelencia f.

except (ik'sept) vt exceptuar. prep excepto, menos, salvo. **exception** n excepción f. **exceptional** adj excepcional.

excerpt (n 'eksəːpt; v ek'səːpt) n extracto m. vt extractar.

excess (n ik'ses; adj 'ekses) n exceso m. adj excedente. **excessive** adj excesivo.

exchange (iks'tʃeindʒ) vt 1 cambiar. 2 canjear. 3 intercambiar. n 1 cambio m. 2 intercambio m. **exchangeable** adj cambiable, canjeable.

exchequer (iks'tʃekə) n hacienda f. tesoro público m.

excise ('eksaiz) n impuestos m pl.

excite (ik'sait) vt 1 entusiasmar. 2 excitar, provocar. 3 poner nervioso. **exciting** adj emocionante, excitante.

exclaim (ik'skleim) vi,vt exclamar. **exclamation** n exclamación f. **exclamation mark** n punto de admiración m.

exclude (ik'skluːd) vt excluir. **exclusion** n exclusión f. **exclusive** adj 1 exclusivo. 2 selecto. **exclusive of** sin contar, excluyendo.

excommunicate (ekskə'mjuːnikeit) vt excomulgar. **excommunication** n excomunión f.

excruciating (ik'skruːʃieitiŋ) adj agudísimo, atroz.

excursion (ik'skəːʒən) n excursión f.

excuse (v ik'skjuːz; n ik'skjuːs) vt 1 excusar, dispensar. 2 disculpar. **excuse me!** ¡perdón! ~n 1 excusa f. 2 disculpa f.

execute ('eksikjuːt) vt 1 ejecutar. 2 law legalizar, otorgar. **execution** n 1 ejecución f. 2 law legalización f. otorgamiento m. **executioner** n verdugo m. **executive** adj ejecutivo. n 1 ejecutivo m. 2 director, gerente m. **executor** n 1 ejecutor m. albacea, ejecutor testamentario m.

exempt (ig'zempt) adj exento. vt exentar, eximir, dispensar. **exemption** n exención f.

exercise ('eksəsaiz) n ejercicio m. vt,vi 1 ejercer. 2 ejercitar.

exert (ig'zəːt) vt ejercer, emplear. **exertion** n esfuerzo m.

exhale (eks'heil) vt 1 exhalar. 2 espirar. **exhalation** n 1 exhalación f. 2 espiración f.

exhaust (ig'zɔːst) vt agotar. n escape m. **exhausting** adj agotador. **exhaustion** n agotamiento m. **exhaustive** adj exhaustivo.

exhibit (ig'zibit) n 1 objeto expuesto m. 2 law documento m. prueba f. vt 1 exhibir. 2 exponer. **exhibition** n 1 exhibición f. 2 exposición f. 3 beca f. **exhibitionism** n exhibicionismo m. **exhibitionist** n,adj exhibicionista m,f. **exhibitor** n expositor m.

exhilarate (ig'ziləreit) vt 1 regocijar. 2 estimular, levantar el ánimo. **exhilarating** adj estimulante. **exhilaration** n 1 regocijo m. 2 excitación f.

exile ('egzail) n 1 exilio, destierro m. 2 exiliado, desterrado m. vt exiliar, desterrar.

exist (ig'zist) vi existir. **existence** n existencia f. **existent** adj existente. **existentialism** n existencialismo m.

exit ('eksit) n 1 salida f. 2 mutis m. vi hacer mutis.

exorbitant (ig'zɔːbitənt) adj exorbitante.

exorcize ('eksɔːsaiz) vt exorcizar. **exorcism** n exorcismo m. **exorcist** n exorcista m,f.

exotic (ig'zɔtik) adj exótico. **exoticism** n exotismo m.

expand (ik'spænd) vt,vi 1 extender, ampliar. 2 dilatar. 3 desarrollar. 4 expansionar.

expanse (ik'spæns) n extensión f. **expansion** n 1 expansión f. 2 dilatación f. **expansive** adj expansivo.

expatriate (eks'pætriit) n expatriado m. adj expatriado.

expect (ik'spekt) vt 1 esperar, contar con. 2 figurarse. **expectancy** n expectación f. **expectant** adj expectante. **expectant mother** futura mamá f. **expectation** n 1 expectación f. 2 esperanza, expectativa f.

expedient (ik'spiːdiənt) adj expeditivo, oportuno. n expediente m. **expedience** also **expediency** n conveniencia f.

expedition (ekspi'diʃən) n expedición f.

expel (ik'spel) vt 1 expulsar. 2 arrojar.

expenditure (ik'spenditʃə) n gasto m. desembolso m. **expendable** adj prescindible.

expense (ik'spens) n 1 gasto m. 2 expensas f pl. **expensive** adj caro, costoso.

experience (ik'spiəriəns) n experiencia f. vt experimentar, sentir.

experiment (ik'sperimənt) n experimento m. vi

experimentar, hacer experimentos. **experimental** *adj* experimental.

expert ('eksp∂:t) *adj* 1 experto. 2 pericial. *n* experto, perito *m*. **expertise** *n* pericia *f*.

expire (ik'spai∂) *vi* 1 expirar. 2 vencer. 3 caducar. **expiration** *n* 1 expiración *f*. 2 vencimiento *m*.

explain (ik'splein) *vt* explicar. **explanation** *n* explicación *f*. **explanatory** *adj* explicativo.

expletive (ik'spli:tiv) *n* 1 expletivo *m*. 2 palabrota *f*.

explicit (ik'splisit) *adj* explícito.

explode (ik'sploud) *vt* 1 volar, hacer saltar. 2 reventar, hacer explotar. 3 *inf* desmentir, refutar. *vi* estallar, hacer explosión.

exploit[1] ('eksploit) *n* hazaña *f*.

exploit[2] (ik'sploit) *vt* explotar. **exploitation** *n* explotación *f*.

explore (ik'splo:) *vt* explorar. **exploration** *n* exploración *f*. **exploratory** *adj* exploratorio, preparatorio. **explorer** *n* explorador *m*.

explosive (ik'splousiv) *n,adj* explosivo *m*. **explosion** *n* explosión *f*.

exponent (ik'spounant) *n* exponente *m,f*.

export (*v* ik'spo:t; *n* 'ekspo:t) *vt* exportar. *n* exportación *f*. **exporter** *n* exportador *m*.

expose (ik'spouz) *vt* 1 exponer. 2 desenmascarar. **exposition** *n* exposición *f*. **exposure** *n* 1 exposición *f*. 2 desenmascaramiento *m*.

express (ik'spres) *adj* 1 expreso. 2 rápido. **express letter** *n* carta urgente *f*. **express train** *n* rápido *m*. ~*vt* 1 expresar. 2 exprimir. **expression** *n* expresión *f*. **expressive** *adj* expresivo.

expulsion (ik'spʌlʃən) *n* expulsión *f*.

exquisite (ek'skwizit) *adj* 1 exquisito. 2 intenso.

extend (ik'stend) *vt,vi* 1 extender. 2 ampliar. 3 prolongar. 4 exigir el máximo. **extension** *n* 1 extensión *f*. 2 ampliación *f*. 3 prolongación *f*. 4 prórroga *f*. **extensive** *adj* 1 extenso. 2 dilatado. 3 frecuente.

extent (ik'stent) *n* 1 extensión *f*. 2 alcance *m*. **to a large extent** en gran parte. **to what extent?** ¿hasta qué punto?

exterior (ek'stiəriə) *adj,n* exterior *m*.

exterminate (ik'stə:mineit) *vt* exterminar. **extermination** *n* exterminio *m*.

external (ek'stə:nl) *adj* externo.

extinct (ik'stiŋkt) *adj* extinto. **extinction** *n* extinción *f*.

extinguish (ik'stiŋgwiʃ) *vt* extinguir. **extinguisher** *n* extintor *m*.

extra ('ekstrə) *adj* 1 adicional. 2 de más, de

sobra. 3 extraordinario, extra. *adv* 1 especialmente. 2 más. *n* extra *m*.

extract (*n* 'ekstrækt; *v* ik'strækt) *n* 1 extracto *m*. 2 trozo *m*. *vt* extraer. **extraction** *n* extracción *f*.

extramural (ekstrə'mjuərəl) *adj* de extramuros.

extraordinary (ik'strɔ:dənri) *adj* extraordinario.

extravagant (ik'strævəgənt) *adj* 1 derrochador, despilfarrador. 2 excesivo. 3 extravagante, estrafalario. **extravagance** *n* 1 derroche, despilfarro *m*. 2 exceso *m*. 3 extravagancia *f*.

extreme (ik'stri:m) *adj* extremo, extremado. *n* extremo *m*. **go to extremes** 1 tomar medidas extremas. 2 propasarse. **extremely** *adv* sumamente. **extremism** *n* extremismo *m*. **extremist** *n* extremista *m,f*. **extremity** *n* 1 extremidad *f*. 2 apuro *m*.

extricate ('ekstrikeit) *vt* 1 desenredar, desembrollar. 2 sacar, librar.

extrovert ('ekstrəvə:t) *adj,n* extrovertido *m*.

exuberant (ig'zju:bərənt) *adj* 1 exuberante. 2 eufórico. **exuberance** *n* 1 exuberancia *f*. 2 euforia *f*.

exult (ig'zʌlt) *vi* exultar.

eye (ai) *n* 1 ojo *m*. 2 *bot* yema *f*. **black eye** ojo amoratado. ~*vt* mirar detenidamente.

eyeball ('aibɔ:l) *n* globo del ojo *m*.

eyebrow ('aibrau) *n* ceja *f*.

eyelash ('ailæʃ) *n* pestaña *f*.

eyelid ('ailid) *n* párpado *m*.

eye shadow *n* sombreador de ojos *m*.

eyesight ('aisait) *n* vista *f*.

eyesore ('aisɔ:) *n* cosa que ofende la vista *f*.

eyestrain ('aistrein) *n* vista cansada *f*.

eye-witness *n* testigo ocular *or* presencial *m*.

F

fable ('feibəl) *n* fábula *f*.

fabric ('fæbrik) *n* 1 tejido, género *m*. 2 estructura *f*. **fabricate** *vt* 1 fabricar. 2 inventar. 3 falsificar. **fabrication** *n* 1 fabricación *f*. 2 invención *f*. 3 falsificación *f*.

fabulous ('fæbjuləs) *adj* fabuloso.

facade (fə'sɑ:d) *n* 1 fachada *f*. 2 apariencia *f*.

face (feis) *n* 1 cara *f*. rostro *m*. 2 mueca *f*. 3 esfera *f*. 4 superficie *f*. 5 apariencias *f pl*. **lose face** desprestigiarse. **save one's face** salvar las apariencias. **show one's face** dejarse ver. ~*vt* 1 encarar. 2 estar enfrente de. 3 arrostrar, hacer frente a. 4 reconocer, aceptar. **be**

faced with presentársele a. **facecloth** n paño m.

facet ('fæsit) n faceta f.

facetious (fə'si:ʃəs) adj chistoso, gracioso.

facile ('fæsail) adj fácil, superficial, ligero. **facilitate** vt facilitar. **facility** n facilidad f.

facing ('feisiŋ) prep frente a.

facsimile (fæk'simili) n, adj facsímil m.

fact (fækt) n 1 hecho m. 2 pl datos m pl. **as a matter of fact** en realidad. **factual** adj basado en hechos, objetivo.

faction ('fækʃən) n facción f.

factor ('fæktə) n factor m.

factory ('fæktri) n fábrica f.

faculty ('fækəlti) n facultad f.

fad (fæd) n 1 manía f. 2 novedad, moda f.

fade (feid) vi,vt 1 descolorar, desteñir. 2 marchitar. 3 apagar, desvanecer.

fag (fæg) n 1 faena f. trabajo penoso m. 2 sl pitillo m.

Fahrenheit ('færənhait) adj referente al termómetro de Fahrenheit.

fail (feil) vi 1 fallar. 2 fracasar. 3 desfallecer. 4 dejar de. vt 1 faltar a. 2 educ suspender. **failure** n 1 fracaso m. 2 fallo m.

faint (feint) adj 1 débil. 2 tenue. **feel faint** estar mareado. ~vi desmayarse, desfallecer. n desmayo m. **faint-hearted** adj pusilánime, medroso.

fair¹ (fɛə) adj 1 justo. 2 imparcial. 3 razonable. 4 hermoso, bello. 5 rubio. **fair-minded** adj imparcial. **fairly** adv 1 justamente, imparcialmente, limpiamente. 2 bastante, medianamente. **fairness** n 1 justicia, imparcialidad f. 2 hermosura f.

fair² (fɛə) n feria f. **fairground** n parque de atracciones m.

fairy ('fɛəri) n hada f. adj de hadas, mágico. **fairytale** n cuento de hadas m.

faith (feiθ) n fe f. **faithful** adj fiel. **faithfulness** n fidelidad f.

fake (feik) n 1 falsificación f. 2 imitación f. 3 impostor m. adj 1 falso. 2 fingido. vt 1 falsificar. 2 fingir.

falcon ('fɔ:lkən) n halcón m.

fall* (fɔ:l) n 1 caída f. 2 baja f. 3 desnivel m. vi 1 caer. 2 bajar. 3 recaer, tocar. 4 amainar. **fall down** 1 caerse. 2 derrumbarse. **fall in love** enamorarse.

fallacy ('fæləsi) n 1 error m. 2 sofisma m. 3 falacia f. 4 mentira f.

fallible ('fæləbəl) adj falible.

fallow ('fælou) adj barbechado.

false (fɔ:ls) adj 1 falso. 2 postizo. **falsehood** n falsedad f. **false teeth** n dentadura postiza f. **falsify** vt falsificar.

falter ('fɔ:ltə) vi 1 titubear, vacilar. 2 desfallecer.

fame (feim) n fama f. **famed** adj famoso.

familiar (fə'miliə) adj familiar. **be familiar with** estar familiarizado con. **familiarity** n familiaridad f. **familiarize** vt familiarizar.

family ('fæmili) n familia f.

famine ('fæmin) n 1 hambre f. 2 escasez f. **famished** adj hambriento, famélico.

famous ('feiməs) adj famoso, célebre.

fan¹ (fæn) n 1 abanico m. 2 ventilador, m. 3 aventadora f. vt 1 abanicar. 2 ventilar. **fanbelt** n correa de ventilador f.

fan² (fæn) n (inf) 1 admirador m. 2 entusiasta, hincha, m,f. **fan club** n club de admiradores m.

fanatic (fə'nætik) adj fanático.

fancy ('fænsi) n 1 quimera f. 2 fantasía f. 3 capricho, antojo m. 4 afición f. adj 1 de fantasía. 2 caprichoso. 3 estrafalario. vt 1 imaginar, figurar. 2 antojar. 3 encaprichar. **fancy dress** n disfraz m. **fanciful** adj 1 caprichoso. 2 fantástico.

fanfare ('fænfɛə) n 1 toque de trompetas m. 2 charanga f.

fang (fæŋ) n colmillo m.

fantastic (fæn'tæstik) adj fantástico.

fantasy ('fæntəsi) n fantasía f.

far (fɑ:) adj lejano. adv lejos. **by far** con mucho. **so far** 1 hasta aquí. 2 hasta ahora. **far-away** adj remoto. **far-fetched** adj inverosímil. **far-off** adj lejano, remoto. **far-reaching** adj 1 trascendental. 2 de mucho alcance.

farce (fɑ:s) n farsa f. **farcical** adj ridículo, absurdo.

fare (fɛə) n 1 precio m. 2 billete m. 3 naut pasaje m. 4 comida f.

farewell (fɛə'wel) interj ¡adiós! n adiós m.

farm (fɑ:m) n 1 hacienda f. 2 granja f. 3 criadero m. vt cultivar, labrar. vi ser agricultor. **farmer** n agricultor, granjero m. **farmhouse** n casa de campo, granja f. **farming** n 1 cultivo m. 2 agricultura f. **farmland** n tierras de labor f pl. **farmyard** n corral m.

farther ('fɑ:ðə) adj más alejado. adv más lejos.

farthest ('fɑ:ðist) adj el más alejado. adv a lo más lejos.

fascinate ('fæsineit) vt fascinar. **fascinating** adj fascinador. **fascination** n fascinación f.

fascism ('fæʃizəm) n fascismo m. **fascist** adj,n fascista.

fashion ('fæʃən) n 1 manera f. modo m. 2 moda f. **after a fashion** en cierto modo. **in fashion** de moda. **out of fashion** pasado de moda. ~vt formar, modelar. **fashionable** adj de moda, elegante.

fast[1] (fɑ:st) adj 1 rápido, veloz. 2 sólido, inalterable. adv 1 rápidamente, de prisa. 2 firmemente.

fast[2] (fɑ:st) n ayuno m. vi ayunar.

fasten ('fɑ:sən) vt 1 fijar, sujetar. 2 abrochar. **fastener** n 1 pestillo m. 2 corchete m. 3 grapa f.

fastidious (fæ'stidiəs) adj 1 quisquilloso. 2 exigente.

fat (fæt) adj 1 gordo, grueso. 2 graso. **get fat** engordar. ~n grasa f. **fatten** vt engordar.

fatal ('feitl) adj fatal, mortal. **fatality** n fatalidad f.

fate (feit) n 1 destino m. 2 suerte f. **fateful** adj fatídico.

father ('fɑ:ðə) n padre m. vt engendrar. **fatherhood** n paternidad f. **father-in-law** n suegro m. **fatherland** n patria f. **fatherly** adj paternal.

fathom ('fæðəm) n braza f. vt 1 sondear. 2 desentrañar. **fathomless** adj insondable.

fatigue (fə'ti:g) n fatiga f. vt fatigar.

fatuous ('fætjuəs) adj fatuo, necio.

fault (fɔ:lt) n 1 falta f. defecto m. 3 culpa f. 4 tech avería f. **be at fault** tener la culpa. **find fault with** criticar, censurar. ~vt tachar, encontrar defectos en.

favour ('feivə) n favor m. **be in favour of** estar a favor de. **be in favour with** gozar del favor de. **fall out of favour** caer en desgracia. ~vt favorecer. **favourable** adj favorable. **favourite** adj,n favorito m.

fawn[1] (fɔ:n) n cervato m.

fawn[2] (fɔ:n) vi adular, lisonjear. **fawning** adj servil, lisonjero.

fear (fiə) n miedo, temor m. vt temer. **fearful** adj 1 temeroso. 2 tímido. 3 espantoso, pavoroso. **fearless** adj intrépido, audaz.

feasible ('fi:zəbəl) adj factible.

feast (fi:st) n 1 fiesta f. 2 festín m. vt 1 festejar. 2 agasajar. **feast-day** n fiesta f.

feat (fi:t) n hazaña f.

feather ('feðə) n pluma f. vt emplumar. **featherbed** n colchón de pluma m.

feature ('fi:tʃə) n 1 rasgo m. característica f. 2 facción f. 3 artículo m. crónica f. 4 número

m. **feature film** n pelicula de largo metraje f. ~vt presentar, destacar.

February ('februəri) n febrero m.

feckless ('fekləs) adj descuidado, atolondrado.

fed (fed) v see **feed**.

federal ('fedərəl) adj federal. **federalism** n federalismo m. **federalist** n federalista m, f. **federate** vt federar. **federation** n federación f.

fee (fi:) n 1 honorarios m pl. 2 cuota f.

feeble ('fi:bəl) adj débil. **feeble-minded** adj imbécil.

feed[*] (fi:d) vt alimentar, dar de comer. vi comer. **be fed up** estar harto. **feedback** n 1 tech realimentación f. 2 reacción f. **feeding** n alimentación f. **feeding-bottle** n biberón m.

feel (fi:l) vt,vi sentirse. vt 1 sentir. 2 tocar, tantear. 3 parecer. **feeler** n 1 zool antena f 2 zool tentáculo m. 3 sondeo m. **feeling** n 1 sensación f. sentimiento m. 2 sensibilidad f. 3 parecer m. 4 presentimiento m. adj sensible.

feign (fein) vt 1 fingir. 2 inventar.

feint[1] (feint) n 1 treta f. 2 sport finta f. vi hacer una finta.

feint[2] (feint) adj tenue.

feline ('fi:lain) adj felino.

fell[1] (fel) vt 1 talar, cortar. 2 derribar.

fell[2] (fel) v see **fall**.

fellow ('felou) n 1 compañero m. 2 miembro, socio m. 3 tipo, sujeto m. **fellowship** n 1 compañerismo m. 2 asociación f.

felony ('felani) n delito grave m.

felt[1] (felt) n fieltro m.

felt[2] (felt) v see **feel**.

female ('fi:meil) adj,n hembra f.

feminine ('feminin) adj femenino. **femininity** n feminidad f.

feminism ('feminizəm) n feminismo m. **feminist** n feminista m,f.

fence (fens) n valla, cerca f. vt cercar. vi esgrimir. **fencing** n esgrima f.

fend (fend) vi 1 defenderse. 2 apañarse.

fennel ('fenl) n hinojo m.

ferment (n 'fə:ment; v fə'ment) n fermento m. vi fermentar.

fern (fə:n) n helecho m.

ferocious (fə'rouʃəs) adj feroz. **ferocity** n ferocidad f.

ferret ('ferit) n hurón m.

ferry ('feri) vt pasar a través del río. n transbordador m. **ferryboat** n transbordador m.

fertile ('fə:tail) adj fértil. **fertility** n fertilidad

f. fertilize vt fecundar, fertilizar. **fertilizer** n fertilizante, abono m.

fervent ('fə:vənt) adj ferviente.

fervour ('fə:və) n fervor m.

fester ('festə) vi enconarse, emponzoñarse.

festival ('festivəl) n 1 festival m. 2 fiesta f. **festive** adj festivo. **festivity** n festividad f.

festoon (fes'tu:n) n festón m. vt festonear.

fetch (fetʃ) vt 1 ir a buscar, ir por, traer. 2 hacer venir. 3 venderse por, alcanzar. **fetching** adj atractivo.

fete (feit) n fiesta f.

fetid ('fetid) adj fétido.

fetish ('fetiʃ) n fetiche m.

fetlock ('fetlɔk) n cerneja f.

fetter ('fetə) n grillete m. vt encadenar.

feud (fju:d) n 1 enemistad heredada f. 2 disputa f. vi reñir, pelear.

feudal ('fju:dl) adj feudal. **feudalism** n feudalismo m.

fever ('fi:və) n fiebre f. **feverish** adj febril.

few (fju:) adj 1 pocos. 2 algunos, unos. **a few** unos cuantos. **fewer** adj menos.

fiancé (fi'ɔnsei) n prometido, novio m.

fiasco (fi'æskou) n fiasco m.

fib (fib) n inf mentirijilla f. vi decir mentirijillas.

fibre ('faibə) n fibra f. **fibreglass** n fibra de vidrio f. **fibrous** adj fibroso.

fickle ('fikəl) adj veleidoso, mudable, inconstante.

fiction ('fikʃən) n ficción f. **fictional** adj novelesco. **fictitious** adj ficticio.

fiddle ('fidl) n 1 violín m. 2 inf trampa, estafa f. vt inf 1 hacer trampa. 2 agenciar. vi tocar el violín. **fiddler** n inf violinista m,f.

fidelity (fi'deliti) n fidelidad f.

fidget ('fidʒit) vi agitar nerviosamente. **fidgety** adj nervioso, azogado.

field (fi:ld) n 1 campo m. 2 prado m. 3 esfera, especialidad f. vt parar, recoger.

fiend (fi:nd) n 1 demonio, diablo m. 2 fanático m. **fiendish** adj diabólico.

fierce (fiəs) adj 1 feroz, fiero. 2 intenso. **fierceness** n ferocidad, furia f.

fiery ('faiəri) adj ardiente, fogoso.

fifteen (fif'ti:n) adj,n quince m. **fifteenth** adj decimoquinto.

fifth (fifθ) adj quinto.

fifty ('fifti) adj,n cincuenta m. **go fifty-fifty** ir a medias. **fiftieth** adj quincuagésimo.

fig (fig) n higo m.

fight (fait) vt luchar contra, combatir. **fight**

back resistir. **fight off** rechazar. ~n lucha, pelea f.

figment ('figmənt) n invención f.

figure ('figə) n 1 figura f. 2 tipo m. vt figurar. **figurative** adj 1 figurado. 2 figurativo.

filament ('filəmənt) n filamento m.

file[1] (fail) n 1 ficha f. 2 carpeta f. 3 fichero, archivo m. 4 fila, hilera f. vt archivar. **filing cabinet** n fichero, archivador m.

file[2] (fail) n lima f. vt limar.

filial ('filiəl) adj filial.

fill (fil) vt 1 llenar. 2 rellenar. 3 ocupar, cubrir. 4 completar. **fill in** llenar, rellenar. **fill up** llenar hasta el tope. ~n 1 hartazgo m. 2 lleno m. **filling** n 1 relleno m. 2 med empaste m.

fillet ('filit) n filete m. vt cortar en filetes.

filly ('fili) n potra f.

film (film) n película f. vt filmar. vi hacer una película. **filmstar** n astro m. estrella f.

filter ('filtə) n filtro m. vt filtrar.

filth (filθ) n inmundicia, porquería f. **filthy** adj sucio, cochino.

fin (fin) n aleta f.

final ('fainl) adj 1 final. 2 decisivo. 3 terminante. n final f. **finalist** n finalista m,f. **finalize** vt ultimar, finalizar.

finance ('fainæns) n finanzas f pl. vt financiar. **financial** adj financiero. **financier** n financiero m.

find (faind) vt encontrar, hallar. **find out** averiguar. 2 descubrir. ~n hallazgo m. **finding** n 1 descubrimiento m. 2 pl recomendaciones f pl.

fine[1] (fain) adj 1 fino. 2 hermoso. 3 bueno, magnífico, excelente. adv muy bien. **feel fine** sentirse estupendamente. **that's fine!** ¡estupendo! **fine arts** n pl bellas artes f pl. **finery** n 1 galas f pl. 2 adornos m pl.

fine[2] (fain) n multa f. vt multar.

finger ('fingə) n dedo m. **little finger** meñique m. **put one's finger on it** poner el dedo en la llaga. **twist someone round one's little finger** hacer con uno lo que le da la gana. ~vt 1 tocar. 2 manosear. **fingernail** n uña f. **fingerprint** n huella dactilar f. **fingertip** n punta del dedo f. **have at one's fingertips** saberse al dedillo.

finish ('finiʃ) vt,vi terminar, acabar. **finish off** rematar. ~n 1 fin, final m. 2 remate m. 3 sport meta f. 4 tech acabado m.

finite ('fainait) adj finito. **finite verb** n verbo, conjugado m.

fir (fə:) n abeto m.

fire (faiə) n 1 fuego m. 2 incendio m. **be on fire** estar ardiendo. **catch fire** encenderse. **set on fire, set fire to** pegar fuego, incendiar. ~vt 1 incendiar. 2 disparar. 3 inf despedir.

fire alarm n alarma de incendios f.

firearm ('faiəra:m) n arma de fuego f.

fire brigade n cuerpo de bomberos m.

fire engine n bomba de incendios f.

fire-escape n escalera de incendios f.

fire extinguisher n extintor m.

fireguard ('faiəga:d) n guardafuego m.

fireman ('faiəmən) n bombero m.

fireplace ('faiəpleis) n chimenea f.

fireside ('faiəsaid) n hogar m.

fire station n parque de bomberos m.

firework ('faiəwə:k) n fuegos artificiales m pl.

firing ('faiəriŋ) n 1 mil disparo m. 2 mil tiroteo m. 3 tech encendido m. **firing squad** n pelotón de ejecución m.

firm[1] (fə:m) adj firme.

firm[2] (fə:m) n empresa, firma comercial f.

first (fə:st) adj,adv primero. **at first** al principio. **first of all** ante todo. ~n primero m. **first aid** n primeros auxilios m pl. **first-born** n primogénito m. **first-class** adj de primera clase. **first-hand** adj de primera mano. **first-name** n nombre de pila m. **first person** n primera persona f. **first-rate** adj de primera.

fiscal ('fiskəl) adj fiscal.

fish (fiʃ) n 1 pez m. 2 pescado m. vt,vi pescar. **fishbowl** n pecera f. **fisherman** n pescador m. **fish finger** n croqueta de pescado f. **fishing** n pesca f. **fishing rod** n caña de pescar f. **fishmonger** n pescadero m. **fishmonger's shop** n pescadería f. **fishy** adj 1 de pescado. 2 inf sospechoso.

fission ('fiʃən) n 1 escisión f. 2 fisión f.

fist (fist) n puño m. **fistful** n puñado m.

fit[1] (fit) vt ajustar, encajar. vi sentar bien, ir bien. adj 1 idóneo, apropiado. 2 digno. 3 med bien de salud. 4 sport en forma. n 1 ajuste m. 2 corte m. **fitness** n 1 idoneidad f. 2 med buena salud f. 3 sport buena forma f. **fitting** adj apropiado, conveniente. n 1 prueba f. 2 talla f. 3 pl accesorios m pl. **fitted** adj 1 hecho a medida. 2 empotrado.

fit[2] (fit) n acceso, ataque m. **fitful** adj espasmódico.

five (faiv) adj,n cinco m.

fix (fiks) vt 1 fijar. 2 arreglar. **fixation** n fijación f. **fixed** adj fijo. **fixture** n 1 cosa fija f. 2 instalación fija f. 3 sport encuentro m.

fizz (fiz) vi estar en efervescencia. n efervescencia f. **fizzy** adj gaseoso, espumoso, efervescente. **fizzle** vi apagarse.

flabbergast ('flæbəga:st) vt pasmar.

flabby ('flæbi) adj 1 flojo. 2 fofo.

flag[1] (flæg) n bandera f. vt hacer señales con una bandera. **flagpole** n asta de bandera f. **flagship** n buque insignia m.

flag[2] (flæg) vi flaquear, languidecer, decaer.

flagon ('flægən) n 1 jarra f. 2 comm garrafa f.

flagrant ('fleigrənt) adj flagrante, notorio.

flair (flɛə) n instinto, don especial m.

flake (fleik) n 1 copo m. 2 escama f. vi descascararse, desconcharse. vt separar en escamas. **flaky** adj 1 en copos. 2 escamoso. 3 desmenuzable.

flamboyant (flæm'bɔiənt) adj 1 extravagante. 2 llamativo.

flame (fleim) n llama, llamarada f. vi llamear. **flame up** enflamarse.

flamingo (flə'miŋgou) n flamenco m.

flan (flæn) n tarta f.

flank (flæŋk) n 1 costado m. 2 flanco m. vt flanquear.

flannel ('flænl) n franela f. **face-flannel** paño de la cara m.

flap (flæp) vt batir, sacudir. n 1 hoja plegadiza f. 2 aleteo m.

flare (flɛə) vi resplandecer, llamear. vt acampanar. **flare up** encenderse. ~n 1 llamarada f. 2 mil bengala f. 3 acampanado m.

flash (flæʃ) n 1 destello m. 2 llamarada f. relámpago m. vi destellar, relampaguear. **flashback** n escena retrospectiva f. **flashbulb** n bombilla de flash f. **flashlight** n 1 flash m. 2 linterna de señales f.

flask (fla:sk) n 1 frasco m. 2 termo m.

flat[1] (flæt) adj 1 llano. 2 plano. 3 soso. 4 terminante. 5 mus bemol. adv de plano. **flatfish** n pez plano m. **flat-footed** adj 1 pies planos. 2 torpe. **flatten** vt allanar, aplanar.

flat[2] (flæt) n piso m.

flatter ('flætə) vt 1 halagar, adular. 2 favorecer. **flatterer** n adulador m. **flattery** n 1 halagos m pl. 2 adulación f.

flaunt (flɔ:nt) vt ostentar, hacer gala de. **flaunt oneself** pavonearse.

flautist ('flɔ:tist) n flautista m,f.

flavour ('fleivə) n 1 sabor m. 2 gustillo m. vt sazonar. **flavouring** n condimento m.

flaw (flɔ:) n 1 grieta f. 2 defecto m. **flawless** adj impecable, perfecto.

flax (flæks) n lino m.

flea (fli:) n pulga f.

fleck (flek) n mota f. punto m. vt motear.

fled (fled) v see **flee.**

flee* (fli:) vi, vt huir.

fleece (fli:s) n vellón m. vt esquilar. **fleecy** adj lanudo.

fleet (fli:t) n flota f.

fleeting ('fli:tiŋ) adj fugaz.

flesh (fleʃ) n carne f. **fleshy** adj carnoso.

flew (flu:) v see **fly .**

flex (fleks) vt flexionar. n cordón eléctrico m. **flexible** adj flexible. **flexibility** n flexibilidad f.

flick (flik) n 1 golpecito m. 2 chasquido m. vt 1 dar un golpecito. 2 chasquear.

flicker ('flika) vi 1 parpadear. 2 vibrar. n parpadeo m.

flight[1] (flait) n vuelo m.

flight[2] (flait) n huída f. **put to flight** ahuyentar.

flimsy ('flimzi) adj 1 endeble. 2 delgado. 3 baladí. **flimsiness** n 1 endeblez f. 2 delgadez f.

flinch (flintʃ) vi arredrarse, acobardarse.

fling* (fliŋ) vt arrojar, echar. n tiro m. bravata f.

flint (flint) n pedernal m.

flip (flip) n capirotazo m. vt echar de un capirotazo. **flipper** n aleta f.

flippant ('flipant) adj frívolo. **flippancy** n falta de seriedad f.

flirt (fla:t) vi coquetear, flirtear. **flirt with** jugar con. ~n coqueta f.

flit (flit) vi 1 revolotear. 2 escurrirse.

float (flout) vi flotar. vt 1 hacer flotar. 2 lanzar, emitir. n 1 flotador m. 2 carroza f.

flock[1] (flok) n 1 rebaño m. 2 bandada f. 3 manada f. vi congregarse, juntarse.

flock[2] (flok) n borra f.

flog (flog) vt azotar.

flood (flʌd) n 1 inundación f. 2 diluvio m. vt inundar. vi desbordar. **floodgate** n compuerta m. **floodlight** n foco m. vt iluminar con focos.

floor (flɔ:) n 1 suelo m. 2 fondo m. 3 pista f. **have the floor** tener la palabra. **take the floor** salir a la palestra. ~vt 1 poner el piso a. 2 derribar. 3 confundir. **floorboard** n tabla f.

flop (flɔp) vi 1 desplomarse. 2 inf venirse abajo, fracasar. n inf fracaso m. **floppy** adj suelto, colgante.

floral ('flɔ:ral) adj 1 floral. 2 de flores. **florist** n florista m,f. **florist's shop** n floristería f.

flounce[1] (flauns) vi brincar de enojo.

flounce[2] (flauns) n (of a dress) volante m.

flounder[1] ('flaunda) vi perder el hilo. **flounder about** forcejear.

flounder[2] ('flaunda) n zool platija f.

flour (flaua) n harina f. vt enharinar.

flourish ('flʌriʃ) vi prosperar, florecer. n 1 rúbrica f. 2 toque de trompeta m. 3 floreo m. **flourishing** adj floreciente.

flout (flaut) vt mofarse de.

flow (flou) vi 1 fluir, correr. 2 ondear.

flower (flaua) n flor f. vi florecer. **flowerbed** n macizo m. **flower pot** n maceta f.

fluctuate ('flʌktʃueit) vi fluctuar.

flue (flu:) n cañón de chimenea m.

fluent ('flu:ant) adj fluido, fácil. **be fluent in a language** dominar un idioma. **fluency** n 1 fluidez, soltura f. 2 dominio m. **fluently** adv con fluidez or soltura.

fluff (flʌf) n pelusa f. **fluffy** adj ahuecado.

fluid ('flu:id) adj,n fluido m. **fluidity** n fluidez f.

flung (flʌŋ) v see **fling.**

fluorescent (flua'resant) adj fluorescente. **fluorescence** n fluorescencia f.

fluoride ('fluaraid) n fluoruro m.

flush[1] (flʌʃ) vi sofocarse. n rubor m.

flush[2] (flʌʃ) adj nivelado, parejo. vt tirar un chorro de agua. vi (of a toilet) funcionar.

fluster ('flʌsta) vt aturdir. n aturdimiento m.

flute (flu:t) n flauta f.

flutter ('flʌta) vi 1 aletear. 2 palpitar. vt agitar. n 1 aleteo m. 2 palpitación f. 3 agitación f.

flux (flʌks) n flujo m.

fly*[1] (flai) vi 1 volar. 2 ir en avión. vt 1 hacer volar. 2 pilotar. 3 transportar en avión. **flyover** n puente de tráfico m.

fly[2] (flai) n 1 mosca f. 2 bragueta f.

foal (foul) n potro m.

foam (foum) n espuma f. vi echar espuma.

focus ('foukas) n, pl **foci** foco m. **in focus** enfocado. **out of focus** desenfocado. ~vt enfocar. **focal** adj focal.

fodder ('foda) n forraje m.

foe (fou) n enemigo m.

foetus ('fi:tas) n feto m.

fog (fog) n niebla f. **foghorn** n sirena de niebla f. **foggy** adj 1 brumoso. 2 velado.

foible ('foibal) n debilidad f.

foil[1] (foil) vt desbaratar, frustrar.

foil[2] (foil) n papel de plata m.

foil[3] (foil) n florete m.

foist (foist) vt encajar con engaño.

fold[1] (fould) vt 1 plegar. 2 envolver. n pliegue m. **folder** n carpeta f. **folding** adj plegable.

fold² (fould) n redil m.

foliage ('fouliidʒ) n follaje m.

folk (fouk) n gente f. **folk dance** n danza folklórica f. **folklore** n folklore m. **folk song** n canción popular f. **folktale** n cuento popular m.

follicle ('fɔlikəl) n folículo m.

follow ('fɔlou) vt,vi seguir. **follow up 1** llevar hasta el fin. **2** proseguir. **3** investigar. **follower** n seguidor m. **following** adj siguiente. n seguidores m pl.

folly ('fɔli) n locura, insensatez f.

fond (fɔnd) adj cariñoso, indulgente. **be fond of 1** ser aficionado a. **2** estar encariñado con. **fondness** n 1 cariño m. **2** afición f.

fondle ('fɔndl) vt acariciar.

font (fɔnt) n pila f.

food (fu:d) n 1 comida f. **2** alimento m.

fool (fu:l) n 1 tonto, insensato m. **2** bufón m. **make a fool of** poner en ridículo. **play the fool** hacer el tonto. ~vt engañar, embaucar. **foolish** adj tonto, insensato. **foolishness** n tontería, insensatez f. **foolproof** adj 1 a prueba de impericia. **2** infalible.

foolscap ('fu:lzkæp) n papel tamaño folio m.

foot (fut) n, pl **feet** pie m. vt inf pagar. **football** n 1 fútbol m. **2** balón m. **football pools** n quinielas f pl. **footbridge** n puente de peatones m. **foothold** n pie firme m. base segura f. **footing** n 1 pie m. **2** posición f. **footlights** n pl candilejas f pl **footnote** n nota f. **footprint** n huella f. **footstep** n paso m. pisada f.

for (fə; stressed fɔ:) prep 1 para. **2** por. **as for** en cuanto a. **be for** estar a favor de. **but for** a no ser por. **for all that** con todo. **for good** definitivamente. ~conj ya que, pues.

forage ('fɔridʒ) n forraje m. vi forrajear. **forage for** rebuscar.

forbear (fə'bɛə) vi contenerse, reprimirse. **forbearance** n 1 paciencia f. **2** dominio propio m.

forbid* (fə'bid) vi prohibir. **forbidding** adj imponente.

force (fɔ:s) n 1 fuerza f. **2** personal m. **3** mil cuerpo m. **by force** a la fuerza. ~vt forzar. **forced** adj forzado. **forcefeed** vt alimentar a la fuerza. **forceful** adj fuerte, vigoroso, enérgico. **forcible** adj 1 forzoso. **2** vigoroso. **3** convincente.

forceps ('fɔ:seps) n fórceps m.

ford (fɔ:d) n vado m. vt vadear.

fore (fɔ:) n frente m. delantera f. adj delantero, anterior.

forearm¹ ('fɔ:rɑ:m) n antebrazo m.

forearm² (fɔ:'rɑ:m) vt armar previamente.

forebear ('fɔ:bɛə) n antepasado m.

forecast ('fɔ:kɑ:st) vt pronosticar. n pronóstico m.

forecourt ('fɔ:kɔ:t) n atrio m.

forefather ('fɔ:fɑ:ðə) n antepasado m.

forefinger ('fɔ:fiŋgə) n dedo índice m.

forefront ('fɔ:frʌnt) n vanguardia f.

foreground ('fɔ:graund) n primer plano m.

forehand ('fɔ:hænd) n directo m.

forehead ('fɔrid) n frente f.

foreign ('fɔrin) adj 1 extranjero. **2** extraño, ajeno. **foreigner** n extranjero m.

foreleg ('fɔ:leg) n pata delantera f.

forelock ('fɔ:lɔk) n guedeja m.

foreman ('fɔ:mən) n 1 capataz m. **2** law presidente del jurado m.

foremost ('fɔ:moust) adj 1 primero. **2** delantero.

forensic (fə'rensik) adj forénsico.

forerunner ('fɔ:rʌnə) n precursor m.

foresee* (fɔ:'si:) vt prever. **foreseeable** adj previsible.

foresight ('fɔ:sait) n previsión, perspicacia f.

forest ('fɔrist) n 1 bosque m. **2** selva f. adj forestal.

forestall (fɔ:'stɔ:l) vt 1 prevenir. **2** anticipar.

foretaste ('fɔ:teist) n anticipo m.

foretell* (fɔ:'tel) vt 1 predecir. **2** presagiar.

forethought ('fɔ:θɔ:t) n 1 prevención f. **2** premeditación f.

forfeit ('fɔ:fit) n 1 pena f. **2** prenda f. vt perder el derecho a.

forge¹ (fɔ:dʒ) vt 1 forjar, fraguar. **2** falsificar, falsear. n 1 fragua f. **2** fundición f. **forger** n falsificador m. **forgery** n falsificación f.

forge² (fɔ:dʒ) vi ir avanzando.

forget* (fə'get) vt olvidar. **forgetful** adj olvidadizo, descuidado. **forgetfulness** n 1 olvido m. **2** descuido m.

forgive* (fə'giv) vt perdonar. **forgiveness** n 1 perdón m. **2** misericordia f.

forgo* (fɔ:'gou) vt privarse de.

fork (fɔ:k) n 1 tenedor m. **2** horquilla f. **3** bifurcación f. vi bifurcarse. **fork out** inf desembolsar.

forlorn (fə'lɔ:n) adj abandonado, desamparado.

form (fɔ:m) n 1 forma f. **2** bulto m. **3** impreso m. **4** educ clase f. vt formar. **formal** adj 1 formal. **2** ceremonioso. **3** protocolario. **4** de etiqueta. **formality** n 1 formalidad f. **2** ceremonia f. **formalize** vt formalizar. **formation** n formación f. **formative** adj formativo.

former ('fɔːmə) adj 1 pasado. 2 anterior. **the former** aquél m.

formidable ('fɔːmidəbəl) adj formidable.

formula ('fɔːmjulə) n fórmula f. **formulate** vt formular.

forsake* (fə'seik) vt abandonar.

fort (fɔːt) n fuerte m.

forte ('fɔːtei) n fuerte m.

forth (fɔːθ) adv 1 adelante. 2 afuera. **and so forth** y así sucesivamente. **forthcoming** adj 1 venidero. 2 en preparación. 3 disponible. 4 comunicativo. **forthright** adj franco, rotundo.

fortify ('fɔːtifai) vt 1 fortalecer. 2 mil fortificar. **fortification** n fortificación f.

fortnight ('fɔːtnait) n quincena f. **fortnightly** adj quincenal. adv cada quince días.

fortress ('fɔːtrəs) n fortaleza f.

fortune ('fɔːtʃən) n fortuna f. **tell one's fortune** decir la buenaventura. **fortune-teller** n adivina f. **fortunate** adj afortunado.

forty ('fɔːti) adj,n cuarenta m. **fortieth** adj cuadragésimo.

forum ('fɔːrəm) n foro m.

forward ('fɔːwəd) adj 1 delantero. 2 adelantado. 3 de avance. 4 desenvuelto, fresco. n sport delantero m. vt 1 enviar. 2 (of a letter) hacer seguir. 3 entregar. **forwards** adv hacia adelante.

fossil ('fɒsəl) adj,n fósil m.

foster ('fɒstə) vt 1 nutrir, favorecer. 2 criar. 3 fomentar. **fostermother** n madre adoptiva f.

fought (fɔːt) v see **fight**.

foul (faul) adj 1 sucio, inmundo. 2 viciado. 3 asqueroso. n sport falta f. vt ensuciar. vi sport cometer una falta. **foulmouthed** adj deslenguado. **foul play** n juego sucio m. **foulsmelling** adj hediondo.

found[1] (faund) v see **find**.

found[2] (faund) vt fundar. **foundation** n 1 fundación f. 2 fundamento m. 3 pl arch cimientos m pl. **founder** n fundador m.

foundry ('faundri) n fundición f.

fountain ('fauntin) n fuente f. **fountain pen** n estilográfica f.

four (fɔː) adj,n cuatro m. **on all fours** a cuatro patas. **fourth** adj cuarto. n 1 cuarta parte f. 2 mus cuarta f. **fourthly** adv en cuarto lugar. **four-poster** n cama de columnas f. **foursome** n grupo de cuatro m.

fourteen (fɔː'tiːn) adj,n catorce m. **fourteenth** adj decimocuarto.

fowl (faul) n ave de corral f.

fox (fɒks) n zorra f. vt despistar. **foxglove** n dedalera f. **foxhound** n perro raposero m. **foxhunting** n caza de la zorra f. **foxy** adj astuto.

foyer ('fɔiei) n vestíbulo, hall m.

fraction ('frækʃən) n fracción f. **fractional** adj fraccionario.

fracture ('fræktʃə) n fractura f. vt fracturar.

fragile ('frædʒail) adj frágil. **fragility** n fragilidad f.

fragment ('frægmənt) n fragmento m. **fragmentary** adj fragmentario.

fragrant ('freigrənt) adj fragante. **fragrance** n fragancia f.

frail (freil) adj 1 frágil. 2 débil. **frailty** n debilidad f.

frame (freim) n 1 marco m. 2 montura. 3 estructura f. esqueleto m. vt 1 enmarcar. 2 construir, modelar. 3 formular. 4 incriminar por medio de una estratagema. **framework** n 1 marco, sistema m. 2 armazón f.

franc (fræŋk) n franco m.

France (frɑːns) n Francia f. **French** adj francés. **French (language)** n francés m. **French bean** n judía verde f. **French dressing** n aliño a la francesa m. **French horn** n trompa f. **French window** n puerta ventana f.

franchise ('fræntʃaiz) n 1 derecho al voto m. 2 franquicia f. 3 concesión f.

frank (fræŋk) adj franco. **frankness** n franqueza f.

frankfurter ('fræŋkfə:tə) n salchicha de Frankfurt f.

frantic ('fræntik) adj frenético m.

fraternal (frə'tɔːnl) adj fraternal. **fraternity** n fraternidad, hermandad f. **fraternize** vi fraternizar.

fraud (frɔːd) n 1 fraude m. 2 impostor m. **fraudulent** adj fraudulento.

fraught (frɔːt) adj cargado, lleno.

fray[1] (frei) n combate m. lucha f.

fray[2] (frei) vt raer, desgastar. vi deshilacharse.

freak (friːk) n 1 monstruo m. 2 fenómeno m. 3 capricho m.

freckle ('frekəl) n peca f. vt motear.

free (friː) adj 1 libre. 2 gratuito. 3 liberal. adv gratis. vt libertar. **freedom** n libertad f. **freehand** adj hecho a pulso. **freehold** n dominio absoluto m. **freelance** adj independiente. n periodista independiente m,f. **free will** n libre albedrío m.

freeze* (friːz) vt 1 helar. 2 congelar. vi helarse.

n helada *f.* **freezing point** *n* punto de congelación *m.*

freight (freit) *n* **1** flete *m.* **2** carga *f.* **3** mercancías *f pl.* **freight train** *n* tren de mercancías *m.*

frenzy ('frenzi) *n* frenesí *m.*

frequency ('fri:kwənsi) *n* frecuencia *f.* **frequent** *adj* frecuente. *vt* frecuentar.

fresco ('freskou) *n* fresco *m.*

fresh (freʃ) *adj* **1** fresco. **2** nuevo. **3** puro. **4** atrevido. **freshness** *n* pureza *f.* **freshwater** *adj* de agua dulce.

fret[1] (fret) *vt* irritar, molestar.

fret[2] (fret) *n* calado *m.* **fretwork** *n* calado *m.*

friar ('fraiə) *n* fraile *m.*

friction ('frikʃən) *n* **1** fricción *f.* **2** rozamiento *m.*

Friday ('fraidi) *n* viernes *m.*

fridge (fridʒ) *n inf* nevera *f.* frigorífico *m.*

friend (frend) *n* amigo *m.* **friendly** *adj* **1** simpático. **2** amistoso. **friendship** *n* amistad *f.*

frieze (fri:z) *n* friso *m.*

fright (frait) *n* susto *m.* **frighten** *vt* **1** asustar. **2** espantar. **be frightened** tener miedo. **frightful** *adj* espantoso.

frigid ('fridʒid) *adj* **1** frío. **2** frígido.

frill (fril) *n* lechuga *f.*

fringe (frindʒ) *n* **1** franja *f.* **2** flequillo *m.* **3** margen *m.*

frisk (frisk) *vt* cachear. *vi* retozar.

fritter[1] ('fritə) *vt* desperdiciar.

fritter[2] ('fritə) *cul n* buñuelo, churro *m.* fruta de sartén *f.*

frivolity (fri'vɔliti) *n* frivolidad *f.* **frivolous** *adj* frívolo.

frizz (friz) *n* rizos pequeños *m pl.* frisado *f.*

frizzle[1] ('frizəl) *vt* rizar, frisar

frizzle[2] ('frizəl) *vi* chisporrotear.

fro (fro) *adv* **to and fro** de un lado a otro.

frock (frɔk) *n* vestido *f.* **frock coat** *n* levita *f.*

frog (frɔg) *n* rana *f.* **have a frog in the throat** tener carraspera.

frolic ('frɔlik) *n* travesura *f.* *vi* juguetear.

from (frəm; *stressed* frɔm) *prep* **1** de. **2** desde. **3** por. **4** de parte de.

front (frʌnt) *adj* delantero. **front door** *n* puerta principal. ～*n* **1** frente *m.* **2** fachada *f.*

frontier ('frʌntiə) *n* frontera *f.* *adj* fronterizo.

frost (frɔst) *n* **1** helada *f.* **2** escarcha *f.* *vt* cubrir de escarcha. **frostbite** *n* congelación *f.*

froth (frɔθ) *n* espuma *f.* *vi* espumar.

frown (fraun) *n* ceño *m.* *vi* fruncir el entrecejo.

froze (frouz) *v see* **freeze.**

frozen ('frouzən) *v see* **freeze.**

frugal ('fru:gəl) *adj* frugal.

fruit (fru:t) *n* fruta *f.* **fruitful** *adj* fructuoso, provechoso. **fruitless** *adj* infructuoso. **fruit machine** *n* máquina tragaperras *f.* **fruit salad** *n* ensalada de frutas *f*

fruition (fru:'iʃən) *n* **1** fruición *f.* **2** cumplimiento *m.*

frustrate (frʌs'treit) *vt* frustrar. **frustration** *n* frustración *f.*

fry (frai) *vt* freír. **frying pan** *n* sartén *f.*

fuchsia ('fju:ʃə) *n* fucsia *f.*

fuel ('fju:əl) *n* combustible *m.* *vt* proveer de combustible.

fugitive ('fju:dʒitiv) *adj,n* fugitivo *m.*

fulcrum ('fʌlkrəm) *n* fulcro *m.*

fulfil (ful'fil) *vt* **1** cumplir con. **2** realizar. **3** llenar. **fulfilment** *n* cumplimiento *m.* realización *f.*

full (ful) *adj* **1** lleno. **2** completo. **3** pleno. **in full** sin abreviar. **full-length** *adj* **1** de tamaño natural. **2** de cuerpo entero. **full moon** *n* luna llena *f.* **full stop** *n* punto *m.* **fully** *adv* completamente.

fumble ('fʌmbəl) *vt* manosear. *vi* **1** titubear. **2** buscar con las manos.

fume (fju:m) *vi* **1** humear. **2** rabiar. *n* **1** vaho *m.* **2** tufo *m.* **3** emanación *f.*

fun (fʌn) *n* **1** diversión *f.* **2** broma *f.* **have fun** divertirse. **make fun of** burlarse de. **funfair** *n* parque de atracciones *m.*

function ('fʌŋkʃən) *n* función *f.* *vi* funcionar.

fund (fʌnd) *n* fondo *m.* *vt* consolidar.

fundamental (fʌndə'mentl) *adj* fundamental.

funeral ('fju:nərəl) *n* entierro, funeral *m.* *adj* fúnebre.

fungus ('fʌŋgəs) *n, pl* **fungi** *bot* hongo *m.*

funnel ('fʌnl) *n* **1** embudo *m.* **2** *naut* chimenea *f.*

funny ('fʌni) *adj* **1** divertido, gracioso. **2** raro.

fur (fə:) *n* piel *f.* **fur coat** *n* abrigo de pieles *m.*

furious ('fjuəriəs) *adj* furioso.

furnace ('fə:nis) *n* horno *m.*

furnish ('fə:niʃ) *vt* **1** amueblar. **2** proporcionar. **furniture** ('fə:nitʃə) *n* mobiliario, mueblaje *m.*

furrow ('fʌrou) *n* surco *m.* *vt* **1** surcar. **2** arrugar.

further ('fə:ðə) *adj* **1** adicional. **2** más lejano. *adv* **1** más lejos. **2** además. *vt* promover. **furthest** *adv* más lejos. *adj* más lejano.

furtive ('fə:tiv) *adj* furtivo.

fury ('fjuəri) *n* furia *f.*

fuse[1] ('fju:z) *n* **1** plomo, fusible *m.* **2** mecha *f.*

fuse[2] (fju:z) *vt* fundir. **fusion** *n* fusión *f.*

fuselage ('fju:zəla:ʒ) n fuselaje m.

fuss (fʌs) n 1 bulla f. 2 lio m. 3 aspaviento m. vi agitarse.

futile ('fju:tail) adj 1 inútil. 2 fútil.

future ('fju:tʃə) adj 1 futuro. 2 venidero. n futuro, porvenir m.

fuzz (fʌz) n 1 pelusa f. 2 vello m. 3 inf policía f.

G

gabble ('gæbəl) n cotorreo m. vi 1 cotorrear. 2 hablar atropelladamente.

gable ('geibəl) n faldón, gablete m.

gadget ('gædʒit) n artilugio, chisme m.

gag[1] (gæg) n mordaza f. vt amordazar.

gag[2] (gæg) n 1 broma f. 2 chiste m.

gaiety ('geiəti) n alegria, jovialidad f.

gain (gein) n 1 ganancia f. 2 provecho m. 3 aumento m. vt ganar. vi avanzar.

gait (geit) n modo de andar m.

gala ('gɑ:lə) n fiesta, gala f.

galaxy ('gæləksi) n 1 galaxia f. 2 grupo brillante m.

gale (geil) n 1 ventarrón m. vendaval f. 2 tempestad, galerna f.

gallant ('gælənt) adj 1 valiente. 2 galante. n galán m.

galleon ('gæliən) n galeón m.

gallery ('gæləri) n 1 galería f. 2 pasadizo m.

galley ('gæli) n 1 galera f. 2 cocina f.

gallon ('gælən) n galón m.

gallop ('gæləp) n galope m. vi galopar.

gallows ('gælouz) n pl horca f.

galore (gə'lɔ:) adv en abundancia.

galvanize ('gælvənaiz) vt galvanizar.

gamble ('gæmbəl) n 1 jugada f. 2 riesgo m. vt, vi jugar. vi especular.

game (geim) n 1 juego m. 2 partido m. 3 (hunting) caza f. adj animoso **gamekeeper** n guardabosque m.

gammon ('gæmən) n jamón m.

gander ('gændə) n ganso m.

gang (gæŋ) n 1 pandilla f. grupo m. 2 brigada f. vi agrupar. **gang up** conspirar. **gangster** n pistolero, gángster m.

gangrene (gæŋ'gri:n) n gangrena f.

gangway ('gæŋwei) n 1 pasillo m. pasarela f.

gap (gæp) n 1 hueco m. 2 desfiladero m. 3 intervalo m. 4 brecha f.

gape (geip) vi 1 abrirse mucho. 2 embobarse, estar boquiabierto.

garage ('gærɑ:ʒ) n garaje m. vt poner en el garaje.

garbage ('gɑ:bidʒ) n basura f. desperdicio m.

garble ('gɑ:bəl) vt mutilar, falsear.

garden ('gɑ:dn) n jardín m. vi cultivar. **gardener** n jardinero m. **gardening** n jardinería f.

gargle ('gɑ:gəl) n gárgaras f pl. vi hacer gárgaras.

garlic ('gɑ:lik) n ajo m.

garment ('gɑ:mənt) n prenda de vestir f.

garnish ('gɑ:niʃ) vt 1 adornar. 2 aderezar. n aderezo m.

garrison ('gærisən) n guarnición f. vt guarnecer.

garter ('gɑ:tə) n 1 ligas f pl. 2 jarretera f.

gas (gæs) n gas m. vt asfixiar con gas. **gas cooker** n cocina de gas f.

gash (gæʃ) n 1 hendedura, raja f. 2 cuchillada f. vt 1 acuchillar. 2 rajar.

gasket ('gæskit) n tech junta f.

gasp (gɑ:sp) n 1 boqueada f. jadeo m. 2 grito sofocado m. vi 1 boquear, jadear. 2 sofocarse.

gastric ('gæstrik) adj gástrico. **gastronomic** adj gastronómico.

gate (geit) n 1 puerta f. 2 verja f. 3 entrada f. **gatecrash** vt, vi asistir sin ser invitado.

gather ('gæðə) vt 1 reunir. 2 coger. 3 recolectar. 4 fruncir. vi 1 reunirse. 2 acumularse.

gauche (gouʃ) adj desmañado.

gaudy ('gɔ:di) adj 1 chillón. 2 cursi.

gauge (geidʒ) n 1 norma de medida f. 2 calibre m. 3 indicador m. vt 1 medir. 2 calibrar.

gaunt (gɔ:nt) adj 1 flaco, desvaído. 2 severo.

gauze (gɔ:z) n gasa f.

gave (geiv) v see **give**.

gay (gei) adj 1 alegre. 2 vistoso. 3 ligero.

gaze (geiz) n mirada fija f. vi mirar con fijeza.

gazelle (gə'zel) n gacela f.

gear (giə) n 1 engranaje m. 2 marcha f. 3 aparato m. 4 aparejos m pl. vt engranar. **gearbox** n caja de cambio f. **gear lever** n palanca de cambio f.

gelatine ('dʒeləti:n) n gelatina f.

gem (dʒem) n 1 joya f. 2 piedra preciosa f.

Gemini ('dʒeminai) n Géminis m.

gender ('dʒendə) n género m.

gene (dʒi:n) n gen m.

genealogy (dʒi:ni'ælədʒi) n genealogía f.

general ('dʒenərəl) adj,n general m. **general election** n elecciones generales f. **general practitioner** n médico general, médico de cabecera m. **generalize** vi generalizar.

207

generate

generate ('dʒenəreit) vt 1 generar. 2 producir. **generation** n generación f.

generic (dʒi'nerik) adj genérico.

generous ('dʒenərəs) adj 1 generoso. 2 amplio. **generosity** n generosidad f.

genetic (dʒi'netik) adj genético. **genetics** n genética f.

genial ('dʒi:niəl) adj simpático, afable.

genital ('dʒenitl) adj,n genital. n pl órganos genitales m pl.

genitive ('dʒenitiv) n genitivo m.

genius ('dʒi:niəs) n 1 genio m. 2 genialidad f.

genteel (dʒen'ti:l) adj fino, elegante, gentil.

gentian ('dʒenʃən) n genciana f.

gentile ('dʒentail) adj,n 1 gentil m. 2 pagano m.

gentle ('dʒentl) adj 1 benévolo. 2 suave. 3 ligero. **gentleman** n caballero m.

genuflect ('dʒenjuflekt) vi doblar la rodilla.

genuine ('dʒenjuin) adj 1 genuino. 2 sincero.

genus ('dʒi:nəs) n, pl **genera** género m.

geography (dʒi'ɔgrəfi) n geografía f. **geographical** adj geográfico. **geographer** n geógrafo m.

geology (dʒi'ɔlədʒi) n geología f.

geometry (dʒi'ɔmətri) n geometría f.

geranium (dʒə'reiniəm) n geranio m.

geriatrics (dʒeri'ætriks) n geriatría f.

germ (dʒə:m) n 1 germen m. 2 bacteria f.

Germany ('dʒə:məni) n Alemania f. **German** adj,n alemán m. **German** (language) n alemán m. **Germanic** adj germánico. **German measles** n rubéola f.

germinate ('dʒə:mineit) vi germinar.

gerund ('dʒerənd) n gerundio m.

gesticulate (dʒis'tikjuleit) vi accionar, gesticular.

gesture ('dʒestʃə) n 1 gesto, ademán m. 2 muestra f.

get* (get) vt 1 obtener. 2 coger. 3 comprender. vi ponerse. **get by** lograr pasar.

geyser ('gi:zə) n 1 géiser m. 2 calentador de agua m.

ghastly ('gɑ:stli) adj 1 horrible. 2 pálido, cadavérico.

gherkin ('gə:kin) n pepinillo m.

ghetto ('getou) n judería f.

ghost (goust) n fantasma m. **Holy Ghost** Espíritu Santo m.

giant ('dʒaiənt) n gigante m. adj gigantesco.

giddy ('gidi) adj 1 vertiginoso. 2 casquivano.

gift (gift) n 1 regalo m. 2 prenda f.

gigantic (dʒai'gæntik) adj gigantesco.

giggle ('gigəl) n risilla tonta f. vi reírse tontamente.

gild (gild) vt dorar.

gill[1] (gil) n agalla f.

gill[2] (dʒil) n cuarta parte de una pinta f.

gilt (gilt) adj,n dorado m.

gimmick ('gimik) n 1 truco publicitario m. 2 artimaña f.

gin (dʒin) n ginebra f.

ginger ('dʒindʒə) n jengibre m. **ginger up** animar. **gingerbread** n pan de jengibre m.

gingham ('giŋəm) n guinga, tela de algodón fino f.

Gipsy ('dʒipsi) adj,n gitano m.

giraffe (dʒi'rɑ:f) n jirafa f.

girder ('gə:də) n viga f.

girdle ('gə:dl) n 1 ceñidor m. 2 faja f. vt ceñir.

girl (gə:l) n 1 chica f. 2 niña f. **girlfriend** n 1 amiga f. 2 novia f.

girth (gə:θ) n 1 cincha f. 2 circunferencia f. 3 gordura f.

give* (giv) vt 1 dar. 2 entregar. 3 ofrecer. **give away** regalar. **give back** devolver. **give in** rendirse. **give up** 1 dejar. 2 renunciar. 3 sacrificar.

glacier ('glæsiə) n glaciar m.

glad (glæd) adj alegre, contento.

glamour ('glæmə) n encanto, atractivo m. **glamorous** adj encantador.

glance (glɑ:ns) n ojeada f. vistazo m. vi 1 mirar. 2 echar un vistazo.

gland (glænd) n glándula f.

glare (glɛə) n 1 brillo m. 2 deslumbramiento m. vi 1 relumbrar. 2 mirar ferozmente.

glass (glɑ:s) n 1 vaso m. 2 vidrio m. 3 artículos de vidrio m pl. 4 espejo m.

glaze (gleiz) n barniz, lustre m. vt 1 vidriar. 2 esmaltar.

gleam (gli:m) n destello m. vi brillar, relucir.

glean (gli:n) vt espigar.

glee (gli:) n 1 alegría f. 2 júbilo m.

glib (glib) adj 1 voluble. 2 engañoso.

glide (glaid) n 1 deslizamiento m. 2 planeo, vuelo sin motor m. vi 1 deslizarse. 2 volar sin motor. **glider** n planeador m.

glimmer ('glimə) n 1 vislumbre m. 2 luz tenue f. vi brillar tenuemente.

glimpse (glimps) n 1 vislumbre m. 2 vista momentánea f. vt vislumbrar.

glint (glint) vi destellar. n destello m.

glisten ('glisən) vi relucir, brillar.

glitter ('glitə) n resplandor m. vi relucir, centellear.

208

gloat (glout) vi relamerse, deleitarse.

globe (gloub) n globo m.

gloom¹ (glu:m) n oscuridad f.

gloom² (glu:m) n melancolía, tristeza f.

glory ('glɔ:ri) n gloria f. vi gloriarse. **glorify** vt glorificar. **glorious** adj glorioso.

gloss¹ (glɔs) n lustre m. vt lustrar.

gloss² (glɔs) n glosa f. vt glosar. **gloss over 1** encubrir. **2** paliar.

glossary ('glɔsəri) n glosario m.

glove (glʌv) n guante m.

glow (glou) n **1** resplandor m. **2** color vivo m. vi brillar, relucir.

glower ('glauə) vi mirar con ceño.

glucose ('glu:kous) n glucosa f.

glue (glu:) n cola f. vt encolar, pegar.

glum (glʌm) adj **1** taciturno. **2** triste. **3** sombrío.

glut (glʌt) n exceso m.

glutton ('glʌtn) n glotón m.

gnarled (nɑ:ld) adj nudoso, retorcido.

gnash (næʃ) vt, vi crujir los dientes.

gnat (næt) n mosquito m.

gnaw (nɔ:) vt roer.

gnome (noum) n gnomo m.

go* (gou) vi **1** ir. **2** marchar. **3** pasar. **4** partir. **go by** pasar. **go on** continuar. ~n **1** energía f. **2** jugada f.

goad (goud) n **1** aguijón m. **2** estímulo m. vt **1** aguijonear. **2** incitar, provocar.

goal (goul) n **1** meta f. **2** ambición f. **3** portería f. **4** gol m. **goalkeeper** n guardameta m.

goat (gout) n cabra, macho cabrío m.

gobble ('gɔbəl) vi (of a turkey) gluglutear. vt engullir.

goblin ('gɔblin) n duende m.

god (gɔd) n dios m. **for God's sake!** ¡por Dios! **goddaughter** n ahijada f. **godfather** n padrino m. **godmother** n madrina f. **godson** n ahijado m.

goddess ('gɔdis) n diosa f.

goggles ('gɔgəlz) n pl **1** anteojos m. **2** gafas submarinas f.

gold (gould) n oro m. **golden** adj de oro, dorado. **goldfish** n carpa dorada f. **goldmine** n mina de oro f. **goldsmith** n orfebre m.

golf (gɔlf) n golf m. **golfball** n pelota de golf f. **golf club** n palo de golf m. **golfcourse** n campo de golf m.

gondola ('gɔndələ) n góndola f. **gondolier** n gondolero m.

gone (gɔn) v see **go**.

gong (gɔŋ) n gong, gongo m.

good (gud) adj bueno. **as good as** tanto como. **feel good** estar satisfecho. ~n **1** bien, provecho m. **2** pl bienes, efectos m pl. **good afternoon** interj buenas tardes f pl. **goodbye** interj, n adiós m. **good evening** interj buenas tardes f pl. **Good Friday** n Viernes Santo m. **good-looking** adj bien parecido, guapo. **good morning** interj buenos días m pl. **good night** interj buenas noches f pl. **good-will** n buena voluntad f.

goose (gu:s) n, pl **geese** ganso m. **gooseberry** n uva espina, grosella f.

gore¹ (gɔ:) n sangre f.

gore² (gɔ:) vt cornear.

gorge (gɔ:dʒ) n **1** garganta f. **2** barranco m. vt engullir. vi hartarse.

gorgeous ('gɔ:dʒəs) adj magnífico, brillante.

gorilla (gə'rilə) n gorila m.

gorse (gɔ:s) n aulaga f. tojo m.

gory ('gɔ:ri) adj **1** ensangrentado. **2** inf desagradable.

gosh (gɔʃ) interj sl ¡caray!

gosling ('gɔzliŋ) n ganso pequeño m.

gospel ('gɔspəl) n evangelio m.

gossip ('gɔsip) n **1** chismoso m. **2** chismes m. **3** comadreo m. vi cotillear.

got (gɔt) v see **get**.

Gothic ('gɔθik) adj, n gótico m.

goulash ('gu:læʃ) n guiso húngaro m.

gourd (guəd) n calabaza f.

gourmet (guə'mei) n gastrónomo m.

govern ('gʌvən) vt, vi **1** gobernar. **2** gram regir. **government** n gobierno m. **governor** n gobernador m.

gown (gaun) n **1** toga f. **2** vestido m.

grab (græb) n agarro m. vt arrebatar.

grace (greis) n **1** gracia f. **2** elegancia f. **3** talante m. vt adornar. **say grace** bendecir la mesa. **graceful** adj elegante, gracioso.

gracious ('greiʃəs) adj **1** cortés. **2** benigno.

grade (greid) n **1** grado m. **2** clase f. vt clasificar, graduar. **gradient** n pendiente f. **gradual** adj **1** gradual. **2** graduado. **graduate** n graduado m.

graffiti (grə'fi:ti) n obras esgrafiadas f.

graft (grɑ:ft) n **1** injerto m. **2** corrupción f.

grain (grein) n **1** grano m. **2** cereal m. **3** fibra f. vt granular.

gram (græm) n gramo m.

grammar ('græmə) n gramática f. **grammar school** n centro de segunda enseñanza m. **grammatical** adj gramatical.

gramophone ('græməfoun) n gramófono m

granary ('grænəri) n granero m.

grand (grænd) adj grandioso, magnífico. **grandeur** n grandeza f. esplendor m.

grandad ('grændæd) n inf also **grandpa** abuelito m.

grandchild ('grænt∫aild) n nieto m.

granddaughter ('grændɔ:tə) n nieta f.

grandfather ('grænfɑ:ðə) n abuelo m.

grandma ('grænmɑ:) n inf also **granny** abuelita f.

grandmother ('grænmʌðə) n abuela f.

grandparent ('grænpɛərənt) n abuelo m.

grand piano n piano de cola m.

grandson ('grænsʌn) n nieto m.

grandstand ('grændstænd) n tribuna f.

granite ('grænit) n granito m.

grant (grɑ:nt) n 1 concesión f. 2 subvención f. 3 beca f. vt conceder. **take for granted** dar por supuesto

grape (greip) n uva f. **grapefruit** n toronja f. pomelo m. **grapevine** n 1 vid f. 2 parra f.

graph (græf) n gráfica f. **graphic** adj gráfico.

grapple ('græpəl) vt agarrar. vi agarrarse.

grasp (grɑ:sp) n 1 agarro m. 2 apretón m. 3 comprensión f. vt 1 agarrar. 2 comprender.

grass (grɑ:s) n 1 hierba f. 2 césped m. **grassroots** adj 1 básico. 2 popular.

grate [1] (greit) n parrilla de hogar f.

grate [2] (greit) vt rallar. vi molestar.

grateful ('greitfəl) adj agradecido

gratify ('grætifai) vt 1 satisfacer. 2 complacer.

gratitude ('grætitju:d) n agradecimiento m.

grave [1] (greiv) n sepultura f. sepulcro m. **gravestone** n lápida sepulcral f. **graveyard** n cementerio m

grave [2] (greiv) adj 1 serio. 2 grave.

gravel ('grævəl) n grava f. cascajo m.

gravity ('græviti) n 1 gravedad f. 2 gravitación f

gravy ('greivi) n salsa f. jugo m.

graze [1] (greiz) vt 1 pacer. 2 apacentar.

graze [2] (greiz) n roce m. vt raspar, raer.

grease (gri:s) n grasa f. vt engrasar. **greaseproof** adj impermeable a la grasa.

great (greit) adj 1 grande. 2 importante.

Great Britain n Gran Bretaña f.

Greece (gri:s) n Grecia f. **Grecian** adj griego. **Greek** adj,n griego m. **Greek (language)** n griego m.

greed (gri:d) n 1 codicia, avaricia f. 2 gula, glotonería f

green (gri:n) adj 1 verde. 2 novato. n 1 verde

m. 2 pl verduras f pl. **greengrocer** n verdulero m. **greenhouse** n invernadero m.

greet (gri:t) vt 1 saludar. 2 presentarse a. **greeting** n salutación f

gregarious (gri'gɛəriəs) adj gregario.

grenade (gri'neid) n granada f

grew (gru:) v see **grow**.

grey (grei) adj,n gris m. vi encanecer. **greyhound** n galgo m

grid (grid) n 1 reja f. 2 parrilla f.

grief (gri:f) n dolor, pesar m

grieve (gri:v) vt dar pena a. vi afligirse. **grievance** n 1 pesar m. 2 agravio m.

grill (gril) n 1 parrilla f. 2 asado a la parrilla m. vt 1 asar en parrilla. 2 interrogar.

grille (gril) n rejilla f.

grim (grim) adj 1 severo. 2 ceñudo. 3 fiero.

grimace (gri'mis) n mueca f. vi hacer muecas.

grime (graim) n mugre f

grin (grin) n 1 sonrisa burlona f. 2 mueca f. vi sonreír mostrando los dientes

grind* (graind) vt 1 moler. 2 afilar. vi rechinar. n trabajo pesado m

grip (grip) n 1 apretón m. 2 asidero m. 3 bolso de mano m. vt agarrar, asir.

gripe (graip) n retorcijón de tripas m. vi inf quejarse

gristle ('grisəl) n cartílago m. ternilla f.

grit (grit) n 1 arena f. 2 polvo m. 3 tesón m. vt apretar los dientes

groan (groun) n gemido m. vi 1 gemir. 2 crujir.

grocer ('grousə) n verdulero, tendero m.

groin (grɔin) n ingle f.

groom (gru:m) n 1 novio m. 2 caballerizo m. vt almohazar

groove (gru:v) n 1 ranura f. 2 surco m. vt estriar

grope (group) vi ir a tientas.

gross (grous) adj 1 grueso. 2 craso. 3 grosero.

grotesque (grou'tesk) adj grotesco.

grotto ('grɔtou) n gruta f

ground [1] (graund) n 1 tierra f. 2 suelo m. 3 terreno m. 4 fundamento m. 5 pl parque, jardín m. **ground floor** n entresuelo m. **groundsheet** n tela impermeable f. **groundsman** n guarda encargado de recinto deportivo m. **groundwork** n trabajo preliminar m.

ground [2] (graund) v see **grind**.

group (gru:p) n grupo m. vt agrupar.

grouse [1] (graus) n invar lagópedo m.

grouse [2] (graus) n rezongo m. vt rezongar.

grove (grouv) n arboleda f

grovel ('grɔvəl) *vi* arrastrarse.

grow* (grou) *vt* 1 cultivar. 2 dejar, crecer. *vi* 1 crecer. 2 aumentarse. **grown-up** *adj* adulto. *n* persona mayor. **growth** *n* crecimiento, aumento *m*.

growl (graul) *n* gruñido *m*. *vi* gruñir.

grub (grʌb) *n* 1 gusano *m*. 2 *inf* comida *f*. *vi* escarbar.

grubby ('grʌbi) *adj* sucio, mugriento.

grudge (grʌdʒ) *n* rencor *m*. *vt* escatimar.

gruelling ('gru:əliŋ) *adj* duro, penoso.

gruesome ('gru:səm) *adj* horrible, horripilante.

gruff (grʌf) *adj* 1 brusco. 2 bronco.

grumble ('grʌmbəl) *n* queja *f*. *vi* refunfuñar.

grumpy ('grʌmpi) *adj* gruñón, malhumorado.

grunt (grʌnt) *n* gruñido *m*. *vi* gruñir.

guarantee (gærən'ti:) *n* garantía *f*. *vt* garantizar. **guarantor** *n* fiador *m*.

guard (ga:d) *n* guardia *f*. *vt* guardar, proteger. **guardian** *n* 1 guardián *m*. 2 tutor *m*.

guerrilla (gə'rilə) *n* guerrillero *m*.

guess (ges) *n* conjetura *f*. *vt,vi* 1 adivinar. 2 suponer. **guesswork** *n* conjeturas *f pl*.

guest (gest) *n* 1 convidado *m*. 2 huésped *m,f*. **guesthouse** *n* casa de huéspedes *f*.

guide (gaid) *n* guía *f*. *vt* 1 guiar. 2 dirigir. **guidance** *n* 1 guía *f*. 2 consejo *m*. **guidebook** *n* guía del viajero *f*.

guild (gild) *n* gremio *m*.

guillotine (gilə'ti:n) *n* guillotina *f*. *vt* guillotinar.

guilt (gilt) *n* culpabilidad *f*. **guilty** *adj* culpable.

guinea ('gini) *n* guinea *f*. **guinea pig** *n* cobayo, conejillo de Indias *m*.

guitar (gi'ta:) *n* guitarra *f*.

gulf (gʌlf) *n* golfo *m*.

gull (gʌl) *n* gaviota *f*. *vt* estafar.

gullet ('gʌlit) *n* gaznate *m*.

gulp (gʌlp) *n* trago *m*. *vt* tragarse. *vi* tragar saliva.

gum¹ (gʌm) *n* goma *f*. *vt* engomar.

gum² (gʌm) *n* encía *f*.

gun (gʌn) *n* 1 fusil *m*. 2 cañón *m*. 3 pistola *f*. *vt* disparar sobre. **gunman** *n* pistolero *m*. **gunpowder** *n* pólvora *f*. **gunshot** *n* escopetazo *m*.

gurgle ('gə:gəl) *n* gorgoteo *m*. *vi* gorgotear.

gush (gʌʃ) *n* chorro *m*. *vi* brotar, chorrear.

gust (gʌst) *n* ráfaga *f*.

gut (gʌt) *n* tripa *f*. **guts** *n inf* valor *m*. valentía *f*.

gutter ('gʌtə) *n* 1 arroyo *m*. 2 gotera *f*. 3 canal, canalera *f*.

guy¹ (gai) *n* mamarracho *m*.

guy² (gai) *n naut* cuerda *f*.

gymnasium (dʒim'neiziəm) *n* gimnasio *m*. **gymnast** *n* gimnasta *m,f*. **gymnastic** *adj* gimnástico.

gynaecology (gaini'kɔlədʒi) *n* ginecología *f*.

gypsum ('dʒipsəm) *n* yeso *m*.

H

haberdasher ('hæbədæʃə) *n* mercero *m*. **haberdashery** *n* mercería *f*.

habit ('hæbit) *n* 1 costumbre *f*. 2 hábito *m*. **habitable** *adj* habitable. **habitual** *adj* habitual.

hack¹ (hæk) *vt* tajar. *n* hachazo *m*.

hack² (hæk) *n* rocín *m*.

hackneyed ('hæknid) *adj* trillado.

had (hæd) *v* see **have.**

haddock ('hædək) *n* eglefino *m*.

haemorrhage ('heməridʒ) *n* hemorragia *f*.

hag (hæg) *n* 1 bruja *f*. 2 vejarrona *f*.

haggard ('hægəd) *adj* ojeroso.

haggle ('hægl) *vi* 1 discutir. 2 regatear.

hail¹ (heil) *vt* 1 llamar. 2 saludar.

hail² (heil) *n* granizo *m*. *vi* granizar. **hailstone** *n* pedrisco *m*. **hailstorm** *n* granizada *f*.

hair (hɛə) *n* pelo, cabello *m*. **grey hair** canas *f pl*. **hairbrush** *n* cepillo para el pelo *m*. **haircut** *n* corte de pelo *m*. **hairdo** *n* peinado *m*. **hairdresser** *n* peluquero *m*. **hairgrip** or **hairpin** *n* horquilla *f*.

half (ha:f) *n,pl* **halves** mitad *f*. *adj* medio. *adv* a medias, semi.

half-back *sport n* medio *m*.

half-breed *adj* mestizo.

half-brother *n* medio hermano *m*.

half-hour *n* media hora *f*.

half-mast *n* **at half-mast** a media asta.

halfpenny ('heipəni) *n* medio penique *m*.

half-pint *n* media pinta *f*.

half-sister *n* media hermana, hermanastra *f*.

half-time *n* descanso *m*.

halftone ('ha:ftoun) *n* media tinta *f*.

halfway (ha:f'wei) *adj* intermedio. *adv* a medio camino.

halfwit ('ha:fwit) *n* imbécil *m,f*.

hall (hɔ:l) *n* 1 vestíbulo *m*. 2 comedor *m*. 3 sala *f*. **town hall** *n* ayuntamiento *m*

hallmark ('hɔ:lma:k) *n* 1 marca de ley *f*. 2 sello *m*.

Halloween (hælou'i:n) *n* víspera de todos los Santos *f*.

hallucination (həlu:si'neiʃən) *n* alucinación *f*.

halo ('heilou) *n pl* **-os** *or* **-oes** 1 halo *m.* 2 aureola *f.*

halt (hɔːlt) *n* alto *m.* parada *f. vt* parar. *vi* hacer alto.

halter ('hɔːltə) *n* cabestro, ronzal *m.*

halve (hɑːv) *vt* partir por mitad.

ham (hæm) *n* 1 jamón *m.* 2 *Th inf* comicastro *m.*

hamburger ('hæmbəːgə) *n* hamburguesa *f.*

hammer ('hæmə) *n* martillo *m. vt* martillar.

hammock ('hæmək) *n* hamaca *f.*

hamper[1] ('hæmpə) *vt* impedir.

hamper[2] ('hæmpə) *n* cesto *m.* canasta *f.*

hand (hænd) *n* 1 mano *f.* 2 manecilla *f.* 3 palmo *m. vt* entregar.

handbag ('hændbæg) *n* bolso *m.*

handbook ('hændbuk) *n* 1 manual *m.* 2 guía *f.*

handbrake ('hændbreik) *n* freno de mano *m.*

handcart ('hændkɑːt) *n* carretilla *f.*

handcuffs ('hændkʌf) *n pl* esposas *f pl.*

handful ('hændful) *n* puñado *m.*

hand grenade *n* granada *f.*

handicap ('hændikæp) *n* desventaja *f.* obstáculo *m. vt* 1 impedir. 2 perjudicar.

handicraft ('hændikrɑːft) *n* artesanía *f.*

handiwork ('hændiwəːk) *n* obra manual *f.*

handkerchief ('hæŋkətʃif) *n* pañuelo *m.*

handle ('hændl) *n* 1 mango *m.* 2 manivela *f.* 3 asa *m. vt* 1 tocar. 2 manipular. 3 manejar. **handlebars** *n pl* manillar *m.*

handmade (hænd'meid) *adj* hecho a mano.

hand-out *n* 1 distribución *f.* 2 limosna *f.*

hand-pick *vt* escoger a mano.

handrail ('hændreil) *n* pasamano *m.*

handshake ('hændʃeik) *n* apretón de manos *m.*

handsome ('hænsəm) *adj* 1 hermoso, guapo. 2 generoso.

handwriting ('hændraitiŋ) *n* escritura *f.*

handy ('hændi) *adj* 1 a mano. 2 hábil. 3 útil.

hang* (hæŋ) *vt* 1 colgar. 2 tender. 3 ahorcar. **hangman** *n* verdugo *m.* **hangover** *n* resaca *f.*

hanker ('hæŋkə) *vi* añorar, anhelar.

haphazard (hæp'hæzəd) *adj* fortuito.

happen ('hæpən) *vi* pasar, suceder, ocurrir. **happening** *n* suceso, acontecimiento *m.*

happy ('hæpi) *adj* 1 feliz. 2 contento. 3 alegre. **happiness** *n* felicidad *f.*

harass ('hærəs) *vt* acosar, hostigar.

harbour ('hɑːbə) *n* puerto *m. vt* 1 abrigar. 2 hospedar.

hard (hɑːd) *adj* 1 duro. 2 penoso. 3 severo. *adv* 1 fuerte. 2 duro. **hardback** *n* libro de tapas

duras *m.* **hardboard** *n* chapa de madera dura *f.* **hardship** *n* 1 trabajos *m pl.* penas *f pl.* 2 apuro económico *m.* **hardware** *n* ferretería, quincalla *f.*

harden ('hɑːdn) *vt* endurecer.

hardly ('hɑːdli) *adv* 1 duramente. 2 apenas.

hardy ('hɑːdi) *adj* 1 fuerte. 2 resistente.

hare ('hɛə) *n* liebre *f.*

haricot ('hærikou) *n* alubia *f.*

harm (hɑːm) *n* daño, perjuicio *m. vt* dañar. **harmful** *adj* perjudicial.

harmonic (hɑː'mɔnik) *adj* armónico. **harmonize** *vt,vi* armonizar. **harmony** *n* armonía *f.*

harness ('hɑːnis) *n* guarniciones *f pl. vt* 1 enjaezar. 2 utilizar.

harp (hɑːp) *n* arpa *f.*

harpoon (hɑː'puːn) *n* arpón *m. vt* arponear.

harpsichord ('hɑːpsikɔːd) *n* arpicordio *m.*

harsh (hɑːʃ) *adj* 1 áspero. 2 cruel.

harvest ('hɑːvist) *n* cosecha *f. vt* cosechar.

has (hæz) *v see* **have.**

hashish ('hæʃiʃ) *n* hachís *m.*

haste (heist) *n* prisa *f.* **hasten** *vt* acelerar. *vi* apresurarse.

hat (hæt) *n* sombrero *m.*

hatch[1] (hætʃ) *vt* empollar. *vi* salir del huevo.

hatch[2] (hætʃ) *n naut* escotilla *f.*

hatchet ('hætʃit) *n* hacha *f.*

hate (heit) *n* odio *m. vt* odiar, aborrecer.

haughty ('hɔːti) *adj* altanero, arrogante.

haul (hɔːl) *n* 1 tirón *m.* 2 trayecto *m.* 3 redada *f. vt* arrastrar.

haunch (hɔːntʃ) *n* 1 anca *f.* 2 pierna *f.*

haunt (hɔːnt) *n* guarida *f. vt* 1 frecuentar. 2 aparecer en. 3 obsesionar.

have* (hæv) *vt* 1 tener. 2 tomar. 3 llevar. *v aux* haber. **have to** tener que.

haven ('heivən) *n* 1 puerto *m.* 2 refugio *m.*

haversack ('hævəsæk) *n* mochila *f.*

havoc ('hævək) *n* estragos *m pl.*

hawk[1] (hɔːk) *n* halcón *m.*

hawk[2] (hɔːk) *vt* pregonar.

hawthorn ('hɔːθɔːn) *n* espino *m.*

hay (hei) *n* heno *m.* **haywire** *adj inf* 1 en desorden. 2 loco.

hazard ('hæzəd) *n* riesgo *m. vt* 1 arriesgar. 2 aventurar.

haze (heiz) *n* bruma, neblina *f.*

hazel ('heizəl) *n* avellano *m.*

he (hiː) *pron 3rd pers s* él.

head (hed) *n* 1 cabeza *f.* 2 cabecera *f.* 3 jefe *m. vt* encabezar. *vi* dirigirse. *adj* principal. **headache** ('hedeik) *n* dolor de cabeza *m.*

heading ('hediŋ) n encabezamiento, título m.
headlamp or **headlight** ('hedlait) n faro m.
headline ('hedlain) n titular m.
headlong ('hedlɔŋ) adj precipitado. adv de cabeza.
headmaster (hed'mɑːstə) n director m.
headquarters ('hedkwɔːtəz) n cuartel general m.
headstrong ('hedstrɔŋ) adj terco, testarudo.
headway ('hedwei) n progreso, avance m.
heal (hiːl) vt curar, sanar. vi cicatrizarse.
health (helθ) n 1 salud f. 2 sanidad f. **healthy** adj sano, saludable.
heap (hiːp) n montón m. vt 1 amontonar. 2 colmar.
hear* (hiə) vt 1 oír. 2 law ver. **hear of** oír hablar de. **hear that** oír decir que. **hearing** n 1 oído m. 2 audición f. **hearing aid** n audífono m.
hearse (hɑːs) n coche fúnebre.
heart (hɑːt) n corazón m. **by heart** de memoria. **heart attack** n ataque cardíaco m. **heartbeat** n latido del corazón m. **heartbroken** adj angustiado, acongojado.
hearty ('hɑːti) adj 1 cordial. 2 fuerte. 3 campechano. 4 (of a meal) copioso.
hearth (hɑːθ) n 1 hogar m. 2 chimenea f.
heat (hiːt) n 1 calor m. 2 ardor . 3 zool celo m. vt calentar. vi calentarse. **heater** n calentador m. **heatwave** n ola de calor f.
heath (hiːθ) n brezal m.
heathen ('hiːðən) adj,n pagano m.
heather ('heðə) n brezo m.
heave* (hiːv) n 1 esfuerzo m. 2 tirón m. 3 empujón m. vt 1 alzar. 2 exhalar.
heaven ('hevən) n 1 cielo m. 2 paraíso m.
heavy ('hevi) adj 1 pesado. 2 denso. 3 grueso.
Hebrew ('hiːbruː) adj,n hebreo m.
heckle ('hekəl) vt,vi interrumpir, importunar.
hectare ('hektɑː) n hectárea f.
hectic ('hektik) adj febril.
hedge (hedʒ) n seto vivo m. vt 1 cercar. 2 rodear. vi contestar con evasivas. **hedgehog** n erizo m.
heed (hiːd) vt hacer caso de. n atención f.
heel (hiːl) n 1 talón m. 2 tacón m.
hefty ('hefti) adj 1 pesado. 2 fuerte.
height (hait) n 1 altura f. 2 estatura f. **heighten** vt 1 elevar. 2 realzar.
heir (εə) n heredero m. **heirloom** n herencia, reliquia f.
held (held) v see **hold**.
helicopter ('helikɔptə) n helicóptero m.

hell (hel) n infierno m.
hello (hə'lou) interj 1 ¡hola! 2 (in calling on telephone) ¡oiga! 3 (in answering telephone) ¡diga!
helm (helm) n timón m.
helmet ('helmit) n casco, yelmo m.
help (help) n 1 ayuda f. 2 socorro m. vt ayudar. **help yourself** sírvase. **helpless** adj 1 desvalido. 2 desmañado.
hem (hem) n dobladillo m.
hemisphere ('hemisfiə) n hemisferio m.
hemp (hemp) n cáñamo m.
hen (hen) n 1 gallina f. 2 hembra f.
hence (hens) adv 1 de aquí. 2 desde ahora. 3 por lo tanto.
her (həː) pron 3rd pers s 1 la. 2 ella. poss adj 3rd pers s su, de ella. **herself** pron 3rd pers s 1 ella misma. 2 se. 3 sí misma.
herald ('herəld) n heraldo m. vt anunciar.
herb (həːb) n hierba f.
herd (həːd) n 1 rebaño m. 2 multitud f. vt guardar. vi reunirse. **herdsman** n 1 vaquero m. 2 pastor m.
here (hiə) adv 1 aquí. 2 acá.
hereditary (hi'reditri) adj hereditario.
heredity (hi'rediti) n herencia f.
heresy ('herəsi) n herejía f.
heritage ('heritidʒ) n 1 herencia f. 2 patrimonio m.
hermit ('həːmit) n ermitaño m.
hero ('hiərou) n, pl **heroes** 1 héroe m. 2 protagonista m.
heroin ('herouin) n heroína f.
heron ('herən) n garza real f.
herring ('heriŋ) n arenque m.
hers (həːz) pron poss 3rd pers s de ella, (el) suyo, (la) suya, (los) suyos, (las) suyas f.
hesitate ('heziteit) vi 1 vacilar. 2 titubear. **hesitation** n vacilación f.
hexagon ('heksəgən) n hexágono m.
hibernate ('haibəneit) vi 1 invernar. 2 hibernar.
hiccup ('hikʌp) n also **hiccough** hipo m. vi hipar.
hide* [1] (haid) vt esconder, ocultar.
hide [2] (haid) n 1 piel f. 2 cuero m.
hideous ('hidiəs) adj horrible, horrendo.
hiding [1] ('haidiŋ) n **be in hiding** estar escondido.
hiding [2] ('haidiŋ) n paliza f.
hierarchy ('haiərɑːki) n jerarquía f.
high (hai) adj 1 alto. 2 mayor. 3 elevado.
highbrow ('haibrau) adj,n intelectual m,f.
high-fidelity adj alta fidelidad.

high frequency adj alta frecuencia.

highlands ('hailands) n pl montañas f pl. meseta montaña f.

highlight ('hailait) n punto más notable m. vt destacar.

Highness ('hainis) n alteza f.

highpitched ('haipitʃt) adj de tono alto.

high tide n pleamar f.

highway ('haiwei) n carretera f.

hijack ('haidʒæk) vt atracar.

hike (haik) n caminata f. vi caminar por el campo.

hilarious (hi'lɛəriəs) adj divertido.

hill (hil) n 1 colina f. cerro m. 2 cuesta f. **hillside** n ladera f. **hilltop** n cumbre f.

him (him) pron 3rd pers s 1 le, lo. 2 él. **himself** pron 3rd pers s 1 el mismo. 2 se. 3 sí mismo.

hind (haind) n 1 cierva f. 2 trasero m. **hindleg** n pata trasera f.

hinder ('hində) vt 1 estorbar. 2 dificultar. **hindrance** n estorbo.

Hindu ('hindu:) adj,n hindú.

hinge (hindʒ) n bisagra f. gozne m. vt engoznar.

hint (hint) n 1 indirecta f. 2 consejo m. 3 señal f. vt insinuar. vi aludir.

hip (hip) n cadera f.

hippopotamus (hipə'pɔtəməs) n hipopótamo m.

hire (haiə) n 1 alquiler m. 2 salario, jornal m. vt alquilar. 2 contratar.

his (hiz) poss adj 3rd pers s su, sus. poss pron 3rd pers s de él, (el) suyo, (la) suya, (los) suyos, (las) suyas.

hiss (his) n silbido, siseo m. vt,vi silbar, sisear.

history ('histri) n historia f. **historian** n historiador m. **historic** adj histórico m.

hit (hit) n 1 golpe m. 2 tiro m. 3 éxito m. vt 1 golpear. 2 dar en, atinar. vi chocar.

hitch (hitʃ) n 1 tirón m. 2 dificultad f. vt 1 atar. 2 mover de un tirón. **hitch-hike** vi hacer autostop.

hive (haiv) n colmena f.

hoard (hɔ:d) n 1 acumulación f. 2 tesoro escondido m. vt amontonar, atesorar, acaparar.

hoarding ('hɔ:diŋ) n cartelera f.

hoarse (hɔ:s) adj ronco.

hoax (houks) n 1 trampa f. truco m. vt engañar, mistificar.

hobble ('hɔbl) n 1 cojera f. 2 maniota, traba f. vi cojear. vt manear.

hobby ('hɔbi) n 1 pasatiempo m. 2 afición f.

hock [1] (hɔk) n anat corvejón m.

hock [2] (hɔk) n vino del Rin m.

hoe (hou) n azadón, sacho m. vt azadonar, sachar.

hog (hɔg) n cerdo m. vt acaparar.

hoist (hɔist) n 1 montacargas m invar. 2 grúa f. vt 1 alzar, levantar. 2 izar.

hold [1] (hould) n 1 agarro m. 2 influencia f. dominio m. vt agarrar, coger. vi 1 mantenerse firme. 2 valer. **holdall** n funda f. neceser m. **holder** n 1 poseedor, tenedor m. 2 inquilino m. 3 titular m. 4 asidero m.

hold [2] (hould) n naut bodega m.

hole (houl) n agujero, hoyo m.

holiday ('hɔlidi) n 1 día de fiesta m. 2 vacación f. vi pasar las vacaciones. **holiday camp** n colonia veraniega f.

Holland ('hɔlənd) n Holanda f.

hollow ('hɔlou) adj hueco, ahuecado. n hueco m. concavidad f. vt ahuecar, excavar.

holly ('hɔli) n acebo m. **hollyhock** n malva loca f.

holster ('houlstə) n pistolera f.

holy ('houli) adj santo, sagrado. **holiness** n santidad f.

homage ('hɔmidʒ) n homenaje m.

home (houm) n casa f. hogar m. adj doméstico. **at home** en casa. **homecoming** n regreso al hogar m. **home-made** adj casero. **homesick** adj nostálgico.

homosexual (houmə'sekʃuəl) adj,n homosexual m,f

honest ('ɔnist) adj 1 honrado. 2 sincero. **honesty** n 1 honradez f. 2 franqueza f.

honey ('hʌni) n miel f. **honeycomb** n panal m. **honeymoon** n luna de miel f. vi pasar la luna de miel. **honeysuckle** n madreselva f.

honour ('ɔnə) n 1 honor m. 2 honradez f. vt honrar. **honorary** adj honorario.

hood (hud) n 1 capucha f. 2 capirote m. 3 mot capota f

hoof (hu:f) n, pl **hooves** casco m. pezuña f.

hook (huk) n 1 gancho m. 2 anzuelo m. vt 1 enganchar. 2 pescar. vi encorvar.

hooligan ('hu:ligən) n gamberro m.

hoop (hu:p) n aro m. argolla f. vt enarcar.

hoot (hu:t) n 1 grito m. 2 bocinazo m. vt abuchear. vi ulular, gritar.

Hoover ('hu:və) n Tdmk aspirador m.

hop [1] (hɔp) n salto, brinco m. vi 1 brincar. 2 cojear.

hop [2] (hɔp) n bot lúpulo m.

hope (houp) n esperanza f. vi esperar. **hopeful** adj esperanzador. **hopefully** adv con optimismo. **hopeless** adj 1 desesperado, sin esperanza. 2 sin remedio.

horde (hɔːd) n horda f.

horizon (həˈraizən) n horizonte m. **horizontal** adj horizontal.

hormone (ˈhɔːmoun) n hormona f.

horn (hɔːn) n 1 cuerno m. 2 mus trompa f. 3 bocina f.

hornet (ˈhɔːnit) n avispón, moscardón m.

horoscope (ˈhɔrəskoup) n horóscopo m.

horrible (ˈhɔrəbl) adj horrible.

horrid (ˈhɔrid) adj horroroso.

horrify (ˈhɔrifai) vt 1 horrorizar. 2 escandalizar.

horror (ˈhɔrə) n horror m.

hors d'oeuvre (ɔː ˈdɜːv) n entremeses m pl.

horse (hɔːs) n caballo m. **horse chestnut** n castaña de Indias f. **horsefly** n tábano m. **horsehair** n crin m. **horseman** n jinete m. **horsepower** n caballo de fuerza m. **horseradish** n rábano picante m. **horseshoe** n herradura f. **on horseback** a caballo.

horticulture (ˈhɔːtikʌltʃə) n horticultura f. **horticulturalist** n horticultor m.

hose (houz) n invar 1 medias, calzas f pl. 2 calceta f. 3 manga f. manguera f. vt regar con manga.

hosiery (ˈhouziəri) n calceta, calcetería f.

hospitable (ˈhɔspitəbəl) adj hospitalario.

hospital (ˈhɔspitl) n hospital m.

hospitality (hɔspiˈtæliti) n hospitalidad f.

host¹ (houst) n 1 huésped m. 2 anfitrión m.

host² (houst) n multitud f.

hostage (ˈhɔstidʒ) n rehén m.

hostel (ˈhɔstl) n parador m. **youth hostel** albergue para jóvenes m.

hostess (ˈhoustis) n 1 huéspeda f. 2 anfitriona f. 3 aviat azafata f. 4 cabaretera f.

hostile (ˈhɔstail) adj enemigo, hostil. **hostility** n hostilidad f.

hot (hɔt) adj 1 caliente. 2 caluroso. 3 picante. **be hot** hacer or tener calor. **hot-blooded** adj apasionado. **hothouse** n invernadero m. **hotplate** n calientaplatos m invar. **hot-water bottle** n bolsa de agua caliente f.

hotel (houˈtel) n hotel m.

hound (haund) n podenco, sabueso m. vt acosar, perseguir.

hour (auə) n hora f.

house (haus) n casa f. vt alojar, hospedar.

houseboat (ˈhausbout) n casa flotante f.

household (ˈhaushould) n 1 casa f. 2 familia f.

housekeeper (ˈhauskiːpə) n ama de casa, ama

de llaves f. **housekeeping** n gobierno doméstico m.

housemaid (ˈhausmeid) n criada f.

houseman (hausmən) n médico interno m.

House of Commons n Cámara de los Comunes f.

House of Lords n Cámara de los Lores f.

housewife (ˈhauswaif) n, pl **housewives** 1 ama de casa f. 2 madre de familia f.

housework (ˈhauswɜːk) n quehacer doméstico m.

housing (hauziŋ) n alojamiento m.

hover (ˈhɔvə) vi 1 cernerse. 2 rondar. **hovercraft** n hidroala m.

how (hau) adv como, de que modo. **however** adv como, de cualquier modo. conj sin embargo.

howl (haul) n alarido, aullido m. vi 1 gritar. 2 reírse a carcajadas.

hub (hʌb) n cubo, centro m.

huddle (ˈhʌdl) n montón, grupo m. vi acurrucarse, amontonarse.

huff (hʌf) n rabieta f. enojo m. vt enojar.

hug (hʌg) n abrazo m. vt abrazar, apretar.

huge (hjuːdʒ) adj enorme, inmenso, vasto.

hulk (hʌlk) n 1 barco viejo, casco m. 2 carraca f. 3 bulto m.

hull¹ (hʌl) n vaina, cáscara f.

hull² (hʌl) n naut casco m.

hullo (haˈlou) interj ¡hola!

hum (hʌm) n 1 zumbido m. 2 tarareo m. vt canturrear. vi zumbar.

human (ˈhjuːmən) adj,n humano m. **human nature** n naturaleza humana f. **humane** adj humano, humanitario. **humanism** n humanismo m. **humanitarian** adj,n humanitario m,f. **humanity** n humanidad f.

humble (ˈhʌmbəl) adj humilde. vt humillar.

humdrum (ˈhʌmdrʌm) adj 1 monótono, aburrido. 2 rutinario.

humid (ˈhjuːmid) adj húmedo. **humidity** n humedad f.

humiliate (hjuːˈmilieit) vt humillar.

humility (hjuːˈmiliti) n humildad f.

humour (ˈhjuːmə) n humor m. vt complacer, seguir el humor a. **humorist** n humorista m,f. **humorous** adj chistoso, divertido.

hump (hʌmp) n joroba, corcova, giba f. vt llevar.

hunch (hʌntʃ) n presentimiento m. **hunchback** adj,n jorobado, corcovado.

hundred (ˈhʌndrəd) adj,n ciento, cien. n centenar m. centena f. **hundredth** adj centésimo. **hundredweight** n quintal m.

hung (hʌŋ) v see **hang**.

Hungary ('hʌŋgəri) n Hungría f. **Hungarian** adj,n húngaro m. **Hungarian** (language) n húngaro m.

hunger ('hʌŋgə) n hambre m. vi tener hambre. **hungry** adj hambriento. **be hungry** tener hambre. **go hungry** pasar hambre.

hunt (hʌnt) n 1 caza, cacería f. 2 búsqueda f. vt 1 cazar. 2 perseguir. **hunting** n cacería, montería f. **huntsman** n cazador, montero m.

hurdle ('hə:dl) n 1 zarzo m. 2 obstáculo m.

hurl (hə:l) vt lanzar, arrojar.

hurrah (hu'rɑː) interj ¡viva!

hurricane ('hʌrikein) n huracán m.

hurry ('hʌri) n prisa f. **be in a hurry** tener prisa. vt apresurar, dar prisa a. vi darse prisa.

hurt (hə:t) n 1 herida f. 2 daño m. vt 1 lastimar. 2 herir. vi doler.

husband ('hʌzbənd) n marido, esposo m. vt economizar.

hush (hʌʃ) n silencio m. vt hacer callar. vi callarse. **hush!** ¡chitón!

husk (hʌsk) n cáscara, vaina f.

husky ('hʌski) adj 1 ronco. 2 fornido. n perro esquimal m.

hustle ('hʌsəl) n bullicio m. vt empujar, dar prisa a. vi darse prisa.

hut (hʌt) n 1 cabaña f. 2 cobertizo m. 3 choza f.

hutch (hʌtʃ) n 1 conejera f. 2 cabaña f.

hyacinth ('haiəsinθ) n jacinto m.

hybrid ('haibrid) n,adj híbrido m.

hydraulic (hai'drɔːlik) adj hidráulico.

hydro-electric adj hidroeléctrico.

hydrogen ('haidrədʒən) n hidrógeno m.

hyena (hai'iːnə) n hiena f.

hygiene ('haidʒiːn) n higiene f. **hygienic** adj higiénico.

hymn (him) n himno m. **hymnbook** n himnario m.

hyphen ('haifən) n guión m.

hypnosis (hip'nousis) n hipnosis f. **hypnotic** adj hipnótico. **hypnotism** n hipnotismo m.

hypochondria (haipə'kɔndriə) n hipocondría f.

hypocrisy (hi'pɔkrəsi) n hipocresía f. **hypocrite** n hipócrita m,f.

hypodermic (haipə'də:mik) n aguja hipodérmica f.

hypothesis (hai'pɔθəsis) n, pl **hypotheses** hipótesis f.

hysterectomy (histə'rektəmi) n histerectomía f.

hysteria (his'tiəriə) n histerismo m. histeria f.

I

I (ai) pron 1st pers s yo.

Iberia (ai'biəriə) n Iberia f. **Iberian** adj,n ibero.

ice (ais) n hielo m. vt helar. **iceberg** n témpano de hielo m. **ice-cream** n helado m. **ice hockey** n hockey sobre hielo m. **ice rink** n pista de hielo f. **ice-skate** vi patinar sobre hielo. **icicle** n carámbano m. **icing** n cul garapiña f. **icy** adj helado, glacial.

icon ('aikɔn) n icono m.

idea (ai'diə) n 1 idea f. 2 concepto m. 3 ocurrencia f.

ideal (ai'diəl) adj,n ideal m. **idealist** n idealista m,f. **idealize** vt idealizar.

identify (ai'dentifai) vt identificar.

identity (ai'dentiti) n identidad f. **identity card** n carnet de identidad m. **identical** adj idéntico.

ideology (aidi'ɔlədʒi) n ideología f.

idiom ('idiəm) n 1 modismo m. locución f. 2 lenguaje m.

idiosyncrasy (idiə'siŋkrəsi) n idiosincrasia f.

idiot ('idiət) n idiota m,f. tonto m.

idle ('aidl) adj 1 ocioso. 2 perezoso. 3 frívolo. vi mot marchar en vacío.

idol ('aidl) n ídolo m. **idolatry** n idolatría f. **idolize** vt idolatrar.

idyllic (i'dilik) adj idílico.

if (if) conj si.

ignite (ig'nait) vt encender, incendiar. vi encenderse. **ignition** n ignición f.

ignore (ig'nɔ:) vt no hacer caso de, desconocer. **ignorant** adj ignorante. **be ignorant of** ignorar, desconocer.

ill (il) adj enfermo, malo. adv mal. **ill-bred** adj mal educado. **illness** n enfermedad f. **ill-treat** vt maltratar. **ill will** n 1 mala voluntad f. 2 rencor m.

illegal (i'liːgəl) adj ilegal.

illegible (i'ledʒəbəl) adj ilegible.

illegitimate (ili'dʒitimət) adj ilegítimo.

illicit (i'lisit) adj ilícito.

illiterate (i'litərət) adj,n analfabeto m.

illogical (i'lɔdʒikəl) adj ilógico.

illuminate (i'luːmineit) vt iluminar.

illusion (i'luːʒən) n ilusión f.

illustrate ('iləstreit) vt ilustrar.

illustrious (i'lʌstriəs) adj ilustre.

image ('imidʒ) n 1 imagen f. 2 reputación f. **imagery** n 1 imagen f. 2 metáfora f.

imagine (i'mædʒin) vt imaginar. **imaginary** adj imaginario. **Imagination** n imaginación f. **imaginative** adj imaginativo.

imitate ('imiteit) vt **1** imitar. **2** remedar. **imitation** n imitación f.

immaculate (i'mækjulət) adj inmaculado.

immature (imə'tjuə) adj **1** inmaturo. **2** juvenil.

immediate (i'mi:diət) adj **1** inmediato. **2** urgente.

immense (i'mens) adj enorme, inmenso.

immerse (i'mə:s) vt sumergir, hundir.

immigrate ('imigreit) vi inmigrar. **immigrant** adj,n inmigrante m,f.

imminent ('iminənt) adj inminente.

immobile (i'moubail) adj inmóvil. **immobilize** vt inmovilizar.

immoral (i'mɔrəl) adj inmoral.

immortal (i'mɔ:tl) adj,n inmortal m,f.

immovable (i'mu:vəbəl) adj **1** inmóvil, inmoble. **2** inconmovible, inmovible.

immune (i'mju:n) adj inmune. **immunize** vt inmunizar.

imp (imp) n diablillo, duende m.

impact ('impækt) n choque, impacto m.

impair (im'peə) vt **1** perjudicar, dañar. **2** empeorar, deteriorar.

impart (im'pɑ:t) vt comunicar.

impartial (im'pɑ:ʃəl) adj imparcial.

impatient (im'peiʃənt) adj **1** impaciente. **2** intolerante.

impeach (im'pi:tʃ) vt **1** acusar. **2** procesar.

impeccable (im'pekəbəl) adj impecable.

impediment (im'pedimənt) n **1** obstáculo m. **2** impedimento m. **3** defecto del habla m.

impel (im'pel) vt impulsar, impeler.

imperative (im'perativ) adj,n imperativo m.

imperfect (im'pə:fikt) adj imperfecto, defectuoso.

imperial (im'piəriəl) adj imperial.

impersonal (im'pə:sənl) adj impersonal.

impersonate (im'pə:səneit) vt **1** hacerse pasar por. **2** imitar.

impertinent (im'pə:tinənt) adj impertinente.

impetuous (im'petʃuəs) adj impetuoso.

impetus ('impitəs) n impetu m.

impinge (im'pindʒ) vi **impinge on** afectar a.

implement ('impləmənt) n **1** herramienta f. **2** apero m. vt poner en obra.

implicit (im'plisit) adj **1** implícito. **2** absoluto.

implore (im'plɔ:) vt implorar, suplicar.

imply (im'plai) vt **1** implicar. **2** querer decir. **3** insinuar.

import (n 'impɔ:t; v im'pɔ:t) n **1** importación m. **2** sentido m. **3** importancia f. vt importar.

importance (im'pɔ:tns) n importancia f.

impose (im'pouz) vt imponer. vi **1** embaucar. **2** abusar. **imposing** adj imponente.

impossible (im'posabəl) adj imposible.

impostor (im'postə) n impostor m.

impotent ('impətənt) adj impotente.

impound (im'paund) vt embargar.

impoverish (im'povəriʃ) vt empobrecer.

impress (im'pres) vt **1** estampar. **2** impresionar. vi hacer buena impresión. **impression** n impresión f.

imprint (n 'imprint; v im'print) n **1** impresión, huella f. **2** pie de imprenta m. vt imprimir, grabar.

imprison (im'prizən) vt encarcelar.

improbable (im'probəbəl) adj improbable.

impromptu (im'promptju:) adj **1** improvisado. **2** impremeditado. adv de improviso.

improper (im'propə) adj **1** impropio. **2** indecoroso.

improve (im'pru:v) vt **1** mejorar. **2** perfeccionar. **improvement** n mejoramiento.

improvise ('imprəvaiz) vt,vi improvisar.

impudent ('impjudənt) adj impudente, descarado.

impulse ('impʌls) n impulso m.

impure (im'pjuə) adj impuro.

in (in) prep **1** en. **2** dentro de. **3** de. adv dentro, adentro.

inability (inə'biliti) n **1** inhabilidad f. **2** incapacidad f.

inaccurate (in'ækjurət) adj inexacto, incorrecto. **inaccuracy** n inexactitud f.

inadequate (in'ædikwit) adj inadecuado, insuficiente.

inadvertent (inəd'və:tnt) adj inadvertido.

inane (i'nein) adj necio, fatuo.

inanimate (in'ænimit) adj inanimado.

inarticulate (inɑ:'tikjulət) adj incapaz de expresarse.

inasmuch (inəz'mʌtʃ) conj puesto que.

inaudible (in'ɔ:dəbəl) adj inaudible.

inaugurate (i'nɔ:gjureit) vt inaugurar.

incapable (in'keipəbəl) adj incapaz.

incense [1] ('insens) n incienso m.

incense [2] (in'sens) vt indignar.

incessant (in'sesənt) adj incesante.

incest ('insest) n incesto m.

inch (intʃ) n pulgada f. **inch by inch** palmo a palmo. vi moverse poco a poco.

incident ('insidənt) n incidente m. **incidental** adj incidental.

incite (in'sait) vt incitar.

incline (in'klain) n declive m. vt inclinar.

include (in'klu:d) vt incluir. **inclusion** n inclusión f

incoherent (inkou'hiərənt) adj incoherente.

income ('inkʌm) n 1 renta f. 2 rédito m.

incompatible (inkəm'pætibəl) adj incompatible.

incompetent (in'kɔmpətənt) adj incompetente. **incompetence** n incompetencia f.

incomplete (inkəm'pli:t) adj incompleto.

incomprehensible (inkɔmpri'hensəbəl) adj incomprensible.

inconceivable (inkən'si:vəbəl) adj inconcebible.

inconclusive (inkən'klu:siv) adj inconcluso.

incongruous (in'kɔŋgruəs) adj incongruo.

inconsiderate (inkən'sidərit) adj desconsiderado.

inconsistent (inkən'sistənt) adj inconsistente.

inconvenient (inkən'vi:niənt) adj 1 incómodo, molesto. 2 inoportuno. **inconvenience** n incomodidad f.

incorporate (in'kɔ:pəreit) vt 1 incorporar. 2 agregar.

incorrect (inkə'rekt) adj incorrecto.

increase (v in'kri:s; n 'inkri:s) n aumento, incremento m. vt aumentar.

incredible (in'kredəbəl) adj increíble.

incubate ('inkjubeit) vt incubar, empollar. **incubator** n incubadora f.

incur (in'kə:) vt 1 incurrir en. 2 contraer.

indecent (in'di:sənt) adj indecente.

indeed (in'di:d) adv de veras. **yes indeed!** ¡claro que sí!

indefinite (in'defənit) adj indefinido.

independent (indi'pendənt) adj independiente. **independence** n independencia f.

index ('indeks) n, pl **indices** índice m. **index finger** n dedo índice m.

India ('indiə) n la India f. **Indian** adj,n indio m.

indicate ('indikeit) vt indicar. **indicator** n indicador m.

indifferent (in'difrənt) adj indiferente.

indigestion (indi'dʒestʃən) n indigestión f.

indignant (in'dignənt) adj indignado.

indirect (indi'rekt) adj indirecto.

indiscreet (indi'skri:t) adj indiscreto.

indiscriminate (indi'skriminit) adj 1 indistinto. 2 que no hace distinción.

indispensable (indi'spensəbəl) adj indispensable, imprescindible.

individual (indi'vidʒuəl) adj individual. n individuo m.

indoctrinate (in'dɔktrineit) vt adoctrinar.

indolent ('indələnt) adj indolente.

indoor ('indɔ:) adj 1 de puerta adentro. 2 interior. **indoors** adv 1 en casa. 2 dentro.

induce (in'dju:s) vt 1 inducir. 2 ocasionar.

indulge (in'dʌldʒ) vt 1 satisfacer. 2 complacer. vi abandonarse a

industry ('indəstri) n industria f. **industrial** adj industrial. **industrious** adj trabajador, industrioso.

inefficient (ini'fiʃənt) adj ineficaz. **inefficiency** n ineficacia f.

inept (i'nept) adj inepto.

inequality (ini'kwɔliti) n desigualdad f.

inert (i'nə:t) adj inerte. **inertia** n 1 inercia f. 2 pereza f.

inevitable (in'evitəbəl) adj inevitable, ineludible.

infallible (in'fæləbəl) adj infalible.

infamous ('infəməs) adj infame.

infant ('infənt) n 1 niño m. 2 educ párvulo m. **infancy** n infancia f.

infantry ('infəntri) n infantería f.

infatuate (in'fætʃueit) vt 1 apasionar. 2 engreír.

infect (in'fekt) vt infectar, contagiar. **infection** n infección f.

infer (in'fə:) vt inferir, deducir.

inferior (in'fiəriə) adj,n inferior m,f.

infernal (in'fə:nl) adj infernal.

infest (in'fest) vt infestar.

infidelity (infi'deliti) n infidelidad f.

infiltrate ('infiltreit) vt infiltrarse en.

infinite ('infinit) adj,n infinito m. **infinity** n 1 infinidad f. 2 math infinito m.

infinitive (in'finitiv) adj,n infinitivo m.

infirm (in'fə:m) adj enfermizo, débil.

inflame (in'fleim) vt inflamar, encender.

inflammable (in'flæməbəl) adj inflamable.

inflate (in'fleit) vt hinchar, inflar. **inflation** n inflación f.

inflection (in'flekʃən) n inflexión f

inflict (in'flikt) vt 1 infligir, inferir. 2 imponer.

influence ('influəns) n influencia f. vt influenciar. **influential** adj influyente.

influenza (influ'enzə) n gripe f.

inform (in'fɔ:m) vt informar, avisar. **information** n 1 información f. 2 conocimientos m pl.

informal (in'fɔ:məl) adj familiar, poco ceremonioso.

infringe (in'frindʒ) vt infringir, violar.

infuriate (in'fjuərieit) vt enfurecer

ingenious (in'dʒi:niəs) adj ingenioso, genial.
ingredient (in'gri:diənt) n ingrediente m.
inhabit (in'hæbit) vt habitar.
inhale (in'heil) vt aspirar, inhalar.
inherent (in'hiərənt) adj 1 inherente. 2 innato.
inherit (in'herit) vt heredar. **inheritance** n herencia f.
inhibit (in'hibit) vt inhibir, impedir. **inhibition** n inhibición f.
inhuman (in'hju:mən) adj inhumano.
initial (i'niʃəl) adj,n inicial. vt marcar, rubricar.
initiate (i'niʃieit) vt iniciar.
initiative (i'niʃətiv) n iniciativa f.
inject (in'dʒekt) vt inyectar. **injection** n inyección f.
injure ('indʒə) vt 1 herir, lastimar. 2 perjudicar. **injury** n 1 herida, lesión f. 2 daño m.
injustice (in'dʒʌstis) n injusticia f.
ink (iŋk) n tinta f. vt entintar.
inkling ('iŋkliŋ) n 1 indicio m. 2 sospecha f.
inland (adj 'inlənd; adv in'lænd) adj interior. adv tierra adentro. **Inland Revenue** n Delegación de Contribuciones f.
inmate ('inmeit) n 1 residente m,f. 2 asilado m. 3 preso m.
inn (in) n posada f. mesón m. taberna f.
innate (i'neit) adj innato.
inner ('inə) adj interior.
innocent ('inəsənt) adj,n inocente.
innocuous (i'nɔkjuəs) adj innocuo.
innovation (inə'veiʃən) n innovación f.
innuendo (inju'endou) n insinuación f.
inoculate (i'nɔkjuleit) vt inocular.
inquest ('inkwest) n indagación judicial f.
inquire (in'kwaiə) vt preguntar, informarse de. **inquire into** investigar. **inquiry** n 1 pregunta f. 2 pesquisa f. 3 investigación f.
inquisition (inkwi'ziʃən) n inquisición f.
inquisitive (in'kwizitiv) adj inquiridor, curioso.
insane (in'sein) adj loco, demente.
insatiable (in'seiʃəbəl) adj insaciable.
inscribe (in'skraib) vt 1 inscribir 2 dedicar. **inscription** n inscripción f.
insect ('insekt) n insecto m. **insecticide** n insecticida m.
insecure (insi'kjuə) adj inseguro.
inseminate (in'semineit) vt inseminar.
insert (in'sə:t) vt insertar.
inside (in'said) adv dentro. prep dentro de. adj,n interior m.
insidious (in'sidiəs) adj 1 insidioso. 2 maligno.
insight ('insait) n perspicacia f.
insignificant (insig'nifikənt) adj insignificante.

insinuate (in'sinjueit) vt insinuar.
insist (in'sist) vi insistir.
insolent ('insələnt) adj insolente, descarado. **insolence** n insolencia f.
insomnia (in'sɔmniə) n insomnio m.
inspect (in'spekt) vt inspeccionar. **inspector** n inspector m.
inspire (in'spaiə) vt inspirar, infundir. **inspiration** n inspiración f.
instability (instə'biliti) n instabilidad f.
install (in'stɔ:l) vt instalar. **installation** n instalación f.
instalment (in'stɔ:lmənt) n 1 entrega f. 2 comm plazo m.
instance ('instəns) n ejemplo m. vt poner por caso. **instant** adj inmediato, instantáneo. n instante m. **instantaneous** adj instantáneo.
instead (in'sted) adv en lugar de. **instead of** en vez de.
instep ('instep) n empeine m.
instigate ('instigeit) vt instigar.
instil (in'stil) vt infundir, inculcar.
instinct ('instiŋkt) n instinto m. **instinctive** adj instintivo.
institute ('institju:t) n instituto m. vt instituir. **institution** n 1 institución f. 2 tradición f. 3 asilo m. 4 manicomio m.
instruct (in'strʌkt) vt 1 instruir. 2 mandar. **instruction** n 1 instrucción f. 2 indicación f.
instrument ('instrumənt) n instrumento m. **instrumental** adj instrumental.
insubordinate (insə'bɔ:dinət) adj insubordinado.
insular ('insjulə) adj insular.
insulate ('insjuleit) vt aislar.
insulin ('insjulin) n insulina f.
insult (v in'sʌlt; n 'insʌlt) n insulto m. vt insultar.
insure (in'ʃuə) vt asegurar. **insurance** n seguro m.
intact (in'tækt) adj 1 intacto. 2 ileso.
integral ('intigrəl) adj íntegro. n math integral f.
integrate ('intigreit) vt integrar.
integrity (in'tegriti) n integridad f.
intellect ('intəlekt) n intelecto m. **intellectual** adj,n intelectual.
intelligent (in'telidʒənt) adj inteligente. **intelligence** n 1 inteligencia f. 2 información f. **intelligible** adj inteligible.
intend (in'tend) vt proponerse, pensar.
intense (in'tens) adj intenso. **intensify** vt intensificar. **intensity** n intensidad f. **intensive** adj intensivo.

intent[1] (in'tent) n intento, propósito m.

intent[2] (in'tent) adj 1 absorto. 2 resuelto.

intention (in'tenʃən) n 1 intención f. 2 propósito m.

inter (in'tə:) vt enterrar.

interact (intə'rækt) vi obrar recíprocamente.

intercept (intə'sept) vt interceptar.

interchange (intə'tʃeindʒ) vt intercambiar.

intercourse ('intəkɔ:s) n 1 trato m. 2 comercio m. 3 coito m.

interest ('intrəst) n 1 interés m. 2 beneficio m. vt interesar.

interfere (intə'fiə) vi 1 intervenir. 2 interferir.

interim ('intərim) adj interino, provisional.

interior (in'tiəriə) adj,n interior m.

interjection (intə'dʒekʃn) n interjección f.

interlude ('intəlu:d) n intervalo m.

intermediate (intə'mi:diət) adj intermedio, intermediario. **intermediary** adj,n intermediario m.

intermission (intə'miʃən) n intermisión f. intervalo m.

intermittent (intə'mitnt) adj intermitente.

intern (in'tə:n) vt internar, recluir.

internal (in'tə:nl) adj interno, interior.

international (intə'næʃnl) adj internacional.

interpose (intə'pouz) vt interponer.

interpret (in'tə:prit) vt interpretar. **interpretation** n interpretación f. **interpreter** n intérprete m,f.

interrogate (in'terəgeit) vt interrogar. **interrogative** adj interrogativo.

interrupt (intə'rʌpt) vt,vi interrumpir. **interruption** n interrupción f.

intersect (intə'sekt) vt cruzar.

interval ('intəvəl) n 1 intervalo m. 2 descanso m.

intervene (intə'vi:n) vi intervenir.

interview ('intəvju:) n entrevista f. vt entrevistarse con.

intestine (in'testin) n intestino m.

intimate[1] ('intimit) adj íntimo.

intimate[2] ('intimeit) vt dar a entender, intimar.

intimidate (in'timideit) vt intimidar.

into ('intə; stressed 'intu:) prep 1 en. 2 dentro de. 3 hacia el interior de.

intolerable (in'tɔlərəbəl) adj intolerable. **intolerant** adj intolerante.

intonation (intə'neiʃən) n entonación f.

intoxicate (in'tɔksikeit) vt embriagar.

intransitive (in'trænsitiv) adj intransitivo.

intrepid (in'trepid) adj intrépido.

intricate ('intrikət) adj intrincado.

intrigue (in'tri:g) n intriga f. vt fascinar. vi intrigar.

intrinsic (in'trinsik) adj intrínseco.

introduce (intrə'dju:s) vt 1 introducir. 2 presentar. **introduction** n 1 introducción f. 2 presentación f.

introspective (intrə'spektiv) adj introspectivo.

introvert ('intrəvə:t) adj,n introvertido m.

intrude (in'tru:d) vi 1 estorbar. 2 entrometerse.

intuition (intju'iʃən) n intuición f. **intuitive** adj intuitivo.

inundate ('inʌndeit) vt inundar.

invade (in'veid) vt invadir. **invasion** n invasión f.

invalid[1] ('invali:d) adj,n inválido m.

invalid[2] (in'vælid) adj inválido, nulo.

invaluable (in'væljuəbl) adj inestimable.

invariable (in'vɛəriəbəl) adj invariable.

invent (in'vent) vt inventar. **invention** n 1 invención f. 2 inventiva f.

inventory ('invəntəri) n inventario m.

invert (in'və:t) vt invertir, trastocar.

invertebrate (in'və:təbreit) adj,n invertebrado m.

invest (in'vest) vt invertir. **investment** n comm inversión f.

investigate (in'vestigeit) vt investigar.

invincible (in'vinsəbl) adj invencible.

invisible (in'vizəbl) adj invisible.

invite (in'vait) vt invitar. **invitation** n invitación f. convite m.

invoice ('invɔis) n factura f. vt facturar.

invoke (in'vouk) vt invocar.

involve (in'vɔlv) vt 1 implicar. 2 enredar. 3 suponer, implicar.

inward ('inwəd) adj interior.

inwards ('inwədz) adv hacia dentro.

iodine ('aiədi:n) n yodo m.

Ireland ('aiələnd) n Irlanda f. **Irish** adj,n irlandés m. **Irish** (language) n irlandés m.

iris ('airis) n 1 anat iris m. 2 bot lirio m.

iron ('aiən) n 1 hierro m. 2 plancha f. vt 1 planchar. 2 allanar. **Iron Curtain** n telón de acero m. **ironmonger** n ferretero m.

irony ('airəni) n ironía f. **ironic** adj irónico.

irrational (i'ræʃənl) adj irracional.

irregular (i'regjulə) adj irregular.

irrelevant (i'reləvənt) adj inaplicable, fuera de lugar.

irresistible (iri'zistəbəl) adj irresistible.

irrespective (iri'spektiv) adj aparte, sin hacer caso de.

irresponsible (iri'spɔnsəbəl) adj irresponsable.

irrevocable (i'revɔkəbəl) *adj* irrevocable.

irrigate ('irigeit) *vt* regar.

irritate ('iriteit) *vt* irritar.

is (iz) *v* see **be.**

Islam ('izlɑ:m) *n* Islam *m*. **Islamic** *adj* islámico.

island ('ailənd) *n* isla *f*.

isolate ('aisəleit) *vt* aislar. **Isolation** *n* aislamiento *m*.

issue ('iʃu:) *n* 1 resultado *m*. 2 cuestión *f*. 3 emisión *f*. 4 edición *f*. 5 descendencia *f*. *vt* 1 emitir. 2 distribuir. 3 expedir. *vi* salir.

it (it) *pron 3rd pers s* 1 ello. 2 lo. 3 la. 4 le. **itself** *pron 3rd pers s* él mismo *m*. ellos mismos *m pl*. ella misma *f*. ellas mismas *f pl*.

italic (i'tælik) *adj* 1 en bastardilla. 2 itálico.

Italy ('itəli) *n* Italia *f*. **Italian** *adj,n* italiano *m*. **Italian** (language) *n* italiano *m*.

itch (itʃ) *n* picazón *m*. *vi* picar, sentir comezón.

item ('aitəm) *n* 1 artículo *m*. 2 detalle, punto *m*.

itinerary (ai'tinərəri) *n* itinerario *m*.

its (its) *poss adj 3rd pers s* su, sus. *poss pron 3rd pers s* (el) suyo, (la) suya, (los) suyos, (las) suyas.

ivory ('aivəri) *n* marfil *m*.

ivy ('aivi) *n* hiedra, yedra *f*.

J

jab (dʒæb) *n* pinchazo *m*. *vt* pinchar.

jack (dʒæk) *n* 1 *mot* gato *m*. 2 *game* valet *m*.

jackal ('dʒækəl) *n* chacal *m*.

jackdaw ('dʒækdɔ:) *n* chova *f*.

jacket ('dʒækit) *n* 1 chaqueta *f*. 2 cazadora *f*. 3 forro de un libro *m*. cubierta *f*.

jackpot ('dʒækpɔt) *n* premio gordo *m*.

jade (dʒeid) *n* min jade *m*.

jaded ('dʒeidid) *adj* cansado, agotado.

jagged ('dʒægid) *adj* dentado.

jaguar ('dʒægjuə) *n* jaguar *m*.

jail (dʒeil) *n* cárcel *f*. calabozo *m*. *vt* encarcelar.

jam ¹ (dʒæm) *n* 1 aprieto, atasco, apiñamiento *m*. 2 *mot* embotellamiento *m*. congestión *f*. *vt* apretar, obstruir, atascar.

jam ² (dʒæm) *n* mermelada *f*.

January ('dʒænjuəri) *n* enero *m*.

Japan (dʒə'pæn) *n* Japón *m*. **Japanese** *adj,n* japonés. **Japanese** (language) *n* japonés *m*.

jar ¹ (dʒɑ:) *n* 1 jarra *f*. 2 tarro *m*.

jar ² (dʒɑ:) *n* 1 choque *m*. 2 sacudida *f*. 3 vibración *f*. *vt* 1 sacudir. 2 tocar. *vi* 1 vibrar. 2 chirriar.

jargon ('dʒɑ:gən) *n* jerga *f*.

jasmine ('dʒæzmin) *n* jazmín *m*.

jaundice ('dʒɔ:ndis) *n med* ictericia *f*.

jaunt (dʒɔ:nt) *n* paseo *m*. caminata *f*. **jaunty** *adj* garboso.

javelin ('dʒævlin) *n* jabalina *f*.

jaw (dʒɔ:) *n* 1 mandíbula, quijada *f*. 2 garras *f pl*. 3 boca *f*. **jawbone** *n* mandíbula *f*.

jazz (dʒæz) *n* jazz *m*.

jealous ('dʒeləs) *adj* envidioso, celoso. **jealousy** *n* envidia *f*. celos *m pl*.

jeans (dʒi:nz) *n* pantalones vaqueros *m pl*.

jeep (dʒi:p) *n* jeep *m*.

jeer (dʒiə) *n* 1 insulto *m*. 2 abucheo *m*. *vt* abuchear. *vi* mofarse.

jelly ('dʒeli) *n* gelatina, jalea *f*. **jellyfish** *n* medusa *f*.

jeopardize ('dʒepədaiz) *vt* arriesgar.

jerk (dʒə:k) *n* sacudida *f*. tirón *m*. *vt* sacudir, dar sacudidas a.

jersey ('dʒə:zi) *n* jersey *m*.

jest (dʒest) *n* burla, broma, chanza *f*. *vi* burlarse, bromear.

Jesus ('dʒi:zəs) *n* Jesús *m*.

jet ¹ (dʒet) *n* 1 *aviat* avión a reacción *m*. 2 chorro, surtidor *m*. *vi inf* salir a chorro.

jet ² (dʒet) *n min* azabache *m*.

jetty ('dʒeti) *n* muelle, malecón *m*.

Jew (dʒu:) *n,adj* judío *m*.

jewel ('dʒu:əl) *n* 1 joya *f*. 2 rubí *m*. **jeweller** *n* joyero *m*. **jeweller's** *n* joyería *f*.

jig ¹ (dʒig) *n tech* plantilla de guía *f*. **jigsaw** *n* 1 rompecabezas *m invar*. 2 sierra de vaivén *f*.

jig ² (dʒig) *n* jiga *f*. *vi* bailar la jiga.

jiggle ('dʒigəl) *vt* zarandear. *n* zarandeo *m*.

jilt (dʒilt) *vt* plantar, dejar.

jingle ('dʒiŋgəl) *n* 1 cascabeleo, tintineo *m*. 2 verso popular *m*. *vi* cascabelear, tintinear.

job (dʒɔb) *n* 1 trabajo *m*. 2 tarea, obra *f*. 3 empleo *m*.

jockey ('dʒɔki) *n* jockey *m*.

jodhpurs ('dʒɔdpəz) *n* pantalones de montar *m pl*.

jog (dʒɔg) *n* 1 golpecito, codazo *m*. 2 estímulo *m*. 3 trote *m*. *vt* 1 empujar. 2 estimular. *vi* trotar.

join (dʒɔin) *vt* juntar, unir. *vi* asociarse. **joint** *n* 1 juntura *f*. empalme *m*. 2 articulación *f*. nudillo *m*. *adj* común, colectivo.

joist (dʒɔist) *n* viga *f*.

joke (dʒouk) *n* chiste *m*. broma *f*. *vi* bromear.

jolly ('dʒɔli) *adj* alegre, divertido. *adv inf* muy, extremadamente.

jolt (dʒoult) *n* sacudida *f*. traqueteo *m*. *vt* dar sacudidas a. *vi* traquetear.

jostle ('dʒɔsəl) *n* empellón, empujón *m*. *vt* empujar.

journal ('dʒɔ:nl) *n* 1 periódico *m*. 2 revista *f*. 3 diario *m*. **journalism** *n* periodismo *m*. **journalist** *n* periodista *m*.

journey ('dʒɔ:ni) *n* viaje *m*. *vi* viajar.

jovial ('dʒouviəl) *adj* jovial, alegre.

joy (dʒɔi) *n* alegría, felicidad *f*.

jubilee ('dʒu:bili:) *n* jubileo *m*.

Judaism ('dʒu:deiizəm) *n* judaísmo *m*.

judge (dʒʌdʒ) *n* juez *m*. *vt*,*vi* juzgar, estimar. **judgment** *n* juicio *m*.

judicial (dʒu:'diʃəl) *adj* judicial.

judicious (dʒu:'diʃəs) *adj* juicioso, sensato, prudente.

judo ('dʒu:dou) *n sport* judo *m*.

jug (dʒʌg) *n* jarro *m*.

juggle ('dʒʌgəl) *vi* hacer juego de manos. **juggler** *n* malabarista *m,f*.

juice (dʒu:s) *n* jugo, zumo *m*. **juicy** *adj* jugoso, suculento.

jukebox ('dʒu:kbɔks) *n* tocadiscos automático *m invar*.

July (dʒu'lai) *n* julio *m*.

jumble ('dʒʌmbəl) *n* confusión, mezcla, desorden *m*. *vt* mezclar, amontonar. **jumble sale** *n* venta de objetos usados *f*.

jump (dʒʌmp) *n* salto, brinco *m*. *vi* saltar, dar saltos, brincar.

jumper ('dʒʌmpə) *n* 1 saltador *m*. 2 jersey *m*.

junction ('dʒʌŋkʃən) *n* 1 cruce *m*. 2 unión *f*. 3 empalme *m*.

June (dʒu:n) *n* junio *m*.

jungle ('dʒʌŋgəl) *n* selva *f*.

junior ('dʒu:niə) *adj* 1 menor. 2 subalterno.

juniper ('dʒu:nipə) *n* junípero *m*.

junk (dʒʌŋk) *n* 1 chatarra *f*. 2 baratijas *f pl*.

junta ('dʒʌntə) *n* junta *f*.

Jupiter ('dʒu:pitə) *n* Júpiter *m*.

jurisdiction (dʒuəris'dikʃən) *n* jurisdicción *f*.

jury ('dʒuəri) *n* jurado *m*. **juror** *n* jurado *m*.

just (dʒʌst) *adj* 1 justo. 2 imparcial. *adv* 1 justamente, precisamente. 2 recién. 3 sólo 4 poco más o menos, casi.

justice ('dʒʌstis) *n* 1 justicia *f*. 2 juez *m*.

justify ('dʒʌstifai) *vt* justificar.

jut (dʒʌt) *vi* sobresalir, proyectarse.

jute (dʒu:t) *n* yute *m*.

juvenile ('dʒu:vənail) *adj* juvenil, joven. *n* joven *m,f*. **juvenile delinquency** *n* delincuencia juvenil *f*.

juxtapose (dʒʌkstə'pouz) *vt* yuxtaponer.

K

kaleidoscope (kə'laidəskoup) *n* calidoscopio *m*.

kangaroo (kæŋgə'ru:) *n* canguro *m*.

keel (ki:l) *n* quilla *f*. *v* **keel over** 1 *naut* zozobrar. 2 *inf* desplomarse.

keen (ki:n) *adj* 1 agudo, afilado. 2 penetrante, intenso. 3 deseoso, ansioso. 4 entusiasta.

keep* (ki:p) *vt* 1 tener. 2 mantener. 3 observar. 4 guardar. 5 detener. *vi* continuar, seguir. **keepsake** *n* recuerdo, regalo *m*.

keg (keg) *n* barril, barrilete *m*.

kennel ('kenl) *n* perrera *f*.

kept (kept) *v see* **keep.**

kerb (kə:b) *n* bordillo de la acera *m*.

kernel ('kə:nl) *n* 1 grano *m*. 2 almendra *f*. piñón *m*. 3 meollo *m*.

kettle ('ketl) *n* 1 olla, marmita, caldera *f*. 2 pava *f*. **kettledrum** *n* timbal *m*.

key (ki:) *n* 1 llave *f*. 2 tecla *f*. 3 *tech* chaveta *f*. 4 *mus* tono *m*. **keyboard** *n* teclado *m*. **keyhole** *n* ojo de la cerradura *m*. **keyring** *n* llavero *m*.

khaki ('kɑ:ki) *n* caqui *m*.

kick (kik) *n* 1 patada *f*. 2 puntapié *m*. 3 coz *f*. 4 culatazo *m*. *vt* 1 dar un puntapié a. 2 dar una patada a. *vi* dar coces. **kick-off** *n sport* saque *m*.

kid[1] (kid) *n* 1 *zool* cabrito *m*. 2 carne de cabrito *f*. 3 niño, muchacho *m*.

kid[2] (kid) *vt* tomar el pelo a, embromar.

kidnap ('kidnæp) *vt* raptar, secuestrar **kidnapping** *n* rapto, secuestro *m*.

kidney ('kidni) *n* riñón *m*. **kidney bean** *n* alubia *f*. fríjol *m*.

kill (kil) *vt* matar, destruir. **kill time** pasar el tiempo, matar el tiempo

kiln (kiln) *n* horno *m*.

kilo ('ki:lou) *n* kilo *m*.

kilogram ('kiləgræm) *n* kilogramo *m*.

kilometre (ki'lɔmitə) *n* kilómetro *m*.

kilowatt ('kiləwɔt) *n* kilovatio *m*.

kilt (kilt) *n* falda escocesa *f*.

kimono (ki'mounou) *n* kimono *m*.

kin (kin) *n* parientes *m pl*.

kind[1] (kaind) *adj* bueno, benévolo, bondadoso, amable.

kind[2] (kaind) *n* clase, especie, suerte *f*. género, tipo *m*.

kindergarten ('kindəgɑːtn) n jardín de infancia m.

kindle ('kindl) vt encender.

kinetic (ki'netik) adj cinético.

king (kiŋ) n rey m. **kingdom** n reino m. **kingfisher** n martin pescador m.

kink (kiŋk) n 1 enroscadura f. 2 rizo m. **kinky** adj 1 rizado. 2 arrugado. 3 inf pervertido.

kiosk ('kiɔsk) n quiosco m.

kipper ('kipə) n arenque ahumado m.

kiss (kis) n beso m. vt besar.

kit (kit) n 1 equipo m. 2 caja para herramientas f. 3 med botiquín m.

kitchen ('kitʃin) n cocina f.

kite (kait) n 1 cometa m. 2 zool milano m.

kitten ('kitn) n gatito m.

kitty ('kiti) n 1 gatito m. 2 game polla, puesta f. bote m.

kleptomania (kleptə'meiniə) n cleptomanía f.

knack (næk) n 1 habilidad, maña f. 2 truco, artificio m.

knapsack ('næpsæk) n mochila f.

knave (neiv) n 1 bellaco m. 2 game sota f.

knead (niːd) vt amasar.

knee (niː) n rodilla f. **kneecap** n rótula f.

kneel (niːl) vi arrodillarse, hincar la rodilla.

knew (nuː) v see **know**.

knickers ('nikəz) n bragas f pl.

knife (naif) n, pl **knives** 1 cuchillo m. 2 navaja f. vt acuchillar.

knight (nait) n 1 caballero m. 2 game caballo m. **knighthood** n orden de caballería m.

knit* (nit) vt hacer a punto de aguja. vi hacer punto.

knob (nɔb) n 1 tirador m. 2 bulto m. 3 protuberancia f. **knobbly** adj nudoso.

knock (nɔk) n 1 golpe m. 2 llamada a la puerta f. vt 1 golpear. 2 inf denigrar. vi llamar a la puerta.

knot (nɔt) n 1 nudo, lazo m. 2 enredo m. vt 1 anudar. 2 atar, enlazar.

know* (nou) vt,vi 1 conocer. 2 saber.

knowledge ('nɔlidʒ) n 1 conocimiento m. 2 saber m. erudición, ciencia f.

knuckle ('nʌkəl) n 1 nudillo m. 2 cul jarrete m.

L

label ('leibəl) n etiqueta, marca f. rótulo, marbete m. vt 1 poner etiqueta. 2 clasificar, designar.

laboratory (lə'bɔrətri) n laboratorio m.

labour ('leibə) n 1 trabajo m. 2 labor f. 3 esfuerzo m. 4 parto m. **be in labour** estar de parto. ~vi trabajar. **Labour Party** n Partido Laborista m. **labour-saving** adj que ahorra trabajo. **laborious** adj penoso, pesado.

labyrinth ('læbarinθ) n laberinto m. **labyrinthine** adj laberíntico, intrincado.

lace (leis) n 1 cordón m. 2 encaje m. puntilla f. vt atar.

lack (læk) n falta, carencia f. vi faltar. vt carecer de.

lacquer ('lækə) n laca f. barniz m. vt laquear, barnizar.

lad (læd) n muchacho, mozalbete, chico m.

ladder ('lædə) n 1 escalera, escala f. 2 (of stockings) carrera f.

laden ('leidn) adj cargado.

ladle ('leidl) n cazo, cucharón m.

lady ('leidi) n señora f. **ladybird** n mariquita f.

lag[1] (læg) vi rezagarse, retrasarse.

lag[2] (læg) vt tech forrar, revestir.

lager ('lɑːgə) n cerveza f.

laid (leid) v see **lay**[1].

lain (lein) v see **lie**[2].

laity ('leiəti) n laicado m.

lake (leik) n lago m.

lamb (læm) n cordero m.

lame (leim) adj 1 cojo, lisiado. 2 inf débil.

lament (lə'ment) n lamento m. queja f. vt lamentar.

lamp (læmp) n 1 lámpara f. 2 mot faro m. 3 bombilla f.

lance (lɑːns) n lanza f. vt med abrir con lanceta.

land (lænd) n 1 tierra f. 2 país m. 3 terreno m. vt,vi desembarcar. **landing** n 1 desembarco m. 2 desembarque m. 3 aviat aterrizaje m. 4 (of stairs) descanso m. **landlady** n 1 patrona f. 2 dueña f. **landlord** n 1 patrón m. 2 dueño m.

lane (lein) n 1 camino m. vereda f. 2 mot carril m.

language ('læŋgwidʒ) n 1 lenguaje m. 2 lengua, habla, idioma f.

lanky ('læŋki) adj larguirucho.

lantern ('læntən) n 1 linterna f. 2 farol m.

lap[1] (læp) n anat regazo m.

lap[2] (læp) vt envolver, plegar. n 1 sport etapa f. 2 traslapo m.

lap[3] (læp) vt lamer. vi chapalear. n 1 lamedura f. 2 chapaleteo m.

lapel (lə'pel) n solapa f. lapón m.

lapse (læps) n 1 lapso, error, desliz m. 2 período m. vi 1 pasar, transcurrir. 2 caer en error.

larceny ('lɑːsəni) n latrocinio m.

lard (lɑːd) n manteca de cerdo f.

larder ('lɑːdə) n despensa f.

large (lɑːdʒ) adj 1 grande. 2 amplio. 3 extenso. **largely** adv en gran parte.

lark[1] (lɑːk) n alondra f.

lark[2] (lɑːk) n broma f. vi divertirse.

larva ('lɑːvə) n, pl **larvae** larva f.

larynx ('læriŋks) n laringe f. **laryngitis** n laringitis f.

laser ('leizə) n láser m.

lash (læʃ) n 1 látigo, azote m. 2 latigazo m. 3 anat pestaña f. vt 1 azotar, dar latigazos a, flagelar. 2 atar.

lass (læs) n chica, joven, moza, muchacha f.

lasso (læˈsuː) n lazo m.

last[1] (lɑːst) adj 1 último, final. 2 pasado. n último m. adv por último.

last[2] (lɑːst) vi durar, permanecer, conservarse.

latch (lætʃ) n picaporte, pestillo m. aldaba f. vt cerrar con picaporte.

late (leit) adj 1 tarde. 2 difunto. adv tarde. **latecomer** n recién llegado, retrasado m. **later** adv 1 más tarde. 2 después. adj 1 más tardío. 2 más reciente. 3 ulterior. **latest** adj,adv último, más reciente, más tarde.

latent ('leitnt) adj latente, oculto.

lateral ('lætərəl) adj lateral.

lathe (leið) n torno m.

lather ('lɑːðə) n espuma f. vt 1 espumar. 2 enjabonar.

Latin ('lætin) adj latino. n latín m. **Latin America** América Latina. **Latin American** adj,n latinoamericano.

latitude ('lætitjuːd) n latitud f.

latter ('lætə) adj más reciente. n éste, este último, el segundo.

laugh (lɑːf) n risa f. vi reir, reirse.

launch[1] (lɔːntʃ) n 1 botadura f. 2 lancha, chalupa f.

launch[2] (lɔːntʃ) vt 1 botar. 2 lanzar. 3 emprender.

launder ('lɔːndə) vt lavar. **laundry** n 1 lavandería f. lavadero m. 2 ropa por lavar f.

laurel ('lɔrəl) n laurel m.

lavatory ('lævətri) n lavabo m.

lavender ('lævində) n espliego m. lavanda f.

lavish ('læviʃ) adj pródigo, profuso, copioso. vt prodigar, dar con profusión.

law (lɔː) n 1 ley f. 2 derecho m. 3 jurisprudencia f. 4 justicia f. **lawsuit** n proceso, pleito, litigio m. **lawyer** n abogado m.

lawn (lɔːn) n césped m. **lawn-mower** n cortadora de césped f.

lax (læks) adj 1 decuidado, negligente. 2 (of morals) laxo.

laxative ('læksətiv) adj,n laxativo m.

lay[1] (lei) vt poner, dejar. **layer** n 1 capa f. 2 estrato. 3 acodo m. vt acodar.

lay[2] (lei) v see **lie**[2].

lay[3] (lei) adj lego, seglar. **layman** n lego, seglar, laico m.

laze (leiz) vi holgazanear. **lazy** adj perezoso, holgazán, gandul, ocioso.

lead[1] (liːd) n 1 mando m. guía f. 2 primer lugar m. 3 tech conductor m. vt llevar, conducir, guiar, inducir. **leader** n 1 jefe, líder m. 2 guía, conductor m. **leadership** n dirección, jefatura f.

lead[2] (led) n min plomo m.

leaf (liːf) n, pl **leaves** bot hoja f. **leaflet** n prospecto, folleto m.

league (liːg) n liga, alianza, confederación f.

leak (liːk) n 1 fuga f. escape m. 2 gotera f. 3 pérdida f. vt dejar perderse. vi 1 tener fugas, escaparse. 2 naut hacer agua.

lean[1] vi inclinarse, ladearse. **leaning** n inclinación, tendencia f.

lean[2] (liːn) adj 1 delgado, enjuto. 2 magro.

leap (liːp) n salto, brinco m. vi saltar, brincar. **leapfrog** n pídola f. vi saltar a la rana. **leap year** n año bisiesto m.

learn (ləːn) vt,vi 1 aprender. 2 enterarse de, oír decir. **learned** adj erudito, docto, versado.

lease (liːs) n arriendo, arrendamiento m. vt arrendar. **leasehold** n tenencia en arriendo f.

leash (liːʃ) n cuerda f.

least (liːst) adj mínimo, menor. n lo menos, lo más pequeño. **at least** al menos, por lo menos.

leather ('leðə) n cuero m.

leave[1] (liːv) vi 1 partir, salir, marcharse. vt dejar.

leave[2] (liːv) n permiso m.

Lebanon ('lebənən) n Líbano m. **Lebanese** n,adj libanés m.

lecherous ('letʃərəs) adj lascivo. **lechery** n lascivia, lujuria f.

lectern ('lektən) n atril, facistol m.

lecture ('lektʃə) n conferencia, lección f. **lecturer** n conferenciante m.

led (led) v see **lead**[1].

ledge (ledʒ) n 1 repisa f. 2 saliente m. 3 antepecho, alféizar m. 4 anaquel m.

ledger ('ledʒə) n comm libro mayor m.

leech (li:tʃ) n sanguijuela f.

leek (li:k) n puerro m.

leer (liə) n mirada impúdica f. vi mirar impúdicamente.

leeward (li:wəd) adj,adv naut sotavento m.

left[1] (left) n izquierda f. adj izquierdo. **left-handed** adj zurdo. **left-wing** adj pol izquierdista.

left[2] (left) v see **leave**[1]. **left-luggage office** n consigna f.

leg (leg) n 1 pierna f. 2 pata f. 3 pernera f.

legacy (legəsi) n legado m. herencia f.

legal (li:gəl) adj 1 legal. 2 de derecho. 3 legítimo, lícito. **legalize** vt 1 legalizar. 2 autorizar.

legend (ledʒənd) n leyenda f.

legible (ledʒibl) adj legible.

legion (li:dʒən) n legión f.

legislate (ledʒisleit) vi legislar. **legislation** n legislación f.

legitimate (li'dʒitimət) adj legítimo. vt also **legitimize** legitimar.

leisure (leʒə) n tiempo libre, ocio m.

lemon (lemən) n limón m. **lemonade** n limonada f.

lend* (lend) vt prestar, proporcionar. **lend a hand** echar una mano. **lend oneself to** prestarse a, entregarse a.

length (leŋθ) n 1 longitud, largura f. largo m. 2 espacio m. **at length** por extenso. **lengthen** vt prolongar, extender.

lenient (li:niənt) adj indulgente, clemente.

lens (lenz) n 1 lente m. 2 anat cristalino m. 3 phot objetivo m.

lent (lent) v see **lend**.

Lent (lent) n Cuaresma f.

lentil (lentjl) n lenteja f.

Leo (li:ou) n Leo m.

leopard (lepəd) n leopardo m.

leper (lepə) n leproso m. **leprosy** n lepra f.

lesbian (lezbiən) n 1 lesbiana f. 2 inf tortillera f. adj lesbiano, lesbico.

less (les) adj menor, menos, inferior. adv menos. prep menos. **lessen** vt disminuir, achicar, mermar, quitar importancia.

lesson (lesən) n lección f.

lest (lest) conj para que no.

let* (let) vt 1 dejar, permitir. 2 arrendar, alquilar. **let on** inf revelar.

lethal (li:θəl) adj letal, mortífero.

lethargy (leθədʒi) n letargo m.

letter (letə) n 1 letra f. 2 carta f. vt inscribir, rotular. **letterbox** n buzón m.

lettuce (letis) n lechuga f.

leukaemia (lu:ki:miə) n med leucemia f.

level (levəl) adj 1 llano, plano. 2 uniforme. 3 a nivel. adv a nivel. n nivel m. vt 1 nivelar, allanar, aplanar. 2 derribar. **level crossing** n paso a nivel m. **level-headed** adj sensato, juicioso.

lever (li:və) n palanca, barra f.

levy (levi) n 1 exacción f. 2 impuesto m. 3 mil leva f. vt 1 recaudar, imponer. 2 mil reclutar.

lewd (lu:d) adj lúbrico, obsceno.

liable (laiəbəl) adj 1 propenso, expuesto. 2 responsable, obligado. **liability** n 1 riesgo m. exposición f. 2 responsabilidad f.

liaison (li'eizɔn) n enlace m.

liar (laiə) n mentiroso, embustero m.

libel (laibəl) n libelo m. difamación f.

liberal (libərəl) adj liberal. n pol liberal m,f.

liberate (libəreit) vt librar, liberar, libertar. **liberator** n libertador m.

liberty (libəti) n libertad f. **take liberties** tomarse libertades.

Libra (li:brə) n Libra f.

library (laibrəri) n biblioteca f. **librarian** n bibliotecario m.

libretto (li'bretou) n libreto m.

licence (laisəns) n 1 licencia f. 2 permiso m. 3 libertinaje m. **license** vt autorizar. **licensee** n titular de una licencia m.

lichen (laikən) n liquen m.

lick (lik) n lamedura, lengüetada f. vt lamer.

lid (lid) n tapa f.

lie[1] (lai) n mentira, falsedad f. embuste m. vi mentir.

lie* [2] (lai) vi acostarse, tenderse, echarse, tumbarse.

lieutenant (lef'tenənt) n teniente, lugarteniente m.

life (laif) n, pl **lives** vida f. **lifebelt** n cinturón salvavidas m. **lifeboat** n bote salvavidas m. **lifebuoy** n boya salvavidas f. **lifeguard** n vigilante m.

lift (lift) n 1 ascensor m. montacargas m invar. 2 elevación f. alzamiento m. 3 fuerza elevadora f. 4 inf viaje gratuito m. 5 estímulo m. vt alzar, levantar, izar.

light[1] (lait) n 1 luz, lumbre f. 2 lámpara f. adj claro, con mucha luz. vt iluminar, alumbrar. 2 encender. **lighthouse** n faro m. **lighting** n alumbrado m. iluminación f.

light[2] (lait) adj 1 ligero, ágil. 2 leve. 3 liviano. 4 alegre. **light-headed** adj aturdido, delirante, mareado. **light-hearted** adj alegre, despreocupado. **lightweight** adj ligero, de poco peso.

light[3] (lait) vi descender, posarse, caer.

lighten[1] ('laitņ) vt 1 iluminar, alumbrar. 2 aclarar.

lighten[2] ('laitņ) vt 1 aligerar, aliviar. 2 descargar.

lightning ('laitniņ) n relámpago m.

like[1] (laik) adj igual, similar, semejante. **be like** parecerse a. ~prep como, igual que. conj como. **like-minded** adj de la misma mentalidad. **likeness** n parecido m. semejanza f. **likewise** adv 1 asimismo, también. 2 lo mismo, parecidamente.

like[2] (laik) vt 1 querer. 2 gustar.

likely ('laikli) adj 1 probable. 2 apropiado, adecuado. 3 creíble, verosímil.

lilac ('lailək) n lila f.

lily ('lili) n lirio m. azucena f. **lily-of-the-valley** n lirio de los valles, muguete m.

limb (lim) n 1 anat miembro m. 2 bot rama f.

limbo ('limbou) n limbo m.

lime[1] (laim) n min cal f. **limelight** n luz de calcio m. **be in the limelight** estar a la vista del público. **limestone** n piedra caliza f.

lime[2] (laim) n bot 1 lima f. 2 limero m.

limerick ('limərik) n quintilla jocosa f.

limit ('limit) n límite m. vt limitar. **limitation** n limitación f.

limp[1] (limp) n cojera f. vi cojear.

limp[2] (limp) adj fláccido, blando, lacio.

limpet ('limpit) n lapa f.

linden ('lindən) n tilo m.

line[1] (lain) n 1 línea f. 2 cuerda, cinta f. cable m. 3 raya f. 4 linaje m. vt 1 linear. 2 rayar. 3 alinear. **lineage** n linaje, abolengo m. **linear** adj lineal.

line[2] (lain) vt forrar, revestir, guarnecer.

linen ('linin) n 1 lino, lienzo m. 2 ropa blanca f. 3 mantelería f.

liner ('lainə) n naut vapor, trasatlántico m.

linger ('liņgə) vi 1 entretenerse, demorar, vacilar. 2 prolongarse, durar.

lingerie ('lɔnʒəri:) n ropa interior de mujer f.

linguist ('liņgwist) n lingüista m,f. **linguistic** adj lingüístico. **linguistics** n lingüística f.

lining ('lainiņ) n 1 forro m. 2 revestimiento m.

link (liņk) n 1 enlace, vínculo m. 2 eslabón m. vt unir, enlazar.

linoleum (li'nouliəm) n linóleo m.

linseed ('linsi:d) n linaza f.

lion ('laiən) n león m.

lip (lip) n labio m. **lip-read** vi leer el movemiento de los labios. **lipstick** n barra de labios f.

liqueur (li'kjuə) n licor m.

liquid ('likwid) adj,n líquido m. **liquidate** vt 1 liquidar. 2 matar. **liquidize** vt licuar, hacer líquido.

liquor ('likə) n 1 licor m. 2 bebida f.

liquorice ('likəris) n regaliz m.

lira ('liərə) n lira f.

lisp (lisp) n ceceo m. vt,vi cecear.

list[1] (list) n lista f. catálogo m. vt 1 registrar, catalogar. 2 alistar.

list[2] (list) naut escora f. vi escorar.

listen ('lisən) vt,vi escuchar, oír, prestar atención.

listless ('listləs) adj apático, sin interés.

lit (lit) v see **light**[1].

litany ('litəni) n letanía f.

literal ('litərəl) adj literal.

literary ('litərəri) adj literario.

literate ('litərət) adj que sabe leer y escribir.

literature ('litərətʃə) n literatura f.

litre ('li:tə) n litro m.

litter ('litə) n 1 basura f. escombros m pl. 2 cama para animales f. 3 litera f. 4 zool camada, cría f. vt esparcir papeles por. **litter-bin** n papelera f.

little ('litļ) adj 1 pequeño, chico, menor. 2 poco, escaso, corto. adv poco. n poco m. **little finger** n dedo meñique m. **little toe** n dedo meñique del pie m.

liturgy ('litədʒi) n liturgia f.

live[1] (liv) vi vivir, existir.

live[2] (laiv) adj 1 vivo. 2 ardiente, encendido. 3 cargado con corriente eléctrica.

livelihood ('laivlihud) n mantenimiento m.

lively ('laivli) adj 1 vivo. 2 vigoroso, fogoso. 3 alegre, animado.

liver ('livə) n anat hígado m.

livestock ('laivstɔk) n ganado m.

livid ('livid) adj lívido, pálido.

living ('liviņ) adj vivo, viviente. n sustento m. vida f. **earn** or **make a living** ganarse la vida. **living room** n sala de estar f.

lizard ('lizəd) n lagarto m.

llama ('la:mə) n llama f.

load (loud) n 1 carga f. 2 peso, fardo m. 3 tech resistencia f. vt 1 cargar. 2 oprimir, agobiar.

loaf[1] (louf) n, pl **loaves** pan m. hogaza f.

loaf[2] (louf) vi pasearse, holgazanear.

loan (loun) n préstamo, empréstito m.

loathe (louð) vt detestar, abominar. **loathsome** adj aborrecible, detestable, odioso.

lob (lɔb) n sport voleo alto m. vt,vi volear por alto.

lobby ('lɔbi) n 1 antecámara f. 2 pasillo m. 3 vestíbulo m. 4 grupo de presión m. vt ejercer influencia sobre.

lobe (loub) n lóbulo m.

lobster ('lɔbstə) n langosta f.

local ('loukəl) adj 1 local. 2 regional. **locality** n localidad f. **localize** vt localizar. **locate** vt situar, colocar. **location** n 1 posición f. 2 localización f.

lock[1] (lɔk) n 1 cerradura, cerraja f. 2 esclusa f. 3 tech chaveta f. vt cerrar con llave. **locker** n armario, cajón que se cierra con llave m.

lock[2] (lɔk) n rizo, mechón m.

locket ('lɔkit) n medallón, relicario m.

locomotive (loukə'moutiv) n locomotora f. adj locomotor.

locust ('loukəst) n langosta f.

lodge (lɔdʒ) n 1 portería f. 2 logia masónica f. vt alojar, hospedar. vi 1 alojarse, hospedarse. 2 quedarse. **lodgings** n pl alojamiento, hospedaje m.

loft (lɔft) n desván m.

log (lɔg) n 1 leño, tronco m. 2 naut diario de navegación m. vt registrar.

logarithm ('lɔgəriðəm) n logaritmo m.

logic ('lɔdʒik) n lógica f. **logical** adj lógico.

loin (lɔin) n 1 ijada f. 2 lomo m.

loiter ('lɔitə) vi ir despacio, vagar.

lollipop ('lɔlipɔp) n piruli m.

London ('lʌndən) n Londres m. **Londoner** adj,n londinense m,f.

lonely ('lounli) adj 1 solo, solitario. 2 triste, desolado.

long[1] (lɔŋ) vi anhelar. **longing** n ansia f. anhelo m.

long[2] (lɔŋ) adj 1 largo. 2 prolongado. adv largo or mucho tiempo. **long-distance** adj de larga distancia. **long-distance call** n conferencia interurbana f. **long jump** n salto de longitud m. **long-playing** adj de larga duración. **long-range** adj de largo alcance. **long-sighted** adj 1 présbita. 2 sagaz, precavido. **longstanding** adj de mucho tiempo. **long wave** n onda larga f. **longwinded** adj latoso, pesado, fastidioso.

longevity (lɔn'dʒeviti) n longevidad f.

longitude ('lɔndʒitju:d) n longitud f.

look (luk) n 1 mirada f. vistazo m. 2 apariencia f. aspecto m. vi 1 mirar. 2 parecer. **look after** encargarse de.

loom[1] (lu:m) n telar m.

loom[2] (lu:m) vi asomar, aparecer confusamente.

loop (lu:p) n vuelta, curva f. lazo m. vt formar curva. 2 asegurar con presilla. **loophole** n inf escapatoria, salida f.

loose (lu:s) adj 1 suelto. 2 flojo. 3 ancho, holgado. 4 vago, indeterminado. 5 libre, relajado. **loosen** vt soltar, desatar, aflojar.

loot (lu:t) n botín m. presa f. vt saquear.

lop (lɔp) vt 1 podar. 2 desmochar.

lopsided (lɔp'saidid) adj inclinado, mal equilibrado, asimétrico.

lord (lɔ:d) n señor m.

lorry ('lɔri) n camión m.

lose* (lu:z) vt perder.

loss (lɔs) n 1 pérdida f. 2 perdición f.

lost (lɔst) v see **lose**.

lot (lɔt) n 1 lote m. 2 parte, cuota f. 3 solar m. porción f.

lotion ('louʃən) n loción f.

lottery ('lɔtəri) n lotería f.

lotus ('loutəs) n loto m.

loud (laud) adj fuerte, ruidoso. **loud-mouthed** adj gritón. **loudspeaker** n altavoz m.

lounge (laundʒ) n salón m. vi pasar el tiempo holgazaneando.

louse (laus) n, pl **lice** piojo m. **lousy** adj 1 piojoso. 2 inf miserable, asqueroso.

love (lʌv) n amor, cariño m. devoción f. **be in love** estar enamorado. **fall in love** enamorarse. **make love** 1 hacer amor. 2 cortejar. ~vt amar, querer. **lovesick** adj enfermo de amor. **lovely** adj 1 bello, hermoso. 2 encantador.

low[1] (lou) adj 1 bajo. 2 grave. 3 ruin, vil. **lowbrow** n persona poco intelectual f. **low frequency** adj de baja frecuencia. **lowland** n tierra baja f. **low-necked** adj escotado. **low-pitched** adj sonido grave. **low tide** n marea baja f.

low[2] (lou) n mugido m. vi mugir.

lower ('louə) adj,adv más bajo. vt 1 bajar, inclinar hacia abajo. 2 naut arriar. 3 reducir, abatir, disminuir, rebajar.

loyal ('lɔiəl) adj leal, fiel.

lozenge ('lɔzindʒ) n 1 rombo m. 2 pastilla f.

lubricate ('lu:brikeit) vt lubricar.

lucid ('lu:sid) adj lúcido.

luck (lʌk) n suerte, fortuna f. **lucky** adj de suerte, afortunado.

lucrative ('lu:krətiv) adj lucrativo.

ludicrous ('lu:dikrəs) adj absurdo, ridículo.

lug (lʌg) n 1 asa f. 2 arrastre, tirón m. vt tirar de, arrastrar.

luggage ('lʌgidʒ) n equipaje m.
lukewarm (lu:k'wɔ:m) adj templado, tibio.
lull (lʌl) n momento de calma m. vt 1 arrullar. 2 sosegar, calmar. **lullaby** n canción de cuna f.
lumbago (lʌm'beigou) n lumbago m.
lumber[1] ('lʌmbə) n madera f. tablas f pl. tablones m pl. **lumberjack** n leñador m.
lumber[2] ('lʌmbə) vi moverse pesadamente.
luminous ('lu:minəs) adj luminoso.
lump (lʌmp) n 1 pedazo, trozo, terrón m. 2 nudo m. 3 bulto, chinchón m. vt amontonar, apelotonar.
lunacy ('lu:nəsi) n locura, demencia f.
lunar ('lu:nə) adj lunar.
lunatic ('lu:nətik) adj,n lunático m.
lunch (lʌntʃ) n almuerzo m.vi almorzar.
lung (lʌŋ) n pulmón m.
lunge (lʌndʒ) n 1 estocada f. 2 salto hacia adelante m. embestida f. vi abalanzarse, arremeter.
lurch[1] (lə:tʃ) n **leave in the lurch** dejar plantado.
lurch[2] (lə:tʃ) n sacudida f. tumbo m. vi 1 dar sacudidas. 2 tambalearse.
lure (luə) n 1 reclamo m. 2 cebo m. 3 engaño m. tentación f. vt atraer, inducir, tentar.
lurid ('luərid) adj 1 sensacional. 2 espeluznante.
lurk (lə:k) vi ocultarse, esconderse, estar en acecho.
luscious ('lʌʃəs) adj 1 dulce, sabroso. 2 delicioso, meloso.
lush (lʌʃ) adj exuberante, rico.
lust (lʌst) n 1 sensualidad, lujuria f. 2 deseo vehemente m. vt anhelar, desear con lujuria.
lustre ('lʌstə) n lustre, brillo m.
lute (lu:t) n mus laúd m.
Luxembourg ('lʌksəmbə:g) n Luxemburgo m.
luxury ('lʌkʃəri) n lujo m. **luxurious** adj lujoso.
lynch (lintʃ) vt linchar. **lynching** n linchamiento m.
lynx (liŋks) n lince m.
lyre ('laiə) n lira f.
lyrical ('lirikəl) adj 1 lírico. 2 elocuente, entusiasmado.
lyrics ('liriks) n pl letras de una canción f pl. **lyricism** n lirismo m.

M

mac (mæk) n impermeable m.
macabre (mə'kɑ:b) adj macabro.
macaroni (mækə'rouni) n macarrones m pl.

mace[1] (meis) n maza f.
mace[2] (meis) n bot macis f.
machine (mə'ʃi:n) n 1 máquina f. 2 aparato m. 3 pol organización f. vt 1 trabajar a máquina. 2 coser a máquina. **machine-made** adj hecho a máquina. **machine-gun** n ametralladora f. vt ametrallar. **machinery** n 1 maquinaria f. 2 mecanismo m. 3 organización f. sistema m. **machinist** n operario de máquina, mecánico m.
mackerel ('mækrəl) n caballa f.
mackintosh ('mækintɔʃ) n impermeable m.
mad (mæd) adj 1 loco, demente. 2 rabioso. 3 furioso. **maddening** adj desesperante.
madam ('mædəm) n señora f.
made (meid) v see **make**.
Madonna (mə'dɔnə) n Virgen, Madona f.
Madrid (mə'drid) n Madrid.
magazine (mægə'zi:n) n 1 revista f. 2 depósito de cartuchos m. recámara f. 3 almacén m.
maggot ('mægət) n cresa f. gusano m.
magic ('mædʒik) adj mágico. n magia f. **magical** adj mágico. **magician** n 1 mago, mágico, brujo m. 2 prestidigitador m.
magistrate ('mædʒistreit) n 1 magistrado m. 2 juez municipal m.
magnanimous (mæg'næniməs) adj magnánimo.
magnate ('mægneit) n magnate, potentado m.
magnet ('mægnit) n imán m. **magnetic** adj magnético. **magnetism** n magnetismo m. **magnetize** vt magnetizar, imantar.
magnificent (mæg'nifisənt) adj magnífico. **magnificence** n magnificencia f.
magnify ('mægnifai) vt 1 aumentar, magnificar. 2 agrandar, exagerar. **magnifying glass** n lupa, lente de aumento f.
magnitude ('mægnitju:d) n magnitud f.
magnolia (mæg'nouliə) n magnolia f.
magpie ('mægpai) n urraca f.
mahogany (mə'hɔgəni) n caoba f.
maid (meid) n 1 criada, doncella f. 2 camarera f. 3 muchacha f. **old maid** n solterona f. **maiden** n 1 doncella f. 2 muchacha f. **maiden name** n apellido de soltera m.
mail (meil) n 1· malla f. 2 correo m. cartas f pl. correspondencia f. vt echar al correo. **mailbag** n saca de correos f. **mail order** n pedido postal m.
maim (meim) vt mutilar.
main (mein) adj 1 principal. 2 mayor. n cañería principal f. **in the main** en general. **mainland** n tierra firme f. continente m. **mainsail**

n vela mayor *f*. **mainspring** *n* muelle real *m*. *n* corriente principal *f*.

maintain (mein'tein) *vt* 1 mantener. 2 guardar. **maintenance** *n* 1 mantenimiento *m*. 2 conservación *f*.

maize (meiz) *n* maíz *m*.

majesty ('mædʒisti) *n* majestad *f*. **majestic** *adj* majestuoso.

major ('meidʒə) *adj* mayor, principal. *n mil* comandante *m*. **major general** general de división *m*. **majority** *adj* mayoritario. *n* 1 mayoría *f*. 2 mayor edad *f*.

Majorca (mə'dʒɔːkə) *n* Mallorca *f*.

make (meik) *vt* 1 hacer. 2 crear, formar, construir. 3 creer, deducir, calcular. 4 ganar, obtener. 5 forzar, obligar. **make away** or **off** largarse, huir, escaparse. **make off with** llevarse, escaparse con. **make out** salir bien. ~*n* 1 marca *f*. 2 tipo, modelo *m*. **making** *n* fabricación *f*. **make-believe** *adj* fingido, simulado. *vi* fingir. **makeshift** *adj* 1 improvisado. 2 provisional. *n* improvisación *f*. **make-up** *n* 1 composición *f*. 2 estructura *f*. 3 maquillaje *m*.

maladjusted (mælə'dʒʌstid) *adj* inadaptado.

malaria (mə'lɛəriə) *n* malaria *f*.

male (meil) *adj* 1 macho. 2 masculino. 3 viril. *n* 1 macho *m*. 2 varón *m*.

malfunction (mæl'fʌŋkʃən) *n* funcionamiento defectuoso *m*.

malice ('mælis) *n* malicia, mala voluntad *f*.

malignant (mə'lignənt) *adj* maligno. **malign** *adj* maligno. *vt* difamar.

mallet ('mælət) *n* mazo *m*.

malnutrition (mælnju'triʃən) *n* desnutrición *f*.

malt (mɔːlt) *n* malta *f*.

Malta ('mɔːltə) *n* Malta *f*. **Maltese** *adj,n* maltés *m*.

maltreat (mæl'triːt) *vt* tratar mal. **maltreatment** *n* maltrato *m*.

mammal ('mæməl) *n* mamífero *m*.

mammoth ('mæməθ) *adj* gigantesco. *n* mamut *m*.

man (mæn) *n, pl* **men** 1 hombre *m*. 2 el género humano *m*. *vt* tripular. **manly** *adj* varonil. **man-handle** *vt* maltratar. **manhole** *n* abertura de inspección *f*. **man-made** *adj* artificial. **manpower** *n* mano de obra *f*. **manslaughter** *n* homicidio sin premeditación *m*.

Man, Isle of *n* Isla de Man *f*.

manage ('mænidʒ) *vt* 1 manejar. 2 dirigir, administrar, llevar. **management** *n* 1 manejo *m*. dirección, gerencia *f*. 2 junta de directores

f. **manager** *n* 1 *comm* director, gerente *m*. administrador *m*. 3 empresario *m*.

mandarin ('mændərin) *n* mandarín *m*.

mandate ('mændeit) *n* 1 mandato *m*. 2 territorio bajo mandato *m*. *vt* asignar por mandato.

mane (mein) *n* 1 melena *f*. 2 crin *f*.

mange (meindʒ) *n* roña sarna *f*.

mangle[1] ('mæŋgəl) *n* rodillo, exprimidor *m*.

mangle[2] ('mæŋgəl) *vt* magullar, mutilar, estropear.

mango ('mæŋgou) *n, pl* **-oes** or **-os** mango *m*.

mania ('meiniə) *n* manía *f*. **maniac** *adj,n* maníaco *m*. **manic** *adj* maníaco.

manicure ('mænikjuə) *n* manicura *f*. *vt* hacer la manicura a.

manifest ('mænifest) *adj* manifiesto, evidente. *vt* mostrar, manifestar. **manifestation** *n* manifestación *f*.

manifesto (mæni'festou) *n* manifiesto *m*.

manifold ('mænifould) *adj* múltiple, numeroso.

manipulate (mə'nipjuleit) *vt* manipular. **manipulation** *n* manipulación *f*.

mankind ('mænkaind) *n* género humano *m*.

manner ('mænə) *n* 1 manera *f*. modo *m*. 2 conducta *f*. 3 clase, especie *f*. **manners** *n pl* 1 costumbres *f pl*. 2 modales *m pl*. 3 educación *f*. **mannerism** *n* 1 amaneramiento *m*. 2 manerismo *m*. 3 hábito *m*. peculiaridad *f*.

manoeuvre (mə'nuːvə) *n* maniobra *f*. *vt* hacer maniobrar. *vi* maniobrar.

manor ('mænə) *n* 1 finca *f*. 2 señorío *m*. **manor house** *n* casa señorial *f*.

mansion ('mænʃən) *n* 1 casa grande *f*. 2 casa solariega *f*.

mantelpiece ('mæntəlpiːs) *n* repisa de chimenea *f*.

mantilla (mæn'tilə) *n* mantilla *f*.

mantle ('mæntl) *n* manto *m*. capa *f*.

manual ('mænjuəl) *adj,n* manual *m*.

manufacture (mænju'fæktʃə) *n* 1 fabricación *f*. 2 manufactura *f*. producto *m*. *vt* fabricar. **manufacturer** *n* fabricante *m*.

manure (mə'njuə) *n* estiércol, abono *m*. *vt* estercolar, abonar.

manuscript ('mænjuskript) *n* manuscrito *m*.

many ('meni) *adj* muchos *pl*. **how many?** ¿cuántos? **so** or **as many** tanto. **many-sided** *adj* 1 multilátero. 2 polifacético.

map (mæp) *n* 1 mapa *m*. 2 plano *m*. *vt* trazar el mapa de. **map out** proyectar.

maple ('meipəl) *n* arce *m*.

mar (mɑː) *vt* 1 desfigurar. 2 aguar.

marathon ('mærəθən) *n* carrera de maratón *f*

marble ('ma:bəl) *adj* marmóreo, de mármol. *n* 1 mármol *m*. 2 canica *f*.

march (ma:tʃ) *n* marcha *f*. *vt* hacer marchar, llevar. *vi* 1 marchar. 2 ir a pie.

March (ma:tʃ) *n* marzo *m*.

marchioness ('ma:ʃənis) *n* marquesa *f*.

mare (mɛə) *n* yegua *f*.

margarine (ma:dʒə'ri:n) *n* margarina *f*.

margin ('ma:dʒin) *n* 1 margen *m*. 2 *comm* reserva *f*. 3 borde *m*. **marginal** *adj* marginal.

marguerite (ma:gə'ri:t) *n* margarita *f*.

marigold ('mærigould) *n* caléndula *f*.

marinade (mæri'neid) *n* escabeche *m*. **marinate** *vt* escabechar.

marine (mə'ri:n) *adj* marino. *n* soldado de marina *m*. **maritime** *adj* marítimo.

marital ('mærit|) *adj* marital.

marjoram ('ma:dʒərəm) *n* mejorana *f*. orégano *m*.

mark[1] (ma:k) *n* 1 señal, marca *f*. 2 mancha. 3 huella. 4 etiqueta *f*. 5 blanco *m*. 6 calificación, nota *f*. *vt* 1 señalar, marcar. 2 manchar. **marked** *adj* 1 fuerte. 2 notable. **marksman** *n* tirador *m*. **marksmanship** *n* buena puntería *f*.

mark[2] (ma:k) *n* marco *m*.

market ('ma:kit) *n* mercado *m*. **stock market** *n* bolsa *f*. *vt* llevar al mercado. **market garden** *n* huerto *m*. **market research** *n* análisis de mercados *f*.

marmalade ('ma:məleid) *n* mermelada *f*.

maroon[1] (mə'ru:n) *adj,n* marrón *m*.

maroon[2] (mə'ru:n) *vt* abandonar.

marquee (ma:'ki:) *n* entoldado *m*.

marquess ('ma:kwis) *n* marqués *m*.

marriage ('mæridʒ) *n* 1 matrimonio *m*. 2 casamiento *m*. 3 boda *f*. **marriage certificate** *n* partida de casamiento *f*.

marrow ('mærou) *n* 1 *anat* médula *f*. tuétano *m*. 2 *inf* meollo *m*. 3 *bot* calabacín *m*. **marrowbone** *n* hueso medular *m*.

marry ('mæri) *vt* casar.

Mars (ma:z) *n* Marte *m*.

marsh (ma:ʃ) *n* 1 pantano *m*. ciénaga *f*. 2 marisma *f*. **marshy** *adj* pantanoso.

marshal ('ma:ʃəl) *n* 1 mariscal *m*. *vt* 1 ordenar. 2 formar.

martial ('ma:ʃəl) *adj* marcial.

martin ('ma:tin) *n* *zool* avión, vencejo *m*.

martyr ('ma:tə) *n* mártir *m,f*. *vt* martirizar. **martyrdom** *n* martirio *m*.

marvel ('ma:vəl) *n* maravilla *f*. *vi* maravillarse.

marvellous ('ma:vələs) *adj* maravilloso.

Marxism ('ma:ksizəm) *n* marxismo *m*. **Marxist** *adj,n* marxista *m,f*.

mascara (mæ'ska:rə) *n* rimel *m*.

mascot ('mæskɔt) *n* mascota *f*.

masculine ('mæskjulin) *adj,n* masculino *m*. **masculinity** *n* masculinidad *f*.

mash (mæʃ) *n* 1 mezcla *f*. 2 amasijo *m*. **mashed potatoes** puré de patatas. ~*vt* 1 mezclar. 2 amasar. 3 hacer un puré de.

mask (ma:sk) *n* 1 máscara *f*. 2 disfraz *m*. 3 careta *f*. antifaz *m*. *vt* enmascarar.

mason ('meisən) *n* 1 albañil, cantero *m*. 2 masón, francmasón *m*. **masonry** *n* 1 albañilería *f*. 2 masonería *f*.

masquerade (mæskə'reid) *n* baile de máscaras *m*. mascarada *f*.

mass[1] (mæs) *n* 1 masa *f*. 2 bulto *m*. 3 macizo *m*. **the masses** las masas *f pl*. **mass media** *n pl* medios de comunicación con las masas *m pl*. **mass-produce** *vt* producir en serie. **mass-production** producción en serie *f*.

mass[2] (mæs) *n rel* misa *f*. **high mass** misa mayor. **low mass** misa rezada.

massacre ('mæsəkə) *n* carnicería, matanza *f*. *vt* hacer una carnicería de, masacrar.

massage ('mæsa:ʒ) *n* masaje *m*. *vt* dar masaje a. **masseur** *n* masajista *m*.

massive ('mæsiv) *adj* 1 macizo, sólido, abultado. 2 impresionante.

mast (ma:st) *n* palo, mástil *m*. **masthead** *n* tope *m*.

master ('ma:stə) *n* 1 amo *m*. 2 señor *m*. 3 dueño *m*. 4 maestro, profesor *m*. **master of ceremonies** maestro de ceremonias *m*. ~*vt* 1 dominar. 2 vencer, derrotar. **masterful** *adj* imperioso, dominante. **masterpiece** *n* obra maestra *f*.

masturbate ('mæstəbeit) *vi* masturbarse. **masturbation** *n* masturbación *f*.

mat (mæt) *n* 1 estera, esterilla *f*. 2 felpudo *m*. 3 salvamanteles *m*.

match[1] (mætʃ) *n* 1 cerilla *f*. fósforo *m*. 2 mecha *f*. **matchbox** *n* caja de cerillas *f*. **matchstick** *n* fósforo *m*.

match[2] (mætʃ) *n* 1 igual *m,f*. 2 compañero *m*. 3 casamiento *m*. 4 *sport* partido *m*. *vt* 1 emparejar. 2 igualar. 3 hacer juego con. *vi* armonizar.

mate (meit) *n* 1 compañero, camarada *m*. 2 cónyuge *m,f*. 3 ayudante *m,f*. 4 *naut* primer oficial *m*. *vt zool* parear.

material (mə'tiəriəl) *adj* material, importante. *n* 1 material *m*. materia *f*. 2 tejido *m*. tela *f*.

materialist adj,n materialista. **materialistic** adj materialista. **materialism** n materialismo m.

maternal (mə'tə:nl̩) adj 1 materno. 2 maternal. **maternity** n maternidad f.

mathematics (mæθə'mætiks) n matemáticas f pl. **mathematician** n matemático m.

matinee ('mætinei) n función de tarde, matiné f.

matins ('mætinz) n pl maitines m pl.

matrimony ('mætriməni) n matrimonio m.

matrix ('meitriks) n, pl **matrices** matriz f.

matron ('meitrən) n matrona f.

matter ('mætə) n 1 materia f. material m. 2 tema m. 3 asunto m. cuestión f. 4 cosa f. **a matter of course** por rutina. **as a matter of fact** en realidad, el caso es que. **no matter** no importa. **what's the matter?** ¿qué hay? ¿qué pasa? ~vi importar. **it doesn't matter** no importa, da lo mismo, es igual. **matter-of-fact** adj prosaico, práctico.

mattress ('mætrəs) n colchón m.

mature (mə'tjuə) adj 1 maduro. 2 comm vencido. vt,vi madurar. **maturity** n 1 madurez f. 2 comm vencimiento m.

maudlin ('mɔ:dlin) adj 1 sensiblero. 2 llorón.

maul (mɔ:l) vt 1 magullar. 2 maltratar.

mausoleum (mɔ:sə'liəm) n mausoleo m.

mauve (mouv) adj,n color malva m.

maxim ('mæksim) n máxima f.

maximum ('mæksiməm) adj máximo. n máximo, máximum m. **maximize** vt llevar al máximum, extremar.

may* (mei) v mod aux 1 poder. 2 ser posible. 3 tener permiso para. **maybe** adv quizá, tal vez.

May (mei) n mayo m. **May Day** n primero de mayo. **maypole** n mayo m.

mayonnaise (meiə'neiz) n mayonesa f.

mayor ('mɛə) n alcalde m.

maze (meiz) n 1 laberinto m. 2 enredo m.

me (mi:) pron 1st pers s 1 me. 2 mí. **with me** conmigo.

meadow ('medou) n prado m. pradera f.

meagre ('mi:gə) adj escaso, exiguo.

meal¹ (mi:l) n comida f.

meal² (mi:l) n harina f. **mealy** adj harinoso.

mean*¹ (mi:n) vt 1 querer decir. 2 significar. **mean well** tener buenas intenciones. **meaning** n 1 intención f. propósito m. 2 sentido, significado m.

mean² (mi:n) adj mezquino, tacaño.

meander (mi'ændə) n meandro m. vi 1 serpentear. 2 errar, vagar.

means (mi:nz) n, pl 1 medios, recursos m pl. 2 manera f. 3 dinero m. **by all means** ¡claro que sí! **by means of** por medio de.

meanwhile ('mi:nwail) adv entretanto, mientras tanto.

measles ('mi:zəlz) n sarampión m.

measure ('meʒə) n 1 medida f. 2 mus compás m. **made to measure** hecho a medida. ~vt 1 medir. 2 tallar. 3 tomar las medidas a. **measurement** n medida, medición f.

meat (mi:t) n carne f. **cold meat** fiambre m.

mechanic (mi'kænik) n mecánico m. **mechanical** adj 1 mecánico. 2 maquinal. **mechanical engineering** n ingeniería mecánica f. **mechanism** n mecanismo m. **mechanize** vt mecanizar.

medal ('medl̩) n medalla f. **medallion** n medallón m.

meddle ('medl̩) vi entrometerse. **meddler** n entrometido m. **meddlesome** adj entrometido.

media ('mi:diə) n pl medios m pl.

medial ('mi:diəl) adj medial.

median ('mi:diən) adj mediano. n número medio, punto medio m.

mediate ('mi:dieit) vi mediar. **mediation** n mediación f.

medical ('medikəl) adj 1 médico. 2 de medicina. n reconocimiento médico m. **medicine** n medicación f. n medicina f. medicamento m. **medicine chest** n botiquín m. **medicinal** adj medicinal.

medieval (medi'i:vəl) adj medieval.

mediocre (mi:di'oukə) adj mediocre, mediano. **mediocrity** n mediocridad f.

meditate ('mediteit) vi meditar, reflexionar. **meditation** n meditación, reflexión f.

Mediterranean (meditə'reiniən) adj mediterráneo. **Mediterranean Sea** n Mar Mediterráneo m. n Mediterráneo m.

medium ('mi:diəm) adj mediano, regular, intermedio. n 1 medio m. 2 médium m,f.

meek (mi:k) adj dócil, humilde, manso.

meet* (mi:t) vt 1 encontrar. 2 encontrarse con. 3 tropezar con. 4 conocer. 5 pagar, satisfacer. vi 1 encontrarse, verse. 2 conocerse. **meeting** n 1 reunión f. 2 encuentro m. 3 mitin m. 4 sport concurso m.

megaphone ('megəfoun) n megáfono m.

melancholy ('melənkəli) adj melancólico f.

mellow ('melou) adj 1 maduro, sazonado. 2

231

blando, suave, meloso. *vt* madurar. *vi* madurarse, suavizarse.

melodrama ('melədrɑ:mə) *n* melodrama *m*. **melodramatic** *adj* melodramático.

melody ('melədi) *n* melodía *f*.

melon ('melən) *n* melón *m*.

melt (melt) *vt* 1 fundir. 2 derretir. 3 disolver. 4 ablandar. **melting point** *n* punto de fusión *m*.

member ('membə) *n* 1 miembro *m*. 2 socio *m*. 3 *anat* miembro *m*. **member of parliament** diputado *m*. **membership** *n* calidad de miembro *f*.

membrane ('membrein) *n* membrana *f*.

memento (mə'mentou) *n* recuerdo *m*.

memo ('memou) *n inf* memorándum *m*.

memoir ('memwɑː) *n* memoria *f*.

memorandum (memə'rændəm) *n* 1 memorándum, memorando *m*. 2 apunte *m*. nota *f*. memo *m*.

memory ('meməri) *n* 1 memoria *f*. 2 recuerdo *m*. **from memory** de memoria. **in memory of** en memoria de. **memorable** *adj* memorable. **memorial** *adj* conmemorativo. *n* 1 monumento *m*. 2 memorial *m*. **memorize** *vt* aprender de memoria.

menace ('menəs) *n* 1 amenaza *f*. 2 *inf* persona peligrosa *f*. *vt* amenazar.

menagerie (mə'nædʒəri) *n* casa de fieras, colección de fieras *f*.

mend (mend) *vt* 1 remendar. 2 zurcir. 3 reparar, componer. *vi* mejorar, reponerse.

menial ('mi:niəl) *adj* 1 doméstico. 2 bajo, servil.

menopause ('menəpɔ:z) *n* menopausia *f*.

menstrual ('menstruəl) *adj* menstrual. **menstruate** *vi* menstruar. **menstruation** *n* menstruación *f*. periodo *m*.

mental ('mentl) *adj* mental. **mentality** *n* mentalidad *f*.

menthol ('menθɔl) *n* mentol *m*. **mentholated** *adj* mentolado.

mention ('menʃən) *n* mención *f*. *vt* mencionar, aludir a. **don't mention it!** ¡no hay de qué! **not to mention** sin contar, además de.

menu ('menju:) *n* lista *f*. menú *m*.

mercantile ('mə:kəntail) *adj* mercantil, comercial.

mercenary ('mə:sənəri) *adj,n* mercenario *m*.

merchant ('mə:tʃənt) *adj* mercante, mercantil. *n* comerciante, negociante *m*. **merchant bank** *n* banco mercante *f*. **merchant navy** *n* marina mercante *f*. **merchandise** *n* mercancías *f pl*. géneros *m pl*.

mercury ('mə:kjuri) *n* mercurio *m*.

mercy ('mə:si) *n* misericordia, merced *f*.

mere (miə) *adj* mero, simple, solo, no más que.

merge (mə:dʒ) *vt* 1 unir, combinar. 2 fundir. 3 *comm* fusionar. **merger** *n* fusión, consolidación *f*.

meridian (mə'ridiən) *n geog* meridiano *m*.

meringue (mə'ræŋ) *n* merengue *m*.

merit ('merit) *n* mérito *m*. *vt* merecer, ser digno de. **meritorious** *adj* meritorio.

merry ('meri) *adj* alegre, regocijado.

mesh (meʃ) *n* 1 malla *f*. 2 *tech* engrane, engranaje *m*. *vt* enredar. *vi* engranar.

mesmerize ('mezməraiz) *vt* hipnotizar.

mess (mes) *n* 1 confusión *f*. lío *m*. 2 asco *m*. suciedad *f*. 3 *mil* comedor, rancho *m*. **make a mess of** desordenar, ensuciar. *v* **mess about** perder el tiempo. **mess up** 1 desordenar. 2 ensuciar. **messy** *adj* 1 sucio. 2 en desorden.

message ('mesidʒ) *n* mensaje, recado *m*.

messenger ('mesindʒə) *n* mensajero *m*.

met (met) *v* see **meet**.

metabolism (mi'tæbəlizəm) *n* metabolismo *m*.

metal ('metl) *n* metal *m*. *adj* metálico. **metallurgy** *n* metalurgia *f*.

metamorphosis (metə'mɔ:fəsis) *n* metamorfosis *f*.

metaphor ('metəfə) *n* metáfora *f*. **metaphorical** *adj* metafórico.

metaphysics (metə'fiziks) *n* metafísica *f*. **metaphysical** *adj* metafísico.

meteor ('mi:tiə) *n* meteorito, meteoro *m*. **meteorology** *n* meteorología *f*.

meter ('mi:tə) *n* contador *m*.

method ('meθəd) *n* método *m*. **methodical** *adj* metódico. **methodology** *n* metodología *f*.

Methodist ('meθədist) *adj,n* metodista *m,f*. **Methodism** *n* metodismo *m*.

meticulous (mi'tikjuləs) *adj* meticuloso.

metre ('mi:tə) *n* metro *m*. **metric** *adj* métrico. **metric system** *n* sistema métrico *m*.

metropolis (mə'trɔpəlis) *n* metrópoli *f*. **metropolitan** *adj,n* metropolitano *m*.

Mexico ('meksikou) *n* Méjico, México *m*. **Mexican** *adj,n* mejicano, mexicano.

miaow (mi'au) *n* miau *m*. *vi* maullar.

microbe ('maikroub) *n* microbio *m*.

microphone ('maikrəfoun) *n* micrófono *m*.

microscope ('maikrəskoup) *n* microscopio *m*. **microscopic** *adj* microscópico.

mid (mid) *adj* medio, medio. **midday** *n* mediodía *m*. **midland** *adj* del interior, del centro. **midmorning** *n* media mañana *f*. **midnight** *n* medianoche *f*. **midsummer** *n* pleno verano

m. **midway** adj,adv a medio camino. **midweek** adj de entre semana.

middle ('midl) adj 1 medio, central. 2 intermedio. 3 mediano, medio. n 1 medio, centro m. mitad f. 2 cintura f. **middle-aged** adj de edad madura. **Middle Ages** n pl Edad Media f. **middle class** n clase media f.

midget ('midʒit) n enano m.

midst (midst) n **in the midst of** entre, en medio de.

midwife ('midwaif) n partera, comadrona f. .

might[1] (mait) n fuerza f. poder, poderío m. **mighty** adj fuerte, poderoso, potente.

might[2] (mait) v see **may**.

migraine ('mi:grein) n jaqueca f.

migrate (mai'greit) vi emigrar. **migration** n migración f.

mike (maik) n inf micrófono m.

mild (maild) adj 1 manso. 2 blando. 3 suave, dulce. 4 leve, ligero.

mildew ('mildju:) n moho m.

mile (mail) n milla f. **mileage** n kilometraje m. **mileometer** n mot cuentakilómetros m invar.

militant ('militənt) adj,n militante.

military ('militri) adj militar.

milk (milk) n leche f. vt 1 ordeñar. 2 chupar. **milky** adj lácteo. **milkman** n lechero m. **Milky Way** n Vía Láctea f.

mill (mil) n 1 molino m. 2 fábrica f. taller m. vt moler. **miller** n molinero m. **millstone** n 1 piedra de molino, muela f. 2 inf gran estorbo m.

millennium (mi'leniəm) n milenio, milenario m.

milligram ('miligræm) n miligramo m.

millilitre ('milili:tə) n mililitro m.

millimetre ('milimi:tə) n milímetro m.

million ('miliən) n millón m. **millionaire** n millonario m. **millionth** adj,n millonésimo m.

mime (maim) n 1 pantomima, mímica f. 2 mimo m. vt hacer en pantomima, representar con gestos. **mimic** adj 1 mímico. 2 fingido. n remedador m. vt remedar, imitar. **mimicry** n mímica, imitación f. remedo m.

minaret (minə'ret) n alminar m.

mince (mins) n carne picada f. **mincemeat** n conserva de picadillo de fruta f. ~vt picar, desmenuzar. vi 1 andar con pasos menuditos. 2 hablar remilgadamente. **mincer** n molinillo de picar m. **mincing** adj 1 remilgado, afectado. 2 menudito.

mind (maind) n 1 mente f. 2 inteligencia, entendimiento m. 3 parecer m. 4 memoria f.

vt 1 sentir molestia por. 2 hacer caso de. 3 tener cuidado con.

mine[1] (main) pron 1st pers s el mío, la mía.

mine[2] (main) n mina f. vt extraer. vi extraer minerales. **miner** n minero m.

mineral ('minərəl) adj,n mineral m. **mineral water** n agua mineral f.

minestrone (mini'strouni) n sopa juliana f.

mingle ('miŋgəl) vt mezclar. vi 1 mezclarse. 2 confundirse.

miniature ('miniətʃə) n,adj miniatura f.

minim ('minim) n mus blanca f.

minimum ('miniməm) adj mínimo. n mínimo, minimum m. **minimal** adj mínimo. **minimize** vt minimizar.

mining ('mainiŋ) n 1 minería f. 2 extracción f. **mining engineer** n ingeniero de minas m.

minister ('ministə) n 1 ministro m. 2 rel pastor m. vi 1 ministrar. 2 atender. **ministerial** adj ministerial, de ministro. **ministry** n ministerio m.

mink (miŋk) n 1 zool visón m. 2 piel de visón f.

minor ('mainə) adj 1 menor. 2 secundario. 3 pequeño. n menor de edad m,f. **minority** n minoría f. adj minoritario.

Minorca (mi'nɔ:kə) n Menorca f.

minstrel ('minstrəl) n 1 juglar m. 2 cantor m.

mint[1] (mint) n 1 bot menta f. 2 pastilla de menta f.

mint[2] (mint) n casa de moneda f. adj nuevo, sin usar. **in mint condition** en perfecto estado. ~vt acuñar.

minuet (minju'et) n minué m.

minus ('mainəs) adj menos, negativo. n cantidad negativa f. **minus sign** n signo menos m. ~prep 1 menos. 2 sin.

minute[1] ('minit) n 1 minuto m. 2 minuta, nota f. 3 pl acta f. vt levantar acta de.

minute[2] (mai'nju:t) adj diminuto, menudo, pequeño. **minutely** adv minuciosamente.

miracle ('mirəkəl) n milagro m. **miraculous** adj milagroso.

mirage ('mira:ʒ) n espejismo m.

mirror ('mirə) n 1 espejo m. 2 mot retrovisor m. vt reflejar.

mirth (mə:θ) n alegría f. regocijo m.

misbehave (misbi'heiv) vi 1 portarse mal. 2 ser malo. **misbehaviour** n mala conducta f.

miscarriage (mis'kæridʒ) n med aborto, malparto m. **miscarry** vi 1 med abortar, malparir. 2 fracasar, salir mal.

miscellaneous (misə'leiniəs) adj misceláneo, vario, diverso. **miscellany** n miscelánea f

233

mischance (mis'tʃɑːns) n desgracia, mala suerte f

mischief ('mistʃif) n 1 mal, daño m. 2 malicia f. **mischief-maker** n revoltoso m. **mischievous** adj 1 dañoso, malo. 2 malicioso. 3 travieso.

misconceive (miskən'siːv) vt entender mal. **misconception** n concepto erróneo m.

misconduct (mis'kɔndʌkt) n mala conducta f.

misdeed (mis'diːd) n delito, crimen m.

miser ('maizə) n avaro, tacaño m. **miserly** adj avariento, tacaño.

miserable ('mizərəbəl) adj 1 triste. 2 vil. 3 lastimoso. 4 despreciable. **miserably** adv tristemente. **misery** n 1 sufrimiento m. 2 miseria f.

misfire (mis'faiə) vi fallar.

misfit ('misfit) n persona inadaptada, persona mal ajustada f.

misfortune (mis'fɔːtʃən) n desgracia, desventura f. infortunio m.

misgiving (mis'giviŋ) n recelo m. duda f.

misguided (mis'gaidid) adj equivocado.

mishap ('mishæp) n contratiempo, accidente m.

mislay (mis'lei) vt perder.

mislead (mis'liːd) vt 1 despistar. 2 engañar. **misleading** adj 1 erróneo. 2 engañoso.

misprint ('misprint) n errata f. error de imprenta m.

miss[1] (mis) n 1 tiro errado, tiro perdido m. 2 error, desacierto m. 3 fracaso m. vt 1 errar. 2 perder. 3 no acertar. 4 no entender. 5 omitir. 6 no encontrar. 7 echar de menos. vi 1 errar el blanco. 2 fallar, salir mal. **missing** adj 1 ausente. 2 perdido. 3 mil desaparecido.

miss[2] (mis) n señorita f.

missile ('misail) n proyectil m.

mission ('miʃən) n misión f. **missionary** n misionero m

mist (mist) n 1 niebla f. 2 neblina f. 3 bruma f. vt empañar, velar. **misty** adj nebuloso, brumoso.

mistake* (mis'teik) n equivocación, falta f. error m. **make a mistake** equivocarse. ~vt entender mal, equivocarse sobre. **mistake for** equivocar con, confundir por. **mistaken** adj 1 equivocado, erróneo. 2 incorrecto. **be mistaken** equivocarse, estar equivocado.

mister ('mistə) n señor m.

mistletoe ('misəltou) n muérdago m.

mistress ('mistrəs) n 1 señora, ama de casa f. 2 dueña f. 3 amante, querida f.

mistrust (mis'trʌst) n desconfianza f. recelo m

vt desconfiar de. **mistrustful** adj desconfiado, receloso.

misunderstand* (misʌndə'stænd) vt entender mal, comprender mal, equivocación f. error m. **misunderstanding** n equivocación f. error m.

misuse (n mis'juːs; v mis'juːz) n 1 abuso, mal uso m. 2 empleo erróneo. 3 maltratamiento m. vt 1 abusar de. 2 emplear de. 3 maltratar.

mitre ('maitə) n rel mitra f.

mitten ('mitn) n mitón f.

mix (miks) vt 1 mezclar. 2 combinar, unir. 3 confundir. 4 amasar. **mixture** n 1 mezcla f. 2 med medicina f. **mix-up** n 1 confusión f. 2 inf lío, enredo m.

moan (moun) n 1 gemido, quejido m. 2 queja, protesta f. vt lamentar. vi 1 gemir. 2 quejarse, protestar.

moat (mout) n foso m.

mob (mɔb) n 1 gentío m. muchedumbre, multitud f. 2 populacho m. vt acosar, atropellar.

mobile ('moubail) adj móvil, movible. **mobility** n movilidad f. **mobilize** vt movilizar.

mock (mɔk) adj fingido, simulado. vt 1 ridiculizar. 2 burlarse de, mofarse de. **mockery** n mofa, burla f. **make a mockery of** hacer ridículo. **mocking** adj burlón.

mode (moud) n 1 modo m. 2 manera f. 3 moda f.

model ('mɔdl) adj,n modelo m. vt modelar. vi 1 servir de modelo. 2 ejercer la profesión de modelo.

moderate ('mɔdərət) adj,n moderado m. vt 1 moderar. 2 mitigar. **moderation** n moderación f. **in moderation** con moderación.

modern ('mɔdən) adj moderno. **modernize** vt modernizar. **modernization** n modernización f

modest ('mɔdist) adj 1 modesto. 2 pudoroso. **modesty** n 1 modestia f. 2 pudor m.

modify ('mɔdifai) vt modificar. **modification** n modificación f.

modulate ('mɔdjuleit) vt,vi modular.

module ('mɔdjuːl) n módulo m.

moist (mɔist) adj húmedo, mojado. **moisten** vt humedecer, mojar. **moisture** n humedad f. **moisturize** vt humedecer, mojar.

mole[1] (moul) n anat lunar m.

mole[2] (moul) n zool topo m.

molecule ('mɔlikjuːl) n molécula f. **molecular** adj molecular.

molest (mə'lest) vt importunar, meterse con.

mollusc ('mɔləsk) n molusco m.

molten ('moultən) adj fundido, líquido.

moment ('moumənt) n 1 momento, instante m. 2 importancia f. **momentary** adj momentáneo. **momentous** adj grave, de suma importancia. **momentum** n 1 momento m. 2 ímpetu m.

monarch ('monək) n monarca m. **monarchy** n monarquía f.

monastery ('monəstri) n monasterio m. **monastic** adj monástico.

Monday ('mʌndi) n lunes m.

money ('mʌni) n 1 dinero m. 2 moneda f. **moneybox** n hucha f. **money order** n giro postal m. **monetary** adj monetario.

mongrel ('mʌngrəl) n 1 perro mestizo, perro callejero. 2 mestizo m. adj 1 mestizo. 2 cruzado, callejero.

monitor ('monitə) n monitor m. vt 1 escuchar. 2 controlar.

monk (mʌŋk) n monje m.

monkey ('mʌŋki) n 1 mono m. **make a monkey out of** poner en ridículo. **monkey about with** manosear.

monogamy (mə'nɔgəmi) n monogamia f.

monologue ('monəlɔg) n monólogo m.

monopoly (mə'nɔpəli) n monopolio m. **monopolize** vt monopolizar.

monosyllable ('monəsiləbəl) n monosílabo m.

monotone ('monətoun) n monotonía f. **monotonous** adj monótono.

monsoon (mon'su:n) n monzón m,f.

monster ('monstə) n monstruo m. **monstrosity** n monstruosidad f. **monstrous** adj monstruoso, enorme.

month (mʌnθ) n mes m. **monthly** adj mensual. n revista mensual f.

monument ('monjumənt) n monumento m. **monumental** adj monumental.

moo (mu:) n mugido m. vi mugir.

mood[1] (mu:d) n 1 humor m. 2 capricho m. **moody** adj de mal humor.

mood[2] (mu:d) n gram modo m.

moon (mu:n) n luna f. **full moon** luna llena. **new moon** luna nueva. **once in a blue moon** de Pascuas a Ramos. **moonlight** n luz de la luna f.

moor[1] (muə) n páramo, brezal m. **moorhen** n polla de agua f.

moor[2] (muə) vt amarrar. vi echar las amarras.

Moor (muə) n moro m.

mop (mɔp) n 1 fregasuelos m invar. 2 mata, greña f. vt fregar, limpiar.

mope (moup) vi estar deprimido or abatido.

moped ('mouped) n ciclomotor m.

moral ('morəl) adj 1 moral, ético. 2 virtuoso. n 1 moraleja f. sentido moral m. 2 moral, ética, moralidad f. **morale** n moral f. **morality** n moralidad f. **moralize** vt,vi moralizar.

morbid ('mo:bid) adj 1 mórbido, morboso. 2 malsano. **morbidity** n morbosidad f.

more (mo:r) adj, adv más. **all the more** tanto más. **no more** ya no, no más. **once more** otra vez. **moreover** adv además, por otra parte.

morgue (mo:g) n depósito de cadáveres m. morgue f.

morning ('mo:niŋ) n 1 mañana f. 2 madrugada f. **good morning!** ¡buenos días! **in the morning** por la mañana. **tomorrow morning** mañana por la mañana.

Morocco (mə'rɔkou) n Marruecos m.

moron ('mo:rɔn) n imbécil m,f. **moronic** adj imbécil.

morose (mə'rous) adj malhumorado, hosco.

morphine ('mo:fi:n) n morfina f.

Morse Code (mo:s) n alfabeto Morse m.

mortal ('mo:tl) adj,n mortal. **mortality** n mortalidad f.

mortar[1] ('mo:tə) n mortero m.

mortar[2] ('mo:tə) n argamasa f.

mortgage ('mo:gidʒ) n hipoteca f. vt hipotecar.

mortify ('mo:tifai) vt 1 mortificar. 2 humillar.

mortuary ('mo:tjuəri) n depósito de cadáveres m.

mosaic (mou'zeiik) n mosaico m.

mosque (mɔsk) n mezquita f.

mosquito (mə'ski:tou) n mosquito m. **mosquito net** n mosquitero m.

moss (mɔs) n bot musgo m. **mossy** adj musgoso.

most (moust) adj 1 más. 2 la mayor parte de, los más, la mayoría de, casi todos. adv 1 más. 2 sumamente, de lo más. **most of all** sobre todo. ~n la mayor parte, el mayor número, los más. **at most** a lo más, a lo sumo, todo lo más. **make the most of** sacar el mejor partido de. **mostly** adv por la mayor parte, en general.

motel (mou'tel) n motel m.

moth (mɔθ) n 1 polilla f. 2 mariposa nocturna f. **mothball** n bola de naftalina f. **motheaten** adj apolillado.

mother ('mʌðə) n madre f. vt servir de madre a. **motherhood** n maternidad f. **mother-in-law** n suegra f. **mother superior** n madre superiora f.

motion ('mouʃən) n 1 movimiento m. 2 marcha

f. **3** moción, proposición f. **set in motion** poner en marcha.

motive ('moutiv) n motivo m. **ulterior motive** motivo oculto.

motor ('mouta) n **1** motor m. **2** coche, automóvil m. vi ir en coche o automóvil. **motor car** n coche, automóvil m. **motor cycle** n motocicleta f. **motorist** n automovilista m,f. **motorway** n autopista f.

motto ('motou) n, pl **-os** or **-oes** f **1** lema f. **2** divisa f.

mould[1] (mould) n **1** molde m. **2** cosa moldeada f. vt moldear.

mould[2] (mould) n moho m. **mouldy** adj mohoso, enmohecido.

moult (moult) n muda f. vi mudar.

mound (maund) n **1** montón m. **2** terraplén m.

mount[1] (maunt) vt montar, subir a. vi **1** subir. **2** montar. **3** aumentar.

mount[2] (maunt) n montón, montículo, monte m.

mountain ('mauntin) n **1** montaña f. **2** montón m. **mountain range** n sierra f. **mountainous** adj montañoso. **mountaineer** n montañero m. **2** alpinista m. **mountaineering** adj,n montañismo, alpinismo m.

mourn (mɔ:n) vt llorar, lamentar. **mourner** n **1** doliente m,f. **2** plañidero m. **mournful** adj triste, afligido. **mourning** n **1** luto m. **2** lamentación f.

mouse (maus) n, pl **mice** ratón m. **mousetrap** n ratonera f. **mousy** adj **1** tímido. **2** pardusco.

mousse (mu:s) n postre de crema m.

moustache (mə'sta:ʃ) n bigote m. bigotes m pl. **wear a moustache** tener bigote.

mouth (mauθ) n boca f. **mouthful** n bocado m. **mouthpiece** n **1** mus boquilla f. **2** inf portavoz m. **mouth-watering** adj sumamente apetitoso.

move (mu:v) n **1** movimiento m. **2** game jugada, movida f. **3** paso m. acción f. **4** mudanza f. traslado m. vt **1** mover. **2** trasladar. **3** conmover. **4** proponer. **movable** adj movible. **movement** n **1** movimiento m. juego m. **2** mus tiempo m. **moving** adj **1** movedor. **2** móvil. **3** conmovedor.

mow (mou) vt **1** segar. **2** cortar. **lawn-mower** n cortacésped m.

Mr ('mistə) n señor, don m.

Mrs ('misiz) n señora, doña f.

much (mʌtʃ) adj,adv **1** mucho. **2** casi, más o menos. **3** con mucho. **as much, so much**

tanto. **how much?** ¿cuánto? **however much** por mucho que.

muck (mʌk) n **1** estiércol m. **2** suciedad f. **mucky** adj sucio.

mud (mʌd) n lodo, barro, fango m. **mudguard** n guardabarros m invar.

muddle ('mʌdl) n **1** desorden m. confusión f. **2** embrollo, lío m. **get into a muddle** embrollarse. ~vt **1** embrollar, confundir. **2** aturdir, confundir.

muff (mʌf) n manguito m.

muffle ('mʌfəl) vt **1** envolver. **2** embozar, tapar. **3** amortiguar, apagar. **muffled** adj sordo, apagado.

mug (mʌg) n **1** taza f. **2** jarra f.

mulberry ('mʌlbəri) n mora, morera f. adj morado.

mule[1] (mju:l) n zool mulo m.

mule[2] (mju:l) n babucha f.

multiple ('mʌltipəl) adj múltiple, múltiplo. n múltiplo m.

multiply ('mʌltiplai) vt multiplicar. **multiplication** n multiplicación f.

multitude ('mʌltitju:d) n multitud f.

mum[1] (mʌm) adj callado. **keep mum** callarse.

mum[2] (mʌm) n inf mamá f.

mumble ('mʌmbəl) vt decir entre dientes. vi musitar, refunfuñar. **speak in a mumble** hablar entrer dientes.

mummy[1] ('mʌmi) n momia f.

mummy[2] ('mʌmi) n inf mamá f.

mumps (mʌmps) n paperas, parótidas f pl.

munch (mʌntʃ) vt mascar, ronzar.

mundane ('mʌndein) adj **1** mundano. **2** vulgar, trivial.

municipal (mju'nisipəl) adj municipal. **municipality** n municipio m.

mural ('mjuərəl) n pintura mural f.

murder ('mɔ:də) n asesinato, homicidio m. vt **1** asesinar. **2** matar. **murderer** n asesino m.

murmur ('mɔ:mə) n **1** murmullo, murmurio m. **2** susurro. vt,vi murmurar.

muscle ('mʌsəl) n **1** músculo m. **2** inf fuerza muscular f. v **muscle in** entrar por fuerza. **muscular** adj **1** muscular. **2** musculoso. **3** fornido.

muse (mju:z) n musa f.

museum (mju:'ziəm) n museo m.

mushroom ('mʌʃrum) n **1** seta f. hongo m. **2** champiñón m. vi inf crecer como los hongos.

music ('mu:zik) n **1** música f. **face the music** pagar el pato. **set to music** poner música a.

musicar. **musical** adj musical, músico. n comedia musical f. **musician** n músico m.

musk (mʌsk) n 1 almizcle m. 2 bot almizcleña f.

musket ('mʌskit) n mosquete m.

Muslim ('muzlim) adj,n musulmán m.

muslin ('mʌzlin) n muselina f.

mussel ('mʌsəl) n mejillón m.

must[*] (mʌst) v aux deber, tener que, haber de.

mustard ('mʌstəd) n mostaza f.

mute (mju:t) adj mudo, silencioso. n 1 mudo m. 2 mus sordina f.

mutilate ('mju:tileit) vt mutilar.

mutiny ('mju:tini) n motín m. sublevación f. vi amotinarse, sublevarse.

mutter ('mʌtə) n murmullo m. vt,vi murmurar.

mutton ('mʌtn) n carne de carnero f.

mutual ('mju:tjuəl) adj 1 mútuo. 2 común.

muzzle ('mʌzəl) n 1 hocico m. 2 bozal m. 3 boca f. vt 1 abozalar. 2 amordazar.

my (mai) poss adj 1st pers s mi, mis. **myself** pron 1st pers s 1 yo mismo, yo misma. 2 me. 3 mí.

myopia (mai'oupiə) n miopia f.

myrrh (mə:) n mirra f.

myrtle ('mə:tl) n arrayán, mirto m.

mystery ('mistəri) n misterio m. **mysterious** adj misterioso.

mystic ('mistik) adj,n místico. **mysticism** n misticismo m. mística f.

mystify ('mistifai) vt dejar perplejo, desconcertar.

mystique (mi'sti:k) n misterio m.

myth (miθ) n mito m. **mythical** adj mítico. **mythology** n mitología f.

N

nag[1] (næg) vt regañar, importunar, machacar. **nagging** adj 1 regañón. 2 persistente.

nag[2] (næg) n jaca f. rocín m.

nail (neil) n 1 anat uña f. 2 zool garra f. 3 clavo m. vt clavar, enclavar. **nailfile** n lima f. **nail varnish** n esmalte para las uñas m.

naive (nai'i:v) adj ingenuo.

naked ('neikid) adj desnudo. **nakedness** n desnudez f.

name (neim) n nombre m. **what is your name?** ¿cómo se llama? ~vt nombrar. **namely** adv a saber **namesake** n tocayo, homónimo m.

nanny ('næni) n niñera f.

nap (næp) n sueño ligero m. **have** or **take a nap** descabezar un sueño. ~vi dormitar.

napkin ('næpkin) n 1 servilleta f. 2 pañal m.

nappy ('næpi) n inf pañal m.

narcotic adj,n narcótico m.

narrate (nə'reit) vt narrar. **narration** n narración f. **narrative** n narrativa f. adj narrativo. **narrator** n narrador m.

narrow ('nærou) adj 1 estrecho, angosto. 2 reducido, justo. vt 1 estrechar. 2 reducir. **narrowly** adv 1 estrechamente. 2 por poco. **narrow-minded** adj intolerante, estrecho de conciencia.

nasal ('neizəl) adj nasal.

nasty ('nɑ:sti) adj 1 asqueroso. 2 horrible. 3 grosero. 4 odioso, malo. 5 desagradable.

nation ('neiʃən) n nación f. **national** adj nacional. **national anthem** n himno nacional m. **national insurance** n seguro obligatorio m. **national service** n servicio nacional m. **nationalism** n nacionalismo m. **nationalist** adj,n nacionalista m,f. **nationality** n nacionalidad f. **nationalize** vt nacionalizar.

native ('neitiv) n 1 natural m,f. 2 indígena m,f. adj 1 nativo. 2 natal.

nativity (nə'tiviti) n natividad f.

natural ('nætʃərəl) adj 1 natural. 2 innato. **natural history** n historia natural f. **naturalize** vt naturalizar.

nature ('neitʃə) n 1 naturaleza f. 2 natural, carácter m.

naughty ('nɔ:ti) adj 1 malo, travieso, pícaro. 2 picante.

nausea ('nɔ:siə, -ziə) n náusea f. **nauseate** vt dar náuseas. **nauseating** adj nauseabundo.

nautical ('nɔ:tikəl) adj 1 náutico. 2 marino.

naval ('neivəl) adj naval, de marina.

nave (neiv) n nave f.

navel ('neivəl) n ombligo m.

navigate ('nævigeit) vi navegar. vt guiar. **navigator** n 1 navegante m. 2 piloto m.

navy ('neivi) n marina f. **navy blue** adj azul marino.

near (niə) adv cerca. prep 1 cerca de. 2 hacia. adj 1 cercano, próximo. 2 aproximado. vi acercarse, aproximarse. **nearby** adv cerca. adj cercano, próximo. **nearly** adv 1 casi. 2 de cerca.

neat (ni:t) adj 1 pulcro. 2 hábil. 3 puro.

nebulous ('nebjuləs) adj nebuloso.

necessary ('nesəsəri) adj necesario **necessity** n necesidad f.

neck (nek) n cuello m. **neck and neck** al

mismo nivel. ~*vi inf* besuquearse. **necklace** *n* collar *m*. **neckline** *n* escote *m*.

need (ni:d) *n* necesidad *f*. **if need be** si fuera necesario. ~*vt* **1** necesitar. **2** tener que. **needless** *adj* innecesario, inútil.

needle ('ni:dl) *n* aguja *f*. *vt* provocar.

negate (ni'geit) *vt* anular. **negative** *adj* negativo. *n* **1** negativa *f*. **2** *phot* negativo *m*.

neglect (ni'glekt) *vt* **1** descuidar, desatender. **2** abandonar, arrinconar. *n* **1** abandono *m*. **2** desatención *f*. **negligence** *n* negligencia *f*. **negligent** *adj* negligente. **negligible** *adj* insignificante, despreciable.

negotiate (ni'goufieit) *vt* **1** negociar, gestionar. **2** salvar. **negotiation** *n* negociación, gestión *f*.

Negro ('ni:grou) *n, pl* **-oes**, *adj* negro.

neigh (nei) *vi* relinchar. *n* relincho *m*.

neighbour ('neibə) *n* vecino *m*. **neighbourhood** *n* **1** vecindario *m*. **2** vecindad *f*. **neighbourly** *adj* de buen vecino.

neither ('naiðə) *adv* ni. **neither...nor** ni...ni. ~*conj* **1** ni. **2** tampoco. **3** ni tampoco. *adj* ninguno. *pron* ninguno *m*.

nephew ('nevju:) *n* sobrino *m*.

nepotism ('nepətizəm) *n* nepotismo *m*.

Neptune ('neptju:n) *n* Neptuno *m*.

nerve (nə:v) *n* **1** nervio *m*. **2** *inf* caradura *f*. **get on one's nerves** crispar los nervios. **nervous** *adj* nervioso. **nervous breakdown** *n* crisis nerviosa *f*. **nervous system** *n* sistema nervioso *m*. **nervousness** *n* nerviosismo *m*. **nervy** *adj* nervioso.

nest (nest) *n* **1** nido *m*. **2** hogar *m*. *vi* **1** anidar. **2** buscar nidos.

nestle ('nesəl) *vi* **1** abrigarse, arrimarse. **2** anidarse.

net[1] (net) *n* **1** red *f*. **2** malla *f*. **3** tul *m*. *vt* **1** prender con red, cubrir con red. **netball** *n* balonvolea *f*. **network** *n* red *f*.

net[2] (net) *adj* neto. *vt* sacar un neto de.

nettle ('netl) *n* ortiga *f*. *vt* irritar.

neurosis (njuə'rousis) *n* neurosis *f*. **neurotic** *adj,n* neurótico.

neuter ('nju:tə) *adj* **1** neutro. **2** castrado. *vt* castrar

neutral ('nju:trəl) *adj* **1** neutral. **2** *tech* neutro. **in neutral** *mot* en punto muerto. **neutralize** *vt* neutralizar

never ('nevə) *adv* nunca, jamás. **never-ending** *adj* interminable. **nevertheless** *adv* no obstante.

new (nju:) *adj* nuevo. **newcomer** *n* recién llegado *m*. **newly** *adv* **1** recién. **2** nuevamente.

New Testament *n* Nuevo Testamento *m*.

New Year *n* Año Nuevo *m*.

news (nju:z) *n* noticias *f pl*. **a piece of news** una noticia *f*. **what's the news?** ¿qué hay de nuevo? **newsagent** *n* vendedor de periódicos *m*. **newspaper** *n* periódico *m*. *adj* periodístico. **newsreel** *n* noticiario *m*.

New Zealand ('zi:land) *n* Nueva Zelanda *f*. **New Zealander** *n* neozelandés *m*.

next (nekst) *adj* **1** próximo, que viene. **2** siguiente. **3** contiguo, de al lado. *adv* **1** después, luego. **2** otra vez. **next to 1** junto a, al lado de. **2** cerca. ~*n* próximo, siguiente *m*.

nib (nib) *n* punta *f*.

nibble ('nibəl) *vt* mordisquear. *n* mordisco *m*.

nice (nais) *adj* **1** bueno, agradable. **2** bonito, mono. **3** simpático. **4** fino. **nicety** *n* **1** detalle *m*. exactitud *f*. **2** refinamiento *m*.

niche (nitʃ) *n* **1** nicho *m*. **2** hornacina *f*.

nick (nik) *vt* **1** mellar, hacer muescas en. **2** *inf* birlar. **3** *inf* trincar. *n* **1** mella, muesca *f*. **2** *sl* cárcel *f*. **in the nick of time** en el momento justo.

nickel ('nikəl) *n* níquel *m*.

nickname ('nikneim) *n* apodo *m*. *vt* apodar.

nicotine ('nikəti:n) *n* nicotina *f*.

niece (ni:s) *n* sobrina *f*.

nigger ('nigə) *n derog* negro *m*.

night (nait) *n* **1** noche *f*. **good night!** ¡buenas noches! **last night** anoche. ~*adj* nocturno. **nightdress** *n* camisón *m*. **nightfall** *n* anochecer *m*. **nightly** *adv* todas las noches. **nightmare** *n* pesadilla *f*. **night-time** *n* noche *f*. **in the night-time** de noche.

nightingale ('naitiŋgeil) *n* ruiseñor *m*.

nil (nil) *n* cero *m*. nada *f*.

nimble ('nimbəl) *adj* ágil, ligero.

nine (nain) *adj,n* nueve *m*. **ninth** *adj* noveno.

nineteen (nain'ti:n) *adj,n* diecinueve *m*. **nineteenth** *adj* decimonoveno, decimonono.

ninety ('nainti) *adj,n* noventa *m*. **ninetieth** *adj* nonagésimo.

nip[1] (nip) *vt* **1** dar un mordisco a. **2** pellizcar. **3** helar. *n* **1** mordisco *m*. **2** pellizco *m*. **3** frío *m*.

nip[2] (nip) *n* trago *m*.

nipple ('nipəl) *n* **1** pezón *m*. **2** tetilla *f*.

nit (nit) *n* **1** liendre *m*. **2** *inf* imbécil *m*.

nitrogen ('naitrədʒən) *n* nitrógeno *m*.

no[1] (nou) *adv* no.

no[2] (nou) *adj* **1** ninguno. **2** sin.

noble ('noubəl) adj noble. **nobility** n nobleza f. **nobleman** n noble m.

nobody ('noubədi) pron nadie.

nocturnal (nɔk'tə:nl) adj nocturno.

nod (nɔd) vi 1 inclinar la cabeza. 2 asentir con la cabeza. 3 cabecear. n 1 inclinación de cabeza f. 2 cabezada f.

node (noud) n 1 bot nudo m. 2 med,tech nódulo, nodo m.

noise (nɔiz) n ruido m. **noisy** adj ruidoso, estrepitoso.

nomad ('noumæd) n nómada m,f. **nomadic** adj nómada.

nominal ('nɔminl) adj nominal.

nominate ('nɔmineit) vt nominar, nombrar. **nomination** n nominación f. nombramiento m. **nominee** n candidato m.

nominative ('nɔminətiv) n nominativo m.

non- pref no, des-, in-.

nonchalant ('nɔnʃələnt) adj 1 indiferente. 2 descuidado.

nondescript ('nɔndiskript) adj 1 indefinible. 2 indefinido. 3 mediocre.

none (nʌn) pron ninguno m. **none of that** nada de eso. ~adv de ningún modo, nada. **none the less** no obstante.

nonentity (nɔn'entiti) n nulidad f.

nonsense ('nɔnsəns) n disparate, desatino m. interj ¡tonterías! **nonsensical** adj disparatado, absurdo.

noon (nu:n) n mediodía m.

no-one pron nadie.

noose (nu:s) n lazo corredizo m. vt cazar con lazo.

nor (nɔ:) conj ni.

norm (nɔ:m) n norma, pauta f. **normal** adj normal. **normality** n normalidad f. **normalize** vt normalizar.

north (nɔ:θ) n norte m. adj del norte, septentrional. adv al norte. **northeast** adj,n nordeste m. **northeasterly** adj nordeste. **northeastern** adj nordeste. **northerly** adj del norte, septentrional. **northern** adj del norte, norteño, septentrional. **northwest** adj,n noroeste m. **northwesterly** adj del noroeste. **northwestern** adj del noroeste.

Northern Ireland n Irlanda del Norte f.

Norway ('nɔ:wei) n Noruega f. **Norwegian** adj,n noruego m. **Norwegian** (language) n noruego m.

nose (nɔuz) n 1 nariz f. inf narices f pl. 2 hocico m. 3 olfato m. **nosy** adj inf fisgón, curioso.

nostalgia (nɔ'stældʒiə) n nostalgia f. **nostalgic** adj nostálgico.

nostril ('nɔstril) n nariz, ventana de la nariz f.

not (nɔt) adv no. **not at all** de ningún modo.

notch (nɔtʃ) n muesca f. corte m. vt cortar muescas en.

note (nout) n 1 nota f. 2 comm vale. vt 1 notar. 2 anotar. **notebook** n cuaderno m. **notable** adj notable. **notation** n notación f. **noteworthy** adj digno de ser notado.

nothing ('nʌθiŋ) n nada f. **for nothing** de balde. **nothing much** poca cosa. ~adv en nada.

notice ('noutis) n 1 aviso m. 2 anuncio m. 3 letrero m. 4 plazo m. 5 atención m. **notice board** n tablero de anuncios m. ~vt notar, advertir, fijarse. **noticeable** adj 1 perceptible. 2 notable.

notify ('noutifai) vt notificar. **notification** n notificación f.

notion ('nouʃən) n noción, idea f.

notorious (nou'tɔ:riəs) adj 1 notorio, muy conocido. 2 escandaloso. **notoriety** n notoriedad f. 2 mala fama f.

notwithstanding (,nɔtwiθ'stændiŋ) adv no obstante. prep a pesar de. conj a pesar de que.

nougat ('nu:ga:) n turrón m.

nought (nɔ:t) n 1 nada f. 2 cero m.

noun (naun) n nombre, sustantivo m.

nourish ('nʌriʃ) vt nutrir, alimentar, sustentar. **nourishing** adj nutritivo, alimenticio. **nourishment** n alimento, sustento m.

novel[1] ('nɔvəl) n novela f. **novelist** n novelista m,f.

novel[2] ('nɔvəl) adj 1 nuevo. 2 original. **novelty** n novedad f.

November (nou'vembə) n noviembre m.

novice ('nɔvis) n novicio m.

now (nau) adv ahora. **from now on** de aquí en adelante. **just now** hace un momento. ~conj ahora bien. **nowadays** adv hoy día, hoy en día.

nowhere ('nouwɛə) adv en or a ninguna parte.

noxious ('nɔkʃəs) adj nocivo.

nozzle ('nɔzəl) n boquilla f.

nuance ('nju:əns) n matiz m.

nucleus ('nju:kliəs) n, pl -clei or -cleuses núcleo m. **nuclear** adj nuclear.

nude (nju:d) adj,n desnudo m. **in the nude** desnudo. **nudism** n nudismo m. **nudist** n nudista m,f. **nudity** n desnudez f.

nudge (nʌdʒ) vt dar un codazo. n codazo m.

nugget ('nʌgit) n pepita de oro f.
nuisance ('nju:səns) n 1 molestia, fastidio m. 2 pesado m.
null (nʌl) adj nulo. **nullify** vt anular. **nullity** n nulidad f.
numb (nʌm) adj 1 entumecido. 2 insensible. vt 1 entumecer. 2 paralizar. **numbness** n 1 entumecimiento m. 2 insensibilidad f.
number ('nʌmbə) n número m. vt 1 numerar. 2 contar. **number plate** n mot placa de matrícula f. **numeral** adj numeral. n cifra f. **numerical** adj numérico. **numerous** adj 1 numeroso. 2 muchos.
nun (nʌn) n monja f.
nurse (nə:s) n 1 enfermera f. 2 nodriza f. 3 niñera f. vt 1 cuidar. 2 criar. 3 fomentar. vi hacer de enfermera. **nursing home** n clínica privada f. **nursery** n 1 cuarto de los niños m. 2 vivero, plantel m. **nursery rhyme** n rima infantil f.
nurture ('nə:tʃə) vt 1 nutrir. 2 criar. 3 educar. n crianza f.
nut (nʌt) n 1 nuez f. 2 tech tuerca f. **be nuts** inf estar chiflado. **nutcrackers** n often pl cascanueces m invar. **nutmeg** n nuez moscada f.
nutrition (nju:'triʃən) n nutrición f. **nutritional** adj nutritivo.
nuzzle ('nʌzəl) vt 1 hociquear. 2 arrimar.
nylon ('nailən) n nilón, nylón m.

O

oak (ouk) n roble m.
oar (ɔ:) n remo m. **oarsman** n remero m.
oasis (ou'eisis) n, pl **oases** oasis m.
oath (ouθ) n juramento m. **take an oath** prestar juramento.
oatmeal ('outmi:l) n harina de avena f.
oats (outs) n pl avena f.
obedient (ə'bi:diənt) adj obediente. **obedience** n obediencia f.
obese (ou'bi:s) adj obeso. **obesity** n obesidad f.
obey (ə'bei) vt,vi obedecer.
obituary (ə'bitjuəri) n obituario m.
object (n 'ɔbdʒikt; v əb'dʒekt) n 1 objeto m. 2 gram complemento m. vt objetar vi 1 hacer objeciones, oponerse. 2 protestar. **objection** n objeción f. **objectionable** adj 1 discutible. 2 desagradable. **objective** adj,n objetivo f. **objectivity** n objetividad f.

oblige (ə'blaidʒ) vt 1 obligar. 2 complacer. **be obliged (for)** estar agradecido (por). **obligation** n 1 obligación f. 2 compromiso m. **obligatory** adj obligatorio. **obliging** adj complaciente, servicial.
oblique (ə'bli:k) adj oblicuo.
obliterate (ə'blitəreit) vt 1 borrar. 2 aniquilar. **obliteration** n 1 borradura f. 2 aniquilación f.
oblivion (ə'bliviən) n olvido m. **oblivious** adj abstraído, inconsciente.
oblong ('ɔblɔŋ) adj rectangular.
obnoxious (əb'nɔkʃəs) adj detestable, odioso.
oboe ('oubou) n oboe m.
obscene (əb'si:n) adj obsceno. **obscenity** n obscenidad f.
obscure (əb'skjuə) adj oscuro. vt oscurecer. **obscurity** n oscuridad f.
observe (əb'zə:v) vt observar. **observance** n observancia f. **observant** adj observador. **observation** n observación f. **observatory** n observatorio m. **observer** n observador m.
obsess (əb'ses) vt obsesionar. **obsession** n obsesión f.
obsolete ('ɔbsəli:t) adj obsoleto, en desuso.
obstacle ('ɔbstəkəl) n obstáculo m.
obstinate ('ɔbstinət) adj obstinado. **obstinacy** n obstinación, terquedad f.
obstruct (əb'strʌkt) vt obstruir. **obstruction** n obstrucción f. **obstructive** adj obstructivo.
obtain (əb'tein) vt obtener. vi prevalecer. **obtainable** adj 1 asequible. 2 en venta.
obtrusive (əb'tru:siv) adj 1 importuno. 2 que salta a la vista. 3 penetrante. **obtrusion** n imposición, importunidad f.
obtuse (əb'tju:s) adj obtuso.
obvious ('ɔbviəs) adj obvio.
occasion (ə'keiʒən) n 1 ocasión f. 2 acontecimiento m. vt ocasionar. **occasional** adj 1 ocasional. 2 poco frecuente. **occasionally** adv de vez en cuando.
Occident ('ɔksidənt) n occidente m. **occidental** adj occidental.
occult (ɔ'kʌlt) adj oculto. n lo sobrenatural, lo oculto neu.
occupy ('ɔkjupai) vt ocupar. **occupation** n 1 ocupación f. 2 profesión f. 3 inquilinato m. **occupant** n 1 ocupante m,f. 2 inquilino m.
occur (ə'kə:) vi 1 ocurrir. 2 encontrarse. **occurrence** n 1 acontecimiento m. 2 aparición f. 3 ocurrencia f.
ocean ('ouʃən) n océano m. **oceanic** adj oceánico.

ochre (' oukə) *n* ocre *m.*

octagon ('ɔktəgən) *n* octágono *m.* **octagonal** *adj* octagonal.

octane ('ɔktein) *n* octano *m.*

octave ('ɔktiv) *n* octava *f.*

October (ɔk'toubə) *n* octubre *m.*

octopus ('ɔktəpəs) *n* pulpo *m.*

oculist ('ɔkjulist) *n* oculista *m.f.*

odd (ɔd) *adj* 1 impar. 2 suelto. 3 sobrante. 4 raro, estrambótico. **oddity** *n* rareza, singularidad *f.* **oddment** *n* 1 artículo suelto *m.* 2 resto de serie *m.* 3 retal *m.* **odds** *n pl* 1 ventaja *f.* 2 probabilidades *f pl.* **odds and ends** 1 retazos *m pl.* 2 chismes *m pl.*

ode (oud) *n* oda *f.*

odious ('oudiəs) *adj* odioso.

odour ('oudə) *n* olor *m.*

oesophagus (i'sɔfəgəs) *n* esófago *m.*

oestrogen ('i:strədʒən) *n* ostrógeno *m.*

of (əv; *stressed* ɔv) *prep* de.

off (ɔf) *adv* 1 lejos, a distancia. 2 fuera. **be off** 1 marcharse. 2 estar desconectado. 3 estar pasado. 4 quedar cancelado. ~*prep* 1 lejos de. 2 fuera de. 3 que sale de.

offal ('ɔfəl) *n* 1 asadura *f.* 2 despojos *m pl.*

offend (ə'fend) *vt* ofender. **offend against** pecar contra. **offence** *n* 1 ofensa *f.* 2 *law* delito *m.* **give offence** ofender. **take offence** ofenderse. **offender** *n* 1 ofensor *n.* 2 *law* delincuente *m,f.* **offensive** *adj* ofensivo. *n* ofensiva *f.*

offer ('ɔfə) *n* oferta *f.* *vt* ofrecer.

offhand (ɔf'hænd) *adj* 1 brusco. 2 informal. *adv* de improviso.

office ('ɔfis) *n* 1 oficina *f.* 2 cargo *m.* 3 oficio *m.* **officer** *n* 1 oficial *m.* 2 policía *m.* **office-worker** *n* oficinista *m,f.* **official** *adj* 1 oficial. 2 autorizado. *n* 1 oficial *m.* 2 funcionario *m.*

officious (ə'fiʃəs) *adj* oficioso.

offing ('ɔfiŋ) *n* **be in the offing** estar a la vista.

off-licence *n* tienda de bebidas alcohólicas *f.*

off-peak *adj* fuera de las horas punta.

off-putting *adj* 1 disuasivo. 2 distante, frío.

off-season *adv* fuera de temporada.

offset ('ɔfset) *vt* compensar.

offshore (ɔf'ʃɔ:) *adj* 1 poco distante de la costa. 2 de tierra.

offside (ɔf'said) *adv* fuera de juego.

offspring ('ɔfspriŋ) *n* vástago *m.*

offstage (ɔf'steidʒ) *adv* entre bastidores.

often ('ɔfən) *adv* a menudo. **how often?** ¿cuántas veces?

ogre ('ougə) *n* ogro *m.*

oil (ɔil) *n* 1 aceite *m.* 2 petróleo *m.* 3 óleo *m.* *vt* engrasar. **oilfield** *n* campo petrolífero *m.* **oil painting** *n* pintura al óleo *f.* **oilskin** *n* hule, impermeable *m.*

ointment ('ɔintmənt) *n* ungüento *m.*

old (ould) *adj* 1 viejo *m.* 2 antiguo. **how old is he?** ¿cuántos años tiene? ¿qué edad tiene? **old age** *n* vejez *f.* **old-fashioned** *adj* anticuado.

Old Testament *n* Antiguo Testamento *m.*

olive ('ɔliv) *n* aceituna, oliva *f.* *adj* aceitunado, oliváceo. **olive grove** *n* olivar *m.* **olive oil** *n* aceite de oliva *m.* **olive tree** *n* olivo *m.*

omelette ('ɔmlət) *n* tortilla *f.*

omen ('oumen) *n* agüero, presagio *m.*

ominous ('ɔminəs) *adj* amenazador.

omit (ə'mit) *vt* omitir. **omission** *n* omisión *f.*

omnibus ('ɔmnibəs) *n* ómnibus *m.*

omnipotent (ɔm'nipətənt) *adj* omnipotente. **omnipotence** *n* omnipotencia *f.*

on (ɔn) *prep* en, encima de, sobre. *adv* 1 adelante. 2 encima. 3 en marcha. **and so on** y así sucesivamente. **on and off** intermitentemente.

once (wʌns) *adv* 1 una vez. 2 antes, antiguamente. **at once** de una vez. **once in a while** de tarde en tarde. ~*conj* una vez que.

one (wʌn) *adj* 1 uno. 2 único. *n* uno *m.* *pron* uno, una. **oneself** *pron* 1 uno mismo, una misma. 2 se. 3 sí. **by oneself** solo. **one-way** *adj* de dirección única.

onion ('ʌniən) *n* cebolla *f.*

onlooker ('ɔnlukə) *n* espectador, mirón *m.*

only ('ounli) *adj* único. *adv* sólo, solamente, únicamente. *conj* sólo que.

onset ('ɔnset) *n* comienzo *m.*

onslaught ('ɔnslɔ:t) *n* arremetida *f.*

onus ('ounəs) *n* responsabilidad, carga *f.*

onward ('ɔnwəd) *adj* hacia adelante, progresivo. **onwards** *adv* adelante. **from now onwards** desde ahora en adelante.

ooze (u:z) *vi* rezumar.

opal ('oupəl) *n* ópalo *m.*

opaque (ou'peik) *adj* opaco.

open ('oupən) *adj* 1 abierto. 2 expuesto. 3 susceptible de. 4 público. *vt* 1 abrir. 2 inaugurar. 3 iniciar. **open air** *n* aire libre *m.* **opening** *n* 1 abertura *f.* 2 salida *f.* 3 apertura *f.* *adj* 1 primero. 2 de apertura. **open-minded** *adj* 1 imparcial. 2 receptivo. 3 sin decidir. **open-mouthed** *adj* boquiabierto.

opera ('ɔprə) *n* ópera *f.* **opera house** *n* teatro de la ópera *m.* **operetta** *n* opereta *f.*

operate ('ɔpəreit) vi operar vt **1** funcionar. **2** hacer funcionar. **operating** adj **1** operante. **2** de explotación. **operating theatre** n quirófano m. **operation** n **1** operación f. **2** funcionamiento m. **3** explotación m. **operator** n **1** maquinista m,f. **2** operador m. **3** telefonista m,f. **4** agente m,f.

opinion (ə'piniən) n opinión f. **opinionated** adj **1** pertinaz. **2** dogmático. **opinion poll** n encuesta f.

opium ('oupiəm) n opio m.

opponent (ə'pounənt) n contrincante m.

opportune (ɔpə'tu:n) adj oportuno.

opportunity (ɔpə'tju:niti) n oportunidad f.

oppose (ə'pouz) vt oponer.

opposite ('ɔpəzit) adj **1** opuesto. **2** de enfrente. adv **1** en frente. **2** frente a frente. prep frente a, enfrente de. n lo contrario neu. **opposition** n **1** oposición f. **2** resistencia f.

oppress (ə'pres) vt **1** oprimir. **2** agobiar. **oppression** n **1** opresión f. **2** agobio m. **oppressive** adj opresivo, agobiante. **oppressor** n opresor m.

opt (ɔpt) vi optar.

optical ('ɔptikəl) adj óptico. **optician** n óptico m

optimism ('ɔptimizəm) n optimismo m. **optimist** n optimista m,f. **optimistic** adj optimista

option ('ɔpʃən) n opción f. **optional** adj opcional.

opulent ('ɔpjulənt) adj opulento. **opulence** n opulencia f

or (ɔ:) conj **1** o. **2** u.

oral ('ɔ:rəl) adj oral.

orange ('ɔrindʒ) n naranja f. adj color naranja. **orange blossom** n azahar m. **orange grove** n naranjal m. **orange tree** n naranjo m.

oration (ə'reiʃən) n oración f. discurso m. **orator** n orador m.

orbit ('ɔ:bit) n órbita f. vt,vi orbitar.

orchard ('ɔ:tʃəd) n huerta f.

orchestra ('ɔ:kistrə) n **1** orquesta f. **2** Th platea f. **orchestral** adj orquestal. **orchestrate** vt orquestar. **orchestration** n orquestación f.

orchid ('ɔ:kid) n orquídea f.

ordain (ɔ:'dein) vt **1** ordenar. **2** disponer.

ordeal (ɔ:'di:l) n **1** prueba f. **2** sufrimiento m.

order ('ɔ:də) n **1** orden m. **2** orden f. **3** comm pedido m. **in order** en regla. **in order that** para que. **in order to** para. ~vt **1** ordenar. **2** mandar. **3** encargar. **4** comm pedir. **orderly** adj **1** ordenado. **2** pacífico. n ordenanza m.

ordinal ('ɔ:dinl) adj,n ordinal m.

ordinary ('ɔ:dənri) adj ordinario.

ore (ɔ:) n mena f. mineral metalífero m.

oregano (ɔri'gɑ:nou) n orégano m.

organ ('ɔ:gən) n órgano m. **organist** n organista m,f. **organic** adj orgánico.

organism ('ɔ:gənizəm) n organismo m.

organize ('ɔ:gənaiz) vt organizar. **organization** n organización f. organismo m. **organizer** n organizador m.

orgasm ('ɔ:gæzəm) n orgasmo m.

orgy ('ɔ:dʒi) n orgía f

Orient ('ɔ:riənt) n Oriente m. **oriental** adj,n oriental m,f.

orientate ('ɔ:rienteit) vt orientar. **orientation** n orientación f.

origin ('ɔridʒin) n origen m. **original** adj,n original m. **originality** n originalidad f. **originate** vt originar.

ornament ('ɔ:nəmənt) n **1** adorno m. **2** ornamento m. vt adornar, ornamentar. **ornamental** adj ornamental.

ornate (ɔ:'neit) adj recargado, ornado.

ornithology (ɔ:ni'θɔlədʒi) n ornitología f. **ornithologist** n ornitólogo m.

orphan ('ɔ:fən) n huérfano m. **orphanage** n orfanato m.

orthodox ('ɔ:θədɔks) adj ortodoxo. **orthodoxy** n ortodoxia f

orthography (ɔ:'θɔgrəfi) n ortografía f.

orthopaedic (ɔ:θə'pi:dik) adj ortopédico. **orthopaedics** n ortopedia f.

oscillate ('ɔsəleit) vi oscilar.

ostensible (ɔ'stensəbəl) adj pretendido.

ostentatious (ɔsten'teiʃəs) adj ostentoso.

osteopath ('ɔstiəpæθ) n osteópata m. **osteopathy** n osteoplastia f.

ostracize ('ɔstrəsaiz) vt condenar al ostracismo.

ostrich ('ɔstritʃ) n avestruz m.

other ('ʌðə) adj otro. pron **1** el otro m. **2** los demás m pl. las demás f pl. **otherwise** adv **1** de otro modo. **2** por lo demás.

otter ('ɔtə) n nutria f.

ought (ɔ:t) v aux deber.

ounce (auns) n **1** onza f. **2** pizca f.

our (auə) poss adj 1st pers pl nuestro, nuestra, nuestros, nuestras. **ours** poss pron 1st pers pl el nuestro, la nuestra, los nuestros, las nuestras. **ourselves** pron 1st pers pl **1** nosotros mismos m pl. **2** nos.

oust (aust) vt desalojar, echar.

out (aut) adv fuera, a fuera, hacia fuera. **out**

of 1 fuera de. **2** entre, de entre. **3** de. **4** por. **5** sin.

outboard ('autbɔːd) *adj* fuera de borda.

outbreak ('autbreik) *n* **1** estallido *m*. erupción *f*. **3** epidemia *f*. **4** ola *f*.

outburst ('autbɜːst) *n* **1** explosión *f*. **2** arranque *m*.

outcast ('autkɑːst) *n* paria *m,f*.

outcome ('autkʌm) *n* resultado *m*.

outcry ('autkrai) *n* clamor *m*. protesta vehemente *f*.

outdo* (aut'duː) *vt* exceder, eclipsar.

outdoor ('autdɔː) *adj* al aire libre, exterior. **outdoors** *adv also* **out-of-doors 1** fuera de casa. **2** al aire libre.

outer ('autə) *adj* exterior, externo.

outfit ('autfit) *n* **1** equipo *m*. **2** conjunto *m*.

outgoing ('autgouiŋ) *adj* saliente.

outgrow* (aut'grou) *vt* **1** crecer más que. **2** hacerse demasiado mayor para. **3** superar.

outhouse ('authaus) *n* dependencia *f*. cobertizo *m*.

outing ('autiŋ) *n* excursión, salida *f*. paseo *m*.

outlandish (aut'lændiʃ) *adj* disparatado, extravagante.

outlaw ('autlɔː) *vt* proscribir. *n* **1** proscrito *m*. **2** forajido *m*.

outlay ('autlei) *n* desembolso *m*. inversión *f*.

outlet ('autlet) *n* salida *f*.

outline ('autlain) *n* **1** contorno *m*. **2** esbozo *m*. **in outline** a grandes rasgos. ~*vt* **1** perfilar. **2** esbozar.

outlive (aut'liv) *vt* **1** sobrevivir a. **2** durar más que.

outlook ('autluk) *n* **1** perspectiva *f*. **2** actitud *f*. **3** punto de vista *m*.

outlying ('autlaiiŋ) *adj* **1** lejano, remoto. **2** exterior.

outnumber (aut'nʌmbə) *vt* exceder en número.

outpatient ('autpeiʃənt) *n med* paciente externo *m,f*.

outpost ('autpoust) *n* avanzada *f*.

output ('autput) *n* **1** producción *f*. **2** *tech* rendimiento *m*.

outrage (aut'reidʒ) *n* **1** atrocidad *f*. **2** ultraje, atropello *m*. *vt* ultrajar, atropellar. **outrageous** *adj* **1** inaudito. **2** escandaloso.

outright ('autrait) *adj* **1** completo. **2** cabal, acabado. *adv* **1** de un golpe. **2** de plano.

outside (aut'said) *adv* fuera. *prep* fuera de. *adj* **1** exterior. **2** extremo. *n* exterior *m*. **at the outside** a lo sumo. **outsider** *n* **1** desconocido *m*. **2** independiente *m,f*.

outsize ('autsaiz) *adj* de tamaño fuera de serie.

outskirts ('autskɜːts) *n pl* afueras *f pl*.

outspoken (aut'spoukən) *adj* franco, abierto.

outstanding (aut'stændiŋ) *adj* **1** destacado. **2** *comm* pendiente.

outstrip (aut'strip) *vt* dejar atrás, aventajar.

outward ('autwəd) *adj* exterior, externo. **outwards** *adv* hacia fuera.

outweigh (aut'wei) *vt* pesar más que.

outwit (aut'wit) *vt* **1** ser más listo que. **2** burlar.

outworn (aut'wɔːn) *adj* gastado.

oval ('ouvəl) *adj* ovalado. *n* óvalo *m*.

ovary ('ouvəri) *n* ovario *m*.

ovation (ou'veiʃən) *n* ovación *f*.

oven ('ʌvən) *n* horno *m*.

over ('ouvə) *adv* **1** encima, por encima. **2** al otro lado. **3** al revés, patas arriba. **4** demasiado. **be over** estar terminado. **over and over again** repetidas veces. ~*prep* **1** por encima de, sobre. **2** al otro lado de. **3** más allá de. **4** a través de.

overall I ('ouvərɔːl) *adj* de conjunto. **overalls** *n pl* bata *f*.

overbalance (ouvə'bæləns) *vt* hacer perder el equilibrio.

overboard ('ouvəbɔːd) *adv* por la borda.

overcast ('ouvəkɑːst) *adj* encapotado.

overcharge (ouvə'tʃɑːdʒ) *vt* **1** sobrecargar. **2** *comm* cobrar más de la cuenta.

overcoat ('ouvəkout) *n* abrigo *m*.

overcome* (ouvə'kʌm) *vt* vencer, superar.

overdo* (ouvə'duː) *vt* **1** excederse. **2** exagerar. **overdone** *adj* **1** exagerado. **2** *cul* muy hecho, pasado.

overdose ('ouvədous) *n* dosis excesiva *f*.

overdraft ('ouvədrɑːft) *n* **1** giro en descubierto *m*. **2** saldo deudor *m*. **3** préstamo bancario *m*.

overdraw* (ouvə'drɔː) *vt* girar en descubierto.

overdue (ouvə'djuː) *adj* **1** atrasado. **2** *comm* vencido y por pagar.

overestimate (*v* ouvər'estimeit; *n* ouvər'estimit) *vt* sobreestimar. *n* **1** sobreestimación *f*. **2** *comm* presupuesto excesivo *m*.

overfill (ouvə'fil) *vt* hacer rebosar.

overflow (*v* ouvə'flou; *n* 'ouvəflou) *vi* **1** rebosar. **2** desbordarse. *n* **1** desbordamiento *m*. **2** desagüe *m*. **overflowing** *adj* rebosante.

overhang* (ouvə'hæŋ) *vi* sobresalir. *vt* colgar sobre.

overhaul (ouvə'hɔːl) *vt* revisar, repasar. *n* revisión *f*. repaso general *m*.

overhead (*adv* ouvə'hed; *adj,n* 'ouvəhed) *adv*

243

por arriba, por lo alto. *adj* **1** de arriba. **2** aéreo. **3** suspendido. *n pl* gastos generales *m pl*.

overhear* (ouvə'hiə) *vt* oír por casualidad.

overheat (ouvə'hi:t) *vt* recalentar.

overjoyed (ouvə'dʒɔid) *adj* lleno de alegría.

overland (*adv* ouvə'lænd; *adj* 'ouvəlænd) *adv, adj* por vía terrestre.

overlap (*v* ouvə'læp; *n* 'ouvəlæp) *vt* traslapar, coincidir en parte, cubrir en parte. *n* traslapo *m*. coincidencia parcial *f*.

overlay* (*v* ouvə'lei; *n* 'ouvəlei) *vt* **1** cubrir con. **2** incrustar. *n* **1** capa *f*. **2** cobertura *f*. **3** incrustación *f*.

overleaf (ouvə'li:f) *adv* al dorso.

overload (*v* ouvə'loud; *n* 'ouvəloud) *vt* sobrecargar. *n* sobrecarga *f*.

overlook (ouvə'luk) *vt* **1** dominar. **2** dar a. **3** vigilar. **4** pasar por alto.

overnight (*adv* ouvə'nait; *adj* 'ouvənait) *adv* **1** durante la noche. **2** de la noche a la mañana. *adj* de (una) noche.

overpower (ouvə'pauə) *vt* **1** vencer. **2** dominar. **overpowering** *adj* abrumador, arrollador.

overrate (ouvə'reit) *vt* exagerar el valor de.

overreach (ouvə'ri:tʃ) *vt* **overreach oneself 1** excederse. **2** pasarse de listo.

overrule (ouvə'ru:l) *vt* **1** anular. **2** denegar.

overrun (ouvə'rʌn) *vt* **1** arrollar. **2** infestar, invadir. **3** rebasar.

overseas (ouvə'si:z) *adv* en ultramar, allende el mar. *adj* de ultramar, extranjero.

overshadow (ouvə'ʃædou) *vt* **1** sombrear. **2** hacer sombra. **3** eclipsar.

overshoot* (ouvə'ʃu:t) *vt* **1** sobrepasar. **2** pasar de largo.

oversight ('ouvəsait) *n* **1** descuido *m*. **2** equivocación *f*.

oversleep* (ouvə'sli:p) *vi* dormir más de la cuenta.

overspill ('ouvəspil) *n* exceso *m*.

overt ('ouvə:t) *adj* **1** abierto. **2** patente.

overtake* (ouvə'teik) *vt* **1** alcanzar. **2** mot adelantar.

overthrow* (*v* ouvə'θrou; *n* 'ouvəθrou) *vt* derrocar. *n* derrocamiento *m*.

overtime ('ouvətaim) *n* horas extraordinarias *f pl*.

overtone ('ouvətoun) *n* **1** sugestión, implicación *f*. **2** *mus* armónico *m*.

overture ('ouvətʃə) *n* **1** *mus* obertura *f*. **2** proposición *f*.

overturn (ouvə'tə:n) *vt, vi* **1** volcar. **2** trastornar. **3** derrocar.

overweight (ouvə'weit) *adj* que excede el peso reglamentario. **be overweight** estar demasiado gordo.

overwhelm (ouvə'welm) *vt* **1** abrumar. **2** aplastar. **3** inundar. **overwhelming** *adj* abrumador, aplastante.

overwork (*v* ouvə'wə:k; *n* 'ouvəwə:k) *vi* trabajar demasiado. *vt* hacer trabajar demasiado. *n* trabajo excesivo *m*.

overwrought (ouvə'rɔ:t) *adj* sobreexcitado.

ovulate ('ɔvjuleit) *vi* ovular. **ovulation** *n* ovulación *f*.

owe (ou) *vt* deber. *vi* estar en deuda. **owing** *adj* debido. **owing to** debido a.

owl (aul) *n* lechuza *f*. mochuelo, búho *m*.

own (oun) *adj* propio. *vt* **1** ser dueño de, poseer. **2** reconocer. **owner** *n* dueño, propietario *m*. **ownership** *n* propiedad *f*.

ox (ɔks) *n*, *pl* **oxen** buey *m*. **oxtail** *n* cola de buey *f*.

oxygen ('ɔksidʒən) *n* oxígeno *m*. **oxygenate** *vt* oxigenar.

oyster ('ɔistə) *n* ostra *f*.

P

pace (peis) *n* **1** paso *m*. **2** ritmo *m*. **keep pace with** mantenerse a la par con. *vi* pasearse. *vt* medir a pasos.

Pacific (pə'sifik) *n* (Océano) Pacífico *m*.

pacify ('pæsifai) *vt* **1** apaciguar. **2** pacificar. **pacifism** *n* pacifismo *m*. **pacifist** *n* pacifista *m, f*.

pack (pæk) *n* **1** fardo *m*. **2** paquete *m*. **3** manada *f*. **4** baraja *f*. *vt* **1** empaquetar. **2** envasar. **3** llenar. **4** atestar. *vi* hacer las maletas. **package** *n* **1** paquete, bulto *m*. **2** embalaje *m*. **packet** *n* paquete *m*.

pact (pækt) *n* pacto *m*.

pad¹ (pæd) *n* **1** almohadilla *f*. **2** bloc (of paper) *m*. *vt* **1** almohadillar. **2** rellenar. **padding** *n* relleno *m*.

pad² (pæd) *vi* pisar sin hacer ruido.

paddle¹ ('pædl) *n* paleta *f*. remo *m*. *vt* remar.

paddle² ('pædl) *vi* chapotear.

padlock ('pædlɔk) *n* candado *m*. *vt* cerrar con candado.

paediatric (pi:di'ætrik) *adj* pediátrico. **paediatrician** *n* pediatra *m, f*. **paediatrics** *n* pediatría *f*.

pagan ('peigən) *adj, n* pagano *m*.

page[1] (peidʒ) n 1 página f. 2 plana f. vt paginar.

page[2] (peidʒ) n paje m.

pageant ('pædʒənt) n 1 espectáculo brillante m. 2 desfile m. **pageantry** n pompa f.

paid (peid) v see **pay.**

pain (pein) n 1 dolor m. 2 pl esfuerzos m pl. cuidados m pl. vt 1 doler. 2 dar lástima a. **painful** adj 1 doloroso. 2 penoso. **painstaking** adj esmerado, cuidadoso.

paint (peint) n pintura f. vt,vi pintar. **paintbrush** n 1 pincel m. 2 brocha f. **painter** n pintor m. **painting** n pintura f.

pair (pɛə) n 1 par m. 2 pareja f. vt emparejar.

pal (pæl) n compañero, amigo m.

palace ('pælis) n palacio m.

palate ('pælət) n paladar m. **palatable** adj 1 apetitoso. 2 aceptable.

pale (peil) adj pálido. vi palidecer. **paleness** n palidez f.

palette ('pælit) n paleta f. **palette knife** n espátula f.

pall (pɔːl) vi 1 perder su sabor. 2 empalagar.

palm[1] (pɑːm) n anat palma f. **palmistry** n quiromancia f.

palm[2] (pɑːm) n bot 1 palma f. 2 palmera f. **Palm Sunday** n Domingo de Ramos m.

pamper ('pæmpə) vt 1 mimar. 2 regalar.

pamphlet ('pæmflət) n folleto m.

pan (pæn) n cazuela f. cazo m. **frying pan** sartén f. **pancake** n hojuela, tortita f.

Panama ('pænəmɑː) n Panamá m. **Panamanian** adj,n panameño m.

pancreas ('pæŋkriəs) n páncreas m.

pane (pein) n cristal m.

panel ('pænl) n 1 panel m. 2 jurado m. 3 registro m.

pang (pæŋ) n punzada f.

panic* ('pænik) n pánico m. vi llenarse de pánico. vt aterrar.

panorama (pænə'rɑːmə) n panorama m. **panoramic** adj panorámico.

pansy ('pænzi) n bot pensamiento m.

pant (pænt) vi jadear.

panther ('pænθə) n pantera f.

pantomime ('pæntəmaim) n pantomima f.

pantry ('pæntri) n despensa f.

pants (pænts) n pl calzoncillos m pl. **panties** n pl bragas f pl.

papal ('peipəl) adj papal.

paper ('peipə) n 1 papel m. 2 periódico m. 3 exámen escrito m. 4 artículo m. 5 ponencia f. 6 pl documentación f. vt empapelar. **paper-**
back n libro en rústica m. **paperclip** n sujetapapeles m invar. **paperweight** n pisapapeles m invar.

papier-mâché (pæpiei'mæʃei) n cartón piedra m. pasta f.

paprika ('pæprikə) n pimentón m.

par (pɑː) n par f. **at par** a la par. ~adj nominal.

parable ('pærəbəl) n parábola f.

parachute ('pærəʃuːt) n paracaídas m invar. vi lanzarse en paracaídas.

parade (pə'reid) n 1 desfile m. 2 parada f. 3 alarde m. vi desfilar. vt lucir.

paradise ('pærədais) n paraíso m.

paradox ('pærədɒks) n paradoja f. **paradoxical** adj paradójico.

paraffin ('pærəfin) n 1 petróleo m. 2 (wax) parafina f.

paragraph ('pærəgrɑːf) n párrafo m.

Paraguay ('pærəgwai) n Paraguay m. **Paraguayan** adj,n paraguayo m.

parallel ('pærəlel) adj,n paralelo m. vt ser paralelo a. **parallelism** n paralelismo m.

paralyse ('pærəlaiz) vt paralizar. **paralysis** n,pl **paralyses** parálisis f. **paralytic** adj,n paralítico m.

paramount ('pærəmaunt) adj supremo, primordial.

paranoia (pærə'nɔiə) n paranoia f.

parapet ('pærəpit) n parapeto m.

paraphernalia (pærəfə'neiliə) n.inf avíos m pl.

paraphrase ('pærəfreiz) n paráfrasis f. vt parafrasear.

parasite ('pærəsait) n parásito m. **parasitic** adj parasítico.

parcel ('pɑːsəl) n 1 paquete m. 2 parcela f. vt parcelar, dividir.

parch (pɑːtʃ) vt resecar.

parchment ('pɑːtʃmənt) n pergamino m.

pardon ('pɑːdən) n 1 perdón m. 2 law indulto m. **I beg your pardon** Vd perdone. **I beg your pardon?** ¿cómo? ~vt 1 perdonar. 2 law indultar.

pare (pɛə) vt 1 cortar. 2 mondar.

parent ('pɛərənt) n 1 padre m. 2 madre f. 3 pl padres m pl. adj madre, matriz. **parentage** n 1 familia f. linaje m. 2 nacimiento m. **parental** adj 1 de los padres. 2 paternal. 3 maternal.

parenthesis (pə'renθəsis) n, pl **parentheses** paréntesis m.

parish ('pæriʃ) n parroquia f. adj parroquial. **parishioner** n feligrés m.

parity ('pæriti) n paridad f.

park (pɑːk) n parque m. **car park** aparcamiento, parking m. ~vt 1 estacionar. 2 aparcar. vi estacionarse. **parking** n estacionamiento, aparcamiento m. **parking meter** n parquímetro m.

parliament ('pɑ:ləmənt) n parlamento m. **parliamentarian** n parlamentario m. **parliamentary** adj parlamentario.

parlour ('pɑ:lə) n 1 salón m. 2 locutorio m.

parochial (pə'roukiəl) adj 1 parroquial. 2 de miras estrechas, limitado.

parody ('pærədi) n parodia f. vt parodiar.

parole (pə'roul) n 1 palabra de honor f. 2 law libertad bajo palabra f. vt poner en libertad bajo palabra.

parquet ('pɑ:kei) n entarimado, parquet m.

parrot ('pærət) n loro, papagayo m.

parsley ('pɑ:sli) n perejil m.

parsnip ('pɑ:snip) n chirivía f.

parson ('pɑ:sən) n 1 cura m. 2 párroco m. **parsonage** n casa parroquial f.

part (pɑ:t) n 1 parte f. 2 tech pieza f. 3 Th papel m. vt 1 separar. 2 dividir, partir. **part from** despedirse. **part with** 1 ceder. 2 desprenderse de. ~adj parcial. adv en parte. **parting** n 1 separación f. 2 despedida f. 3 (of hair) raya f. **part-time** adj,adv por horas.

partake* (pɑ:'teik) vi 1 participar en. 2 aceptar.

partial ('pɑ:ʃəl) adj parcial. **be partial to** sentir inclinación por. **partiality** n 1 parcialidad f. 2 inclinación f

participate (pɑ:'tisipeit) vi participar. **participant** n partícipe m,f. **participation** n participación f

participle ('pɑ:tisəpəl) n participio m.

particle ('pɑ:tikəl) n 1 partícula f. 2 pizca f.

particular (pə'tikjulə) adj 1 particular. 2 exigente. n pl informe detallado m.

partisan (pɑ:ti'zæn) n 1 partidario m. 2 partisano, guerrillero m. adj 1 partidista. 2 de partisanos.

partition (pɑ:'tiʃən) n 1 partición f. 2 tabique m. vt repartir, dividir.

partner ('pɑ:tnə) n 1 comm socio m. 2 pareja f. 3 compañero m. vt acompañar. **partnership** n 1 comm sociedad f. 2 asociación f.

partridge ('pɑ:tridʒ) n perdiz f.

party ('pɑ:ti) n 1 partido m. 2 partida f. 3 reunión f. 4 fiesta f. 5 law parte f. **be a party to** 1 subscribir a. 2 ser cómplice de.

pass (pɑ:s) vt 1 pasar. 2 cruzarse con. 3 aprobar. n 1 pase m. 2 aprobado m. 3 educ paso m. 4 geog puerto m. 5 inf requiebro m.

passage ('pæsidʒ) n 1 paso m. 2 pasaje m. 3 pasillo m.

passenger ('pæsindʒə) n pasajero m.

passion ('pæʃən) n pasión f. **passionate** adj apasionado.

passive ('pæsiv) adj pasivo. **passivity** n pasividad f.

passport ('pɑ:spɔ:t) n pasaporte m.

past (pɑ:st) adj pasado. n 1 pasado m. 2 historia f. adv por delante. prep 1 más allá de. 2 más de. 3 por delante de.

pasta ('pæstə) n macarrones, fideos m pl.

paste (peist) n 1 pasta f. 2 engrudo m. vt 1 pegar. 2 empastar.

pastel ('pæstəl) adj,n pastel m.

pasteurize ('pæstəraiz) vt pasteurizar.

pastime ('pɑ:staim) n pasatiempo m.

pastoral ('pæstərəl) adj,n pastoral f.

pastry ('peistri) n 1 pasta f. 2 repostería f.

pasture ('pɑ:stʃə) n pasto m.

pasty[1] ('peisti) adj pastoso.

pasty[2] ('pæsti) n empanada f.

pat[1] (pæt) vt 1 dar una palmadita a. 2 pasar la mano por. n 1 palmadita, palmada f. 2 golpecito m.

pat[2] (pæt) adj oportuno, justo. adv al dedillo.

patch (pætʃ) n 1 remiendo m. 2 parche m. 3 retazo m. vt 1 remendar. 2 componer. **patchwork** n labor de retazos m. **patchy** adj 1 desigual. 2 manchado.

pate (peit) n inf mollera f

patent ('peitnt) adj 1 patente. 2 comm patentado, de patente. n patente f. vt patentar. **patent leather** n charol m.

paternal (pə'tə:nl) adj 1 paternal. 2 paterno. **paternity** n paternidad f.

path (pɑ:θ) n 1 senda f. 2 camino m. 3 trayectoria f. 4 pista f

pathetic (pə'θetik) adj 1 patético, conmovedor. 2 que da pena.

pathology (pə'θɔlədʒi) n patología f. **pathological** adj patológico. **pathologist** n patólogo m.

patience ('peiʃəns) n paciencia f. **patient** adj,n paciente.

patio ('pætiou) n patio m.

patrician (pə'triʃən) adj,n patricio m.

patriot ('peitriət) n patriota m,f. **patriotic** adj patriótico. **patriotism** n patriotismo m.

patrol (pə'troul) n patrulla f. vt,vi patrullar.

patron ('peitrən) n 1 comm parroquiano m. 2 patrono m. 3 patrón m. **patronage** n 1 patrocinio m. 2 patronazgo m. **patronize** vt 1 patrocinar. **2** tratar con aire condescendiente. **patronizing** adj condescendiente.

patter[1] ('pætə) vi andar con pasos ligeros. n pasos ligeros m pl.

patter[2] ('pætə) n **1** jerga f. **2** parloteo m.

pattern ('pætən) n **1** modelo m. **2** muestra f. **3** (for clothes) patrón m. **4** diseño m. vt modelar.

paunch (pɔ:ntʃ) n panza, barriga f. **paunchy** adj panzudo.

pauper ('pɔ:pə) n pobre m,f.

pause (pɔ:z) n pausa f. vi hacer una pausa.

pave (peiv) vt pavimentar. **pavement** n **1** acera f. **2** pavimento m.

pavilion (pə'viliən) n pabellón m.

paw (pɔ:) n **1** pata f. **2** garra f. vt **1** dar zarpazos a. **2** piafar.

pawn[1] (pɔ:n) n prenda f. vt empeñar, dejar en prenda. **pawnbroker** n prestamista m.

pawn[2] (pɔ:n) n game peón m.

pay* (pei) vt **1** pagar. **2** salir a cuenta. **3** prestar (attention). n paga f. **payroll** n nómina f.

pea (pi:) n guisante m.

peace (pi:s) n **1** paz f. **2** tranquilidad f. **make peace** hacer las paces. **peaceful** adj **1** tranquilo. **2** pacífico.

peach (pi:tʃ) n melocotón m.

peacock ('pi:kɔk) n pavo real m.

peak (pi:k) n **1** pico m. **2** cumbre f. **3** punta f. **4** visera f.

peal (pi:l) n repiqueteo m. vt,vi repicar.

peanut ('pi:nʌt) n cacahuete m.

pear (pɛə) n pera f.

pearl ('pə:l) n perla f.

peasant ('pezənt) n,adj campesino m.

peat (pi:t) n turba f.

pebble ('pebəl) n guijarro m.

peck (pek) n picotazo m. vt picotear.

peculiar (pi'kju:liə) adj peculiar. **peculiarity** n peculiaridad f.

pedal ('pedl) n pedal m. vt,vi pedalear.

peddle ('pedl) vt andar vendiendo. **pedlar** n vendedor ambulante m.

pedestal ('pedistəl) n pedestal m.

pedestrian (pi'destriən) n peatón m. adj pedestre.

pedigree ('pedigri:) n árbol genealógico m. adj de raza.

peel (pi:l) n piel f. vt pelar.

peep (pi:p) vi **1** atisbar, espiar. **2** asomar. n atisbo m. mirada furtiva f. **peephole** m mirilla f.

peer[1] (piə) n par m. **peerage** n **1** dignidad de par f. **2** nobleza f.

peer[2] (piə) vi **1** escudriñar. **2** asomar.

peevish ('pi:viʃ) adj malhumorado, enojadizo.

peg (peg) n **1** colgador m. **2** pinza f. **3** clavija f. **4** estaca f. vt fijar con estacas.

pejorative (pi'dʒɔrətiv) adj peyorativo.

pelican ('pelikən) n pelícano m.

pellet ('pelit) n **1** bolita f. **2** perdigón m.

pelt[1] (pelt) vt **1** arrojar. **2** apedrear.

pelt[2] (pelt) n pellejo m.

pelvis ('peivis) n pelvis m.

pen[1] (pen) n pluma f. **fountain pen** n estilográfica f. vt escribir, redactar. **penknife** n cortaplumas m invar. **pen-nib** n **1** plumilla f. **2** plumín m.

pen[2] (pen) n corral, redil m. vt acorralar.

penal ('pi:nl) adj **1** penal. **2** gravoso. **penalize** vt penalizar. **penalty** n **1** pena f. castigo m. **2** sport penalty m.

penance ('penəns) n penitencia f.

pencil ('pensəl) n lápiz m.

pendant ('pendənt) n medallón, pendiente m.

pending ('pendiŋ) adj pendiente. prep **1** durante. **2** hasta.

pendulum ('pendjuləm) n péndulo m.

penetrate ('penitreit) vt penetrar. **penetration** n penetración f.

penguin ('peŋgwin) n pingüino m.

penicillin (peni'silin) n penicilina f.

peninsula (pə'ninsjulə) n península f. **peninsular** adj peninsular.

penis ('pi:nis) n pene m.

penitent ('penitənt) adj,n penitente.

pennant ('penənt) n gallardete m.

penny ('peni) n, pl **pence** penique m. **penniless** adj sin un céntimo.

pension ('penʃən) n pensión f. vt pensionar. **pension off** jubilar.

pensive ('pensiv) adj pensativo, meditabundo.

pent (pent) adj **pent-up 1** reprimido. **2** encerrado.

Pentecost ('pentikɔst) n Pentecostés m invar.

penthouse ('penthaus) n ático m.

people ('pi:pəl) n **1** gente f. **2** pueblo m. vt poblar.

pepper ('pepə) n **1** pimienta f. **2** pimiento m. vt **1** sazonar con pimienta. **2** salpicar. **peppercorn** n grano de pimienta m. **peppermill** n molinillo de pimienta m. **peppermint** n **1** menta f. **2** pastilla de menta f.

per (pə:) prep por. **per annum** al año.

perceive (pə'si:v) vt 1 percibir, notar. 2 apercibirse de.

per cent (pə 'sent) adv por ciento.

percentage (pə'sentidʒ) n porcentaje m.

perception (pə'sepʃən) n 1 percepción f. 2 perspicacia f. **perceptible** adj perceptible. **perceptive** adj 1 perspicaz, agudo. 2 perceptivo.

perch (pə:tʃ) vi 1 posarse. 2 encaramarse. n 1 percha f. 2 posición elevada f.

percolate ('pə:kəleit) vi filtrarse. **percolator** n cafetera de filtro f.

percussion (pə'kʌʃən) n percusión f.

perennial (pə'reniəl) adj perenne. n planta perenne f.

perfect (adj,n 'pə:fikt; v pə'fekt) adj,n perfecto m. vt perfeccionar. **perfection** n perfección f. **perfectionist** n perfeccionista m,f.

perforate ('pə:fəreit) vt perforar. **perforation** n perforación f.

perform (pə'fɔ:m) vt 1 realizar, cumplir. 2 desempeñar. 3 ejecutar. 4 Th representar. vi 1 actuar. 2 tech funcionar. **performance** n 1 ejecución f. 2 desempeño m. 3 representación f. 4 actuación f. 5 tech rendimiento m. **performer** n 1 actor m. 2 mus intérprete m,f.

perfume (n 'pə:fju:m; v pə'fju:m) n perfume m. vt perfumar.

perhaps (pə'hæps) adv tal vez.

peril ('perəl) n peligro m.

perimeter (pə'rimitə) n perímetro m.

period ('piəriəd) n período m. adj de época. **periodic** adj periódico. **periodical** adj periódico. n publicación periódica, revista f.

peripheral (pə'rifərəl) adj periférico. **periphery** n periferia f.

periscope ('periskoup) n periscopio m.

perish ('periʃ) vi perecer. **perishable** adj 1 perecedero. 2 corruptible.

perjure ('pə:dʒə) vt perjurar. **perjurer** n perjuro m. **perjury** n perjurio m.

perk (pə:k) vi **perk up** 1 erguir la cabeza. 2 reanimarse, cobrar ánimo. **perky** adj 1 despabilado. 2 alegre.

permanent ('pə:mənənt) adj permanente. **permanence** n permanencia f.

permeate ('pə:mieit) vt 1 penetrar. 2 impregnar. **permeability** n permeabilidad f. **permeable** adj permeable.

permit (v pə'mit; n 'pə:mit) vt permitir. n permiso m. licencia f. **permission** n permiso m. **permissible** adj permisible. **permissive** adj permisivo.

permutation (pə:mju'teiʃən) n permutación f.

peroxide (pə'rɔksaid) n peróxido m.

perpendicular (pə:pən'dikjulə) adj,n perpendicular f.

perpetual (pə'petʃuəl) adj perpetuo.

perpetuate (pə'petʃueit) vt perpetuar. **perpetuation** n perpetuación f. **perpetuity** n perpetuidad f.

perplex (pə'pleks) vt dejar perplejo, confundir. **perplexed** adj perplejo. **perplexing** adj desconcertante. **perplexity** n perplejidad f.

persecute ('pə:sikju:t) vt 1 perseguir. 2 importunar. **persecution** n persecución f. **persecutor** n perseguidor m.

persevere (pə:si'viə) vi perseverar. **perseverance** n perseverancia f. **persevering** adj perseverante.

persist (pə'sist) vi 1 persistir. 2 empeñarse. **persistence** n persistencia f. **persistent** adj persistente.

person ('pə:sən) n persona f. **personable** adj bien parecido. **personal** adj personal. **personality** n personalidad f.

personify (pə'sɔnifai) vt personificar. **personification** n personificación f.

personnel (pə:sə'nel) n personal m.

perspective (pə'spektiv) n perspectiva f.

perspire (pə'spaiə) vi transpirar, sudar. **perspiration** n sudor m.

persuade (pə'sweid) vt persuadir. **persuasion** n persuasión f. **persuasive** adj persuasivo.

pert (pə:t) adj 1 vivaracho. 2 descarado, fresco.

pertain (pə'tein) vi atañer.

pertinent ('pə:tinənt) adj pertinente. **pertinence** n pertinencia f.

perturb (pə'tə:b) vt perturbar. **perturbation** n perturbación f.

Peru (pə'ru:) n Perú m. **Peruvian** adj,n peruano.

pervade (pə'veid) vt 1 extenderse por. 2 impregnar. **pervasive** adj penetrante.

perverse (pə'və:s) adj 1 perverso. 2 contumaz. 3 díscolo. **perversion** n perversión f. **perversity** n 1 perversidad f. 2 contumacia f.

pervert ('pə:və:t) n pervertido m. vt pervertir.

pessimism ('pesimizəm) n pesimismo m. **pessimist** n pesimista m,f. **pessimistic** adj pesimista.

pest (pest) n 1 plaga f. 2 parásito m. **pesticide** n pesticida m.

pester ('pestə) vt importunar, molestar.

pet [1] (pet) n 1 animal domesticado m. 2 favorito m. 3 inf encanto m. adj 1 domesticado. 2 favorito. 3 (of a name) cariñoso. vt acariciar.

pet [2] (pet) n malhumor m.

petal ('petl) n pétalo m.

peter out ('pi:tə) vi **1** agotarse. **2** desvanecerse.

petition (pi'tiʃən) n petición f. vt dirigir una instancia, solicitar.

petrify ('petrifai) vt petrificar.

petrol ('petrəl) n gasolina f. **petrol pump** n **1** surtidor de gasolina m. **2** tech bomba de gasolina f.

petroleum (pi'trouliəm) n petróleo m.

petticoat ('petikout) n enaguas f pl.

petty ('peti) adj **1** insignificante, nimio. **2** quisquilloso, intransigente. **petty cash** n dinero para gastos menores m.

petulant ('petjulənt) adj irritable, malhumorado. **petulance** n mal humor m.

pew (pju:) n banco de iglesia m.

pewter ('pju:tə) n peltre m. adj de peltre.

phantom ('fæntəm) n fantasma m. adj fantasmal.

pharmacy ('fa:məsi) n farmacia f. **pharmaceutical** adj farmacéutico. **pharmacist** n farmacéutico m.

pharynx ('færiŋks) n faringe f.

phase (feiz) n fase f. vt organizar por etapas.

pheasant ('fezənt) n faisán m.

phenomenon (fi'nɔminən) n, pl **phenomena** fenómeno m. **phenomenal** adj fenomenal.

philanthropy (fi'lænθrəpi) n filantropía f. **philanthropic** adj filantrópico. **philanthropist** n filántropo m.

philately (fi'lætəli) n filatelia f.

Philippines ('filipi:nz) n pl Islas Filipinas f pl.

Philistine ('filistain) adj,n filisteo m.

philosophy (fi'lɔsəfi) n filosofía f. **philosopher** n filósofo m. **philosophical** adj filosófico.

phlegm (flem) n flema f. **phlegmatic** adj flemático.

phobia ('foubiə) n fobia f.

phone (foun) n inf teléfono m. vt,vi telefonear.

phonetic (fə'netik) adj fonético.

phoney ('founi) adj inf **1** falso. **2** postizo.

phosphate ('fɔsfeit) n fosfato m.

phosphorescence (fɔsfə'resəns) n fosforescencia f.

phosphorus ('fɔsfərəs) n fósforo m. **phosphorous** adj fosforoso.

photo ('foutou) n foto f.

photocopy ('foutoukɔpi) n fotocopia f. vt fotocopiar.

photogenic (foutə'dʒenik) adj fotogénico.

photograph ('foutəgra:f) n fotografía f. vt fotografiar. **photographer** n fotógrafo m.

photographic adj fotográfico. **photography** n fotografía f.

phrase (freiz) n frase f. vt expresar. **phrasebook** n manual de conversación m.

physical ('fizikəl) adj físico.

physician (fi'ziʃən) n médico m.

physics ('fiziks) n física f. **physicist** n físico m.

physiology (fizi'ɔlədʒi) n fisiología f. **physiologist** n fisiólogo m.

physiotherapy (fiziou'θerəpi) n fisioterapia f. **physiotherapist** n fisioterapeuta m,f.

physique (fi'zi:k) n físico m.

piano (pi'ænou) n piano m. **pianist** n pianista m,f.

picador ('pikadɔ:) n picador m.

pick [1] (pik) vt **1** escoger, seleccionar. **2** recoger. **3** coger. n **1** elección f. **2** selección f. **3** lo más selecto, lo mejor neu. **pickpocket** n carterista, ratero m.

pick [2] (pik) n pico m.

picket ('pikit) n **1** piquete m. **2** estaca f. vt,vi hacer guardia.

pickle ('pikəl) n escabeche m. vt escabechar.

picnic* ('piknik) n excursión campestre f. vi **1** ir de picnic. **2** hacer un picnic.

pictorial (pik'tɔ:riəl) adj ilustrado.

picture ('piktʃə) n **1** cuadro m. **2** imagen f. **3** retrato m.

picturesque (piktʃə'resk) adj pintoresco.

pie (pai) n pastel m.

piece (pi:s) n **1** trozo, pedazo m. **2** pieza f. **piece together 1** juntar. **2** atar cabos. **piecemeal** adv a trozos. adj fragmentario. **piecework** n trabajo a destajo m.

pier (piə) n embarcadero m.

pierce (piəs) vt,vi **1** penetrar. **2** atravesar. **3** perforar. **piercing** adj penetrante.

piety ('paiəti) n piedad, devoción f.

pig (pig) n cerdo m. **pig-headed** adj testarudc. **pig-iron** n hierro en lingotes m. **pigskin** n piel de cerdo f. **pigsty** n pocilga f. **pigtail** n coleta f.

pigeon ('pidʒən) n paloma f. **pigeonhole** n casilla f. vt archivar. **pigeon-toed** adj patituerto.

pigment ('pigmənt) n pigmento m.

pike (paik) n zool lucio m.

pilchard ('piltʃəd) n sardina arenque f.

pile [1] (pail) n montón m. pila f. vt amontonar, apilar. **pile-up** n accidente múltiple m.

pile [2] (pail) n arch pilote m. **piledriver** n martinete m.

pile [3] (pail) n pelo, pelillo m.

piles (pailz) *n pl* hemorroides, almorranas *f pl.*

pilfer (´pilfə) *vt,vi* sisar, ratear.

pilgrim (´pilgrim) *n* peregrino *m.* **pilgrimage** *n* peregrinación *f.*

pill (pil) *n* píldora *f.*

pillage (´pilidʒ) *n* pillaje *m. vt* pillar, saquear.

pillar (´pilə) *n* pilar *m.* **pillar-box** *n* buzón *m.*

pillion (´piliən) *n* asiento de atrás *m.*

pillow (´pilou) *n* almohada *f.* **pillowcase** *n* funda de almohada *f.*

pilot (´pailət) *n* piloto *m. vt* pilotar.

pimento (pi´mentou) *n* pimiento *m.*

pimple (´pimpəl) *n* grano *m.*

pin (pin) *n* 1 alfiler *m.* 2 clavija *f.* 3 *tech* perno *m. vt* 1 prender, sujetar. 2 clavar. **pinball** *n* billar automático *m.* **pincushion** *n* acerico *m.* **pin-money** *n* alfileres *m pl.* **pinpoint** *vt* precisar, determinar. **pinstripe** *adj* a rayas, rayado.

pinafore (´pinəfɔ:) *n* delantal *m.*

pincers (´pinsəz) *n pl* tenazas, pinzas *f pl.*

pinch (pintʃ) *n* 1 pellizco *m.* 2 pizca *f.* 3 aprieto *m. vt* 1 pellizcar. 2 apretar. 3 *inf* birlar. *vi* privarse, economizar.

pine[1] (pain) *n* pino *m.* **pinecone** *n* piña *f.* **pinewood** *n* pinar *m.*

pine[2] (pain) *vi* languidecer. **pine for** suspirar por.

pineapple (´painæpəl) *n* ananás *m.*

pinion (´piniən) *n* piñón *m. vt* atar los brazos a.

pink (piŋk) *n bot* clavellina *f. adj* rosa.

pinnacle (´pinəkəl) *n* pináculo *m.*

pint (paint) *n* pinta *f.*

pioneer (paiə´niə) *n* 1 explorador, pionero *m.* 2 zapador *m. vt* iniciar.

pious (´paiəs) *adj* piadoso, devoto.

pip[1] (pip) *n* 1 *game* punto *m.* 2 *mil* estrella *f.*

pip[2] (pip) *n bot* pepita *f.*

pipe (paip) *n* 1 tubo, caño *m.* 2 *mus* cañón *m.* 3 *mus* caramillo *m.* 4 pipa *f. vt* 1 conducir en cañerías. 2 *mus* tocar. **pipeline** *n* tubería, cañería *f.*

piquant (´pi:kənt) *adj* picante.

pirate (´pairət) *n* pirata *m. vt* pillar, robar. **piracy** *n* piratería *f.* **piratical** *adj* pirático.

Pisces (´pisi:z) *n* Piscis.

pistachio (pis´tæʃiou) *n* pistacho *m.*

pistol (´pistəl) *n* pistola *f.* revólver *m.*

piston (´pistən) *n* pistón, émbolo *m.*

pit (pit) *n* 1 hoyo, foso *m.* hoya *f.* 2 mina *f. vt* 1 marcar (con hoyas). 2 oponer (a). **pitfall** *n* escollo *m.* trampa *f.*

pitch[1] (pitʃ) *n* 1 lanzamiento *m.* 2 *sport* campo,

terreno *m.* 3 punto, extremo *m. vt* 1 arrojar, lanzar, tirar. 2 armar (a tent).

pitch[2] (pitʃ) *n* pez, brea *f. vt* embrear.

pith (piθ) *n* 1 *bot* médula *f.* 2 *inf* meollo, jugo *m.* esencia *f.*

pittance (´pitns) *n* miseria, renta miserable *f.*

pity (´piti) *n* 1 compasión, piedad *f.* 2 lástima *f. vt* compadecer, tener lástima a.

pivot (´pivət) *n* 1 pivote *m.* 2 *inf* eje, punto central *m. vt* montar sobre un pivote. *vi* girar.

placard (´plækɑ:d) *n* 1 cartel, letrero *m.* 2 pancarta *f.*

placate (plə´keit) *vt* aplacar.

place (pleis) *n* 1 sitio, lugar *m.* 2 local *m.* 3 puesto, empleo *m.* 4 lugar, puesto *m.* 5 plaza *f.* 6 (table) cubierto *m.* **take place** tener lugar. ~*vt* 1 colocar, poner. 2 acordarse bien de. 3 identificar. **placename** *n* topónimo *m.*

placenta (plə´sentə) *n* placenta *f.*

placid (´plæsid) *adj* plácido.

plagiarize (´pleidʒəraiz) *vt* plagiar. **plagiarism** *n* plagio *m.*

plague (pleig) *n med* peste, plaga *f. vt* 1 plagar, infestar. 2 *inf* acosar, atormentar.

plaice (pleis) *n invar* platija *f.*

plaid (plæd) *n* 1 tela a cuadros *f.* 2 manta escocesa *f.*

plain (plein) *adj* 1 claro, evidente. 2 sencillo, llano, sin adornos. 3 natural, puro. 4 sin atractivo, ordinario. *adv* claro, claramente. *n* llano *m.* llanura *f.* **plainly** *adv* 1 claramente, evidentemente. 2 francamente. **plain-clothes man** *n* policía vestido de paisano *m.* **plain sailing** coser y cantar.

plaintiff (´pleintif) *n* demandante *m,f.*

plaintive (´pleintiv) *adj* dolorido.

plait (plæt) *n* trenza *f. vt* trenzar.

plan (plæn) *n* 1 proyecto, plan *m.* 2 *arch* plano *m.* 3 programa *m. vt* 1 proyectar. 2 planear, planificar. *vi* hacer proyectos. **plan to** proponerse.

plane[1] (plein) *adj* plano. *n* 1 nivel *m.* esfera *f.* 2 avión *m.*

plane[2] (plein) *n* cepillo (de carpintero) *m. vt* acepillar.

planet (´plænit) *n* planeta *m.*

plank (plæŋk) *n* tablón *m.* tabla *f. vt* entablar, entarimar.

plankton (´plæŋktən) *n* plankton *m.*

plant (plɑ:nt) *n* 1 *bot* planta *f.* 2 *tech* instalación, maquinaria *f.* 3 fábrica *f. vt* 1 plantar, sembrar. 2 poner, colocar. **plantation** *n* 1 plantación *f.* 2 hacienda *f.*

plaque (plɑːk) *n* placa *f.*

plasma ('plæzmə) *n* plasma *m.*

plaster ('plɑːstə) *n* 1 yeso *m.* 2 argamasa *f.* 3 *med* parche *m.* escayola *f.* **adhesive plaster** esparadrapo *m.* ~*vt* 1 enyesar, enlucir. 2 *med* emplastar. **plaster cast** *n* vaciado *m.* **plaster of Paris** *n* yeso mate *m.*

plastic ('plæstik) *adj,n* plástico *m.* **plastic surgery** *n* cirugía estética or plástica *f.*

Plasticine ('plæstisiːn) *n Tdmk* plasticina *f*

plate (pleit) *n* 1 plato *m.* 2 placa *f.* 3 lámina, chapa, plancha *f.* 4 *phot* placa *f.* 5 vajilla de plata *f. vt* planchear, chapear. **plate glass** *n* vidrio cilindrado or en planchas *m.*

plateau ('plætou) *n* meseta *f.*

platform ('plætfɔːm) *n* 1 plataforma *f.* 2 andén *m.* **platform ticket** *n* billete de andén *m.*

platinum ('plætnəm) *n* platino *m.*

platonic (plə'tɔnik) *adj* platónico.

plausible ('plɔːzəbl) *adj* verosímil.

play (plei) *n* 1 juego, recreo *m.* 2 obra dramática *f.* **fair play** juego limpio *m.* ~*vt* 1 jugar a or contra. 2 *mus* tocar. 3 representar. *vi* 1 jugar, divertirse. 2 *mus* tocar. **player** *n* 1 actor *m.* actriz *f.* 2 músico *m.* 3 jugador *m.* **playground** *n* patio de recreo *m.* **playhouse** *n* teatro *m.* **playing card** *n* carta *f.* **playing field** *n* campo de deportes *m.* **playmate** *n* compañero de juego *m.* **playschool** *n* guardería *f.* **playwright** *n* dramaturgo *m.*

plea (pliː) *n* 1 pretexto *m.* disculpa *f.* 2 *law* alegato *m.* defensa *f.* 3 contestación a la demanda, declaración *f.*

plead (pliːd) *vi* 1 suplicar, rogar. 2 *law* abogar. 3 declarar. **plead guilty** declararse or confesarse culpable. **plead not guilty** negar la acusación.

please (pliːz) *vt* gustar. *vi* dar satisfacción. **please!** ¡por favor! **pleasing** *adj* grato. **be pleased** estar contento. **be pleased to** complacerse en. **pleasant** *adj* agradable, ameno, simpático. **pleasantry** *n* chiste *m.* agudeza *f.* **pleasure** *n* 1 placer, gusto *m.* 2 voluntad *f.* **with pleasure** con mucho gusto.

pleat (pliːt) *n* pliegue *m. vt* plegar, plisar.

pledge (pledʒ) *n* 1 prenda *f.* 2 promesa *f. vt* 1 empeñar, dejar en prenda. 2 prometer. 3 brindar por.

plenty ('plenti) *adv inf* bastante, muchísimo. *n* abundancia *f.* **plentiful** *adj* abundante, copioso.

pliable ('plaiəbl) *adj* flexible, pegable.

pliers ('plaiəz) *n pl* tenazas *f pl.* alicates *m pl.*

plight (plait) *n* apuro, aprieto *m.* condición inquietante, situación difícil *f.*

plimsoll ('plimsəl) *n* zapatilla de goma *f.*

plod (plɔd) *vi* 1 avanzar laboriosamente, caminar despacio. 2 trabajar laboriosamente.

plonk (plɔŋk) *n* 1 golpe seco *m.* 2 *inf* vino barato *m.*

plot[1] (plɔt) *n* 1 complot *m.* conspiración *f.* 2 *Th* argumento *m.* trama, intriga *f. vt* 1 trazar. 2 tramar, maquinar. *vi* conspirar, intrigar.

plot[2] (plɔt) *n* parcela *f.* terreno *m.*

plough (plau) *n* arado *m. vt* arar.

pluck (plʌk) *n* valor, ánimo *m. vt* 1 coger, arrancar. 2 desplumar. 3 *mus* puntear. **plucky** *adj* valiente, animoso.

plug (plʌg) *n* 1 tapón, taco *m.* 2 *tech* enchufe *m.* 3 *inf* anuncio incidental *m.* publicidad incidental *f. vt* tapar, llenar, obturar. **plug in** enchufar.

plum (plʌm) *n* ciruela *f.* **plum tree** *n* ciruelo *m.*

plumage ('pluːmidʒ) *n* plumaje *m.*

plumb (plʌm) *n* plomada *f. adj* vertical. *vt* sondar, sondear. **plumber** *n* fontanero *m.* **plumbing** *n* fontanería *f.*

plume (pluːm) *n* pluma *f.* **plumed** *adj* plumado.

plump[1] (plʌmp) *adj* rechoncho, rollizo, gordo.

plump[2] (plʌmp) *vi* caer pesadamente.

plunder ('plʌndə) *n* botín, pillaje *m. vt* 1 saquear, pillar. 2 robar. **plunderer** *n* saqueador *m.*

plunge (plʌndʒ) *n* salto *m.* zambullida *f. vt* sumergir, hundir. **plunger** *n* émbolo *m.*

pluperfect (pluː'pəːfikt) *n* pluscuamperfecto *m.*

plural ('pluərəl) *adj,n* plural *m.*

plus (plʌs) *adj* positivo. *n math* 1 signo más *m.* 2 cantidad positiva *f. prep inf* más, y, además de.

plush (plʌʃ) *adj* 1 de felpa. 2 lujoso, de buen tono.

Pluto ('pluːtou) *n* Plutón *m.*

ply[1] (plai) *vt* 1 manejar, menear. 2 ejercer. 3 emplear. **ply between** hacer el servico entre.

ply[2] (plai) *n* 1 cabo (of wool) *m.* 2 capa *f.* **plywood** *n* madera contrachapeada *f.*

pneumatic (njuː'mætik) *adj* neumático. **pneumatic drill** *n* perforadora *f.* martillo picador *m.*

pneumonia (njuː'mouniə) *n* pulmonía *f.*

poach[1] (poutʃ) *vt cul* escalfar.

poach[2] (poutʃ) *vt* 1 cazar en vedado. 2 robar. *vi* cazar en finca ajena.

pocket ('pɔkit) *n* 1 bolsillo *m.* 2 bolsa *f. vt* 1 meter en el bolsillo. 2 ganar. **pocket-knife** *n*

navaja f. **pocket-money** n dinero para pequeños gastos personales m.
pod (pɔd) n vaina f.
poem ('pouim) n poesía f. poema m.
poet ('pouit) n poeta m. **poet laureate** poeta
laureado m. **poetic** adj poético. **poetry** n
poesía f.
poignant ('pɔinjənt) adj 1 conmovedor, patético.
2 intenso, agudo.
point (pɔint) n 1 punto m. 2 punta f. 3 lo
significativo, lo importante neu. 4 fin, objeto
m. 5 utilidad f. **point of view** punto de vista
m. ~vt 1 afilar, aguzar. 2 apuntar. vt,vi
señalar con el dedo, indicar. **pointed** adj 1
puntiagudo. 2 afilado, agudo. 3 lleno de
intención, enfático. **pointless** adj 1 inútil. 2
sin motivo.
poise (pɔiz) n 1 equilibrio m. 2 porte m. 3
confianza en sí mismo f. vt equilibrar. **poised**
adj confiado en sí mismo.
poison ('pɔizən) n veneno m. vt envenenar.
poisonous adj venenoso, tóxico.
poke (pouk) n empuje, empujón, codazo, hur-
gonazo m. vt 1 empujar. 2 hurgar. **poke fun
at** burlarse de. **poky** adj 1 estrecho, muy
pequeño. 2 mezquino.
poker¹ ('poukə) n atizador m. badila f.
poker² ('poukə) n game póquer m.
Poland ('pouland) n Polonia f. **Pole** n polaco
m. **Polish** adj polaco. **Polish** (language) n
polaco m.
polar ('poulə) adj polar. **polar bear** n oso
blanco m. **polarize** vt polarizar.
pole¹ (poul) n 1 palo m. 2 mástil m. 3 poste m.
4 pértiga f. **pole-vault** n salto con pértiga m.
pole² (poul) n polo m. **Pole Star** n estrella
polar f.
polemic (pə'lemik) adj polémico. n polémica f.
police (pə'liːs) n policía f. vt vigilar, patrullar.
policeman n policía, guardia m. **police
station** n comisaria f.
policy¹ ('pɔlisi) n política f.
policy² ('pɔlisi) n (insurance) póliza f.
polish ('pɔliʃ) n 1 lustre, brillo m. 2 betún m. 3
cera de lustrar f. 4 pulimento m. 5 inf finura,
cultura f. vt 1 limpiar. 2 encerar, sacar brillo a.
3 pulir. **polished** adj 1 pulido. 2 limado,
elegante. 3 culto, distinguido.
polite (pə'lait) adj cortés, atento, fino.
politics ('pɔlitiks) n pl política f. **political** adj
político. **politician** n político m.
polka ('pɔlkə) n polca f. **polka dot** n punto,
lunar m.

poll (poul) n 1 votación, elección f. 2 votos m pl.
vt recibir. **polling booth** n cabina de votar
f. **polling station** n colegio electoral m. urnas
electorales f pl.
pollen ('pɔlən) n polen m. **pollinate** vt fecundar. **pollination** n polinización f.
pollute (pə'luːt) vt 1 contaminar. 2 corromper.
pollution n contaminación f.
polygamy (pə'ligəmi) n poligamia f. **polyga-
mist** n polígamo m.
polygon ('pɔligən) n polígono m.
polytechnic (pɔli'teknik) n escuela politécnica
f.
polythene ('pɔliθiːn) n politene m.
pomegranate ('pɔmigrænət) n granada
f. **pomegranate tree** n granado m.
pomp (pɔmp) n pompa f. **pompous** adj pom-
poso.
pond (pɔnd) n 1 charca f. 2 estanque m.
ponder ('pɔndə) vt ponderar. vi reflexionar,
pensar. **ponderous** adj pesado.
pony ('pouni) n caballito m. jaca f.
poodle ('puːdl) n perro de lanas m.
pool¹ (puːl) n 1 charca, balsa f. 2 estanque m. 3
piscina f.
pool² (puːl) n 1 game trucos m pl. 2 mancomunidad f. 3 reserva f. **football pools**
quinielas f pl. ~vt mancomunar.
poor (puə, pɔː) adj 1 pobre. 2 malo. 3 mezquino.
pop¹ (pɔp) n taponazo m. vi estallar, reventar.
popcorn n palomitas, rosetas f pl.
pop² (pɔp) adj popular. **pop music** n música
moderna y popular f.
pope (poup) n papa m.
poplar ('pɔplə) n chopo m.
poppy ('pɔpi) n amapola f.
popular ('pɔpjulə) adj popular. **popularity** n
popularidad f.
population (pɔpju'leiʃən) n población f.
porcelain ('pɔːslin) n porcelana f.
porch (pɔːtʃ) n pórtico m.
porcupine ('pɔːkjupain) n puerco espín m.
pore¹ (pɔː) vi **pore over** estudiar con atención.
pore² (pɔː) n poro m.
pork (pɔːk) n carne de cerdo m.
pornography (pɔː'nɔgrəfi) n pornografía
f. **pornographic** adj pornográfico.
porous ('pɔːrəs) adj poroso.
porpoise ('pɔːpəs) n marsopa f.
porridge ('pɔridʒ) n gachas de avena f pl.
port¹ (pɔːt) n puerto m. **port of call** n puerto
de escala m.

port² (pɔ:t) n naut babor m.

port³ (pɔ:t) n oporto m.

portable ('pɔ:tabal) adj portátil.

porter¹ ('pɔ:tə) n mozo de estación, mozo de equipajes m.

porter² ('pɔ:tə) n portero, conserje m.

portfolio (pɔ:t'fouliou) n cartera, carpeta f. **minister without portfolio** n ministro sin cartera m.

porthole ('pɔ:thoul) n portilla f.

portion ('pɔ:ʃən) n porción, parte f.

portrait ('pɔ:trit) n retrato m.

portray (pɔ:'trei) vt 1 art retratar. 2 describir. **portrayal** n descripción f.

Portugal ('pɔ:tjugəl) n Portugal m. **Portuguese** adj,n portugués m. **Portuguese** (language) n portugués m.

pose (pouz) n 1 postura, actitud f. 2 afectación f. vt 1 colocar. 2 plantear. 3 formular. vi 1 posar. 2 darse tono.

posh (pɔʃ) adj inf elegante, lujoso.

position (pə'ziʃən) n 1 posición f. 2 categoría f. 3 puesto m.

positive ('pɔzitiv) adj 1 positivo. 2 enfático, categórico. 3 enérgico. 4 afirmativo. n phot positiva f. **positively** adv 1 absolutamente. 2 con énfasis.

possess (pə'zes) vt poseer. **possessed** adj poseso. **possession** n 1 posesión f. 2 pl bienes m pl. **take possession of** tomar posesión de. **possessive** adj 1 gram posesivo. 2 dominante. n gram posesivo m.

possible ('pɔsəbəl) adj posible. **possibility** n posibilidad f.

post¹ (poust) n poste m.

post² (poust) n puesto, empleo m. vt 1 apostar, situar. 2 destinar.

post³ (poust) n correo m. **by post** por correo. **by return post** a vuelta de correo. **registered post** correo certificado. ~vt mandar por correos, despachar. **postage** n franqueo, porte m. **postage stamp** n sello de correo m. **postal order** n giro postal m. **postbox** n buzón m. **postcard** n tarjeta postal f. **postman** n cartero m. **postmark** n matasellos m invar. **post office** n (casa de) correos f.

poster ('poustə) n cartel m.

posterior (pɔs'tiəriə) adj posterior. n inf culo m.

posterity (pɔs'teriti) n posteridad f.

postgraduate ('poust'grædjuət) adj,n postgraduado m.

posthumous ('pɔstjuməs) adj póstumo. **posthumously** adv después de la muerte.

post-mortem (poust'mɔ:təm) n autopsia f.

postpone (pəs'poun) vt aplazar. **postponement** n aplazamiento m.

postscript ('pousskript) n posdata f.

postulate (v 'pɔstjuleit; n 'pɔstjulət) vt postular. n postulado m.

posture ('pɔstʃə) n postura f. vi adoptar una actitud.

pot (pɔt) n 1 cul olla, marmita f. puchero m. 2 pote m. 3 tiesto m. **go to pot** echarse a perder, arruinarse. ~vt 1 cul conservar. 2 plantar en tiesto. **pothole** n bache m.

potassium (pə'tæsiəm) n potasio m.

potato (pə'teitou) n, pl **potatoes** patata f.

potent ('poutnt) adj 1 potente. 2 fuerte.

potential (pə'tenʃəl) adj,n potencial m,f.

potion ('pouʃən) n poción f.

potter¹ ('pɔtə) vi hacer bagatelas.

pottery ('pɔtəri) n 1 alfarería f. 2 art cerámica f. 3 cacharros m pl. 4 cerámicas f pl. **potter** n alfarero m.

pouch (pautʃ) n bolsa f.

poultice ('poultis) n cataplasma f. emplasto m.

poultry ('poultri) n aves de corral f pl.

pounce (pauns) n salto m. vi atacar súbitamente. **pounce on** saltar sobre.

pound¹ (paund) vt 1 golpear repetidamente, machacar. vi dar golpes.

pound² (paund) n 1 libra f. 2 libra esterlina f.

pour (pɔ:) vt 1 echar, derramar. 2 servir. vi 1 llover mucho, llover a cántaros. 2 correr a raudales, fluir.

pout (paut) n puchero m. vi hacer pucheros.

poverty ('pɔvəti) n pobreza f. **poverty-stricken** adj menesteroso.

powder ('paudə) n 1 polvo, m. 2 polvos m pl. 3 pólvora f. vt reducir a polvo. **powdery** adj polvoriento. **powder room** n aseos m pl. tocador m.

power ('pauə) n 1 poder m. 2 empuje m. vt accionar, impulsar. **powerful** adj poderoso, potente. **powerless** adj impotente, ineficaz.

practicable ('præktikəbəl) adj factible, practicable.

practical ('præktikəl) adj práctico. **practicality** n factibilidad f.

practice ('præktis) n 1 costumbre, uso m. 2 práctica f. 3 ejercicio m. 4 med clientela f. 5 law bufete m. **be out of practice** haber perdido la costumbre.

practise ('præktis) vt 1 practicar. 2 ejercitar, ejercer. 3 sport entrenarse en. 4 hacer prácticas de. *vi* **1** *mus* tocar, estudiar. **2** *sport* entrenarse. **practised** *adj* experto.

practitioner (præk'tiʃənə) *n* **1** practicante *m,f.* **2** *med* médico *m.* **general practitioner** *n* médico general *m.*

pragmatic (præg'mætik) *adj* pragmático.

prairie ('prɛəri) *n* pradera, llanura *f.*

praise (preiz) *n* alabanza *f.* elogio *m. vt* alabar, elogiar. **praiseworthy** *adj* digno de alabanza *or* elogio.

pram (præm) *n inf* cochecito de niño *m.*

prance (prɑːns) *vi* saltar, hacer cabriolas.

prank (præŋk) *n* broma *f.*

prattle ('prætl) *n* **1** parloteo *m.* **2** balbuceo *m. vi* **1** parlotear. **2** balbucear.

prawn (prɔːn) *n* gamba *f.*

pray (prei) *vt* suplicar. *vi* orar. **prayer** *n* **1** *rel* oración *f.* rezo *m.* **2** ruego *m.* súplica *f.* **say one's prayers** rezar. **prayerbook** *n* misal *m.*

preach (priːtʃ) *vi* predicar. **preacher** *n* predicador *m.*

precarious (pri'kɛəriəs) *adj* precario.

precaution (pri'kɔːʃən) *n* precaución *f.* **precautionary** *adj* de precaución, preventivo.

precede (pri'siːd) *vt,vi* preceder. **preceding** *adj* precedente. **precedence** *n* precedencia *f.* **precedent** *n* precedente *m.* **without precedent** sin precedentes.

precinct ('priːsiŋkt) *n* recinto *m.*

precious ('preʃəs) *adj* **1** precioso. **2** amado, querido. **3** afectado. *adv inf* muy.

precipice ('presipis) *n* precipicio *m.*

precipitate (prə'sipiteit) *vt* **1** precipitar. **2** acelerar. *n sci* precipitado *m.*

precis ('preisi) *n* resumen *m.*

precise (pri'sais) *adj* preciso, exacto. **precisely** *adv* precisamente, con precisión. **precisely!** ¡perfectamente!, ¡eso es! **precision** *n* precisión *f.*

precocious (pri'kouʃəs) *adj* precoz. **precocity** *n* precocidad *f.*

preconceive (priːkən'siːv) *vt* preconcebir. **preconception** *n* preconcepción *f.*

predatory ('predətəri) *adj* rapaz, de rapiña. **predator** *n* predador *m.*

predecessor ('priːdisesə) *n* predecesor *m.*

predestine (priː'destin) *vt* predestinar. **predestination** *n* predestinación *f.*

predicament (pri'dikəmənt) *n* apuro *m.*

predicate (*n* 'predikit; *v* 'predikeit) *n* predicado *m. vt* predicar.

predict (pri'dikt) *vt* pronosticar, predecir. **prediction** *n* pronóstico *m.* predicción *f.*

predominate (pri'dɔmineit) *vi* predominar. **predominant** *adj* predominante. **predominantly** *adv* por la mayor parte.

pre-eminent *adj* preeminente.

preen (priːn) *vt* arreglar con el pico. **preen oneself** *inf* pavonearse. **preen oneself on** jactarse de.

prefabricate (priː'fæbrikeit) *vt* prefabricar.

preface ('prefis) *n* prefacio *m. vt* prologar, introducir.

prefect ('priːfekt) *n* prefecto *m.*

prefer (pri'fəː) *vt* **1** preferir. **2** promover. **prefer a charge against** acusar a. **preferable** *adj* preferible. **preferably** *adv* más bien. **preference** *n* preferencia *f.* **preferential** *adj* preferente.

prefix ('priːfiks) *n* prefijo *m. vt* prefijar.

pregnant ('pregnənt) *adj* embarazada, encinta. **pregnancy** *n* embarazo *m.*

prehistoric (priːhis'tɔrik) *adj* prehistórico.

prejudice ('predʒədis) *n* prejuicio *m.* **have a prejudice against** estar predispuesto contra. **without prejudice to** sin perjuicio de. ~*vt* **1** predisponer. **2** perjudicar. **prejudiced** *adj* **1** parcial, interesado. **2** lleno de prejuicios. **prejudicial** *adj* perjudicial.

preliminary (pri'liminəri) *adj,n* preliminar *m.*

prelude ('preljuːd) *n* preludio *m.*

premarital (priː'mæritl) *adj* premarital.

premature ('premətʃə) *adj* prematuro.

premeditate (priː'mediteit) *vt* premeditar. **premeditation** *n* premeditación *f.*

premier ('premiə) *adj* primero, principal. *n* primer ministro *m.*

premiere ('premiɛə) *n* estreno *m.*

premise ('premis) *n* premisa *f.* **on the premises** en el local.

premium ('priːmiəm) *n* **1** *comm* prima *f.* **2** premio *m.* **be at a premium** tener mucha demanda.

preoccupied (priː'ɔkjupaid) *adj* preocupado. **preoccupation** *n* preocupación *f.*

prepare (pri'pɛə) *vt* preparar. **be prepared to** disponerse a. **preparation** *n.* preparación *f.* **preparations** preparativos *m pl.*

preposition (prepə'ziʃən) *n* preposición *f.*

preposterous (pri'pɔstərəs) *adj* absurdo, prepóstero.

prerogative (pri'rɔgətiv) *n* prerrogativa *f.*

Presbyterian (prezbi'tiəriən) *adj,n* presbiteriano.

prescribe (pri'skraib) *vt,vi* **1** prescribir. **2** *med* recetar. **prescription** n 1 prescripción f. 2 med receta f.

presence ('prezəns) n presencia f. **in the presence of** ante, en presencia de.

present¹ ('prezənt) adj presente, actual. **be present** asistir. ~n 1 presente m. actualidad f. 2 gram tiempo presente m. **at present** actualmente. **for the present** por ahora. **present participle** n participio de presente m.

present² (v pri'zent; n 'prezənt) n regalo, presente m. vt 1 presentar. 2 exponer. **presentable** adj presentable. **presentation** n presentación f. **presently** adv dentro de poco, luego.

preserve (pri'zə:v) n 1 cul conserva, confitura f. 2 coto m. vt 1 conservar. 2 cul hacer una conserva de. **preservation** n conservación, preservación f. **preservative** adj,n preservativo m.

preside (pri'zaid) vi presidir.

president ('prezidənt) n presidente m. **presidency** n presidencia f. **presidential** adj presidencial.

press (pres) n 1 prensa f. 2 imprenta f. 3 presión f. apretón m. 4 apiñamiento m. vt 1 apretar, pulsar. 2 planchar. 3 insistir en. vi 1 apretar, hacer presión. 2 urgir, apremiar. **pressing** adj urgente. **press conference** n conferencia de prensa f. **press-gang** n ronda de enganche f. **press-up** n flexión f.

pressure ('preʃə) n 1 presión f. 2 urgencia f. 3 med tensión nerviosa f. **pressure cooker** n olla a presión f. **pressurize** vt presionar.

prestige (pres'ti:ʒ) n prestigio m.

presume (pri'zju:m) vt,vi presumir, suponer. **presume to** atreverse a. **presumably** adv según cabe presumir. **presumption** n 1 presunción f. 2 atrevimiento m.

pretend (pri'tend) vt 1 fingir. 2 pretender. **pretence** n 1 pretensión f. 2 afectación f. **false pretences** fraude m. **pretension** n 1 pretensión f. 2 afectación f. **pretentious** adj pretencioso, presumido.

pretext ('pri:tekst) n pretexto m.

pretty ('priti) adj 1 bonito, guapo, lindo. 2 considerable. **prettily** adv con gracia.

prevail (pri'veil) vi 1 prevalecer. 2 predominar. **prevail upon** persuadir. **prevailing** adj reinante, imperante, predominante. **prevalent** adj corriente, frecuente, predominante. **prevalence** n uso corriente m. costumbre f.

prevent (pri'vent) vt 1 impedir, estorbar. 2

evitar. **prevention** n prevención f. el impedir m.

preview ('pri:vju:) n 1 pre-estreno m. 2 vista anticipada f.

previous ('pri:viəs) adj previo, anterior. **previous to** antes de.

prey (prei) n presa, víctima f. **bird of prey** ave de rapiña f. **prey on** 1 atacar, alimentarse de, pillar. 2 preocupar, remorder.

price (prais) n precio m. **at any price** a toda costa. **not at any price** de ningún modo. ~vt estimar, valuar, fijar el precio de. **priceless** adj 1 inapreciable. 2 inf divertidísimo.

prick (prik) n pinchazo, alfilerazo m. punzada f. vt pinchar, picar. **prick up one's ears** aguzar el oído. **prickle** n 1 espina, púa f. 2 picazón m. **prickly** adj 1 espinoso, lleno de espinas. 2 malhumorado, difícil.

pride (praid) n orgullo m. **pride oneself on** enorgullecerse de.

priest (pri:st) n sacerdote, cura m. **parish priest** n párroco m. **priesthood** n sacerdocio, clero m. **priestly** adj sacerdotal.

prim (prim) adj 1 remilgado. 2 etiquetero.

primary ('praiməri) adj primario, principal. **primary school** n escuela primaria f.

primate n 1 ('praimit) rel primado m. 2 ('praimeit) zool primate m.

prime (praim) adj 1 primero, principal, fundamental. 2 selecto, de primera clase. n flor f. vt 1 cebar. 2 preparar. **prime minister** n primer ministro m.

primitive ('primitiv) adj 1 primitivo. 2 rudimentario.

primrose ('primrouz) n primavera f.

prince (prins) n príncipe m. **princely** adj principesco, magnífico.

princess (prin'ses) n princesa f.

principal ('prinsəpəl) adj principal, mayor. n 1 principal, jefe m. 2 educ director m.

principality (prinsi'pæliti) n principado m.

principle ('prinsəpəl) n principio m.

print (print) n 1 marca f. 2 tipo m. 3 art estampa f. grabado m. 4 phot positiva f. **be in print** estar impreso. **printer** n impresor m. **printing** n 1 imprenta, tipografía. 2 impresión f. 3 tirada f.

prior ('praiə) adj anterior, previo. adv **prior to** antes de. **priority** n prioridad f.

prise (praiz) vt prise open abrir por fuerza.

prism ('prizəm) n prisma m.

prison ('prizən) n cárcel, prisión f. **prisoner** n detenido, prisionero m.

private ('praivit) *adj* **1** privado, particular. **2** confidencial. **3** íntimo. *n mil* soldado raso *m*. **in private** confidencialmente. **privacy** *n* soledad *f*. retiro, aislamiento *m*.

privet ('privit) *n* ligustro *m*.

privilege ('privilidʒ) *n* privilegio *m*. prerrogativa *f*. **privileged** *adj* privilegiado.

prize[1] (praiz) *n* premio *m*. *adj* premiado.

prize[2] (praiz) *vt* apreciar, estimar.

probable ('probabəl) *adj* probable. **probability** *n* probabilidad *f*.

probation (prə'beiʃən) *n law* libertad condicional *f*.

probe (proub) *n* **1** *med* sonda *f*. **2** *inf* investigación, encuesta *f*. *vt* **1** *med* sondar, tentar. **2** investigar. **probing** *n* **1** sondeo *m*. **2** investigación *f*.

problem ('probləm) *n* problema *m*.

proceed (prə'si:d) *vi* **1** proceder. **2** continuar. **proceed against** procesar. **proceed with** proseguir. **proceeds** *n pl* ganancias *f pl*. **procedure** *n* procedimiento *m*. **proceeding** *n* procedimiento *m*. **proceedings** *n pl* **1** actos *m pl*. **2** medidas *f pl*.

process ('prouses) *n* procedimiento, proceso *m*. *vt* preparar, tratar.

procession (prə'seʃən) *n* **1** desfile *m*. **2** *rel* procesión *f*.

proclaim (prə'kleim) *vt* proclamar. **proclamation** *n* proclamación *f*.

procreate ('proukrieit) *vt* procrear. **procreation** *n* procreación *f*.

procure (prə'kjuə) *vt* **1** obtener, conseguir. **2** lograr. **procurement** *n* obtención *f*.

prod (prod) *n* **1** empuje *m*. **2** codazo *m*. *vt* **1** empujar. **2** codear.

prodigy ('prodidʒi) *n* prodigio *m*. **prodigal** *adj*, *n* pródigo *m*.

produce (*v* prə'dju:s, *n* 'prodju:s) *n* producto. *vt* **1** producir, presentar, mostrar. **2** fabricar. **3** causar. **4** *Th* poner en escena. **producer** *n* **1** productor *m*. **2** *Th* director de escena *m*. **product** *n* **1** producto *m*. **2** resultado *m*. consecuencia *f*. **waste products** desperdicios *n pl*. **production** *n* **1** producción *f*. **2** *Th* presentación *f*. **production line** línea de montaje *f*. **productive** *adj* productivo. **productivity** *n* productividad *f*.

profane (prə'fein) *adj* profano. *vt* profanar. **profanity** *n* **1** profanidad *f*. **2** lenguaje indecente *m*.

profess (prə'fes) *vt* **1** profesar. **2** manifestar. **profession** *n* profesión *f*. **professional** *adj* **1** profesional. **2** experto. *n* profesional *m,f*. **professor** *n* profesor *m*.

proficient (prə'fiʃənt) *adj* perito, hábil. **proficiency** *n* pericia, habilidad *f*.

profile ('proufail) *n* perfil *m*.

profit ('profit) *n comm* ganancia *f*. **gross profit** ganancia bruta *f*. **net profit** ganancia neta *f*. **profit and loss** ganancias y pérdidas *f pl*. ~*vt* servir a, aprovechar. *vi* ganar, sacar ganancia. **profitable** *adj* **1** provechoso, útil. **2** lucrativo. **profitably** *adv* **1** con provecho. **2** *comm* lucrativamente.

profound (prə'faund) *adj* profundo.

profuse (prə'fju:s) *adj* **1** profuso. **2** pródigo. **profusion** *n* profusión *f*.

programme ('prougræm) *n* programa *m*. *vt* programar. **program** (in computers) *n* programa *f*. *vt* programar.

progress (*n* 'prougres; *v* prə'gres) *n* **1** progreso *m*. **2** marcha *f*. desarrollo *m*. *vi* **1** hacer progresos, progresar. **2** avanzar. **progression** *n* progresión *f*.

progressive (prə'gresiv) *adj* **1** progresivo. **2** *pol* progresista. *n pol* progresista *m,f*.

prohibit (prə'hibit) *vt* prohibir. **prohibition** *n* prohibición *f*. **prohibitive** *adj* prohibitivo.

project (*n* 'prodʒekt; *v* prə'dʒekt) *n* proyecto *m*. *vt* proyectar. *vi* salir, resaltar. **projectile** *n* proyectil *m*. **projecting** *adj* saliente. **projection** *n* **1** proyección *f*. **2** saliente, resalto *m*. **projector** *n* proyector *m*.

proletariat (prouli'tɛəriət) *n* proletariado *m*.

proliferate (prə'lifəreit) *vt* multiplicar, extender. *vi* proliferar, extenderse.

prolific (prə'lifik) *adj* prolífico.

prologue ('proulog) *n* prólogo *m*.

prolong (prə'loŋ) *vt* prolongar. **prolongation** *n* prolongación *f*.

promenade (promə'na:d) *n* paseo *m*. *vi* pasear.

prominent ('prominənt) *adj* **1** saliente, prominente. **2** (of eyes) saltón. **3** eminente, importante. **prominence** *n* **1** prominencia *f*. **2** eminencia, importancia *f*.

promiscuous (prə'miskjuəs) *adj* promiscuo. **promiscuity** *n* libertinaje *m*. promiscuidad *f*.

promise ('promis) *n* **1** promesa *f*. **2** esperanza *f*. porvenir *m*. **keep one's promise** cumplir su promesa. ~*vt* **1** prometer. **2** augurar. **promising** *adj* prometedor, que promete.

promote (prə'mout) *vt* **1** promover, fomentar. **2** estimular. **3** dar publicidad a. **4** apoyar. **promotion** *n* **1** promoción *f*. fomento *m*. **2** facilitación *f*. **3** ascenso *m*.

prompt (prɔmpt) *adj* pronto, puntual. *adv* puntualmente. *vt* **1** mover, incitar. **2** *Th* apuntar. **prompter** *n Th* apuntador *m*.

prone (proun) *adj* postrado. **be prone to** ser propenso a.

prong (prɔŋ) *n* punta, púa *f*.

pronoun ('prounaun) *n* pronombre *m*. **personal pronoun** pronombre personal. **possessive pronoun** pronombre posesivo.

pronounce (prə'nauns) *vt* pronunciar. **pronounce on** expresar una opinión sobre. **pronounced** *adj* fuerte. **pronouncement** *n* declaración, opinión *f*. **pronunciation** *n* pronunciación *f*.

proof (pru:f) *n* **1** prueba *f*. **2** (of alcohol) graduación normal *f*. **give proof** dar prueba de. **proofread** *vt* corregir las pruebas de.

prop[1] (prɔp) *n* apoyo *m*. *vt* apoyar. **prop up** apuntalar, sostener.

prop[2] (prɔp) *n Th* accesorio *m*.

propaganda (prɔpə'gændə) *n* propaganda *f*.

propagate ('prɔpəgeit) *vt* propagar.

propel (prə'pel) *vt* impulsar, propulsar. **propeller** *n* hélice *f*.

proper ('prɔpə) *adj* **1** propio. **2** apropiado, conveniente. **3** decente, correcto. **4** etiquetero. **5** *inf* verdadero. **properly** *adv* correctamente, debidamente. **proper noun** *n* nombre propio *m*.

property ('prɔpəti) *n* propiedad *f*.

prophecy ('prɔfisi) *n* profecía *f*. **prophesy** *vt* **1** profetizar. **2** *inf* predecir, prever.

prophet ('prɔfit) *n* profeta *m*.

proportion (prə'pɔ:ʃən) *n* proporción *f*.

propose (prə'pouz) *vt* proponer, ofrecer. *vi* **propose to** proponerse. **proposal** *n* propuesta, proposición, oferta *f*. **proposition** *n* proposición, propuesta *f*.

proprietor (prə'praiətə) *n* propietario, dueño *m*.

propriety (prə'praiəti) *n* decoro *m*. corrección *f*. **proprieties** convenciones *f pl*.

propulsion (prə'pʌlʃən) *n* propulsión *f*.

prose (prouz) *n* prosa *f*.

prosecute ('prɔsikju:t) *vt law* procesar, llevar a juicio. **prosecution 1** *law* proceso, juicio *m*. **2** prosecución *f*. cumplimiento *m*.

prospect ('prɔspekt) *n* **1** perspectiva *f*. **2** vista *f*. **3** probabilidad *f*. *vt* explorar. **prospect for** buscar. **prospective** *adj* anticipado, esperado. **prospectus** *n* prospecto *m*.

prosper ('prɔspə) *vi* prosperar. **prosperity** *n* prosperidad *f*. **prosperous** *adj* próspero.

prostitute ('prɔstitju:t) *n* prostituta *f*. **prostitution** *n* prostitución *f*.

prostrate (*v* prɔ'treit; *adj* 'prɔstreit) *adj* postrado. *vt* postrar. **prostration** *n* postración *f*.

protagonist (prə'tægənist) *n* protagonista *m,f*.

protect (prə'tekt) *vt* proteger. **protection** *n* protección *f*. **protective** *adj* protector.

protégé ('prɔtiʒei) *n* protegido *m*.

protein ('prouti:n) *n* proteína *f*.

protest (*n* 'proutest; *v* prə'test) *n* protesta *f*. **under protest** bajo protesta. ~*vt,vi* protestar.

Protestant ('prɔtistənt) *adj,n* protestante.

protocol ('proutəkɔl) *n* protocolo *m*.

proton ('prouton) *n* protón *m*.

prototype ('proutətaip) *n* prototipo *m*.

protrude (prə'tru:d) *vt* sacar fuera. *vi* sobresalir, salir fuera. **protruding** *adj* saliente. **protrusion** *n* protuberancia *f*.

proud (praud) *adj* **1** orgulloso. **2** soberbio, engreído. **be proud of** enorgullecerse de. **be proud to** tener el honor de.

prove (pru:v) *vt* **1** probar, demostrar. **2** confirmar. **3** verificar. *vi* resultar.

proverb ('prɔvə:b) *n* refrán, proverbio *m*. **proverbial** *adj* proverbial.

provide (prə'vaid) *vt* **1** surtir. **2** proporcionar. **provide for** proveer. **provide that** disponer que. **provided that** con tal que. **provision** *n* **1** provisión *f*. abastecimiento *m*. **2** disposición, estipulación *f*. *vt* abastecer. **provisional** *adj* provisional.

province ('prɔvins) *n* **1** provincia *f*. **2** jurisdicción *f*.

proviso (prə'vaizou) *n* **1** condición, estipulación *f*.

provoke (prə'vouk) *vt* **1** provocar, irritar. **2** mover, incitar. **provocation** *n* provocación *f*. **provocative** *adj* provocador, provocativo.

prow (prau) *n* proa *f*.

prowess ('prauis) *n* **1** valor *m*. **2** destreza *f*.

prowl (praul) *vi* rondar. *n* ronda *f*.

proximity (prɔk'simiti) *n* proximidad *f*.

prude (pru:d) *n* remilgado, gazmoño *m*. **prudery** *n* remilgo *m*. gazmoñería *f*. **prudish** *adj* remilgado, gazmoño.

prudent ('pru:dnt) *adj* prudente. **prudence** *n* prudencia *f*.

prune[1] (pru:n) *n* ciruela pasa *f*.

prune[2] (pru:n) *vt* **1** podar. **2** reducir, escamondar. **pruning** *n* poda *f*.

pry (prai) *vi* **1** fisgonear **2** entrometerse. **prying** *adj* **1** fisgón, curioso. **2** entrometido.

psalm (sa:m) *n* salmo *m*.

257

pseudonym ('sju:dənim) n seudónimo m.

psychedelic (saiki'delik) adj psiquedélico.

psychiatry (sai'kaiətri) n psiquiatría f. **psychiatrist** n psiquiatra m,f.

psychic ('saikik) adj psíquico.

psychoanalysis (saikouə'nælisis) n psicoanálisis m. **psychoanalyse** vt psicoanalizar. **psychoanalyst** n psicoanalista m,f.

psychology (sai'kɔlədʒi) n psicología f. **psychologist** n psicólogo m. **psychological** adj psicológico.

psychopathic (saikə'pæθik) adj psicopático. **psychopath** n psicópata m,f.

psychosomatic (saikousə'mætik) adj psicosomático.

pub (pʌb) n taberna f. **publican** n inf tabernero m.

puberty ('pju:bəti) n pubertad f.

public ('pʌblik) adj,n público m. **public house** n taberna f. **public relations** n pl relaciones públicas f pl. **public school** n internado privado m.

publication (pʌbli'keiʃən) n publicación f.

publicity (pʌb'lisiti) n publicidad f.

publicize ('pʌblisaiz) vt publicar, dar publicidad a.

publish ('pʌbliʃ) vt publicar. **publisher** n editor m. **publishing** n publicación f. **publishing firm** or **house** n casa editorial f.

pucker ('pʌkə) vt arrugar. n arruga f.

pudding ('pudiŋ) n pudín m.

puddle ('pʌdl) n charco m.

puff (pʌf) n 1 soplo m. 2 borla (for powder) f. vt,vi soplar. **puffy** adj hinchado. **puff pastry** n hojaldre m.

pull (pul) n 1 tirón, estirón m. 2 inf influencia f. 3 cuerda f. vt 1 tirar de. 2 arrastrar. 3 torcerse, dislocarse. vi tirar, dar un tirón. **pullover** n jersey m.

pulley ('puli) n polea f.

pulp (pʌlp) n pulpa, pasta f. vt hacer pulpa. **pulpy** adj pulposo.

pulpit ('pʌlpit) n púlpito m.

pulsate (pʌl'seit) vi pulsar, latir. **pulsation** n pulsación f, latido m.

pulse (pʌls) n 1 anat pulso m. 2 pulsación f. **take someone's pulse** tomar el pulso a uno. ~vi pulsar, latir.

pulverize ('pʌlvəraiz) vt 1 pulverizar. 2 cascar. **pulverization** n pulverización f.

pummel ('pʌməl) vt apuñear, cascar.

pump (pʌmp) n 1 bomba f. 2 pompa f. vt 1 sacar con bomba. 2 sonsacar. **pump up** inflar.

pumpkin ('pʌmpkin) n calabaza f.

pun (pʌn) n juego de palabras m. vi hacer un juego de palabras.

punch[1] (pʌntʃ) n puñetazo, golpe m. vt dar un puñetazo a, golpear.

punch[2] (pʌntʃ) n 1 punzón m. 2 taladro m. vt 1 punzar, taladrar. 2 picar.

punch[3] (pʌntʃ) n ponche m.

punctual ('pʌŋktʃuəl) adj punctual. **punctuality** n puntualidad f.

punctuate ('pʌŋktʃueit) vt puntuar.

punctuation (pʌŋktʃu'eiʃən) n puntuación f.

puncture ('pʌŋktʃə) n 1 perforación, puntura f. 2 pinchazo m. vt 1 perforar. 2 pinchar.

pungent ('pʌndʒənt) adj 1 acre. 2 picante. 3 mordaz, acerbo. **pungency** 1 lo acre neu. 2 picante m. 3 mordacidad, acerbidad f.

punish ('pʌniʃ) vt 1 castigar. 2 maltratar. **punishment** n 1 castigo m. 2 tratamiento severo m. **capital punishment** pena de muerte f. **corporal punishment** castigo corporal m.

punt[1] (pʌnt) n batea f. vt sport dar un puntapié a.

punt[2] (pʌnt) vi jugar, hacer apuestas.

pupil[1] ('pju:pəl) n alumno m.

pupil[2] ('pju:pəl) n anat pupila f.

puppet ('pʌpit) n títere m. marioneta m,f.

puppy ('pʌpi) n perrito, cachorro m.

purchase ('pə:tʃis) n 1 compra f. 2 adquisición f. vt comprar.

pure (pjuə) adj puro. **purity** n pureza f.

purgatory ('pə:gətri) n purgatorio m.

purge (pə:dʒ) n purga f. purgante m. vt purgar, purificar.

purify ('pjuərifai) vt purificar, depurar. **purification** n purificación, depuración f.

Puritan ('pjuəritən) adj,n puritano m.

purple ('pə:pəl) adj purpúreo. n púrpura f. **purplish** adj purpurino.

purpose ('pə:pəs) n propósito, objeto m. intención f. vt proponerse, proyectar. **purposeful** adj resuelto, determinado. **purposely** adv adrede, a propósito.

purr (pə:) n ronroneo m. vi ronronear.

purse (pə:s) n bolsa f. **purse one's lips** fruncir los labios.

pursue (pə'sju:) vt 1 seguir, perseguir, cazar. 2 dedicarse a. 3 proceder de acuerdo con. 4 ejercer. **pursuit** n 1 caza, busca f. 2 ocupación f. 3 pasatiempo m.

pus (pʌs) n pus m.

push (puʃ) n empuje, empujón m. **get the push** ser despedido. ~vt **1** empujar. **2** proseguir. **pushchair** n sillita de ruedas f.

pussy (ˈpusi) n minino, micho m.

put* (put) vt **1** poner, colocar, meter. **2** hacer, proponer. **put in for** presentarse a, solicitar. **put on 1** (clothes) ponerse. **2** afectar. **put up with** aguantar, resignarse a.

putrid (ˈpjuːtrid) adj podrido.

putty (ˈpʌti) n masilla f.

puzzle (ˈpʌzəl) n **1** game rompecabezas m. **2** problema, enigma m. **crossword puzzle** crucigrama m. ~vt confundir, dejar perplejo. **puzzled** adj perplejo. **puzzling 1** extraño. **2** enigmático.

PVC n (una especie de) impermeable plástico m.

pyjamas (pəˈdʒɑːməz) n pl pijama m.

pylon (ˈpailən) n pilón m.

pyramid (ˈpirəmid) n pirámide f.

Pyrenees (pirəˈniːz) n pl Pirineos m pl.

python (ˈpaiθən) n pitón m.

Q

quack[1] (kwæk) n (of a duck) graznido m. vi graznar.

quack[2] (kwæk) n inf curandero m.

quadrangle (ˈkwɔdræŋgəl) n **1** cuadrángulo m. **2** patio m.

quadrant (ˈkwɔdrənt) n cuadrante m.

quadrilateral (kwɔdriˈlætərəl) adj,n cuadrilátero m.

quadruped (ˈkwɔdruped) n cuadrúpedo m.

quadruple (ˈkwɔdrupəl) vt cuadruplicar **quadruplet** n cuatrillizo m.

quail[1] (kweil) n codorniz f.

quail[2] (kweil) vi acobardarse, descorazonarse.

quaint (kweint) adj singular, típico.

quake (kweik) vi temblar, estremecerse.

qualify (ˈkwɔlifai) vt **1** calificar. **2** habilitar. **3** modificar. vi **1** habilitarse, capacitarse. **2** obtener el título, graduarse. **qualification** n **1** calificación f. **2** requisito m. **3** reserva, modificación f. **4** pl aptitud, capacidad f. títulos m pl. **qualified** adj **1** calificado, competente. **2** modificado, limitado.

quality (ˈkwɔliti) n calidad f.

qualm (kwɑːm) n escrúpulo m. **have no qualms about doing** hacer sin escrúpulos.

quandary (ˈkwɔndəri) n apuro, dilema m.

quantity (ˈkwɔntiti) n cantidad f.

quarantine (ˈkwɔrəntiːn) n cuarentena f.

quarrel (ˈkwɔrəl) n **1** riña f. **2** reyerta, pelea f. **pick a quarrel** buscar camorra. ~vi **1** reñir. **2** pelear.

quarry[1] (ˈkwɔri) n cantera f. vt extraer.

quarry[2] (ˈkwɔri) n presa f.

quart (kwɔːt) n cuarto de galón m.

quarter (ˈkwɔːtə) n **1** cuarto m,f. **2** trimestre m. **3** barrio m. **4** pl mil alojamiento, cuartel m. **at close quarters** de cerca. ~vt **1** cuartear. **2** descuartizar. **3** mil acuartelar, alojar. **quarterly** adj trimestral. n publicación trimestral f.

quartet (kwɔːˈtet) n cuarteto m.

quash[1] (kwɔʃ) vt reprimir.

quash[2] (kwɔʃ) vt anular, invalidar.

quaver (ˈkweivə) n **1** temblor m. **2** mus corchea f. vi temblar, vibrar.

quay (kiː) n muelle m.

queasy (ˈkwiːzi) adj **1** bascoso. **2** escrupuloso.

queen (kwiːn) n **1** reina f. **2** game dama, reina f. caballo m. **queen mother** reina madre.

queer (kwiə) adj **1** raro, extraño, excéntrico. **2** inf med enfermo. **3** sl maricón. n sl maricón, marica m. vt estropear.

quell (kwel) vt reprimir, aquietar.

quench (kwentʃ) vt apagar.

query (ˈkwiəri) n **1** pregunta f. **2** duda f. **3** interrogante m. vt, vi preguntar.

quest (kwest) n busca, búsqueda f.

question (ˈkwestʃən) n **1** pregunta f. **2** asunto, problema m. cuestión f. **be a question of** tratarse de. **question mark** n signo de interrogación m. ~vt **1** hacer preguntas a, interrogar. **2** poner en duda. **questionable** adj cuestionable. **questionnaire** n cuestionario m.

queue (kjuː) n cola f. **jump the queue** salirse de su turno. ~vi hacer cola.

quibble (ˈkwibəl) n sofistería, sutileza f. vi sutilizar, argüir.

quick (kwik) adj rápido, veloz, pronto, vivo, ágil, inteligente. **quicken** vt acelerar, apresurar. vi acelerarse, apresurarse. **quicksand** n arena movediza f. **quickstep** n paso doble m. **quick-tempered** adj de genio vivo. **quick-witted** adj agudo, perspicaz.

quiet[1] (ˈkwaiət) n silencio, reposo m. paz, tranquilidad f. **on the quiet** a hurtadillas.

quiet[2] (ˈkwaiət) adj silencioso, callado, quieto, inactivo. **quiet** or **quieten** vt calmar, hacer callar.

quill (kwil) n **1** zool pluma de ave f. **2** cañón de pluma m. **3** pluma de ganso f.

quilt ('kwilt) *n* edredón *m*. *vt* acolchar.
quince (kwins) *n* membrillo *m*.
quinine (kwi'ni:n) *n* quinina *f*.
quintessence (kwin'tesəns) *n* quinta esencia *f*.
quintet (kwin'tet) *n* quinteto *m*.
quirk (kwə:k) *n* **1** capricho *m*. **2** peculiaridad *f*.
quit (kwit) *vt* **1** dejar, renunciar. **2** salir de. *vi* **1** irse, marcharse. **2** retirarse. **3** dimitir. **quits** *adj inf* en paz.
quite (kwait) *adv* completamente.
quiver [1] ('kwivə) *n* temblor *m*. *vi* temblar.
quiver [2] ('kwivə) *n* carcaj *m*. aljaba *f*.
quiz (kwiz) *n, pl* **-zes,** acertijo *m*. encuesta *f*. *vt* interrogar.
quizzical ('kwizikəl) *adj* burlón.
quota ('kwoutə) *n* cuota *f*.
quote (kwout) *vt* **1** citar. **2** *comm* cotizar. **quotation** *n* **1** citación. **2** *comm* cotización *f*. **quotation marks** *n pl* comillas *f pl*.

R

rabbi ('ræbai) *n* rabino, rabí *m*.
rabbit ('ræbit) *n* conejo *m*.
rabble ('ræbəl) *n* canalla, gentualla *f*.
rabies ('reibi:z) *n* rabia *f*. **rabid** *adj* **1** *med* rabioso. **2** *inf* fanático.
race [1] (reis) *n sport* carrera, regata *f*. *vt* hacer correr, presentar. *vi* **1** correr de prisa. **2** competir, presentarse. **racecourse** *n* hipódromo *m*.
race [2] (reis) *n* raza, casta, estirpe, familia *f*. **human race** *n* género humano *m*. **racial** *adj* racial, racista. **racialism** *n* racismo *m*.
rack (ræk) *n* **1** estante, anaquel *m*. **2** percha *f*. **3** potro *m*. *vt* atormentar.
racket [1] ('rækit) *n* **1** ruido, estrépito *m*. **2** barahunda *f*. **3** *inf* trampa, estafa *f*.
racket [2] ('rækit) *n sport* raqueta *f*.
radar ('reidə:) *n* radar *m*.
radial ('reidiəl) *adj* radial.
radiant ('reidiənt) *adj* radiante. **radiance** *n* brillantez *f*.
radiate ('reidieit) *vt* irradiar. **radiation** *n* radiación *f*. **radiator** *n* radiador *m*.
radical ('rædikəl) *adj,n* radical *m*.
radio ('reidiou) *n* radio *f*. **radio station** *n* emisora *f*. ~*vt* radiar, transmitir por radio.
radioactivity (reidiouæk'tiviti) *n* radiactividad *f*.
radish ('rædiʃ) *n* rábano *m*.
radium ('reidiəm) *n* radio *m*.
radius ('reidiəs) *n, pl* **-dii** *or* **-diuses** radio *m*.

raffle ('ræfəl) *n* rifa *f*. sorteo *m*. *vt* rifar, sortear.
raft (rɑ:ft) *n* balsa *f*.
rafter ('rɑ:ftə) *n* cabrio *m*.
rag [1] (ræg) *n* **1** trapo *m*. **2** *sl* periodicucho *m*. **ragged** *adj* harapiento, andrajoso.
rag [2] (ræg) *vt* tomar el pelo a. *n* broma pesada *f*.
rage (reidʒ) *n* **1** rabia *f*. furor *m*. **2** manía *f*. *vi* rabiar.
raid (reid) *n* **1** correría, incursión *f*. **2** *aviat* bombardeo *m*. *vt* **1** invadir, atacar. **2** bombardear.
rail (reil) *n* **1** barandilla *f*. **2** carril *m*. **railway** *n* ferrocarril *m*. **railway station** *n* estación de ferrocarril *f*.
rain (rein) *n* lluvia *f*. *vi* llover. **rainbow** *n* arco iris *m*. **raindrop** *n* gota de lluvia *f*.
raise (reiz) *vt* **1** levantar, alzar. **2** criar. **3** aumentar. **4** reunir.
raisin ('reizən) *n* pasa *f*.
rake (reik) *n* **1** rastrillo, rastro *m*. **2** libertino *m*. *vt* rastillar.
rally ('ræli) *n* **1** reunión, manifestación *f*. **2** *comm* recuperación *f*. *vt* reunir.
ram (ræm) *n* **1** *zool* carnero *m*. **2** *mil* ariete *m*. *vt* **1** apisonar, apretar. **2** dar contra.
ramble ('ræmbəl) *n* paseo *m*. excursión *f*. *vi* **1** salir de excursión a pie. **2** divagar. **rambling** *adj* divagador, errante.
ramp (ræmp) *n* rampa *f*.
rampage ('ræmpeidʒ) *n* alboroto *m*. *vi* alborotar, desbocarse.
rampant ('ræmpənt) *adj* prevaleciente, desenfrenado.
rampart ('ræmpɑ:t) *n* muralla *f*. terraplén *m*.
ramshackle ('ræmʃækəl) *adj* destartalado.
ran (ræn) *v see* **run.**
ranch (rɑ:ntʃ) *n* rancho *m*.
rancid ('rænsid) *adj* rancio.
rancour ('ræŋkə) *n* rencor *m*.
random ('rændəm) *adj* casual, fortuito. **at random** al azar.
rang (ræŋ) *v see* **ring** [2].
range (reindʒ) *n* **1** alcance *m*. **2** gama *f*. **3** línea, sierra *f*. *vt* ordenar, clasificar. *vi* extenderse.
rank [1] (ræŋk) *n* **1** rango, grado *m*. **2** fila, línea *f*. *vt* clasificar, ordenar. *vi* clasificarse. **rank and file** *n* masas *f pl*.
rank [2] (ræŋk) *adj* **1** lozano. **2** rancio.
rankle ('ræŋkəl) *v* roer.
ransack ('rænsæk) *vt* **1** saquear. **2** rebuscar, registrar.
ransom ('rænsəm) *n* rescate. *vt* rescatar.
rap (ræp) *n* golpecito *m*. *vt* golpear, tocar.

rape (reip) n violación f. vt violar, forzar.

rapid ('ræpid) adj rápido. **rapids** n pl rápidos m pl.

rapier ('reipiə) n estoque m.

rapture ('ræptʃə) n rapto, éxtasis m.

rare[1] (rɛə) adj raro, poco común. **rarity** n rareza f

rare[2] (rɛə) adj cul poco hecho.

rascal ('rɑːskəl) n pícaro m.

rash[1] (ræʃ) adj precipitado, inconsiderado.

rash[2] (ræʃ) n med erupción f.

raspberry ('rɑːzbri) n frambuesa f.

rat (ræt) n rata f

rate (reit) n 1 proporción, razón f. 2 precio m. tarifa, tasa f. 3 clase f. orden m. **at any rate** de todos modos. **first-rate** de primer orden. ~vt 1 valuar, apreciar. 2 clasificar.

rather ('rɑːðə) adv 1 más bien. 2 bastante.

ratio ('reiʃiou) n 1 relación f. 2 math razón f.

ration ('ræʃən) n ración f. vt racionar.

rational ('ræʃənəl) adj racional. **rationalize** vt racionalizar.

rattle ('rætl) n ruido, golpeteo m. vt 1 sacudir. 2 hacer sonar. 3 desconcertar. vi hacer ruido.

raucous ('rɔːkəs) adj ronco.

ravage ('rævidʒ) n 1 estrago, destrozo m. 2 saqueo m. vt asolar, arruinar, saquear.

rave (reiv) vi 1 delirar, desvariar. 2 declamar con violencia.

raven ('reivən) n cuervo m. **ravenous** adj 1 voraz. 2 famélico, hambriento.

ravine (rə'viːn) n barranco m.

ravioli (rævi'ouli) n canalones m pl.

ravish ('ræviʃ) vt 1 forzar, violar. 2 raptar.

raw (rɔː) adj crudo.

ray (rei) n 1 rayo m. 2 zool raya f.

rayon ('reiɔn) n rayón m.

razor ('reizə) n navaja de afeitar f. **razor blade** n hoja de afeitar f.

reach (riːtʃ) n 1 alcance, poder m. 2 distancia, extensión f. vt 1 alargar. 2 alcanzar, llegar a. vi llegar, extenderse.

react (ri'ækt) vi reaccionar. **reaction** n reacción f. **reactionary** adj,n reaccionario m.

read[*] (riːd) vt 1 leer. 2 descifrar, interpretar. 3 estudiar, aprender. **reader** n 1 lector m. 2 libro de lectura m.

readjust (riːə'dʒʌst) vt reajustar. **readjustment** n reajuste m.

ready ('redi) adj 1 preparado, listo, dispuesto. 2 disponible, a la mano. vt preparar, aprestar.

real (riəl) adj real. **realism** n realismo

m. **realize** vt 1 comprender, darse cuenta de. 2 realizar, llevar a cabo. **reality** n realidad f.

realm (relm) n 1 reino m. 2 esfera f.

reap (riːp) vt 1 segar. 2 cosechar, recoger. 3 obtener, sacar fruto.

reappear (riːə'piə) vi reaparecer.

rear[1] (riə) adj trasero, de atrás, de cola, posterior. n 1 trasera, espalda, parte de atras f. 2 mil retaguardia f. **rear admiral** n contralmirante m. **rearguard** n retaguardia f.

rear[2] (riə) vt 1 criar, educar. 2 levantar, erguir. 3 erigir.

rearrange (riːə'reindʒ) vt volver a arreglar, volver a ordenar.

reason ('riːzən) n 1 razón f. 2 causa f. motivo m. 3 cordura f. buen sentido m. vi razonar, raciocinar. **reasonable** adj 1 racional. 2 razonable.

reassure (riːə'ʃuə) vt tranquilizar, devolver la confianza.

rebate ('riːbeit) n rebaja f.

rebel (n,adj 'rebəl; v ri'bel) adj,n rebelde m. vi rebelarse, insurreccionarse.

rebound (n 'riːbaund; v ri'baund) n rebote, resalto m. vi rebotar.

rebuff (ri'bʌf) n desaire m. repulsa f. vt desairar.

rebuild (riː'bild) vt reedificar.

rebuke (ri'bjuːk) n reproche m. reprimenda f. vt reñir, reprender.

recall (ri'kɔːl) vt 1 llamar, hacer volver. 2 hacer revivir, rememorar. n 1 llamada para hacer volver f. 2 recordación f. 3 revocación f.

recede (ri'siːd) vi retroceder.

receipt (ri'siːt) n 1 recibo m. 2 quitanza f. **receipts** n pl ingresos m pl.

receive (ri'siːv) vt 1 recibir. 2 aceptar, tomar. 3 cobrar. **receiver** n 1 receptor m. 2 law liquidador m. 3 tech auricular m.

recent (ri'sənt) adj reciente, moderno.

receptacle (ri'septəkəl) n receptáculo, recipiente m.

reception (ri'sepʃən) n 1 recepción f. 2 recibimiento m. acogida f. **receptive** adj receptivo.

recess (ri'ses) n 1 vacación f. recreo m. 2 lugar apartado, retiro m. 3 hueco m. alcoba f. **recession** n retroceso m. recesión f.

recipe ('resipi) n récipe m. receta f.

recipient (ri'sipiənt) n recibidor m.

reciprocate (ri'siprəkeit) vt reciprocar, devolver. **reciprocal** adj recíproco.

recite (ri'sait) vt,vi 1 recitar. 2 narrar, contar. 3 declamar.

reckless ('reklǝs) adj **1** descuidado. **2** atrevido, atolondrado.

reckon ('rekǝn) vt **1** contrar, calcular. **2** suponer, creer. **reckoning** n **1** cuenta f. cálculo m. **2** ajuste de cuentas m.

reclaim (ri'kleim) vt **1** reclamar. **2** reformar, civilizar. **3** recuperar, volver a hacer útil.

recline (ri'klain) vt reclinar. vi rechinarse, recostarse.

recluse (ri'klu:s) n solitario, recluso m.

recognize ('rekǝgnaiz) vt **1** reconocer. **2** admitir, aceptar. **recognition** n reconocimiento m.

recoil (ri'kɔil) n retroceso m. vi retroceder, retirarse.

recollect (rekǝ'lekt) vt recordar, acordarse de. **recollection** n recuerdo m.

recommence (ri:kǝ'mens) vt, vi volver a comenzar.

recommend (rekǝ'mend) vt recomendar. **recommendation** n recomendación f.

recompense ('rekǝmpens) n recompensa f. vt recompensar.

reconcile ('rekǝnsail) vt reconciliar. **reconciliation** n reconciliación f.

reconstruct (ri:kǝn'strʌkt) vt reconstruir. **reconstruction** n reconstrucción f.

record (n 'rekɔ:d; v ri'kɔ:d) n **1** anotación f. registro m. **2** acta, crónica f. anales m pl. **3** mus disco m. **4** récord m. marca f. vt **1** registrar. **2** apuntar. **3** marcar. **record-player** n tocadiscos m invar.

recount (ri'kaunt) vt referir, narrar, detallar.

recover (ri'kʌvǝ) vt recobrar, recuperar. vi recobrar la salud. **recovery** n recobro m. recuperación f.

recreation (rekri'eiʃǝn) n recreación f. recreo m.

recruit (ri'kru:t) n recluta m. vt reclutar, alistar.

rectangle ('rektæŋgǝl) n rectángulo m. **rectangular** adj rectangular.

rectify ('rektifai) vt rectificar.

recuperate (ri'kju:pǝreit) vt recuperar. vi reponerse, convalecer.

recur (ri'kǝ:) vi repetirse.

red (red) adj **1** rojo. **2** colorado. **redcurrant** n grosella roja f.

redeem (ri'di:m) vt **1** redimir. **2** rescatar. **3** desempeñar. **redemption** n **1** redención f. rescate m. **2** desempeño m.

redevelop (ri:di'velǝp) vt volver a desarroller.

red-handed adj con las manos en la masa.

redress (ri'dres) n **1** reparación f. desagravio m. **2** satisfacción f. vt **1** enderezar. **2** compensar. **3** corregir.

reduce (ri'dju:s) vt reducir.

redundant (ri'dʌndǝnt) adj redundante, de más. **be made redundant** quedar sin trabajo.

reed (ri:d) n caña f. junco m.

reef (ri:f) n arrecife, escollo m.

reek (ri:k) n humo, tufo, vaho m. vi humear, oler mal.

reel[1] (ri:l) n **1** carrete de pesca m. **2** phot rollo, carrete m. **3** broca, bobina f.

reel[2] (ri:l) vi tambalearse, andar haciendo eses, vacilar.

refectory (ri'fektǝri) n refectorio m.

refer (ri'fǝ:) vt referir, remitir, aludir. **referee** n árbitro m. vt arbitrar. **reference** n **1** referencia, relación f. **2** remisión, alusión f. **referendum** n referéndum m.

refill (v ri:'fil; n 'ri:fil) vt rellenar. n repuesto m.

refine (ri'fain) vt refinar, purificar. **refinement** n refinamiento m. **refinery** n refinería f.

reflect (ri'flekt) vt reflejar. vi reflexionar, pensar. **reflection** n **1** reflexión f. **2** reflejo m. **reflector** n reflector m.

reflex ('ri:fleks) adj,n reflejo m. **reflexive** adj reflexivo.

reform (ri'fɔ:m) n reforma f. vt reformar. vi reformarse. **reformation** n reforma, reformación f.

refract (ri'frækt) vt refractar.

refrain[1] (ri'frein) vi abstenerse.

refrain[2] (ri'frein) n estribillo m.

refresh (ri'freʃ) vt refrescar. **refreshment** n refresco m.

refrigerator (ri'fridʒǝreitǝ) n refrigerador, frigorífico m. nevera f.

refuge ('refju:dʒ) n refugio, asilo m. **refugee** n refugiado m.

refund (n 'rifʌnd; v ri'fʌnd) n reembolso m. vt reintegrar, reembolsar.

refuse[1] (ri'fju:z) vt **1** rehusar, rechazar. **2** negarse a. **refusal** n **1** repulsa f. **2** denegación f.

refuse[2] ('refju:s) n basura f.

refute (ri'fju:t) vt refutar.

regain (ri'gein) vt recobrar, recuperar.

regal ('ri:gǝl) adj real, regio.

regard (ri'gɑ:d) n **1** miramiento m. consideración f. **2** relación f. respecto m. **with regard to** con respecto a. ~vt **1** mirar. **2** considerar, tener en cuenta. **3** estimar, apreciar. **4** concernir. **regardless** adj indiferente, que no hace caso. adv a pesar de todo.

regatta (ri'gɑ:tǝ) n regata f.

regent ('ri:dʒǝnt) adj,n regente m.

regime (rei'ʒi:m) *n* régimen *m*.

regiment ('redʒimənt) *n* regimiento *m*.

region ('ri:dʒən) *n* región *f*.

register ('redʒistə) *n* registro *m. vt* **1** registrar, inscribir, matricular. **2** (of a letter) certificar. **3** indicar. **registrar** *n* **1** registrador, archivero *m.* **2** secretario *m.* **3** (in a hospital) doctor *m.*

regress (ri'gres) *vi* retroceder. **regression** *n* regresión *f.* **regressive** *adj* regresivo.

regret (ri'gret) *n* **1** pesar, sentimiento *m.* pena *f.* **2** *pl* excusa *f. vt* lamentar, sentir. **regretful** *adj* pesaroso.

regular ('regjulə) *adj* **1** regular. **2** metódico, ordenado. **3** normal, corriente. *n* parroquiano *m.*

regulate ('regjuleit) *vt* regular, regularizar, ajustar. **regulation** *n* **1** regulación *f.* **2** reglamentación *f.* **regulations** *n pl* ordenanzas *f pl.*

rehabilitate (ri:ə'biliteit) *vt* rehabilitar. **rehabilitation** *n* rehabilitación *f.*

rehearse (ri'hə:s) *vt* ensayar, repasar. **rehearsal** *n* ensayo *m.* repetición *f.*

reheat (ri:'hi:t) *vt* volver a calentar.

reign (rein) *n* reino, reinado *m. vi* reinar.

reimburse (ri:im'bə:s) *vt* reembolsar, indemnizar.

rein (rein) *n* rienda *f.*

reincarnation (ri:inkɑ:'neiʃən) *n* reencarnación *f.*

reindeer ('reindiə) *n* reno *m.*

reinforce (ri:in'fɔ:s) *vt* reforzar. **reinforcement** *n* refuerzo *m.*

reinstate (ri:in'steit) *vt* reinstalar, rehabilitar.

reinvest (ri:in'vest) *vt* reinvertir.

reissue (ri:'iʃu:) *vt* **1** reimprimir. **2** emitir de nuevo. *n* reimpresión, nueva emisión *f.*

reject (*v* ri'dʒekt; *n* 'ri:dʒekt) *vt* rechazar, desechar, expeler. *n* desecho *m.*

rejoice (ri'dʒɔis) *vi* regocijarse, alegrarse.

rejuvenate (ri'dʒu:vəneit) *vt* rejuvenecer.

relapse (ri'læps) *n* recaída, reincidencia *f. vi* recaer, reincidir.

relate (ri'leit) *vt* **1** relatar, contar. **2** relacionar. **relation** *n* **1** relato *m.* narración *f.* relación *f.* **3** parentesco *m.* afinidad *f.* **in relation to** en relación con. **relations** *n pl* parientes *m pl.* **relationship** *n* relación, afinidad *f.* parentesco *m.* **relative** *adj, n* relativo *m.* **relativity** *n* relatividad *f.*

relax (ri'læks) *vt* **1** relajar. **2** aliviar, mitigar. *vi* **1** relajarse. **2** descansar, esparcirse, calmarse.

relaxation *n* **1** relajación *f.* **2** descanso, esparcimiento *m.* **3** mitigación *f.*

relay (*n* 'ri:lei; *v* ri'lei) *n* tanda *f. vt* **1** *tech* retransmitir. **2** pasar.

release (ri'li:s) *n* **1** liberación *f.* **2** emisión *f.* lanzamiento, descargo, disparo *m. vt* **1** emitir. **2** libertar. **3** lanzar, disparar. **4** estrenar, publicar. **5** aflojar.

relent (ri'lent) *vi* **1** ablandarse, aplacarse. **2** enternecerse.

relevant ('relavənt) *adj* pertinente, a propósito, al caso.

reliable (ri'laiəbəl) *adj* **1** digno de confianza. **2** fidedigno.

relic ('relik) *n* reliquia *f.*

relief (ri'li:f) *n* **1** ayuda *f.* socorro *m.* **2** consuelo, alivio *m.* **3** relevo *m.* **4** relieve *m.*

relieve (ri'li:v) *vt* **1** aliviar. **2** relevar, socorrer. **3** realzar, dar relieve.

religion (ri'lidʒən) *n* religión *f.* **religious** *adj* religioso.

relinquish (ri'liŋkwiʃ) *vt* **1** abandonar, desistir de. **2** ceder.

relish ('reliʃ) *n* **1** buen sabor *m.* **2** gusto, goce *m.* **3** condimento *m. vt* **1** saborear. **2** apreciar con gusto.

reluctant (ri'lʌktənt) *adj* reluctante, reacio.

rely (ri'lai) *vi* confiar. **rely on** contar con.

remain (ri'mein) *vi* **1** quedar. **2** restar. **3** permanecer. **remainder** *n* **1** resto, sobrante, restante *m.* **2** *math* residuo *m.*

remand (ri'mɑ:nd) *vt* mandar de nuevo a la cárcel.

remark (ri'mɑ:k) *n* **1** observación *f.* **2** nota *f.* comentario *m. vt* **1** advertir. **2** hacer notar, observar. **remarkable** *adj* **1** considerable, señalado. **2** observable, notable.

remedy ('remədi) *n* remedio *m. vt* remediar.

remember (ri'membə) *vt* acordarse de, recordar. **remembrance** *n* recuerdo *m.* memoria, conmemoración *f.*

remind (ri'maind) *vt* recordar, hacer presente. **reminder** *n* **1** recordatorio *m.* **2** advertencia *f.*

reminiscence (remi'nisəns) *n* reminiscencia *f.* **reminiscent** *adj* **1** recordativo, evocador. **2** lleno de recuerdos.

remiss (ri'mis) *adj* remiso, descuidado. **remission** *n* remisión *f.* perdón *m.*

remit (ri'mit) *vt* **1** remitir. **2** perdonar. **remittance** *n* giro *m.* remesa *f.*

remnant ('remnənt) *n* **1** remanente *m.* **2** resto *m.* **3** retazo *m.*

remorse (ri'mɔ:s) *n* remordimiento *m.*

remote (ri'mout) *adj* remoto.
remove (ri'mu:v) *vt* **1** quitar. **2** eliminar. **3** extirpar. **4** deponer, destituir. **removal** *n* **1** remoción *f.* **2** extirpación *f.* **3** mudanza *f.* **4** destitución *f.*
remunerate (ri'mju:nəreit) *vt* renumerar.
renaissance (ri'neisəns) *n* renacimiento *m.*
render ('rendə) *vt* **1** dar, rendir. **2** pagar, devolver. **3** hacer. **4** entregar.
rendezvous ('rɔndivu:) *n invar* cita *f. vi* acudir a una cita.
renew (ri'nju:) *vt* **1** renovar. **2** reanudar. **3** *comm* extender. **renewal** *n* **1** renovación *f.* **2** reanudación *f.* **3** prórroga *f.*
renounce (ri'nauns) *vt* renunciar.
renovate ('renəveit) *vt* renovar.
renown (ri'naun) *n* renombre *m.*
rent[1] (rent) *n* **1** alquiler, arrendar. **2** hacer pagar la renta. *n* alquiler *m.* arrendamiento *m.* renta *f.* **rental** *n* renta *f.* alquiler *m.*
rent[2] (rent) *n* rasgadura *f.*
reorganize (ri:'ɔ:gənaiz) *vt* reorganizar.
rep (rep) *n comm inf* agente, viajante *m.*
repair (ri'pɛə) *n* reparación *f.* arreglo, reparo *m. vt* reparar.
repartee (repə'ti:) *n* agudeza *f.*
repatriate (ri'pætrieit) *vt* repatriar.
repay (ri'pei) *vt* volver a pagar, recompensar.
repeal (ri'pi:l) *n* abrogación, anulación *f. vt* abrogar, anular.
repeat (ri'pi:t) *vt* repetir.
repel (ri'pel) *vt* repeler, rechazar. **repellent** *adj* repelente.
repent (ri'pent) *vt* arrepentirse de.
repercussion (ri:pə'kʌʃən) *n* repercusión *f.*
repertory ('repətri) *n also* **repertoire** repertorio *m.*
repetition (repə'tiʃən) *n* repetición *f.*
replace (ri'pleis) *vt* reemplazar, substituir. **replacement** *n* reemplazo *m.*
replay (ri:'plei) *vt, vi* **1** volver a jugar. **2** volver a tocar.
replenish (ri'pleniʃ) *vt* rellenar.
replica ('replikə) *n* reproducción, copia, réplica *f.*
reply (ri'plai) *n* respuesta *f. vt* responder, contestar.
report (re'pɔ:t) *n* **1** relato *m.* **2** informe *m.* memoria *f.* **3** reportaje *m.* noticia, información *f.* **4** detonación *f. vt* **1** relatar, dar cuenta. **2** denunciar. **3** rumorear, propalar. **4** hacer reportaje. **reporter** *n* periodista, reportero *m.*

repose (ri'pouz) *n* reposo, descanso *m. vi* reclinarse, tenderse, descansar, reposar.
reposition (ri:pə'ziʃən) *n* reposición *f.*
represent (repri'zent) *vt* representar. **representation** *n* representación *f.* **representative** *adj* representativo. *n* representante, delegado *m.*
repress (ri'pres) *vt* reprimir.
reprieve (ri'pri:v) *n* **1** *law* indulto *m.* **2** alivio *m. vt* **1** indultar. **2** aliviar.
reprimand ('reprimɑ:nd) *n* reprimenda *f. vt* reprender.
reprint (*v* ri:'print; *n* 'ri:print) *n* reimpresión *f. vt* reimprimir.
reprisal (ri'praizəl) *n* represalia *f.*
reproach (ri'proutʃ) *n* **1** reproche *m.* **2** tacha *f. vt* reprochar, reprender.
reproduce (ri:prə'dju:s) *vt* reproducir. **reproduction** *n* reproducción *f.*
reptile ('reptail) *n* reptil *m.*
republic (ri'pʌblik) *n* república *f.* **republican** *adj,n* republicano *m.*
repudiate (ri'pju:dieit) *vt* repudiar.
repugnant (ri'pʌgnənt) *adj* repugnante.
repulsion (ri'pʌlʃən) *n* repulsión *f.* **repulsive** *adj* repelente, repulsivo, repugnante.
repute (ri'pju:t) *n* **1** reputación, fama *f.* **2** opinión *f.* **reputable** *adj* de buena reputación. **reputation** *n* reputación, fama *f.*
request (ri'kwest) *n* **1** petición, súplica *f.* **2** demanda *f. vt* pedir, solicitar, rogar.
requiem ('rekwiəm) *n* réquiem *m.*
require (ri'kwaiə) *vt* requerir, demandar, necesitar. **requirement** *n* requisito *m.* demanda, exigencia *f.*
rescue ('reskju:) *n* rescate, socorro *m. vt* rescatar, socorrer, librar.
research (ri'sə:tʃ) *n* investigación, indagación *f. vt* investigar, indagar.
resemble (ri'zembəl) *vt* parecerse a. **resemblance** *n* parecido *m.* semejanza *f.*
resent (ri'zent) *vt* resentirse de, ofenderse por.
reserve (ri'zə:v) *vt* **1** reservar. **2** preservar, conservar. **3** retener. *n* reserva *f.* **reservation** *n* reserva, reservación *f.* **reserved** *adj* **1** reservado. **2** frío, poco efusivo.
reservoir ('rezəvwɑ:) *n* **1** depósito *m.* **2** embalse *m.* presa *f.*
reside (ri'zaid) *vi* residir. **residence** *n* residencia, morada *f.* **resident** *adj,n* residente *m.*
residue ('rezidju:) *n* residuo *m.*
resign (ri'zain) *vt, vi* dimitir, resignar. **resignation** *n* dimisión, renuncia *f.*
resilient (ri'ziliənt) *adj* **1** elástico. **2** resistente. **3**

con poder de adaptarse. **resilience** n 1 elasticidad f. 2 resistencia f.

resin ('rezin) n resina f.

resist (ri'zist) vt resistir. **resistance** n resistencia f.

resolute ('rezəlu:t) adj resuelto, determinado.

resolution (rezə'lu:ʃən) n 1 resolución f. 2 propósito m. 3 decisión f. acuerdo m.

resolve (ri'zɔlv) vt resolver. n 1 resolución f. 2 propósito m. ·

resonant ('rezənənt) adj resonante.

resort (ri'zɔ:t) n 1 recurso, medio m. 2 lugar de recreo m. vi 1 acudir, frecuentar. 2 acudir, recurrir.

resound (ri'zaund) vi resonar, repercutir.

resource (ri'zɔ:s) n recurso, remedio, medio m. **resourceful** adj ingenioso.

respect (ri'spekt) n respeto m. estima f. vt respetar. **respectable** adj respetable. **respective** adj respectivo.

respite ('respit) n respiro, descanso m. tregua, prórroga f.

respond (ri'spɔnd) vi responder. **response** n respuesta f. **responsive** adj sensible, que responde.

responsibility (rispɔnsə'biliti) n responsabilidad f. **responsible** adj responsable.

rest[1] (rest) n 1 descanso, reposo m. 2 pausa f. 3 tranquilidad, paz f. **at rest** en reposo. ~vi descansar, reposar.

rest[2] (rest) n resto, restante m.

restaurant ('restərɔnt) n restaurante m.

restless ('restləs) adj 1 inquieto, intranquilo. 2 revoltoso, bullicioso.

restore (ri'stɔ:) vt 1 restaurar. 2 reconstruir. 3 instaurar. 4 restituir, devolver. **restoration** n 1 restauración f. 2 restitución, devolución f. renovación f.

restrain (ri'strein) vt 1 refrenar, cohibir, contener. 2 privar, encerrar. 3 limitar, restringir. **restraint** n 1 freno m. restricción, limitación f. 2 moderación f. dominio m.

restrict (ri'strikt) vt restringir, limitar, contener.

result (ri'zʌlt) n resultado m. consecuencia f. **as a result** por consiguiente, debido a. **result in** terminar en, producir.

resume (ri'zju:m) vt 1 continuar, reasumir. 2 resumir.

résumé ('rezumei) n resumen m.

resurrect (rezə'rekt) vt resucitar.

retail ('ri:teil) n venta al por menor f. vt vender al por menor.

retain (ri'tein) vt retener.

retaliate (ri'tælieit) vi vengarse de.

retard (ri'tɑ:d) vt retardar, retrasar.

reticent ('retisənt) adj reticente.

retina ('retinə) n retina f.

retire (ri'taiə) vi 1 jubilarse. 2 mil retirarse. **retirement** n retiro m.

retort[1] (ri'tɔ:t) n réplica, respuesta aguda f. vi replicar.

retort[2] (ri'tɔ:t) n sci retorta f.

retrace (ri'treis) vt 1 retroceder sobre los pasos. 2 volver a trazar.

retract (ri'trækt) vt 1 revocar, retractar. 2 retraer.

retreat (ri'tri:t) n 1 rel retiro m. 2 refugio m. 3 mil retirada f. vi retirarse.

retrieve (ri'tri:v) vt recobrar, recuperar, salvar.

retrograde ('retrəgreid) adj retrógrado.

retrogress (retrə'gres) vi retroceder. **retrogressive** adj retrógrado.

retrospect ('retrəspekt) n retrospección f. **in retrospect** retrospectivamente.

return (ri'tə:n) n 1 vuelta f. regreso m. 2 comm ganancia f. **in return for** a cambio de. **many happy returns** feliz cumpleaños m invar. **return ticket** billete de ida y vuelta m. ~vt 1 volver, regresar. 2 devolver.

reunite (ri:ju:'nait) vt reunir.

reveal (ri'vi:l) vt revelar. **revelation** n revelación f.

revel ('revəl) vi jaranear. **revel in** deleitarse en or con.

revenge (ri'vendʒ) n venganza f. vt vengar.

revenue ('revənju:) n rentas f pl.

reverberate (ri'və:bəreit) vi reverberar, resonar.

reverence ('revərəns) n reverencia f. vt reverenciar. **reverent** adj reverente.

reverse (ri'və:s) adj opuesto, inverso. n 1 revés m. 2 mot marcha atrás f. 3 contrario m. vt 1 mot poner en marcha atrás. 2 revocar. 3 invertir.

revert (ri'və:t) vi volver a, revertir.

review (ri'vju:) n 1 lit,mil revista f. 2 reseña f. vt 1 repasar, examinar, analizar. 2 (journalism) reseñar. 3 mil pasar revista.

revise (ri'vaiz) vt 1 revisar, volver a mirar. 2 (correct) corregir, modificar.

revive (ri'vaiv) vi reponerse, revivir, resucitar. vt 1 resucitar. 2 reanimar.

revoke (ri'vouk) vt revocar, anular.

revolt (ri'voult) n rebelión f. vi rebelarse. vt dar asco a, repugnar. **revolting** adj repugnante, asqueroso, repelente. **revolution** n 1 revolución, sublevación f. 2 vuelta f. giro m.

revolve (ri'vɔlv) vt girar, revolver. **revolver** n revólver m.

revue (ri'vju:) n Th revista f.

revulsion (ri'vʌlʃən) n asco m. repugnancia f.

reward (ri'wɔːd) n premio, pago m. recompensa f. vt premiar, pagar, recompensar.

rhetoric ('retərik) n retórica f. **rhetorical** adj retórico.

rheumatism ('ruːmətizəm) n reumatismo m.

rhinoceros (rai'nɔsərəs) n rinoceronte m.

rhyme (raim) n rima, poesía f. verso m. vt, vi rimar.

rhythm ('riðəm) n ritmo m.

rib (rib) n 1 anat costilla f. 2 varilla f. vt inf tomar el pelo.

ribbon ('ribən) n cinta f.

rice (rais) n arroz m.

rich (ritʃ) adj 1 rico. 2 lujoso, suntuoso. 3 sabroso, delicioso. 4 fértil.

rickety ('rikiti) adj inseguro, inestable, peligroso.

rid* (rid) vt librar, desembarazar. **get rid of** desembarazarse de.

riddance ('ridns) n libramiento m. **good riddance!** ¡menos mal!

riddle[1] ('ridl) n problema, misterio, acertijo m.

riddle[2] ('ridl) vt cribar.

ride* (raid) n 1 excursión f. paseo a caballo, paseo en coche m. 2 recorrido m. vi 1 montar. 2 viajar, ir.

ridge (ridʒ) n 1 (of mountains) sierra f. 2 arruga f.

ridicule ('ridikjuːl) n ridículo m. burla f. vt ridiculizar. **ridiculous** adj ridículo, absurdo, grotesco.

rife (raif) adj muy común.

rifle[1] ('raifəl) n fusil m.

rifle[2] ('raifəl) vt robar, saquear.

rift (rift) n grieta, rendija f.

rig (rig) n naut aparejo m. vt 1 naut aparejar. 2 construir. **rigging** n naut cordaje, aparejo m.

right (rait) adj 1 justo. 2 exacto, preciso. 3 debido. 4 verdadero. 5 ideal. adv 1 bien. 2 exactamente. 3 a la derecha. n 1 derecha f. law derecho m. 3 bien m. n pl derechos m pl. **all right** ¡conforme! ¡está bien! **be right** tener razón. **right angle** n ángulo recto m. **right-hand** adj a la derecha, por la derecha. **right-handed** adj que usa la mano derecha. **right now** ahora mismo. **right of way** n derecho de paso m. **right-wing** adj derechista.

righteous ('raitʃəs) adj honrado, virtuoso, justo.

rigid ('ridʒid) adj rígido, firme.

rigour ('rigə) n rigor m.

rim (rim) n borde, extremo, canto m.

rind (raind) n piel, corteza, cáscara f.

ring[1] (riŋ) n 1 círculo m. 2 anillo m. vt 1 rodear. 2 anillar. **ringleader** n cabecilla f. **ring-road** n carretera de circunvalación f.

ring[2] (riŋ) n 1 resonancia f. 2 repique, campaneo m. 3 llamada f. vt 1 hacer sonar. 2 repicar.

rink (riŋk) n pista f. patinadero m.

rinse (rins) n 1 aclarado m. 2 reflejos m pl. vt enjuagar, aclarar.

riot ('raiət) n alboroto, tumulto, disturbio m. vi alborotar, rebelarse.

rip (rip) n rasgadura f. rasgón m. vt rasgar.

ripe (raip) adj 1 maduro. 2 listo, dispuesto, preparado. **ripen** vt, vi madurar.

ripple ('ripəl) n onda, ola f. rizo m. vi rizarse.

rise* (raiz) n 1 subida, elevación f. 2 aumento m. 3 salida f. vi 1 levantarse. 2 subir, elevar. 3 aumentar.

risk (risk) n riesgo m. vt arriesgar.

rite (rait) n rito m. **last rites** exequias f pl.

ritual ('ritjuəl) adj,n ritual m.

rival ('raivəl) adj,n rival m. vt competir con, rivalizar con.

river ('rivə) n río m. **riverside** adj ribereño. n orilla, margen, ribera f.

rivet ('rivit) n remache, roblón m. vt remachar, clavar.

road (roud) n camino m. carretera, calle, calzada f.

roam (roum) vt vagar por, errar por. vi vagar, errar.

roar (rɔː) n rugido, bramido m. vi rugir, bramar.

roast (roust) n carne asada f. adj asado. vt asar.

rob (rɔb) vt robar, hurtar.

robe (roub) n 1 manto m. vestidura, túnica f. 2 rel hábito m. sotana f.

robin ('rɔbin) n petirrojo m.

robot ('roubɔt) n autómata, robot m.

robust (rou'bʌst) adj robusto.

rock[1] (rɔk) n roca, piedra, peña f.

rock[2] (rɔk) vi 1 bambolear, tambalear. 2 mecerse, balancearse. **rocker** n 1 tech balancín m. 2 mecedora f. **rocking-chair** n mecedora f. **rocking-horse** n caballo mecedor, caballo de balancín m.

rocket ('rɔkit) n cohete m.

rod (rɔd) n 1 palo m. vara, varilla f. 2 tech barra f. **fishing rod** n caña f.

rode (roud) v see ride.

rodent (´roudṇt) n roedor m.

roe (rou) n 1 (hard) hueva f. 2 (soft) lecha f.

roe deer n corzo m.

rogue (roug) n 1 pillo, gamberro, bribón, pícaro m.

role (roul) n papel m.

roll (roul) n 1 panecillo, bollo m. 2 lista f. catálogo m. 3 bamboleo m. 4 redoble m. vt 1 hacer rodar, dar vueltas. 2 liar. 3 tambalear. **roller** n 1 tech rodillo m. 2 rueda, ruedecilla f. 3 naut ola grande. **roller-skate** n patín de ruedas m. **rolling pin** n rodillo m.

Roman Catholic adj,n católico romano m.

romance (rǝ´mæns) adj romance. n 1 lit novela sentimental f. 2 amores m pl. **romantic** adj romántico, sentimental. n romántico m.

Rome (roum) n Roma f. **Roman** adj,n romano m.

romp (rɔmp) n juego, retozo m. vi 1 retozar, hacer cabriolas. 2 jugar, juguetear.

roof (ru:f) n 1 techa, tejado m. techumbre f. 2 anat paladar m. 3 hogar m. morada f. vt techar.

rook (ruk) n 1 zool grajo m. 2 game torre f. vt engañar, defraudar.

room (ru:m) n 1 cuarto m. habitación, pieza f. 2 lugar, sitio m. n pl alojamiento m. vi alojarse. **roomy** adj espacioso, amplio.

roost (ru:st) n percha f. gallinero m. vi descansar en la percha.

root[1] (ru:t) n 1 bot,math raíz f. 2 origen m. base f. **root out** vt arrancar, desarraigar. **take root** vi bot echar raíces.

root[2] (ru:t) vi hocicar.

rope (roup) n cuerda, soga f. cordel m.

rosary (´rouzǝri) n rosario m.

rose[1] (rouz) n bot rosa f. **rosebush** n rosal m. **rose garden** n rosaleda f. **rosy** adj 1 rosado, color de rosa. 2 inf prometedor, alegre.

rose[2] (rouz) v see **rise**.

rosemary (´rouzmǝri) n romero m.

rot (rɔt) n 1 podredumbre f. 2 decadencia, ruina f. 3 inf disparate m. tontería f. vt pudrir, descomponer. **rotten** adj 1 podrido, descompuesto, fétido, corrompido. 2 vil, desagradable, fatal.

rota (´routǝ) n lista f. **rotary** adj rotativo. **rotate** vt 1 hacer girar, dar vueltas a.

rouge (ru:ʒ) n carmín m.

rough (rʌf) adj 1 áspero, escabroso. 2 brutal, abrupto. 3 tempestuoso, violento. 4 borroso,

aproximado. n 1 bruto m. 2 aspereza, dureza f.

round (raund) adj 1 redondo, circular. 2 rotundo. adv alrededor. n 1 esfera f. círculo m. 2 circuito m. vuelta f. 3 rodaja f. 4 tiro m. 5 ronda f. prep alrededor de. vt doblar, circundar, rodear. **roundabout** adj indirecto. n 1 tiovivo m. 2 mot redondel m.

rouse (rauz) vt 1 despertar. 2 excitar, estimular, provocar. 3 animar.

route (ru:t) n ruta, vía f.

routine (ru:´ti:n) adj rutinario, acostumbrado. n rutina, costumbre f.

rove (rouv) vt errar por, vagar por.

row[1] (rou) n fila, línea, hilera f. **in a row** seguido.

row[2] (rou) vt,vi remar.

row[3] (rau) n 1 alboroto, ruido, tumulto, estrépito m. 2 disputa, querella, riña f. vi reñir, querellar, pelear.

rowdy (´raudi) adj ruidoso, alborotador, estrepitoso.

royal (´rɔiǝl) adj 1 real. 2 espléndido, magnífico. **royalty** n 1 realeza f. 2 familia real f. 3 pl derechos m pl.

rub (rʌb) n frotamiento, roce m. vt frotar, estregar, rozar, raer.

rubber (´rʌbǝ) n 1 goma f. caucho m. 2 goma de borrar. 3 game partida f. adj de goma, de caucho. **rubber band** n liga de goma, gomita f.

rubbish (´rʌbiʃ) n 1 basura, suciedad f. 2 inf tontería, necedad f. disparate m.

rubble (´rʌbǝl) n escombros m pl.

ruby (´ru:bi) n rubí m.

rucksack (´rʌksæk) n mochila f. morral m.

rudder (´rʌdǝ) n naut timón, gobernalle m.

rude (ru:d) adj 1 grosero, descortés, insolente. 2 rudo, inculto.

rudiment (´ru:dimǝnt) n rudimento m.

rueful (´ru:fǝl) adj triste, afligido, melancólico.

ruff (rʌf) n gorguera f.

ruffian (´rʌfiǝn) n gamberro, pícaro, pillo m.

ruffle (´rʌfǝl) n volante m. vt 1 arrugar, perturbar, agitar.

rug (rʌg) n alfombra f.

rugby (´rʌgbi) n rugby m.

rugged (´rʌgid) adj 1 robusto, vigoroso. 2 duro, tosco. 3 fuerte. 4 áspero, escabroso.

ruin (´ru:in) n ruina f. vt arruinar, destrozar.

rule (ru:l) n 1 gobierno, mando m. 2 regla, ley f. 3 costumbre f. hábito m. vt 1 gobernar, mandar, regir. 2 math reglar, rayar. **ruler** n 1 monarca, soberano, gobernante m. 2 *math* regla f.

rum (rʌm) n ron m.

Rumania (ruːˈmeiniə) n Rumania f. **Rumanian** adj,n rumano. **Rumanian** (language) n rumano m.

rumble (ˈrʌmbəl) n retumbo, rumor, trueno m. vi retumbar, tronar.

rummage (ˈrʌmidʒ) vi **rummage in** revolver en. **rummage sale** n venta de prendas usadas f.

rumour (ˈruːmə) n.rumor m.

rump (rʌmp) n 1 *anat* trasero, culo m. nalgas f pl. 2 *cul* cuarto trasero m. 3 anca f.

run (rʌn) n 1 carrera f. 2 serie, sucesión f. vt 1 correr. 2 dirigir, gobernar. **run away** huir. **runner** n 1 corredor, competidor m. 2 patín m. 3 corredera f. **runner bean** n judía f. fríjol m. **runner-up** n subcampeón m. **running** adj 1 corriente, corredor. 2 *med* supurante. n 1 funcionamiento m. marcha f. 2 carrera, corrida f. 3 dirección f. gobierno m. **runway** n *aviat* pista de aterrizaje f.

rung[1] (rʌŋ) v see **ring**[2].

rung[2] (rʌŋ) n escalón, peldaño m.

rupture (ˈrʌptʃə) n ruptura f. vt causar una hernia en, quebrar, romper.

rural (ˈruərəl) adj rural, campestre, rústico.

rush[1] (rʌʃ) adj urgente, apremiante. n prisa f. apuro m. vi darse prisa, apresurarse, precipitarse, apurar. vt mil asaltar, atacar de repente.

rush[2] (rʌʃ) n *bot* junco m.

Russia (ˈrʌʃə) n Rusia f. **Russian** adj,n ruso. **Russian** (language) n ruso m.

rust (rʌst) n herrumbre, oxidación f. vi oxidarse. **rusty** adj herrumbroso, oxidado.

rustic (ˈrʌstik) adj 1 rústico, campesino, campestre, pastoral. 2 palurdo, toso, rudo. n rústico, palurdo m.

rustle (ˈrʌsəl) n murmullo, susurro m. vi murmurar, susurrar.

rut (rʌt) n 1 bache, carril, surco m. rodera f. 2 rutina f. 3 *zool* celo m. **be in a rut** de esclavo ser la rutina.

ruthless (ˈruːθləs) adj despiadado, desalmado.

rye (rai) n centeno m.

S

Sabbath (ˈsæbəθ) n 1 sábado m. 2 domingo m.

sable (ˈseibəl) n *zool* cebellina.

sabotage (ˈsæbətɑːʒ) n sabotaje m. vt sabotear.

sabre (ˈseibə) n sable m.

saccharin (ˈsækərin) n sacarina f. adj sacarino.

sachet (ˈsæʃei) n *bol*sita f. saquito m.

sack[1] (sæk) n 1 costal, saco, zurrón m. 2 *inf* despedida f. vt *inf* despedir.

sack[2] (sæk) n saqueo. vt saquear.

sacrament (ˈsækrəmənt) n sacramento m.

sacred (ˈseikrid) adj sagrado, santo.

sacrifice (ˈsækrifais) n sacrificio m. vt,vi sacrificar.

sacrilege (ˈsækrilidʒ) n sacrilegio m.

sad (sæd) adj triste, sombrío, melancólico. **sadden** vt entristecer.

saddle (ˈsædl) n 1 silla de montar f. 2 sillín m. 3 (of meat) cuarto trasero m. vt ensillar.

sadism (ˈseidizəm) n sadismo m.

safari (səˈfɑːri) n safari m.

safe (seif) adj 1 seguro. 2 salvo. 3 cierto. n caja fuerte f. **safely** adv con seguridad. **safeguard** n salvaguardia f. vt salvaguardar. **safety** n seguridad f. **safety belt** n cinturón de seguridad m. **safety pin** n imperdible m.

saffron (ˈsæfrən) n *bot* azafrán m.

sag (sæg) vi 1 ceder. 2 combarse. n comba f.

saga (ˈsɑːgə) n saga f.

sage[1] (seidʒ) adj,n sabio.

sage[2] (seidʒ) n *bot* salvia f.

Sagittarius (sædʒiˈtɛəriəs) n Sagitario m.

sago (ˈseigou) n sagú m.

said (sed) v see **say.**

sail (seil) n 1 *naut* vela f. 2 aspa f. vt *naut* gobernar. vi *naut* 1 navegar. 2 flotar, volar. **sailor** n marinero, marino m.

saint (seint) n santo m.

sake (seik) n causa f. motivo m. **for the sake of** por motivo de, por.

salad (ˈsæləd) n ensalada f. **salad dressing** n 1 aliño m. 2 mayonesa f.

salami (səˈlɑːmi) n salchichón m.

salary (ˈsæləri) n salario, sueldo m.

sale (seil) n 1 venta f. 2 liquidación f. saldo m. **for sale** se vende. **on sale** de venta. **salesman** n vendedor m. **salesmanship** n arte de vender m. **travelling salesman** n viajante m.

saliva (səˈlaivə) n saliva f. **salivate** vi salivar.

sallow (ˈsælou) adj amarillento, cetrino.

salmon (ˈsæmən) n invar salmón m.

salon (ˈsælɔn) n salón m.

saloon (səˈluːn) n 1 salón m. 2 *mot* turismo m.

salt (sɔːlt) n sal f. **salt-cellar** n salero m. **salty** adj salado.

salute (səˈluːt) n saludo m. vt saludar.

scene

salvage ('sælvidʒ) n salvamento m. vt salvar.
salvation (sæl'veiʃən) n salvación f.
salve (sælv) n ungüento m.
same (seim) adj 1 mismo, idéntico. igual. 2 monótono. **all the same** a pesar de todo.
sample ('sɑ:mpəl) n muestra f. vt probar, ensayar.
sanatorium (sænə'tɔ:riəm) n sanatorio m.
sanction ('sæŋkʃən) n 1 sanción f. 2 autorización f. vt 1 sancionar. 2 autorizar.
sanctity ('sæŋktiti) n santidad f.
sanctuary ('sæŋktʃuəri) n santuario m.
sand (sænd) n arena f. **sandpaper** n papel de lija m. vt lijar. **sandpit** n arenal, hoyo de arena m.
sandal ('sændl) n sandalia, alpargata f.
sandwich ('sænwidʒ) n bocadillo, sándwich m. vt intercalar.
sane (sein) adj 1 cuerdo, juicioso. 2 prudente. **sanity** n cordura, sensatez f.
sang (sæŋ) v see **sing**.
sanitary ('sænitri) adj higiénico, sanitario. **sanitary towel** n compresa higiénica f. **sanitation** n sanidad f.
sank (sæŋk) v see **sink**.
sap (sæp) n bot savia f. vt agotar, desgastar.
sapphire ('sæfaiə) n zafiro m.
sarcasm ('sɑ:kæzəm) n sarcasmo m. **sarcastic** adj sarcástico.
sardine (sɑ:'di:n) n sardina f.
sardonic (sɑ:'dɔnik) adj sardónico.
sash[1] (sæʃ) n banda, faja f.
sash[2] (sæʃ) n marco corredizo de ventana m.
sat (sæt) v see **sit**.
Satan ('seitn) n Satán m. **satanic** adj satánico.
satchel ('sætʃəl) n cartera f. cartapacio m.
satellite ('sætəlait) n satélite m.
satin ('sætin) n raso m.
satire ('sætaiə) n sátira f. **satirical** adj satírico. **satirize** vt satirizar.
satisfy ('sætisfai) vt satisfacer. **satisfactory** adj satisfactorio. **satisfaction** n satisfacción f.
saturate ('sætʃəreit) vt saturar.
Saturday ('sætədi) n sábado m.
Saturn ('sætən) n Saturno m.
sauce (sɔ:s) n salsa f. **saucepan** n cacerola f. **saucer** n platillo m. **saucy** adj impertinente, fresco.
Saudi Arabia ('saudi) n Arabia Saudita, Arabia Saudí f.
sauerkraut ('sauəkraut) n chucruta f.
sauna ('sɔ:nə) n sauna f.

saunter ('sɔ:ntə) vi pasearse lentamente. n paseo lento m.
sausage ('sɔsidʒ) n salchicha f. embutido m.
savage ('sævidʒ) adj,n salvaje. vt atacar, embestir.
save[1] (seiv) vt 1 salvar. 2 ahorrar, economizar. 3 guardar.
save[2] (seiv) prep, conj salvo, excepto.
saviour ('seiviə) n salvador m.
savoury ('seivəri) adj 1 sabroso. 2 no dulce, salado.
saw[1] (sɔ:) n sierra f. vt 1 serrar, aserrar. 2 talar. **sawdust** n serrín m.
saw[2] (sɔ:) v see **see**[1].
Saxon ('sæksən) n,adj sajón m.
saxophone ('sæksəfoun) n saxofón m.
say* (sei) vt decir, afirmar. **saying** n dicho, refrán m.
scab (skæb) n costra f.
scaffold ('skæfəld) n cadalso m. **scaffolding** n andamio m.
scald (skɔ:ld) vt escaldar.
scale[1] (skeil) n escama f.
scale[2] (skeil) n 1 escala f. 2 mus pentagrama m. vt escalar.
scale[3] (skeil) n balanza f.
scallop ('skɔləp) n 1 zool venera f. 2 festón m.
scalp (skælp) n cuero cabelludo m.
scalpel ('skælpəl) n 1 escalpelo m. 2 bisturí m.
scampi ('skæmpi) n gamba grande f.
scan (skæn) vt examinar, medir.
scandal ('skændl) n escándalo m. **scandalous** adj escandaloso, vergonzoso.
Scandinavia (skændi'neiviə) n Escandinavia f. **Scandinavian** adj,n escandinavo.
scant (skænt) adj escaso.
scapegoat ('skeipgout) n víctima f.
scar (skɑ:) n cicatriz, señal f. vt señalar, marcar.
scarce (skɛəs) adj escaso. **scarcity** n escasez f. **scarcely** adv escasamente, apenas.
scare (skɛə) vt 1 asustar, atemorizar. 2 ahuyentar. n susto m. **scarecrow** n espantapájaros m invar.
scarf (skɑ:f) n, pl **scarfs** or **scarves** 1 bufanda f. 2 pañuelo de cabeza m.
scarlet ('skɑ:lit) n escarlata, grana f. adj de color escarlata, grana. **scarlet fever** n escarlatina f.
scathing ('skeiðiŋ) adj mordaz.
scatter ('skætə) vt dispersar, esparcir. **scatterbrain** n cabeza loca f.
scavenge ('skævindʒ) vi recoger la basura.
scene (si:n) n 1 Th escena f. 2 paisaje m

269

scenery ('si:nəri) n 1 paisaje m. 2 Th decorado m.

scent (sent) n 1 perfume m. 2 rastro m.

sceptic ('skeptik) adj,n escéptico m. **scepticism** n escepticismo m.

sceptre ('septə) n cetro m.

schedule ('ʃedju:l) n 1 lista f. 2 horario m. vt fijar la hora.

scheme (ski:m) n esquema, plan m. vt planear, proyectar.

schizophrenia (skitsou'fri:niə) n esquizofrenia f. **schizophrenic** n esquizofrénico m.

scholar ('skɔlə) n 1 colegial, escolar m. 2 sabio m. **scholarship** n 1 beca f. 2 erudición f.

scholastic (skə'læstik) adj escolástico.

school[1] (sku:l) n colegio m. escuela f. **schoolboy** n colegial m. **schoolmaster** n profesor, maestro m.

school[2] (sku:l) n escuela f. grupo m.

schooner ('sku:nə) n goleta f.

science ('saiəns) n ciencia f. **scientist** n científico m. **science fiction** n ciencia ficción f. **scientific** adj científico.

scissors ('sizəz) n pl tijeras f pl.

scoff[1] (skɔf) vi mofarse de.

scoff[2] (skɔf) inf vt engullir. n comida f.

scold (skould) vt reñir, regañar.

scoop (sku:p) vt 1 recoger. 2 sacar, excavar. n pala, cuchara f.

scooter ('sku:tə) n 1 escuter, moto m. 2 patinete m.

scope (skoup) n extensión f. alcance m.

scorch (skɔ:tʃ) vt chamuscar, abrasar.

score (skɔ:) vt 1 sport marcar. 2 rayar. n 1 mus partitura f. 2 sport tanteo m. 3 veintena f. **scoreboard** n tanteador m.

scorn (skɔ:n) vt desdeñar. n desdén, desprecio m.

Scorpio ('skɔ:piou) n Escorpión m.

scorpion ('skɔ:piən) n escorpión, alacrán m.

Scotland ('skɔtlənd) n Escocia f. **Scot** n escocés m. **Scotch** adj escocés. n wisky m. **Scottish** adj escocés.

scoundrel ('skaundrəl) n canalla m. sinvergüenza m.

scour[1] ('skauə) vt limpiar, fregar.

scour[2] ('skauə) vt buscar, registrar.

scout (skaut) n explorador, adelantado m. vt explorar, reconocer.

scowl (skaul) vi fruncir el ceño. n mueca f. ceño m.

scramble ('skræmbəl) vt revolver. **scrambled eggs** n pl huevos revueltos m pl.

scrap[1] (skræp) n 1 resto m. 2 pizca f. vt desechar. **scrapbook** n libro de recortes m. **scrap iron** n hierro viejo m. chatarra f.

scrap[2] (skræp) inf n riña. vi riñar.

scrape (skreip) vt 1 raspar. 2 rebañar.

scratch (skrætʃ) vt rascar, arañar. n rasguño, arañazo m.

scrawl (skrɔ:l) vt garabatear. n garabato m.

scream (skri:m) vi chillar. n chillido m.

screech (skri:tʃ) vi 1 chillar. 2 chirriar.

screen (skri:n) n 1 biombo m. 2 pantalla f. vt 1 ocultar. 2 examinar. 3 proyectar.

screw (skru:) n tornillo m. vt atornillar, fijar. **screwdriver** n destornillador m.

scribble ('skribəl) vt garabatear, emborronar. n garabato m.

script (skript) n 1 letra f. 2 guión m.

Scripture ('skriptʃə) n Sagrada Escritura f.

scroll (skroul) n rollo de pergamino m.

scrounge (skraundʒ) vt gorronear.

scrub[1] (skrʌb) vt fregar, estregar. **scrubbing brush** n estregadera f

scrub[2] (skrʌb) n matorral m.

scruffy ('skrʌfi) adj desaliñado.

scruple ('skru:pəl) n escrúpulo m. **scrupulous** adj escrupuloso.

scrutinize ('skru:tinaiz) vt escudriñar. **scrutiny** n escrutinio, examen m.

scuffle ('skʌfəl) n riña, pelea f. vi reñir, pelearse.

scullery ('skʌləri) n fregadero, office m.

sculpt (skʌlpt) vt esculpir. **sculptor** n escultor m. **sculpture** n escultura f.

scum (skʌm) n 1 espuma f. 2 canalla f. 3 heces m pl.

scythe (saið) n guadaña f. vt guadañar.

sea (si:) n mar m. f.

seabed ('si:bed) n fondo del mar m.

seafaring ('si:fɛəriŋ) adj marinero.

seafront ('si:frʌnt) n paseo marítimo m.

seagull ('si:gʌl) n gaviota f.

seahorse ('si:hɔ:s) n caballito de mar m.

seal[1] (si:l) n sello m. vt 1 sellar. 2 cerrar. 3 lacrar. **sealing-wax** n lacre m.

seal[2] (si:l) n zool foca f. **sealskin** n piel de foca f

sea-level n nivel del mar m.

sea-lion n león marino m.

seam (si:m) n 1 dom costura f. 2 junta f. 3 veta, vena f. vt coser.

seaman ('si:mən) n marinero m. **seamanship** n náutica, marinería f.

search (sə:tʃ) vt 1 buscar. 2 registrar. 3 examinar. n 1 búsqueda f. 2 registro m. **searchlight** n proyector m.

seashore ('si:ʃɔ:) n costa del mar, orilla del mar f.

seasick ('si:sik) adj mareado. **become seasick** marearse.

seaside ('si:said) n playa del mar, orilla del mar f.

season ('si:zən) n 1 estación f. 2 temporada f. vt 1 cul sazonar. 2 curar. **seasonable** adj propio de la estación. **seasoning** n condimento m. **season ticket** n abono m.

seat (si:t) n 1 asiento m. 2 pol escaño m. 3 Th localidad f. **seat-belt** n cinturón de seguridad m.

sea water n agua de mar f.

seaweed ('si:wi:d) n alga marina f.

secluded (si'klu:did) adj aislado, retirado.

second[1] ('sekənd) adj,n segundo m. **second best** n sustituto m. adj de segunda categoría. **second class** n segunda clase f. **secondhand** adj de segunda mano. **second-rate** adj de baja calidad. ~vt apoyar. **secondary** adj secundario. **secondary school** n instituto de enseñanza media m.

second[2] ('sekənd) n segundo m.

secret ('si:krət) adj,n secreto m. **secret agent** n agente secreto m. **secrecy** n secreto. **secretive** adj reservado.

secretary ('sekrətri) n secretario m.

secrete (si'kri:t) vt 1 esconder. 2 secretar.

sect (sekt) n secta f. **sectarian** adj sectario.

section ('sekʃən) n sección f.

sector ('sektə) n sector m.

secular ('sekjulə) adj invar secular.

secure (si'kjuə) vt 1 conseguir. 2 asegurar. adj seguro. **security** n 1 seguridad f. 2 comm fianza f. 3 pl comm valores m pl.

sedate (si'deit) adj sosegado. **sedation** n sedación f. tratamiento con calmantes m. **sedative** n,adj calmante, sedante m.

sediment ('sedimənt) n sedimento m. **sedimentary** adj sedimentario.

seduce (si'dju:s) vt seducir. **seduction** n seducción f. **seductive** adj seductor.

see[1] (si:) vt ver, percibir. **see about** encargarse de. **see to** atender a.

see[2] (si:) n rel sede f.

seed (si:d) n semilla f. **seedling** n planta de semillero f. **seedy** adj inf 1 ojeroso. 2 asqueroso.

seek[*] (si:k) vt buscar. **seek to** intentar.

seem (si:m) vi parecer.

seen (si:n) v see **see**[1].

seep (si:p) vi filtrarse.

seesaw ('si:sɔ:) n columpio de balancín m. vi columpiarse.

seethe (si:ð) vi hervir.

segment ('segmənt) n segmento m.

segregate ('segrigeit) vt segregar. **segregation** n segregación f.

seize (si:z) vt 1 coger. 2 apoderarse de.

seldom ('seldəm) adv raramente.

select (si'lekt) vt seleccionar. adj selecto. **selection** n selección f. **selective** adj selectivo.

self (self) n, pl **selves** uno mismo, una misma. pron 1 se. 2 sí mismo.

self-assured adj seguro de sí mismo.

self-aware adj consciente de sí mismo.

self-centred adj egocéntrico.

self-confident adj seguro de sí mismo.

self-conscious adj cohibido.

self-contained adj independiente.

self-defence n defensa propia f.

self-discipline n autodisciplina f.

self-employed adj que trabaja por cuenta propia.

self-expression n autoexpresión f.

self-indulgent adj inmoderado.

self-interest n egoísmo m.

selfish ('selfiʃ) adj egoísta.

self-pity n compasión de sí mismo f.

self-portrait n autorretrato m.

self-respect n dignidad f.

self-righteous adj santurrón.

self-sacrifice n abnegación f.

selfsame ('selfseim) adj mismísimo.

self-satisfied adj pagado de sí mismo.

self-service n autoservicio m.

self-sufficient adj independiente.

self-will n obstinación f.

sell[*] (sel) vt vender.

Sellotape ('seləteip) n Tdmk cinta adhesiva f.

semantic (si'mæntik) adj semántico. **semantics** n semántica f.

semaphore ('seməfɔ:) n semáforo m.

semibreve ('semibri:v) n semibreve f.

semicircle ('semisə:kəl) n semicírculo m.

semicolon (semi'koulən) n punto y coma m.

semidetached (semidi'tætʃt) adj semiseparado. **semidetached house** n casa parcialmente separada f.

semifinal (semi'fainl) n semifinal f.

seminar ('seminɑ:) n seminario m. **seminary** n seminario m.

271

semiprecious (semi'preʃəs) adj semiprecioso.

semiquaver (semi'kweivə) n semicorchea f.

semivowel ('semivauəl) n semivocal f.

semolina (seməli:nə) n sémola f.

senate ('senət) n senado m.

send' ('send) vt **1** enviar. **2** despachar. **3** lanzar.

senile ('si:nail) adj senil. **senility** n debilidad senil f.

senior ('si:niə) adj mayor, más antiguo.

sensation (sen'seiʃən) n sensación f. **sensational** adj sensacional.

sense (sens) n **1** sentido m. **2** juicio m.

sensible ('sensəbəl) adj sensato. **sensibility** n sensibilidad f.

sensitive ('sensitiv) adj sensible, impresionable. **sensitivity** n lo impresionable, neu. delicadeza f.

sensual ('senʃuəl) adj sensual. **sensuality** n sensualidad f.

sensuous ('senʃuəs) adj sensual.

sentence ('sentəns) n **1** gram oración f. **2** law sentencia, condena f. vt sentenciar.

sentiment ('sentimənt) n sentimiento m. **sentimental** adj sentimental.

sentry ('sentri) n centinela m.

separate (adj 'seprit; v 'sepəreit) adj separado. vt separar. **separation** n separación f.

September (sep'tembə) n septiembre m.

septet (sep'tet) n septeto m.

septic ('septik) adj séptico.

sequel ('si:kwəl) n **1** lit continuación f. **2** resultado m.

sequence ('si:kwəns) n **1** orden m. **2** secuencia f.

sequin ('si:kwin) n lentejuela f.

serenade (serə'neid) n serenata f.

serene (si'ri:n) adj sereno. **serenity** n serenidad f.

serf (sə:f) n siervo m.

sergeant (sa:dʒənt) n sargento m. **sergeant major** n sargento major m.

serial ('siəriəl) adj consecutivo. n **serial number** n número de serie m. **serialize** vt convertir en serial.

series ('siəri:z) n invar serie f.

serious ('siəriəs) adj serio. **seriousness** n seriedad f.

sermon ('sə:mən) n sermón m.

serpent ('sə:pənt) n sierpe, serpiente f.

serve (sə:v) vt servir. vi sport sacar. **servant** n sirviente, criado m.

service ('sə:vis) n servicio m. **service station** n estación de servicio f.

serviette (sə:vi'et) n servilleta f.

servile ('sə:vail) adj servil.

session ('seʃən) n sesión f.

set' (set) n **1** juego m. **2** grupo m. **3** colección f. vt colocar, poner. adj **1** resuelto. **2** rígido. **setback** n contratiempo m. **setting** n **1** alrededores m pl. **2** puesta f.

settee (se'ti·) n sofá m.

settle ('setl) vt **1** arreglar. **2** ajustar. **3** calmar. **settlement** n **1** colonia f. **2** convenio m.

seven ('sevən) n,adj siete m. **seventh** n,adj séptimo m.

seventeen (sevən'ti:n) n,adj diecisiete m. **seventeenth** adj decimoséptimo.

seventy ('sevənti) n,adj setenta m. **seventieth** adj septuagésimo.

several ('sevrəl) adj varios pl.

severe (si'viə) adj severo. **severity** n severidad f.

Seville (sə'vil) n Sevilla f.

sew' (sou) vt coser. **sewing machine** n máquina de coser f.

sewage ('su:idʒ) n aguas residuales f pl.

sewer ('su:ə) n alcantarilla f. **sewerage** n alcantarillado m.

sex (seks) n sexo m. **sexual** adj sexual. **sexuality** n sexualidad f. **sexy** adj sensual.

sextet (seks'tet) n sexteto m.

shabby ('ʃæbi) adj raido, gastado.

shack (ʃæk) n choza, chabola f.

shade (ʃeid) n **1** sombra f. **2** tonalidad f. vt dar sombra a.

shadow ('ʃædou) n sombra f. vt seguir. **shadow cabinet** n gabinete de oposición m.

shaft (ʃɑ:ft) n **1** rayo m. **2** mot eje m. **3** pozo m.

shaggy ('ʃægi) adj velludo, peludo.

shake' (ʃeik) vt sacudir, agitar. n sacudida f. meneo m. **shake hands** estrecharse la mano.

shall' (ʃəl; stressed ʃæl) v aux used in forming the future.

shallot (ʃə'lɔt) n chalote m.

shallow ('ʃælou) adj poco profundo, vadoso.

sham (ʃæm) vt,vi fingir. n engaño m. adj falso.

shame (ʃeim) n vergüenza f. vt avergonzar. **shameless** adj descarado. **shamefaced** adj avergonzado.

shampoo (ʃæm'pu:) n champú m. vi lavarse la cabeza.

shamrock ('ʃæmrɔk) n trébol m.

shandy ('ʃændi) n bebida de cerveza mezclada con limonada f.

shanty[1] ('ʃænti) n choza f.

shanty[2] ('ʃænti) n naut saloma f.

shape (ʃeip) vt formar. n forma f. **take shape** tomar forma.

share (ʃɛə) vt compartir. **share out** repartir. ~n 1 parte f. 2 comm acción f. **shareholder** n accionista f.

shark (ʃɑːk) n 1 tiburón m. 2 inf estafador m.

sharp (ʃɑːp) adj 1 agudo. 2 afilado. 3 definido. 4 mus sostenido. **sharp-sighted** adj de vista aguda or penetrante. **sharpen** vt afilar.

shatter ('ʃætə) vt estrellar, romper.

shave (ʃeiv) vt afeitar. n afeitado m. **shavings** n pl virutas f pl.

shawl (ʃɔːl) n mantón m.

she (ʃiː) pron 3rd pers s ella f.

sheaf (ʃiːf) n, pl **sheaves** 1 bot gavilla f. 2 haz m.

shear* (ʃiə) vt 1 cortar. 2 esquilar.

sheath (ʃiːθ) n vaina, funda f. **sheathe** vt envainar, enfundar.

shed¹ (ʃed) n 1 cobertizo m. 2 nave f.

shed*² (ʃed) vt 1 verter. 2 mudarse de.

sheen (ʃiːn) n brillo m.

sheep (ʃiːp) n invar oveja f. **sheepish** adj tímido. **sheepdog** n perro pastor m. **sheepskin** n zamarra f.

sheer¹ (ʃiə) adj diáfano, fino.

sheer² (ʃiə) vi desviarse. adv completamente.

sheet (ʃiːt) n 1 dom sábana f. 2 lámina f.

sheikh (ʃeik) n jeque m.

shelf (ʃelf) n, pl **shelves** 1 estante m. 2 geog banco m.

shell (ʃel) n 1 zool concha f. 2 mil granada f. projectil m. 3 bot cáscara f. vt 1 descascarar. 2 mil bombardear. **shellfish** n mariscos m pl.

shelter ('ʃeltə) n refugio m. vt proteger, abrigar.

shelve (ʃelv) vt aplazar.

shepherd ('ʃepəd) n pastor m.

sherbet ('ʃəːbət) n sorbete m.

sheriff ('ʃerif) n sheriff m.

sherry ('ʃeri) n jerez m.

shield (ʃiːld) n escudo m. vt proteger, escudar.

shift (ʃift) vt cambiar. n 1 cambio m. 2 turno m. **shifty** adj furtivo, sospecho.

shilling ('ʃiliŋ) n chelín m.

shimmer ('ʃimə) vi rielar. n resplandor, reflejo m.

shin (ʃin) n anat espinilla f.

shine* (ʃain) vi brillar. n brillo m.

ship (ʃip) n buque, barco m. vt transportar. **shipbuilding** n construcción naval f. **shipment** n 1 envío m. 2 transporte m. **shipshape**

adj en buen orden, en buena forma. **shipwreck** n naufragio m. **shipyard** n astillero m.

shirk (ʃəːk) vt eludir. **shirker** n gandul m.

shirt (ʃəːt) n camisa f.

shiver ('ʃivə) vi 1 tiritar. 2 temblar. n 1 tiritón m. 2 temblor m.

shock¹ (ʃɔk) n choque, sobresalto m. vt chocar, sobresaltar. **shocking** adj chocante. **shock absorber** n amortiguador m.

shock² (ʃɔk) n (of hair) greña f.

shoddy ('ʃɔdi) adj de pésima calidad.

shoe* (ʃuː) n 1 zapato m. 2 herradura f. vt 1 calzar. 2 herrar. **shoe-shop** n zapatería f. **shoelace** n cordón m.

shone (ʃɔn) v see **shine**.

shook (ʃuk) v see **shake**.

shoot* (ʃuːt) n 1 bot brote, renuevo m. 2 sport partida de caza f. vi 1 tirar, disparar. 2 fusilar. vi lanzarse.

shop (ʃɔp) n 1 tienda f. 2 taller m. vi ir de compras. **shop assistant** n dependiente m. dependienta f. **shop floor** n taller m. **shopkeeper** n tendero m. **shoplifter** n mechera f. ratero m. **shopping** n compras f pl. **shopwindow** n escaparate m.

shore¹ (ʃɔː) n orilla, ribesa f.

shore² (ʃɔː) vt apuntalar. **shore up** sostener.

shorn (ʃɔːn) v see **shear**.

short (ʃɔːt) adj 1 corto. 2 brusco. **shorten** vt acortar.

shortage ('ʃɔːtidʒ) n escasez f.

shortcoming ('ʃɔːtkʌmiŋ) n defecto m.

shorthand ('ʃɔːthænd) n taquigrafía f.

short-handed adv falto de personal.

shortlived ('ʃɔːtlivd) adj efímero.

short-sighted adj miope.

short-tempered adj enojadizo.

short-term adj a corto plazo.

short-wave n onda corta f.

shot¹ (ʃɔt) n 1 disparo m. 2 sport tiro m. **shotgun** n escopeta f.

shot² (ʃɔt) v see **shoot**.

should (ʃəd; stressed ʃud) v aux see **shall**.

shoulder ('ʃouldə) n 1 hombro m. 2 geog lomo m. vt 1 llevar al hombro. 2 cargar con. **shoulder-blade** n omóplato m. paletilla f.

shout (ʃaut) n grito m. vt, vi gritar.

shove (ʃʌv) vt empujar. n empujón m.

shovel ('ʃʌvəl) n pala f. vt traspalar.

show* (ʃou) n 1 exhibición f. 2 Th función f. vt exhibir. **show off** hacer gala de. **show business** n negocio del espectáculo m. **showcase** n vitrina f. **showdown** n momento decisivo, momento de la verdad m. **show-jumping** n concurso hípico m. **showmanship** n teatralidad f. **showroom** n sala de exposiciones f.

shower ('ʃauə) n 1 ducha f. 2 chubasco m. vi 1 ducharse. 2 llover. **showerproof** adj impermeable

shrank (ʃræŋk) v see **shrink**.

shred (ʃred) n triza f. vt hacer trizas.

shrewd (ʃruːd) adj astuto. **shrewdness** n astucia f

shriek (ʃriːk) vt chillar. n chillido m.

shrill (ʃril) adj agudo, chillón.

shrimp (ʃrimp) n camarón m.

shrine (ʃrain) n 1 capilla f. 2 santuario m./

shrink* (ʃriŋk) vt encoger. **shrinkage** n encogimiento m.

shrivel ('ʃrivəl) vt arrugar.

shroud (ʃraud) n mortaja f. vt amortajar.

Shrove Tuesday (ʃrouv) n martes de carnaval m

shrub (ʃrʌb) n arbusto m. **shrubbery** n plantío de arbustos m.

shrug (ʃrʌg) vi encogerse de hombros. n encogimiento de hombros m.

shrunk (ʃrʌŋk) v see **shrink**.

shudder ('ʃʌdə) vi estremecerse. n estremecimiento m.

shuffle ('ʃʌfəl) vi arrastrar los pies. vt game barajar. n game barajadura f.

shun (ʃʌn) vt evitar, esquivar.

shunt (ʃʌnt) vt maniobrar.

shut* (ʃʌt) vt cerrar, obstruir. **shut up!** ¡cállate!

shutter ('ʃʌtə) n 1 contraventana f. 2 phot obturador m.

shuttlecock ('ʃʌtlkɔk) n volante m.

shy (ʃai) adj tímido. vi espantarse. **shyness** n timidez f.

Sicily ('sisəli) n Sicilia f.

sick (sik) adj enfermo. **be sick** vomitar, estar enfermo. **be sick of** inf estar harto de. **sicken** vt dar asco a. vi enfermar. **sickness** n enfermedad, náusea f.

side (said) n lado, costado m. **sideboard** n aparador m. **side effect** n efecto secundario m. **sidelight** n luz de costado f. **sideline** n 1 sport línea lateral f. 2 comm empleo secundario m. **sideshow** n caseta de feria f. **sidestep** vt esquivar. **sidetrack** vt apartar, desviar. **sideways** adv de lado, hacia un lado. **siding** n mot apartadero m.

sidle ('saidl) vi acercarse cautelosamente.

siege (siːdʒ) n sitio m. **lay seige to** sitiar.

sieve (siv) n colador, tamiz m. vt colar.

sift (sift) vt tamizar, colar.

sigh (sai) n suspiro m. vi suspirar.

sight (sait) n 1 vista f. 2 mira f. 3 espectáculo m. vt 1 divisar. 2 apuntar. **catch sight of** alcanzar a ver. **sightread** vt ejecutar a la primera lectura. **sightseeing** n excursionismo m.

sign (sain) n 1 señal f. indicio m. 2 signo m vt firmar. **signpost** n poste indicador m.

signal ('signl) n señal f. vt señalar, comunicar por señales. adj insigne, señalado.

signature ('signətʃə) n firma f. **signatory** n firmante m.

signify ('signifai) vt significar. **significant** adj significante, significativo. **significance** n significación f.

silence ('sailəns) n silencio m. vt imponer silencio. **silencer** n tech silenciador m. **silent** adj silencioso.

silhouette (silu'et) n silueta f.

silk (silk) n seda f. **silky** adj sedoso. **silkworm** n gusano de seda m.

sill (sil) n 1 umbral m. 2 alféizar m.

silly ('sili) adj tonto. **silliness** n tontería f.

silt (silt) n sedimento m.

silver ('silvə) n plata f. adj de plata.

similar ('similə) adj semejante, parecido. **similarity** n parecido m.

simile ('simili) n símil m.

simmer ('simə) vt cocer a fuego lento. vi hervir a fuego lento

simple ('simpəl) adj sencillo. **simple-minded** adj inocente. **simplify** vt simplificar.

simultaneous (siməl'teiniəs) adj simultáneo.

sin (sin) n pecado m. vi pecar. **sinful** adj pecador.

since (sins) prep desde. conj 1 desde que. 2 puesto que. adv desde entonces, después.

sincere (sin'siə) adj sincero. **sincerity** n sinceridad f.

sinew ('sinjuː) n tendón m.

sing* (siŋ) vt 1 cantar. 2 (of birds) trinar.

singe (sindʒ) vt chamuscar.

single ('siŋgəl) adj único, solo. v **single out** señalar, escoger. **single person** n soltero m. **single-handed** adj sin ayuda.

singular ('siŋgjulə) adj singular, extraordinario. adj,n gram singular m.

sinister ('sinistə) adj siniestro.

sink* (siŋk) vt hundir. vi 1 hundirse. 2 sumergirse. 3 declinar. **sink in** penetrar. ~n pila f. fregadero m.

sinner (´sinə) n pecador m.

sinus (´sainəs) n seno m.

sip (sip) n sorbo m. vt sorber.

siphon (´saifən) n sifón. vt sacar con sifón.

sir (sə:) n señor m. **dear sir** muy señor mío.

siren (´sairən) n sirena f.

sirloin (´sə:bin) n solomillo m.

sister (´sistə) n hermana f. **sisterhood** n hermandad f. **sister-in-law** n cuñada f.

sit* (sit) vi sentarse. **sit-in** n huelga de brazos caídos f. **sitting** n sesión f. **sitting room** n sala de estar f.

site (sait) n sitio, solar m. vt situar.

situation (sitju´eiʃən) n 1 situación f. 2 colocación f.

six (siks) n,adj seis m. **sixth** adj sexto.

sixteen (siks´ti:n) n,adj diecisis m. **sixteenth** adj decimosexto.

sixty (´siksti) n,adj sesenta m. **sixtieth** adj sexagésimo.

size (saiz) n tamaño m. **sizeable** adj considerable.

sizzle (´sizəl) vi chisporrotear.

skate[1] (skeit) n patín m. vi patinar. **skating-rink** n pista de patinaje f.

skate[2] (skeit) n zool raya f.

skeleton (´skelətn) n 1 anat esqueleto m. 2 esquema m.

sketch (sketʃ) n 1 boceto m. 2 Th pieza corta f. vt bosquejar. **sketchy** adj incompleto.

skewer (´skjuə) n broqueta f. pincho m. vt espetar.

ski (ski:) vi esquiar. **ski-lift** n teleski m.

skid (skid) vi mot patinar. n mot patinazo m.

skill (skil) n destreza f. **skillful** adj diestro. **skilled** adj hábil, experto.

skim (skim) vt espumar. vi pasar rasando. **skim through a book** hojear. **skimmed milk** n leche descremada f.

skimp (skimp) vt escatimar. vi economizar. **skimpy** adj escaso.

skin (skin) n 1 piel f. 2 cuero m. 3 cutis m. vt 1 zool despellejar. 2 bot peler. **skin-diving** n natación submarina f. **skinny** adj flaco. **skintight** adj ajustado.

skip (skip) vi saltar. n salto m.

skipper (´skipə) n naut capitán m.

skirmish (´skə:miʃ) n escaramuza f.

skirt (skə:t) n falda f. vt bordear.

skittle (´skitl) n bolo m.

skull (skʌl) n 1 calavera f. 2 anat cráneo m.

skunk (skʌŋk) n 1 zool mofeta f. 2 canella m.

sky (skai) n cielo m. **sky-high** adj por las nubes. **skylark** n alondra f. **skyline** n línea del horizonte f. **skyscraper** n rascacielos m invar.

slab (slæb) n 1 plancha f. 2 losa f.

slack (slæk) adj flojo. **slacken** vt aflojar.

slacks (slæks) n pl pantalones m pl.

slam (slæm) vt 1 cerrar de golpe. 2 golpear. n 1 golpe m. 2 game slam m.

slander (´slændə) vt calumniar, difamar. n calumnia, difamación f.

slang (slæŋ) n argot m. jerga f.

slant (slɑ:nt) n inclinación f. vt inclinar.

slap (slæp) n 1 palmada f. 2 bofetada f. vt dar una palmada or bofetada a. **slapdash** adj descuidado. **slapstick** adj payaso.

slash (slæʃ) vt 1 azotar. 2 acuchillar. n 1 latigazo m. 2 cuchillada f.

slat (slæt) n tablilla f.

slate (sleit) n pizarra f. vt 1 cubrir de pizarra. 2 inf criticar.

slaughter (´slɔ:tə) n matanza f. vt matar. **slaughterhouse** n matadero m.

slave (sleiv) n esclavo m. vi trabajar duro. **slavery** n esclavitud f.

sledge (sledʒ) n trineo m.

sledgehammer (´sledʒhæmə) n mazo m.

sleek (sli:k) adj liso, pulido. vt alisar.

sleep* (sli:p) vi dormir. n sueño m. **sleeper** n 1 durmiente m,f. 2 (railway) traviesa f. **sleeping-bag** n saco de dormir m. **sleeping-car** n coche-cama m. **sleeping-pill** n somnífero m. **sleepwalk** vi sonambulear. **sleepwalker** n sonámbulo m.

sleet (sli:t) n aguanieve m. vi caer aguanieve.

sleeve (sli:v) n manga f.

sleigh (slei) n see **sledge.**

slender (´slendə) adj delgado.

slept (slept) v see **sleep.**

slice (slais) n 1 tajada f. 2 rebanada f. vt tajar, rebanar.

slick (slik) adj listo, hábil.

slide* (slaid) vt deslizar. n 1 resbaladero m. 2 corredera f. 3 phot diapositiva f. **slide-rule** n regla de cálculo f.

slight (slait) adj leve, ligero. n desaire m. vt desairar. **slightly** adv un poco.

slim (slim) adj delgado. vi adelgazar.

slime (slaim) n 1 limo, légamo m. 2 (of a snail) baba f. **slimy** adj limoso, legamoso.

sling* (sliŋ) n 1 honda f. 2 med cabestrillo m. vt lanzar, tirar.

slink* (sliŋk) vi andar furtivamente.

slip[1] (slip) vt resbalar. n 1 resbalón m. 2 desliz

m. 3 falta, equivocación *f.* 4 (garment) combinación *f.* **slippery** *adj* resbaladizo.

slip² (slip) *n* (cutting) tira *f.*

slipper ('slipə) *n* zapatilla *f.*

slit (slit) *vt* rajar. *n* raja *f.*

slobber ('slɔbə) *n* baba *f.* *vi* babear.

slog (slɔg) *vi* 1 afanarse. 2 andar penosamente.

slogan ('slougən) *n* slogan *m.*

slop (slɔp) *n* gachas *f pl.* **sloppy** *adj* 1 desaliñado. 2 poco sólido. 3 descuidado.

slope (sloup) *n* 1 inclinación *f.* 2 cuesta *f.* 3 pendiente *f.* 4 ladera *f.* *vi* inclinarse.

slot (slɔt) *n* ranura *f.*

slovenly ('slʌvənli) *adj* descuidado.

slow (slou) *adj* lento. *vi* atrasarse. **slow down** reducir la marcha de, retardar.

slug¹ (slʌg) *n* babosa *f.* **sluggish** *adj* lento, inactivo.

slug² (slʌg) *vt inf* aporrear.

sluice (slu:s) *n* compuerta *f.*

slum (slʌm) *n* barrio bajo, barrio pobre *m.*

slump (slʌmp) *n comm* depresión *f.* *vi* hundirse, desplomarse.

slung (slʌŋ) *v see* **sling**.

slur (slə:) *n* 1 calumnia *f.* 2 *mus* ligado *m.* *vt* 1 omitir. 2 pronunciar con poca claridad.

slush (slʌʃ) *n* fango *m.*

sly (slai) *adj* astuto.

smack¹ (smæk) *vi* **smack of** saber a.

smack² (smæk) *vt* pegar. *n* golpe *m.*

small (smɔ:l) *adj* pequeño, chico. **smallholding** *n* minifundio *m.* **small-minded** *adj* de miras estrechas. **smallpox** *n* viruela *f.*

smart (sma:t) *adj* 1 pulcro, elegante. 2 *inf* listo. 3 rápido. *vi* escocer. **smarten up** *vt* arreglar.

smash (smæʃ) *vt* 1 romper. 2 hacer pedazos. *n* 1 colisión *f.* 2 rotura *f.*

smear (smiə) *vt* 1 untar. 2 difamar. *n* mancha *f.*

smell (smel) *n* 1 olor *m.* 2 olfato *m.* *vt* oler. **smelly** *adj* maloliente.

smile (smail) *n* sonrisa *f.* *vi* sonreir.

smirk (smə:k) *n* sonrisa afectada *f.* *vi* sonreir afectadamente.

smock (smɔk) *n* 1 blusa *f.* 2 bata corta *f.*

smog (smɔg) *n* niebla y humo *f.*

smoke (smouk) *n* 1 humo *m.* 2 pitillo *m.* *vi* humear. *vt* 1 fumar. 2 ahumar. **smoker** *n* fumador *m.*

smooth (smu:ð) *adj* 1 liso. 2 zalamero. *vt* 1 alisar. 2 allanar. 3 suavizar.

smother ('smʌðə) *vt,vi* ahogar, sofocar.

smoulder ('smouldə) *vi* arder sin llama.

smudge (smʌdʒ) *vt* manchar, tiznar. *n* mancha *f.* tiznón *m.*

smug (smʌg) *adj* pagado de sí mismo.

smuggle ('smʌgəl) *vt* pasar de contrabando. **smuggler** *n* contrabandista *m,f.* **smuggling** *n* contrabando *m.*

snack (snæk) *n* bocado, tentempié *m.* **snack-bar** *n* cafetería *f.*

snag (snæg) *n* 1 dificultad, pega *f.* 2 muñón *m.* 3 raigón *m.*

snail (sneil) *n* caracol *m.*

snake (sneik) *n* serpiente *f.*

snap (snæp) *vt,vi* 1 romper. 2 hacer saltar. 3 chasquear. *n* 1 chasquido *m.* 2 cierre *m.* 3 *inf* foto *f.* *adj* repentino. **snapshot** *n* instantánea *f.* foto *m.*

snarl (sna:l) *vi* gruñir. *n* gruñido *m.*

snatch (snætʃ) *vt* 1 arrebatar. 2 coger al vuelo. *n* 1 arrebatamiento *m.* 2 fragmento *m.*

sneak (sni:k) *n* soplón *m.* *vi* andar a hurtadillas. **sneak away** escabullirse.

sneer (sniə) *vi* mofarse. *n* sonrisa despreciativa *f.*

sneeze (sni:z) *vi* estornudar. *n* estornudo *m.*

sniff (snif) *vt* husmear, olfatear. *n* husmeo, olfateo *m.*

snip (snip) *vt* tijeretear. *n* tijeretazo *m.*

snipe (snaip) *vi* disparar desde un escondite. *n* *zool* agachadiza *f.* **sniper** *n* tirador escondido *m.*

snivel ('snivəl) *vi* lloriquear.

snob (snɔb) *n* esnob *m,f.* **snobbery** *n* esnobismo *m.*

snooker ('snu:kə) *n* billar *m.*

snoop (snu:p) *vi* fisgonear.

snooty ('snu:ti) *adj* arrogante, engreído.

snooze (snu:z) *vi* dormitar. *n* siestecita *f.*

snore (snɔ:) *vi* roncar. *n* ronquido *m.*

snort (snɔ:t) *vi* bufar, resoplar. *n* bufido, resoplido *m.*

snout (snaut) *n* hocico, morro *m.*

snow (snou) *n* nieve *f.* *vi* nevar. **snowball** *n* bola de nieve *f.* **snowdrift** *n* amontonamiento de nieve, ventisquero *m.* **snowdrop** *n* campanilla de invierno *f.* **snowfall** *n* nevada *f.* **snowflake** *n* copo de nieve *m.* **snowman** *n* muñeco de nieve *m.* **snowplough** *n* quitanieves *m invar.* **snowstorm** *n* ventisca *f.* temporal de nieve *m.*

snub (snʌb) *vt* desairar. *n* desaire *m.* **snub-nosed** *adj* chato.

snuff (snʌf) *n* rapé *m.* *vt* 1 aspirar. 2 extinguir.

snug (snʌg) adj 1 abrigado. 2 cómodo. 3 ajustado:

snuggle ('snʌgəl) vi acurrucarse.

so (sou) adv 1 tan. 2 así, de este modo. **so that** de modo que. ~conj 1 por consiguiente. 2 conque. **so-and-so** n fulano de tal m. **so-called** adj llamado. **so-so** adv así así, regular.

soak (souk) vt empapar, remojar, chupar.

soap (soup) n jabón m. vt enjabonar. **soap powder** n jabón en polvo m. **soapy** adj jabonoso.

soar (sɔː) vi remontarse, elevarse.

sob (sɔb) vi sollozar. n sollozo m.

sober ('soubə) adj 1 sobrio, serio. 2 sereno.

social ('souʃəl) adj social. **sociable** adj sociable. **socialism** n socialismo m. **socialist** adj,n socialista.

society (sə'saiəti) n 1 sociedad f. 2 asociación f.

sociology (sousi'ɔlədʒi) n sociología f. **sociological** adj sociológico. **sociologist** n sociólogo m.

sock[1] (sɔk) n calcetín m.

sock[2] (sɔk) inf vt pegar, cascar. n castaña f.

socket ('sɔkit) n 1 cavidad f. 2 tech enchufe m.

soda ('soudə) n 1 soda f. 2 sosa f. **soda-water** n sifón m.

sofa ('soufə) n sofá m.

soft (sɔft) adj 1 blando. 2 muelle. 3 suave. 4 inf tonto. **soften** vt 1 ablandar. 2 suavizar. **soft-hearted** adj bondadoso, compasivo.

soggy ('sɔgi) adj empapado, mojado.

soil[1] (sɔil) n suelo m.

soil[2] (sɔil) vt ensuciar.

solar ('soulə) adj solar.

sold (sould) v see **sell.**

solder ('sɔldə) vt soldar. n soldadura f.

soldier ('souldʒə) n soldado m. vi ser soldado, servir.

sole[1] (soul) adj único, exclusivo.

sole[2] (soul) n 1 anat planta f. 2 suela f.

sole[3] (soul) n zool lenguado m.

solemn ('sɔləm) adj solemne.

solicitor (sə'lisitə) n 1 abogado m. 2 notario m.

solid ('sɔlid) adj 1 sólido. 2 macizo. n sólido m. **solidarity** n solidaridad f. **solidify** vt solidificar. n solidez f.

solitary ('sɔlitri) adj solitario, solo.

solitude ('sɔlitjuːd) n soledad f.

solo ('soulou) n solo m. adj 1 a solas. 2 para solo. **soloist** n solista m,f.

solstice ('sɔlstis) n solsticio m.

soluble ('sɔljubəl) adj soluble.

solution (sə'luːʃən) n solución f.

solve (sɔlv) vt resolver, solucionar. **solvent** adj,n solvente m. **solvency** n solvencia f.

sombre ('sɔmbə) adj sombrío.

some (sʌm) adj 1 alguno, algún. 2 unos. 3 un poco de, algo de. pron 1 algunos m pl. algunas f pl. 2 algo neut. adv aproximadamente. **somebody** pron alguien. **somebody else** algún otro, otra persona. **somehow** adv de algún modo. **someone** pron alguien. **something** pron algo. **something else** otra cosa. **sometime** adv algún día, alguna vez. adj antiguo. **sometimes** adv algunas veces, a veces. **somewhat** adv algo, un tanto. **somewhere** adv en or a alguna parte. **somewhere else** en or a otra parte.

somersault ('sʌməsɔːlt) n salto mortal m. vi dar un salto mortal.

son (sʌn) n hijo m. **son-in-law** n yerno, hijo político m.

song (sɔŋ) n 1 canción f. 2 canto m. 3 cantar m.

sonic ('sɔnik) adj sónico.

sonnet ('sɔnit) n soneto m.

soon (suːn) adv 1 pronto. 2 temprano. **as soon as possible** cuanto antes, lo antes possible. **how soon?** ¿para cuándo? **soon after** poco después. **sooner** adv más temprano, antes. **no sooner...than** apenas. **the sooner the better** cuanto antes mejor.

soot (sut) n hollín m.

soothe (suːð) vt calmar. **soothing** adj calmante.

sophisticated (sə'fistikeitid) adj sofisticado.

soprano (sə'prɑːnou) n soprano, tiple f.

sorbet ('sɔːbit) n sorbete m.

sordid ('sɔːdid) adj sórdido.

sore (sɔː) adj inflamado. **be sore** doler. ~n llaga f.

sorrow ('sɔrou) n dolor m. pena f. vi apenarse.

sorry ('sɔri) adj 1 arrepentido. 2 apenado. 3 lastimoso, triste. **be sorry** 1 sentirlo. 2 saber mal. ~interj ¡perdón!

sort (sɔːt) n clase, especie f. tipo m. vt,vi clasificar. **sort out** 1 arreglar. 2 solucionar.

soufflé ('suːflei) n suflé m.

sought (sɔːt) v see **seek.**

soul (soul) n alma f.

sound[1] (saund) n 1 sonido m. 2 son m. 3 ruido m. 4 tech sonda f. vt 1 sonar. 2 tocar. 3 entonar. **soundproof** adj insonorizado.

sound[2] (saund) adj 1 sano, robusto. 2 firme, sólido. 3 razonable. 4 profundo. 5 comm solvente. **safe and sound** sano y salvo.

soup (suːp) n sopa f.

sour (sauə) adj 1 agrio. 2 acre.

source (sɔ:s) n fuente f.

south (sauθ) n sur, mediodía m. adj del sur, meridional. adv hacia el sur. **south-east** adj,n sudeste m. **southerly** adj sudeste, del sudeste. **southern** adj del sur, meridional. **southward** adv hacia el sur. **south-west** adj,n sudoeste m.

South Africa n Africa del Sur f. **South African** adj,n sudafricano.

South America n América del Sur, Sudamérica f. **South American** adj,n sudamericano.

South Pole n Polo Sur m.

souvenir (su:vəˈniə) n recuerdo m.

sovereign (ˈsɔvrin) adj,n soberano m. **sovereignty** n soberanía f.

Soviet Union (ˈsouviət) n Unión Soviética f. **Soviet** adj soviético. n soviet m.

sow*[1] (sou) vt sembrar. **sowing** n siembra f.

sow[2] (sau) n cerda f.

soya bean (ˈsɔiə) n semilla de soja f.

spa (spɑ:) n balneario m.

space (speis) n espacio m. adj espacial. vt espaciar. **spacious** adj espacioso.

spade[1] (speid) n pala f. **call a spade a spade** llamar al pan pan y al vino vino. **spade-work** n desbaste m.

spade[2] (speid) n game 1 picos m pl. 2 espadas f pl.

Spain (spein) n España f. **Spaniard** n español m. **Spanish** adj español. **Spanish** (language) n español m.

span (spæn) n 1 envergadura f. 2 arco m. 3 extensión, duración f. vt 1 extenderse sobre. 2 abarcar

spaniel (ˈspæniəl) n perro de aguas, pachón m.

spank (spæŋk) vt azotar, zurrar. n azote m. nalgada f

spanner (ˈspænə) n llave inglesa f.

spare (spɛə) adj 1 sobrante, de sobra. 2 disponible. 3 tech de recambio, de repuesto. n pieza de recambio f. vt 1 escatimar. 2 ahorrar. 3 perdonar. **sparing** adj 1 escaso. 2 económico

spark (spɑ:k) n chispa f. chispazo m. vi echar chispas, chispear.

sparkle (ˈspɑːkəl) n 1 destello, centelleo m. 2 vivacidad f. vi centellear. **sparkling** adj centelleante.

sparrow (ˈspærou) n gorrión m.

sparse (spɑ:s) adj 1 disperso. 2 escaso.

spasm (ˈspæzəm) n espasmo m. **spasmodic** adj espasmódico. **spastic** adj,n espástico.

spat (spæt) v see **spit.**

spatial (ˈspeiʃəl) adj espacial.

spatula (ˈspætjulə) n espátula f.

spawn (spɔ:n) vi 1 desovar. 2 engendrar, procrear. n 1 huevas f pl. 2 semillas f pl.

speak* (spi:k) vt,vi hablar. **so to speak** por así decirlo. **speak up** hablar alto. **speaker** n 1 el que habla. 2 orador m.

spear (spiə) n 1 lanza f. 2 arpón m. vt 1 dar una lanzada a. 2 arponear

special (ˈspeʃəl) adj especial, particular. **specialist** n especialista m,f. **speciality** n especialidad f. **specialize** vi especializarse.

species (ˈspi:ʃi:z) n especie f.

specify (ˈspesifai) vt especificar. **specific** adj específico.

specimen (ˈspesimən) n ejemplar, espécimen m.

speck (spek) n 1 mota f. 2 partícula f.

spectacle (ˈspektəkəl) n 1 espectáculo m. 2 pl gafas f pl. **spectacular** adj espectacular.

spectator (spekˈteitə) n espectador m.

spectrum (ˈspektrəm) n, pl -tra or -trums espectro m.

speculate (ˈspekjuleit) vi especular. **speculation** n especulación f. **speculative** adj especulativo. **speculator** n especulador m.

speech (spi:tʃ) n 1 discurso m. 2 habla f. 3 palabra f. 4 lenguaje m. **speechless** adj mudo, cortado.

speed* (spi:d) n 1 velocidad f. 2 rapidez f. vi mot exceder la velocidad permitida. **speedboat** n lancha rápida f.

spell*[1] (spel) vt,vi escribir correctamente. **spelling** n ortografía f.

spell[2] (spel) n hechizo m. **cast a spell** hechizar. **spellbound** adj hechizado.

spell[3] (spel) n 1 rato m. 2 temporada f. 3 período m.

spend* (spend) vt,vi 1 gastar. 2 pasar. **spendthrift** adj,n derrochador.

sperm (spə:m) n esperma f.

sphere (sfiə) n esfera f. **spherical** adj esférico.

spice (spais) n 1 especia f. 2 picante m. 3 aliciente m. vt especiar, condimentar. **spicy** adj 1 especiado. 2 picante. 3 sabroso.

spider (ˈspaidə) n araña f.

spike (spaik) n 1 pincho m. púa f. 2 clavo m. 3 bot espiga f. vt sujetar con un pincho, clavar. **spiked** adj claveteado.

spill* (spil) vt 1 derramar, verter. 2 desarzonar. **spill over** desbordarse. ~n caída f.

spin* (spin) vt 1 hacer girar. 2 tech hilar. n

vuelta f. **spin-dry** vt secar con centrífuga. **spin-drier** n secadora centrífuga f.

spinach (´spinidʒ) n espinaca f.

spindle (´spindḷ) n 1 huso m. 2 tech eje m.

spine (spain) n 1 anat espinazo m. 2 zool espina f. **spineless** adj flojo, débil.

spinster (´spinstə) n solterona f.

spire [1] (spaiə) n arch aguja f. chapitel m.

spire [2] (spaiə) n espiral f. **spiral** adj,n espiral f. vi dar vueltas en espiral.

spirit (´spirit) n 1 espíritu m. 2 ánimo m. 3 pl alcohol m. licores m pl. **spirited** adj animoso, fogoso. **spiritual** adj espiritual. **spiritualism** n espiritismo m.

spit [1] (spit) vt,vi escupir. 2 bufar. n saliva f.

spit [2] (spit) n cul asador m.

spite (spait) n rencor, despecho m. **in spite of** a pesar de, a despecho de. ~vt mortificar. **spiteful** adj rencoroso.

splash (splæʃ) vt salpicar. vi chapotear. n 1 salpicadura, rociada f. 2 chapoteo m.

splendid (´splendid) adj espléndido. **splendour** n esplendor m.

splint (splint) n tablilla f. **splinter** n astilla f. vt astillar.

split* (split) vt 1 partir, hender. 2 dividir. 3 separar. n 1 hendedura f. 2 división f. adj 1 partido, hendido. 2 dividido.

splutter (´splʌtə) vi 1 chisporrotear. 2 balbucear. n 1 chisporroteo m. 2 balbuceo m.

spoil (spɔil) vt 1 echar a perder, estropear. 2 malograr. 3 mimar. **spoilt** adj 1 estropeado. 2 mimado. **spoilsport** n aguafiestas m,f invar.

spoke [1] (spouk) v see **speak**.

spoke [2] (spouk) n rayo m.

spoken (´spoukən) v see **speak**.

spokesman (´spouksmən) n portavoz m.

sponge (spʌndʒ) n esponja f. vt pasar la esponja por. **sponge on** inf gorrear.

sponsor (´spɔnsə) n 1 patrocinador m. 2 comm fiador m. vt patrocinar. **sponsorship** n patrocinio m.

spontaneous (spɔn´teiniəs) adj espontáneo.

spool (spu:l) n carrete m.

spoon (spu:n) n cuchara f. vt coger a cucharadas. **spoonful** n cucharada f.

sport (spɔ:t) n 1 deporte m. 2 juego m. diversión f. **sporting** adj 1 deportivo. 2 arriesgado. **sportsman** n deportista m. **sportsmanship** n deportividad f.

spot (spɔt) n 1 punto m. 2 mancha f. 3 grano, lunar m. vt 1 manchar, salpicar. 2 notar. 3 encontrar, descubrir. **spotless** adj nítido, inmaculado. **spotlight** n foco, reflector m.

spouse (spaus) n cónyuge m,f.

spout (spaut) n 1 pitón m. 2 caño m. 3 canalón m. 4 chorro m. vt 1 arrojar en chorro. 2 recitar.

sprain (sprein) vt torcer. n torcedura f.

sprang (spræŋ) v see **spring**.

sprawl (sprɔ:l) vi desparramarse.

spray [1] (sprei) vt 1 rociar. 2 regar. 3 aplicar con pulverizador. n 1 rociada f. 2 (of the sea) espuma f. 3 atomizador m.

spray [2] (sprei) n ramita con hojas y flores f.

spread* (spred) vt 1 extender. 2 esparcir, diseminar. 3 difundir. n 1 extensión f. 2 envergadura f. 3 difusión f.

spree (spri:) n parranda, juerga f.

sprig (sprig) n ramita f.

sprightly (´spraitli) adj animado.

spring* (spriŋ) n 1 primavera f. 2 manantial m. 3 brinco m. vi 1 brotar, nacer. 2 saltar, brincar. **springboard** n trampolín m. **spring-clean** vt hacer limpieza general. **springtime** n primavera f.

sprinkle (´spriŋkəl) vt salpicar, rociar. n 1 rociada f. 2 salpicadura f.

sprint (sprint) n esprint m. vi esprintar.

sprout (spraut) vi brotar. vt echar. n brote m.

sprung (sprʌŋ) v see **spring**.

spun (spʌn) v see **spin**.

spur (spə:) n 1 espuela f. 2 estímulo, aguijón m. vt espolear. **spur on** estimular.

spurt (spə:t) n 1 esfuerzo supremo m. 2 chorro m. vi 1 hacer un esfuerzo supremo. 2 surgir.

spy (spai) vt,vi 1 espiar. 2 divisar. n espía m,f.

squabble (´skwɔbəl) vi reñir. n riña.

squad (skwɔd) n pelotón m. brigada f.

squadron (´skwɔdrən) n 1 escuadrón m. 2 escuadrilla f.

squalid (´skwɔlid) adj escuálido.

squander (´skwɔndə) vt despilfarrar.

square (skwɛə) adj cuadrado. n 1 cuadrado m. 2 plaza f. vt 1 cuadrar. 2 ajustar.

squash (skwɔʃ) vt 1 aplastar. 2 apretar. n 1 zumo m. 2 inf apretujamiento m.

squat (skwɔt) vi 1 agacharse. 2 apropiarse de un edificio. adj 1 rechoncho. 2 achaparrado.

squawk (skwɔ:k) vi graznar. n graznido m.

squeak (skwi:k) vi chirriar. n chirrido m.

squeal (skwi:l) vi chillar. n chillido m.

squeamish (´skwi:miʃ) adj 1 delicado. 2 aprensivo.

279

squeeze (skwi:z) *vt* **1** apretar, estrujar. **2** exprimir. **3** oprimir. *n* apretón, estrujón *m*.

squid (skwid) *n* calamar *m*.

squiggle ('skwigəl) *n* garabato *m*.

squint (skwint) *vi* bizquear, ser bizco. *n* estrabismo *m*.

squire ('skwaiə) *n* **1** hacendado *m*. **2** escudero *m*.

squirm (skwə:m) *vi* retorcerse.

squirrel ('skwirl) *n* ardilla *f*.

squirt (skwə:t) *vt* arrojar un chorro de. *vi* salir a chorro. *n* chorro *m*.

stab (stæb) *vt* apuñalar. *n* puñalada *f*.

stable[1] ('steibəl) *n* cuadra *f*.

stable[2] ('steibəl) *adj* estable. **stability** *n* estabilidad *f*. **stabilize** *vt* estabilizar. **stabilizer** *n* estabilizador *m*.

stack (stæk) *n* montón *m*. pila *f*. *vt* amontonar, apilar.

stadium ('steidiəm) *n*, *pl* **-dia** *or* **-diums** estadio *m*.

staff (sta:f) *n* **1** bastón *m*. **2** palo *m*. **3** personal *m*.

stag (stæg) *n* ciervo, venado *m*.

stage (steidʒ) *n* **1** *Th* escena *f*. **2** estrado *m*. **3** etapa *f*. **4** tramo *m*. *vt* **1** *Th* representar. **2** efectuar. **3** organizar. **stage manager** *n* director de escena *m*.

stagger ('stægə) *vi* tambalearse. *vt* **1** asombrar. **2** hacer vacilar. *n* tambaleo *m*. **staggering** *adj* asombroso.

stagnate (stæg'neit) *vi* estancarse. **stagnant** *adj* estancado.

stain (stein) *n* mancha *f*. *vt* **1** manchar. **2** teñir.

stair (steə) *n* **1** escalón *m*. **2** *pl* escalera *f*. **staircase** *n* escalera *f*.

stake[1] (steik) *n* estaca *f*. poste *m*. *vt* estacar.

stake[2] (steik) *n game* **1** apuesta *f*. **2** *pl* premio *m*. **at stake** en juego. ~*vt* **1** apostar. **2** aventurar, arriesgar.

stale (steil) *adj* **1** pasado, viejo. **2** viciado.

stalemate ('steilmeit) *n* **1** *game* tablas *f pl*. **2** estancamiento *m*.

stalk[1] (stɔ:k) *n bot* tallo *m*.

stalk[2] (stɔ:k) *vt* seguir los pasos a. *vi* andar con paso majestuoso.

stall[1] (stɔ:l) *n* **1** casilla de establo *f*. **2** puesto *m*. **3** *Th* butacas *f pl*.

stall[2] (stɔ:l) *vt* parar, atascar. *vi* **1** pararse. **2** andar con evasivas.

stallion ('stæliən) *n* semental *m*.

stamina ('stæminə) *n* vigor *m*.

stammer ('stæmə) *vt, vi* tartamudear. *n* tartamudeo *m*.

stamp (stæmp) *n* **1** sello *m*. **2** marca *f*. **3** cuño *m*. **4** pataleo *m*. *vt* **1** franquear. **2** sellar. **3** estampar. **4** marcar. *vi* patalear.

stampede (stæm'pi:d) *n* estampida *f*. *vi* salir de estampida.

stand[*] (stænd) *vi* **1** estar de pie. **2** encontrarse. **4** mantenerse en vigor. *vt* **1** colocar, poner. **2** soportar. *n* **1** posición *f*. **2** soporte *m*. **standing** *adj* **1** en pie. **2** permanente. *n* **1** posición *f*. **2** importancia *f*. **3** categoría *f*. **4** reputación *f*.

standard ('stændəd) *n* **1** modelo *m*. **2** nivel *m*. *adj* **1** corriente, standard. **2** patrón, tipo. **standardize** *vt* regularizar.

stanza ('stænzə) *n* estrofa *f*.

stank (stæŋk) *v see* **stink.**

staple[1] ('steipəl) *n* grapa *f*. *vt* sujetar con grapas.

staple[2] ('steipəl) *adj* principal. *n* **1** producto principal *m*. **2** elemento esencial *m*.

star (sta:) *n* estrella *f*. astro *m*. *adj* **1** estelar. **2** destacado, especial. *vi* ser la estrella *or* el astro. **stardom** *n* estrellato *m*. **starfish** *n* estrella de mar *f*.

starboard ('sta:bəd) *n* estribor *m*.

starch (sta:tʃ) *n* **1** almidón *m*. **2** fécula *f*. *vt* almidonar.

stare (steə) *vi* mirar fijamente. *n* mirada fija *f*.

stark (sta:k) *adj* **1** rígido. **2** severo.

starling ('sta:liŋ) *n* estornino *m*.

start (sta:t) *vt* **1** empezar, iniciar. **2** poner en marcha. *vi* sobresaltarse. *n* **1** principio *m*. **2** salida *f*. **3** sobresalto *m*.

startle ('sta:tl) *vt* asustar, dar un susto, sobresaltar. **startling** *adj* **1** asombroso. **2** sobrecogedor.

starve (sta:v) *vi* **1** morir de hambre. **2** pasar hambre. *vt* **1** hacer morir de hambre. **2** hacer pasar hambre. **starvation** *n* hambre *f*. **starving** *adj* hambriento.

state (steit) *n* estado *m*. *adj* **1** estatal. **2** de gala. *vt* **1** declarar. **2** exponer, formular. **stately** *adj* majestuoso, imponente. **statement** *n* **1** declaración *f*. **2** informe *m*. **statesman** *n* estadista *m*. **statesmanship** *n* arte de gobernar *m*.

static ('stætik) *adj* **1** estático. **2** estancado.

station ('steiʃən) *n* **1** estación *f*. **2** puesto *m*. **3** condición *f*. *vt* **1** estacionar. **2** situar. **stationmaster** *n* jefe de estación *m*.

stationary ('steiʃənri) *adj* estacionario.

stationer ('steiʃənə) *n* papelero *m*. **stationer's**

shop n papelería f. **stationery** n papel de escribir m.

statistics (stə'tistiks) n estadística f.

statue ('stætju:) n estatua f.

stature ('stætʃə) n estatura f.

status ('steitəs) n 1 estado m. condición f. 2 categoría, posición f. rango m.

statute ('stætju:t) n estatuto m. **statutory** adj estatutario, obligatorio.

stay[1] (stei) vi 1 quedar, quedarse, permanecer. 2 hospedarse. n estancia f.

stay[2] (stei) n (prop) sostén, puntal m. vt sostener, apuntalar.

steadfast ('stedfɑ:st) adj resuelto, firme.

steady ('stedi) adj 1 firme, fijo. 2 estable. 3 constante. 4 formal. vt 1 estabilizar. 2 calmar.

steak (steik) n 1 bistec, biftec m. 2 tajada f.

steal[*] (sti:l) vt robar.

steam (sti:m) n vapor m. vt 1 empañar. 2 cul cocer al vapor. vi echar vapor. **steam-engine** n máquina de vapor f. **steamer** n vapor m. **steamroller** n apisonadora f.

steel (sti:l) n acero m.

steep[1] (sti:p) adj 1 empinado. 2 escarpado, abrupto.

steep[2] (sti:p) vt empapar, remojar.

steeple ('sti:pəl) n campanario m. torre f. **steeplechase** n carrera de obstáculos f.

steer (stiə) vt 1 conducir, dirigir, guiar. 2 naut gobernar. **steer clear of** evitar. **steering-wheel** n volante m.

stem[1] (stem) n tallo m.

stem[2] (stem) vt refrenar. **stem from** provenir de.

stencil ('stensəl) n 1 cliché m. 2 patrón picado m. vt estarcir.

step (step) n 1 paso m. 2 peldaño, escalón m. 3 medida f. vi 1 dar un paso. 2 pisar. **step aside** hacerse a un lado. **step down** 1 bajar. 2 renunciar. **stepladder** n escalera de mano f

stepbrother ('stepbrʌðə) n hermanastro m.

stepdaughter ('stepdɔ:tə) n hijastra f.

stepfather ('stepfɑ:ðə) n padrastro m.

stepmother ('stepmʌðə) n madrastra f.

stepsister ('stepsistə) n hermanastra f.

stepson ('stepsʌn) n hijastro m.

stereo ('steriou) adj estéreo.

stereophonic (steriə'fɔnik) adj estereofónico, estéreo.

stereotype ('steriətaip) n cliché, estereotipo m. vt estereotipar.

sterile ('sterail) adj estéril. **sterilize** vt esterilizar.

sterling ('stə:liŋ) adj genuino, de ley. **pound sterling** n libra esterlina f.

stern[1] (stə:n) adj severo, austero.

stern[2] (stə:n) n naut popa f.

stethoscope ('steθəskoup) n estetoscopio m.

stew (stju:) vt, vi estofar, guisar. n estofado, guiso m.

steward ('stju:əd) n 1 camarero, mozo m. 2 administrador m. 3 mayordomo m. **stewardess** n azafata f.

stick[1] (stik) n 1 bastón m. 2 palo m. 3 barra f.

stick[*2] (stik) vt 1 pegar. 2 clavar. 3 meter. 4 inf aguantar. vi 1 atascarse. 2 quedarse, pararse. **stick to** 1 persistir. 2 ser fiel a. **sticker** n etiqueta engomada f.

sticky ('stiki) adj 1 pegajoso. 2 inf difícil.

stiff (stif) adj 1 tieso, rígido. 2 duro. 3 entumecido. 4 fuerte. **stiffness** n tiesura, rigidez, inflexibilidad f. **stiffen** vt 1 poner rígido. 2 endurecer. 3 entumecer.

stifle ('staifəl) vt ahogar, sofocar. **stifling** adj sofocante.

stigma ('stigmə) n, pl -mas or -mata estigma m. **stigmatize** vt estigmatizar.

stile (stail) n portillo con escalones m.

still[1] (stil) adj inmóvil, quieto. adv todavía, aún. conj con todo, a pesar de todo. vt calmar, aquietar. **stillborn** adj nacido muerto. **still life** n bodegón m.

still[2] (stil) n alambique m.

stilt (stilt) n zanco m. **stilted** adj afectado, amanerado.

stimulate ('stimjuleit) vt estimular. **stimulant** n estimulante m. **stimulating** adj 1 estimulador. 2 estimulante.

stimulus ('stimjuləs) n, pl -ii or -luses estímulo m.

sting[*] (stiŋ) n 1 zool aguijón m. 2 picadura f. 3 punzada f. 4 escozor m. vt 1 picar. 2 punzar. 3 escocer.

stink[*] (stiŋk) vi oler mal. n mal olor m.

stint (stint) vt escatimar. n (of work) destajo m.

stipulate ('stipjuleit) vt estipular.

stir (stə:) vt 1 revolver. 2 agitar. 3 remover. 4 despertar. **stir up** excitar. ~n 1 agitación f. 2 conmoción f. **stirring** adj emocionante, conmovedor.

stirrup ('stirəp) n estribo m.

stitch (stitʃ) n 1 punto m. puntada f. 2 punzada f. vt 1 coser. 2 hilvanar.

stoat (stout) n zool armiño m.

stock (stɔk) n 1 provisión f. 2 comm existencias f pl. surtido m. 3 valores m pl. 4 cepa f. tronco m. 5 culata f. 6 estirpe f. 7 cul caldo m. **take stock** 1 comm hacer inventario. 2 asesorarse. ~adj 1 acostumbrado. 2 corriente, normal. vt 1 proveer. 2 comm tener en existencia. **stockbreeding** n ganadería f. **stockbreeder** n ganadero m. **stockbroker** n agente de bolsa m. **stock exchange** n bolsa f. **stockholder** n accionista m,f. **stockpile** vt acumular. **stocktaking** n inventario m.

stocking ('stɔkiŋ) n media f.

stodge (stɔdʒ) n inf comida pesada f. **stodgy** adj indigesto, pesado.

stoic ('stouik) n estoico m. **stoical** adj estoico. **stoicism** n estoicismo m.

stoke (stouk) vt cargar, echar carbón a, cebar.

stole¹ (stoul) n estola f.

stole² (stoul) v see **steal**.

stolen ('stoulan) v see **steal**.

stomach ('stʌmək) n 1 estómago m. 2 vientre m. vt aguantar, tragar. **stomach-ache** n dolor de estómago m.

stone (stoun) n 1 piedra f. 2 hueso m. vt 1 apedrear. 2 deshuesar. **stony** adj pedregoso.

stood (stud) v see **stand**.

stool (stu:l) n taburete m.

stoop (stu:p) vi inclinarse, agacharse, encorvarse. **stoop to** rebajarse a. ~n inclinación f.

stop (stɔp) vt 1 parar, detener. 2 impedir. 3 tapar. vi alojarse. n 1 parada f. 2 alto m. **put a stop to** poner fin a. **stopgap** n recurso provisional m. **stoppage** n 1 parada, interrupción f. 2 paro m. 3 obstrucción f. **stopper** n tapón m. **stopwatch** n cronómetro m.

store (stɔ:) n 1 provisión f. 2 almacén m. 3 reserva f. vt 1 almacenar. 2 abastecer. **store up** acumular. **storage** n almacenaje m.

storey ('stɔ:ri) n piso m.

stork (stɔ:k) n cigüeña f.

storm (stɔ:m) n 1 tormenta, tempestad f. vi enfurecerse, rabiar. vt tomar por asalto. **stormy** adj tempestuoso.

story ('stɔ:ri) n 1 historia f. 2 cuento m.

stout (staut) adj 1 macizo, sólido, recio. 2 robusto, corpulento. n cerveza negra f.

stove (stouv) n 1 estufa f. 2 hornillo, fogón m.

stow (stou) vt colocar, meter. **stowaway** n polizón m.

straddle ('strædļ) vt 1 montar a horcajadas. 2 caer a ambos lados de.

straggle ('strægəl) vi 1 desparramarse. 2 rezagarse. **straggler** n rezagado m.

straight (streit) adj 1 recto, derecho. 2 franco, honrado. 3 en órden. adv 1 en línea recta. 2 directamente. 3 francamente. **straight away** en seguida. **straight on** or **ahead** todo seguido. ~n recta f. **straighten** vt 1 enderezar. 2 arreglar. **straightforward** adj 1 franco, honrado. 2 sencillo.

strain¹ (strein) vt 1 estirar, tender. 2 torcer. 3 forzar. 4 cul colar. n 1 tensión, tirantez f. 2 torcedura f. 3 esfuerzo m.

strain² (strein) n 1 estirpe, raza f. 2 tendencia, vena f. 3 variedad f.

strand¹ (strænd) vt encallar. **be stranded** quedarse colgado.

strand² (strænd) n cabo, ramal m. hebra f.

strange (streindʒ) adj 1 extraño. 2 desconocido. **stranger** n 1 desconocido m. 2 forastero m.

strangle ('stræŋgəl) vt estrangular.

strap (stræp) n 1 correa f. 2 tira f. vt sujetar con una correa.

strategy ('strætidʒi) n estrategia f. **strategic** adj estratégico.

straw (strɔ:) n paja f. **strawberry** n fresa f. fresón m.

stray (strei) vi extraviarse. adj 1 extraviado, perdido. 2 aislado. 3 errante. n animal extraviado m.

streak (stri:k) n 1 veta, vena f. 2 racha f. vt listar, rayar. vi pasar como un rayo. **streaky** adj 1 listado. 2 entreverado.

stream (stri:m) n 1 arroyo m. 2 corriente f. 3 raudal m. vi 1 correr, fluir. 2 brotar, manar. 3 ondear. **streamer** n serpentina f. **streamline** vt 1 aerodinamizar. 2 hacer más eficiente, coordinar.

street (stri:t) n calle f.

strength (streŋθ) n 1 fuerza f. 2 resistencia f. **strengthen** vt fortalecer, reforzar, fortificar.

strenuous ('strenjuəs) adj 1 enérgico. 2 tenaz. 3 arduo.

stress (stres) n 1 presión f. 2 tensión f. 3 acento m. 4 énfasis m. vt 1 insistir en. 2 acentuar.

stretch (stretʃ) vt 1 extender, estirar. 2 ensanchar. 3 tender. n 1 extensión f. 2 trecho m. **stretcher** n camilla f.

strict (strikt) adj 1 estricto. 2 severo.

stride* (straid) vi andar a trancos, dar zancadas. vt cruzar de un tranco. n zancada f. tranco m.

strike* (straik) vt 1 golpear, pegar. 2 asestar. 3 alcanzar. 4 dar con. 5 tocar. 6 naut arriar. vi 1 hacer impresión. 2 hacer huelga. 3 dar la hora. 4 atacar. n huelga f. **go on strike**

declararse en huelga. **striker** n huelguista m,f.

string (striŋ) n 1 cordel m. 2 cuerda f. 3 sarta f. 4 **hilera** f. **pull strings** inf mover palancas. ~vt 1 ensartar. 2 mus encordar.

stringent ('strindʒənt) adj riguroso, severo. **stringency** n rigor m. severidad f.

strip[1] (strip) vt 1 despojar. 2 desnudar. 3 tech desmontar. **striptease** n strip-tease, estriptis m.

strip[2] (strip) n 1 tira f. 2 faja f. 3 franja f.

stripe (straip) n 1 raya, lista f. 2 banda f. 3 mil galón m. vt rayar, listar.

strive* (straiv) vi esforzarse.

strode (stroud) v see **stride**.

stroke[1] (strouk) n 1 golpe m. 2 med apoplejía f.

stroke[2] (strouk) vt acariciar. n caricia f.

stroll (stroul) vi pasear. n paseo m.

strong (strɔŋ) adj fuerte. **stronghold** n 1 plaza fuerte f. 2 baluarte m. **strong-minded** adj resuelto.

strove (strouv) v see **strive**.

struck (strʌk) v see **strike**.

structure ('strʌktʃə) n estructura f.

struggle ('strʌgəl) vi luchar. n lucha f.

strum (strʌm) vt rasguear.

strung (strʌŋ) v see **string**.

strut[1] (strʌt) vi pavonearse. n contoneo m.

strut[2] (strʌt) n puntal m.

stub (stʌb) n 1 cabo m. 2 talón m. 3 colilla f. vt 1 desarraigar. 2 apagar.

stubborn ('stʌbən) adj tenaz. **stubbornness** n tenacidad f.

stud[1] (stʌd) n 1 botón de pasador m. 2 tachón m. tachuela f.

stud[2] (stʌd) n caballeriza f.

student ('stju:dnt) n estudiante m,f.

studio ('stju:diou) n estudio m.

study ('stʌdi) n estudio m. vt,vi estudiar. **studious** adj estudioso.

stuff (stʌf) n 1 materia f. 2 tela f. 3 inf cosa f. vt 1 llenar. 2 tapar. 3 cul rellenar. **stuffing** n relleno m. **stuffy** adj 1 sofocante. 2 inf remilgado, estirado. 3 inf de miras estrechas.

stumble ('stʌmbəl) vi tropezar. n tropezón, traspié m. **stumbling block** n obstáculo m.

stump (stʌmp) n 1 tocón m. 2 muñón m. 3 raigón m. vi pisar fuerte, cojear. vt inf confundir.

stun (stʌn) vt 1 aturdir. 2 pasmar.

stung (stʌŋ) v see **sting**.

stunk (stʌŋk) v see **stink**.

stunt[1] (stʌnt) vt atrofiar.

stunt[2] (stʌnt) n 1 acrobacia f. 2 truco m.

stupid ('stju:pid) adj estúpido. **stupidity** n estupidez f.

sturdy ('stə:di) adj 1 robusto, fuerte. 2 vigoroso.

sturgeon ('stə:dʒən) n esturión m.

stutter ('stʌtə) vi tartamudear. n tartamudeo m. **stutterer** n tartamudo m.

sty (stai) n pocilga f.

style (stail) n estilo m. vt cortar a la moda. **stylish** adj elegante, a la moda. **stylist** n estilista m,f. **stylized** adj estilizado.

stylus ('stailəs) n 1 aguja f. 2 estilo m.

subconscious (sʌb'kɔnʃəs) adj,n subconsciente m.

subcontract (sʌbkən'trækt) vt subcontratar.

subdue (səb'dju:) vt 1 dominar. 2 suavizar. 3 amansar.

subject (n,adj 'sʌbdʒikt; v səb'dʒekt) n 1 gram sujeto m. 2 tema, asunto m. 3 educ asignatura f. adj 1 sujeto. 2 sometido, supeditado. vt someter. **subjective** adj subjetivo.

subjunctive (səb'dʒʌŋktiv) adj,n subjuntivo m.

sublime (sə'blaim) adj sublime.

submachine gun (sʌbmə'ʃi:ŋgʌn) n metralleta f.

submarine (sʌbmə'ri:n) adj,n submarino m.

submerge (səb'mə:dʒ) vt sumergir.

submit (səb'mit) vt 1 someter. 2 presentar. 3 proponer. vi someterse, rendirse. **submission** n sumisión f. **submissive** adj sumiso.

subnormal (sʌb'nɔ:məl) adj subnormal.

subordinate (adj,n sə'bɔ:dinət; v sə'bɔ:dineit) adj,n subordinado m. vt subordinar.

subscribe (səb'skraib) vi suscribirse. **subscriber** n suscriptor, abonado m. **subscription** n 1 suscripción m. 2 cuota f.

subsequent ('sʌbsikwint) adj subsiguiente.

subservient (səb'sə:viənt) adj 1 subordinado. 2 servil.

subside (səb'said) vi 1 bajar. 2 amainar. 3 hundirse.

subsidiary (səb'sidiəri) adj 1 subsidiario, auxiliar. 2 comm filial. n filial, sucursal f.

subsidize ('sʌbsidaiz) vt subvencionar. **subsidy** n subvención f. subsidio m.

subsist (səb'sist) vi subsistir. **subsistence** n subsistencia f.

substance ('sʌbstəns) n sustancia f. **substantial** adj 1 sustancial. 2 considerable. 3 sólido. **substantive** adj,n sustantivo m.

substitute ('sʌbstitju:t) vt 1 sustituir. 2 reemplazar. n sustituto m. adj 1 sucedáneo. 2 suplente.

subtitle ('sʌbtaitļ) n subtítulo m.

subtle ('sʌtļ) adj 1 sutil. 2 fino. **subtlety** n 1 sutileza f. 2 astucia f.

subtract (səb'trækt) vt sustraer. **subtraction** n sustracción f.

suburb ('sʌbə:b) n barrio de las afueras, extrarradio m. **suburban** adj suburbano.

subvert (sʌb'və:t) vt subvertir. **subversion** n subversión f. **subversive** adj subversivo.

subway ('sʌbwei) n paso subterráneo m.

succeed (sək'si:d) vi lograr, conseguir. vt 1 suceder. 2 seguir. **success** n éxito m. **successful** adj 1 afortunado. 2 próspero. 3 feliz. **be successful** 1 tener éxito. 2 prosperar. **succession** n sucesión f. **successive** adj sucesivo. **successor** n sucesor m.

succulent ('sʌkjulənt) adj suculento.

succumb (sə'kʌm) vi sucumbir.

such (sʌtʃ) adj tal, semejante. adv tan. pron tal. **suchlike** adj tal. pron otros tales m pl. otras tales f pl.

suck (sʌk) vt 1 chupar. 2 mamar. 3 sorber.

sucker ('sʌkə) n 1 zool ventosa f. 2 bot serpollo m. 3 sl primo m.

suction ('sʌkʃən) n succión f.

Sudan (su:'dæn) n Sudán m. **Sudanese** adj,n sudanés.

sudden ('sʌdņ) adj repentino, súbito. **all of a sudden** de repente. **suddenly** adv de repente, pronto.

suds (sʌdz) n pl jabonaduras f pl.

sue (su:) vt,vi demandar, poner pleito.

suede (sweid) n ante m. gamuza f.

suet ('su:it) n sebo m.

suffer ('sʌfə) vt,vi 1 sufrir. 2 padecer. 3 aguantar. 4 adolecer de. **sufferer** n 1 enfermo m. 2 víctima f. **suffering** n sufrimiento, dolor m.

suffice (sə'fais) vi bastar, ser suficiente. **sufficient** adj suficiente.

suffix ('sʌfiks) n sufijo m.

suffocate ('sʌfəkeit) vt ahogar, asfixiar. **suffocating** adj sofocante, asfixiante. **suffocation** n sofocación, asfixia f.

sugar ('ʃugə) n azúcar m. vt azucarar. **sugar cane** n caña de azúcar f. **sugary** adj 1 azucarado. 2 almibarado.

suggest (sə'dʒest) vt sugerir. **suggestion** n 1 sugerencia f. 2 sugestión f. 3 indicación f. **suggestive** adj 1 sugestivo. 2 sugerente.

suicide ('sju:isaid) n 1 suicidio m. 2 suicida m,f. **commit suicide** suicidarse. **suicidal** adj suicida.

suit (sju:t) n 1 traje m. 2 pleito m. 3 petición f. 4

game palo m. **follow suit** 1 jugar el mismo palo. 2 hacer lo mismo. ~vt 1 adaptar, ajustar. 2 convenir, ir bien. **suitable** adj conveniente, apropiado, adecuado. **suitcase** n maleta f.

suite (swi:t) n 1 juego m. 2 séquito m. 3 suite f.

sulk (sʌlk) vi estar mohino. **sulky** adj mohino, malhumorado.

sullen ('sʌlən) adj hosco, malhumorado.

sulphur ('sʌlfə) n azufre m.

sultan ('sʌltən) n sultán m.

sultana (sʌl'tɑ:nə) n pasa de Esmirna f.

sultry ('sʌltri) adj bochornoso.

sum (sʌm) n 1 suma f. 2 problema m. 3 cantidad f. vt sumar. **sum up** resumir.

summarize ('sʌməraiz) vt resumir, compendiar.

summer ('sʌmə) n verano, estío m. adj de verano. **summertime** n verano m.

summit ('sʌmit) n cima, cumbre f.

summon ('sʌmən) vt 1 llamar. 2 convocar. 3 citar. **summon up** 1 evocar. 2 (courage, energy, etc.) colorar. **summons** n 1 citación f. 2 requerimiento m.

sun (sʌn) n sol m.

sunbathe ('sʌnbeið) vi tomar el sol.

sunburn ('sʌnbə:n) n quemadura del sol f.

Sunday ('sʌndi) n domingo m. adj dominical.

sundial ('sʌndaiəl) n reloj de sol m.

sundry ('sʌndri) adj varios. **sundries** n pl géneros diversos m pl.

sunflower ('sʌnflauə) n girasol m.

sung (sʌŋ) v see **sing.**

sunglasses ('sʌnglɑ:siz) n pl gafas de sol f pl.

sunk (sʌŋk) v see **sink.**

sunlight ('sʌnlait) n luz del sol f.

sunny ('sʌni) adj soleado.

sunrise ('sʌnraiz) n salida del sol f.

sunset ('sʌnset) n puesta del sol f.

sunshine ('sʌnʃain) n sol m. luz del sol f.

sunstroke ('sʌnstrouk) n insolación f.

suntan ('sʌntæn) n bronceado m.

super ('su:pə) adj inf estupendo. interj ¡qué bien!

superannuation (su:pərænju'eiʃən) n jubilación f.

superb (su:'pə:b) adj magnífico, espléndido.

superficial (su:pə'fiʃəl) adj superficial.

superfluous (su:'pə:fluəs) adj 1 superfluo. 2 sobrante.

superhuman (su:pə'hju:mən) adj sobrehumano.

superimpose (su:pərim'pouz) vt sobreponer.

superintendent (su:pərin'tendənt) n superintendente m,f

superior (su'piəriə) *adj,n* superior *m*.

superlative (su'pə:lətiv) *adj,n* superlativo *m*.

supermarket ('su:pəma:kit) *n* supermercado *m*.

supernatural (su:pə'nætʃrəl) *adj* sobrenatural.

supersonic (su:pə'sɔnik) *adj* supersónico.

superstition (su:pə'stiʃən) *n* superstición *f*.

supervise ('su:pəvaiz) *vt* supervisar.

supper ('sʌpə) *n* cena *f*. **have supper** cenar.

supple ('sʌpəl) *adj* 1 flexible. 2 dócil. 3 servil.

supplement ('sʌplimənt) *n* 1 suplemento *m*. 2 apéndice *m*.

supply (sə'plai) *n* 1 suministro *m*. 2 *pl* provisiones *f pl*. **supply and demand** oferta y demanda. ~*vt* 1 proveer. 2 suplir.

support (sə'pɔ:t) *n* 1 soporte *m*. 2 apoyo *m*. *vt* 1 sostener. 2 aguantar. **support oneself** ganarse la vida.

suppose (sə'pouz) *vt,vi* 1 suponer. 2 imaginarse.

suppress (sə'pres) *vt* 1 suprimir. 2 contener. 3 reprimir.

supreme (sə'pri:m) *adj* 1 supremo. 2 sumo.

surcharge ('sə:tʃɑ:dʒ) *n* sobrecarga *f*.

sure (ʃuə) *adj* 1 seguro. 2 cierto. **make sure** comprobar. ~*adv* ciertamente. **surely** *adj* 1 seguramente. 2 por supuesto. **surety** *n* 1 garantía *f*. 2 fianza *f*. 3 fiador *m*.

surf (sə:f) *n* 1 espuma *f*. 2 rompiente *m*. 3 oleaje *m*.

surface ('sə:fis) *n* superficie *f*. *adj* de la superficie. *vt* recubrir. *vi* emerger.

surfeit ('sə:fit) *n* 1 hartura *f*. 2 empacho *m*. 3 exceso *m*. *vt* hartar. *vi* saciarse.

surge (sə:dʒ) *n* oleada *f*. *vi* agitarse, hervir.

surgeon ('sə:dʒən) *n* cirujano *m*. **surgery** *n* 1 cirugía *f*. 2 consultorio *m*.

surly ('sə:li) *adj* malhumorado, hosco.

surmise (sə:'maiz) *n* conjetura, suposición *f*. *vt* conjeturar.

surmount (sə'maunt) *vt* 1 superar, vencer. 2 coronar.

surname ('sə:neim) *n* apellido *m*. *vt* apellidar.

surpass (sə'pɑ:s) *vt* 1 superar. 2 exceder.

surplus ('sə:plis) *n* 1 excedente *m*. 2 superávit *m*. *adj* sobrante, de sobra.

surprise (sə'praiz) *n* sorpresa *f*. asombro *m*. *vt* asombrar, sorprender.

surrealism (sʌ'riəlizəm) *n* surrealismo *m*.

surrender (sə'rendə) *n* 1 rendición *f*. 2 entrega *f*. *vt* rendir. *vi* entregarse.

surreptitious (sʌrəp'tiʃəs) *adj* subrepticio, clandestino.

surround (sə'raund) *n* borde *m*. *vt* 1 rodear. 2 sitiar.

survey (*v* sə'vei; *n* 'sə:vei) *vt* 1 mirar. 2 inspeccionar. *n* vista, inspección *f*. **surveyor** *n* 1 agrimensor *m*. 2 inspector *m*.

survive (sə'vaiv) *vt,vi* 1 sobrevivir. 2 subsistir. **survival** *n* supervivencia *f*.

susceptible (sə'septəbəl) *adj* 1 susceptible. 2 impresionable. 3 enamoradizo.

suspect (*v* sə'spekt; *n,adj* 'sʌspekt) *vt* 1 sospechar. 2 recelar. *adj,n* sospechoso *m*.

suspend (sə'spend) *vt* suspender. **suspense** *n* incertidumbre *f*. suspense *m*. **suspension** *n* suspensión *f*.

suspicion (sə'spiʃən) *n* 1 sospecha *f*. 2 recelo *m*. 3 dejo *m*. **suspicious** *adj* 1 sospechoso. 2 receloso.

sustain (sə'stein) *vt* 1 sostener. 2 sustentar. 3 sufrir. 4 confirmar.

swab (swɔb) *n* med algodón *m*. *vt* med limpiar con algodón.

swagger ('swægə) *n* contoneo *m*. *vi* contonearse.

swallow[1] ('swolou) *n* trago *m*. *vt* 1 tragar. 2 engullir.

swallow[2] ('swolou) *n* golondrina *f*.

swam (swæm) *v see* **swim**.

swamp (swomp) *n* pantano *m*. *vt* 1 sumergir. 2 hundir. 3 abrumar.

swan (swon) *n* cisne *m*.

swank (swæŋk) *n* 1 fachenda *f*. 2 ostentación *f*. fachendón *m*. *vi* darse humos.

swap (swop) *n* intercambio *m*. *vt* intercambiar, canjear.

swarm (swo:m) *n* 1 enjambre *m*. 2 multitud *f*. *vi* 1 enjambrar. 2 pulular.

swastika ('swostikə) *n* esvástica, cruz gamada *f*.

swat (swot) *vt* aplastar, matar.

sway (swei) *n* 1 balanceo *m*. 2 dominio *m*. 3 influencia *f*. *vt* 1 balancear. 2 influir. *vi* oscilar.

swear* (swɛə) *vt* 1 jurar. 2 declarar bajo juramento. *vi* 1 jurar. 2 decir tacos. 3 blasfemar.

sweat (swet) *n* 1 sudor *m*. 2 trabajo duro *m*. *vt,vi* sudar. **sweater** *n* suéter *m*.

swede (swi:d) *n* nabo sueco *m*.

Sweden ('swi:dn) *n* Suecia *f*. **Swede** *n* sueco *m*. **Swedish** *adj* sueco. **Swedish** (language) *n* sueco *m*.

sweep* (swi:p) *n* 1 barredura *f*. 2 redada *f*. *vt* barrer. **sweep along** arrastrar. **sweep by** pasar rápidamente.

sweet (swi:t) *adj* 1 dulce. 2 melodioso. 3 amable. *n* 1 dulce *m*. 2 postre *m*. **sweet-**

bread n lechecilla f. **sweet corn** n maíz tierno m. **sweeten** vt 1 endulzar. 2 azucarar. **sweetheart** n novio m. **sweet pea** n guisante de olor m.

swell* (swel) n mar de fondo m. vt hinchar. vi abultarse.

swept (swept) v see **sweep.**

swerve (swɔːv) n desvío brusco m. vt,vi desviar bruscamente.

swift (swift) adj 1 rápido. 2 repentino. n vencejo m.

swig (swig) n trago m. vt beber a grandes tragos.

swill (swil) n bazofia f. vt limpiar con agua.

swim (swim) n nadadura f. vt pasar a nado. vi nadar. **swimming** n natación f. **swimming costume** n traje de baño m. **swimming pool** n piscina f.

swindle ('swindl) n estafa f. vt estafar, timar.

swine (swain) n puerco, cerdo m.

swing* (swiŋ) n 1 balanceo m. 2 columpio m. vt balancear. vi 1 columpiarse. 2 cambiar de dirección.

swipe (swaip) n golpe fuerte m. vt pegar, golpear.

swirl (swɔːl) vi arremolinarse. n remolino m.

swish (swiʃ) vi silbar, crujir.

switch (switʃ) n 1 varilla f. 2 látigo m. 3 interruptor m. vt desviar. vi cambiar. **switch on** encender. **switchboard** n cuadro de mandos m.

Switzerland ('switsələnd) n Suiza f. **Swiss** adj,n suizo m.

swivel ('swivəl) n pivote m. vt girar sobre un eje.

swollen ('swoulən) v see **swell.**

swoop (swuːp) n 1 calada f. 2 redada f. vi precipitarse.

swop (swɔp) n intercambio m. vt intercambiar.

sword (sɔːd) n espada f. **swordfish** n pez espada m. **swordsman** n espadachín m.

swore (swɔː) v see **swear.**

sworn (swɔːn) v see **swear.**

swot (swɔt) n inf empollón m. vt inf empollar.

swum (swʌm) v see **swim.**

swung (swʌŋ) v see **swing.**

sycamore ('sikəmɔː) n sicomoro m.

syllable ('siləbəl) n sílaba f.

syllabus ('siləbəs) n programa f.

symbol ('simbəl) n símbolo m. **symbolism** n simbolismo m. **symbolize** vt simbolizar.

symmetry ('simitri) n simetría f.

sympathy ('simpəθi) n 1 simpatía f. 2 com-

pasión f. **sympathize** vi 1 simpatizar. 2 compadecerse. 3 comprender.

symphony ('simfəni) n sinfonía f.

symposium (sim'pouziəm) n, pl **symposia** simposio m.

symptom ('simptəm) n 1 síntoma m. 2 indicio m.

synagogue ('sinəgɔg) n sinagoga f.

synchronize ('siŋkrənaiz) vt sincronizar.

syndicate (n 'sindikit; v 'sindikeit) n sindicato m. vt sindicar.

syndrome ('sindroum) n síndrome m.

synonym ('sinənim) n sinónimo m.

synopsis (si'nɔpsis) n, pl **synopses** sinopsis f.

syntax ('sintæks) n sintaxis f.

synthesis ('sinθəsis) n, pl **syntheses** síntesis f. **synthetic** adj sintético.

syphilis ('sifəlis) n sífilis f.

Syria ('siriə) n Siria f. **Syrian** adj,n sirio.

syringe (si'rindʒ) n jeringa f. vt jeringar.

syrup ('sirəp) n 1 jarabe m. 2 almíbar m.

system ('sistəm) n 1 sistema m. 2 método m. **systematic** adj sistemático, metódico.

T

tab (tæb) n 1 oreja f. 2 etiqueta f. **keep tabs on** irgilar a.

tabby ('tæbi) n gato atigrado m.

table ('teibəl) n 1 mesa f. 2 math tabla f. vt presentar. **tablecloth** n mantel m. **tablemat** n salvamanteles m invar. **tablespoon** n cuchara grande f. **table tennis** n tenis de mesa m.

tablet ('tæblət) n 1 tableta f. 2 píldora f. 3 pastilla f.

taboo (tə'buː) adj,n tabú m.

tack (tæk) n 1 tachuela f. 2 hilván m. vt clavar con tachuelas. vi naut virar.

tackle ('tækəl) n 1 aparejo m. 2 equipo m. vt 1 agarrar. 2 emprender.

tact (tækt) n tacto m. discreción f. **tactful** adj discreto.

tactic ('tæktik) n 1 táctica f. 2 maniobra f.

tadpole ('tædpoul) n renacuajo m.

taffeta ('tæfitə, n tafetán f.

tag (tæg) n 1 etiqueta f. 2 cabo m. 3 herrete m. vt pegar una etiqueta a. **tag along** ir también.

tail (teil) n 1 cola f. 2 faldón m. vt inf seguir de cerca a. **tail off** disminuir.

tailor ('teilə) n sastre m. **tailor's shop** n sastrería f. vt confeccionar.

taint (teint) n **1** infección f. **2** mancha f. vt corromper, viciar.

take* (teik) vt **1** tomar. **2** coger. **take aback** desconcertar. vi **1** pegar. **2** tener éxito. **take after** parecerse a. **take-off** n **1** despegue m. **2** caricatura f. **take-over** n tomar posesión f.

talcum powder ('tælkəm) n polvos de talco m pl.

tale (teil) n **1** cuento m. **2** patraña f. **tell tales** chismear, contar cuentos.

talent ('tælənt) n talento m.

talk (tɔ:k) n **1** conversación f. **2** charla f. vi,vt hablar. **talk into** persuadir. **talk over** discutir. **talkative** adj locuaz, hablador.

tall (tɔ:l) adj alto.

tally ('tæli) n **1** tarja f. **2** cuenta f. vi concordar.

talon ('tælən) n garra, uña f.

tambourine (tæmbə'ri:n) n pandereta f.

tame (teim) adj **1** domesticado. **2** manso. **3** soso. vt **1** amansar. **2** reprimir.

tamper ('tæmpə) vi **tamper with 1** estropear. **2** falsificar. **3** entrometerse.

tampon ('tæmpon) n **1** tapón m. **2** tampón m.

tan (tæn) n bronceado m. vt **1** broncear. **2** curtir.

tangent ('tændʒənt) n tangente f.

tangerine (tændʒə'ri:n) n mandarina f.

tangible ('tændʒəbəl) adj **1** tangible. **2** palpable.

tangle ('tæŋgəl) n enredo m. maraña f. vt enredar.

tango ('tæŋgou) n tango m. vi bailar el tango.

tank (tæŋk) n **1** tanque m. **2** cisterna f. **3** carro de combate m. **tanker** n **1** petrolero m. **2** camión-tanque m.

tankard ('tæŋkəd) n pichel m.

tantalize ('tæntəlaiz) vt,vi atormentar, tentar.

tantrum ('tæntrəm) n rabieta f.

tap¹ (tæp) n **1** palmadita f. **2** golpecito m. vt golpear ligeramente.

tap² (tæp) n grifo m. **on tap** de tonel. ~vt **1** espitar. **2** sangrar.

tape (teip) n cinta f. vt grabar en cinta. **tape-measure** n cinta métrica f. **tape-recorder** n magnetofón m.

taper ('teipə) n **1** bujía f. **2** cirio m. vt afilar. vi rematar en punta.

tapestry ('tæpistri) n **1** tapiz m. **2** tapicería f.

tar (tɑ:) n alquitrán m. brea f. vt alquitranar. **tarmac** n alquitranado m.

tarantula (tə'ræntjulə) n tarántula f.

target ('tɑ:git) n **1** blanco m. **2** objetivo m.

tariff ('tærif) n tarifa f.

tarnish ('tɑ:niʃ) vt deslustrar.

tarragon ('tærəgən) n estragón m.

tart¹ (tɑ:t) adj ácido, agrio.

tart² (tɑ:t) n **1** tarta f. **2** pastelillo m. **3** inf fulana f.

tartan ('tɑ:tn) n tartán m.

task (tɑ:sk) n **1** tarea f. **2** empresa f. **take to task** reprender.

tassel ('tæsəl) n borla f.

taste (teist) n **1** sabor m. **2** gusto m. **3** afición f. vt probar. vi saber.

tattoo¹ (tə'tu:) n **1** retreta f. **2** espectáculo militar m.

tattoo² (tə'tu:) n tatuaje m. vt tatuar.

taught (tɔ:t) v see **teach.**

taunt (tɔ:nt) n **1** mofa f. **2** sarcasmo m vt **1** mofarse de. **2** reprochar.

Taurus ('tɔ:rəs) n Tauro m.

taut (tɔ:t) adj tieso, tirante.

tautology (tɔ:'tɒlədʒi) n tautología f.

tavern ('tævən) n taberna f.

tax (tæks) n **1** impuesto m. **2** carga f. vt **1** imponer contribuciones a. **2** tasar. **3** acusar.

taxi ('tæksi) n taxi m. vi aviat rodar de suelo.

tea (ti:) n **1** té m. **2** merienda f. **high tea** merienda-cena f. **tea-bag** n sobre de té m. **tea-break** n descanso para té m. **tea-cloth** n paño de cocina m. **teacup** n taza para té f. **teapot** n tetera f. **teaspoon** n cucharilla f.

teach* (ti:tʃ) vt enseñar. vi ser profesor.

teak (ti:k) n teca f.

team (ti:m) n **1** equipo m. **2** yunta f. v **team up with** asociarse con.

tear¹ (tiə) n lágrima f. **shed tears** llorar. **tear-drop** n lágrima f. **tear-gas** n gas lacrimógeno m.

tear*² (tɛə) n rasgón m. vt **1** rasgar. **2** arrancar. **tear up** romper.

tease (ti:z) vt **1** fastidiar. **2** tormar el pelo a. **3** cardar. n guasón m.

teat (ti:t) n **1** pezón m. **2** teta f.

technical ('teknikəl) adj **1** técnico. **2** laboral. **technician** n **1** técnico m. **2** ayudante de laboratorio m. **technique** n técnica f. **technology** n tecnología f.

tedious ('ti:diəs) adj aburrido, tedioso.

tee (ti:) n meta f.

teenage ('ti:neidʒ) adj,n adolescente.

teetotal (ti:'toutl) adj abstemio.

telegram ('teligræm) n telegrama m.

telegraph ('teligrɑ:f) n telégrafo m. vt,vi telegrafiar. **telegraph pole** n poste telegráfico m.

telepathy (ti'lepəθi) n telepatía f.

287

telephone ('telifoun) n teléfono m. vt,vi telefonear. **be on the telephone** tener teléfono.

telescope ('teliskoup) n telescopio m. vt 1 enchufar. 2 telescopar.

television ('teləviʒən) n televisión f. **televize** vt televisar.

telex ('teleks) n télex m.

tell* (tel) vt 1 decir. 2 contar. 3 anunciar. **tell off** regañar. vi 1 hablar. 2 distinguir. **telltale** adj revelador.

temper ('tempə) n 1 genio, humor m. 2 temple m. vi templar. **temperament** n temperamento m. **temperate** adj 1 templado. 2 moderado. **temperature** n 1 temperatura f. 2 fiebre f.

tempest ('tempist) n tempestad f.

tempestuous (tem'pestjuəs) adj tempestuoso.

temple¹ ('tempəl) n templo m.

temple² ('tempəl) n anat sien f.

tempo ('tempou) n, pl **tempi** 1 tempo m. 2 ritmo m.

temporal ('tempərəl) adj temporal. **temporary** adj 1 provisional. 2 interino.

tempt (tempt) vt 1 tentar. 2 atraer.

ten (ten) adj,n diez m. **tenth** adj,n décimo m.

tenacious (tə'neiʃəs) adj 1 tenaz. 2 porfiado. **tenacity** n tenacidad f.

tenant ('tenənt) n 1 inquilino m. 2 morador m. **tenancy** n 1 tenencia f. 2 arriendo m.

tend¹ (tend) vi 1 tender. 2 inclinarse a. **tendency** n tendencia, propensión f.

tend² (tend) vt cuidar, atender.

tender¹ ('tendə) adj 1 tierno. 2 delicado. 3 blando.

tender² ('tendə) n oferta f. **legal tender** moneda de curso legal f. vt 1 ofrecer. 2 presentar.

tendon ('tendən) n tendón m.

tendril ('tendril) n zarcillo m.

tenement ('tenəmənt) n 1 vivienda f. 2 casa de vecindad f.

tennis ('tenis) n tenis m. **tennis court** n pista de tenis f.

tenor ('tenə) n 1 tenor m. 2 curso m.

tense¹ (tens) adj 1 tirante. 2 tieso. 3 tenso. **tension** n 1 tirantez f. 2 tensión f.

tense² (tens) n gram tiempo m.

tent (tent) n tienda de campaña f.

tentacle ('tentəkəl) n tentáculo m.

tentative ('tentətiv) adj 1 provisional. 2 experimental.

tenuous ('tenjuəs) adj 1 tenue. 2 sutil.

tepid ('tepid) adj tibio.

term (tə:m) n 1 término m. 2 período m. 3 trimestre m. 4 pl condiciones f pl.

terminal ('tə:minl) adj terminal. n 1 término m. 2 borne m.

terminate ('tə:mineit) vt,vi terminar.

terminology (tə:mi'nolədʒi) n terminología f.

terminus ('tə:minəs) n, pl **termini** 1 término m. 2 estación terminal f.

terrace ('terəs) n 1 terraza f. 2 terraplén m. vt terraplenar.

terrestrial (tə'restriəl) adj terrestre.

terrible ('terəbl) adj terrible.

terrify ('terifai) vt aterrar, aterrorizar. **terrific** adj 1 tremendo. 2 inf fabuloso.

territory ('teritri) n territorio m.

terror ('terə) n terror, espanto m. **terrorist** adj,n terrorista m. **terrorize** vt aterrorizar.

Terylene ('terili:n) n Tdmk terylene m.

test (test) n 1 prueba f. 2 examen m. 3 ensayo m. vt probar, poner a prueba.

testament ('testəmənt) n testamento m.

testicle ('testikəl) n testículo m.

testify ('testifai) vi declarar. vt atestiguar.

testimony ('testiməni) n testimonio m. **testimonial** n 1 certificado m. 2 recomendación f

tether ('teθə) n atadura, cuerda f. vt atar.

Teutonic (tju:'tonik) adj teutónico.

text (tekst) n 1 texto m. 2 tema m. **textbook** n libro de texto m.

textile ('tekstail) adj textil. **textiles** n pl tejidos m pl.

texture ('tekstʃə) n textura f.

Thames (temz) n Támesis m.

than (ðən; stressed ðæn) conj 1 que. 2 de. 3 del que. 4 de lo que.

thank (θæŋk) vt dar las gracias a. **thank for** agradecer. **thanks** n pl gracias f pl.

that (ðæt) adj 1 ese, aquel. 2 esa, aquella. pron 1 ése, aquél. 2 ésa, aquélla. 3 que, el cual. conj que.

thatch (θætʃ) n 1 paja f. 2 barda f. vt bardar.

thaw (θɔ:) n deshielo m. vt deshelar, derretir. vi deshelarse.

the (ðə; stressed ði:) def art el, la, lo, los, las. adv cuanto.

theatre ('θiətə) n 1 teatro m. 2 quirófano m.

theft (θeft) n hurto, robo m.

their (ðeə) poss adj 3rd pers pl su, sus. **theirs** poss pron 3rd pers pl el suyo, la suya, los suyos, las suyas, de ellos, de ellas.

them (ðəm; stressed ðem) pron 3rd pers pl 1 los, las. 2 les. 3 ellos, ellas. **themselves** pron

3rd pers pl 1 ellos mismos, ellas mismas. **2** se. **3** sí mismos, ellas mismas.

theme (θi:m) n tema m.

then (ðen; stressed ðen) adv **1** entonces. **2** después. **now and then** de vez en cuando. conj **1** pues. **2** por tanto.

theology (θi'ɔlədʒi) n teología f. **theologian** n teólogo m.

theorem ('θiərəm) n teorema m.

theory ('θiəri) n teoría f. **theoretical** adj teórico. **theorize** vi teorizar.

therapy ('θerəpi) n terapia f. **therapeutic** adj terapéutico.

there (ðeə) adv **1** ahí. **2** allí. **3** allá. **there is or are** hay. ~interj ¡vaya! ¡llvamos! **thereabouts** adv **1** por ahí. **2** aproximadamente. **thereafter** adv después de eso. **thereby** adv **1** por eso. **2** por esa razón. **therefore** adv por tanto, por consiguiente. **thereupon** adv **1** en eso. **2** en seguida. **3** por tanto. **therewith** adv con eso, con lo mismo.

thermal ('θə:məl) adj termal.

thermodynamics (θə:moudai'næmiks) n termodinámica f.

thermometer (θə'mɔmitə) n termómetro m.

thermonuclear (θə:mou'nju:kliə) adj termonuclear.

Thermos ('θə:məs) n Tdmk termo m.

thermostat ('θə:məstæt) n termostato m.

these (ði:z) adj estos, estas. pron éstos, éstas.

thesis ('θi:sis) n, pl **theses** tesis f.

they (ðei) pron 3rd pers pl ellos, ellas.

thick (θik) adj **1** espeso. **2** grueso. **3** denso. **4** turbio. **5** inf estúpido. **thicken** vt espesar. **thick-skinned** adj insensible, duro.

thief (θi:f) n, pl **thieves** ladrón m.

thigh (θai) n muslo m.

thimble ('θimbəl) n **1** dedal m. **2** guardacabo m.

thin (θin) adj **1** delgado. **2** escaso. **3** flaco. vi **1** adelgazar. **2** reducirse. **thin-skinned** adj **1** de piel fina. **2** sensible.

thing (θiŋ) n **1** cosa f. **2** asunto m.

think* (θiŋk) vt **1** pensar. **2** imaginar. **3** considerar. **4** creer. **think of 1** considerar. **2** pensar en. **think over** reflexionar.

third (θə:d) adj tercero. n tercio m. tercera parte f. **third party** adj tercera persona. **third-rate** adj de baja categoría.

thirst (θə:st) n **1** sed f. **2** ansia m. vi tener sed. **thirsty** adj **1** sediento. **2** árido. **be thirsty** tener sed.

thirteen (θə:'ti:n) adj,n trece m. **thirteenth** adj decimotercio.

thirty ('θə:ti) adj,n treinta m. **thirtieth** adj trigésimo.

this (ðis) adj este, esta. pron éste, ésta, esto.

thistle ('θisəl) n cardo m.

thorn (θɔ:n) n espina f.

thorough ('θʌrə) adj **1** completo. **2** concienzudo. **thoroughbred** adj de pura sangre. **thoroughfare** n vía pública f.

those (ðouz) adj esos, aquellos, esas, aquellas. pron ésos, aquéllos, ésas, aquéllas.

though (ðou) conj aunque. adv sin embargo.

thought¹ (θɔ:t) n **1** pensamiento m. **2** concepto m. **3** reflexión f. **on second thoughts** después de pensarlo bien. **thoughtful** adj **1** pensativo. **2** atento. **3** serio. **thoughtless** adj **1** irreflexivo. **2** inconsiderado.

thought² (θɔ:t) v see **think**.

thousand ('θauzənd) adj,n mil m. **thousandth** adj,n milésimo m.

thrash (θræʃ) vt **1** golpear. **2** azotar. **3** derrotar. **thrash about** sacudirse.

thread (θred) n **1** hilo m. **2** hebra f. **3** rosca f. vt enhebrar. **threadbare** adj raído, gastado.

threat (θret) n amenaza f. **threaten** vt, vi amenazar.

three (θri:) adj,n tres m. **three-cornered** adj triangular. **three-dimensional** adj tridimensional.

thresh (θreʃ) vt trillar.

threshold ('θreʃhould) n umbral m.

threw (θru:) v see **throw**.

thrift (θrift) n economía, frugalidad f.

thrill (θril) n **1** emoción f. **2** estremecimiento m. vt emocionar. **thriller** n novela de misterio f.

thrive* ('θraiv) vi **1** prosperar. **2** crecer mucho.

throat (θrout) n garganta f. **clear the throat** aclarar la voz.

throb (θrɔb) n **1** latido m. **2** vibración f. vi **1** latir. **2** vibrar.

throne (θroun) n **1** trono m. **2** corona f.

throng (θrɔŋ) n multitud f. vt atestar. **throng together** reunirse en tropel.

throttle ('θrɔtl) n **1** gaznate m. **2** regulador m. vt ahogar.

through (θru:) adj **1** a través. **2** completamente. prep **1** por. **2** a través de. **3** hasta. **throughout** adv **1** en todas partes. **2** todo el tiempo. prep por todo.

throw* (θrou) n **1** tirada f. **2** lance m. vt echar, tirar. **throw up** vomitar.

thrush (θrʌʃ) n zool zorzal, tordo m.

thrust

thrust (θrʌst) n 1 empuje m. 2 avance m. 3 puñalada f. vt empujar. vi 1 acometer. 2 meterse.

thud (θʌd) n ruido sordo m. vi hacer un ruido sordo.

thumb (θʌm) n pulgar m. vt manosear.

thump (θʌmp) n golpazo m. vt golpear.

thunder (ˈθʌndə) n 1 trueno m. 2 estruendo m. vi tronar. **thunderstorm** n tormenta, tronada f.

Thursday (ˈθəːzdi) n jueves m.

thus (ðʌs) adv 1 así. 2 de este modo. **thus far** hasta aquí.

thwart (θwɔːt) n bancada f. vt frustrar.

thyme (taim) n tomillo m.

thyroid (ˈθairoid) n tiroides m. adj tiroideo.

tiara (tiˈɑːrə) n diadema f.

tick¹ (tik) n 1 tictac m. 2 momento m. 3 señal f.

tick² (tik) n zool garrapata f.

ticket (ˈtikit) n 1 billete m. 2 entrada f. 3 etiqueta f. **ticket-collector** n revisor m. **ticket-office** n 1 despacho de billetes m. 2 Th taquilla f.

tickle (ˈtikəl) vt 1 hacer cosquillas a. 2 divertir. n cosquillas f pl. **ticklish** adj 1 cosquilloso. 2 delicado.

tide (taid) n 1 marea f. 2 corriente f. **tidemark** n lengua del agua f.

tidy (ˈtaidi) adj 1 ordenado. 2 aseado. 3 considerable. vt asear, limpiar.

tie (tai) n 1 lazo m. 2 corbata f. 3 empate m. vt 1 atar. 2 anudar. **tie up** atracar.

tier (tiə) n grada, fila f.

tiger (ˈtaigə) n tigre m.

tight (tait) adj 1 tieso, apretado. 2 escaso. 3 inf borracho. **tighten** vt 1 apretar. 2 estirar. **tight-fisted** adj agarrado, tacaño. **tightrope** n cuerda de volatinero f. **tights** n pl mallas f pl. leotardos m pl.

tilde (ˈtildə) n tilde f.

tile (tail) n 1 teja f. 2 baldosa f. 3 azulejo m. vt tejar.

till¹ (til) prep hasta. conj hasta que.

till² (til) vt cultivar, labrar.

till³ (til) n caja registradora f.

tiller (ˈtilə) n naut caña del timón f.

tilt (tilt) n 1 inclinación f. 2 ladeo m. 3 torneo m. vt inclinar.

timber (ˈtimbə) n 1 madera f. 2 bosque m. 3 madero m.

time (taim) n 1 tiempo m. 2 período m. 3 época f. 4 hora f. **from time to time** de vez en

cuando. **time bomb** n bomba de relojería f. **timetable** n 1 horario m. 2 programa f.

timid (ˈtimid) adj tímido.

timpani (ˈtimpəni) n pl tímpanos m pl.

tin (tin) n 1 estaño m. 2 lata f. 3 hojalata f. vt 1 estañar. 2 envasar en lata. **tin-opener** n abrelatas m invar.

tinge (tindʒ) n 1 tinte m. 2 matiz m. vt 1 teñir. 2 matizar.

tingle (ˈtiŋgəl) n 1 picazón f. 2 hormigueo m. vi sentir hormigueo.

tinker (ˈtiŋkə) n calderero m. vt remendar. vi tratar de reparar.

tinkle (ˈtiŋkəl) n 1 retintín m. 2 campanilleo m. vi campanillear.

tinsel (ˈtinsəl) n oropel m.

tint (tint) n 1 tinte m. vt teñir, matizar.

tiny (ˈtaini) adj pequeñito, diminuto.

tip¹ (tip) n punta f. cabo m. **from tip to toe** de pies a cabeza. **tiptoe** vi ir de puntillas. **on tiptoe** de puntillas f.

tip² (tip) vt inclinar, ladear.

tip³ (tip) n propina f.

tipsy (ˈtipsi) adj achispado.

tire (ˈtaiə) vt 1 cansar. 2 aburrir. **tired** adj cansado.

tissue (ˈtiʃuː) n 1 tejido m. 2 tisú m. 3 pañuelo de papel m.

title (ˈtaitl) n 1 título m. 2 derecho m. vt titular.

to (tə; stressed tuː) prep 1 a. 2 hacia. 3 hasta. 4 para. **to-do** inf lío, follón m.

toad (toud) n sapo m. **toadstool** n hongo venenoso m.

toast¹ (toust) n pan tostado m. vt tostar.

toast² (toust) n brindis m. vt brindar por.

tobacco (təˈbækou) n tabaco m.

toboggan (təˈbɔgən) n tobogán m.

today (təˈdei) adv 1 hoy. 2 hoy en día.

toddler (ˈtɔdlə) n niño aprendiendo a andar m.

toe (tou) n dedo del pie m. **toenail** n uña del dedo del pie f.

toffee (ˈtɔfi) n caramelo m.

together (təˈgeðə) adv 1 junto. 2 juntamente. 3 a la vez.

toil (tɔil) n 1 labor f. 2 fatiga f. 3 esfuerzo m. vi 1 trabajar. 2 fatigarse.

toilet (ˈtɔilət) n 1 tocado m. 2 lavabo m. 3 tocador m. 4 wáter m. **toilet paper** n papel higiénico m. **toilet water** n agua de colonia m.

token (ˈtoukən) n 1 signo m. 2 prenda f. 3 recuerdo m.

told (tould) v see **tell**.

290

tolerate ('tɔləreit) vt tolerar. **tolerance** n tolerancia f.

toll[1] (toul) vt tañer, doblar.

toll[2] (toul) n 1 peaje m. 2 portazgo m. **tollgate** n barrera de peaje f.

tomato (tə'mɑ:tou) n, pl **-oes** tomate m.

tomb (tu:m) n tumba f. sepulcro m. **tombstone** n lápida sepulcral f.

tomorrow (tə'mɔrou) adv mañana f. **the day after tomorrow** pasado mañana.

ton (tʌn) n tonelada f.

tone (toun) n 1 tono m. 2 acento m. 3 matiz m. vt entonar. vi armonizar.

tongs (tɔgz) n pl tenacillas, tenazas f pl.

tongue (tʌŋ) n 1 lengua f. 2 badajo m. **hold one's tongue** callarse. **tongue-tied** adj premioso. **tongue-twister** n trabalenguas m invar.

tonic ('tɔnik) adj,n tónico m. n mus tónica f. **tonic water** n agua tónica m.

tonight (tə'nait) adv esta noche.

tonsil ('tɔnsəl) n amígdala f. **tonsilitis** n amigdalitis f.

too (tu:) adv 1 demasiado. 2 también. 3 además.

took (tuk) v see **take.**

tool (tu:l) n herramienta f. 2 instrumento m.

tooth (tu:θ) n, pl **teeth** 1 diente m. 2 muela f. **have a sweet tooth** ser goloso. **toothache** n dolor de muelas m. **toothbrush** n cepillo de dientes m. **toothpaste** n pasta dentífrica f. **toothpick** n mondadientes m invar.

top[1] (tɔp) n 1 cumbre f. 2 parte superior f. adj 1 más alto. 2 superior. vt encabezar. **top hat** n chistera f. **top-heavy** adj mal equilibrado.

top[2] (tɔp) n peonza f.

topaz ('toupæz) n topacio m.

topic ('tɔpik) n asunto, tema m. **topical** adj actual.

topography (tə'pɔgrəfi) n topografía f.

topple ('tɔpəl) vt 1 derribar. 2 hacer caer. vi caerse.

topsoil ('tɔpsɔil) n capa superficial del suelo f.

topsy-turvy (tɔpsi'tə:vi) adj confuso, desordenado. adv en desorden.

torch (tɔ:tʃ) n 1 antorcha f. 2 linterna f.

tore (tɔ:) v see **tear**[2].

toreador ('tɔriədɔ:) n torero m.

torment (v tɔ:'ment; n 'tɔ:ment) vt atormentar. n tormento m. tortura f.

torn (tɔ:n) v see **tear**[2].

tornado (tɔ:'neidou) n, pl **-dos** or **-does** tornado m.

torpedo (tɔ:'pi:dou) n, pl **-does** torpedo m. vt torpedear.

torrent ('tɔrənt) n torrente m.

torso ('tɔ:sou) n torso m.

tortilla (tɔ:'ti:jə) n tortilla f.

tortoise ('tɔ:təs) n tortuga f.

tortuous ('tɔ:tʃuəs) adj tortuoso.

torture ('tɔ:tʃə) n 1 tortura f. 2 tormento m. vt torturar.

Tory ('tɔ:ri) adj,n conservador m.

toss (tɔs) vt 1 sacudir. 2 echar. **toss up** echar a cara or cruz. ~n 1 sacudida f. 2 echada f.

tot[1] (tɔt) n nene m.

tot[2] (tɔt) vt **tot up** sumar.

total ('toutl) adj 1 total. 2 completo. n total m. vt sumar. **totalitarian** adj totalitario.

totem ('toutəm) n tótem m. **totem pole** n poste totémico f.

totter ('tɔtə) vi 1 bambolearse. 2 estar para caerse.

touch (tʌtʃ) n 1 tacto m. 2 contacto m. 3 pizca m. vt 1 tocar. 2 conmover. **touch off** estallar. **touchy** adj susceptible.

tough (tʌf) adj 1 duro. 2 resistente. 3 tenaz. **toughen** vt.endurecer.

toupee ('tu:pei) n peluca f. pelo postizo m.

tour (tuə) n 1 viaje m. 2 gira f. vt viajar por. vi viajar. **tourism** n turismo m. **tourist** n turista m,f.

tournament ('tuənəmənt) n 1 torneo m. 2 concurso m.

tow (tou) n remolque m. vt remolcar. **towrope** n cable de remolque m.

towards (tə'wɔ:dz) prep also **toward** 1 hacia. 2 cerca de. 3 para con.

towel ('tauəl) n toalla f.

tower ('tauə) n torre f. **tower-block** n alto bloque de pisos m. v **tower above** destacarse sobre.

town (taun) n 1 ciudad f. 2 pueblo m. **town clerk** n secretario del ayuntamiento m. **town hall** n ayuntamiento m. **town-planning** n urbanismo m.

toxic ('tɔksik) adj tóxico.

toy (tɔi) n juguete m. v **toy with** jugar con.

trace (treis) n 1 rastro m. 2 vestigio m. 3 señal f. vt 1 trazar. 2 calcar.

track (træk) n 1 huella f. 2 sport pista f. 3 senda f. 4 vía f. vt rastrear. **tracksuit** n mono de entrenamiento m.

tract[1] (trækt) n zona, región f. **digestive tract** canal digestivo m.

tract[2] (trækt) n tratado, folleto m.

tractor ('træktə) n tractor m.

trade (treid) n comercio m. **trademark** n marca registrada f. **tradesman** n tendero, artesano m. **trade union** n sindicato, gremio m. **trade unionism** n sindicalismo m. **trade unionist** n sindicalista m,f.

tradition (trə'diʃən) n tradición f. **traditional** adj tradicional. **traditionalism** n tradicionalismo m.

traffic ('træfik) n 1 mot circulación f. 2 comm tráfico, comercio m. trata f. **traffic jam** n embotellamiento m. **traffic lights** n pl semáforo m. luces de tráfico f pl. **traffic warden** n guardián del tráfico m.

tragedy ('trædʒədi) n tragedia f. **tragic** adj trágico.

trail (treil) n 1 rastro m. pista f. 2 estela, cola f. 3 camino, sendero m. vt 1 arrastrar. 2 rastrear, seguir la pista de. **trailer** n 1 mot remolque m. 2 trailer, avance m.

train (trein) n 1 mot tren m. 2 serie f. **train of thought** hilo del pensamiento m. ~vt 1 adiestrar, preparar. 2 apuntar. **trained** adj capacitado, amaestrado. **trainee** n aprendiz m. **trainer** n entrenador m.

traitor ('treitə) n traidor m. **traitorous** adj traidor, traicionero.

tram (træm) n tranvía m.

tramp (træmp) n 1 marcha pesada f. 2 paseo largo m. 3 vagabundo m. vi marchar pesadamente.

trample ('træmpəl) vt pisar, pisotear.

trampoline ('træmpəli:n) n trampolín m.

trance (trɑːns) n 1 arrobamiento, éxtasis m. 2 trance m.

tranquil ('træŋkwil) adj tranquilo. **tranquillity** n tranquilidad f. **tranquillizer** n tranquilizante m.

transact (træn'zækt) vt tramitar, despachar. **transaction** n negocio m. transacción f.

transatlantic (trænzət'læntik) adj transatlántico.

transcend (træn'send) vt exceder, superar.

transcribe (træn'skraib) vt transcribir.

transfer (v træns'fə:; n 'trænsfə:) vt transferir, traspasar. vi trasladarse. n 1 transferencia f. 2 traspaso m. 3 traslado m.

transform (træns'fɔ:m) vt transformar. **transformation** n transformación f.

transfuse (træns'fju:z) vt transfundir. **transfusion** n transfusión f.

transistor (træn'zistə) n transistor m.

transit ('trænsit) n tránsito m. **in transit** de tránsito.

transition (træn'ziʃən) n transición f. **transitional** adj transicional.

transitive ('trænsitiv) adj transitivo.

translate (trænz'leit) vt 1 traducir. 2 interpretar. **translation** n traducción f. **translator** n traductor m.

translucent (trænz'lu:sənt) adj translúcido.

transmit (trænz'mit) vt transmitir. **transmission** n transmisión f. **transmitter** n 1 transmisor m. 2 transmisora, emisora f.

transparent (træns'pærənt) adj transparente.

transplant (v træns'plɑ:nt; n 'trænsplɑ:nt) vt trasplantar. n trasplante m.

transport (v træns'pɔ:t; n 'trænspɔ:t) vt transportar. n transporte m. **transportation** n transportación f.

transpose (træns'pouz) vt transponer.

trap (træp) n 1 trampa f. 2 coche m. vt entrampar, atrapar. **trapdoor** n 1 escotilla f. 2 Th escotillón m.

trapeze (trə'pi:z) n trapecio m.

trash (træʃ) n 1 hojarasca f. 2 trastos viejos m pl.

trauma ('trɔ:mə) n trauma m. **traumatic** adj traumático.

travel ('trævəl) vi 1 viajar. 2 ir. n turismo m. viajes m pl. **travel agency** n agencia de turismo f. **traveller** n 1 viajero m. 2 comm viajante n. **traveller's cheque** n cheque de viajeros m.

trawl (trɔ:l) vi pescar a la rastra. vt rastrear. **trawler** n barco rastreador m.

tray (trei) n bandeja f.

treachery ('tretʃəri) n traición f. **treacherous** adj 1 traidor. 2 engañoso.

treacle ('tri:kəl) n melado m. melaza f.

tread* (tred) n 1 paso m. 2 huella f. vt pisar.

treason ('tri:zən) n traición f. **high treason** alta traición f.

treasure ('treʒə) n 1 tesoro m. 2 inf joya f. **treasure trove** n tesoro hallado m. ~vt atesorar. **treasurer** n tesorero m. **treasury** n tesoro m. hacienda f.

treat (tri:t) vt 1 tratar. 2 invitar. n convite m. **treatment** n tratamiento m.

treatise ('tri:tiz) n tratado m. disertación f.

treatment ('tri:tmənt) n tratamiento m.

treaty ('tri:ti) n tratado m.

treble ('trebəl) adj 1 triple. 2 mus de tiple. **treble clef** n clave de sol f. tiple m, f. ~vt triplicar.

tree (tri:) n árbol m.

trek (trek) n 1 viaje m. 2 migración f. 3 jornada f. vi emigrar, viajar.

trellis ('trelis) n enrejado m.

tremble ('trembǝl) vi temblar, estremecerse. n temblor m. **trembling** adj tembloroso. n temblar, temblor m.

tremendous (tri'mendǝs) adj tremendo, imponente, formidable.

tremor ('tremǝ) n 1 temblor m. 2 vibración f.

trench (trentʃ) n zanja f. foso m.

trend (trend) n 1 tendencia, dirección f. 2 moda f. **trendy** adj elegante, modernísimo.

trespass ('trespǝs) n 1 intrusión, entrada sin permiso f. 2 ofensa f. vi entrar sin derecho. **no trespassing** prohibida la entrada. **trespasser** n intruso m.

trestle ('tresǝl) n caballete m.

trial ('traiǝl) n 1 law proceso, juicio m. 2 prueba f. 3 adversidad f. **trial run** n viaje de ensayo m.

triangle ('traiæŋgǝl) n triángulo m. **triangular** adj triangular.

tribe (traib) n tribu f. **tribal** adj tribal. **tribesman** n miembro de una tribu m.

tribunal (trai'bju:nl) n tribunal m.

tributary ('tribju:tǝri) n 1 tributario m. 2 geog afluente m.

tribute ('tribju:t) n 1 tributo m. 2 homenaje m.

trick (trik) n 1 truco m. trampa f. 2 burla f. 3 peculiaridad f. vt engañar, trampear, burlar. **trickery** n astucia f. fraude m. **tricky** adj 1 astuto. 2 delicado, difícil.

trickle ('trikǝl) n chorro delgado, gotos m. vi gotear.

tricycle ('traisikǝl) n triciclo m.

trifle ('traifǝl) n 1 bagatela, fruslería f. 2 pizca f. 3 cul dulce de bizcocho, fruta y natillas o crema. v **trifle away** malgastar. **trifle with** jugar con. **trifling** adj insignificante.

trigger ('trigǝ) n gatillo m. v **trigger off** 1 hacer estallar. 2 provocar.

trill (tril) n 1 trino m. 2 vibración f. vt pronunciar con vibración. vi trinar.

trim (trim) adj aseado. n recorte m. vt 1 cortar. 2 adornar. 3 ordenar.

trio ('triou) n trío m.

trip (trip) n 1 viaje m. 2 tropiezo m. vi 1 andar con paso ligero. 2 tropezar. **trip up** 1 hacer tropezar. 2 coger en la falta.

tripe (traip) n 1 cul callos m pl. 2 inf tonterías f pl.

triple ('tripǝl) adj,n triple m. vt triplicar. **triplet** n 1 mus tresillo m. 2 pl trillizos m pl. **triplicate** adj,n triplicado m.

tripod ('traipɔd) n trípode m.

trite (trait) adj vulgar, trivial.

triumph ('traiʌmf) n triunfo m. vi triunfar. **triumphant** adj triunfante. **triumphantly** adv triunfalmente.

trivial ('trivial) adj trivial.

trod (trɔd) v see **tread.**

trodden ('trɔdn) v see **tread.**

trolley ('trɔli) n carretilla f. **tea trolley** mesita de ruedas f.

trombone (trɔm'boun) n trombón m.

troop (tru:p) n 1 mil tropa f. 2 grupo m. vi marchar.

trophy ('troufi) n trofeo m.

tropic ('trɔpik) n trópico m. **tropical** adj trópico.

trot (trɔt) n trote m. vi trotar. **trotter** n cul pata de cerdo f.

trouble ('trʌbǝl) n 1 aflicción f. 2 dificultad f. 3 conflicto m. vt 1 afligir. 2 molestar. **troublemaker** n alborotador m.

trough (trɔf) n abrevadero, comedero m.

troupe (tru:p) n Th compañía f.

trousers ('trauzǝz) n pl pantalones m pl.

trout (traut) n trucha f.

trowel ('trauǝl) n 1 desplantador m. 2 paleta f.

truant ('truǝnt) n novillero m. **play truant** hacer novillos. **truancy** n ausencia sin permiso f.

truce (tru:s) n tregua f.

truck (trʌk) n 1 camión m. 2 carretilla f. **truck driver** n camionero m.

trudge (trʌdʒ) vi caminar con pena. n caminata f.

true (tru:) adj 1 verdadero. 2 auténtico. 3 fiel, leal. 4 conforme. **be true** ser verdad. **truly** adv verdaderamente. **yours truly** le saluda atentamente.

truffle ('trʌfǝl) n trufa f.

trump (trʌmp) n triunfo m. vt game fallar, inventar. vi triunfar, poner un triunfo.

trumpet ('trʌmpit) n trompeta f. vt trompetear. vi barritar. **trumpet blast** n trompetazo m.

truncheon ('trʌntʃǝn) n porra f.

trunk (trʌŋk) n 1 anat tronco m. 2 baúl m. 3 zool trompa f.

trust (trʌst) n 1 confianza f. 2 comm crédito m. 3 cargo m. obligación f. **on trust** al fiado. ~vt 1 confiar en. 2 confiar dar al fiado. 3 esperar. vi esperar, confiar. **trusted** adj leal, de confianza. **trustee** n 1 síndico m. 2 depositario *m*. **trustworthy** *adj* 1 confiable, de confianza. 2 fidedigno.

truth (truːθ) *n* verdad *f*. **truthful** *adj* verídico, veraz.

try (trai) *n* 1 tentativa *f*. 2 *game* ensayo *m*. *vt* 1 intentar, probar. 2 ensayar. 3 *law* procesar. *vi* probar. **try on** probarse. **try out** someter a prueba. **trying** *adj* molesto.

tsar (tsɑː) *n* zar *m*. **tsarina** *n* zarina *f*.

T-shirt *n* camiseta *f*.

tub (tʌb) *n* cubo *m*. tina, cuba *f*.

tuba ('tjuːbə) *n* tuba *f*.

tube (tjuːb) *n* 1 tubo *m*. 2 *mot* metro *m*. **tube station** *n* estación de metro *f*.

tuber ('tjuːbə) *n* tubérculo *m*.

tuberculosis (tjuːbəːkjuˈlousis) *n* tuberculosis *f*.

tuck (tʌk) *n* alforza *f*. pliegue *m*. *vt* alforzar, plegar.

Tuesday ('tjuːzdi) *n* martes *m*.

tuft (tʌft) *n* 1 copete, mechón *m*. 2 manojo *m*.

tug (tʌg) *n* 1 tirón, estirón *m*. 2 *naut* remolcador *m*. **tug of war** *n* lucha de cuerda *f*. ~*vt* tirar de, arrastrar.

tuition (tjuːˈiʃən) *n* enseñanza *f*.

tulip ('tuːlip) *n* tulipán *m*.

tumble ('tʌmbəl) *n* caída, voltereta *f*. *vi* caer, tropezar. **tumbler** *n* vaso *m*.

tummy ('tʌmi) *n* estómago, vientre *m*.

tumour ('tjuːmə) *n* tumor *m*.

tumult ('tumʌlt) *n* tumulto *m*.

tuna ('tjuːnə) *n* atún *m*.

tune (tjuːn) *n* 1 aire *m*. melodía *f*. 2 tono *m*. **change one's tune** mudar de. tono. ~*vt,vi* afinar, acordar, templar. **tune in** sintonizar. **tuneful** *adj* melodioso.

tunic ('tjuːnik) *n* túnica *f*.

Tunisia (tjuːˈniziə) *n* Túnez *m*. **Tunisian** *adj,n* tunecino *m*.

tunnel ('tʌnl) *n* túnel *m*. *vi* construir un túnel.

tunny ('tʌni) *n* atún *m*.

turban ('təːbən) *n* turbante *m*.

turbine ('təːbain) *n* turbina *f*.

turbot ('təːbət) *n* rodaballo *m*.

turbulent ('təːbjulənt) *adj* turbulento. **turbulence** *n* turbulencia *f*.

turf (təːf) *n* 1 césped *m*. 2 turba *f*. *vt* encespedar. **turf out** echar.

turkey ('təːki) *n* pavo *m*.

Turkey ('təːki) *n* Turquía *f*. **Turk** *n* turco *m*. **Turkish** *adj* turco.

turmeric ('təːmərik) *n* cúrcuma *f*.

turmoil ('təːmɔil) *n* desorden *m*. confusión *f*.

turn (təːn) *n* 1 vuelta *f*. 2 giro, cambio de

dirección *m*. 3 vez *f*. turno *m*. **good turn** favor *m*. ~*vt* volver, girar. *vi* girar, dar vueltas. **turning** *n* vuelta *f*. **turnover** *n* 1 volumen de ventas *m*. 2 *cul* empanada de fruta *f*. **turnstile** *n* torniquete *m*. **turntable** *n* placa giratoria *f*.

turnip ('təːnip) *n* nabo *m*.

turpentine ('təːpəntain) *n* 1 aguarrás *m* invar. 2 trementina *f*.

turquoise ('təːkwɔiz) *n* turquesa *f*.

turret ('tʌrət) *n* 1 *arch* torreón *m*. 2 torre *f*.

turtle ('təːtl) *n* tortuga marina *f*.

tusk (tʌsk) *n* colmillo *m*.

tussle ('tʌsəl) *n* lucha, pelea *f*. *vi* luchar.

tutor ('tjuːtə) *n* preceptor, profesor particular *m*. *vt* enseñar. **tutorial** *adj* preceptoral. *n* clase particular *f*.

tweed (twiːd) *n* tela de lana escocesa *f*.

tweezers ('twiːzəz) *n pl* pinzas *f pl*.

twelve (twelv) *adj,n* doce *m*. **twelfth** *adj* duodécimo.

twenty ('twenti) *adj,n* veinte *m*. **twentieth** *adj* vigésimo.

twice (twais) *adv* dos veces.

twiddle ('twidl) *n* vuelta *f*. *vt* girar, hacer girar. **twiddle one's thumbs** voltear los pulgares.

twig (twig) *n* ramita *f*.

twilight ('twailait) *n* crepúsculo *m*. *adj* crepuscular.

twin (twin) *n* gemelo *m*.

twine (twain) *n* guita *f*. bramante *m*. *vt* 1 tejer. 2 ceñir. *vi* enroscarse, trepar.

twinge (twindʒ) *n* punzada *f*.

twinkle ('twiŋkəl) *n* centelleo *m*. *vi* centellear. **twinkling** *adj* centelleante, risueño.

twirl (twəːl) *n* vuelta *f*. giro *m*. *vt* volver rápidamente.

twist (twist) *vt* torcer, retorcer. *n* 1 torsión *f*. 2 torzal *m*. 3 vuelta *f*. 4 sesgo *m*.

twitch (twitʃ) *n* contracción nerviosa *f*. tic *m*. *vt* tirar ligeramente de. *vi* crisparse.

twitter ('twitə) *vi* gorjear. *n* gorjeo *m*.

two (tuː) *adj,n* dos *m*. **two-faced** *adj* doble, falso. **twosome** *n* pareja *f*. **two-way** *adj* de dos direcciones.

tycoon (taiˈkuːn) *n* magnate *m*.

type (taip) *n* tipo *m*. *vt,vi* escribir a máquina. **typewriter** *n* máquina de escribir *f*. **typist** *n* mecanógrafo *m*.

typhoid ('taifɔid) *n* fiebre tifoidea *f*.

typhoon (taiˈfuːn) *n* tifón *m*.

typical ('tipikəl) *adj* típico.

tyrant ('tairənt) n tirano m. **tyranny** n tiranía f.

tyre ('taiə) n neumático m. **spare tyre** neumático de recambio m.

U

ubiquitous (ju:'bikwitəs) adj omnipresente. **ubiquity** n omnipresencia f.

udder ('ʌdə) n ubre f.

ugly ('ʌgli) adj feo.

ulcer ('ʌlsə) n úlcera f.

ulterior (ʌl'tiəriə) adj ulterior. **ulterior motive** motivo oculto m.

ultimate ('ʌltimət) adj último, final. **ultimatum** n, pl **-tums** or **-ta** ultimátum m.

ultraviolet (ʌltrə'vaiələt) adj ultravioleta.

umbrella (ʌm'brelə) n paraguas m invar.

umpire ('ʌmpaiə) n árbitro m. vt, vi arbitrar.

unable (ʌn'eibəl) adj incapaz. **be unable** no poder.

unacceptable (ʌnək'septəbəl) adj inaceptable.

unaccompanied (ʌnə'kʌmpnid) adj sin acompañamiento.

unanimous (ju:'naniməs) adj unánime.

unarmed (ʌn'ɑ:md) adj desarmado.

unattractive (ʌnə'træktiv) adj poco atractivo.

unavoidable (ʌnə'vɔidəbəl) adj inevitable.

unaware (ʌnə'wɛə) adj ignorante. **be unaware** ignorar, no saber. **unawares** adv de improviso.

unbalanced (ʌn'bælənst) adj desequilibrado.

unbearable (ʌn'bɛərəbəl) adj inaguantable, insoportable.

unbelievable (ʌnbi'li:vəbəl) adj increíble.

unbend (ʌn'bend) vt endevezar. vi inf suavizarse.

unbreakable (ʌn'breikəbəl) adj irrompible.

unbutton (ʌn'bʌtn) vt desabotonar.

uncalled-for (ʌn'kʌmftəbəl) adj 1 gratuito. 2 impertinente.

uncanny (ʌn'kæni) adj misterioso.

uncertain (ʌn'sə:tn) adj incierto. **be uncertain of** no estar seguro de.

uncle ('ʌŋkəl) n tío m.

unclear (ʌn'kliə) adj oscuro.

uncomfortable (ʌn'kʌmftəbəl) adj incómodo.

unconscious (ʌn'kɔnʃəs) adj 1 inconsciente. 2 med sin sentido. n **the unconscious** lo inconsciente neu.

unconventional (ʌnkən'venʃnəl) adj poco convencional.

uncooked (ʌn'kukt) adj crudo.

uncouth (ʌn'ku:θ) adj grosero.

uncover (ʌn'kʌvə) vt descubrir, destapar.

undecided (ʌndi'saidid) adj indeciso.

undeniable (ʌndi'naiəbəl) adj innegable.

under ('ʌndə) adv debajo, abajo. prep 1 debajo de, bajo. 2 inferior a.

undercharge (ʌndə'tʃɑ:dʒ) vt cobrar menos del precio justo a.

undercoat ('ʌndəkout) n primera capa f.

undercover ('ʌndəkʌvə) adj secreto.

undercut (ʌndə'kʌt) vt competir con (rebajando los precios).

underdeveloped (ʌndədi'veləpd) adj subdesarrollado.

underdone (ʌndə'dʌn) adj poco hecho, medio asado.

underestimate (ʌndər'estimeit) vt menospreciar.

undergo (ʌndə'gou) vt sufrir, someterse a.

undergraduate (ʌndə'grædjuət) adj de licenciatura. n inf estudiante no graduado m, f.

underground (adv ʌndə'graund; adj, n 'ʌndə-graund) adv bajo tierra. adj 1 subterráneo. 2 clandestino. n metro m.

undergrowth ('ʌndəgrouθ) n maleza f.

underhand (ʌndə'hænd) adj secreto, clandestino.

underline (ʌndə'lain) vt subrayar.

undermine (ʌndə'main) vt socavar, minar.

underneath (ʌndə'ni:θ) adj inferior, de abajo. adv debajo. prep bajo, debajo de.

underpants ('ʌndəpænts) n pl calzoncillos m pl.

underpass ('ʌndəpɑ:s) n paso inferior m.

underrate (ʌndə'reit) vt menospreciar, subestimar.

understand (ʌndə'stænd) vt, vi 1 comprender, entender. 2 sobreentender. **understanding** n 1 entendimiento m, comprensión f. 2 acuerdo m. adj comprensivo, compasivo.

understate (ʌndə'steit) vt exponer incompletamente, subestimar.

understudy ('ʌndəstʌdi) n suplente m, f.

undertake (ʌndə'teik) vt emprender. **undertake to** comprometerse a. **undertaker** n director de pompas fúnebres m. **undertaker's** n funeraria f. **undertaking** n 1 empresa, tarea f. 2 compromiso m.

undertone ('ʌndətoun) n 1 voz baja. 2 trasfondo m.

underwater (ʌndə'wɔ:tə) adj submarino.

underwear ('ʌndəwɛə) n ropa interior f.

underwent (ʌndə'went) v see **undergo.**

underworld ('ʌndəwə:ld) n 1 infierno m. 2 hampa f.

295

underwrite (' ʌndərait) vt asegurar.

undesirable (ʌndi'zaiərəbəl) adj,n indeseable m,f.

undo (ʌn'du:) vt deshacer, desatar.

undoubted (ʌn'dautid) adj indudable.

undress (ʌn'dres) vt desnudar.

undue ('ʌndju:) adj indebido.

undulate ('ʌndʒəleit) vi ondular.

unearth (ʌn'ə:θ) vt 1 desenterrar. 2 inf descubrir. **unearthly** adj sobrenatural, misterioso.

uneasy (ʌn'i:zi) adj inquieto.

unemployed (ʌnim'plɔid) adj sin empleo. **unemployment** n paro, desempleo m. desocupación f.

unequal (ʌn'i:kwəl) adj desigual. **unequalled** adj sin par.

uneven (ʌn'i:vən) adj 1 desigual. 2 ondulado.

unfair (ʌn'feə) adj injusto.

unfaithful (ʌn'feiθfəl) adj infiel.

unfamiliar (ʌnfə'miliə) adj desconocido. **be unfamiliar with** desconocer.

unfit (ʌn'fit) adj incapaz.

unfold (ʌn'fould) vt 1 desplegar. 2 exponer.

unfortunate (ʌn'fɔ:tʃunət) adj,n desgraciado m.

unfurnished (ʌn'fə:niʃt) adj desamueblado.

ungrateful (ʌn'greitfəl) adj ingrato.

unhappy (ʌn'hæpi) adj infeliz, desdichado.

unhealthy (ʌn'helθi) adj enfermizo.

unicorn ('ju:nikɔ:n) n unicornio m.

uniform ('ju:nifɔ:m) adj,n uniforme m.

unify ('ju:nifai) vt unificar, unir.

unilateral (ju:ni'lætərəl) adj unilateral.

uninterested (ʌn'intrəstid) adj sin interés. **uninteresting** adj poco interesante.

union ('ju:niən) n 1 unión f. 2 enlace m. 3 pol sindicato m.

unique (ju:'ni:k) adj único.

unison ('ju:nizən) n armonía f. **in unison** mus al unísono. **in unison with** de acuerdo con.

unit ('ju:nit) n unidad f. grupo m.

unite (ju:'nait) vt unir, juntar. **united** adj unido. **unity** n unidad f.

United Kingdom n Reino Unido m.

United States of America n Estados Unidos de América m pl.

universe ('ju:nivə:s) n universo m. **universal** adj universal.

university (ju:ni'və:siti) n universidad f. adj universitario.

unkempt (ʌn'kempt) adj 1 desaseado. 2 despeinado.

unkind (ʌn'kaind) adj poco amable.

unlawful (ʌn'lɔ:fəl) adj ilegal.

unless (ən'les) conj a menos que, a no ser que.

unlike (ʌn'laik) adj desemejante, diferente. prep a diferencia de. **unlikely** adj improbable.

unload (ʌn'loud) vt,vi descargar.

unlucky (ʌn'lʌki) adj desgraciado, nefasto. **be unlucky** tener mala suerte.

unnatural (ʌn'nætʃərəl) adj innatural, anormal.

unnecessary (ʌn'nesəsri) adj innecesario.

unofficial (ʌnə'fiʃəl) adj extraoficial, no oficial.

unorthodox (ʌn'ɔ:θədɔks) adj 1 poco ortodoxo. 2 rel heterodoxo.

unpack (ʌn'pæk) vt 1 desembalar. 2 deshacer. vi deshacer las maletas.

unpleasant (ʌn'plezənt) adj desagradable. **unpleasantness** n lo desagradable neu.

unpopular (ʌn'pɔpjulə) adj impopular. **unpopularity** n impopularidad f.

unravel (ʌnrævəl) vt desenmarañar.

unreasonable (ʌn'ri:zənəbəl) adj irrazonable. **unreasoning** adj irracional.

unreliable (ʌnri'laiəbəl) adj de poca confianza.

unrest (ʌn'rest) n 1 malestar m. inquietud f. 2 pol desorden m.

unruly (ʌn'ru:li) adj ingobernable.

unscrew (ʌn'skru:) vt destornillar.

unsettle (ʌn'setl) vt perturbar, agitar. **unsettled** 1 inquieto. 2 variable. 3 inhabitado. **unsettling** adj perturbador.

unsightly (ʌn'saitli) adj feo.

unsound (ʌn'saund) adj 1 falso. 2 defectuoso.

unsteady (ʌn'stedi) adj inestable.

unsuccessful (ʌnsək'sesfəl) adj fracasado. **be unsuccessful in** no lograr. **unsuccessfully** adv en vano.

untangle (ʌn'tæŋgəl) vt desenmarañar.

untidy (ʌn'taidi) adj desaliñado, en desorden.

untie (ʌn'tai) vt desatar.

until (ʌn'til) conj hasta que. prep hasta.

untrue (ʌn'tru:) adj falso, infiel.

unusual (ʌn'ju:ʒuəl) adj insólito.

unwanted (ʌn'wɔntid) adj no deseado.

unwell (ʌn'wel) adj indispuesto.

unwind (ʌn'waind) vt desenvolver. vi 1 desenvolverse. 2 inf esparcirse.

unwrap (ʌn'ræp) vt desenvolver.

up (ʌp) adv arriba, hacia arriba, de pie. prep en lo alto de. **be up to** ser capaz de.

upbringing ('ʌpbriŋiŋ) n educación f.

upheaval (ʌp'hi:vəl) n 1 solevantamiento m. 2 inf cataclismo, trastorno m.

uphill (ʌp'hil) adj arduo. adv cuesta arriba.

uphold (ʌp'hould) vt sostener, defender.

upholstery (ʌp'houlstəri) n tapicería f.
upholster vt tapizar, entapizar.

upkeep ('ʌpki:p) n conservación f.

uplift (ʌp'lift) n 1 sustentación f. 2 inf edificación f. vt edificar.

upon (ə'pɔn) prep en, sobre.

upper ('ʌpə) adj superior, más alto, de arriba.
upper class adj de la clase alta. n clase alta f. **uppermost** adj 1 más alto. 2 principal.

upright ('ʌprait) adj 1 vertical. 2 honrado. adv erguido. n montante m.

uprising ('ʌpraiziŋ) n alzamiento m.

uproar ('ʌprɔ:) n alboroto m. **uproarious** adj tumultuoso.

uproot (ʌp'ru:t) vt arrancar.

upset (v,adj ʌp'set; n 'ʌpset) adj perturbado. n 1 vuelco m. 2 contratiempo m. vt 1 volcar, trastornar. 2 perturbar.

upshot ('ʌpʃɔt) n resultado m.

upside down (ʌpsaid 'daun) adj al revés.

upstairs (ʌp'stɛəz) adv arriba. adj de arriba.

upstream (ʌp'stri:m) adv río arriba.

upward ('ʌpwəd) adj ascendente. **upwards** adv hacia arriba.

Uranus (juə'reinəs) n Urano m.

urban ('ə:bən) adj urbano.

urge (ə:dʒ) n impulso, instinto m. vt animar, impeler, incitar.

urgent ('ə:dʒənt) adj urgente. **urgency** n urgencia f.

urine ('juərin) n orina f. **urinate** vi orinar.

urn (ə:n) n urna f.

us (ʌs) pron 1st pers pl 1 nos. 2 nosotros.

use (v ju:z; n ju:s) n uso, empleo m. **usage** n uso, tratamiento m. costumbre f. ~vt usar, emplear, utilizar. **use up** consumir. **be used to** estar acostumbrado a. **get used to** acostumbrarse a. **used** adj usado, gastado. **useful** adj útil, provechoso. **useless** adj inútil.

usher ('ʌʃə) n 1 ujier m. 2 Th acomodador m.

usual ('ju:ʒuəl) adj usual, acostumbrado, corriente. **as usual** como de costumbre.

usurp (ju'zə:p) vt usurpar.

utensil (ju:'tensəl) n utensilio m.

uterus ('ju:tərəs) n útero m.

utility (ju:'tiliti) adj utilitario. n utilidad f.

utmost ('ʌtmoust) adj mayor, supremo. **do one's utmost** hacer todo lo posible. **to the utmost** hasta más no poder.

utter[1] ('ʌtə) vt pronunciar, proferir.

utter[2] ('ʌtə) adj completo, total, absoluto. **utterly** adv completamente.

V

vacant ('veikənt) adj libre, desocupado. **vacancy** n 1 vacío m. vaciedad f. 2 cuarto vacante m. 3 vacante f.

vacate (və'keit) vt desocupar, dejar vacante.

vacation (və'keiʃən) n vacación f.

vaccine ('væksi:n) n vacuna f. **vaccinate** vt vacunar. **vaccination** n vacunación f.

vacillate ('væsəleit) vi 1 vacilar. 2 oscilar.

vacuum ('vækjuəm) n vacío m. **vacuum cleaner** n aspirador m. **vacuum flask** n termo or termos m.

vagina (və'dʒainə) n vagina f.

vagrant ('veigrənt) adj vagabundo, vagante. n vagabundo m.

vague (veig) adj vago. **vagueness** n vaguedad f.

vain (vein) adj vano. **in vain** en vano.

Valencia (və'lensiə) n Valencia f. **Valencian** adj,n valenciano m.

valiant ('væliənt) adj valiente.

valid ('vælid) adj válido, valedero. **validity** n validez f.

valley ('væli) n valle m.

value ('vælju:) n valor m. vt 1 valorar. 2 estimar, apreciar. **valuable** adj valioso, estimable. **valuables** n pl objetos de valor m pl.

valve ('vælv) n válvula f.

vampire ('væmpaiə) n vampiro m.

van (væn) n mot camioneta f.

vandal ('vændl) n vándalo m. **vandalism** n vandalismo m.

vanilla (və'nilə) n vainilla f.

vanish ('væniʃ) vi desaparecer.

vanity ('væniti) n vanidad f. **vanity case** n neceser de belleza m.

vapour ('veipə) n vapor m.

varnish ('vɑ:niʃ) n barniz m. vt 1 barnizar. 2 esmaltar.

variety (və'raiəti) n variedad f.

various ('vɛəriəs) adj vario, diverso.

vary ('vɛəri) vt,vi variar. **varying** adj diverso, cambiante. **variable** adj,n variable f. **variant** adj,n variante f. **variation** n variación f.

vase (vɑ:z) n jarrón m.

vasectomy (væ'sektəmi) n vasectomía f.

vast (vɑ:st) adj vasto. **vastly** adv sumamente.

vat (væt) n tina f.

Vatican ('vætikən) n Vaticano m.

vault[1] (vɔ:lt) n **1** bóveda f. **2** bodega f. **3** tumba f. vt abovedar.

vault[2] (vɔ:lt) n salto m. vt,vi saltar.

veal (vi:l) n ternera f.

veer (viə) vi virar, cambiar.

vegetable ('vedʒtəbəl) n **1** bot vegetal m. **2** legumbre, hortaliza f. **3** pl cul verduras f pl. ~adj vegetal. **vegetable garden** n huerto m. **vegetarian** adj,n vegetariano m. **vegetation** n vegetación f.

vehement ('viəmənt) adj vehemente. **vehemence** n vehemencia f.

vehicle ('vi:ikəl) n vehículo m.

veil (veil) n velo m. vt velar.

vein (vein) n vena f.

velocity (və'lɒsiti) n velocidad f.

velvet ('velvit) n terciopelo m.

vendetta (ven'detə) n disputa f.

veneer (vi'niə) n **1** chapa f. enchapado m. **2** apariencia f. vt chapear.

venerate ('venəreit) vt venerar. **venerable** adj venerable. **veneration** n veneración f.

venereal disease (vi'niəriəl) n enfermedad venérea f.

Venezuela (veni'zweilə) n Venezuela f. **Venezuelan** adj,n venezolano m.

vengeance ('vendʒəns) n venganza f. **with a vengeance** con creces. **vengeful** adj vengativo.

venison ('venisən) n carne de venado f.

venom ('venəm) n **1** veneno m. **2** virulencia, malignidad f. **venomous** adj **1** venenoso. **2** virulento, maligno.

vent[1] (vent) n abertura f. respiradero m.

vent[2] (vent) vt descargar, desahogar. **give vent to** dar salida a.

ventilate ('ventileit) vt ventilar. **ventilation** n ventilación f.

venture ('ventʃə) n aventura, empresa f. vt aventurar. **venture to** atreverse a.

Venus ('vi:nəs) n Venus f.

veranda (və'rændə) n veranda, terraza f.

verb (və:b) n verbo m. **verbal** adj verbal.

verdict ('və:dikt) n **1** law veredicto m. **2** juicio m. sentencia f. **3** opinión f.

verge (və:dʒ) n borde, margen m. **on the verge of** al borde de. v **verge on** acercarse a.

verify ('verifai) vt verificar.

vermicelli (və:mi'seli) n fideos m pl.

vermin ('və:min) n sabandija f.

vermouth ('və:məθ) n vermut m.

vernacular (və'nækjulə) adj vernáculo, vulgar. n **1** lengua vernácula f. **2** inf idioma corriente m.

versatile ('və:sətail) adj versátil. **versatility** n versatilidad f.

verse (və:s) n **1** estrofa f. **2** versículo m **3** poesías f pl. versos m pl. **4** verso m.

version ('və:ʃən) n versión f.

vertebrate ('və:tibreit) adj,n vertebrado m.

vertical ('və:tikəl) adj,n vertical f.

verve (və:v) n brío m. energía f.

very ('veri) adj mismo. adv muy, mucho. **very much** mucho, muchísimo.

vessel ('vesəl) n **1** anat vaso m. **2** vasija f. **3** barco m.

vest (vest) n camiseta f.

vestment ('vestmənt) n vestidura f.

vestry ('vestri) n sacristía f.

vet (vet) n veterinario m. vt examinar, investigar.

veteran ('vetərən) adj,n veterano m.

veterinary surgeon ('vetrinəri) n veterinario m.

veto ('vi:tou) n, pl **vetoes** veto m. vt vedar, vetar.

vex (veks) vt vejar, fastidiar, enojar. **vexation** n vejación f. **vexatious** adj vejatorio, fastidioso. **vexed** adj **1** vejado, enojado, enfadado. **2** debatido. **vexing** adj fastidioso, molesto.

via (vaiə) prep por, por vía de.

viable ('vaiəbəl) adj viable. **viability** n viabilidad f.

viaduct ('vaiədʌkt) n viaducto m.

vibrate (vai'breit) vt,vi vibrar. **vibration** n vibración f.

vicar ('vikə) n **1** vicario m. **2** párroco, cura m.

vicarious (vi'kɛəriəs) adj experimentado por otro, vicario.

vice[1] (vais) n vicio m.

vice[2] (vais) n torno de banco m.

vice versa ('vaisə) adv viceversa.

vicinity (vi'siniti) n vecindad f. **in the vicinity** cerca.

vicious ('viʃəs) adj **1** vicioso. **2** virulento, rencoroso.

victim ('viktim) n víctima f. **victimize** vt hacer víctima de, escoger y castigar. **victimization** n persecución f.

victory ('viktri) n victoria f. **victorious** adj victorioso.

video-tape ('vidiouteip) n cinta de vídeo f.

view (vju:) n **1** vista f. **2** opinión f. **in view of** en vista de. ~vt mirar, examinar, contemplar. **view-finder** n visor de imagen m.

vigil ('vidʒil) n vigilia f. **keep vigil** velar. **vigilant** adj vigilante. **vigilance** n vigilancia f.

vigour ('vigə) n vigor m. **vigorous** adj vigoroso.

vile (vail) adj vil.

villa ('vilə) n **1** villa f. **2** chalet m. **3** casa de campo f.

village ('vilidʒ) n aldea f. pueblecito m. **villager** n aldeano m.

villain ('vilən) n **1** malvado m. **2** Th malo m. **villainous** adj malvado.

vindictive (vin'diktiv) adj vengativo. **vindictively** adv rencorosamente. **vindictiveness** n deseo de venganza m.

vine (vain) n **1** vid f. **2** parra f. **vineyard** n viña f.

vinegar ('vinigə) n vinagre m.

vintage ('vintidʒ) n **1** vendimia f. **2** cosecha f. adj clásico. **vintage wine** n vino añejo, vino de calidad m.

vinyl ('vainil) n vinilo m.

viola (vi'oulə) n viola f.

violate ('vaiəleit) vt volar. **violation** n violación f.

violence ('vaiələns) n violencia f. **violent** adj violento.

violet ('vaiələt) adj violado. n **1** bot violeta f. **2** violado m.

violin (vaiə'lin) n violín m.

viper ('vaipə) n víbora f.

virgin ('və:dʒin) adj,n virgen f. **virginal** adj virginal. **virginity** n virginidad f.

Virgo ('və:gou) n Virgo.

virile ('virail) adj viril. **virility** n virilidad f.

virtue ('və:tju:) n virtud f. **virtuous** adj virtuoso. **virtual** adj virtual.

virus ('vairəs) n virus m.

visa ('vi:zə) n visado m.

viscount ('vaikaunt) n vizconde m.

vision ('viʒən) n **1** visión f. **2** clarividencia f. **visible** adj visible. **visibility** n visibilidad f.

visit ('vizit) n visita f. vt visitar. vi hacer visitas.

visual ('vizjuəl) adj visual. **visualize** vt **1** imaginarse. **2** prever.

vital ('vaitl) adj **1** indispensable, esencial. **2** enérgico. **3** vital. **vitals** n pl partes vitales f pl. **vitality** n vitalidad f.

vitamin ('vitəmin) n vitamina f.

vivacious (vai'veiʃəs) adj vivaz.

vivid ('vivid) adj **1** intenso. **2** vivo.

vocabulary (və'kæbjuləri) n vocabulario m.

vocal ('voukəl) adj vocal. **vocal chords** n pl cuerdas vocales f pl.

vocation (vou'keiʃən) n vocación f.

vocative ('vɔkətiv) n vocativo m.

vodka ('vɔdkə) n vodka f.

voice (vɔis) n voz f. vt expresar.

void (vɔid) adj **1** vacío. **2** law inválido. n vacío, hueco m. vt **1** evacuar, vaciar. **2** law anular.

volatile ('vɔlətail) adj volátil.

volcano (vɔl'keinou) n volcán m. **volcanic** adj volcánico.

volley ('vɔli) n **1** descarga f. **2** sport voleo m. vt **1** dirigir. **2** sport volear.

volt (voult) n voltio m. **voltage** n voltaje m.

volume ('vɔlju:m) n **1** volumen m. **2** tomo m.

voluntary ('vɔləntri) n voluntario m. vt ofrecer. **voluntary** adj voluntario.

voluptuous (və'lʌptʃuəs) adj voluptuoso.

vomit ('vɔmit) n vómito m. vt,vi vomitar.

voodoo ('vu:du:) n vudú m.

vote (vout) n voto m. votación f. vt,vi votar.

vouch (vautʃ) v **vouch for** responder de, responder por, confirmar. **vouch that** asegurar que, afirmar que.

voucher ('vautʃə) n **1** documento justificativo m. **2** comm comprobante m. **3** vale m.

vow (vau) n voto m. vt jurar. vi hacer voto de.

vowel ('vauəl) n vocal f.

voyage ('vɔiidʒ) n viaje m. vi viajar.

vulgar ('vʌlgə) adj **1** vulgar. **2** grosero. **vulgarity** n vulgaridad f.

vulnerable ('vʌlnrəbl) adj vulnerable. **vulnerability** n vulnerabilidad f.

vulture ('vʌltʃə) n buitre m.

W

wad (wɔd) n **1** taco m. **2** lío m. vt rellenar. **wadding** n **1** taco m. **2** relleno m.

waddle ('wɔdl) n anadeo m. vi anadear.

wade (weid) vi vadear.

wafer ('weifə) n **1** galleta f. barquillo m.

waft (wɔft) vt llevar por el aire. vi flotar. n soplo m.

wag (wæg) vt menear. n meneo m.

wage (weidʒ) n salario, jornal m.

waggle ('wægəl) vt menear. n meneo m.

wagon ('wægən) n carro, vagón m.

waif (weif) n niño abandonado m.

wail (weil) n lamento m. vi lamentarse, gemir.

waist (weist) n cintura f. talle m. **waistband** n cinturilla f. **waistcoat** n chaleco m.

wait (weit) vt,vi esperar. **wait on** servir. **waiter** n camarero m. **waiting list** n lista de aspirantes f. **waiting room** n sala de espera f. **waitress** n camarera f.

waive (weiv) vt renunciar a.

wake (weik) vt,vi despertar. n vela f. **waken** vt,vi despertar.

Wales (weilz) n Gales f. **Welsh** adj,n galés. **Welsh** (language) n galés m.

walk (wɔ:k) n 1 paseo, andar, paso m. 2 alameda f. 3 caminata f. **go for a walk** dar un paseo. ~vt llevar a paseo. vi andar, pasear, pasearse. **walking stick** n bastón m. **walkout** n 1 salida f. 2 huelga f. **walkover** n triunfo fácil m.

wall (wɔ:l) n pared, tapia f. muro m. **wallflower** n alhelí m. **be a wallflower** comer pavo. **wallpaper** n papel de empapelar m. ~vt murar.

wallet ('wɔlit) n cartera f.

wallow ('wɔlou) vi revolcarse.

walnut ('wɔ:lnʌt) n nuez f. **walnut tree** n nogal m.

walrus ('wɔ:lrəs) n morsa f.

waltz (wɔ:ls) n vals m. vi valsar.

wand (wɔnd) n vara f.

wander ('wɔndə) vt vagar por. vi 1 vagar. 2 extraviarse.

wane (wein) vi 1 disminuir. 2 menguar. n disminución f.

wangle ('wæŋgəl) n chanchullo m. trampa f. vt agenciarse.

want (wɔnt) n 1 falta f. 2 miseria f. 3 necesidad f. vt 1 necesitar. 2 querer. vi carecer de.

war (wɔ:) n guerra f. vi guerrear.

warble ('wɔ:bəl) n trino, gorjeo m. vi trinar.

ward (wɔ:d) n 1 tutela f. 2 pupilo m. 3 sala f. v **ward off** desviar. **warden** n 1 guardián m. 2 director m. 3 alcaide m. **warder** n guardián, vigilante m. **wardrobe** n 1 vestidos m pl. 2 vestuario m. 3 armario m.

warehouse ('wɛəhaus) n almacén, depósito m.

warm (wɔ:m) adj 1 caliente. 2 cálido. 3 caluroso. **be warm** tener calor. ~vt 1 calentar. 2 alegrar. **warm-blooded** adj 1 de sangre caliente. 2 apasionado. **warm-hearted** adj bondadoso, afectuoso. **warm-up** n 1 sport ejercicios m pl. 2 preparativos m pl.

warn (wɔ:n) vt 1 advertir. 2 amonestar. 3 prevenir. **warning** n 1 aviso m. 2 advertencia f.

warp (wɔ:p) n 1 urdimbre f. 2 deformación f. v 1 deformar. 2 pervertir. vi deformarse.

warrant ('wɔrənt) n 1 autorización f. 2 cédula f. 3 garantía f. vt 1 autorizar. 2 garantizar.

warrant officer n suboficial m. **warranty** n garantía f.

warren ('wɔrən) n 1 madriguera f. 2 conejera f.

warrior ('wɔriə) n guerrero m.

wart (wɔ:t) n verruga f.

wary ('wɛəri) adj cauteloso, cauto.

was (wɔz; stressed wɔz) v see **be**.

wash (wɔʃ) n 1 lavado m. 2 ropa sucia f. 3 remolino m. vt 1 lavar. 2 fregar. vi lavarse. **washbasin** n 1 palangana f. 2 lavabo m. **washer** n tech arandela f. **washing** n 1 lavado m. 2 colada f. 3 ropa sucia f. **washing machine** n lavadora f. **wash-out** n fracaso m. **washroom** n aseos m pl.

wasp (wɔsp) n avispa f.

waste (weist) adj 1 desechado. 2 inútil. 3 yermo. n 1 despilfarro m. 2 desperdicio m. 3 pérdida f. 4 desierto m. vt despilfarrar. **wastepaper bin** or **basket** n papelera f.

watch (wɔtʃ) n 1 vigilancia f. 2 guardia f. 3 reloj m. vt 1 guardar. 2 observar. vi velar. **watchdog** n perro guardián m. **watchful** adj 1 vigilante. 2 desvelado.

water ('wɔ:tə) n agua m. vt 1 regar. 2 mojar. **water-closet** n retrete m. **watercolour** n acuarela f. **watercress** n berro m. **waterfall** n cascada f. **waterlogged** adj 1 anegado. 2 empapado. **watermark** n filigrana f. **watermelon** n sandía f. **waterproof** adj,n impermeable m. vt impermeabilizar. **watertight** adj 1 impermeable. 2 inf irrefutable. **waterworks** n central depuradora f. **watery** adj 1 acuoso. 2 húmedo. 3 lloroso.

watt (wɔt) n vatio m.

wave (weiv) n 1 ola f. 2 onda f. 3 ademán m. vt 1 ondear. 2 agitar. vi hacer señales. **waveband** n banda de ondas f. **wavelength** n longitud de onda f. **wavy** adj ondulado.

waver ('weivə) vi 1 oscilar. 2 vacilar.

wax[1] (wæks) n cera. vt encerar.

wax[2] (wæks) vi crecer.

way (wei) n 1 camino m. 2 ruta f. 3 vía f. 4 modo m. **by the way** a propósito. **give way** ceder el paso.

waylay (wei'lei) vt acechar.

wayward ('weiwəd) adj 1 travieso. 2 caprichoso. 3 voluntarioso.

we (wi:) pron 1st pers pl nosotros, nosotras.

weak (wi:k) adj 1 débil. 2 flojo. 3 tenue. **weaken** vt 1 debilitar. 2 disminuir. **weakling** n 1 persona débil f. 2 cobarde m. **weak-minded** adj 1 vacilante. 2 imbécil. **weakwilled** adj de voluntad débil.

wealth (welθ) n 1 riqueza f. 2 abundancia f. **wealthy** adj rico.

weapon ('wepən) n arma f.

wear* (wɛə) n 1 uso m. 2 deterioro m. vt 1 llevar. 2 usar. **wear away**, desgastar. ~vi durar.

weary ('wiəri) adj 1 cansado. 2 aburrido. vt cansar.

weasel ('wi:zəl) n comadreja f.

weather ('weðə) n tiempo m. **under the weather** destemplado. ~vt 1 aguantar. 2 curtir. vi desgastarse.

weave* (wi:v) n 1 tejido m. 2 textura f. vt,vi tejer.

web (web) n 1 tela f. 2 telaraña f. 3 membrana f.

wedding ('wediŋ) n 1 boda f. 2 casamiento m. **wedding ring** n anillo de boda m.

wedge (wedʒ) n 1 cuña f. 2 calza f. vi 1 acuñar, calzar. 2 sujetar.

Wednesday ('wenzdi) n miércoles m.

weed (wi:d) n hierba mala f. vt 1 escardar. 2 suprimir.

week (wi:k) n semana f. **weekday** n día laborable m. **weekend** n fin de semana m.

weep* (wi:p) vt,vi llorar.

weigh (wei) vt 1 pesar. 2 ponderar. 3 agobiar. vi pesar. **weighbridge** n báscula de puente f. **weight** n 1 peso m. 2 pesa f. 3 carga f. **put on weight** engordar. **weight-lifting** n levantamiento de pesos m.

weird ('wiəd) adj 1 misterioso. 2 raro.

welcome ('welkəm) adj 1 bienvenido. 2 grato. **you are welcome!** ¡de nada! ~n bienvenida f. vt dar la bienvenida a.

weld (weld) vt 1 soldar. 2 unir.

welfare ('welfɛə) n 1 bienestar m. 2 prosperidad f. 3 asistencia social f.

well[1] (wel) n 1 pozo m. 2 hueco m. vi brotar.

well[2] (wel) adv bien. **as well** también. **well!** ¡vaya! ~adj 1 bien. 2 sano.

well-bred adj 1 bien educado. 2 de pura raza.

well-built adj 1 de construcción sólida. 2 fornido.

well-known adj conocido.

well-off adj 1 acomodado. 2 adinerado.

well-paid adj bien pagado.

well-spoken adj bien hablado.

well-to-do adj pudiente.

well-worn adj 1 raído. 2 trillado.

went (went) v see **go**.

wept (wept) v see **weep**.

were (wə:) v see **be**.

west (west) n oeste, occidente m. adj occidental. **westerly** adj del oeste. **western** adj occidental, del oeste. n novela or película del oeste f. **westward** adj al oeste, occidental. adv hacia el oeste. **westwards** adv hacia el oeste.

West Indies ('indiz) n Antillas f.

wet (wet) adj 1 mojado. 2 húmedo. 3 lluvioso. n lluvia f. vt mojar.

whack (wæk) n 1 golpe m. 2 tentativa f. 3 inf porción f. vt golpear.

whale (weil) n ballena f.

wharf (wɔ:f) n, pl **wharves** or **wharfs** muelle m.

what (wɔt) adj 1 que. 2 qué, cuál de. pron 1 el que, la que, lo que. 2 ¿qué? ¿cómo? 3 ¡cómo! **whatever** pron 1 lo que. 2 todo lo que. adj cualquier.

wheat (wi:t) n trigo m.

wheedle ('wi:dl) vt engatusar.

wheel (wi:l) n 1 rueda f. 2 volante m. vt hacer girar. vi 1 girar. 2 dar vueltas. **wheelbarrow** n carretilla f. **wheelchair** n silla de ruedas f.

wheeze (wi:z) n respiración silbante f. vt,vi jadear, respirar con dificultad.

whelk (welk) n caracol de mar, buccino m.

when (wen) adv cuándo. conj cuando. **whenever** adv 1 siempre que. 2 cuando quiera que.

where (wɛə) adv 1 ¿dónde? 2 donde. 3 adonde. **whereabouts** adv ¿dónde? n paradero m. **whereas** conj 1 visto que, mientras. 2 considerando que. **whereby** adv por lo cual, por donde. **whereupon** adv con lo cual, sobre lo cual. **wherever** adv dondequiera que.

whether ('weðə) conj 1 si. 2 que.

which (witʃ) adj ¿que? ¿cuál? pron 1 ¿cuál? 2 que, lo que. 3 el que, el cual, lo cual. **whichever** adj cualquier. pron 1 cualquiera. 2 el que, la que.

whiff (wif) n 1 soplo m. 2 olorcillo m. vt soplar.

while (wail) conj also **whilst** 1 mientras. 2 aunque. n tiempo, rato m.

whim (wim) n capricho, antojo m. **whimsical** adj 1 caprichoso. 2 fantástico.

whimper ('wimpə) n quejido, gemido m. vi 1 lloriquear. 2 gemir.

whine (wain) n quejido, gimoteo m. vi gimotear.

whip (wip) vt 1 azotar. 2 cul batir. **whip up** avivar. ~n 1 látigo m. 2 azote m. **whip-round** n colecta f.

whippet ('wipit) n perro lebrel m.

whir (wə:l) vi zumbar, runrunear.

whirl (wə:l) n 1 giro m. 2 rotación f. 3 remolino m. vt hacer girar. vi girar. **whirlwind** n torbellino m.

whisk¹ (wisk) n movimiento brusco m. vi moverse rápidamente.

whisk² (wisk) n batidor m. vt batir.

whisker ('wiskə) n 1 pelo de la barba m. 2 pl barbas f pl. 3 pl bigotes m pl.

whisky ('wiski) n whisky m.

whisper ('wispə) n 1 cuchicheo m. 2 susurro m. 3 rumor m. vt susurrar. vi cuchichear.

whistle ('wisəl) n 1 silbido m. 2 silbato m. vt, vi silbar.

white (wait) adj, n blanco m. **whitewash** n 1 jalbegue m. 2 excusas f pl. vt 1 enjalbegar. 2 encubrir.

whiting ('waitiŋ) n pescadilla f.

Whitsun ('witsən) n Pentecostés m invar.

whiz (wiz) vi silbar, zumbar. n silbido, zumbido m.

who (hu:) pron 1 quién. 2 quiénes. 3 que. 4 el que, quien. **whoever** pron 1 quienquiera que, cualquiera que. 2 ¿quién?

whole (houl) adj 1 todo. 2 entero. 3 sano. n 1 todo m. 2 conjunto m. **on the whole** en general. **wholehearted** adj entusiasta. **wholemeal** adj íntegro. n harina integral f. **wholesale** n venta al por mayor f. adj 1 mayorista. 2 en masa. **wholesome** adj saludable, sano. **wholly** adv completamente, enteramente.

whom (hu:m) pron 1 a quién. 2 que, a quien, quienes.

whooping cough ('hu:piŋ) n tos ferina f.

whore (hɔ:) n puta f.

whose (hu:z) pron 1 ¿de quién? 2 cuyo, cuya, cuyos, cuyas.

why (wai) adv por qué. interj ¡cómo! ¡toma!

wick (wik) n mecha f.

wicked ('wikid) adj 1 malo. 2 perverso. 3 inicuo.

wicket ('wikit) n sport palos m pl. rastrillo m.

wide (waid) adj 1 ancho. 2 extenso. 3 amplio. adv lejos. **far and wide** por todas partes. **widen** vt ensanchar. **widespread** adj 1 extendido. 2 difuso. 3 general.

widow ('widou) n viuda f.

width (widθ) n 1 anchura f. 2 ancho m. 3 amplitud f.

wield (wi:ld) vt 1 manejar. 2 empuñar. 3 ejercer.

wife (waif) n, pl **wives** esposa, mujer f.

wig (wig) n peluca f.

wiggle ('wigəl) n meneo rápido m. vt menear rápidamente.

wild (waild) adj 1 salvaje. 2 silvestre. 3 feroz. 4 furioso. 5 loco. n yermo m. **wildlife** n fauna f.

wilderness ('wildənəs) n desierto, yermo m.

wilful ('wilfəl) adj 1 voluntarioso. 2 testarudo.

will¹ (wil) v aux 1 used in forming the future tense. 2 querer.

will² (wil) n 1 voluntad f. 2 albedrío m. 3 testamento m. vt ordenar. **willpower** n fuerza de voluntad f.

willing ('wiliŋ) adj 1 dispuesto. 2 servicial.

willow ('wilou) n sauce m.

wilt (wilt) vt marchitar.

win (win) vt ganar. vi 1 ganar. 2 triunfar. n triunfo m.

wince (wins) vi 1 hacer una mueca de dolor. 2 retroceder. n mueca de dolor f.

winch (wintʃ) n torno m.

wind¹ (wind) n 1 viento m. 2 flatulencia f. 3 aliento m. **windfall** n ganancia inesperada f. **windmill** n molino de viento m. **windpipe** n tráquea f. **windscreen** n parabrisas m invar. **windscreen wiper** n limpiaparabrisas m invar. **windswept** adj azotado por el viento. **windy** adj ventoso.

wind²² (waind) vt 1 enrollar. 2 devanar. 3 dar vueltas a. **wind up** 1 liquidar. 2 serpentear.

windlass ('windləs) n 1 torno m. 2 cabestrante m.

window ('windou) n 1 ventana f. 2 ventanilla f. 3 escaparate m. **window-shop** vi mirar los escaparates.

wine (wain) n vino m. **wineglass** n copa para vino f.

wing (wiŋ) n 1 ala f. 2 Th bastidores m pl. vt herir en el ala. vi volar. **wing commander** n teniente coronel de aviación m. **wingspan** n envergadura f.

wink (wiŋk) n 1 pestañeo m. 2 guiño m. vt guiñar. vi pestañear.

winkle ('wiŋkəl) n 1 bígaro m. 2 zool caracolillo m.

winter ('wintə) n invierno m. vi invernar.

wipe (waip) vt 1 limpiar. 2 enjugar. **wipe out** borrar. ~n limpión m.

wire ('waiə) n 1 alambre m. 2 telegrama m. vt alambrar. vi poner un telegrama.

wise (waiz) adj 1 sabio. 2 prudente.

wish (wiʃ) n 1 deseo m. 2 ruego m. vt desear, querer. vi desear.

wisp (wisp) n 1 mechón m. 2 vestigio m.

wisteria (wis'tiəriə) n vistaria f.

wistful ('wistfəl) adj 1 triste. 2 pensativo. 3 ansioso.

wit (wit) n 1 inteligencia f. entendimiento m. 2 talento m. 3 ingenio m. 4 gracia f.

witch (witʃ) n bruja f. **witchcraft** n brujería f.

with (wið) prep 1 con. 2 según. 3 de.

withdraw* (wið'drɔ:) vt retirar, sacar.

wither ('wiðə) vi marchitarse. vt 1 marchitar. 2 aplastar.

withhold* (wið'hould) vt 1 retener. 2 ocultar. 3 negar.

within (wið'in) adv dentro. prep 1 dentro de. 2 al alcance de.

without (wið'aut) adv 1 fuera. 2 por fuera. prep 1 sin. 2 a falta de.

withstand* (wið'stænd) vt 1 resistir a. 2 oponerse. 3 aguantar.

witness ('witnəs) n 1 testimonio m. 2 testigo m. **bear witness** atestiguar. vt 1 asistir a, presenciar. 2 ver.

witty ('witi) adj 1 ingenioso. 2 gracioso.

wizard ('wizəd) n 1 hechicero, brujo m. 2 genio m.

wobble ('wɔbəl) vi 1 bambolear. 2 vacilar. n bamboleo m.

woke (wouk) v see **wake**.

woken (woukən) v see **wake**.

wolf (wulf) n, pl **wolves** 1 lobo m. 2 inf tenorio m.

woman ('wumən) n, pl **women** mujer f. **womanhood** n 1 feminidad f. 2 sexo femenino m.

womb (wu:m) n 1 matriz f. utero m. 2 seno m.

won (wʌn) v see **win**.

wonder ('wʌndə) n 1 maravilla f. 2 admiración f. 3 prodigio m. vt,vi 1 preguntarse. 2 admirarse. **wonderful** adj 1 maravilloso. 2 estupendo.

wonky ('wɔŋki) adj poco firme, poco seguro.

wood (wud) n 1 bosque m. 2 madera f. 3 leña f. **woodcock** n chochaperdiz f. **wooden** adj 1 de madera. 2 inexpresivo. **woodland** n bosque, arbolado m. **woodpecker** n pájaro carpintero m. **woodpigeon** n paloma torcaz f. **woodwind** n mus instrumento de viento de madera m. **woodwork** n 1 maderaje m. 2 carpintería f. **woodworm** n carcoma f.

wool (wul) n lana f. adj lanar. **woollen** adj 1 de lana. 2 lanar. **woolly** adj 1 lanudo, lanoso. 2 borroso.

word (wə:d) n 1 palabra f. 2 vocablo m. 3 aviso m. 4 orden f. vt redactar.

wore (wɔ:) v see **wear**.

work (wə:k) n 1 trabajo m. 2 labor f. 3 obra f. vt 1 trabajar. 2 bordar. vi funcionar. **worker** n trabajador, obrero m. **working class** adj clase obrera. **workman** n 1 obrero m. 2 trabajador m. **workmanship** n habilidad f. **workshop** n taller m.

world (wə:ld) n mundo m. **worldly** adj mundano. **worldwide** adj mundial, universal.

worm (wə:m) n 1 gusano m. 2 lombriz f. 3 inf canalla m.

wormwood ('wə:mwud) n ajenjo m.

worn (wɔ:n) v see **wear**. adj 1 gastado. 2 estropeado. **worry** ('wʌri) n 1 preocupación f. 2 cuidado m. vt 1 preocupar. 2 molestar. vi preocuparse.

worse ('wə:s) adj 1 peor. 2 inferior. **so much the worse** tanto peor. ~adv peor. **worsen** vt agravar, hacer peor. vi empeorar.

worship ('wə:ʃip) n 1 adoración f. 2 veneración f. 3 culto m. vt adorar. vi 1 adorar. 2 dar culto.

worst (wə:st) adj el peor. n lo peor neu. **get the worst of it** salir perdiendo.

worsted ('wustid) n estambre m.

worth (wə:θ) adj 1 digno de. 2 que vale. **be worth** valer. ~n 1 valor m. 2 mérito m. **worthwhile** adj 1 valioso. 2 que vale la pena. **worthy** adj 1 meritorio. 2 honesto. **worthy of** digno de.

would* (wəd; stressed wud) v see **will**[1].

wound[1] (wu:nd) n herida f. vt herir.

wound[2] (waund) v see **wind**[2].

wove (wouv) v see **weave**.

woven ('wouvn) v see **weave**.

wrangle ('ræŋgəl) n altercado m. riña f. vi 1 reñir. 2 regatear.

wrap (ræp) n bata f. abrigo m. vt 1 envolver. 2 arropar.

wrath (rɔθ) n ira f.

wreath (ri:θ) n 1 guirnalda f. 2 corona f. 3 (of smoke) espiral f.

wreathe (ri:ð) vt 1 ceñir. 2 trenzar. 3 enguirnaldar.

wreck (rek) n 1 naufragio m. 2 buque naufragado m. 3 destrucción f. 4 ruina f. vt hundir, naufragar. **wreckage** n 1 naufragio m. 2 restos m pl.

wren (ren) n chochín m.

wrench (rentʃ) n 1 torcedura f. 2 tirón m. 3 llave inglesa f. vt 1 arrancar. 2 torcer.

wrestle ('resəl) n lucha f. vi luchar.

wretch (retʃ) n desgraciado, infeliz m. **wretched** adj 1 desgraciado. 2 miserable. 3 horrible.

wriggle ('rigəl) n 1 meneo m. 2 serpenteo m. vt menear. vi culebrear.

wring* (riŋ) vt 1 torcer. 2 exprimir. 3 acongojar.

wrinkle ('riŋkəl) n 1 arruga f. 2 pliegue m. vt arrugar. vi plegarse.

wrist (rist) n muñeca f.

writ (rit) n 1 escritura f. 2 mandato m. 3 autoridad f.

write* (rait) vt,vi escribir. **write down** apuntar. **write out** copiar. **write up** redactar. **writing paper** n papel de escribir m.

writhe (raið) vi 1 retorcerse. 2 debatirse.

wrong (rɔŋ) adj 1 malo. 2 injusto. 3 erróneo. 4 impropio. n 1 mal m. 2 injusticia f. vt agraviar.

wrote (rout) v see **write**.

wrought iron (rɔːt) n hierro forjado m.

wrung (rʌŋ) v see **wring**.

wry (rai) adj 1 torcido. 2 irónico. **wry face** mueca.

X

xenophobia (zenə'foubiə) n xenofobia f.

Xerox ('ziərɔks) n Tdmk xérox m.

X-ray n radiografía f. **x-rays** rayos x m pl. vt radiografiar.

xylophone ('zailəfoun) n xilófono m.

Y

yacht (jɔt) n yate m. vi navegar en yate. **yachtsman** n deportista náutico m.

yank (jæŋk) n tirón m. vt tirar de.

yap (jæp) n ladrido agudo m. vi 1 ladrar. 2 inf charlar.

yard[1] (jɑːd) n yarda f. **yardstick** n criterio m. norma f.

yard[2] (jɑːd) n 1 patio m. 2 corral m.

yarn (jɑːn) n 1 hilo m. 2 cuento m. vi contar historias.

yawn (jɔːn) n bostezo m. vi bostezar.

year (jiə) n año m.

yearn (jəːn) vi suspirar. **yearn for** anhelar.

yeast (jiːst) n levadura f.

yell (jel) n grito, alarido m. vt gritar, vociferar. vi gritar.

yellow ('jelou) adj 1 amarillo. 2 inf cobarde. n amarillo m.

yelp (jelp) n gañido m. vi 1 gañir. 2 gritar.

yes (jes) adv sí.

yesterday ('jestədi) adv,n ayer m. **the day before yesterday** anteayer.

yet (jet) adv todavía, aún. **as yet** hasta ahora. ~conj con todo, sin embargo.

yew (juː) n tejo m.

Yiddish ('jidiʃ) adj judío. n lengua alemán-hebreo usado por algunos judíos f.

yield (jiːld) n 1 producción f. 2 cosecha f. 3 rédito m. vt 1 producir. 2 rendir. vi rendirse.

yoghurt ('jɔgət) n yogur m.

yoke (jouk) n 1 yunta f. 2 canesú m. 3 yugo m. vt uncir.

yolk (jouk) n yema f.

yonder ('jɔndə) adj aquel. adv allá, a lo lejos.

you (juː) pron 2nd pers 1 s fam tú. with **you** contigo. 2 s fml usted, le, la. with **you** consigo. 3 pl fam vosotros, vosotras, os. 4 pl fml ustedes, los, las, les.

young (jʌŋ) adj 1 joven. 2 nuevo. 3 menor. n cría f. **youngster** n joven, jovencito m.

your (jɔː, juə) poss adj 2nd pers 1 s fam tu, tus. 2 pl fam vuestro, vuestra, vuestros, vuestras. 3 fml su, sus. **yours** poss pron 2nd pers 1 s fam (el) tuyo, (la) tuya, (los) tuyos, (las) tuyas. 2 fam pl (el) vuestro, (la) vuestra, (los) vuestros, (las) vuestras. 3 fml (el) suyo, (la) suya, (los) suyos, (las) suyas. **yours faithfully** le saluda atentamente. **yourself** pron 1 s fam tu mismo, tu misma. 2 s fml usted mismo. **yourselves** 1 pl fam vosotros mismos. 2 pl fml ustedes mismos.

youth (juːθ) n 1 juventud f. 2 joven m.

Yugoslavia (juːgou'slɑːviə) n Yugoslavia f. **Yugoslav** adj,n yugoslavo m.

Z

zeal (ziːl) n celo, entusiasmo m.

zebra ('zebrə) n cebra f. **zebra crossing** n paso de peatones m.

zenith ('zeniθ) n cenit m.

zero ('ziərou) adj,n cero m.

zest (zest) n gusto, entusiasmo m.

zigzag ('zigzæg) n zigzag m. vi zigzaguear.

zinc (ziŋk) n cinc m.

Zionism ('zaiənizəm) n sionismo m.

zip (zip) n **1** cremallera f. **2** energía f. **3** silbido m. v **zip up** cerrar la cremallera de.

zither ('ziðə) n cítara f.

zodiac ('zoudiæk) n zodíaco m.

zone (zoun) n zona f.

zoo (zu:) n zoo m.

zoology (zou'ɔlədʒi) n zoología f.

zoom (zu:m) n zumbido. vi **1** zumbar. **2** empinarse.